Public Relations

A MANAGERIAL PERSPECTIVE

Public Relations

A MANAGERIAL PERSPECTIVE

Danny Moss
Barbara DeSanto

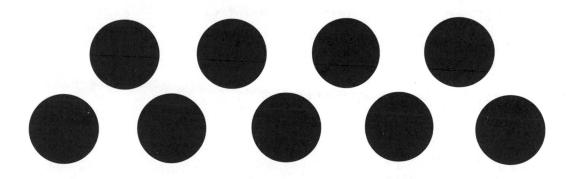

Los Angeles | London | New Delhi
Singapore | Washington DC

SAGE Publications Ltd
1 Oliver's Yard
55 City Road
London EC1Y 1SP

SAGE Publications Inc.
2455 Teller Road
Thousand Oaks, California 91320

SAGE Publications India Pvt Ltd
B 1/I 1 Mohan Cooperative Industrial Area
Mathura Road
New Delhi 110 044

SAGE Publications Asia-Pacific Pte Ltd
3 Church Street
#10-04 Samsung Hub
Singapore 049483

Library of Congress Control Number: 2011929935

British Library Cataloguing in Publication data

A catalogue record for this book is available from the British Library

ISBN 978-0-7619-4856-8
ISBN 978-0-7619-4857-5 (pbk)

Typeset by C&M Digitals (P) Ltd, Chennai, India
Printed by MPG Books Group, Bodmin, Cornwall
Printed on paper from sustainable resources

Dedications

DANNY MOSS

This book is dedicated, like all my works, to the memory of my much loved and now sadly missed golden retriever Angus, who was a wonderfully uncritical listener to my ideas and plans for this book. I also have to thank my wife Eunice for putting up with many lonely hours while I was locked away typing the manuscript.

Finally, both Barbara and I want to thank our commissioning editor Delia Martinez Alfonso for her patience and support for this much delayed book, during the writing of which she has managed to give birth to two children!

BARBARA DESANTO

This book is dedicated to all of my graduate students from Oklahoma State University, the University of North Carolina at Charlotte, and Maryville University, St Louis. Thank you for all of your challenges and inspiration. To my co-author and colleague, Dr Danny Moss, thank you for being a superb colleague through the years. To my husband, Dr Robert John DeSanto, APR, Fellow PRSA, and Rosie Hoover, Frederick the Great, and Winky, thank all of you for strategically knowing how to bring joy to my life.

Contents

Notes on Contributors

DANNY MOSS, CO-EDITOR

Danny Moss is Professor of Corporate and Public Affairs at the University of Chester. Prior to moving to Chester, he was Co-director of the Centre for Corporate and Public Affairs at the Manchester Metropolitan University Business School, and Programme Leader for the University's master's degree in International Public Relations. He also held the post of Director of Public Relations programmes at the University of Stirling where he established the first dedicated master's degree in Public Relations in the UK. He is also the co-organiser of 'Bledcom', the annual global public relations research symposium which is held at Lake Bled, Slovenia. Danny Moss is co-editor of *the Journal of Public Affairs* and author of over 80 journal articles and books, including *Public Relations Research: An International Perspective* (co-edited with Toby MacManus and Dejan Vercic), *Perspectives on Public Relations Research* (co-edited with Dejan Vercic and Gary Warnaby) and *Public Relations Cases: International Perspectives* (co-edited with Barbara DeSanto).

BARBARA DESANTO, CO-EDITOR

Barbara DeSanto, Ed.D, APR, Fellow PRSA, is Professor of Communication and Communication Program Director and Graduate Program director for the strategic communication and organizational leadership masters degrees at Maryville University, St Louis, Missouri. DeSanto's professional media career includes three years as a newspaper reporter, three years as Lee County, Florida, public relations assistant tourism publicity director, and two years as the Lee County, Florida, Chief Public Information Officer. Since earning her doctorate from Oklahoma State University in 1995, she has created and taught more than 20 domestic and international public relations courses in the United States and the United Kingdom. She has guest-lectured in universities in the UK, Sweden, Germany, the Netherlands, and New Zealand. She has more than 12 years of experience in creating and leading public relations and strategic communication study abroad programs and courses.

JOHN ARTHUR

Dr John Arthur has a background in Occupational Psychology, specialising in high-risk professions (fire, police, pharmacy, surgeons, air traffic control). His research covers the human factors of the conceptualisation, measurement and behavioural outcomes of 'risk' as a social construct. He has a PhD from Warwick University on the development of 'for expert systems', comparing heuristic risk reasoning platforms with their formal counterparts such as Bayesian decision analysis.

John works for Unilever, where he is currently the Global Public Affairs Manager. He has been with the company for the last eight years in applied roles looking at risk perception, the conceptualisation of issues management and stakeholder modelling and, latterly, the redevelopment of Unilever's crisis prevention and response governance systems.

When not at work John rides unfeasibly high-powered motorbikes and enjoys working for his local church.

MICHAEL BOARD

Michael Board works as the Director of Marketing & Advertising for James River Equipment Company, headquartered in Richmond, Virginia, and has held this position since January 2004. His experience with employee communication began with a smaller, family-owned operation that merged with James River Equipment in August 2006, and continues today. Board also teaches as an Adjunct Faculty member at the University of North Carolina Charlotte (UNCC) in the Department of Communication Studies, and has held this position since August 2005. Specific undergraduate courses taught include Public Speaking and Communication Campaigns. He earned a BA in Communication Studies in 2000 and an MA in Communication Studies in 2005 from UNC Charlotte, both with emphasis in Public Relations. He lives in Salisbury, North Carolina, with his wife, Jennifer, and cat, Harley.

DAVE H. BRADIN

Dave Bradin has more than ten years of professional experience in communication and investment advisory services. Currently, he serves as a product manager and client services professional for a multinational asset management firm with locations in New York, Boston, Charlotte, NC, London and Australia. In his current role, he is responsible for structuring investment vehicles and developing strategic marketing and investor communication plans for both US and global investment products. In addition to his current role within the financial services industry, he has experience in both merger and acquisitions advisory services and private equity capital raises within the biotechnology industry. Additionally, he has served as a marketing professional for a WB and UPN affiliate, where he was responsible for providing advertising and marketing advisory to a variety of national and regional advertisers.

Dave holds a BA in Mediated Communication from North Carolina State University, an MA in Communication from the University of North Carolina Charlotte (UNCC) and an MBA from Wake Forest University's Babcock Graduate School of Management. While at UNC Charlotte, he studied strategic and risk communication, where he developed a strategic communication plan for a multinational asset manager during the height of the financial crisis of 2008. His research led to the development of a communication strategy that has been instituted for communicating to investors domiciled in the USA, Europe and Asia.

ROB BROWN

Rob Brown graduated in Economics and Politics and spent a year in radio before going into public relations. He set up his own company in the 1990s, working with ITV, Channel Four and Endemol, which he sold to Leedex. In 1999 he left Leedex to join McCann Erickson as Public Relations Director. In 2008 he joined Staniforth as UK Managing Director. Clients include Marks & Spencer, Nissan and Kellogg's. He is the author of *Public Relations and the Social Web* (Kogan Page, 2009).

ANNE GREGORY

Anne Gregory is Professor of Public Relations and Director of the Centre for Public Relations Studies at Leeds Business School, part of Leeds Metropolitan University. Her focus is on academic and commercially funded research as well as consultancy. She works with large clients such as the Department of Health and the Cabinet Office. She is an internationally recognised speaker and researcher, has written and edited books, book chapters and journal articles and appears regularly in the media. Anne was President of the UK Chartered Institute of Public Relations in 2004, edits the Institute's *Public Relations in Practice* series of 17 books and is editor of the *Journal of Communication Management*.

IAN GRIME

Dr Ian Grime is a Principal Lecturer at Manchester Metropolitan University Business School. He has a first degree in Retail Management and a PhD focusing on brand personality and the impact of brand extensions. He is now investigating a variety of research topics in the area of brand management, including brand personality, brand extensions and corporate reputation, identity and image. He has published work in journals such as the *European Journal of Marketing*.

MEL POWELL

Mel Powell is a Senior Lecturer at Manchester Metropolitan University Business School, where she is Programme Leader for the MSc in International Public Relations, as well as leading units in marketing communications theory and creative brand strategy at undergraduate level. Previously she was a Senior Lecturer in public relations at Leeds Metropolitan University Business School. Before becoming an academic in 1996, she spent 14 years as a practitioner in local authority public relations and in arts marketing. Her publications include the recently published *Public Relations Cases: International Perspectives*, which she co-edited with Danny Moss.

RENEE ROBINSON

With more than 13 years experience in public relations, Renee serves as public relations management supervisor at Nicholson Kovac, an integrated marketing communications agency headquartered in Kansas City, MO. Her public relations expertise spans strategic planning, media relations, media training, event planning, and crisis, internal and online communications, including social media.

Prior to joining Nicholson Kovac, Renee worked in corporate communications for Williams, a Fortune 500 energy company headquartered in Tulsa, OK. Renee also worked as the public relations and marketing specialist in the Tulsa office of BKD, one of the largest CPA and advisory firms in the USA. She has been a member of PRSA for more than 12 years and is the 2009–2010 Midwest District chair. She has also served on the boards of directors for both the Kansas City and Tulsa chapters. She was recognised as the Tulsa chapter's Young Professional of the Year in 2002 and was accredited in 2003.

She has also volunteered in a public relations and communications capacity for various not-for-profit organisations, including Camp Fire USA, The Nature Conservancy and Komen Race for the Cure. Renee graduated from Oklahoma State University with bachelor's degrees in English and journalism and broadcasting with a public relations emphasis, as well as a master's degree in mass communications/media management.

ANN RODRIQUEZ

Ann H. Rodriguez, JD, is an Assistant Professor in the College of Mass Communications at Texas Tech University. Dr Rodriguez earned an MBA from Boston University and a law degree from the University of Florida. As a practising attorney she represented a diverse client base, including sports and entertainment management, marketing and sales, toxic torts and general business. She also worked as an Advertising Compliance Officer at GE Capital Corporation and is an active member of the Connecticut State Bar. She was one of the founding editors of the *Florida Entertainment, Art & Sport Law Journal* and earned membership in the Phi Delta Phi legal association in 1994. Dr Rodriguez teaches a variety of public relations and advertising classes, including writing, media planning and public relations management, and has earned the L.U. Kaiser Innovative Teaching Award and the Texas

Tech university-wide Mortar Board Faculty Recognition Award. Her research interests include advertising, public relations, education, sports, and the law.

IAN SOMERVILLE

Dr Ian Somerville is a lecturer in the School of Communication at the University of Ulster, where he is Course Director for the BSc in Public Relations. He has previously published in the areas of public relations ethics, political public relations and the impact on and use of new media technologies in the public relations industry. Current research interests include human rights lobbying and public relations in conflict and post-conflict societies.

DAVID J. THERKELSEN

David J. Therkelsen was a public relations manager for 23 years, most of them in American Red Cross organisations, went on to a general management career, including serving as CEO of two Red Cross units, and currently heads a mental health counselling agency. He is a past president of Minnesota Chapter, PRSA, and past national chair of the Social Services Section. He teaches public relations courses at the University of Minnesota School of Journalism and Mass Communication. He has authored or co-authored 20 articles, including the much-cited message to action model.

JANE TONGE

Dr. Jane Tonge is a Senior Lecturer in Marketing Communications at Manchester Metropolitan University Business School, where she gained her doctorate. She also holds an honours degree in History from Cambridge University and an MA in Public Relations from Manchester Metropolitan University, where she focused on the strategic role of public relations in local government. Jane's research interests are public relations, networks and networking, small and medium-sized enterprises, gender issues and arts marketing. Jane is a former public relations practitioner, working in-house for a housing association and in local government, and as a manager in a business-to-business public relations consultancy with a range of national and international clients. She also set up and ran her own freelance public relations consultancy business.

ROBERT I. WAKEFIELD

Dr Robert I. Wakefield is associate professor of communication at Brigham Young University. He concentrates his research on stakeholder relations and reputation in transnational entities, examining the impacts of globalisation, culture, activism, and other factors on these global practices of public relations. His publications include 'Public relations contingencies in a globalized world where even "glocalization" is not sufficient' in *Public Relations Journal*; 'World-class public relations: a model for effective public relations in the multinational' in *Journal of Communication Management*; and 'Theory of international public relations, the internet, and activism' in *Journal of Public Relations Research*. Before becoming a full-time scholar, Professor Wakefield practised and consulted on strategic public relations in 25 nations between 1990 and 2005. He received a PhD from the University of Maryland in 1997.

RICHARD WARREN

Richard C. Warren is principal lecturer in the HRM & OB Division in the Manchester Metropolitan University Business School. He was a merchant seaman for five years before working in the Commercial Department of the shipowners A.P. Moller-Maersk. His research interests are business ethics, corporate social resonsibility, corporate governance and industrial relations, and he has published articles in a variety of journals and the book *Corporate Governance and Accountability* (Liverpool Academic Press, 2000).

Frameworks and Contexts

1

This opening part of the book comprises five chapters that define the disciplinary boundaries and scope of the subject matters that this book focuses on. More specifically, in this opening part we examine and set out the core managerial framework that we have developed, drawing on management and public relations theory, to inform our understanding of the managerial responsibilities and management processes as applied in the communication/public relations context. Here we also explore the management skills and competencies required of practitioners working at a managerial level within the public relations functional area, and conclude by examining the concept and process of strategy-making and planning in the communication/public relations context.

Introduction

In writing this book, we did not set out to produce another introductory public relations textbook – there are far too many excellent textbooks of this nature already available to readers, whether they are students or practitioners. Rather, the aim of this book was to explore the managerial dimension of public relations and communication practice. All too often the term 'management' or 'managerial' is used within the communication/public relations field without sufficient thought or clarity as to what it means. We also sought to develop a framework that will enable both students and practitioners to identify and make sense of the key elements in managing any particular aspect of communication/public relations practice, and to improve the management of communication/public relations departments. The starting point in thinking about this textbook was a recognition that, despite the claim that public relations should be treated as a managerial function and should have a seat at the senior management table in many organisations, much of the writing about communication/public relations shows little recognition of how thinking about management and managerial practice has evolved in recent years. An examination of the bibliography in many contemporary communication/public relations textbooks reveals few references to contemporary managerial texts, and all too often references to management based on rather dated sources. Thus, we wanted not only to write a textbook that would re-examine how managerial practice could be applied to the communication/public relations field, but also to ensure that we drew on contemporary thinking about management and managerial practice.

In Part One of the book, we sought to examine the core of managerial framework that we believe could be applied to most areas of communication/public relations practice. Establishing a managerial framework for the communication/public relations function also led us to consider other important dimensions of the management function that might apply equally to communication/public relations domain, namely managerial skills and competencies and how they might manifest themselves in terms of communication practice and leadership as applied to the communication function. The final important area we considered in Part One of the book was that of strategy and planning for communication/public relations. Here again a review of the existing literature suggested some confusion, or at least ambiguity, in the use of the terms 'strategy' and 'planning' in this context.

Having established our managerial framework and considered how some of the dimensions of management might apply to communication/public relations in Part One, in the remaining chapters of the book we examine a number of specialist areas of public relations practice, in each case examining not only the issues and considerations surrounding that area of practice, but also drawing on the common managerial framework to explore the management of communication practice in that particular field. In Part Three, we also examine some of the professional considerations that impinge upon the management of communication/public relations departments, notably ethical and legal considerations.

The writing of this book has involved bringing together a number of experts in specific areas of communication/public relations practice, each of whom added their specific insights and knowledge of these specialist areas. In each case, however, we have asked these experts also to examine their subject area through the lens of our managerial framework and to consider the managerial implications for practice in their area. Here we have assembled a team of contributors from both the academic and professional worlds, which we believe provides the appropriate mix of academic and professional perspectives on the subject.

CHAPTER GUIDE AND CONTRIBUTORS

Chapter 1 sets the scene for the rest of the book, examining the current operating environment in which public relations practitioners work, and environmental forces which shape the working environment and the challenges that contemporary organisations face. Chapter 2 sets our underlying managerial framework, which informs much of the discussion of managerial practice in the communication/public relations context in the rest of the book. Here we also explore the development of managerial thinking and managerial theory over the years and set this in context with the way management has been discussed in the public relations literature. In Chapter 3 we explore the area of practitioner competencies, attributes and skills, relating these to both the managerial and technical work that practitioners perform. Chapter 4 examines the concept of leadership and its application to the communication/public relations field and considers the key attributes of leaders and their role in the communication/public relations context. Chapter 5, which concludes Part One, focuses on the concepts of strategy and planning and explores the development of thinking about these concepts from a managerial and communication/public relations perspective.

Part Two draws on the managerial framework advanced in Part One, and begins to explore a number of communication/public relations functions or contexts from a managerial perspective. Chapter 6 looks at the area of corporate branding and corporate reputation management and explores the way in which corporate brands are developed, sustained and defended, and the managerial process involved in developing and sustaining corporate brand/reputation. Chapter 7 looks at the area of government relations and public affairs, and examines the specialist area of communication practice and the important role it plays in managing the interface between organisations and businesses and government and government bodies. Chapter 8 looks specifically at government communication – at how government departments develop their own communication programmes and manage the communication process with citizens and businesses and other bodies. Chapter 9 focuses on consumer and business-to-business communication and explores the way in which organisations and businesses manage the communication process with key customer and business partners. Chapter 10 looks at the specialist area of financial communication and financial public relations, the most regulated and perhaps the most controversial areas of communication. Chapter 11 shifts the focus away from business communication to the not-for-profit sector, and looks at the important role played by communication/public relations for charities and voluntary bodies as well as in fundraising and other areas. Chapter 12 looks at the important area of internal or employee communication and the important role that communication plays in achieving organisational missions and goals. Chapter 13 is concerned with the world of agency/consultancy work; it examines the way in which public relations agencies/ consultancies interact with clients and client organisations and explores the process of managing consultancy operations. Chapter 14 focuses on the increasingly important area of the internet and the impact of Web 2.0 communication, exploring how the increasing prevalence of the internet has changed the business communication model that many organisations rely upon and the way individuals obtain information, supply information and interact in an e-commerce-based trading environment. Chapter 15 focuses on the area of issues management, exploring the way in which organisations monitor, analyse and attempt to manage the impact of issues of public policy and business on their operations.

In Part Three we look at three specialist areas impinging on the work of other functions. In Chapter 16 we examine the ethical dimension of communication/public relations management, exploring the ethical and moral dilemmas that practitioners face, the importance of professionalisation of the practice and how these influences affect the role of practitioners in their day-to-day operations. Chapter 17 examines the increasing emphasis given to corporate social responsibility within the corporate sector and explores the ways in which organisations are attempting to respond to the changing social environment and the changing expectations of corporate behaviour in countries around the world. Chapter 18 examines the legal dimension of public relations/mediation practice, examining the legal constraints on and considerations that must affect both organisational behaviour and communication/public relations practice. Chapter 19 turns the focus to the international/global arena and explores the key considerations that any organisation wishing to expand its organisational operations internationally/globally needs to take into account.

Public Relations Journey into Management: Building Bridges between Public Relations and other Managerial Functions

1

Barbara DeSanto

Key Themes

- Reviewing the main categories of public relations literature to understand why and how public relations history has internally and externally contributed to the definition of what the profession is today
- Understanding the implications of public relations history in the profession's quest to be recognized at the managerial level
- Considering eight challenges facing public relations professionals as they move into and work in management positions at different organizational levels

---

INTRODUCTION

Through the Looking Glass: Turning an Inward Focus into Outward Relationships

When Grunig and Hunt (1984) described public relations as 'the management of communication between an organization and its publics' (p. 6), their intention was undoubtedly one of seeking to position public relations as a mainstream 'managerial' function within organizations, to be treated on a par with the other more traditional organizational functions such as human resource management, finance, production, and marketing. While perhaps recognizing that such a claim for equal status in the functional hierarchy within organizations might prove controversial, it is highly unlikely that Grunig and Hunt would have forecast the degree of debate and controversy that has gradually emerged around the use of the term 'management' to describe the function and practice of public relations. Indeed, public relations scholars perhaps saw little reason to view the use of the term 'management' *per se* as at all controversial; yet as we will show later, by the time that Grunig and Hunt's book was published, a long-running debate was already well under way among management scholars about the nature of management and managerial work. It is not, however, our intention to challenge the basic premise contained in Grunig and Hunt's definition or any of the many other definitions of public relations, namely, that public relations should be treated as a 'managerial function' as opposed to a largely communication oriented, technical function. Moreover, we acknowledge and support the arguments that for public relations to be fully effective in a managerial role, practitioners need to have access to and influence among the senior management team within organizations. However, as a number of academic and professional commentators have pointed out, such access and influence has to be earned, and here we argue that this demands that practitioners demonstrate the necessary skills and business acumen to deserve their place at the 'top table' within organizations. What we intend to do within this book is to examine in more depth what the 'management' of public relations involves, what management practices and processes are involved, and what skills and competences those aspiring to be communication/public relations 'managers' need to possess or develop.

The Excellence Concept

Perhaps the single most influential piece of extended research that has been conducted into public relations practice over the past two decades has been the so-called Excellence Study conducted by James and Larissa Grunig and their co-researchers, which set out to address the fundamental question of 'How, why, and to what extent does communication affect the achievement of organizational objectives?' (Grunig, Grunig, & Dozier, 1992: 2). In articulating some 14 principles of 'excellent' public relations, the research team emphasized the importance of having public relations recognized as a distinctive 'management function' in its own right, and argued that senior practitioners should have access to and participate in the strategic decision-making process within their respective organizations. However, it clear that in advancing their theoretical framework, the excellence team was concerned almost exclusively with the most senior levels of management and with the ability of public relations to function effectively at that level by contributing to strategy and policy making within organizations. While acknowledging the importance of such senior level involvement for public relations, as many studies have shown, such involvement remains far from the 'norm' found in most organizations where public relations is often still treated as a largely functionary and tactical function. Moreover, we also believe that this emphasis on public relations involvement at the 'strategic decision-making level' within organizations tends to overlook the need to also examine public relations 'management' as manifested at the operational/departmental levels. In fact, if we are to develop a comprehensive theory of communication/public relations management there is a need to explain and understand both the strategic and operational dimensions of management as manifest in different levels of public relations practice. Indeed, management scholars (e.g. Hales, 1986, 1999; Mintzberg, 1994; Stewart, 1976, 1982) have acknowledged that much management time is spent on what is often quite 'messy', largely tactical and operational activities, rather than dealing with the more rarefied levels of policy and strategy formulation. This distinction between tactical and strategic management work is something again which we intend to clarify, examining how these terms apply in the context of public relations work.

The Public Relations Society of America's Manager Description

An interesting perspective on the application of the management concept in the public relations context can be seen in the Public Relations Society of America (PRSA) *Professional Career Guide* (1993) (see Figure 1.1), which describes the interpretation of the various career levels in public relations work. Here, the term 'manager' is identified as the middle level of the five career levels, which like Grunig et al.'s excellence model, suggests that some time and experience in the practice are needed before it is possible for practitioners to assume managerial responsibility. The PRSA's description of managerial work provides a useful reference point in developing our explication of managerial work and managerial responsibilities at different levels within organizations, and in particular, how they apply in public relations work.

The *Career Guide*'s description of a public relations manager focuses on skills and knowledge needed to be a manager, including responsibility for 'planning, organizing, directing, and motivating staff, budgeting, problem-solving and problem identification. Managers must be able to 'sell' programs, both inside the department and in other areas of the organization. They often conduct meetings and make presentations or speeches, analyze situations and develop plans of action' (PRSA, 1993: 4).

Thus, in developing our perspective of the manager's role and managerial work in the communication/public relations context, we have drawn on both the existing academic and professional literature to help formulate what we believe is a more comprehensive and effective framework for examining the work of practitioners operating at different levels within organizations and therefore, by implication, having different levels of responsibility in terms of both tactical/operational and more strategic managerial tasks and challenges.

Here, the PRSA *Professional Career Guide* provides a useful basis for examining the types of tasks typically performed as a combination of strategic and tactical, representative of both the levels below and above the managerial level (see Figure 1.2).

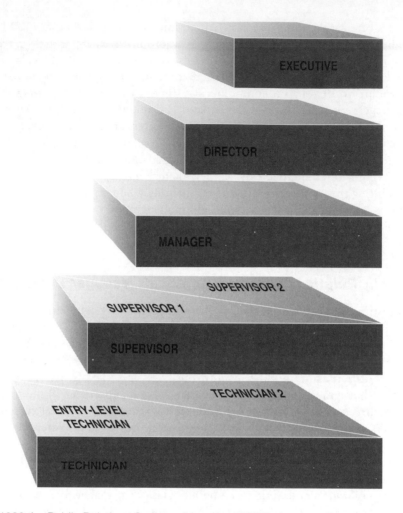

Note: In 1993 the Public Relations Society of America (PRSA) developed a career progression structure for practitioners. Each step was defined by roles and responsibilities. The emphasis in this book is on the manager/director levels.

FIGURE 1.1   The PRSA Five Levels of Career Practice

Source: Public Relations Professional Career Guide © 1993 by The PRSA Foundation.

In this book we attempt to provide insights into how public relations practitioners can address such managerial challenges, which will enhance not only the individual practitioner's status, but also the status of the profession. Armed with this knowledge, we believe practitioners will be better equipped to manage the communication/public relations function more effectively while also demonstrating a general level of managerial competence comparable to that of managerial-level staff from other functions within the organization.

MANAGER

GENERAL RESPONSIBILITIES:

Responsible for departmental operations and for constituency and issue trend analysis. Necessary skills include planning, organizing, leading, evaluating, problem solving and consulting.

TITLES AND JOB DESCRIPTIONS:

Manager of Internal Communications

The person in this position manages all "mass" communications with employees. The function often includes periodical publications, newsletters, magazines, video programs, speeches and specialized materials designed to communicate with employees.

Manager of Member Relations

This title is used in membership organizations such as associations and societies, where members are a special constituency and are as important as customers or shareholders in other types of organizations. The function usually includes responsibility for newsletters, magazines, issues papers, the organization's annual report, audiovisual presentations, and (sometimes) special materials related to the organization's annual membership conference.

Manager of Investor Relations

Manages activities related to communicating the company's financial matters to investors, stock brokers and financial analysts.

Manager of Marketing Communications

Manages the preparation of marketing-related communications materials, public relations and promotions. In consumer product organizations marketing activities may dominate the public relations function, and corporate public relations may serve primarily in the area of investor relations.

Community Relations Manager

Manages public relations activities related to the locations where the organization has a major presence. This includes the city where the organization is headquartered as well as locations regional/district offices, distribution and manufacturing facilities. In corporations, this function generally includes liaison with local news media, the management of the company's corporate contributions program, and planning and conducting major special events.

Manager of Research

Responsible for managing all activities related to the gathering of information needed in management decision-making, as well as in the production of publications, audiovisual presentations and speeches.

Manager of Audiovisual Communications

Manages all activities and personnel involved in planning and producing videotape and multimedia presentations intended to convey specific messages to a precisely/defined constituency.

Issues Manager

Manages the function responsible for gathering information on political, economic and social trends that may affect the future of the organization and its products. The function may be staffed, or services may be provided by outside sources.

OTHER TITLES:

Typical titles in public relations and advertising agencies;
    Director of Public Relations
    Director of Account Services
In management consulting firms:
    Director of Communication Services
    Director of Media Relations

FIGURE 1.2   PRSA Descriptions of Managerial Responsibilities

Source: Public Relations Professional Career Guide © 1993 by The PRSA Foundation.

Developing an Identity and Finding an Organizational Home: Learning from the Past

Things often make more sense when we understand what has preceded the position/ situation we find ourselves in right now. So it is with public relations. Only when we fully appreciate how public relations itself has come to be understood, including how professionals and academics think about it as a concept, function, or discipline, is it possible to carry out a meaningful examination of what it means to manage in the public relations context and what the challenges are that public relations managers face. This section looks back at the last four decades of public relations research by academics and professionals to identify the main perceptions of public relations as a starting point to use in moving into the managerial ranks.

By the time that Grunig and Hunt's (1984) book was published, public relations had begun to emerge from journalism and communication studies curricula as an academic discipline in its own right. By the latter quarter of twentieth century, public relations had become established as a full-fledged, stand-alone major course of study in colleges and universities, beginning in the United States in the 1970s and 1980s, followed by rapid curriculum growth in many parts of Europe in the late 1980s and 1990s. Now, in the twenty-first century, academic programs of study in public relations can be found in countries around the world. Such rapid growth in the number and sophistication of academic and professional training programs in public relations can be seen as an indicator of the growing recognition afforded to public relations as an established 'management-level' discipline within the business world, albeit that such recognition may vary from sector to sector, between organizations, as well as varying across cultures and contexts around the world.

The establishment of formal academic programs in public relations has generated a plethora of academic research focusing on public relations from a variety of perspectives, including the ongoing development and maturing of the profession and practice as it earned its way into different management levels. Perspectives ranged from the effects of gender on managerial or technical roles (e.g., Toth & Grunig, 1993; Creedon, 1991; Choi & Hon, 2002), through the development of the four-step process at different levels of management (e.g., Cutlip & Center, 1971) and the boundary-spanning capabilities of public relations practitioners (e.g. Aldrich & Herker, 1977; Jackson & Center, 1975), to the concept of relationship management as a function of public relations (Ledingham & Bruning, 2000; Grunig & Repper, 1992).

A FRAMEWORK FOR REVIEWING THE PUBLIC RELATIONS LITERATURE

Understanding what research has been completed in the public relations field provides a useful framework within which to develop this book on public relations management. Pavlik (1987) produced one of the first assessments of what research had been done and what research directions might be useful, and *Public Relations Review*, one of the leading public relations academic journals devotes one of its issues to an annual index of research articles and publications in the field. I have developed a framework for categorizing the public relations literature into a number of core thematic areas which, although used primarily as a teaching aid, also serves as a useful way of framing the literature.

I reviewed a wide range of sources along with other indices covering more than 30 years of public relations research, dividing the identified material into four broad thematic categories (see Figure 1.3): (1) public relations as a concept or idea; (2) public relations as a function; (3) public relations as a process; and (4) public relations as a role. These four distinct but related areas are important because each contributes to building an overall perspective of what public relations is and what it should and can do. Moreover, arguably each of these thematic areas also contribute to building an understanding of the 'messy' work of public relations *management*, where functions, departments, and managers overlap in their work.

The outer four areas of the model represent four interrelated areas of research that, when viewed together, reveal something of the contested nature of our understanding

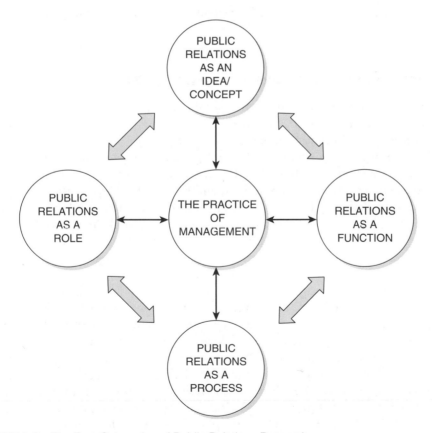

FIGURE 1.3   The Four Categories of Public Relations Research

of public relations as a discipline, as a form of professional practice, and as a set of work-related roles that practitioners perform. Here I have pointed to the strong self-reflecting inward focus of much of this research, with little attention paid to exploring the external context and/or environment outside of the public relations field itself. The concept of 'management' in the public relations context has admittedly been discussed in some depth, particularly within the roles literature, but often without drawing comparisons with how management is understood in other functional disciplines, most notably within the mainstream management literature.

For the purposes of this book, we have placed the concept and practice of management at the center of this model to focus attention on understanding what might constitute the tasks and responsibilities of those practitioners occupying 'managerial level' roles within organizations; this may also help to highlight where and how practitioners can make substantial contributions to the achievement of broader organizational objectives at all levels of management, not just at the most senior level. Public relations practitioners who begin to think beyond their own functional area and link their communication objectives to the business/organizational objectives of other managers are then in a position to demonstrate the impact that communication/public relations can and should have in organizations. In short, they can participate in the conversation where strategy is developed and implemented.

Category 1: Public Relations as a Concept/Idea

The first of these categories or areas contains literature concerned with public relations as a 'concept or idea', and here researchers have sought to uncover a single universal definition of public relations. In essence, agreeing on one definition has the potential benefit of facilitating clearer recognition of what public relations is and stands for. In the 1940s, American practitioner and PRSA founding member Rex Harlow (Cutlip, Center, and Broom, 1985) undertook the monumental task of gathering together all of the definitions of public relations he could find. From the nearly 500 definitions that he catalogued, he worked with the fledgling PRSA to create one 'official' definition that he hoped would be sufficiently broad yet sufficiently definitive to be universally recognized and accepted. The resulting definition (see Figure 1.4), while comprehensive, was not terribly memorable or useful as a shorthand way of explaining public relations to a wider audience. And, of course, while the PRSA and other professional bodies may have similar official definitions, this has not stopped academics and professionals from continuing to devise new definitions, which may add to the lack of clarity about what the term 'public relations' stands for. Of course, the challenge of identifying one universal definition is made all the more difficult by the realization that public relations practice and people's understanding of it may well vary in different environmental or organizational contexts, as well as over time and in different cultures, all of which suggests there may be a need to at least adapt how public relations is defined.

OFFICIAL STATEMENT ON PUBLIC RELATIONS

(Formally adopted by PRSA Assembly, November, 1982)

Public relations helps our complex, pluralistic society to reach decisions and function more effectively by contributing to mutual understanding among groups and institutions. It serves to bring private and public policies into harmony.

Public relations serves a wide variety of institutions in society such as businesses, trade unions, government agencies, voluntary associations, foundations, hospitals, schools, colleges and religious institutions. To achieve their goals, these institutions must develop effective relationships with many different audiences or publics such as employees, members, customers, local communities, shareholders, and other institutions, and with society at large.

The managements of institutions need to understand the attitudes and values of their publics in order to achieve institutional goals. the goals themselves are shaped by the external environment. The public relations practitioner acts as a counselor to management and as a mediator, helping to translate private aims into reasonable, publicly acceptable policy and action.

As a management function, public relations encompasses the following:

- Anticipating, analyzing and interpreting public opinion, attitudes, and issues that might impact, for good or ill, the operations and plans of the organization.
- Counseling management at all levels in the organization with regard to policy decisions, courses of action, and communication, taking into account their public ramifications and the organization's social or citizenship responsibilities.
- Researching, conducting, and evaluating, on a continuing basis, programs of action and communication to achieve the informed public understanding necessary to the success of an organization's aims. These may include marketing, financial, fundraising, employee, community or government relations, and other programs.
- Planning and implementing the organization's efforts to influence or change public policy.
- Setting objectives, planning, budgeting, recruiting and training staff, developing facilities – in short, managing the resources needed to perform all of the above.
- Examples of the knowledge that may be required in the professional practice of public relations include communication arts, psychology, social psychology, sociology, political science, economics, and the principles of management and ethics. Technical knowledge and skills are required for opinion research, public-issues analysis, media relations, direct mail, institutional advertising, publications, film/video productions, special events, speeches, and presentations.

In helping to define and implement policy, the public relations practitioner uses a variety of professional communication skills and plays an integrative role both within the organization and between the organization and the external environment.

FIGURE 1.4 PRSA Statement of Public Relations

Source: Formally adopted by PRSA Assembly, November 6, 1982 http://www.prsa.org/official statementonpublicrelations.

On the other hand, scholars such as Hutton (1999) have warned that unless public relations finds a way to develop one recognizable identity, it will continue to be relegated to the more technical ranks of practice charged with carrying out the decisions largely taken by others.

While the idea of finding one universally acceptable definition of public relations may prove an impossible challenge, what seems a more logical and achievable goal is

Characteristic of Excellent Public Relations Programs

I.   Program Level

    1. Managed strategically

II. Departmental Level

    2. A single or integrated public relations department
    3. Separate function from marketing
    4. Direct reporting relationship to senior management
    5. Two-way symmetrical model
    6. Senior public relations person in the managerial role
    7. Potential for excellent public relations, as indicated by:

        a. Knowledge of symmetrical model
        b. Knowledge of managerial role
        c. Academic training in public relations
        d. Professionalism

    8. Equal opportunity for men and women in public relations

III. Organizational Level

    9. Worldview for public relations in the organization reflects the two-way symmetrical model
    10. Public relations director has power in or with the dominant coalition
    11. Participative rather than authoritarian organizational culture
    12. Symmetrical system of internal communication
    13. Organic rather than mechanical organizational structure
    14. Turbulent, complex environment with pressure from activist groups

IV. Effects of Excellent Public Relations

    15. Programs meet communication objectives
    16. Reduces costs of regulation, pressure, and litigation
    17. Job satisfaction is high among employees

From *Excellence in Public Relations and Communication Management* (1992), edited by James E. Grunig, Lawrence Erlbaum Associates. Hillsdale, NJ, p. 28.

FIGURE 1.5   Grunig, Grunig, and Dozier's Characteristics of Excellent Organizations

to move toward the idea of identifying some more or less common core characteristics of public relations practice and the associated professional skills required of practitioners. For example, Guth and Marsh (2003) propose that the elements of 'management function', 'two-way communication', 'planned activity', 'research-based social science', and 'socially responsible' behavior form the core elements of any definition of public relations (p. 7). Wilcox, Cameron, Ault, and Agee (2003) identify the key words to defining public relations as including: 'deliberate, planned, performance, public interest, two-way communication, and management function.' (p. 5). Clearly these examples show that while the context and environment can greatly vary, the concept displays consistent elements and values. Similarly, as we have already pointed to earlier, one of the key outcomes of the 'excellence study' was the identification of a set of key characteristics of excellent communication and public relations practice, as shown in Figure 1.5 (Grunig, 1992; Grunig et al., 1992).

Category 2: Public Relations as a Function

The second category of literature focuses on the idea of public relations as a function that relates to the purpose for which public relations exists. Here the literature looks at what public relations should or can contribute to the organization's overall goals and objectives and in what specific and general ways. Examples include public relations as the conscience of the organization (social responsibility and reputation management), the organizational mouthpiece (media relations), the environmental scanner (issues management or environmental interpreter), or, one of the most often cited, the boundary spanner. Grunig et al. (1992) maintained that the level at which these functions are performed affects whether the practitioner is thought of as a 'manager' or a 'technician', although their focus was limited to identifying the truly excellent organizations and the senior executives in them. Nevertheless, the logic here is that the location of the function within the organizational hierarchy is likely to reflect the dominant coalition's perceptions of public relations which, in turn, will have a significant influence on how far practitioners are able to enact a predominantly managerial rather than technical role. In addition to its relationship with the dominant coalition, public relations must also define its position and contribution in relation to other mainstream organizational functions and levels, such as marketing, human resources, legal, and finance.

Interestingly, 'crisis management' is the one of the areas that appears fairly well defined as the responsibility of the public relations function. One plausible explanation for this link between public relations and crisis management is the often very strong media component present in crisis situations. This harkens back to public relations roots as a 'journalist-in-residence' function (Grunig & Hunt, 1984: 22), when organizations attracted journalists into becoming advocates for them because of their well-developed understanding of the media and how to use it for organizational objectives. Even in crisis situations, however, the level at which the function is carried out depends on the organization's understanding of the public relations function. At one extreme public relations might operate simply as a 'mouthpiece' for disseminating the company line supplied by dominant coalition members, while at the other extreme public relations practitioners may play an active part in helping to construct strategically important messages that might impact significantly on the organization's short- and long-term objectives. Crisis management also provides an interesting insight into how fluid yet crucial the functional level of public relations can be. During a crisis, public relations is often sought out by dominant coalition members for ideas and input, yet once the crisis declines in intensity, public relations may often be relegated to fulfilling a much more routine role within the organization until the next crisis flares up. Figure 1.6 shows typical titles and responsibilities the PRSA has identified as functions of public relations managers.

Category 3: Public Relations as a Process

The third category/area of literature concerns the view of public relations as a 'process'. This area has attracted significant research interest over the years as scholars have attempted to map, explain and conceptualize the public relations process. Here,

MANAGER

TYPICAL TITLES:

Issues Manager

Manager of Audiovisual Communications
Manager of Community Relations
Manager of Corporate Communications
Manager of Internal Communications
Manager of Investor Relations
Manager of Marketing Communications
Manager of Media Relations
Manager of Member Relations
Manager of Public Relations/Public Information
Manager of Publications
Manager of Research

USUAL RESPONSIBILITIES AT THIS LEVEL:

Using advanced skills to provide constituency and issue trend analysis; departmental management including planning, organizing, budgeting, leading, controlling, evaluating and problem solving,

SKILLS & KNOWLEDGE TYPICALLY REQUIRED AT THIS LEVEL:

For each item, rank your competency on a scale from 1–10 where 1 = Poor, 5 = Average and 10 = Outstanding
— **Managing research projects**
— **Managing internal communications**
— **Managing media relations**
— **Managing external communications**
— **Developing strategics for actions**
— **Writing objectives**
— **Reviewing proposals and plans**
— **Analyzing proposed budgets**
— **Selling public relations programs to internal/external clients**
— **Presenting to groups**
— **Managing speakers bureaus**
— **Conducting staff conferences**
— **Giving media interviews**
— **Interviewing, selecting personnel**
— **Training staff members**
— **Coordinating the writing of public relations plans**
— **Measuring results**
— **Directing contributions programs**
— **Supporting marketing with public relations activities**
— **Selecting, preparing spokespersons**
— **Supporting fundraising with public relations activities**

FIGURE 1.6 The Public Relations Professional Career Guide Description of Managerial Titles Knowledge and Skills

Source: Public Relations Professional Career Guide © 1993 by The PRSA Foundation.

for example, perhaps the best-recognized model of the public relations process is the ubiquitous four-step process model, consisting of research, planning, communication, and evaluation, pioneered by Cutlip and Center (1971) in the fourth edition of their classic textbook, *Effective Public Relations*. Indeed, the four-step process has spawned a plethora of models describing the sequence of actions to achieve communication/public relations objectives. One possible suggestion for the wealth of literature in this area is that is perhaps the easiest or most visible area to study because researchers can, in effect, observe the sequence of actions as they unfold, producing results that can be relatively straightforward. Indeed, the majority of public relations textbooks tend to adopt a 'process perspective' in examining the field and tend to portray the process as essentially a 'linear one' in which activities and actions follow in a logical sequential way, which of course is not always the case in reality. Moreover, the examination of 'process' generally tends to be rather superficial and inward-looking rather than seeking to explore where and how public relations might interlink with other managerial functions and processes that contribute to the realization of organizational objectives.

Finally, a common theme in the public relations literature is the exhortation that that practitioners should be involved in the strategic management process within organizations (part of the dominant coalition) and should contribute to such decisions. In reality, as we have suggested earlier, public relations tends to be omitted from the top policy-making/decision-making work of the dominant coalition and is often only called in to help implement and communicate strategic decisions developed at a higher level in the absence of any public relations input (White & Dozier, 1992). The implementation of strategic decisions made without public relations input simply reinforces the tactical emphasis found in much of the process of public relations work. Moreover, if one examines the management literature, little if any reference can be found to a role for public relations, particularly in the context of any discussion of strategic decision-making (e.g., Mintzberg, 1994; Johnson & Scholes, 1993). This mutual lack of acknowledgement on the part of public relations and management scholars reflects the difficulty in practice of integrating public relations into the mainstream management processes in the majority of organizations.

Category 4: Public Relations as a Role

The final major category of literature identified in this model centers around the concept of public relations as a 'role' enacted within an organizational setting. The emergence of practitioner roles theory has provided the basis for explaining the recurring patterns of behavior adopted by practitioners in response to the situations they face and, importantly, the expectations of others as to how they should conduct themselves in their jobs. Research into practitioner role enactment is particularly relevant to our examination of the managerial dimensions of public relations work as it has provided the basis for identifying the managerial and technical profiles and specific responsibilities of practitioners working within different organizational structures. Although we will examine the application of roles theory to public relations in greater depth in Chapter 2, where it will be used to inform and underpin our own model of public relations management, here it may be useful to briefly outline the principal practitioner role typologies advanced by Glen Broom (Broom, 1982, Broom & Smith, 1979) and subsequently by David Dozier (Dozier,

TABLE 1.1 The Traditional Four- and Two-Role Typology Models

Four-Role Public Relations Typology	Two-Role Public Relations Typology
Expert Prescriber	
Problem-solving Facilitator	Manager
Communication Facilitator	
Communication Technician	Communication Technician

1984; Broom & Dozier, 1986, Dozier & Broom, 1995). The two dominant roles frameworks that have emerged from roles research, Broom and Smith's four-role typology and Dozier's manager–technician dual typology, are outlined in Table 1.1.

As will be examined further in Chapter 2, Broom and Smith's four-role typology and, more particularly, Dozier's (1984) manager–technician role dichotomy have provided a quite robust framework for broadly explaining practitioner work patterns within the industry. However, these role typologies are acknowledged to be simplifications of the range of activities that practitioners may perform in the course of their jobs and as such are open to a variety of criticisms, not the least being the way in which they conceptualize the essential components of managerial work in the public relations context – a weakness we will explore further in Chapter 2.

Despite such criticisms, roles research has provided some valuable insights into a range of influences on the way practitioners perform their jobs as well as into the status and influence of public relations within organizations. Here, in particular, roles researchers (e.g. Broom & Dozier, 1995; Toth, Serini, Wright, & Emig, 1998; Cline, Toth, Turk, Walters, Johnson, & Smith 1986; Choi & Hon, 2002) have established a strong link between role enactment and gender, arguing that women have traditionally been under-represented within managerial ranks and paid less than their male counterparts for performing similar work. One further comment worth making at this stage is that the vast majority of practitioner roles studies have been conducted among samples of practitioners themselves, rather than gathering data about how other functions and, in particular, how senior management see the role performed by practitioners. Only a few studies, such as Wright (1995) and Hon (1998), have attempted gather this 'outside-in' perspective, which can provide a valuable reality check on how the function is really perceived by powerful elites and others within the organizational setting.

CHALLENGES FACING PUBLIC RELATIONS MANAGERS

This brief overview and classification of key areas of public relations literature helps to highlight some key challenges that we believe public relations practitioners and academics have to address if they are, first, to develop a better appreciation of the managerial dimensions of the work practitioners perform, and second, to secure both externally and internally the recognition and respect for the public relations function. Here we have identified eight key challenges that public relations faces in gaining wider recognition as a mainstream organizational function working alongside other organizational functions, rather than operating in isolation. Each challenge represents an opportunity for professionals and academics to explore public relations as a management function. Considering these eight challenges individually and collectively provides insights into why current thinking about the management function in the communication/public relations context often remains poorly developed and, in many senses, ambiguous. It also suggests areas in which progress needs to be made if public relations is to be recognized widely as a serious and important management function. The eight challenges identified are:

1. The ongoing challenge of defining public relations.
2. Organizational and social ignorance of the value of public relations efforts to organizational efforts.
3. The lack of a formally recognized managerial-level function for public relations within the organization.
4. The overlap and/or encroachment of other managerial functions on public relations functions and roles.
5. The size of the public relations function/presence in most organizations.
6. The breadth and variety of public relations practitioner roles.
7. The varied background of public relations practitioners.
8. The lack of general managerial/business education for public relations technicians and managers.

Challenge #1: *Defining public relations*

As mentioned earlier, how public relations is defined continues to be a problem for both practitioners and academics. Despite a veritable explosion of academic and professional textbooks and publications devoted to the subject, there has been, if anything, even more controversy over how the boundaries of the discipline or function should be defined. The growth of concern over ethics and corporate social responsibility, the emergence of debates about terminological distinctions such as 'corporate communications' or 'public affairs' and 'public relations', and the increasing use of controversial terms such as 'spin' and 'propaganda' have all added to the confusion. Naturally, the lack of consensus merely adds to the difficulty in establishing a clear understanding of what the term 'public relations' comprises and, hence, what needs to be managed. Ironically, a common theme found in many of the often-cited definitions of public relations is the notion of a function that is primarily concerned with the 'the management of communication between organizations and their publics or stakeholders'. However, while many of the definitions make reference to the idea of public relations having responsibility for 'managing' communication and relationships with organizational stakeholders, there is little elaboration of what such management processes involve, and equally, at what level within organizations this 'managerial function' occurs.

Challenge #2: *Organizational and social ignorance of the value of public relations to organizational and societal efforts*

Partly because of the lack of a widely accepted and understood definition of public relations, and partly because of the very diverse nature of public relations practice itself, understanding what value public relations can add to social causes, organizational objectives, or corporate outputs is also often confused, and at worst, completely misunderstood. Indeed, public relations has been seen as a form of propaganda, designed to mislead people for the greed of some organizational entity or to persuade people to behave in ways they might otherwise resist. The profession's failure to devise ways to communicate effectively what public relations is and what it can achieve has allowed commentators outside the profession to fill the vacuum and propagate the image of public relations as a manipulative force, working to obscure or cover up government blunders or corporate malfeasance, or engage in rather frivolous publicity stunts. Public relations receives very little recognition for its role in promoting important social change such as reductions in smoking and poor dietary practice, partly at least because much of this work is low visibility, taking place through the media or other third-party entities or venues. Clearly, in so far as the value of public relations continues to be misunderstood, it makes it all the more difficult for practitioners to gain recognition as performing a significant managerial function.

Challenge #3: *The lack of a commonly recognized place for public relations within the organizational structure*

A frequently cited complaint from practitioners is that public relations often does not have the appropriate access and reporting relationship it deserves and needs within organizations to be fully effective. Again such complaints can be traced at least in part to the lack of clear understanding of what public relations is and how it contributes to organizational goals. The authors' earlier research (e.g. DeSanto & Moss, 2004) found a range of reporting relationships and locations for the public relations function within organizations, in some cases reporting to marketing or even finance directors. Where public relations is positioned as subordinate to other managerial functions, it is impossible for public relations practitioners to be recognized as having equal status to other managers. As a consequence, public relations is unlikely to be working to its full potential as a contributor at the managerial level.

Challenge #4: *The overlap and/or encroachment of other managerial functions on public relations*

Linked to the previous challenge, because public relations is considered a subordinate function with a limited scope for operation, there is always the danger of other *organizational* functions, such as human resource management or marketing, encroaching into what might traditionally be recognized as the domain of public relations. This is particularly the case with marketing that has tended to annex the publicity element of public relations as a part of the marketing communications and has increasing sought to annex other elements of public relations work, particularly those concerned with stakeholder relationship-building activities. The emergence of concepts such as 'Marketing–PR' (Harris, 1993) typify this attempt by marketers to encroach into traditional public relations territory. The consequence of such encroachment is to often to diminish the standing of public relations and hence handicap its ability to realize fully the managerial potential of its role.

Challenge #5: *The size of the public relations function in most organizations*
The size of the department matters, because the more senior practitioners in small public relations departments with relatively few employees tend to find themselves stretched to serve the range of issues, from day-to-day activities to long-term efforts, that may confront them, the more difficult it becomes to free themselves to concentrate on those issues that may enable them to make a more significant contribution at the managerial level. Also, because there has been a noticeable trend toward 'downsizing' the number of staff employed in in-house communication/public relations departments over the past 15 years, it has been increasingly the case that in-house teams are often hard pressed simply to cope with all the routine communication work, let alone have time contemplate how they might make a more strategic contribution to their organizations. However, even in the face of such downsizing, the most talented practitioners have continued to participate as members of the senior management team (dominant coalition) within organizations. Here the key to retaining such a 'seat at the top table' is undoubtedly the practitioner's comprehension of the business and industry, and his/her ability to contribute effectively to business decision-making. Here the obvious challenge for practitioners is to maintain their understanding of business developments and issues as well as how communication affects the business perspective, not simply keep up with and address issues from a communication perspective.

Challenge #6: *The breadth and variety of public relations practitioner roles*
Linked to the previous issue of department size and recognition of the public relations in an organization is a further challenge for practitioners aspiring to operate at the managerial level, namely the breadth and variety of roles that practitioners may have to perform on a regular basis. The ability of public relations practitioners to turn their hand to a wide variety of problems and challenges is recognized as one of their strengths; but equally, in becoming generalists, practitioners may struggle to gain the depth of understanding of some aspect of management necessary to play a full working part in the eyes of the dominant coalition. In effect, practitioners may have to wear 'many hats', not all of which may fit comfortably on the head of someone wishing to operate at the most senior management level within the organization. Communication is part of all areas, whereas other managers

tend to operate in relatively specific, well-defined areas (human resources, marketing, operations); this presence in all organizational areas poses the special challenge for public relations managers to develop a wide and varied understanding of all organizational functions.

Challenge #7: *The varied background of public relations practitioners*
A further related challenge for those practitioners wishing to be accepted as members of the senior managerial team in organizations and wishing to develop their managerial competence lies in the varied background of most practitioners. In the main, practitioners have traditionally tended to enter the public relations profession from a journalistic background or from a variety of other fields, and rarely from a mainstream managerial background. While the lack of a mainstream management background need not prove an insurmountable barrier to practitioners participating in the work of the senior management team, clearly where practitioners lack such previous experience they are going to have to work at bridging any gaps in their knowledge, particularly in terms of their understanding not only of the relevant industry and business issues affecting their organizations, but also the key operational issues that determine the success of the business. While many practitioners have bridged this knowledge gap and assumed influential positions within their organization's senior management team, others continue to emphasize their media and publication production knowledge and skills and then bemoan their lack of inclusion at the most senior management levels.

Challenge #8: *The lack of general managerial/business training/education for public relations practitioners*
The fact that most practitioners typically have entered the public relations profession from journalism partly explains the lack of business knowledge and acumen shown by many practitioners. However, with the growth of public relations education both in the US and in the UK, and increasingly in other parts of the world, there are a growing number of well-qualified young practitioners entering the field each year. The problem with many of these educational programs, however, is that they tend to have been designed to develop the basic knowledge and skills required for entry-level jobs, often excluding anything other than a superficial examination of management theory and practice. This is particularly true of many of the public relations programs offered at US institutions, which have historically tended to be located in journalism or speech communication schools, rather than in business schools. The challenge here is to bring about some change in the balance of the curriculum offered to public relations students, exposing them to a greater degree of relevant management theory in addition to mainstream communication and public relations theories, and thereby helping those graduating to be better prepared to assume more managerial-level positions.

Viewed collectively as well as individually, these eight challenges help explain to a large degree why it has often proved difficult for public relations to be accepted as a mainstream 'management' function within organizations, and hence, why it is that senior practitioners have often struggled to gain acceptance as members of the dominant coalition within organizations. In the course of this book we will examine how such challenges impact on the way communication/public relations practitioners perform their roles within organizations, are viewed by other managerial and senior-level functions within their organizations, and also how, in some cases, practitioners have effectively addressed these challenges and, as a result, are able to perform a mainstream managerial role within their organizations. Our aim is that by helping public relations managers gain an awareness of the importance of understanding and drawing on relevant management theories and principles in performing their roles, they will be better able to earn the recognition and respect of their managerial counterparts within other areas of their organizations. This recognition, in turn, will enhance the understanding of the value of public relations in accomplishing organizational objectives.

SUMMARY

To summarize, this book's purpose is to demonstrate that the management of communication/public relations takes place at all levels within organizations, not just at the most senior strategic levels. Hence, our theories and examples will blend both the strategic and the operational elements of management practice. Through our new framework, described in the next chapter, we intend to set out an explanatory framework that will provide a platform for holistically explicating communication management as a function, process, and role at all organizational levels, as well as providing a basis for understanding how and why management practices in the communication/public relations context may differ between organizations and cultures.

REFERENCES

Aldrich, H., & Herker, D. (1977) Boundary spanning roles and organization structure. *Academy of Management Review*, 2, 217–230.

Broom, G.M. (1982) A comparison on sex roles in public relations. *Public Relations Review*, 5, 17–22.

Broom, G.M., & Dozier, D.M. (1986) Advancement for public relations role models. *Public Relations Review*, 12, 37–56.

Broom, G.M., & Smith G.D. (1979) Testing the practitioner's impact on clients. *Public Relations Review*, 5(3), 47–59.

Choi, Y., & Hon, L.C. (2002) The influence of gender composition in powerful positions on public relations practitioners' gender-related perceptions. *Journal of Public Relations Research*, 14, 229–63.

Cline, C.G., Toth, E.L., Turk, J.V., Walters, L.M., Johnson, N., & Smith, H. (1986) *The Velvet Ghetto: The Impact of the Increasing Percentage of Women in Public Relations and Business Communication*. San Francisco: IABC Foundation.

Creedon, P. J. (1991) Public Relations and women's work: Towards a feminist analysis of public relations roles. In L.A. Grunig & J.E. Grunig (eds), *The Public Relations Research Annual* (pp. 67–84). Hillsdale, NJ: Erlbaum.

(Continued)

(Continued)

Cutlip, S.M., & Center, A.H. (1971) *Effective Public Relations*, 4th ed. Englewood Cliffs, NJ: Prentice Hall.

Cutlip, S.M., Center, A.H., & Broom, G.M. (1985) *Effective Public Relations*, 5th ed. Englewood Cliffs, NJ: Prentice Hall.

DeSanto, B.J., & Moss, D.A. (2004) Rediscovering what PR managers do: Rethinking the measurement of managerial behavior in the public relations context. *Journal of Communication Management*, *19*, 179–96.

Dozier, D.M. (1984) Program evaluation and roles of practitioners. *Public Relations Review*, *10*, 13–21.

Dozier, D.M., & Broom, G.M. (1995) Evolution of the manager role in public relations practice. *Journal of Public Relations Research*, *7*, 3–26.

Grunig, J.E. (1992) Excellence in Public Relations and Communication Management. Hillsdate, NJ: Erlbaum.

Grunig, J.E., & Hunt, T. (1984) *Managing Public Relations*. Fort Worth, TX: Harcourt Brace.

Grunig, J.E., & Repper, F.C. (2002) Strategic management, publics, and issues. In J.E. Grunig (ed.), *Excellence in Public Relations and Communication Management* (pp. 117–58). Hillsdale, NJ: Erlbaum.

Grunig, L.A., Grunig, J.E., & Dozier, D.M. (2002) *Excellent Public Relations and Effective Organizations*. Mahwah, NJ: Erlbaum.

Guth, D.W., & Marsh, C. (2003) *Public Relations: A Values-Driven Approach*, 2nd ed. Boston: Allyn & Bacon.

Hales. C. (1986) What do managers do? A critical review of the evidence. *Journal of Management Studies*, *23*, 88–115.

Hales, C. (1999) Why do managers do what they do? Reconciling evidence and theory in accounts of managerial work. *British Journal of Management*, *10*, 335–50.

Harris, T.L. (1993) *The Marketer's Guide to Public Relations*. New York: Wiley

Hon, L.C. (1998) Demonstrating effectiveness in public relations: Goals, objectives, evaluation. *Journal of Public Relations Research*, *10*, 103–35.

Hutton, J.G. (1999) The definition, dimensions, and domain of public relations. *Public Relations Review*, *25*(2), 199–214.

Jackson, P., & Center, A.H. (1975) *Public Relations Practices: Managerial Case Studies and Problems*. Upper Saddle River, NJ: Prentice Hall.

Johnson, G., & Scholes, K. (1993) *Exploring Corporate Strategy*, 3rd ed. London: Prentice Hall.

Ledingham, J.A., & Bruning, S.D. (eds) (2000) *Public Relations as Relationship Management*. Hillsdale, NJ: Erlbaum.

Mintzberg, H. (1994) *The Rise and Fall of Strategic Planning*. New York: Free Press.

Pavlik, J.V. (1987) *Public Relations: What Research Tells Us*. Newbury Park, CA: Sage Publications Ltd.

PRSA (1993) *Public Relations Professional Career Guide*. New York: PRSA Foundation.

Stewart, R. (1976) *Contrasts in Management*. Maidenhead: McGraw-Hill.

Stewart, R. (1982) *Choices for the Manager*. Englewood Cliffs, NJ: Prentice Hall.

Toth, E.L., & Grunig, L.A. (1993) The missing story of women in public relations. *Journal of Public Relations Research*, *5*, 153–75.

Toth, E.L., Serini, S.A., Wright, D.K., & Emig, A.G. (1998) Trends in public relations roles: 1990–1995. *Public Relations Review*, *24*, 145–63.

White, J., & Dozier, D.M. (1992) Public relations and management decision making. In J.E. Grunig (ed.), *Excellence in Public Relations and Communication Management* (pp. 91–108). Hillsdale, NJ: Erlbaum.

Wilcox, D.L., Cameron, G.T., Ault, P.H., & Agee, W.K. (2003) *Public Relations: Strategies and Tactics*, 7th ed. Boston: Allyn & Bacon.

Wright, D.K. (1995) The role of corporate public relations executives in the future of employee communication. *Public Relations Review*, *21*(3), 181–98.

A Managerial Perspective of Public Relations: Locating the Function and Analysing the Environmental and Organisational Context

2

Danny Moss

Key Themes

- Understanding the application of the concept of management in the communication/public relations context
- Understanding the nature and practice of management
- A framework for understanding the management process in the communication/public relations context: C-MACIE
- The importance of external and internal context analysis
- Introduction to the key tools for conducting external and internal context and stakeholder analysis
- Understanding the process of management choices in terms of key communication policy and operational decisions
- Implementing communication policies and programmes
- Evaluating communication programmes and outcomes

A COMMUNICATION MANAGEMENT FRAMEWORK

As was outlined in the introduction, in writing this book we set out to develop an effective framework for understanding the concept and process of management as applied to organisational communication/public relations departments or functions. As we have already acknowledged, there is still considerable confusion over the terminology used in the organisational communications field, with a healthy debate continuing about how to distinguish between terms such as 'public relations' 'corporate communication(s)', 'organisational communication', 'public affairs', 'strategic communications', etc. In recent years, a number of strong schools of thought have emerged, perhaps most notably those calling for a reinterpretation of how the concept of corporate communications and public relations, in particular, should be understood (Cornelissen, 2004; van Riel, 1995; Schultz, Hatch, & Larsen, 2000). Rather than becoming embroiled in this ongoing debate about functional definitions and terminology, for the purposes of this book we have chosen to refer to all external and internal communications undertaken on behalf of an organisation as *organisational communications*, and we use the term *communication management* to refer to the application of management principles and practices in the organisational communications context. However, where appropriate, the distinctions are drawn between specialist areas of communication practice, or specialist sub-functions such as public affairs or issues management, in order to identify particular characteristics and process associated with specialist areas of organisational communications that may have particular implications or pose particular challenges for communications management processes.

Definitions

One of the main reasons why we are interested in the application of managerial concepts to the area of organisational communication is that among the numerous definitions of public relations and corporate communication (see Chapter 1) there is a strong emphasis on the positioning of public relations as essentially a function that sits within the management domain. We can see this emphasis in the following well-known definitions of public relations. According to Cutlip, Center, and Broom (2000: 6), 'Public relations is the *management* function that establishes and maintains mutually beneficial relationships between an organization and the publics on whom its success or failure depends' (emphasis added). For Grunig and Hunt (1984: 6), 'Public relations is the *management* of communication between an organisation and its publics' (emphasis added).

A similar managerial emphasis can be found in definitions of corporate communication(s): 'Corporate communications is a *management* function that offers a framework for the effective coordination of all internal and external communication with the overall purpose of establishing and maintaining favourable reputations with stakeholder groups.' (Cornelissen, 2008: 5).

However, it is one thing to describe the communication/public relations function as a *managerial* function, but what is often not questioned sufficiently is how far the term 'management' is universally understood, particularly within the communications field. While superficially, at least, there may be a more or less common understanding of what the term 'management' means, if one probes below the surface there appears to be little depth of understanding of what constitutes the core elements of management, or of managerial processes, particularly among communication scholars and professionals. Indeed, even amongst management scholars a healthy debate continues about how the concept and practice of management should be understood (see Hales, 1986, 2001).

Thus in order to advance an effective framework for understanding the nature and practice of 'communications management' in organisations – the management of all forms of internal and externally-directed communications on behalf of an organisation – it is first necessary to clarify our fundamental understanding of the term 'management' before going on to examine how it can be applied in the organisational communications context.

The Origins of the Concept of Management and the Manager's Role

The origins of the term 'management' can be traced to the Latin word *manus* (hand) and also to the French terms *ménage* (to handle or direct) and *ménager* (to use carefully, to husband). Thus, managers are, by definition, those people within organisations who hold and exercise responsibility for certain resources and/or other people within an organisation that need to be directed towards the achievement of specified goals. This largely directive view of management is reflected in work of classical management theorists such as Fayol (1949) who identified the key elements of management as comprising *planning, organising, coordinating, commanding* and *controlling* activities within an organisation. Similarly, Gulick and Urwick (1937) advanced the acronym 'POSDCORB' to represent what they suggested to be the primary elements of managerial responsibility: *planning, organising, staffing, directing, coordinating, reporting* and *budgeting*.

While popular at the time, this type of 'classical' perspective of management has come under strong criticism from management scholars on a number of grounds:

1. It represents an inward-looking, largely *administrative* view of management which reflects an early emphasis on the drive for efficiency through the 'control' of the workforce and the effective utilisation of resources.
2. It portrays management as largely 'the passive informational control of subordinates' – a view that has been replaced by a more 'participative view' of management with a emphasis on motivating employees through empowerment, co-determination and team working (see Mintzberg, 1994).
3. It places too much emphasis on the internal role of management, and fails to recognise that managers tend to spend as much time dealing with a wide range of *external* stakeholders as they do dealing with internal audiences.
4. However, perhaps the strongest criticisms of the classical perspective of management have focused on the argument that it fails to reflect accurately what it is that managers actually do (e.g. Mintzberg, 1973; Stewart, 1983).

While it is perhaps easy to label the classical perspective of management as a some-what outdated and essentially reductionist view of management (Mintzberg, 1973; Stewart, 1983), more recent reinterpretations of research into managerial work have questioned whether the classical model of management can be so readily dismissed, suggesting that it might, in fact, still broadly encapsulate many of the *core tasks and responsibilities* performed by managers (Hales, 1986).

What Do Managers Actually Do?

Research over the past three or more decades has focused on uncovering the main work activities of managers (Kotter, 1982; Mintzberg, 1973, 1990; Stewart, 1967, 1982, 1988). Here, for example, Kotter suggested that 'agenda setting', 'network building' and 'task execution' are among the most important elements of the manager and, in particular, senior manager roles. In his earlier work, Mintzberg (1973) identi-fied a set of ten related management work roles which he suggested can be grouped into three broad categories – *interpersonal, informational* and *decisional* roles (see Figure 2.1). These ten roles, Mintzberg argued at that time, *broadly* described the main areas of management activity and responsibility in organisations. Reflecting crit-ically on this earlier work, Mintzberg (2009) acknowledged that his list of manager work roles, 'while not without merit, was often criticised by practising managers as essentially too abstract and lifeless'. Mintzberg argued that the difficulty with attempt-ing to generalise about managerial roles and work is that so much managerial work is context-specific – to a specific organisation, function and situation. However, not-withstanding this criticism, Mintzberg has argued that some level of abstraction and generalisation is possible about what distinguishes managerial work.

'Indeed in an organization a good deal of what we generally accept as intrinsically "managerial" corresponds to specialised functions in the organization: managers brief subordinates, but their organizations have formal information systems; manag-ers serve as figureheads at ceremonial events despite the presence of public rela-tions specialists; managers have long been described as planners and controllers, while near them can be found planning departments. A good part of the work of managing involves doing what specialists do, but in ways that make use of the man-ager's special contacts, status and information' (Mintzberg, 2009: 43).

Reviewing the accumulated literature and documentation on managerial work, Mintzberg (2009) advanced a further general model intended to capture the essence of what managing involves. Here he argued that the manager has an *inward* respon-sibility for the unit, department or function, ensuring it does what it supposed to do by overseeing, directing, encouraging and controlling the actions of others. The manager relies on information to drive other people to take action. The man-ager also has an *outward*-facing responsibility for the unit/function's actions in

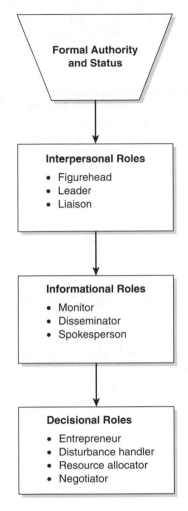

FIGURE 2.1   Mintzberg's (1973) Ten Manager Work Roles, p. 59. Reprinted by permission of Pearson Education Inc., Upper Saddle River, NJ.

relation to the rest of the organisation, or to the relevant stakeholders in the external environment – customers, suppliers, local community, etc. In short, Mintzberg suggested that managerial work takes place *on three planes* – from the conceptual to the concrete; with information transmitted through people; and then translated into action directly (2009: 49). This revised model of managing is shown in Figure 2.2. The model suggests that two core roles are performed on each of the three planes. On the *information plane*, managers *communicate* all around the unit and *control* the actions of others inside the unit. On the *people plane*, they *lead* (inside the unit) and *link* the unit to the outside world. Finally, on the *action plane*, manages *do* (take and direct actions) and *deal* with the outside world. For the individual manager two further roles strongly influence how they perform their overall function – the *framing* and *scheduling* of the work. Framing refers to managers' approach to or perception of

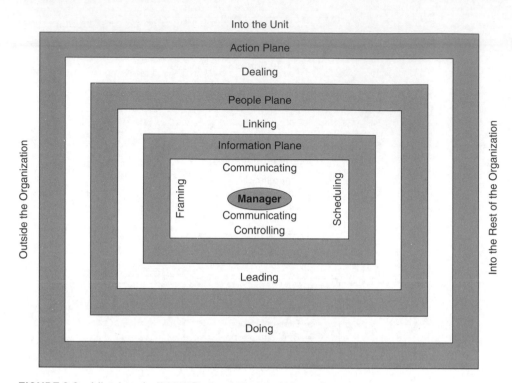

FIGURE 2.2   Mintzberg's (2009) Revised Model of Managing

the job (part of their world-view), and scheduling refers to how they organise their time and that of the rest of the unit to achieve their own and the unit's goals.

In a study published just over ten years after Mintzberg's original model of the manager role appeared, Hales (1986) produced a comprehensive review of some three decades of management research into the nature of managerial work. Hales pointed to the lack of common foci and methodology adopted within the various studies of managerial work which made it very difficult to identify any broad consensus about what might constitute the common elements of managerial work. Hales found that some studies had examined the substantive content of managerial work (what managers do), while others had examined the distribution of managerial time between work elements (how managers work), managerial interactions with others at work (who managers work with), or the informal elements of managerial work (what else do managers do). Moreover, Hales (1986: 93) suggested that there had been a shift in emphasis away from a static analytical approach providing a snapshot-view of managerial work 'towards ... attempts to capture the fluidity of managerial work in its different guises'.

Drawing on this body of evidence, Hales (1986, 2001) concluded that managers appear to perform both *specialist/technical* as well as *general/administrative work*, and the pattern of work will tend to vary, perhaps quite markedly, in different organisational settings and contexts. The latter conclusion may be of particular significance when considering the *manager's role in the organisational communications context*. Notwithstanding such variations and fluidity in managerial work patterns, Hales (2001:50) identified what research has suggested are a number of more less common activities that most managers perform to a greater or lesser degree:

1. Acting as a figurehead and leader for an organisational unit.
2. Networking: the formation and maintenance of contacts.
3. Monitoring and disseminating information.
4. Allocating resources to different work activities.
5. Directing and monitoring the work of subordinates.
6. Problem-solving and handling disturbances to work flows.
7. Negotiating with a broad constituency.
8. Innovating processes and products.
9. Planning and scheduling work.
10. Technical work relating to the manager's professional or functional specialism.

Of course, any attempt to prescribe what might be termed as a broad 'generic' set of managerial activities is always likely to attract criticisms from one quarter or another, as it is unlikely that any one set of activities can hope to adequately explain managerial work in all settings and contexts. Nevertheless, the set of broadly 'common' managerial activities outlined in the above list do seem to capture what appears to be the recurring pattern of activities reported in much of the research into the work of managers, which can be seen to focus around the following core areas:

- Day-to-day people management;
- Management of routine information;
- Day-to-day monitoring and maintenance of work processes;
- Non-managerial activities, such as conducting or assisting with technical work.

In short, as Hales (2001: 51) has observed, managers appear to 'share a common and probably inescapable preoccupation with routine day-to-day maintenance of work processes and people for whom they are responsible'. Here arguably some strong parallels can be drawn between these 'common' elements of managerial work and the 'classical principles' of management identified by early management scholars such as Fayol. However, such inferences need to be treated with a degree of caution since more recent research suggests that aspects of planning, coordinating and commanding-type activities have undergone a number of subtle as well as not so subtle changes over the years in response to changing environmental and organisational conditions.

Managerial Behaviour

Turning to managerial behaviour (how managers do what they do), as has already been suggested, managerial work emerges as essentially 'technical, tactical, reactive and frenetic' in nature (Hales,1986: 96). Indeed, even senior managers appear to have little time for planning and abstract strategy formulation being subject to constant interruption and engaging in frequent face-to-face meetings. Stewart (1983: 96), one of the leading scholars in the field of management research, captures something of the hectic nature of the typical manager's working day, describing a manager as someone who:

> lives in a whirl of activity, in which attention must be switched every few minutes from one subject, problem, and person to another; of an uncertain world where relevant information includes gossip and speculation.... It is a picture not of a manager who sits quietly controlling but who is dependent on many people, other than subordinates, with whom reciprocating relationships should be created; who need to learn how to trade, bargain and compromise.

What this picture of frenetic, fragmentary managerial activity suggests is that the notion of the manager as a strategist, planner and thinker is something of a 'myth' (Mintzberg, 1975), with managers finding themselves constantly diverted from their 'real' work by interruptions and capricious interpersonal contact. However, this apparently rather unstructured and *ad hoc* pattern of managerial work may be somewhat misleading because it may not distinguish clearly between what managers are observed or reported to 'do' (their *behaviour and activities*), and what managers are charged or seek to 'achieve' (their *tasks, responsibilities and functions*). This distinction between managerial 'work' as a set of *actual behaviours* and as a set of *desired* (either by managers or others) *outcomes* may at least in part help to explain why some managerial behaviour may not always seem, in practice or by design, instrumental to the achievement of specific functional responsibilities or intended organisational outcomes. On the other hand, as Brewer and Tomlinson (1964) and others have suggested, this somewhat erratic, verbal and apparently non-decisional character of much managerial work might be consistent with the manager's need to cope with increasing complex and rapidly changing environments through the rapid accumulation and analysis of information and the delegation of decisions. These observations about the characteristics of managerial work can be seen to apply equally to the work of managers operating across the range of organisational functions including communication/public relations.

Managerial Interaction and Communication

Interestingly, studies of managerial behaviour have identified managerial *interaction and communication* as key elements of what managers do and how they perform their roles. Indeed, studies of managerial behaviour have revealed that managers tend to spend 60–80% of their time communicating with others, imparting and receiving information predominantly through face-to-face interaction (Horne & Lupton, 1965; Kotter, 1982; Mintzberg, 1973). Here evidence suggests that managers spend much of their time engaged in *lateral* interaction and communication with other managers of the same status, whereas the degree of *vertical* communication appears to vary considerably among managerial positions within organisations. A good deal of managerial interaction also appears to involve managers responding to requests of others rather than initiating action themselves (Kotter, 1982). Managers also seem to spend a good deal of their time interacting and communicating with others on matters that, on the surface, appear to be wide-ranging and only tenuously connected to business matters, and are often informal in character (Dalton, 1959; Kotter, 1982).

The degree and significance of managerial communication, particularly with external individuals/groups, appears to vary widely by industry, organisation type and managerial position. However, most studies concur that managerial interaction and communication are a central feature of the management process – of what managers do and how they perform their roles. Indeed, Silverman and Jones (1976) have suggested that communication is not simply what managers spend a great deal of time doing, but is the medium through which managerial work *itself* is constituted.

The Informal Aspects of Managerial Work

Not all managerial work is necessarily concerned with the formal purposes of the organisation. Indeed, a number of studies over the years have pointed to the 'informal or unofficial' elements of managerial work (e.g., Dalton, 1959; Stewart, 1967, 1982) which are often associated with the internal power struggles and machinations through which managers attempt to preserve their positions, secure or defend their resources, or implement corporate policies at a local level in a more favourable way *vis-à-vis* local line and staff functions.

Although questions are often raised about whether such informal managerial activity is conducive or detrimental to 'proper' managerial work, one argument advanced is that such informal practices often serve as the 'lubricant' of successful organisational operation and even the preservative of managerial 'sanity'. Others have argued that it is difficult, if not impossible sometimes, to draw a clear distinction between what constitutes *formal* and *informal* practices as such distinctions will often depend on what individual managers perceive to be, or not to be, part of the job.

Kotter (1982) has also highlighted the important distinction between 'informal/unofficial' managerial practices and an 'informal management style' of doing things and of communicating with others. The latter refers to a more 'relaxed' approach to managerial interaction and communication, which can often prove highly effective in encouraging others to contribute to the achievement of the desired outcomes.

Summarising the Evidence about the Characteristics of Managerial Work

Despite the various caveats and cautions highlighted earlier about treating descriptions of managerial work as largely unproblematic, it is possible to distil some more or less common characteristics of managerial work from the body of extant research:

- Managerial work often combines a specialist/professional element and a more general managerial element.
- Managerial work is contingent upon, *inter alia*, function level, organisation (type, structure, size) and environment.
- The substantive elements of managerial work involve day-to-day responsibility for people and work processes and essential liaison, beneath which are subsumed more detailed work elements which in turn are characterised by: short, interrupted and fragmented activities; a preoccupation with the urgent, *ad hoc* and unforeseen, rather than the planned; and an obligation to react to events, problems and the requirements of others.
- Much managerial time is spent on day-to-day troubleshooting and *ad hoc* problems of organisation and regulation.
- Patterns of managerial communication vary in terms of what the communication is about and with whom it takes place.
- Managers appear to spend a lot of time accounting for and explaining what they do, in informal relationships and 'politicking'.
- Little time seems to be spent on any one activity, particularly on the conscious, systematic formulation of plans; rather planning and decision-making seem to take place as part of other activities.
- Managerial activities are subject to constant contradiction, cross-pressures and conflicts: much managerial work involves coping with and reconciling internal social and technical conflicts.
- There is often considerable choice exercised in terms of what is done as well as how things are done: an important part of managerial work involves setting the boundaries and negotiating over the work itself.
- Beyond these common characteristics, managerial work appears to vary considerably in terms of: the balance between different elements; the type of contact patterns; the patterns or rhythms of work; where work is carried out (the work context); the extent of dependency on others; the degree of interaction involved; and the degree of choice available.

Thus perhaps the key conclusion that emerges from this review of previous research into managerial work is that any search for uniformity and consistency in managerial work roles and practices may be misplaced, and that a degree of diversity in work activities and roles that appears to exist can be seen to largely reflect the variety of managerial jobs and contexts.

Of course, managerial practice and scholarly debate about it do not stand still, and even the broad consensus that seems to have emerged about the nature of management and managerial work remains under threat as rapid changes in technology and organisational structures over the past decade or more have resulted in marked changes to both the pattern and scope of managerial work. Indeed, some scholars have suggested there is already evidence of a steady demise of managerial positions, particularly at the 'middle management' level, as organisations change from hierarchical, rule-bound bureaucracies to much more decentralised and empowered networks or 'post-bureaucratic' organisations, in which skilled knowledge workers and smart computers combine in flexible, task or problem-based self-managing teams (Drucker, 1988; Heckcher & Donnellon, 1994; Kanter, 1989).

However, a more detailed examination of such debates is beyond the scope and the purpose of this book, save to acknowledge that such changes in the nature of mainstream managerial jobs and work may well be echoed in patterns of managerial work found in organisational communications departments or functions. We have provided some guidance to further reading for those interested in pursuing these debates with the management literature at the end of the chapter.

This review of the way the thinking about the concept and practice of management has evolved and about the suggested commonalities as well as diversity in managerial work clearly has some interesting implications for our understanding of managerial roles and work in the organisational communications context. Indeed, how this book differs from other books in this field is in the explicit parallels we have attempted to draw with management theory. In fact, we believe that it makes little sense to talk about public relations as a 'management' function unless we have a clear understanding of what this term means and how it is understood by other organisational functions. In the following sections of this chapter we examine how professional and academic thinking about the concept of management and the manager's role in the organisational communications context has developed, and we go on to advance what we believe is a useful framework for examining the managerial process and managerial practice in this context.

AN EVOLVING THEORETICAL DOMAIN

As with virtually all disciplines, thinking and theorising about public relations continue to take place, albeit with the pace and magnitude of change varying over time. Moreover, there has been considerable debate about the disciplinary 'roots' of public relations theory, particularly in terms of whether it should be considered a management- or communications-based discipline. Looking more specifically at research and theorising about the *management* of communication within organisations, Vercic and Grunig (2000) suggested that the origins of public relations theory can be traced back to early 'economic theories of the firm', and in particular to the preoccupation with efficiency of organisational behaviour, perhaps most closely associated with the ground-breaking work of F.W. Taylor in the early twentieth century. Taylor went on to disseminate his ideas in his seminal work, *The Principles of Scientific Management*, published in 1911. Vercic and Grunig suggest that Edward Bernays, who is widely acknowledged as the one of the founding figures of professional public relations, utilised similar principles to Taylor to establish public relations as a 'scientific approach' to the management of firms' relationships with their environments. Bernays (1923, 1928, 1955) saw the key elements of this process as 'crystallizing, manipulation, and ultimately the engineering of public opinion'. Bernays (1928: 44) advanced the idea that public relations operates as a form of social engineering directed towards the 'elimination of the waste and friction that results when industry does things or makes things which its public does not want, or when the public does not understand what is being offered it'.

While theorising about the role and practice of public relations has evolved progressively over the years since Bernays articulated his views, the emphasis he placed on the need for public relations to focus on managing organisational relationships with the external environment and, in particular, with key publics continues to pervade contemporary thinking about the key role and purpose of public relations. Indeed, the concept of *relationship management* (see box below), focusing on key organisational stakeholder relationships, has emerged as a central metaphor in modern theorising about public relations (Ledingham & Bruning, 2000; Grunig, Grunig, & Dozier, 2002). Moreover, this positioning of public relations as having a key functional role in *managing* the relationship between organisations and their environments has been a central pillar in the case for treating public relations as a strategically important function in organisations (Grunig & Repper, 1992). Here arguments have centred around the 'boundary-spanning' capability of public relations practitioners (Aldrich & Herker, 1977) to perform an 'environment scanning' and 'representational function' (see box below), coupled with the growing recognition amongst both public relations and management professionals and scholars of society's demand for organisations to demonstrate greater social responsibility.

RELATIONSHIP/RELATIONAL PERSPECTIVE OF PUBLIC RELATIONS

The *relationship/relational* perspective of public relations, although perhaps implicit in much of the theoretical discussion of the public relations function's role and purpose, has only emerged as a more distinctive and coherent perspective in its own right in recent years (e.g., Ledingham & Bruning, 2000). Whilst the relationship between organisations and stakeholders and publics has always been an important concern for public relations scholars and practitioners, scholars such as Bruning (2002) maintain that, until comparatively recently, the focus within public relations has been on the *managing of communications processes* and outputs, rather than the product or outcome of such communications, namely *relationships*. Indeed, the broad concept of relationships and their importance to the success and survival of organisations not only permeates the public relations literature, but also can be found increasingly in a number of other disciplinary fields, perhaps most notably in marketing. Moreover, this 'relational perspective' of public relations represents an essentially multi-faceted perspective of public relations, embracing elements drawn from a number of other areas of theory development including interpersonal communication theory, inter-organisational theory, and systems theory, which in turn draw on other theoretical ideas, including resource dependency theory and conflict and social exchange theory, among others.

THE BOUNDARY-SPANNING ROLE

The idea of public relations operating as a 'boundary-spanning function' between an organisation and its environment has been a central concept for those arguing that public relations can and should play a strategically important role in organisations, fulfilling an *environmental scanning* function – interpreting the environment for the organisation and representing the organisation to important external stakeholder groups (Aldrich & Herker, 1977; Leifer & Delbecq, 1978). This boundary-spanning role is also seen to empower and enable practitioners to participate in the work of the dominant coalition within organisations, contributing to the strategic decision-making processes (White & Dozier, 1992). This concept of public relations as a boundary-spanning function is an integral part of a broader interpretation of the role of public relations from what has been termed the 'systems-theory' perspective. This systems perspective recognises that all organisations operate as part of a wide network of interacting parts/systems and hence that all organisations are 'open' to a greater or lesser degree to pressures, influences and forces originating within the wider system. The problem is that not all organisations are willing to acknowledge the inevitability of interactions with other members/parties within their 'system' and hence may try to operate as if they were part of a relatively 'closed' system which may lead to tension and conflict with stakeholders and/or other members of the system.

PRACTITIONER ROLES THEORY

While relationship and boundary-spanning theories support the notion of the public relations as an important managerial *function* within organisations, particularly in terms of helping to manage organisational interfaces with the external environment and with key stakeholder groups, it is the emergence of *practitioners roles theory* that has provided the basis for defining and explaining the managerial *profile and specific responsibilities* of those practitioners who are deemed to enact *managerial roles* within organisations.

Four-Role and Dual Typologies

In Chapter 1 we highlighted the fact that research into practitioner roles has built on the pioneering work of Glen Broom (Broom, 1982; Broom & Smith, 1979) and David Dozier (Dozier, 1984; Broom & Dozier, 1986; Dozier & Broom, 1995). Broom and Smith (1979) initially conceptualised a five-role typology drawing on the literature on consulting and organisational roles. Practitioners were conceptualised as consultants to senior managers, with each role type providing a distinct form of assistance. Broom (1982) later reconfigured the five role types, consolidating them into the four-role typology summarised below:

- The *expert prescriber* role, in which practitioners are seen to operate as the primary 'authority' and source of expertise on communication issues/problems, occupying what has been likened to a doctor–patient relationship with management, defining communication/public relations problems and identifying solutions to them.
- The *communication facilitator* role, in which practitioners serve as a liaison, interpreter and/or mediator between the organisation and its publics – acting as a boundary-spanning agent. This role emphasises the notion of maintaining a continuous flow of two-way communication between the organisation and its various stakeholder groups.
- The *problem-solving process facilitation* role, in which practitioners are seen to collaborate with the organisation's senior managers (dominant coalition) to define and solve organisational communication problems. This collaborative problem-solving approach is contrasted with the expert prescriber role, where practitioners often work independently of senior management rather than helping them to think systematically through solutions to organisational communication problems.
- The *communication technician* role, in which practitioners are seen to function primarily as technical service providers, concerned largely with producing communications materials for an organisation's public relations efforts. In this sense, as communication technicians, practitioners are highly unlikely to have any direct involvement in senior management decision-making, and are, in fact, viewed as essentially 'journalists-in-residence'.

Roles research has recognised that practitioners will often enact a number of different roles within their organisations. In fact, researchers have consistently found a close correlation between the expert prescriber, communication facilitator and the problem-solving process facilitator roles in particular, while these tend to be quite distinct from the communication technician role. Building on this earlier stream of research, Dozier (1984) argued that the four-role typology could be effectively reduced to a dual typology of *manager and technician* roles, maintaining that these two role types are both empirically and conceptually distinct. The public relations manager's role is thus defined as essentially a composite role comprising elements of *expert prescription*, *communication facilitation* and *problem-solving process facilitation*. While the manager and technician roles may comprise distinctively different sets of activities, as Dozier and Broom have acknowledged, in practice, 'all practitioners enact elements of both the manager and technician roles, which are themselves only useful *abstractions* for studying the wide range of activities that practitioners perform in their daily lives' (1995: 20). The strengths and limitations of this conceptualisation of the manager's role in the public relations context will be examined further below, but first we need to consider the different influences on practitioner role enactment.

Factors Influencing Role Enactment

The study of practitioner roles has proved useful as a basis not only for identifying dominant patterns of practitioner work-based activity, but also for explaining how role enactment may be affected by individual characteristics and circumstances, as well as varying in differing organisational and situational contexts. Here research into practitioner role enactment has identified two broad sets of factors that to greater or lesser degrees appear to influence the configuration of role activities and role behaviour performed by practitioners. The first set of factors, which can be labelled *personal attributes and characteristics*, comprises such factors as the individual practitioner's gender, educational background and training, professional experience and tenure in the job, as well as, perhaps more subtly, their personality and charisma. The second broad set of influencing factors – *organisational context factors* – comprises a range of contextual factors that serve to shape and/or constrain the type and scope of role that practitioners may perform and also the way that they carry out their roles. These contextual factors include the organisational and industry setting, environmental conditions, size of corporate communication/public relations department, management 'world-views' or expectations, and organisational and societal culture.

These factors are summarised briefly in Table 2.1. Undoubtedly it is the issue of 'gender' that has attracted the bulk of the research roles, with scholars such as Toth and Grunig (1993), Hon (1995) and Creedon (1991) mounting a vociferous attack on gender discrimination in terms of female practitioner career advancement.

Understanding the significance of these various factors, individually and collectively, is crucial in helping to explain the extent to which practitioners are able to assume a more significant *managerial* role within organisations. Enactment of the public relations manager's role is particularly crucial if practitioners are to realise the aspiration of operating as part of the dominant coalition/senior management team within organisations. However, there appears to be little evidence to support the notion that *managerial* role enactment *per se* will necessarily always enable practitioners to participate directly in the work of the top management team within organisations. Indeed, quite the opposite, it appears to be more the exception than the rule to find even senior practitioners operating as active members of their organisation's top management team (Moss, Warnaby, & Newman, 2000; Grunig et al., 2002).

In part, at least, the explanation for the relatively small numbers of practitioners who appear to work as recognised members of the top management team in organisations may lie in the typical background and knowledge and skills profile of the majority of senior practitioners, who may often lack the type of financial and broader business knowledge and experience expected of top management decision-makers. This issue of senior practitioner roles and involvement in senior management decision-making/policy-making will be discussed in more detail in later chapters.

TABLE 2.1 Factors Influencing Public Relations Practitioner Role Enactment

Factors	Description	Authors
Personal Characteristics/Attributes:		
Gender	Gender has been identified as the chief antecedent factor affecting patterns of work, length of employment and opportunities for career advancement. Women often claim to have been disadvantaged in terms of both salary and progression to managerial roles	Cline et al. (1986); Creedon (1991); Dozier and Broom (1995); Toth and Grunig (1993); Toth et al. (1988)
Practitioner education	Entry level and career advancement seen to correlate with level of educational achievement	Lauzen, (1992); Dozier and Broom (1995)
Professional experience	The greater the extent of the practitioner's professional experience the easier it for them to assume managerial role positions	Druck and Hiebert (1979); Dozier and Broom (1995); Toth et al (1998);
Tenure with employer	The longer a practitioner remains with an employer the more likely it is for them to advance to more senior manager level roles	Dozier and Broom (1995)
Personality/charisma	Although little research has been completed into the effects of personality/charisma it seems self-evident that career progression and leadership are closely tied to this factor	Moss, Warnaby, & Newman (2000); DeSanto & Moss (2004)
Organisational/environmental factors:		
Organisation-type/ industry	Organisational structure, culture and systems recognised as a major enabling/ constraining force on practitioner role enactment having a major	Grunig, Grunig, & Dozier (2002); White and Dozier (1992);
Environmental conditions	The extent to which the external/industry environment is threatening/unstable and poses a particular challenge to the achievement of organisational goals likely to determine scope for manager role enactment	Acharya (1985); White and Dozier; (1992)
Communication/PR department size	The larger the size of the communication/PR department the easier it is for more senior practitioners to delegate more routine technical work to other staff and thus concentrate on managerial-type work	Lauzen (1992)
Management worldviews/ expectations	The scope of the communication/PR professional's role is ultimately constrained/ enabled by the prevailing expectations for the function held by the organisation's senior management	White and Dozier (1992); Grunig, Grunig, & Dozier (2002)
Organisational/ societal culture	Roles research to date has been largely confined to US organisations. More recent research has challenged whether the US roles typologies can be applied in other cultures where different values/norms/practices may prevail	Sriramesh and White (1992); Sriramesh (1996); Moss, Warnaby, & Newman (2000)

Critique of Roles Research and Role Typologies

Despite the central place of practitioner roles research in public relations theory building, practitioner roles theory, particularly in terms of the manager–technician dichotomy, has come under criticism on a number of grounds:

- Methodologically, it has been argued that the manager-technician typology represents an essentially reductionist, overly simplified view of the complexities of role enactment which may obscure some of the subtle yet significant differences in the range of tasks that practitioners perform within organisations.
- The traditional four- and two-role typologies have been used largely as static categories into which practitioners are 'pigeonholed' rather than recognising that role enactment is a more dynamic process in which roles may be relatively loosely o tightly defined and may also vary significantly both across organisations and in different situations/contexts (e.g., Culbertson, 1991).
- Liberal feminist scholars (e.g., Creedon, 1991; Hon, 1995; Hon et al., 1992; Toth & Grunig, 1993) have argued that the manager–technician perspective tends to trivialise the technical work often performed to a greater degree by female practitioners. Feminist scholars have also expressed wider concerns over the failure of much of the roles research to examine gender issues in public relations from the perspective of women.
- Role research and role typologies have focused almost exclusively on US-based practitioners and there has been little international comparative research into practitioner role enactment.
- A further major line of criticism which is of specific interest to this book has focused on the limitations of how the managerial dimension of practitioners' work is actually defined and measured (e.g., Leichty & Springston, 1996; Moss et al., 2000).

In reviewing the body of roles research over the past three decades, Grunig et al. (2002) acknowledged that there is no simple answer to the question of which is the best approach to measuring practitioner roles, since roles typologies are essentially abstractions of reality, which makes their measurement inherently problematic. However, given the ongoing evolution of the communication profession, it follows that there is a need to constantly update and reinvent our understanding of what constitutes the main elements of work performed by practitioners operating at both the technician and managerial levels. By implication, this requires intensive observation of *what communicators do*.

The fact that there has been relatively little research based on direct observation of the activities involved in the day-to-day management of communications functions or departments highlights what can be seen as one of the most important weaknesses in the way in which the manager's role in the public relations context has been conceptualised, namely the failure to distinguish clearly between managerial work in terms of a set of *actual behaviours*, and as a set of *intended outcomes or goals*. This type of potential confusion over what amounts to practitioner manager *behaviours* (how they go about managing their departments and processes), and managerial *tasks, responsibilities and goals* (what they set out,to achieve or are charged with achieving) can be seen to echo similar problems identified earlier in the mainstream body of management research. However, whereas in the case of mainstream management the confusion emerges, at least in part, from different streams of research that have been conducted using different methodologies and with different purposes in mind, in the case of public relations roles research there has been little attempt to draw a distinction between manager *tasks* and *responsibilities* and manager *behaviours*. Most roles research has, in fact, focused only on gathering data about the main tasks and responsibilities performed by practitioners, rather than also observing their behaviours. This distinction between managerial behaviours and outcomes is something that requires closer attention if we are to understand more fully the nature of the managerial role in the communications context.

Developing a Managerial Perspective Framework

Despite the criticisms of practitioner roles research and the way the manager's role has been conceptualised within the literature, there is clearly a strong emphasis on positioning communications as a significant management function within organisations. However, no comprehensive and coherent theory of organisational communications *management* has arguably yet emerged. Rather what exists is a rather disjointed set of theories that attempt to explain, on the one hand, how and why the communication/public relations function can contribute to the strategic management of organisations (e.g., Grunig & Repper, 1992; Moss & Warnaby, 2000); and on the other hand, how communications professionals can plan, manage and evaluate organisational communication programmes – how they can enact the 'manager's role' (e.g., Dozier, 1984; Dozier & Broom, 1995; Grunig et al., 2002).

Arguably, what is needed is an integrating framework that is capable of bringing together and helping to explain what might be termed both the more *strategic* (the focus for most of the existing public relations literature) and *functional* dimensions of the 'managerial work' performed by communications professionals. The next section of this chapter outlines a broad conceptual framework that we have developed to help explicate what can be seen as the key elements of managerial *process* in the organisational communications context. We believe that this framework offers a relatively simple but powerful basis for understanding the role of the communications function and communications professionals both at the *operation level* – developing, overseeing the implementation of and evaluating communication/public relations programmes – but also at a more *strategic level* within organisations – helping to advise and even shape communications strategy and perhaps also contributing to the overall organisational strategy and policy decisions.

Of course, any attempt to conceptualise such a potentially complex human process as management will inevitably be open to the criticism of over-simplification, and equally, may fail to reflect the nuances of difference in the way managerial responsibilities and tasks may be performed in different functional and/or organisational contexts. Nevertheless, despite such caveats, we believe that this framework offers a useful starting point in developing a more systematic and coherent insight into the management process in organisational communications context, in terms of the key decisions and actions involved in directing, coordinating and controlling the function's people and resources, and ensuring they are directed effectively towards the achievement the intended communication goals, and ultimately, the organisational goals in question.

THE C-MACIE FRAMEWORK

In line with the broad approach taken in this book of bringing together communication/ public relations and management thinking, the new conceptual framework we have advanced to help explain the managerial role and process in the organisational communication context draws on both public relations and management theory, as well as on the author's own experience and observation of senior communication practitioner practices across a range of organisational contexts. Our framework is based around what management scholars have broadly recognised as the four principle stages or elements in the management process – namely, *management analysis*, *choice*, *implementation* and *evaluation* – and also echoes elements of the traditional public relations planning framework – often known as the RACE model (*research*, *action*, *communication* and *evaluation*). However, while the RACE framework serves primarily as a communication *planning* framework, the communication management framework advanced here goes beyond the role of communication planning, providing a basis for analysing and explaining the principal elements involved in the overall strategic and operational management of the communication function.

Adapting the above generic management process framework for use in the communication context, and to provide an easily memorable and relevant acronym, we have simply added a 'C' – for communication – to each of the four stages, giving rise to the term 'C-MACIE':

- communication management analysis;
- communication management choice;
- communication management implementation;
- communication management evaluation.

These four stages or elements in the management process arguably encompass what can be seen as the key tasks and responsibilities that communication managers perform in most organisational settings – namely, analysing the situation they face, making choices about how best to respond, implementing the chosen set of actions, and evaluating the outcomes. Arguably this four-stage process can be seen to apply to both strategically important decisions and actions as well as dealing with more

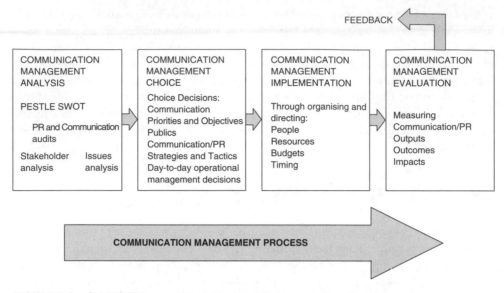

FIGURE 2.3   C-MACIE Framework: A Model of Communication Management

routine operational matters. What this framework does not identify *explicitly*, how-ever, are the specific managerial *behaviours* associated with performance of key tasks at each of these stages. However, as we have discussed earlier, managerial *behaviour* and managerial *work* cannot be so easily separated and, in fact, can be seen as 'two sides of the same coin' – representing the 'what' and the 'how' of managerial work.

This four-element framework is summarised in Figure 2.3, and each element of the framework is discussed briefly below.

Communication Management Analysis

The first element in this framework, *communication management analysis,* repre-sents the essential first step in the communication management process – analysing the particular situation facing the organisation and determining the issues and chal-lenges that need to be tackled. At the more strategic level, such analysis is concerned with the essential work of continually scanning, analysing and interpreting data from the organisation's external and internal environments in order to identify and under-stand and, where possible, anticipate the forces shaping the current (and future) situation the organisation faces, particularly in terms of its relationship with key stakeholder groups and the implications for the organisation's communication strat-egies. On a day-to-day operational level, such analysis involves examining the more immediate challenges that might be faced, analysing how best to husband and utilise resources, how to deploy people and manage available budgets, etc.

Traditionally, communications analysis has been treated as the initial step in the communication/public relations planning process, focusing on identifying the most important and relevant stakeholders and understanding the attitudes, opinions and behaviours of those stakeholders whose support or opposition is crucial to the realisation of the organisation's goals. Of course, analysis of communication-related variables (stakeholder perceptions and behaviour, channel effectiveness, message reception and comprehension, etc.) has to be set in the broader context of the trends and developments affecting the organisation's business/competitive environment as well as looking inside the organisation, exploring the internal systems, culture, values, etc. that influence the way members of the organisation think, behave and respond to challenges and opportunities that they may face. While communication managers are unlikely to be responsible for this broader external and internal environmental analysis, it is essential that they have this broader contextual understanding in order to advise senior management on communication policy issues, identifying the implications of different courses of action for stakeholder relationships and helping to determine the most appropriate communication strategies and tactics to support the organisation's goals.

As was suggested earlier, the task of external environmental analysis – what is often termed *environmental scanning* – is usually claimed to be part of the responsibilities of communication practitioners operating in their *boundary-spanning mode* (see earlier Figure 2.4, Boundary Spanning). However, it is also clear that the organisational communication function does not have any exclusive franchise over boundary-spanning and environmental analysis activities on behalf of organisations. Indeed, marketing and sales and management information systems are often seen as chief architects of organisational intelligence gathering systems, which would normally include some form of environmental scanning as an important source of external intelligence. Arguably, what communication managers can contribute to the task of environmental analysis is a broader and more balanced *total stakeholder* perspective that may differ from the more partial, commercial or financial emphasis normally found in marketing or management information systems analysis. In short, the value of the communication manager's role in environmental analysis arguably lies in their ability to offer a broad '360-degree' view of the organisation's total set of stakeholder relationships and interactions, analysing and balancing the interests of both the organisation and the relevant stakeholder groups. In this sense, communication/public relations managers can reflect the views from 'both sides of the fence' to senior management, analysing the potential consequences of alternative courses of action that the organisation may be considering. It is this ability to provide senior management with this objective broader and more balanced overview of all organisational stakeholder relationships and interactions, and not simply those relationships with customers, suppliers or other commercial partners, that is arguably the communications function's particular value to senior management

Analytical Tools

Although we will return to consider to the process of strategic analysis further as part of our examination of strategy-making and planning in Chapter 5, it is worth briefly outlining a number of the analytical tools that are used most frequently by communication managers (and other managerial functions) in developing an understanding of the communication challenges and issues that their organisation might need to address. Here techniques such as *PEST* or *PESTLE* analysis, *SWOT* analysis, *stakeholder mapping and analysis*, and *communication auditing* are often drawn upon and combined to gain a rounded understanding of an organisation's position, the key challenges and issues it faces, and from a communication perspective, the key stakeholder relationships that need to be maintained or developed further (see Table 2.2 for a summary of the purpose and characteristics of these key analytical tools). The use of these analytical tools will be examined further in Chapter 5.

Communication Management Choice

The work of communication analysis prepares the way for what is often seen as the core task of management, namely the exercising of *management choice* with respect to the appraisal and selection of alternative targets/objectives and strategy options or courses of action that should be undertaken. For communication managers, these choices centre around decisions about which challenges/issues they should focus attention on, what outcomes/objectives should be sought, which stakeholders should be targeted, what communication strategies should be adopted and what specific tactics should be used. Despite the emphasis on *strategic* management choices, 'choice' is, in fact a theme that permeates all aspects of managerial work and not simply the area of strategy-making and planning. Choices have to be made, for example, about the allocation of resources across the function, about the division of responsibilities between staff within the function and the hiring/firing or promotion/demotion of individuals within the department, or the hiring/firing of external agencies. In short, choices exist at virtually every turn for communication managers, ranging from the relatively routine to profound decisions and actions that might affect the function or department's future as well as that of the organisation as a whole. There are often no simple formulas to help communication managers take the 'right' decision, rather it is often a matter of careful judgement, experience and even inspiration or 'gut' feeling in some cases. Indeed, it is arguably the ability to make consistently good or even inspired choice decisions that is one of the key characteristics that separates the 'gifted' manager and leader from the more 'pedestrian' performers.

In this choice dimension of communication management, one recurring area of controversy is the extent to which communication managers participate directly in the broader strategic decision-making process within organisations. As was highlighted earlier, much of the research to date suggests that it is still perhaps more the exception than the rule to find even senior communications practitioners operating as members of the top management team (dominant coalition) within organisations (e.g., DeSanto and Moss, 2004; Grunig et al., 2002). Rather, it appears that even the most senior communications professionals will generally tend to act primarily as advisers to top management, offering a communications perspective on the alternative mainstream managerial policy choices, but in most cases rarely being party to the

TABLE 2.2 Key Environmental Analysis Tools

Analytical Technique	Purpose	Methods/Key Outputs
PEST[LE]	Macro-environmental analysis technique – assesses the key environmental forces, variables and trends likely to impact or constrain the achievement of organisational goals	Draws on a wide range of secondary and primary data and intelligence sources to identify relevant external trends/developments, categorising these in terms of six key areas: • Political • Economic • Social • Technological • Legal • Environmental
SWOT	Technique for analysing and determining an organisation's relative position in terms of both *internal* strengths and weaknesses and *external* opportunities and threats – essentially draws together analysis of internal and external forces	Draws together internal and external intelligence from a range of sources, categorises that data in terms of both *internal* organisational strengths and weaknesses, comparing these with key *externally* identified opportunities and threats
Stakeholder mapping	Identifies and evaluates an organisation's key stakeholder groups and defines the nature of the relationship the organisation has with each of the identified stakeholder groups	Uses visual stakeholder mapping techniques and ranking to identify the network of key stakeholder relationships and assign priorities to them
Communication audits	Periodic and systematic reviews of all organisational communication activities and assessment of the effectiveness each area of activity	Uses a variety data collection tools – surveys, observation and expert opinions, 'scorecards' to periodically review and assess the effectiveness of all current organisational communication activities
Issues analysis	As part of an issues management system, identifies priorities and assesses the potential threat/ opportunity presented by trends, events and developments, both internal and external to an organisation, that may threaten key stakeholder relationships and the organisation's ability to realise its goals	Draws on intelligence gathered from techniques such as PESTLE and SWOT, interpreting such data to identify key communication issues that might threaten organisational stakeholder relationships and the organisation's reputation

mainstream policy choice decisions themselves. We will return to examine further the controversy surrounding the role that communications managers might play in strategic choice decisions within the organisation in Chapter 5.

Communication Choice Tools

Despite the fact that it is difficult, if not impossible, to prescribe a universal formula for successful choice decisions, nevertheless there are some choice decision tools that can aid communication managers in making important decisions. Here the obvious first step in the choice process is to identify what alternative options may be open to decision-makers. In some cases the options may be quite obvious, in other cases it may be necessary to look beyond the obvious – 'think outside the box' – to think creatively about what alternative courses of action might exist that might be worth considering. Although there may be no one universally accepted method of generating alternative options that will work in all circumstances, team *brainstorming* is a widely used means of idea generation and problem-solving, particularly when dealing with particularly complex situations. Here it may be best to bring together people from a number of different backgrounds or with different perspective in order to generate the widest possible range of options/solutions.

Once a number of alternative options have been identified, it is necessary to evaluate and select the one(s) that appear to be most attractive in the situation in question, normally in terms of risk and reward. In some cases this appraisal and choice of options might be done almost intuitively, perhaps with little perceived need for consultation or extended analysis. In other cases, where the situation faced is quite complex and the perceived risk of a wrong decision is high, one might expect to find greater consultation among managers operating at the decision level and greater uses of decision support techniques. Decision support techniques have been developed to help management evaluate the alternative choice options they may be considering. These decision support techniques include such methods as ranking methods, Delphi technques, decision trees, scenario building, balanced score cards and discounted cash flow analysis. Table 2.3 provides a brief summary of the main characteristics and purpose of these techniques, and we will return to this question of decision analysis in Chapter 15 where we examine risk and issues analysis techniques in particular.

Of course, as was suggested earlier, choice decisions, whether about issue prioritisation, strategy options or more routine budget or resource decisions, are fundamental to the management process. In this sense communication managers are no different from managers in other functional areas in their need to confront and resolve choice decisions. What may make such decision-making more problematic, at least for some communications managers, is that many may have had relatively little formal training in these typse of choice decision techniques, as comparatively few communication practitioners have tended to come into the field from a mainstream managerial background. This is not to suggest that most communications managers are not capable of making appropriate choice decisions, rather this is an area of managerial competence that all communication managers (as with any other functional area) need to continually develop and strengthen through on-the-job training and reflective experience in order to be prepared to cope with whatever choice decisions may come their way.

TABLE 2.3 Decision Support Techniques

Technique	Characteristics	Purpose	Limitations
Delphi technique	Pooling of informed/expert opinion in a series of shared rounds of assessment	Helps pool and review collective opinion on issue/decision – useful when there is considerable uncertainty	Opinions shared still be relative subjective and tendency for people to go along with the 'norm' that emerges
Ranking methods	Individual or collective ranking of alternative options against a predetermined set of agreed criteria – costs, risks etc	Helps prioritise the decisions/actions that appear most likely to achieve the desired goals	Relies on relatively subjective judgment both of what criteria are important and of the ranking of each alternative
Decision trees	Creates a visual flowchart of conditions that steer decisions progressively towards particular outcomes based on a series of 'filtering criteria that steer decisions in a particular direction – e.g. risk, cost, timing, etc	Enables multiple criteria to be introduced and considered and satisfied as decisions are refined against each set of criteria	May be complicated to implement. Requires agreement on the prioritised criteria and the assessment made at each stage in the process. Can be fraught with potential conflicts over decision 'routes' selected
Scenario building	Allows alternative options to be matched against a range of possible future scenarios in order to assess the best fit with the organisation's priorities	Attempts to 'future-proof' the decisions strategies chosen by postulating alternative world views of the organisation and its environment	Relies on accurate predictions of the future industry/environmental scenarios and agreement on how such change might affect organisational policies. Potential for considerable conflict amongst management about such predictions
Balanced score card approach	Allows alternative strategy options to be considered from multiple internal and external stakeholder perspectives – creates a 'scorecard' that attempts to integrate and balance financial and other performance measures relevant to different key stakeholder groups	Helps to achieve a 'balanced' outcome that is more likely to satisfy both the organisation and its key stakeholder	Can be relative complex to implement and maintain and requires clear guidelines on how to equate and balance different performance measures
Discounted cash flow	Used to calculate the future value of alternative courses of action/activities in terms of there net present value	Helps to focus attention of the financial value of alternative courses of action	Only considers alternative outcomes in financial terms and ignores other important potential costs/impacts

Communication Management Implementation

Much of the discussion of communication management processes tends to focus on the analysis and strategic and operational decision-making (choice) stages of the process, rather than on *implementation*. However, the way in which communications departments manage the implementation of communication policies/strategies and programmes is arguably is no less important to achieving the intended outcome, since even the best-designed strategies and programmes can fail though poorly managed implementation. It is generally recognised that the key to successful implementation of communication policies and programmes lies in the effective management of *people* and *resources*. Indeed, as management scholars such as Mintzberg (1973, 2009) and Kotter (1982) have highlighted, the way that managers essentially get things done is through the direction and control of people and resources under their responsibility.

People Management

Accounting for and exercising some degree of control and direction over the 'human element' – the people employed – within any organisational function is a fundamental task of management, yet it is also generally acknowledged to be one of the most potentially problematic and unpredictable elements affecting functional performance. Managing implementation of policies and programmes within departments, including communications, essentially requires effective 'people management' skills or what nowadays is often termed *human resource management skills*. In the case of the communication function, these people management skills relate not just to those employed within the organisation's own communication department, but may extend to handling relationships with those employed by external agencies or organisations whose services might be needed to facilitate the implementation of policies. Equally, because communication policies and actions might impact on – or rely on support or collaboration with other organisational functions – successful implementation will often involve a degree of internal cross-functional negotiation and relationship management to navigate through the almost inevitable 'politics' and sensitivities that often exist and even characterise some organisations. These concerns often rise to the surface and become particularly problematic where policies involve some degree of significant change within organisations that may disrupt the existing status quo. Thus, for example, significant restructuring of an organisation's operations and management structures invariably causes uncertainty and disquiet and often triggers opposition from those who perceive their own positions and futures under threat.

Looking more generically at the 'people management' dimension in organisations, scholars such as Johnson and Scholes (2002) have identified three key elements of people management process that impact on the successful implementation of policies: the configuration of organisational *structures*, *processes* and *relationships* (see Figure 2.4). These three elements of the people management dimension are outlined briefly below:

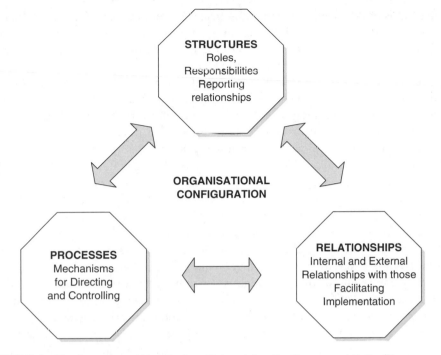

FIGURE 2.4 Configuration of Key Factors Determining the Success of Policy/Programme Implementation

- **Structures.** This term relates to the way people are organised within the organisation as a whole and within the communication function itself. Here, in particular, the focus is on examining the roles, responsibilities and reporting relationships within the organisation.
- **Processes.** This term relates to the formal and informal processes that connect, drive and support people within the organisation. In effect, these processes provide for the control, supervision and direction/encouragement of those actions and behaviours that determine the success of the organisation's operations.
- **Relationships.** This term relates the network of relationships both within and external to the organisation that may have a critical influence on the success of its operations. In case of the communication/public relations function, internal relationships may be with other functions within the organisation whose support is required, whereas external relationships may be with external agencies and freelancers who may contribute significantly to the successful implementation of programmes.

Financial and Material Resources

While the management of people is often critical to successful implementation of policies and programmes, without the necessary financial and other material resources it is impossible to implement policies or programmes effectively. While the need for adequate resource allocation and, in particular, adequate funding might seem obvious, often there are many competing demands on the relatively finite resources available to most organisations. Here resource capabilities relate not only to the availability of *finance*, but increasingly also to access the necessary *technology* and *information* which can be critical success factors in implementing programmes effectively. In an increasingly fast-changing communications environment, timely access to the necessary information about issues and developments affecting the organisation and/or the industry/sector in which it operates may be absolutely crucial to the success of any communication programme. Here the ability to access, analyse and interpret relevant information is often closely tied to the adequacy and sophistication of the information technology systems within the organisation. Indeed, with increased availability of ever more powerful computers and the rapid expansion of information available on the internet, the issue for most organisations is not so much access to information as the ability to sift, process and analyse the information that is relevant to the organisation and its current and future position.

Securing the required funding/budget to enable planned policies and operational programmes to be implemented effectively has always been a somewhat contentious issue, particularly in the field of organisational communication, where budgets are often the first to come under pressure when organisational resources are stretched. The recent severe economic recession that has been felt around the world has seen communications budgets across all sectors of industry come under severe pressure, with many programmes cut back or cancelled as an immediate reaction to the demands of senior management to reign in all 'non-essential' expenditure. Interestingly, it appears that once organisations have had time to reassess the situation, many began to have second thoughts about the advisability of making deep cuts to their communications budgets, and in particular to their public relations activity. As a result, many corporate public relations budgets have been reallocated, albeit with tighter constraints on what exactly the budgets are used to do.

Determining accurately what budget is required to support particular communication/public relations programmes can be extremely difficult because of the many uncertainties that might need to be taken into account, not the least being the amount of time that practitioners may need to devote to implementing the programme. Here, the preferred budgeting approach for communication planners, is normally the *objective-task method* which involves setting objectives and devising an appropriate programme of action which is then costed to arrive at a required a required budget to carry out the planned programme effectively.

In most organisations, however, annual budgets tend to be determined *a priori* using some agreed formula such as a fixed percentage of the previous year's sales or forecast sales. While such budgeting methods are quite crude, they continue to be used because of their simplicity and consistency. Moreover, the percentage of sales or similar approach often appeals to senior management because it ensures that expenditure remains capped within what is seen as an affordable band. Obviously, it is unrealistic to expect that communications manager should be given *carte blanche* to spend whatever they see fit, and yet too rigid a budget formula may mean that there are simply insufficient resources to implement programmes fully as anticipated. In practice, a combination of budgeting methods may be favoured, with simple percentage formulas being used to determine the broad expenditure 'envelope', and more detailed programme costings then being prepared for approval. Here, in general, the greater the level of uncertainty about future developments affecting the organisation, the greater the need for a more flexible budgetary allocation in order to allow for unforeseen contingencies.

Communication Management Evaluation

The final element of this C-MACIE framework focuses on evaluation of the outcomes of the communication programmes undertaken and of the work of communication departments. Here the aim is establish, firstly, the extent to which the immediate programme and longer-term policy objectives have been achieved, and secondly, the significance of external and internal factors affecting the programme outcomes. As suggested above, organisational objectives and targets have become more and more diverse, reflecting the need to balance different stakeholder expectations of organisations – recognising that financial performance may have to be set against other environmental, social, and even political considerations affecting an organisation's longer-term position and success. Where organisations have accepted the need for this type of 'balanced score card approach' to objective and target setting (e.g., Kaplan & Norton, 1992), it follows that any evaluation of performance and outcomes will need to use an appropriate set of quantitative and qualitative performance measures.

While this discussion of balanced score cards and more pluralistic organisational objectives and performance measures has focused mainly on the areas of broader corporate and business policy and strategy-making, the arguments can be applied equally to the area of communications policies and programmes, which of course should take their lead from these higher-level strategies. Moreover, the implementation of corporate and business strategies will invariably have communicative and reputational effects that will need to be assessed and responded to effectively by the organisation's communications function. Indeed, as was argued earlier, communications practitioners are generally seen as advocates and champions of a broader stakeholder perspective of organisational and business strategy and policy-making. Thus it is perhaps only logical to expect communications managers to advocate a balanced score card approach to evaluation of their work, reflecting the potentially varied range of ways in which activities can contribute to organisational success.

Thus, although communication policies and programmes have the potential to impact organisational stakeholders in quite varied ways, once these intended outcomes have been identified, it should in principle be possible to identify an appropriate set of measures to evaluate their success. In practice, however, defining appropriate measures and carrying out the evaluation of the outcomes of designated programmes has proved highly problematic, particularly in terms of isolating and measuring the specific communication effects. Indeed, the evaluation of communication pro-grammes has proved something of an Achilles heel for the communication function and has been the focus of protracted industry debate about how best to measure the results of communication/public relations programmes effectively.

Debates about communication evaluation have tended to crystallise around the distinction between 'process' and 'impact' measurement (Broom & Dozier, 1990; Dozier, 1992; Grunig & Hunt, 1984; Macnamara, 1992). For example, Broom and Dozier (1990) emphasised the need to distinguish between measures of programme output in terms of the number of messages sent, placed and then received, and meas-ures of outcome or impact in terms of how such measures are understood and influ-ence people's attitudes opinions and ultimately behaviours. Macnamara (1992) drew a similar distinction between communication/public relations outputs or process measures and impact measures of results, and advanced a hierarchical model illustrat-ing the typical type of measurement criteria used at each stage along with the types of research methodologies that might be used to assess each criteria.

Despite significant advances in terms of the level of sophistication of understanding about communications and specifically public relations evaluation in recent years, uni-versal understanding and, more important, adoption of what might be recognised as 'best practice' in terms of impact evaluation of communications programmes remains an aspiration rather than a reality. The principal reason for this continued emphasis on media-based evaluation can be attributed largely to issues of cost and convenience. To conduct the type of more sophisticated 'impact'-based evaluation of communication programmes suggested by Macnamara and other scholars inevitably involves more complex and costly research. Moreover, even if such research is undertaken, it is often extremely difficult if not impossible to isolate and 'prove' the extent to which any spe-cific communication programme has been instrumental in bringing about a particular attitudinal or behavioural response. This is particularly the case where the communica-tion programme objectives relate to significant change in social behaviour (e.g., reduc-tion in drink-driving, quitting smoking, reduction in abusive behaviour). In such cases, it may be extremely difficult to determine to what degree any observed behaviour change, which itself may take some time to occur, could be attributed solely or even primarily to a particular communication programme. However, experimental research designs can and have been be set up and used to test and evaluate the 'social' impact of communications programmes. In fact some of the most sophisticated and effective communication evaluations have taken place with social change programmes such as the prevention of drink-driving campaigns in the UK where longer-term tracking stud-ies have been used to compare trends and frequency of drink-driving offences with the level and type of communications activity. Here, in particular, researchers were inter-ested in examining the impact of the type of messages/images used to try to discourage younger drivers, in particularly, from drinking and driving. Of course, such research can be complex and costly to set up and carry out, but illustrates that effective solu-tions to even complex communication programme evaluation do exist.

Cost and convenience appear to remain the overriding obstacles to a move towards a more standardised demand and adoption of impact-based forms of evaluation.

Moreover, the communication/public relations industry's response to demands for 'better' evaluation has largely been to produce ever more sophisticated forms of 'media evaluation' – analysing message placement, tonality, favourability of coverage, etc. – rather than 'encouraging the growth of ever more sophisticated methodologies for 'impact measurement'. The move towards more sophisticated impact-based measurement does seem inevitable, especially as clients become more aware of the fallibility of current evaluation methods and as resources committed to communication continue to increase.

SUMMARY

In this chapter we have sought to explore current understanding of the concept and practice of management in the organisational communication context, highlighting the deficiencies in the way the concept of management has been treated within the communications and public relations literature to date. Here in particular we have highlighted the limitation of the way in which the manager's role has been defined by communication/public relations scholars and we have sought to advance what we believe is a more effective conceptual framework – C-MACIE – to help examine and make sense of the management role and process in the communication context.

This framework will provide the foundation underpinning our examination of different areas of communication practice in the subsequent chapters of the book. In the remaining chapters in Part One, we build on this managerial framework and examine the skills and competencies required by communications managers, explore the distinction between management and leadership in the communication context, and examine the nature of strategy and of strategy formation in the communication context. In this way, Part One attempts to build a strategic and operation management perspective of the organisational communication function and the challenges practitioners face in developing effective management systems for communications.

Parts Two and Three go on to examine a number of specific key areas of communication practice, exploring the challenges that organisations and communication managers face in developing and managing effective communication policies and programmes in each of the areas examined.

REFERENCES

Acharya, L. (1985) Public relations environments. *Journalism Quarterly 62*(3): 577–84.
Aldrich, H., & Herker, D. (1977) Boundary-spanning roles and organisational structure. *Academy of Management Review*, 2, 217–30.
Bernays, E.L. (1923) *Crystallizing Public Opinion*. New York: Boni and Liveright.

(Continued)

(Continued)

Bernays, E.L. (1928) Manipulating public opinion: The why and the how. *American Journal of Sociology* (May), 958–71.

Bernays, E.L. (ed.) (1955) *The Engineering of Consent*. Norman: University of Oklahoma Press.

Brewer, E., & Tomlinson, J.W.C. (1964). The manager's working day. *Journal of Industrial Economics*, *12*, 191–7.

Broom, G.M. (1982) A comparison of sex roles in public relations. *Public Relations Review*, 5, 17–22.

Broom, G.M., & Dozier, D.M. (1986) Advancement for public relations role models. *Public Relations Review*, *12*(1), 37–56.

Broom, G.M., & Smith, G.D. (1979) Testing the practitioner's impact on clients. *Public Relations Review*, *5*, 47–59.

Bruning, S. D. (2002) Relationship building as a retention strategy: Linking relationship attitudes and satisfaction evaluations to behavioural outcomes. *Public Relations Review*, *28*, 39–48.

Cline, C. G., E. L. Toth, et al. (1986) *The Velvet Ghetto: The Impact of the Increasing Percentage of Women in Public Relations and Business Communication*. San Francisco: IABC Foundation.

Cornelissen, J. (2008) *Corporate Communication: Theory and Practice* (2nd ed.). London: Sage.

Creedon, P. J. (1991) Public relations and women's work: Towards a feminist analysis of public relations roles. In L.A. Grunig & J.E. Grunig (eds), *The Public Relations Research Annual* (pp. 67–84). Hillsdale, NJ: Erlbaum.

Culbertson, H. (ed.) (1991) *Role Taking and Sensitivity: Keys to Playing and Making Public Relations Roles* (Vol. 3). Hillsdale, NJ: Erlbaum.

Cutlip, S.M., Center, A.H., & Broom, G.M. (2000) *Effective Public Relations* (8th ed.). Upper Saddle River, NJ: Prentice Hall.

Cutlip, S.M., Center, A.H., & Broom, G.M. (2006) *Effective Public Relations* (9th ed.). Upper Saddle River, NJ: Pearson Prentice Hall.

Dalton, M. (1959) *Men who Manage*. New York: Wiley.

DeSanto, B.J., & Moss, D.A. (2004) Rediscovering what PR managers do: Rethinking the measurement of managerial behavior in the public relations context. *Journal of Communication Management*, *19*, 179–96.

Dozier, D.M. (1984) Program evaluation and roles of practitioners. *Public Relations Review*, *10*(2), 13–21.

Dozier, D. M. (ed.) (1990) *The Innovation of Research in Public Relations Practice*. Public relations research annual. Hillsdale, NJ: Erlbaum.

Dozier, D.M. (1992) The organizational roles of communicators and public relations practitioners. In J. E. Grunig (ed.), *Excellence in Public Relations and Communications Management* (pp. 327–56). Hillsdale, NJ: Erlbaum.

Dozier, D.M., & Broom, G.M. (1995) Evolution of the manager role in public relations practice. *Journal of Public Relations Research*, *7*(1), 3–26.

Druck, K.B. & R.E. Hiebert (1979) Your personal guidebook to help you chart a more successful career in public relations. New York: Public Relations Society of America.

Drucker , P (1988) The coming of the new organization. *Harvard Business Review*, January–February, 45–53.

Fayol, H. (1949) *General and Industrial Management*. London: Pitman.

Grunig, J.E., & Hunt, T. (1984) *Managing Public Relations*. Fort Worth, TX: Harcourt Brace College Publishers.

Grunig, J.E., & Repper, F.C. (1992) Strategic management, publics and issues. In J. E. Grunig (ed.), *Excellence in Public Relations and Communication Management* (pp. 117–57). Hillsdale, NJ: Erlbaum.

Grunig, L.A., Grunig, J.E., & Dozier, D.M. (2002) *Excellent Public Relations and Effective Organisations*. Mahwah, NJ: Erlbaum.

Gulick, H., & Urwick, L.F. (1937) *Paper on the Science of Administration*. Unpublished manuscript, New York.

(Continued)

(Continued)

Hales, C. (1986) What do managers do? A critical review of the evidence. *Journal of Management Studies*, *23*(1), 88–115.

Hales, C. (2001) Does it matter what managers do? *Business Strategy Review*, *12*(2), 50–8.

Heckscher, C., & Donnellon, A. (eds) (1994) *The Post Bureaucratic Organization: New Perspectives on Organizational Change*. Thousand Oaks: Sage.

Hon, L.C. (1995) Towards a feminist theory in public relations. *Journal of Public Relations Research*, *7*(1), 27–88.

Hon, L.C., Grunig, L.A., & Dozier, D.M. (1992) Women in public relations: Problems and opportunities. In J.E. Grunig (ed.), *Excellence in Public Relations and Communication Management* (pp. 419–438). Hillsdale, NJ: Erlbaum.

Horne, J.H. and Lupton, T. (1965) The work activities of middle managers: An exploratory study. *Journal of Management Studies, 2*, 14–33.

Johnson, G., & Scholes, K. (2002) *Exploring Corporate Strategy: Text & Cases* (6th ed.). Harlow: FT Prentice Hall.

Kanter, R.M. (1989) *When Giants Learn to Dance: Mastering the Challenges of Strategy-Management and Careers in the 1990s*. London: Routledge.

Kaplan, R., & Norton, D.(1992) The balanced scorecard: Measures that drive performance. *Harvard Business Review*, *70*(1), 71–9.

Kotter, J. (1982) *The General Manager*. New York: Free Press.

Lauzen, M.M. (1992) Public relations roles, intra-organizational power, and encroachment. *Journal of Public Relations Research 4*(2): 61–80.

Ledingham, J.A., & Bruning, S.D. (eds) (2000) *Public Relations as Relationship Management*. Mahwah, NJ: Erlbaum.

Leichty, G., & Springston, J. (1996) Elaborating public relations roles. *Journalism Quarterly*, *73*, 467–77.

Leifer, R.P., & Delbecq, A. (1978) Organizational/environmental interchange: A model of boundary-spanning activity. *Academy of Management Review*, *3*, 40–50.

Macnamara, J. (1992) Evaluation of public relations; the Achilles heel of the PR profession. *International Public Relations Review*, *15*(4), 17–31.

Mintzberg, H. (1973) *The Nature of Managerial Work*. New York: Harper & Row.

Mintzberg, H. (1975) The manager's job: Folklore and fact. *Harvard Business Review*, *53*(July/August), 49–61.

Mintzberg, H. (1990)The design school: Reconsidering the basic premises of strategic management. *Strategic Management Journal,11*, 171–95.

Mintzberg, H. (1994) Rounding out the manager's job. *Sloan Management Review*, Fall, 11–26.

Mintzberg, H. (2009) *Managing*. San Francisco: Berrett-Koehler.

Moss, D.A., & Warnaby, G. (2000) Strategy and public relations. In D.A. Moss, D. Vercic, and G. Warnaby (eds), *Perspectives on Public Relations Research* (pp. 59–85). London: Routledge.

Moss, D.A., Warnaby, G., & Newman, A. (2000) Public relations practitioner role enactment at the senior management level within UK companies. *Journal of Public Relations Research*, *12*(4), 348–58.

Schultz, S., Hatch, M.J., & Larsen, M.H. (eds) (2000) *The Expressive Organization: Linking Identity, Reputation and the Corporate Brand*. Oxford: Oxford University Press.

Silverman, D., & Jones, J. (1976) *Organizational Work*. London: Macmillan.

Sriramesh, K. (1996) Power distance and public relations: An ethnographic study of southern Indian organizations. In H.M. Culbertson & N. Chen (eds), *International Public Relations: A Comparative Analysis*. NJ: Erlbaum.

Sriramesh, K. and J. White (1992) Societal culture and public relations. In J.E. Grunig (ed.), *Excellence in Public Relations and Communications Management*. Hillsdale, NJ: Erlbaum.

Stewart, R. (1967) *Managers and Their Jobs*. Maidenhead: McGraw-Hill.

Stewart, R. (1976) *Contrasts in Management*. Maidenhead: McGraw-Hill.

Stewart, R. (1982) *Choices for the Manager*. Englewood Cliffs, NJ: Prentice Hall.

(Continued)

(Continued)

Stewart, R. (Ed.) (1983) Managerial behaviour: How research has changed the traditional picture. In M.J. Earl (ed.), *Perspectives on Management* (pp. 82–98). London: Oxford University Press.

Stewart, R. (1988) *Managers and Their Jobs: A Study of the Similarities and Differences in Ways Managers Spend Their Time*. London: Macmillan.

Toth, E.L., & Grunig, L.A. (1993) The missing story of women in public relations. *Journal of Public Relations Research*, 5(3), 153–75.

Toth, E. L., S. A. Serini, et al. (1998) Trends in public relations roles:1990–1995. *Public Relations Review* 24(2), 145–63.

Van Riel, C.B.M. (1995) *Principles of Corporate Communication*. London: Prentice Hall.

Vercic, D., & Grunig, J.E. (2000) The origin of public relations theory in economics and strategic management. In D. A. Moss, G. Vercic, & G. Warnaby (eds), *Perspectives on Public Relations Research* (pp. 1–58). London: Routledge.

White, J., & Dozier, D.M. (1992) Public relations and management decision-making. In J.E. Grunig (ed.), *Excellence in Public Relations and Communications Management* (pp. 91–108). Hillsdale, NJ: Erlbaum.

Moving from Management to Leadership

Barbara DeSanto

Key Themes

- History of the management–leadership debate
- Differences and similarities between management and leadership
- Research on leadership traits, behaviours, and situations
- Public relations scholarship on leadership
- The Arthur W. Page 2007 Authentic Enterprise Report on leadership
- C-MACIE framework applied to leadership

INTRODUCTION: THE CONFUSED WORLD OF MANAGEMENT AND LEADERSHIP

For years, public relations practitioners have been encouraged, pushed, prodded, even exhorted to earn a seat at the management table. The underlying thinking for this move to management is that public relations as a practice has developed into more than the function that you call on when you have a crisis or find the media camped out on your front steps. As the chapters in this book show, public relations contributions to organizational and business success have become more sophisticated, moving from managing press and acting as journalists-in-residence to researching and managing issues, balancing multiple and complex stakeholder relationships, communicating in diverse environments, and functioning as partners with all types of enterprises from not-for-profit to investor relations.

While the move to management is firmly on its way, the next stage of development seems to be aimed at not only performing and being recognized as good managers, but also demonstrating strong leadership ability. During the past few years, public relations scholars and senior-level practitioners have been speaking and writing about not only gaining a seat at the management table, but also earning a place on the executive-levels of organizations. And, overwhelmingly, any discussion about a place on the executive-level clearly demands solid, recognized leadership knowledge and skills.

Through a discussion of the different types of leadership paradigms and a review of the most recent public relations scholarship exploring leadership in public relations practice, this chapter addresses the questions of how leadership is different than management and why public relations practitioners who understand how to take leadership roles will not only contribute to their organizations in meaningful ways, but also contribute to the practice and the reputation of public relations as a legitimate, essential, recognized element of good organizational management.

LEADERSHIP VERSUS MANAGEMENT: MORE THAN A SEMANTIC DIFFERENCE?

Scholars and practitioners line up on both sides of this debate. Whether you conduct an informal Google search or read scholarly articles featuring the terms 'leadership' and 'management', you will often find that while many authors say that leadership and management are 'different' things, halfway through the article the terms start to be used interchangeably, referring to managers as leaders and describing leaders as performing management tasks.

Henry Mintzberg (1973, 1994), one of the leading scholars in the field of management and leadership, takes the view that leadership is not superior to management and actually says that leadership is a component of management. Leadership is seen as sexy and management is desperately mundane in contrast. His main point is that managers display leadership characteristics as part of their management work. 'I want people to recognize one component of management is leadership but there are lots of other components – information, action, how you involve yourself, how you connect, and all sorts of things.'[1]

A 20-year veteran of the executive recruiting industry, Brian M. Sullivan, chief executive officer (CEO) of the executive search firm Christian and Timbers, disagrees with Mintzberg's view.

Let me start by explaining what I mean by these two terms. Leadership is innovative, creative, and, above all else, proactive. When CEOs are effective leaders, they anticipate problems and opportunities; they motivate and develop strategic responses; and they actively involve themselves in the implementation of action-oriented plans.

In contrast, management is a reactive tool to whatever situations happen to crop up … Why settle for a 'manager' whose goal is basically to maintain the status quo? After all, the mission of a 'leader' is to reinvent, so that the organization he or she directs … continuously becomes better.[2]

The picture here is that while managers are maintaining the day-to-day, here-and-now operations, leaders are looking beyond the present to identify and create the next version of the day-to-day for the organization to not only survive, but thrive.

So where do good leaders come from? Is the natural progression from performing as a good manager to becoming a good leader? Not necessarily, according to Marcus Buckingham, a management consultant who works with the Wharton School of Business. 'The chief responsibility of a leader ... is to rally people for a better future ... No matter how bleak his or her mood ... nothing can undermine a leader's belief that things can get better, and must get better.'[3]

Most scholars and researchers agree that leadership has been recognized for centuries, while management is a relatively recent concept which has been around for the last 100 years.

University professors Joyce Heames and Michael Harvey (2006) seem to share some of Mintzberg's philosophy that managers can and must develop into leaders. Using the history of management as their base, they contend that the twentieth-century manager will compare to the twenty-first-century global leader. Their argument, summarized in Table 3.1, is that today's fast-paced, rapidly changing environment and enormous amounts of information delivered 24/7 through hundreds of channels force managers to function as leaders.

Heames and Harvey also contend that personal characteristics and traits of leaders cannot be divorced from the major changes in today's environment, which requires individuals to function much more autonomously, making their own decisions and choices, than managers of old who were primarily charged with carrying out directives from their superiors. The focus today is on delivering results more than following a set process under a superior's watchful eyes. What you deliver, it can be argued, is more important than how you got there.

TABLE 3.1 From Manager to Leader

20th Century Manager (early 1900s)	21st Century Global Leader (early 2000s)
Broad interests, wide imagination and understanding	Open-minded and flexible
Superior intellectual capacities	Value-added technical and business skills
Understanding of the field of human relations	Cultural interest and sensitivity
Appreciate the importance of persuasion in human affairs	Resilient, resourceful, optimistic, and energetic
Understand what constitutes rational behavior toward the unknown and the unknowable	Able to deal with complexity
	Stable personal life
	Possess and engender honesty and integrity
(Barnard, 1948: 195–204)	(McCall & Hollenbeck, 2002: 35)

Source: Heames and Harvey (2006: 36).

Heames and Harvey also cited Harvey's previous work focusing on the environmental and economic evolutions from the twentieth to the twenty-first century, as Table 3.2 illustrates. The emphasis here outlines the sweeping changes that move individual nations into global community members, in great part due to technological advances. These fluid and all-encompassing environments in which individuals are equipped with technology, allow them to perform many different functions and roles as situations demand.

TABLE 3.2 Management Transitions from the Twentieth Century to the Twenty-First Century

20th Century	21st Century
High percentage of manufacturing industries	High percentage of service industries
Emphasis on functional expertise	Emphasis on management processes
Domestic market	Foreign markets and cultures
Legitimate authority in hierarchical organization structure	Virtual team and network organizational structures
Clearly defined operating procedures	Fluid and reactive operating procedures
Well-defined industry boundaries	Ill-defined industry boundaries
Fairly constant market	Turbulent market
Bricks and mortar	Virtual offices
Communication slow and unreliable	Communication instantaneous and continuous
Technology growth emerging	Technology growth exponential
Many employees with similar responsibilities and skills	Many employees with unique responsibilities and skills

Source: Heames and Harvey (2006: 32).

Northouse (2007) created a comparison chart of management and leadership competencies (Table 3.3). His main point focused on the fact that the work of managers and leaders, while similar, produces very different outcomes. The expectations,

TABLE 3.3 Management and Leadership Competencies

Management Produces Order And Consistency	Leadership Produces Change And Movement
• Planning and budgeting	• Establishing direction
• Establishing agendas	• Creating a vision
• Setting timetables	• Clarifying the big picture
• Allocating resources	• Setting strategies
• Organizing & staffing	• Aligning people
• Provide structure	• Communicating goals
• Making job placements	• Seeking commitment
• Establishing rules & procedures	• Building teams & coalitions
• Controlling & problem-solving	• Motivating & inspiring
• Developing incentives	• Inspiring & energize
• Generating creative solutions	• Empowering subordinates
• Taking corrective action	• Satisfying unmet needs

Source: Northouse (2007: 10).

therefore, for managers and leaders are different. While competencies can be demonstrated or overlap in different situations, one of the major differences is that managers are charged with focusing on the status quo and more immediate products, often having to take a shorter-term view, while leaders are expected to work toward the next revision or change, involving a longer-term view.

What can be learned from this discussion of management and leadership is that leadership may be the best vehicle to really 'showcase' the true power of public relations, because people with power make the decisions and determine courses of short- and long-term action.

Yet all attempts to define and study 'leadership' have not resulted in one definitive definition or description. In fact, most scholarship shows more what leadership is *not*, rather than what it is. Therefore, a brief overview of how leadership has been approached by scholars is useful in coping with the different perspectives about leadership.

A BRIEF HISTORY OF LEADERSHIP STUDIES

The academic study of leadership has resulted in three major areas of study: leaders' personal traits and characteristics; leaders' behaviours; and situations in which leaders or behaviours are readily apparent.

When leadership was identified as a major area of study in the social sciences, researchers began by trying to isolate a set of universal traits and characteristics that all leaders would possess to some degree. These traits and characteristics would be readily identifiable with the individual and displayed most of the time. Finding and isolating these common leadership attributes, however, proved futile as the individuals studied displayed a myriad of observable traits and characteristics, but few that seemed to be part of every leader's make-up. And leaders did not display them all of the time. Nor did the characteristics and behaviours appear in any type of regular pattern. Thus, researchers could not come to any common agreement. A list of the original major researchers and studies who pursued traits and characteristics is included in Table 3.4.

The focus then shifted from traits and characteristics to observing and trying to isolate leaders' behaviours. Again, a great number of behaviours were observed, identified, and catalogued, but as in the trait studies, no set of universal behaviours emerged. A list of the initial leader behaviour studies is included in Table 3.5.

After focusing exclusively on either traits and characteristics or leaders' behaviours, the next generation of researchers hypothesized that leadership behaviour or characteristics could not be separated from the situation and/or environment in which the behaviours were taking place and the characteristics displayed. This recognition that the situation affected leadership behaviour earned the name 'contingency theory', because the behaviours and characteristics manifested were influenced by the situation at hand. Different situations called for different types of leadership, and scholars posited that the same individual leader would probably display different types of leadership depending on the situation. These studies were important because they led researchers to combine behaviours with the situation, resulting in contingency theory development.

Contingency theories attempt to consider leaders' behaviours as displayed in specific situational contexts. Fiedler (1967, 1971) suggested that leader traits and behaviour interacted with the specifics of a situation and that leaders with more control over

TABLE 3.4   Selected Research on Leadership Traits

Traits That Distinguish Leaders From Others

1974	R.M. Stogdill	*Handbook of Leadership: A Survey of Theory and Research*	New York: Free Press
1994	D. Simonton	*Greatness: Who Makes History and Why*	New York: Guilford

Measurement of Prosocial Influence Motivation

1979	R.J. House & M.I. Baetz	Leadership: Some empirical generalizations & new research directions in B. Staw (Ed.) *Research in Organizational Behavior*, Vol. 1.	Greenwich, CT: JAI Press

Multiple Intelligences

1983	H. Gardner	*Frames of Mind: The Theory of Multiple Intelligences*	New York: Basic Books
1995	H. Gardner	*Leading Minds: An Anatomy of Leadership*	New York: Basic Books

Triarchic Intelligence

1988	R. Sternberg	*The Triarchic Mind: A New Theory of Intelligence*	New York: Viking-Penguin

Leaders Born or Made?

1990	T.J. Bourchard, D.T. Lykken, M. McGue, N.L. Segal, & A. Tellegen	Source of human psychological differences: the Minnesota Twins study of twins reared apart	*Science*, *250*, 223–8

Source: Adapted from House and Aditya (1997).

situations produced more effective results. Other researchers created and tested variations of Fiedler's original research, but the results provided little consensus and data. One recognized contribution of contingency theory was a rather serendipitous finding about the relationship between effective leaders and their followers, specifically that followers who identify an effective leader are often empowered by that leader, resulting in a relationship where the leader has follower loyalty. A second result of contingency research is that leaders operating in difficult situations tend to rely on their previous experiential behaviours and knowledge, indicating that leaders have a learning curve that provides opportunities to observe their innate abilities and traits. A list of the major contingency studies is included in Table 3.6.

Because of the variety of findings, their inconsistencies, and the inability to bring the streams of trait, behavioural, and contingency research together in any consistent, reliable model, researchers turned to examining relationships, perceptions, and vision to help explain who and what leaders are. This group of theories explores the interaction and relationships between leaders and followers. The discussion became about who is a leader and who identifies a leader. A great deal of leadership research began with the assumption that leaders were identified by followers, with the emphasis

TABLE 3.5 Selected Research on Leader Behaviour

Leader Task and Leader Person Behaviours

1953	R.L. Kahn & D. Katz	Leadership practices in relation to productivity and morale. In D. Cartwright & A. Zander (Eds.), *Group Dynamics*	New York: Harper & Row
1954	R. F. Bales	In conference	Harvard Business Review *32*(2), 44–50
1957	R.M. Stogdill & A.E. Coons	*Leader Behavior: Its Description and Measurement*	Ohio State University Press for Bureau of Business Research
1961	R. Likert	*New Patterns of Management*	New York: McGraw-Hill
1965	F.C. Mann	Toward an understanding of the leadership role in formal organization. In R. Durbin (ed.), *Leadership and Productivity*	San Francisco: Chandler
1966	D.G. Bowers & S.E. Seashore	Predicting organizational effectiveness with a four-factor theory of leadership	*Administrative Science Quarterly, 11*, 238–63
1971	R.J. House	A path goal theory of leader effectiveness	*Administrative Science Quarterly, 16*, 321–38
1974	L.L. Larson, J.G. Hunt, & R.N. Osborne	Correlates of leadership and demographic variables in three organizational settings	*Journal of Business Research, 2*, 335–47

Source: Adapted from House and Aditya (1997).

TABLE 3.6 Leadership Contingency Theories

Fiedler's Contingency Theory

1967	F.E. Fiedler	*A Theory of Leadership Effectiveness*	New York: McGraw-Hill
1971	F.E. Fiedler	Validation & extention of the contingency model of leadership effectiveness: A review of empirical findings	*Psychological Bulletin, 76*: 128–148
1973	A.S. Ashour	Further discussion of Fiedler's contingency model of leadership effectiveness: An evaluation	*Organizational Behavior & Human Performance, 9:* 339–55.
1977	C. Schriesheim & S. Kerr	Theories & measures of leadership: A critical appraisal of present & future directions. In J.C. Hunt & L.L. Larson (eds.), *Leadership: The Cutting Edge*	Carbondale, IL: Southern Illinois University Press
1981	M.J. Strube & J.E. Garcia	A meta-analytical investigation of Fiedler's contingency model of leadership effectiveness	*Psychological Bulletin, 90*: 307–21
1985	L.H. Peters, D.D. Hartke, & J.T.Pohlman	Fiedler's contingency model of leadership: An application of the meta-analysis procedure of Schmidt and Hunter	*Psychological Bulletin, 97:* 274–85

(Continued)

TABLE 3.6　(Continued)

Path-Goal Theory

1971	R.J. House	A path-goal theory of leader effectiveness	*Administrative Science Quarterly, 16:* 321–38
1974	R.J. House & T.R. Mitchell	Path-goal theory of leadership	*Journal of Contemporary Business, 3:* 81–97
1993	J.C. Wofford, & L.Z. Liska	Path-goal theories of leadership: A meta-analysis	*Journal of Management, 19:* 857–76

Life Cycle Theory

1982	P. Hersey & K. Blanchard	*Management of Organizational Behavior: Utilizing Human Resources*	Englewood Cliffs, NJ: Prentice-Hall
1987	R.P. Vecchio	Situational leadership theory: An examination of a prescriptive theory	*Journal of Applied Psychology, 72(3):* 444–51

Cognitive Resource Theory

1987	F.E. Fiedler & J.E. Garcia	*New Approaches to Effective Leadership: Cognitive Resources & Organizational Performance*	New York: Wiley
1995	F.E. Fiedler	Cognitive resources & leadership performance	*Applied Psychology – An International Review 44:* 5–28
1988	V.H. Vroom & A.G. Jago	*The New Leadership: Managing Participation in Organizations*	Englewood Cliffs, NJ: Prentice-Hall

Decision Process Theory

1973	V.H. Vroom & P.W. Yetton	*Leadership and Decision-making*	Pittsburgh, PA: University of Pittsburgh Press
1979	R.H.G. Field	A critique of the Vroom–Yetton contingency model of leadership behavior	*Academy of Management Review, 4:* 249–57
1984	M.E. Heilman, H.A. Hornstein, J.H. Cage, & J.K. Herschlag	Reactions to prescribed leader behavior as a function of role-perspective: The case of the Vroom-Yetton model	*Journal of Applied Science, 69:* 50-60
1988	V.H. Vroom & P.W. Yetton	*The New Leadership: Managing Participation in Organizations*	Englewood Cliffs, NJ: Prentice-Hall

Source: Adapted from House and Aditya (1997).

on the person identified. Little attention was paid to the followers who identified the leader. Now the hypothesis was predicated on the idea of a 'mature superior–subordinate dyadic relationship' (House & Aditya, 1997: 430), with the resulting product an effective relationship between leader and followers, producing more positive situational outcomes. Elements identified in this research included trust, respect and feelings of mutual cooperation between the leaders and followers. The question then emerged: What do the elements of an effective relationship look like? And would these elements look different in different situations?

While researchers found that leaders and followers could and did develop effective relationships, they could not determine exactly what the characteristics of those relationships were over a variety of situations. Trust, respect, and feelings of mutual cooperation between the leaders and followers were identified, but could not be detected in all relationships; researchers concluded that followers, leaders, and situations had too many factors that could influence the results in too many ways. Furthermore, there can be a wide variation in the types and strengths of responses between leaders and followers, which is difficult to measure. A list of the leader–follower theories is included in Table 3.7.

As researchers struggled with dealing with the seemingly endless variables present in contingency theories, the concept of 'charisma' reappeared in what are called the 'new leadership theories'. Bryman (1993) described the four elements of this set of theories as:

- explaining how leaders are able to get their organizations to produce significant accomplishments;
- recognizing that leaders inspire and motivate followers to high levels of performance;
- identifying observable leader behaviours; and
- recognizing follower benefits, such as self-esteem and personal motivation.

One high-profile concept to emerge from this research is transformational leadership, along with the development of the MLQ scale for measuring the difference among situations generated by charismatic leadership studies. What was still missing, however, was the actual measure of leadership behaviour. A list of the major new leadership theories is included in Table 3.8.

TRANSFORMATIONAL OR TRANSACTIONAL LEADERSHIP: ANOTHER VIEW OF THE MANAGEMENT–LEADERSHIP DEBATE?

No consideration of leadership is complete without addressing the transactional and transformational leadership concepts, two of the most recognized styles of leadership in today's contemporary management literature.

TABLE 3.7 Selected Research on Leader–Follower Theories

Leader Member Exchange Theory

1975	F. Dansereau, G.B. Graen, & W. Haga	A vertical dyad linkage approach to leadership in formal organizations	*Organizational Behavior & Human Performance, 13*, 46–78
1975	G. Graen & J.F. Cashman	A role-making model of leadership in formal organizations: A developmental approach. In J.G. Hunt & L.L. Larson (eds), *Leadership frontiers*	Kent, OH: Kent State University Press
1986	G.B. Graen, T. Scandura, & M.R. Graen	A field experimental test of the moderating effects of growth need strength on productivity	*Journal of Applied Psychology, 73*(3), 695–702
1994	A.J. Kinicki & R.P. Vecchio	Influences on the quality of supervisor–subordinate relations: The role of time-pressure, organizational commitment, and locus of control	*Journal of Organizational Behavior, 15*, 75–82
1995	G.B. Graen & M. Uhl-Bien	Relationship-based approach to leadership: Development of leader–member exchange (LMX) theory of leadership over 25 years: Applying a multi-level multi-domain perspective	*Leadership Quarterly, 6*(2), 868–72

Implicit Leadership Theory

1978	R.G. Lord, J.F. Binning, M.C. Rush, & J.C. Thomas	The effects of performance cues and leader behavior on questionnaire ratings of leadership behavior	*Organizational Behavior & Human Performance, 21*(1), 27–39
1984	R.G. Lord, R. Foti, & C.L. DeVader	A test of leadership categorization theory: Internal structure, information processing, & leadership perceptions	*Organizational Behavior & Human Performance, 34*, 343–78
1986	R.G. Lord, C.L. DeVader, & G.M. Alliger	A meta-analysis of the relation between personality traits and leadership perceptions: An application of validity generalizations procedures	*Journal of Applied Psychology 71*(3), 402–10
1991	R.G. Lord & K.J. Maher	*Leadership and Information Processing: Linking Perception and Performance*	Boston: Unwin Hyman

Source: Adapted from House and Aditya (1997).

The two concepts were introduced by Burns (1978) in his political studies research. He describes transactional leadership as a concrete, often short-term resource exchange, while transformational leadership addresses long-term vision and changes. In effect, the two types of leadership are two entirely different things. McWhinney (1997) added authoritative leadership as another moniker for transactional leadership,

TABLE 3.8 Selected New Leadership Theories

Charismatic Leadership Theories and Variations

1977	R.J. House	A 1976 theory of leader effectiveness. In .I.G. Hunt & L.L. Larson (eds), *Leadership: The Cutting Edge*	Carbondale: Southern Illinois University Press
1978	J.M. Burns	*Leadership*	New York: Harper & Row
1985	B.M. Bass	*Leadership and Performance Beyond Expectations*	New York: Free Press
1985	W. Bennis & B. Nanus	*Leaders: The Strategies for Taking Charge*	New York: Harper & Row
1987	J.A. Conger & R.A. Kanungo	Toward a behavioral theory of charismatic leadership in organizational settings	*Academy of Management Review, 12*, 637–47
1987	J.M. Kousnes & B.Z. Posner	The leadership challenge: how to get extraordinary things done in organizations	San Francisco: Jossey-Bass
1991	R. Pillai & J.R. Meindl	The effects of a crisis on the emergence of charismatic leadership: a laboratory study. In *Best Paper Proceedings, Annual Meeting of the Academy of Management*	Miami, FL
1993	R.J. House & B. Shamir	Towards the integration of transformational, charismatic and visionary theories. In M.M. Chemers & R. Ayman (eds), *Leadership Theory and Research: Perspectives and Directions*	San Diego, CA: Academic Press
1993	G. Yukl	A retrospective on Robert House's 1976 theory of charismatic leadership and recent revisions	*Leadership Quarterly 4(3–4)*, 367–73
1996	K.B. Lowe, K.G. Kroeck, & N. Sivasubramaniam	Effectiveness correlates of transformational and transactional leadership: a meta-analytic review of the MLQ literature	*Leadership Quarterly, 7(3):* 385–425
1996	D. Waldman, R.J. House, & G. Ramirez	A Replication of the effects of U.S. CEO charismatic leadership on firm profitability under conditions of certainty and uncertainty based on Canadian executives	Unpublished manuscript, Wharton School of Business
1997	R.J. House, A.L. Delbecq, & T. Taris	Value-based leadership: a theory and an empirical test	Reginald H. Jones Center for Strategic Management, Wharton School of Business

Source: Adapted from House and Aditya (1997).

TABLE 3.9   Transactional and Transformational Leadership: Comparative Summary

Transactional Leader	Transformational Leader
Performance is more reactive than proactive	Performance is more proactive than reactive
Responsive to primary focus of current immediate issues and maintaining the status quo	Primary focus is on envisioning and creating long-term plans to grow and capitalize on organization's strengths
Relies on accepted forms of inducement and compliance; e.g. rewards and punishment	Ability to create learning opportunities and intellectual stimulation for employees, which in turn creates individualized loyalty to cause larger than themselves
Employee self-interest is secondary to immediate organizational goal	Involves employees in making decisions
Aware of the link between specific efforts and and rewards	Instils pride, trust and respect with and among employees
Motivates by setting goals and promising rewards/punishments for specific performance	Possess ability to develop emotional links with employees
Watches and searches for deviations from rules and standards, initiates corrective action	Treats employees individually rather than as collective
Treats employees as collective groups rather than individuals	Motivates employees to work beyond individual self-interest in achieving the current objective

Source: Developed primarily from work by B. Bass, Distinguished Professor of Management and Director of the Center for Leadership Studies at the State University of New York at Binghamton.

which he said is characterized by 'leaders … least supportive of intentional change, and highly reliant on certainty, clear direction, personal oversight' and perceptions of 'right' positions (Aldoory & Toth, 2004: 159). McWhinney (1997) also extended Burns's work on transformational leadership, delineating 'risk taking, goal articulation, high expectations, emphasis on collective identity, self-assertion and vision' as central tenets.

Bass (1985), however, posited that the two types of leadership could not be separated, writing that a leader displays both short- and long-term behaviours, with short-term exchanges functioning as the building blocks to long-term vision necessary to effect change. Table 3.9 outlines a comparison of the transactional and transformational leadership.

One additional way to consider the differences and dependencies between transactional and transformational leadership lies in the status quo differences between management and leadership. Management expectations mirror transactional leadership in that managers are expected to carry out and maintain the status quo through focusing on discrete, often short-term tasks. Completing these tasks maintains a sense of order and stability. Leadership, on the other hand, can be argued to mirror transformational leadership in that the emphasis is on long-term, visionary, change-related ideas and concepts, which will ultimately challenge the stability and order of the organization. Given this line of thinking, public relations is a natural component of leadership because it is concerned with short- and long-term actions and changes in that it constructs the language of actions and changes for organizations.

LEADERSHIP AND PUBLIC RELATIONS

Public relations is developing its own stream of research about leadership in the field. Recent studies show that the topics range from individual elements of public relations to the grand challenge of creating an integrated public relations framework that encompasses all of the components. The one facet that all of the academics in these wide-ranging studies agree on is that it is necessary for public relations to move from management to leadership studies as an important way to become part of an executive-level team or dominant coalition.

Beginning Positions and Assumptions: Definitions of Excellent Leadership in Public Relations

Like other traditional leadership researchers, public relations scholars have chosen different sets of assumptions and starting places to enter the leadership debate.

Aldoory and Toth (2004) were among the first scholars to bring these two leadership styles into the world of public relations practice. Using focus groups, they reported that practitioners strongly preferred transformational over transactional leadership. Although their study also considered the gender implications of different leadership styles, they concluded: 'Focus group responses by men and by women were remarkably similar to each other in terms of preferences for leadership styles. All groups regardless of sex focused on transformational and democratic qualities for leadership' (p. 175).

Meng and Heyman (2009) chose to begin by adapting the major streams of leadership research to traditional public relations concepts of practitioners functioning as strategic communicators developing mutually beneficial relationships with internal and external stakeholders:

> Excellent leadership in public relations is a dynamic process that encompasses public relations executives' personal attributes and efforts in leading the team to facilitate mutual relationships inside and outside of organizations, to participate in the organization's strategic decision-making processes, and to contribute toward the effectiveness and success of the organizations of which they are members (p. 10).

This beginning point sets the stage for including as many positions and elements as possible, and it can be argued from the position quoted above that the language of public relations and leadership is quite similar, suggesting that public relations and leadership are kindred concepts and practices.

Similarly, Zerfass and Huck (2007) began with opening an umbrella concept that describes excellent communication leadership as social, cognitive, affective, and connotative dimensions combined into a new role focusing on innovation. Their explanation includes that innovation requires communication leaders to 'manage meaning' with all relevant stakeholders (p. 107). This overarching definition suggests that innovation or change affects all of these dimensions in varying degrees depending on the context or situation.

Each of these studies and scholars has a different set of assumptions from which to begin their studies. What is the same, however, is that leadership is now an accepted concept in public relations practice, whatever the definition. The important element here is to recognize the starting point and assumptions of each study, elements that determine the direction and conclusions of the different research. What this selection of definitions and assumptions also illustrates is that, like traditional leadership studies in general and leadership studies in other disciplines and professions, leadership in public relations is also fragmented and difficult to generalize into one theory that says it all. What is interesting, however, is that concepts in public relations, ranging from the rather theoretical, such as influence and perceptions, to the more concrete, such as observed behaviours and skills, are parallel in nature to the concepts in leadership in that they are fluid, situational, and contextual, and rely on the individual to decide how to combine the theoretical and the practical to achieve his/her objectives. Perhaps this also suggests that public relations professionals are well suited for leadership tasks because they are conditioned and comfortable dealing with ambiguity and uncertainty.

Selected Public Relations Leadership Studies and Their Implications

It is useful to examine a range of recent public relations leadership studies to understand the variety of leadership results they found because of the way they constructed their studies and what they concluded from their research.

Bowen (2008) chose to explore leadership as one of four paths that lead public relations practitioners to become part of a dominant coalition. Her starting point is an oft-repeated public relations mantra – that public relations practitioners must demonstrate and be recognized for their contributions to earn a seat at the management table. She posits that leadership is not the reward of earning that management seat, but the visible demonstration of the value of public relations to the dominant coalition. In her description, therefore, leadership becomes a manifestation of the contributions and power of public relations to achieve organizational objectives. Her research study, comprised of a worldwide survey of practitioners and focus groups supplemented by 32 long interviews with practitioners who did and did not have access to the dominant coalition in their organizations, identified leadership as one of five routes to membership in the coalition. Important elements of leadership here were moral courage along with the willingness to use that courage to 'offer insightful advice … mak[ing] a crucial decision alone', or taking a strong and steady stand on an issue (p. 11). These quotations speak to the axiological position of values, which the leadership literature emphasizes a great deal. Bowen also concludes that leadership is a method of earning credibility, which in turn, has impact with members of dominant coalitions.

The implication here is that a strong, firm, credible, stance based on sound judgement, defined by Bowen as leadership, is a tool or method to gaining access to an organization's executive-level. This suggests that leadership is not an end point as much of the literature seems to suggest, but ongoing personal development that leads to top positions. Much of the literature reads as though leadership is where a practitioner ends up when he or she reaches 'the top.' In contrast, then, Bowen's conclusion is that leadership is an important component of getting to the top.

Like most leadership scholars, Choi and Choi (2008) acknowledge that defining leadership is a difficult task and has resulted in little consensus, so they begin from the position of concentrating on one dimension they identify as critical: emotional traits and skills. They subscribe to the idea that transformational leadership is best suited to public relations practice because its empathetic base fosters more trust and confidence among employees throughout the organization. They chose to study the value of public relations in an organization-wide context. Their survey of public relations practitioners asked them to rate how much and how often they performed seven leadership behaviours: providing vision; being a change agent; exerting upward influence; networking using interpersonal contacts; combining public relations efforts with other management functions; monitoring internal information; and presenting public relations as a function to other organizational members. Their findings reflected four of the traditional leadership literature elements: that leaders provide vision; that leaders function as change agents; that leaders coordinate efforts among organizational members; and that leaders are influential, particularly in upward communication (p. 18). Choi and Choi conclude that their findings are useful to practitioners working to move into executive-level positions.

What is suggested in this study is that observable leadership behaviours play a large part in public relations practitioners being recognized as leaders and, as with Bowen's study, becoming part of the decision-making or dominant coalition. It further suggests that leadership behaviours are noticed throughout the organization, which can be helpful in other organizational elements understanding the value and power of public relations as part of the dominant coalition. To say that public relations can contribute is one thing, but demonstrating those contributions is what gains credibility with others.

Jin (2010) conducted a national survey of public relations practitioners identified as leaders by their titles in different types of organizations, using Aldoory and Toth's Leadership Preference Index. Her findings indicate that American public relations practitioners prefer transformational leadership as a style because of the humanistic relationship qualities such as trust, participative management, empathy, sensitivity, and relationship-building. Jin concludes that empathy is the most important emotional trait of public relations leaders and suggests that empathy is the best quality to have in conflict-resolution situations.

The findings here suggest that public relations practitioners can and should tap into their emotional sides as a way to build and strengthen relationships, which will help reduce or prevent conflict, and ultimately contribute to a more productive team-centred environment. Jin Gayle and Preiss (1988) the public relations practitioners learn to use creativity and imagination to connect emotionally with stakeholders. An emotion-based strategy will, in turn, foster and create transformations. This way, she contends, transformation can take place.

An axiological approach was taken by Meng, Berger, Gower, and Heyman (2009). Their survey questioned several hundred experienced public relations practitioners about their perceptions of the value of leadership in their practice. Among their findings are that:

- public relations leaders must have the capability to be make strategic decisions, to solve problems, and to communicate effectively;
- public relations leaders must want to be leaders and take the initiative to become leaders; and
- leaders look to others as role models as they develop their own leadership styles.

They also found that public relations leaders identified communication management as a critical component of leadership, especially in creating understanding across the organization and with external stakeholders (p. 21).

This suggests that communication is the vehicle through which an organization makes its leadership known, be it words or actions. In the authors' words, the most important finding of this study is that:

> public relations leaders do not only succeed in the application of technical communication skills; but more importantly, effective public relations leaders practice leadership as a dynamic complex. It encompasses individual traits, attributes, and behaviors. It also relies on the strategic application of comprehensive communication knowledge and expertise and the strategic expansion of the values of public relations to the organization. (p. 22)

Each of the studies above focused on one aspect of public relations leadership, but two studies took on the task of attempting to create one overarching public relations leadership theory. Zerfass and Huck (2007) believed that strategic communication was one of the facets contributing to organizational success, which they define as innovation-based. Their approach was to combine as many of theoretical concepts and research findings into a 'wheel of leadership communication' (p. 107). This circular model, they contend, should replace the traditional linear leadership social science based model, which begins with research, is tested through experimentation, and is then prototyped in best practice.

The premise of communication as creating and managing meaning within and outside of the organization is the foundation of the wheel. Zerfass and Huck argue that 'leaders are managers of meaning' and 'point directions' (p. 113); make sense of words and actions; can envision outcomes on a long-term scale; and use their political skills to deal with stakeholders. In short, they summarize, 'communication is the foundation of the interaction between leaders and followers' (p. 114). Therefore, they constructed their wheel to include cognitive, affective, connotative, and social dimensions. The concept of a wheel allows communicators/leaders to locate their actions by considering the factors involved and plotting a place, while realizing that that actions are dependent on one another.

The major implication here is that communication is at the heart of leadership; in fact, one could argue that communication is leadership because of the many roles it plays in managing perception, meaning, and change. This also suggests that to ignore communication in change management is to ignore an element that can greatly help or hinder all organizational efforts. Therefore, Zerfass and Huck contend that communication, by virtue of its essential contributions, is the essential leadership skill.

Perhaps the most ambitious leadership study in recent public relations scholarship is Meng et al.'s (2009) attempt to create a conceptually integrated public relations leadership framework. Like scholars before them, this was a complicated undertaking combining trait and characteristics research, behavioural research, and situational/contextual research within one idea. From their review of the literature, they identified self-dynamics, ethical orientation, relationship building, strategic decision-making, and communication knowledge management as the most important leadership qualities and facets. The configured result is the 'multilevel theoretical framework of excellent leadership in public relations' (Figure 3.1).

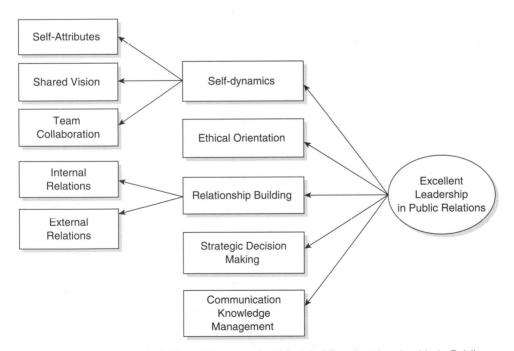

FIGURE 3.1   Meng et al. Multilevel Measurement Model of Excellent Leadership in Public Relations

Source: Meng (2009), p. 44.

The authors describe the conceptual framework thus:

- The attributes and entities associated with a specific culture not only predict organizational structure and culture, but also influence public relations leaders' behaviours that are most frequently enacted to achieve excellent in leadership in that particular culture.
- Within the concept of excellent leadership itself, PR leaders can apply traits and explicit knowledge and take actions to reduce constraints, strengthen internal and external relations, and favorably influence strategic decision-making.
- At the same time, the achievement of excellence in leadership may be overwhelmed by strong situational influences such as the organization structure and culture, as well as the belief and values associated with the society. (p. 20)

The impetus behind creating one theory is that including the traits, behaviours, and situations/context provide a place to begin testing these dimensions in situations where all of the elements might be present in different configurations.

The authors posit that the core dimensions will gain universal understanding, but be applied as appropriate to different situations.

TWENTY-FIRST CENTURY PUBLIC RELATIONS LEADERSHIP CHALLENGES

The preceding discussions focus on the different evolutions of management and leadership through the academic and scholarly lenses of traditional leadership studies from different perspectives. This focus on leadership, the different approaches to developing and testing the strands of leadership characteristics and skills, and some of the latest studies on application of leadership principles and positions to public relations practice is purely academic.

But the professional practitioner voice has also contributed to understanding the development of public relations not only as a maturing and management-level function, but as a critical member of twenty-first-century executive-level leadership teams. The well-researched Arthur W. Page (2007) leadership report provides insightful, realistic, and thoughtful contributions through its research for senior-level practitioners and CEOs describing what public relations leaders should contribute in contemporary organizations.

The first two columns of Table 3.10 summarize the more than six decades of evolution of the profession from a technical service provider developing into a communicator manager with varying degrees of power and responsibility and access to strategic decision-making processes. The third column is what the senior Page Society members see as the roles, characteristics, opportunities, and challenges for today's communicators. The leadership function neatly sums up the new role and status: a chief communication officer reporting directly to the CEO.

TABLE 3.10 The Evolution of the Public Relations Profession

	Yesterday: Public Relations (ca. 1945–1995)	Today: Corporate Communications (1995–2007)	Tommorrow (2008–?)
Mission	Liaison of the enterprise	Strategic planner of enterprise positioning	Shepherd of enterprise reputation and authenticity
Roles and responsibilities	Build and maintain relationships with the media; corporate journalism; internal events; speechwriting	Drive coverage: influence external criteria; change culture; influence strategy and policy	Create and influence ecosystem of advocates; steward company's values, brand and reputation; shape culture and behaviors; create the new, blended physical/virtual work environment; empower employees as communicators
Audiences	Media, employees, shareholders, general public	Media, employees, shareholders, senior management, analysts; in some cases government, NGOs, foundations	Media, employees, shareholders, senior management, analysts; in some cases government, NGOs, foundations, boards of directors and a billion global "publishers" with the means to be heard by mass audiences and to organize quickly
Channels	Print, broadcast, 'house organs,' events	Print, broadcast, events, Web IO (e.g., intranets)	Print, broadcast, interactive partnerships, town halls and Web 2.0 (enabling employees, partners, clients, influencers – a billion 'publishers')
Content	Content controlled by PR: external announcements (products, business actions, etc.); internal news, messaging and morale-building; executive speeches	Some content controlled by Communications, some by HR and marketing, some by stakeholders; the latter includes employee feedback, ecosystem-created ideas and perspectives on company	Content is created by everyone, influenced by Communications: defining values, strategy, brand; collaboratively shaped public policy; new academic curricula
Measurement of Value	Activity-based: e.g., volume and nature of press coverage, readership of employee publications	Attitude-based: e.g., corporate reputation surveys; measures of employee commitment	Impact-based: e.g., changes in policy, behaviour (internal and external); increased revenue, growth; recruitment; social network analysis
Functional Disciplines	Media relations, employee publications, speechwriting	Media, analyst and investor relations, internal and executive communications	Influencer relations and analytics; workforce enablement; values and brand experience; social networking/new media; corporate affairs; CSR
Skills	Writing, design, managing the press, message management, event planning	Driving coverage, organizational culture change, shaping strategic agendas	Building collaborative business ecosystems – engaged, enabled, supportive populations
Talent Pool	Former reporters, freelance writers, graphic designers, PR agencies	Reporters, writers and web experts, information managers (e.g., library science, opinion research)	Reporters, writers, Web experts, information managers, policy wonks, learning and organization development professionals, MBAs and business strategists
Leadership	VP of Public Relations: reports to Marketing, HR, Chief Operations Officer (COO) or Public Affairs	SVP of Corporate Communications: nearly half report to CEO	Chief Communications Officer: reports to CEO

Source: Arthur W. Page Society (2007: 21–2).

The Authentic Enterprise Report's Environment Change Findings

While the academic community has been positing, discussing, and studying leadership, the Page Society used its own historical analysis, outlined in Table 3.10, to conduct research among Chief Executive Officers (CEO) to define and determine the major opportunities and challenges to organizations and businesses in today's fast-paced business, media, and social/cultural environments. The results of this study clearly illustrate the evolution of the public relations manager's role into a public relations leadership role. The report's major findings include:

1. Identification of three ' major drivers of change' (p. 12) in today's environment.
2. A definition of what an authentic enterprise (p. 15) is and why it is important.
3. An explanation of why trust (p. 27) must be the fundamental grounding of the organization.
4. 'A call to action' (p. 29) for communication leaders to recognize, develop, and lead the efforts to address the issues critical not only to success for today's organizations, but also to survival.

The change drivers identified through this research reflect the changes happening not just in communication, but throughout the social, cultural, economic, and political facets of society. Access to digital technology and media is available to anyone able to afford it, and the technology makes anyone with an ordinary cell phone or computer a potential broadcaster or news outlet, as well as a personal communicator. Time and space have been compressed to instant communication that obliterates the time and distance of physical boundaries and technological limitations. While the benefits of instant global-reaching communication can be priceless, its curses can also be immense. Adding the global reality of today's world to this instant communication environment transforms the vertical communication chains into horizontal playing fields, with many more potential participants around the world, providing organizations with opportunities and challenges. Economy of effort through integrated networks makes global or international communication and collaboration possible, resulting in informed and up-to-date organizational components and stakeholders worldwide. That same dynamic holds true for challenging situations, like issues, that can turn into crises as fast as the information spreads. Organizations, therefore, have to be forever alert and in analysis mode.

The new media environment in a global world also brings in what the Authentic Enterprise Report calls 'the appearance and empowerment of myriad new stakeholders' (p. 6). These groups of stakeholders are not mere onlookers, they generally have some vested interest in the organization, as the Page Report describes: 'Many of these new players represent important interests, while others are not legitimate stakeholders, but rather simply adversarial or malicious. Regardless of motive, all are far more able to collaborate among themselves around shared interests and to reach large audiences' (p. 12).

The challenge and the opportunity here are for organizations to be vigilant about these identified change agents, as well as aware of trends and more change agents that in this environment have the potential to greatly – for better and/or worse – impact their survival.

The Authentic Enterprise Report's Authentic Enterprise Definition

The far-reaching changes described above point to what the Authentic Enterprise Report explains as the challenges of trying to exercise control in global, rapidly-changing environments and situations. Simply put, every action can now be shared around the globe, immediately affecting awareness and attitudes. Organizations can no longer say one thing while acting in ways that stakeholders can interpret as opposing what the messages appear to portray. In short, actions can and do speak louder than words, because actions are available with the words. The technology and global network allows actions to be instantly communicated, with the organization only one voice among many. Stakeholder assessments and interpretations take on a new importance in this new integrated landscape as they are communicated alongside the organization's message.

The Authentic Enterprise Report's Emphasis on Trust

In an environment where everyone's voice can be heard and stakeholders can assess actions for themselves, the Authentic Enterprise Report posits that trust is the critical element for organizational survival. Leaders 'today no longer have control – but ultimately [they] still have responsibility' (p. 27). This type of transparency and responsibility creates new challenges for top-level executives, making their first and constant mission to create and maintain internal working environments where all employees in all organizational locations not only understand and share the values, but also live the values. At the same time, the organization's external stakeholders, friend and foe alike, must see that the organizational values realistically make up the fabric of the organization, and are not just window dressing. Trust is painstakingly earned, yet can be quickly destroyed by organizational actions not driven by clearly communicated and understood values.

The Authentic Enterprise Report's Call to Action

The Authentic Enterprise Report outlined four challenges for organizations to recognize and address in the new change environment:

1. That organizations' core values be redefined or defined and put into action in ways relevant to the new environment.
2. That organizations must build and maintain stable congruent stakeholder relationships through one stable, authentic, organizational reputation.

3. That all employees in organizations must master the new technology and media environment conceptually as well as enabling their employees to use it.

4. That organizations have create, implement, and constantly evaluate strategies to build and manage trust with all stakeholders.

CEOs and Executive-Level Communicators: Addressing Today's Environment

The Authentic Enterprise Report concluded its research with in-depth interviews with CEOs who were asked to delineate the roles, tasks and responsibilities they expected high-level, strategic communicators to possess. What emerged from these interviews was 'the ideal communications chief' who possessed the following characteristics:

1. Detailed knowledge of the business.
2. Extensive communications background.
3. A crystal ball.
4. Executive-suite credibility.
5. Extensive internal relationships.
6. A team player.
7. An educator (pp. 44–5).

It is arguably clear from the major global changes and challenges the CEOs identified that all involve clear, value-driven, transparent, flexible, knowledge-based, consistent communication. And for this communication to become an executive-level function, communicators can no longer function as parrots or transmitters of top-down executive orders developed without consideration of the communication effects on the multiplicity of internal and external stakeholders and situations.

The first through sixth characteristics that emerged in this study have been topics of discussion among managerial scholars and practitioners for at least a decade. What is relatively new is the seventh characteristic – that an executive-level communication officer must function as an educator. This means more than just training people to handle tradition media relations; today each organizational employee is expected to be the face and voice of the organization to stakeholders armed with technology not only to form opinions and make judgements about organizations, but also able to explain their research-supported position locally, regionally, nationally, or globally. The potential impact has never been easier to create.

How the C-MACIE Framework Fits with the Enterprise Report

The underlying premise of the C-MACIE model focuses on greater communication input and involvement at all stages of organizational decision- and policy-making, essentially mirroring the Authentic Enterprise Report's findings that communication must be recognized as a critical part of all strategic decision-making. In reality, however, it is often not fully incorporated into the executive-suite for a number of reasons, ranging from reluctance to move from standard business decision-making processes to a lack of understanding about the power of communication and the necessity of having an educated and experienced professional taking charge of and being responsible for communication.

The management of analysis stage of the C-MACIE model speaks directly to the ideal communications chief's abilities to 'see around corners' (Arthur W. Page Society, 2007: 44) and have a great deal of communication experience. Accomplished communication professionals have not only experience to draw upon, but also established information networks, which are continual sources of information that keep practitioners up to date. Similarly, the relationships that professionals have can be called upon for certain types of information needed. The ability to gather information is not in itself a leadership skill; however, the ability to understand, assess, and apply the potential meanings of relevant information are. The concept of communicator as 'boundary spanner' speaks to collecting relevant information; the concept of leader recognizes that communicators have special insights into interpreting what this information means to different stakeholders in different situations, and the experience to weigh in on potential courses of action.

Similarly, the C-MACIE model recognizes that public relations managers use their experience, knowledge, and insights to recommend and/or develop, implement, and measure strategies in harmony with the organization's values, as well as its business objectives. Communication leaders must be able to see beyond the financial consequences to also assess the social, political, cultural, and, most importantly, reputational issues that may arise from specific communication strategies. Developing strategies that rely on communication to preserve or enhance reputation rarely work without the professional communicator being part of the executive-level team analyzing information and planning strategy. The 360-degree view of an experienced communicator provides leadership here.

Managing the implementation of the communication strategy, the third element of the C-MACIE model, is simply that messages and channels do matter. For example, BP's voice had been reduced to paid advertising across the United States because of its actions during the 2010 Gulf of Mexico oil platform disaster. Arguably, the communication neither matched the actions nor satisfied the media. The result has been direct attacks on BP's credibility nearly every news day. It is in this implementation step that communicators have probably earned their most visible role, because these are the channels and the words that can never be retracted. Whatever is released, said, broadcast, tweeted, or e-mailed is immediate public communication to all stakeholders in all locations. So the ramifications of how messages are crafted, who delivers them, in what situations, to whom, and with what intent are even more critical. And in today's digital world, the message does last forever. This again is another opportunity for communication professionals to take a leadership position in their organizations by contributing their expertise throughout the decision and strategy-making processes.

Ongoing evaluation of the organization's reputation, success and/or difficulty or failure in achieving objectives, and the organization's response to its stakeholders offers communication leaders another opportunity to demonstrate their value to the organization. Standard business evaluation models concentrate on profits, losses, customer retention, and other dollar-based measures to provide a picture of the business's financial health. However, financial position is only one indicator of organizational success or reputation. As the Authentic Enterprise Report research concluded, an organization's reputation – an intangible asset – is just as important as a solid financial base. And, arguably, the damage from a tarnished reputation can swiftly impact a company's solid financial base. The 2010 BP Gulf of Mexico oil well disaster provides an example of a company whose drilling in the Gulf results in about 10% of its worldwide oil drilling, but is costing the company far more than 10% of its corporate reputation.[4]

NOTES

1. http://www.management-issues.com/2009/10/5/mentors/henry-mintzberg-on-leadership-vs-management.asp
2. http://www.management-issues.com/2006/6/22/opinion/leadership-vs-management.asp
3. http://www.managementconsultingnews.com/interviews/buckingham_interview.php
4. http://www.bp.com/genericarticle.do?categoryId=2012968&contentId=7065717

SUMMARY

This chapter addressed the step from management to leadership for communication professionals. Forward thinking organizations such as the Arthur W. Page Society and a number of public relations scholars have begun a line of research addressing the issue of communicators as leaders. As the public relations profession continues to demonstrate its power to manage the communication function and to take on more of the tasks and roles that today's revolutionary environment presents, leadership roles are clearly places where communicators can contribute and showcase their expertise as boundary spanners, information providers and analyzers, reputation managers, and organizational voices internally and externally. Perhaps the last decade's call for managers to be recognized as important organizational contributors in all strategic processes will be recognized when communicators become leaders.

REFERENCES

Aldoory, L., & Toth, E.L. (2004) Leadership and gender in public relations: Perceived effectiveness of transformational and transactional leadership styles. *Journal of Public Relations Research*, *16*(2), 157–83.

(Continued)

(Continued)

Arthur W. Page Society. (2007) The CEO View: Opportunities & Challenges for the Senior Communication Executive. The Authentic Enterprise Report. Retrieved from http://www.awpagesociety.com/

Barnard, C.I. (1948) Education for executives. In K. Thompson (ed.), *The Early Sociology of Management and Organizations* (pp. 194–206). New York: Routledge/Taylor & Francis.

Bass, B.M. (1985) *Leadership and Performance Beyond Expectations*. New York: Free Press.

Bowen, S.A. (2008) What public relations practitioners tell us regarding dominant coalition access and gaining membership. Paper presented at the 11th International Public Relations Research Conference, Miami, FL.

Bryman, A. (1993) Charismatic leadership in business organizations: Some neglected issues. *Leadership Quarterly 4*(3–4), 289–304.

Burns, J.M. (1978) *Leadership*. New York: Harper & Row.

Choi, J., & Choi, Y. (2008) Dimensions of leadership in public relations: Exploring an organization-wide perspective. Paper presented at the annual meeting of the International Communication Association, Montreal.

Fiedler, F.E. (1967) *A Theory of Leadership Effectiveness*. New York: McGraw-Hill.

Fiedler, F.E. (1971) Validation and extension of the contingency model of leadership effectiveness: A review of empirical findings. *Psychological Bulletin*, *76*, 128–48.

Gayle, B.M., & Preiss, R.M. (1998) Assessing emotional organizational conflicts. *Management Communication Quarterly*, *12*(2), 280–302.

Heames, J.T., & Harvey, M. (2006) The evolution of the concept of the 'executive' from the 20th century manager to the 21st century global leader. *Journal of Leadership and Organizational Studies*, *13*(2), 29–41.

House, R.J., & Aditya, R.N. (1997) The social scientific study of leadership: Quo vadis? *Journal of Management*, *23*(3), 409–73.

Jin, Y. (2010) Emotional leadership as a key dimension of public relations leadership: A national survey of public relations leaders. *Journal of Public Relations Research*, *22*(2), 159–81.

McCall, M.W. & Hollenbeck, G.P. (2002) *Developing Global Executives: The Lessons of International Experience*. Cambridge, MA: Harvard Business School Press.

McWhinney, W. (1997) *Paths of Change: Strategic Choices for Organizations and Society*. Thousand Oaks, CA: Sage.

Meng, J. (2009) Excellent leadership in public relations: An application of multiple-group CFA models in assessing cross-national measurement invariance. *Unpublished doctoral dissertation*, The University of Alabama, Tuscaloosa (UMI No. 3369756)

Meng, J., Berger, B.K., Gower, K.K., & Heyman, W.C. (2009, May) A test of excellent leadership in public relations: Key qualities, valuable sources, and distinctive leadership. Paper presented at the Public Relations Division of the 59th International Communication Association Convention, Chicago.

Mintzberg, H. (1973) *The Nature of Managerial Work*. New York, Harper & Row.

Mintzberg, H. (1994) Rounding out the manager's job. *Sloan Management Review*, Fall, 11–26.

Mintzberg, H. (2009) *Managing*. San Francisco: Berrett Koehler.

Mintzberg, H., Ahlstrand, B., & Lampel, J. (1998) *Strategy Safari: A Guided Tour Through the Wilds of Strategic Management*. New York: Free Press.

Northouse, P.G. (2007) *Leadership: Theory and Practice*, 4th ed. Thousand Oaks, CA: Sage.

Zerfass, A., & Huck, S. (2007) Innovation, communication, and leadership: New developments in strategic communication. *International Journal of Strategic Communication*, *1*(2), 107–22.

The Capabilities Needed for the Strategic Management Role

4

Anne Gregory

Key Themes

- Understanding the importance of context for determining the capabilities necessary for senior communication/public relations practitioners
- Understanding recent research on roles: a corporate communications perspective; a European perspective; and a management theory perspective
- Implications of roles theory for senior practitioner capabilities
- Identifying the key components of capability: skills, knowledge and competencies
- Defining senior practitioner skills, knowledge and competencies
- Relating skills, knowledge and competencies to the C-MACIE framework

---

INTRODUCTION

As has been already demonstrated in Chapter 2, there has been a great deal written on management roles generally and on communication/public relations roles more specifically. Indeed, it is not an overstatement to say that a discussion on roles is a pervasive and recurring theme in the communication/public relations literature, featuring in all the standard teaching texts (see Grunig & Hunt, 1984; Newsom, Turk, & Kruckeberg, 2000; Cornelissen, 2008; Cutlip, Center, & Broom, 2009; Tench & Yeomans, 2009).

Chapter 2 pointed to the distinction drawn by some scholars (Hales 1986, 1999) between managerial tasks and responsibilities (what managers should or intend to do) and managerial behaviour (how managers do what they do). However, in advancing the C-MACIE we did not explicitly focus on defining the appropriate managerial behaviours for each stage of the model). However, given that this book is at least in part about about the strategic management process of communication/public relations as undertaken by senior practitioners, it is entirely appropriate that their overall capabilities are examined. This chapter will explore practitioner capabilities under three main headings – *knowledge*, *skills* and *competencies* – and then apply them to the C-MACIE framework.

Context

Before a discussion on capabilities can be undertaken, it is worth reflecting on the context in which practitioners currently operate, since that will help to frame the roles that they have to enact. For the purposes of this chapter, 'context' will be separated into external and internal. Both will be addressed in relation to how this impacts on the *role* of the senior practitioner. It will not cover context, or as it is sometimes called, environmental analysis, for strategic communication planning purposes.

External Context

Communication/public relations practitioners are seen to be organisational 'boundary spanners' (Aldrich & Herker, 1977), with one foot inside the organisation and one foot outside. They have a strategic remit of interpreting the outside (and internal) environment for senior management and representing the organisation externally. In that role they encounter the flux and change of that external environment. Hence, they need to develop the skills and knowledge required to gather, sift and interpret both the long-term trends and short-term developments within and turbulence of that external environment, and the shifting positions of their stakeholders within the context of that activity.

As Pearson (2000: 67) concludes: 'Public relations practice is situated at precisely that point where competing issues collide. Indeed, public relations problems can be defined in terms of the collision, or potential collision of these interests'. Indeed, Gollner (1983) asserts that public relations is of growing importance precisely because external issues are 'crowding in' on organisational decision-making and that the shrinking, mutually dependent world is of increasing complexity as often incompatible value systems are forced to interact. The *raison d'être* of communication/public relations is the resultant conflict. The capabilities required to handle this complexity will be further discussed later in this chapter.

So what, in summary, are some of the big issues that are changing the external environment and which in turn have an impact on the role of communication/public relations? The Arthur W. Page Society (2007), in a seminal report called *The Authentic Enterprise*, identified three interlinked factors which it proposes will radically alter chief executive officer (CEO) expectations of chief communication officers (CCOs). They state that today's organisations 'are facing a rapidly changing landscape' (p. 6) which comprises:

- A new digital information sphere that is ubiquitous and accessible to huge numbers of people.
- A globalised economy.
- Stakeholders, many of whom are new to organisations who are empowered because of the first two factors.

They go on to say:

> Together these forces have created a global playing field of unprecedented transparency and radically democratised access to information production, dissemination and consumption. They are overturning the corporation's traditional ability to segment audiences and messages and to manage how it wishes to be perceived.

Alistair Campbell (2008), director of communications for the former UK prime minister Tony Blair, identifies six trends which he believes are transforming the role of communication/public relations:

- The rise of the democratic corporation, where organisations are held to account in new ways as their corporate responsibilities are insisted upon and as new technologies makes their activities more open to scrutiny.
- Participatory media, including the use of citizen journalism, means that the nature of news gathering and presentation is changing and is instant.
- Information has an infinity – new technology means that information is unbounded in time and in place, and also has the potential for infinite existence.
- The press does not reflect what people think – it is increasingly negative and cynical in the pursuit of audiences.
- The merger of the citizen and consumer, where citizens expect private sector standards from the public sector and public sector values from the private sector.
- The task of communication is meaning – given the huge amount of information available, the lack of agreement on or common readership of authoritative information sources, and the lack of recognised authority figures to provide a compass, the task of professional communicators/public relations practitioners is to provide meaning.

Beinhocker, Davis and Mendonca (2009) identify 10 trends that have to be watched over the next few years. A number of them have direct impact on the communicator's role,

- Globalisation: the globalisation of goods, services and talent will grow even if financial globalisation is restrained. The requirement for cross-cultural understanding and communication will remain.
- Trust in business is running out: hence organisational accountabilities will increase and they will have to work harder to rebuild trust.

- A bigger role for government: their involvement in business during the recession of 2007–10 is likely to remain and regulation could increase. The implications for government relations are obvious.
- Shifting consumption patterns and the rise of the Asian economies mean changes in consumer and value chain relationships.
- Ther march of innovation will apply to communication technologies too and the challenges of on-demand responsiveness will increase.

Internal Context

Chapter 12 of this book deals extensively with the challenges of internal communication; so in this chapter only the impact of these challenges on the communication/public relations *role* is discussed. All the external trends that affect organisations also apply internally. Employees are also global citizens, empowered by technology and able to hold their organisations to account by their connection to other networks. They are also increasingly threatened as old ownership and working patterns and practices become obsolete. Jobs for life and paternalistic cultures are rare as organisations have to respond to the challenges of a global economy. Downsizing, rightsizing, outsourcing, mergers and acquisitions, along with social changes such as increased mobility and other lifestyle issues, are changing the nature of organisations and the nature of the contract (physical and psychological) that organisations have with their employees (Yeomans, 2009). Nonetheless, there is general consensus that the old style authoritarian mode of running organisations is no longer appropriate and that harnessing employees' abilities and energy as partners in the enterprise is more fulfilling for them as individuals and helps to contribute to organisational success (Smythe, 2007).

These changes in the way that organisations are organised and managed internally suggest a different kind of relationship with this key stakeholder group which, along with the fact that employees are also citizens of the wider word, has a clear impact on the way that senior communication/public relations practitioners fulfil their internal communication role.

Implications of Context

The Authentic Enterprise Report (Arthur W. Page Society, 2007), alluded to earlier, identifies a number of challenges and opportunities for the senior communication/public relations practitioner. The largest opportunity is that in light of the changing landscape, organisations will need a new way of operating which has communication at its heart. Consistent behaviour and action guided by commonly held values, principles or beliefs will be required for an organisation to be regarded as 'authentic', and authenticity will be the touchstone against which organisations will be judged.

To achieve acceptance and support as an authentic enterprise, CEOs are looking to their CCOs to take a more strategic role because the changes required under this new way of operating involve a far greater emphasis on stakeholder relationships and public perception, or reputation. Furthermore, CEOs will need to develop their collaboration skills as they seek to ensure all their corporate functions work to common values and as they seek to work in partnership with other enterprises and stakeholders with whom they find common cause. They will turn to their CCOs to help them with this.

In conclusion, The Authentic Enterprise Report sets out four new priorities and skills which CCOs must acquire if they are to assume a leadership role:

- Leadership in defining and instilling company values.
- Leadership in building and managing multi-stakeholder relationships.
- Leadership in enabling the enterprise with 'new media' skills and tools.
- Leadership in building and managing trust, in all its dimensions.

A study of the literature on the capabilities of practitioners undertaken by Watson and Sreedharan (2010) concurs with these findings, but also concludes that future senior practitioners will need to:

- Have broader analytical and critical skills in order to become respected at the most senior levels.
- Become closer to trends and policy-making, especially on corporate social resonsibility/sustainability; often participating in the discourse.
- Possess a wider inter-disciplinary set of competencies so they can act as advisors with equal standing to other senior organisational colleagues.
- Have relationship-building, negotiation and management skills.

Finally, a study of European communication directors, called the European Communication Monitor (Zerfass et al., 2009), which sampled 1,524 communication professionals across 34 countries, identified their perceptions of the most important issues facing them in the next 3 years. Figure 4.1 shows the results. Again, it can be seen that there are common themes, which confirm those coming from the other studies cited earlier. The first ranked topic, linking business strategy and communication, is a clear consequence and necessary requirement if communication is to be placed at the heart of the ways organisations operate.

THE ROLE OF COMMUNICATION/ PUBLIC RELATIONS AND SENIOR PRACTITIONERS

Without going over the ground on roles already covered in Chapter 2, it is important to touch briefly on the more recent scholarship on the role of communication/ public relations and senior practitioners within organisations, because without this it is impossible to explain what capabilities are needed to underpin those roles.

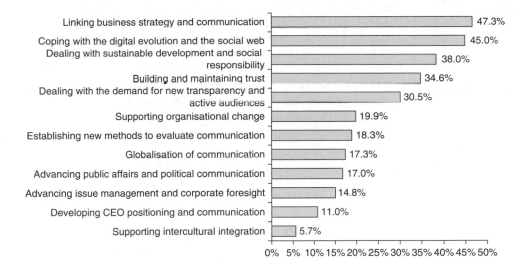

FIGURE 4.1 The Most Important Communications Issues in Detail
Source: Zerfass et al. (2009), p. 66.

Chapter 2 gives an overview of the roles research which has continued to evolve and develop over time.

A Corporate Communications Strategy View

Steyn (2003), drawing on the strategic management literature, mapped the contribution that communication/public relations can make at five levels of strategic management, and related it specifically to the groups of stakeholders that are primarily involved.

Enterprise strategy, the broadest level of strategy, is where the political legitimacy of the organisation is addressed. Here the organisation has to consider its role in society, to decide what values it wants to represent and what the implications are of this in resource allocation and business positioning terms. At this level, the organisation is seeking to reinforce its legitimacy and gather support from a broad range of stakeholders, and it is likely to focus on non-financial goals such as working to increase the reputation of the organisation and ensuring that it fulfils its social responsibilities.

According to Steyn (2003), important stakeholders at this level will be the media, activist groups, community, government and society at large. Tasks for communication/public relations are to ensure that the organisation's reputation is managed, to help clarify and promote its values and ensure that corporate governance principles are adopted. If these things are successfully done, the end result is more likely to be a trusted organisation whose 'licence to operate' is supported.

Corporate strategy is where the portfolio of business forming the organisation's operations is determined and where corporate resources and capabilities are managed. Here strategy is financially orientated and shareholders are the main stakeholders.

The task of communication/public relations will therefore be to ensure that share-holders' views are taken into account in decision-making and that the organisation is represented in a way that will encourage their support.

Business unit strategies relate to the organisation's approach to its industrial sector, market and products. Here the decisions taken at corporate level are operationalised. Given that business unit strategies are usually market orientated, communication/public relations effort is likely to be focused on customers, suppliers, employees and regulators – in other words, on the value chain – with the aim of securing the active support of those stakeholders.

Functional strategy determines how the various functions of the organisation, such as marketing, finance, and human resources, need to work together to achieve higher strategies, and how they, as individual functional areas will make the contribution most appropriate for them.

For example, the marketing function will address the external market, gathering customer and competitor information, and work with the sales force in forging exchange relationships with customers. The job of communication/public relations will be to help equip functions to engage with those stakeholders most relevant to them, either by coaching staff within those functions, or conducting engagement activities on their behalf. Communication/public relations will also build and main-tain relationships with those stakeholders for whom it takes specific responsibility, for example, the media, the local community, and government.

Operational strategy is where strategies are put into action. Here operational plans will be developed and implemented. For communication/public relations, this will mean implementing specific programmes and campaigns.

Steyn (2003) proposes a number of key features in the operationalisation of cor-porate communication strategy (i.e. the corporate communication strategy process) which will support the various levels of organisational strategy outlined above. The task of the corporate communication function is to:

- Analyse and advise on the organisational internal environment – its profile, vision, mission, values, culture and strategies.
- Identify strategic stakeholders and publics in the internal and external environment.
- Identify, describe and differentiate the key issues in both environments.
- Identify the implications of each key issue for each affected stakeholder group.
- Define the communication strategy (i.e., what must be communicated to either solve the problems or grasp the opportunities presented by each key issue).
- Develop appropriate communication plans based on goals which will be determined by the above.

From this it can be deduced that there are various roles for communicators. At the most senior level (Steyn calls this the *strategist*) it will be to advise boards and other senior managers about what is happening in the internal and external environments and about key stakeholder concerns. These are critical elements potentially affecting both the reputation of the organisation and the relationships it depends upon, to secure ongoing support and legitimacy. *Managers* will ensure that plans are developed and implemented in support of the organisation's strategic purpose and *technicians* will undertake the implementation. It follows that different capabilities will be required to undertake these different roles.

A European View

In 2004 the results of a Delphi panel, involving 37 experts in research and/or education, in 25 countries in Europe, were published (van Ruler et al., 2004). Although the study did not claim to be statistically representative, it did point to four characteristics of communication/public relations in Europe which anecdotally have found resonance with the communication/public relations community in Europe. These four characteristics are given in Figure 4.2 and define the contribution that communication/public relations makes to organisations. The similarities between this conceptualisation of the contribution of communication/public relations and the Steyn (2003) conceptualisation can be seen. Again, the capabilities to underpin these contributions will require skills, knowledge and behaviours that are wide-ranging and at strategic, managerial and technical levels.

A Managerial View

Work undertaken by Moss and colleagues (Moss, Warnaby, & Newman, 2000; Moss & Green, 2001; Moss, Newman, & DeSanto, 2005) in the UK and USA, focused on observing and interviewing communication/public relations managers about what

REFLECTIVE	MANAGERIAL
Analysing changing standards, values and standpoints in society and discussing these with members of the organisation in order to adjust the standards, values/ standpoint of the organisation accordingly. Concerned with organisational standards, values and views and aimed at the development of mission and organisational standards.	Developing plans to communicate and maintain relationships with public groups in order to gain public trust and/or mutual understanding. Concerned with commercial and other (internal and external) public groups and with public opinion as a whole, and is aimed at the execution of the organisation's mission and strategies.
OPERATIONAL	EDUCATIONAL
Preparing the means of communication for the organisation (and its members) in order to help the organisation formulate its communications. Concerned with services and aimed at implementation of communication plans developed by others.	Helping all members of the organisation to become communicatively competent in order to respond to societal demands. Concerned with the thinking and behaviour of organisational members and aimed at internal publics.

FIGURE 4.2 The Four Characteristics of European Communication/Public Relations

they actually do. They pointed out that earlier studies had used a deductive, normative approach to conceptualise roles, based on the consulting literature. Moss and colleagues' work was based on empirical work, following the inductive, grounded approach taken by most management researchers.

In summary, the studies in the UK and USA identified five elements to the communication/public relations manager role: four relating to managerial responsibility and one to technical work. The four managerial responsibilities were:

- *Monitor and Evaluator*. This element describes the managerial responsibilities that senior practitioners have for organising, controlling and monitoring the work of communication/public relations departments both internally and externally. Within their departments they are responsible for setting targets, acting within budget and monitoring performance against these targets. Outside their department they have to negotiate with other areas, including senior management, to set their own departmental targets, negotiate resources and commission external agencies.
- *Key Policy and Strategy Advisor*. This aspect relates to the relationship communicators/public relations practitioners should have with senior management, although Moss et al. (2005) found that this was more of an expectation than a reality. In this role practitioners advise on matters such as stakeholder relationships and issues, on how decisions are likely to be perceived and how to present policies and decisions.
- *Issues Management Expert*. This relates to the practitioner's role in diagnosing and responding to external threats posed by major or minor issues and involves not only identifying these threats, but interpreting them.
- *Troubleshooting/Problem-Solver*. This factor relates to the practitioner responding to and dealing with internal and external challenges, threats and crises and they are recognised as the person designated to do so. The difference with this and issues management is that whereas the latter focuses on a predictive and advisory role, this role is operationally focused.

The responsibility relating to technical work is the following:

- *Communication Technician*. This relates to at least overseeing, and in many cases implementing, the technical duties of communication work, including media relations. The level of involvement may depend on departmental size and resources, but also reflects the preference of some senior practitioners to retain involvement in operational work.

Some Conclusions about the Role of Communication/ Public Relations and Senior Practitioners

Drawing together this more recent work on roles shows an emerging picture of the demands on and opportunities for senior practitioners, which suggest the kinds of capabilities that will be required. These include:

- An ability to work with senior management to identify and clarify organisational values, principles of operating, policies and strategies, which will secure the organisation's 'licence to operate', that is, to reinforce its legitimacy.
- Skills and knowledge to scan, interrogate and interpret the external environment, including the disposition of external and internal stakeholders; to identify issues and opportunities pertaining to this analysis and bring these to senior managers' attention, so that they can be factored into organisational decision-making.
- An understanding of business objectives and imperatives and the ability to contribute to these by engaging with a range of internal and external stakeholders, to gather intelligence and support from them and to represent and promote the organisation to and through them.
- Skills and knowledge to plan strategically and to construct communication/ public relations plans which support organisational objectives and which have appropriate resources for their delivery and evaluation.
- An ability to implement these plans effectively and efficiently.
- The capability to work with others in the organisation, including senior managers and other employees, to enable the organisation to be able to understand and handle the complexities of communication in, by and with organisations (communicative competence).

SKILLS, KNOWLEDGE AND COMPETENCIES OF SENIOR PRACTITIONERS

Having considered the context of communication/public relations and the emerging roles of senior practitioners, it is now appropriate to look in depth at the capabilities required of those practitioners. However, before doing so, it is necessary to clarify the meaning of a number of words, since it is clear that there is confusion about how they are used in the literature.

Definitions

Words such as *attributes*, *skills*, *capabilities*, *knowledge*, *experience*, *traits* and *qualities* are used with little definition. In this chapter the following definitions will be used (Gregory, 2008):

- *Knowledge*: what practitioners need to *know* in order to undertake their role competently (PRSA, 2006).
- *Skills*: what practitioners need to be able to *do* to undertake their role competently (PRSA, 2006).
- *Competencies*: behavioural repertoires or sets of *behaviours* that support the attainment of organisational objectives – how knowledge and skills are used in performance (Bartram, 2004).

As indicated earlier, there is much confusion in the literature about what constitutes skills, knowledge and competence, and indeed a level of conflation. For example, skills cover writing, but also departmental management, leadership, and a lively, enquiring mind (Skinner, Von Essen, & Mersham, 2004: 12), 'a good attitude' (PRSA, 2006: 19) and credibility, integrity and flexibility (IPR, 2003).

Lang and Cantor (cited in Cutlip, Center, & Broom, 2000: 53–5) list the personality traits and qualities of those aspiring to a successful career in communication/public relations, which include results, conceptualisation, style, human relations, response to tension, individual initiative, curiosity and learning, energy, drive and ambition, friendliness and a lack of self-consciousness.

It is not always clear whether these lists are based on research or are 'received wisdom', distilled by academics and practitioners with knowledge of the profession. In light of this, personal attributes, character traits and personal qualities are not covered in detail in this chapter, not because they are unimportant, but because they are highly contested, contradictory and often subjective. Skills, knowledge and competencies are not contested and are focused on the basic requirements of performance. If these elements are not present, the senior practitioner will not be competent in their role. Matters to do with personality and qualities may be regarded as less central to the role.

In their research on the competencies and training needs of the senior communicator of the future, Watson and Sreedharan (2010) framed a number of propositions which summarised the literature on the requirements of senior manager roles into the future and then tested these with practitioners. The resultant top 12 competencies and skills are listed in Table 4.1.

Skills

Focusing on the specific skills needed of senior practitioners, there have been a number of studies and reports summarising these, mainly emanating from the public relations professional bodies (IPR, 2003; BP, 2002; PRSA, 2006). Note that, as of May 2010, the 2006 PRSA document remains current for communication/public relations career development planning. Table 4.2 provides an overview of these sources, abstracting senior practitioner skills from them.

As can be seen, this is an eclectic mix of skills, some mapping directly onto managerial roles and responsibilities of senior practitioners, some relating more obviously to the senior technician role. However some of the higher level skills can be summarised as being those identified in the section on conclusions about the role of communication/ public relations and senior practitioners in this chapter, namely environmental scanning (externally and internally) using social scientific research techniques; issues identification and crisis management; working with senior and other managers in policy development and organisational decision-making; planning, monitoring and evaluating strategic communication programmes and campaigns; managing resources and demonstrating technical competence.

TABLE 4.1   Propositions Framing the Senior Practitioner Role into the Future

Rank	Proposition
1	Communication strategy will be ever more tightly linked to overall business strategy and less on organisational publicity. Competencies in strategic management will be part of the senior communicator's portfolios.
2	Senior communicators need to have broader analytical and critiquing skills in order to become trusted senior advisors.
3	A more inter-disciplinary set of skills, knowledge and competencies is needed for senior communicators for them to act as advisors of equal standing with other senior operational colleagues.
4=	Senior communicators will become the cross-discipline chief reputation officers in their organisations. This will involve higher-level internal networking and communication skills and organisational knowledge in order to be effective.
4=	Senior communicators should focus more on engagement with stakeholders and less on media relations. Skills of negotiation and relationship management will need development.
6	Proof of performance (the demonstration of the value of communication strategy to the organisation) will require higher skills of analysis, planning and measurement of outcomes.
7	Future senior communicators need to be able to interpret changes and trends in communication technologies and practices. They will be able to measure and evaluate the real value of evolving media forms, including social media, not just the traffic.
8	The creation of social capital and the maintenance of the organisation's 'operating licence' will be an increasingly important role for senior communicators.
9	The increasing internationalisation of corporations will require greater competence amongst senior communicators in culturally sensitive communication, its management and coordination.
10	Senior communicators will need to be closer to public policy-making, particularly on sustainability and corporate social responsibility issues. This may need additional education in public affairs.
11	Succession planning should involve mentoring for mid-level staff on current and future organisational demands by senior communicators in order to develop them as trusted counsellors, not just superior communications technicians.
12	There should be greater emphasis on senior communications developing coaching and mentoring skills so they can aid senior management in problem-solving and presentation.

Knowledge

Turning to the knowledge that senior practitioners should have to underpin and complement their practical skills uncovers a richer seam of information and research. The sources cited above have also listed their knowledge requirements (see Table 4.3).

However, the academic literature also has insights that supplement these lists. Dozier, Grunig, and Grunig (1995) in their conclusions to a 15-year, three-nation

TABLE 4.2 Skills of Senior Practitioners

PRSA, 1993	PRSA, 2006	IPR, 2003	BP, 2002[1]
Skills of Directors/Executives	Skills in Educational Curricula Underpinning Senior Level Activity	Skills of Practitioners	Skills of Managers/Directors
DIRECTORS:			**MANAGERS:**
• Designing/directing research programmes	• Research methods and analysis	• Written and verbal communication	• Research methods
• Directing external communication/public relations programmes	• Management of information	• Creativity	• Use of research software
• Consulting with internal/external clients	• Mastery of language in written and oral communication	• Media relations	• Presentation of results
• Providing strategic planning	• Problem-solving and negotiation	• Crisis management	• Production, design and dissemination of content for media
• Planning responses to evolving issues	• Management of communication	• Issues management	• Leading and directing others
• Managing organisational development	• Strategic planning	• Credibility and integrity	• Team building and working
• Developing pivotal action, advocacy programmes	• Issues management	• Flexibility	• Monitoring progress
• Planning institutional and issue advertising	• Audience segmentation	• Influence, persuasion and diplomacy	• Motivating and incentivising others
• Planning staff training	• Informative and persuasive writing	• Critical judgement	• Making decisions in complex situations
• Hiring and developing personnel	• Community, consumer and employee relations and other practice areas	• Problem-solving	• Communication planning
	• Technological and visual literacy	• Organisation, planning and task focus	• Budgeting
		• Using information and e-communications	• Evaluating plans

(Continued)

TABLE 4.2 (Continued)

PRSA, 1993 Skills of Directors/Executives	PRSA, 2006 Skills in Educational Curricula Underpinning Senior Level Activity	IPR, 2003 Skills of Practitioners	BP, 2002[1] Skills of Managers/Directors
• Managing community relations programmes • Interacting with other directors **EXECUTIVES:** • Interacting with investors, boards of directors, management teams and other constituencies • Leading industry organisations • Political action committee activities • Leading community organisations • Conducting shareholder meetings • Conducting management conferences • Planning management succession • Representing the organisation as spokesperson	• Managing people, programmes and resources • Sensitive interpersonal communication • Critical listening skills • Fluency in foreign language • Ethical decision-making • Participation in professional communication/public relations community • Managing production • Working with current issues • Environmental monitoring • Public speaking and presentation • Applying cross-cultural and cross-gender sensitivity		**DIRECTORS:** • Research methods • Use of research software • Analysis and presentation of research results • Developing research programmes • Translating research skills into programmes of action • Leading multi-disciplinary teams • Delegating responsibility and tasks • Motivating and incentivising others • Making decisions in complex situations • Developing comprehensive corporate communication strategy and plans • Evaluating programmes and plans

Note: these sources did not separate knowledge and skills: the author has done so for the purpose of this chapter. [1]Cited in Cornelissen (2008).

TABLE 4.3 Knowledge of Senior Practitioners

PRSA, 1993	PRSA, 2006	IPR, 2003	BP, 2002
Knowledge of Director/Executives	Knowledge in Educational Curricula Underpinning Senior Level Activity	Knowledge of Practitioners	Knowledge of Managers/Directors
• Communication and persuasion concepts and strategies • Communication and public relations theories • Relationships and relationship building • Societal trends • Ethical issues • Legal requirements and issues • Marketing and finance • Communication/public relations history • Uses of research and forecasting • Multicultural and global issues • Business case for diversity	**DIRECTORS:** • Organisational policies • Reporting communication/public relations effectiveness • Directing government, regulatory affairs, legislative monitoring • Directing staff and budgets • Serving as a 'conscience' of the organisation • Understanding relevant laws, regulations • Supporting volunteers	• Understanding of business • Corporate strategy • Finance • Corporate governance • Data analysis • Audience research • Management of people and resources • Reflection	**DIRECTORS:** • Understanding of stakeholder, identity and reputation, their theoretical antecedents, practical application and incorporation into communication strategy and communication programmes • History of corporate communication and theoretical developments • Knowledge of how to translate theory into practice • Knowledge of research methods and research software • Knowledge of digital and modern media • Understanding of corporate finance and financial reporting and implications for stakeholders

(Continued)

TABLE 4.3 (Continued)

PRSA, 1993 **Knowledge of Director/Executives**	PRSA, 2006 **Knowledge in Educational Curricula Underpinning Senior Level Activity**	IPR, 2003 **Knowledge of Practitioners**	BP, 2002 **Knowledge of Managers/Directors**
• World social, political, economic and historical frameworks • Organisational change and development • Management concepts and theories • Communication/public relations management • Behavioural science • Communication processes • Publics • Communication/public relations programming and production	**EXECUTIVES:** • Monitoring and predicting consequences of government regulations • Directing development of policies • Directing development of organisational design		**MANAGERS:** • Understanding of stakeholders, identity and reputation, their theoretical antecedents, practical application and operationalisation • History of corporate communications and theoretical developments • Knowledge of how to translate theory into practice • Knowledge of research methods and software • Deep knowledge of all media characteristics and applications • Detailed understanding of corporate finance and financial reporting

Note: these sources did not separate knowledge and skills: the author has done so for the purpose of this chapter. ¹Cited in Cornelissen (2008).

study of excellence in public relations and communication management, provide four areas of knowledge for communication excellence:

- Strategic and operational management knowledge – develop strategies for solving public relations and communication problems; manage the organisation's response to issues; prepare a departmental budget; manage people.
- Research knowledge – perform environmental scanning; determine public reactions to the organisation; use research to segment publics; conduct evaluation research.
- Negotiation knowledge – negotiate with an activist public; help management to understand the opinions of particular publics; use theories of conflict resolution in dealing with publics.
- Persuasive knowledge – persuade a public that the organisation is right on an issue; use attitude theory in a campaign; get publics to act as organisation wants.

More recent work on roles also indicates that practitioners should have an understanding and knowledge of how organisations are structured and operate, how the dominant coalition (or decision-making elite) make decisions, and a knowledge of the basic business functions such as finance, human resources, marketing and operations. Indeed, it is this lack of broader business knowledge that manifests itself as one of the main barriers to practitioners becoming the most senior managers within their organisations (Hogg & Doolan, 1999; Bronn, 2001; PRSA, 2006; Cornelissen, 2008), along with a practitioner preference for tactical involvement (Hogg & Doolan, 1999; Moss et al., 2005).

As can be seen, there is some conflation of skills and knowledge when Tables 4.2 and 4.3 are compared, but that is explainable. For example, a practitioner needs to know how government operates before being able to undertake the design of a government relations programme.

Competencies

It is striking that in all the roles literature, with its calls for senior communicators to enact those roles (e.g., Dozier, Grunig, & Grunig, 1995; Hogg & Doolan, 1999; Murray & White, 2005; Moss et al., 2005), there is no specific itemisation of the competencies or behavioural repertoires that are required. In her discussion of board-level skills and competencies, Bronn (2001) examined the management literature and called for research to look specifically at individual senior communicator competencies in place of the 'constant focus on role enactment' (p. 323). Aldoory and Toth's (2004) research into leadership style and gender in public relations used a number of behaviourally based questions designed to elicit information about leadership styles. However, the number of questions is small and it is not possible to garner a comprehensive assessment of behaviours from it. Indeed, the only comprehensive study of senior practitioners competencies based on empirical research is that under-taken by Gregory (2008). Because little is written on competencies and because behaviours are so important as predictors of performance (Bailey, Bartram, & Kurtz, 2001), more discussion is merited on this area rather than on the more familiar areas of skills and behaviours.

Working with trained occupational psychologists, Gregory's project involved interviewing and testing 17 board-level communicators: 8 from the private sector and 9 from the public sector. The test instrument administered was an accepted pro-prietary competency framework (Bartram, 2004).

The resultant top ten competencies for the private sector (Table 4.4) and the pub-lic sector (Table 4.5) represent an aggregate for the private and public sector groups. Each individual in each group will display all the competencies indicated, but the bal-ance between the individual competencies in their behavioural repertoires will differ between each individual and depending on the situations in which they work. The competencies are not arranged in any particular order.

The interview research also supports the conclusions of a number of earlier studies in identifying a senior advisor role (Dozier & Broom, 1995; Toth, Serini, Wright, & Emig, 1998; Moss et al., 2000; Moss & Green, 2001). The interviews also revealed that 'top' practitioners have tactical responsibilities that can be burdensome (Moss et al., 2005).

For the private sector groups the *understanding others* competence had slightly more importance than others. This involves not only an understanding of people inside and outside the organisation, but also a deep understanding of their motiva-tions and aspirations. It implies a level of contextual intelligence; understanding the environment in which people operate and which frames their aspirations. This understanding is important in defining the requirements and context of organisa-tional decision-making and communications programmes. Additionally, these senior communicators were able to take a holistic view of the opinions expressed to them and to negotiate and integrate positions in order to develop win–win solutions for all involved.

The *strategic/long-term view* competency had a particular emphasis on commercial 'bottom line' impacts and links closely to the *investigating and analysing* and *prepar-ing thoroughly* and *making decisions and acting* competencies. These are associated with a good understanding of the business and business strategy. Senior practitioners show an ability to handle and use information and business intelligence, and a will-ingness to take difficult decisions based on the evidence, leading to decisive actions. Other competencies worth special note are *taking responsibility for high standards*, with its reference to ethical standards, and *maintaining a positive outlook*, referring to remaining calm and in control, especially in crisis situations. In these situations in particular, communicators are able to demonstrate their value to their organisation and gain substantial professional credibility.

For the public sector, the competencies that came out as slightly more important were *building strong relationships* and *consulting and involving*.

UK government directives require consultation by many public sector organisa-tions, but relationship-building and involvement go beyond a statutory requirement

TABLE 4.4 The Ten Competency Titles, Descriptions and Behavioural Indicators for Private Sector Communicators

Strategic/Long-Term View	Leading and Supporting	Making Decisions and Acting	Maintaining a Positive Outlook	Networking
Thinks broadly and strategically. Plans ahead and remains focused on organisational objectives.	Provides direction, advice and coaching to individuals or teams. Supports and encourages others. Fosters openness and information sharing.	Willing to make tough decisions quickly based on the information available. Successfully generates activity and shows confidence in the chosen course of action.	Responds positively to changes or setbacks. Remains calm and in control of own emotions, manages pressure well.	Talks easily to people at all levels both internally and externally. Canvases opinions widely and builds strong infrastructures to receive and disseminate information.
• Develops an agreed understanding of key business issues	• Provides others with a clear direction	• Weighs up the positive and negative outcomes of a decision	• Looks for positive outcomes and remains optimistic	• Seeks opportunities to interact with people at all levels
• Evaluates actions in terms of their potential impact on overall organisational objectives	• Elevates insights to the board	• Makes tough decisions	• Communicates messages of hope	• Builds relationships with 'gatekeepers'
	• Builds a strong team of talented individuals	• Identifies urgent decisions	– Uses humour	• Consults with subject-matter experts
• Thinks ahead and focuses on the future rather than the past	• Gives advice and coaches others	• Makes unpopular decisions	– Shows awareness of the differences between setback and failure	• Talks to people regularly
	• Demonstrates commitment to the development of staff	• Suggests various courses of action		• Canvases suggestions and options
• Shows awareness of long-term benefits over short-term political issues	• Delegates work appropriately to others	• Decides upon a course of action quickly	– Deals with ambiguity, making positive use of the opportunities it presents	• Builds relationships across functions
	• Offers challenging opportunities to staff	• Takes calculated risks on the basis of evidence		• Seeks to build relationships with key individuals
• Maintains a vision of objectives and regularly reviews those objectives	• Acknowledges the contribution of others through formal or informal recognition	• Uses facts and figures when making decisions	– Keeps emotions under control during difficult situations	• Builds relationships externally
		• Acts with confidence when executing decisions	• Works productively in a pressurised environment	• Develops an extended network via team
		• Makes things happen		
		• Implements solutions		

(Continued)

TABLE 4.4 (Continued)

- Thinks broadly beyond immediate issues
- Shows recognition of impact on the bottom line
- Keeps up to date with market and competitor developments
- Considers links between seemingly unrelated issues

- Maintains confidences
- Creates an open culture of information sharing

- Imparts knowledge and expertise to others
- Makes himself/herself visible throughout organisation

Communicating
Communicates verbally and in writing clearly, consistently and convincingly both internally and externally.

- Communicates clearly and concisely to all interested parties
- Sends a consistent message to all

Investigating and Analysing
Gathers, probes and tests information. Shows evidence of clear analytical thinking. Gets to the heart of complex problems and issues.

- Gathers information from a wide variety of sources
- Seeks out different situations to find new information

Taking Responsibility for High Standards
Behaves consistently with clear personal values that support those of the organisation. Takes responsibility for the standard of organisational communication and for their own and team's actions.

- Sets high goals and standards
- Behaves consistently in line with organisational values

Preparing Thoroughly
Spends time understanding tasks and objectives. Prepares carefully and thoroughly for situations that may occur and cause difficulties. Prepares for formal events and meetings.

- Plans how objectives can be achieved
- Involves team in planning process

- Remains buoyant in emotional or difficult situations
- Remains emotionally stable in challenging circumstances

Understanding Others
Remains open-minded when taking into account individual views and needs. Demonstrates interest in others and is empathetic to their concerns. Works towards solutions of mutual benefit.

- Understands the objectives of all parties
- Works towards a win-win situation

(Continued)

TABLE 4.4 (Continued)

• Adapts communication to the needs of the audience	• Uses personal experience to help understand problems	– Clearly defines boundaries for information sharing	• Develops plans that take account of potential changing or difficult circumstances	• Asks questions around individuals' own issues
• Uses probing questions to challenge views	• Probes for further information to clarify vague or confusing issues	• Takes responsibility for the team's actions	• Monitors situations carefully	• Works to understand the motivations of others
• Speaks with conviction	• Breaks information into component parts and relationships	• Accepts that mistakes are made	• Maintains a constant awareness of issues helping or hindering progress	• Keeps an open mind when others are expressing their views
• Support arguments with facts and figures	• Distinguishes the core issues from peripheral issues of a situation	• Admits own mistakes	• Prepares thoroughly for meetings and interviews	• Tolerates differing needs and viewpoints
• Articulates the reasons behind actions	• Identifies similarities between situations	– Handles criticism well and learns from it	• Rehearses arguments	• Picks up on verbal/non-verbal cues
• Communicates internally in an open and direct way	• Rapidly grasps the key facts of a situation	• Acts quickly to overcome errors	• Writes agendas	• Considers the impact of action on other people
• Confronts senior people with difficult issues	• Identifies and highlights key facts and figures	• Seeks help from others when required		• Shows respect and sensitivity to individual needs and cultural differences
• Clarifies that a shared understanding has been received	• Uses numbers and statistics when analysing information	– Stops communication if necessary		• Shows an interest in people
• Writes clearly and engagingly	• Analyses the potential outcomes of a situation			• Responds with sympathy
• Make use of contemporary channels of communication				

(Continued)

TABLE 4.5 The Ten Competency Titles, Descriptions and Behavioural Indicators for Public Sector Communicators

Strategy and Action Understanding the Bigger Picture (essential for all public sector communicators)	Taking Action (essential for all public sector communicators)	Consulting and Involving (not as important in wider public sector – but within top 10)	Presenting and Communicating (not in top 10 for wider public sector)	Creating and Innovating
Demonstrates a comprehensive understanding of the impact of organisational strategy on own responsibilities.	Makes prompt and clear decisions, empowers others to do the same.	Works with staff, patients and the wider community to ensure successful consultation and support.	Ensures audience understanding through the use of an appropriate and interactive communication style.	
• Understands how organisational strategies relate to the bigger picture	• Makes prompt and clear decisions when dealing with contentious issues	• Listens to the views of others	• Communicates clearly and succinctly, both orally and in writing	• Finds ways to innovate
• Considers the impact of organisational strategies on others	• Takes responsibility for people and projects	• Encourages others to contribute	• Translates complex messages into communication that is relevant for the audience	• Seeks out opportunities to change things.
• Ensures plans are aligned to organisational development	• Delivers on promises	• Encourages effective team-working	• Adapts communication style according to individual needs	• Introduces change sensitively, but firmly
• Puts communication at the heart of organisational development	• Involves relevant people in the decision-making process	• Brings people with the right skills into a project	• Develops communication that meet the requirements of the particular situation	
• Prioritises resources and projects according to organisational needs	• Empowers others to make decisions where appropriate	• Shows an awareness of the diverse views of others	• Projects credibility when presenting information to others	
	• Escalates issues when necessary	• Works with people to build acceptable solutions		
		• Develops the skill of individuals and teams		
		• Consults and involves others to gain their support		

(Continued)

TABLE 4.5 (Continued)

				Formulating Strategies and Concepts
• Recognises when it is appropriate to alter plans when strategies change • Takes account of a wide range of issues across, and related to, the organisation • Understands the pros and cons of a solution	• Takes initiative and works under own direction • Gives direction to the decision-making of others	• Provides others with the information they need to present a convincing case • Finds new ways to present information to maintain the interest of the audience • Uses an open and interactive communication style		
Persuading and Influencing (not as important in wider public sector – just within top 10) Gains clear agreement and commitment to an agreed course of action through effective persuasion and negotiation.	**People/Community Upholding the Reputation of the Service (three wider public sector communicators say essential)** Behaves consistently with clear personal values which complement those of the organisation and wider community.	**Personal Communication Building Strong Relationships (essential for all public sector communicators)** Relates well to a broad range of people, building and maintaining an extensive network of contacts.	**Personal Characteristics Managing Under Pressure (essential for all public sector communicators)** Finds ways to enable self and others to cope with difficult challenges, demonstrates clear thinking and keeps problems in perspective.	
• Persuades others to agree course of action • Helps others to understand different viewpoints and find common ground	• Upholds the ethics and values of the service • Demonstrates integrity by acting openly and honestly	• Builds rapport quickly and makes people feel at ease • Establishes strong relationships with people from all backgrounds	– Keeps emotions under control in difficult times – Balances the demands of work and personal life	• Thinks broadly • Approaches most strategies • Sets and develops communications strategy

(Continued)

TABLE 4.5 (Continued)

- Guides conversations to a desired endpoint
- Manages conflict sensitively and diplomatically
- Makes a strong personal impression on others
- Influences the agendas of everyone
- Takes account of the internal and external political climate when persuading others
- Closes discussion with clear commitment to action from both sides

- Promotes and defends equal opportunities
- Builds diverse teams that reflect the wider community
- Deals sensitively with personal information
- Takes pride in delivering a service to the community
- Gains the respect and trust of others
- Gives honest and objective advice to others

- Establishes strong working relationships with people at all levels of the organisation
- Builds and maintains strong people networks
- Knows who to speak to when particular information is required
- Gathers perceptions to increase understanding of underlying organisational issues
- Uses humour appropriately to build relationships
- Creates a safe environment that encourages others to share information with them

– Finds ways to cope with the pressure and expectations that they face
– Draws on personal experiences to help self and others through difficult situations
– Keeps difficult challenges in perspective
– Copes with a changing environment and helps others to feel comfortable with it
– Demonstrates clear and realistic thinking when faced with difficult issues
– Focuses energy on the most important and relevant issues

- Establishes a vision for the communication department

TABLE 4.6 Comparison of Private and Public Sector Competencies

Private Sector	Public Sector
Networking	Building Strong Relationships
Leading and Supporting/Understanding Others	Consulting and Involving
Maintaining a Positive Outlook	Managing Under Pressure
Taking Responsibility for High Standards	Upholding the Reputation of the Service
Communicating	Presenting and Communicating
Decision-Making and Acting	Taking Action
Formulating Strategies and Concepts	Understanding the Bigger Picture
Investigating and Analysing	Formulating Strategies and Concepts
Preparing Thoroughly	
	Persuading and Influencing
	Creating and Innovation

for these practitioners. Public sector communicators are not motivated primarily by power or money, but they do want to make a difference in society. This societal commitment is very pronounced and the desire to build community and cohesion permeates much of their daily activity.

The next two most important competencies were *taking action* and *upholding the reputation of the service*. Although these practitioners work in environments where issues are deeply contested and with many divergent viewpoints, they are clear and transparent in their decision-making and have a defined ethical framework, with 'duty to the public' being a compelling value around which decisions are made.

Notable about public sector competencies is their 'people' emphasis. In this environment, collaborative, consensual working is critical, and although 'the bottom line' is not so apparent as a driver, they do want to deliver good value (sometimes referred to as best value), and that includes social good as well as financial value for money.

It is clear, comparing Tables 4.4 and 4.5, that there are many similarities between the public and private sectors, and some differences (see Table 4.6). Gregory (2008) explains some of these differences and it is not necessary to cover the fine detail here. Suffice to say that *investigating and analysing* and *preparing thoroughly* are necessary to the private sector where competition and shareholder accountability loom large. In the public sector the ability to enact these competencies appears to be pushed down the agenda as operational pressures crowd in. The *formulating strategies and concepts* and *creating and innovating* competencies are exclusive to the public sector and appear to relate to creating operational communication plans within tight resource restraints, often for long-term behavioural change campaigns. These constraints require adept campaigns which rely on creativity and innovation, rather than on money. This might be regarded as a positive feature, but these practitioners are also frustrated because they are rarely allowed into strategic planning circles and their energies are channelled into the tactical by management, but also to a certain extent by themselves.

Having looked in some detail at the skills, knowledge and competencies required of senior communicators, it is now appropriate to see how they support the C-MACIE framework.

APPLICATION TO C-MACIE

As stated in Chapter 2, the C-MACIE framework is a communication planning process. At all points it needs to be supported by appropriate skills, knowledge and behaviours. Some of these, previously described, will underpin more than one part of the process: research, for example, could be regarded as an essential element of each. Table 4.7 takes some of the more common skills and knowledge identified in the literature and applies them to the framework. It also applies all Gregory's (2008) competencies, split into private and public sectors.

SUMMARY

The literature on communication/public relations context, roles, skills and knowledge is large. This chapter has sought to identify the main strands of thinking in order to provide an indication of the capabilities needed to support the C-MACIE framework.

What is apparent from this analysis is that the C-MACIE process demands a plethora of skills, knowledge and competencies. It seems appropriate that these should be acquired in a systematic and consistent way. The most apparent way to do this is for there to be programmes of study provided by both educational institutions and the professional bodies responsible for communication/public relations standards. Thankfully these are now available in most parts of North America, Europe and Australasia and there is growing provision in Asia, Africa, South America, the Middle and Far East. Unfortunately, there are still many consultancies and in-house departments who spend little on ongoing training and development (IPR, 2003), and while this remains the case communication/public relations is in danger of being 'behind the curve' (Watson and Sreedharan, 2010).

However, what is encouraging is that there is growing evidence that communication/public relations is becoming increasingly recognised as a core capability for organisations (Murray and White, 2005; Arthur W. Page Society, 2007), and that planning process frameworks, typified by C-MACIE, are required to demonstrate that communicators are comfortable with working with recognised business planning methodologies. By doing so their professionalism can be demonstrated and the full range of their skills, knowledge and competencies acknowledged.

TABLE 4.7 The Skills, Behaviours and Competencies which Underpin the C-MACIE Process

Competencies		C-MACIE Process	Skills	Knowledge
Private Sector	**Public Sector**			
• Strategic/long-term view • Understanding others • Networking • Investigating and analysing	• Understanding bigger picture	**ANALYSIS**	• Environmental scanning and analysis using a variety of research methods • Stakeholder analysis • Interacting with stakeholders to gain intelligence • Working with senior managers to set organisations' vision, values and strategy • Integrating information	• Societal trends • Legal/regulatory requirements • Business, corporate strategy, finance • Stakeholders, identity, reputation and related theories • Research methods and forecasting • Behavioural and management science • History of communication
• Making decisions and acting • Taking responsibility for high standards • Preparing thoroughly	• Taking action • Consulting and involving • Upholding reputation of the service • Formulating strategies and concepts • Persuading and influencing	**CHOICE**	• Identifying issues • Strategic planning • Developing communication strategy and planning • Organisational/staff development • Problem-solving/critical judgement • Stakeholder prioritisation • Ethical decision-making	• Organisational decision-making • Data analysis and interpretation • Communication and persuasion • Theories and strategies • Audience research • Marketing • Organisational change and development • Decision analysis
• Leading and supporting • Maintaining a positive outlook • Communicating • Networking	• Managing under pressure • Presenting and communicating • Building strong relationships • Persuading and influencing • Creating and innovating	**IMPLEMENTATION**	• Implementing communication programmes and campaigns • Influencing, negotiating, persuading • Designing content, producing and disseminating • Team building and direction • Budgeting and timescales • Creativity	• Communication/public relations management • Management of people and resources • Reflection • Relationship building • Channels, tactics and media • Project management
• Investigating and analysing • Taking responsibility for high standards	• Understanding bigger picture	**EVALUATION**	• Monitoring progress • Evaluating programmes • Using research results	• Evaluation and monitoring techniques • Research methods

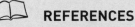

REFERENCES

Aldoory, L., & Toth, E.L. (2004) Leadership and gender in public relations: Perceived effectiveness of transformational and transactional leadership styles. *Journal of Public Relations Research*, *16*(2), 157–83.

Aldrich, H., & Herker, D. (1977) Boundary-spanning roles and organisational structure. *Academy of Management Review*, *2*, 217–30.

Arthur W. Page Society (2007) *The Authentic Enterprise*. New York: Arthur W. Page Society.

Bailey, R., Bartram, D. and Kurz, R. (2001) *Cracking Competencies: Development of the SHL Competency Framework*. Poster at the British Psychological Society Centennial Conference, Glasgow, U.K.

Bartram, D. (2004) *The SHL Competency Framework*, SHL Business Series 4. Thames Ditton: SHL.

Beinhocker, E., Davis, I., & Mendonca, L. (2009) The 10 trends you have to watch. *Harvard Business Review*, July–August.

BP (2002) *Beroeps Niveau Profiles*. Amsterdam: Beroepsvereniging voor Communicatie.

Bronn, P.S. (2001) Communication managers as strategists? Can they make the grade? *Journal of Communication Management*, *5*(4), 313–26.

Campbell, A. (2008) Strategic communication in the 24 hour media age. Speech given at Communicate 08, National NHS Communications Conference, London, 5 November.

Cornelissen, J. (2008) *Corporate Communication* (2nd ed.). London: Sage.

Cutlip, S. M., Center, A. H., and Broom, G. M. (2000) *Effective Public Relations* (8th ed.). Englewood Cliffs, NJ: Prentice Hall.

Cutlip, S. M., Center, A. H., and Broom, G. M. (2009) *Effective Public Relations* (10th ed.). Upper Saddle River, NJ: Prentice Hall.

Dozier, D.M., & Broom, G.M. (1995) Evolution of the manager role in public relations practice. *Journal of Public Relations Research*, *7*(1), 3 –26.

Dozier, D.M., Grunig, L.A. and Grunig, J.E. (1995) *Manager's Guide to Excellence in Public Relations and Communication Management*. Mahwah, NJ: Erlbaum.

Gollner, A.B. (1983) *Social Change and Corporate Strategy: The Expanding Role of Public Affairs*. Stanford, CT: Issues Action Press.

Gregory, A. (2008) Competencies of senior communication practitioners in the UK: An initial study. *Public Relations Review*, *34*, 215–23

Grunig, J.E., & Hunt, T. (1984) *Managing Public Relations*. New York: Holt, Rinehart and Winston.

Hales, C. (1986) What do managers do? A critical review of the evidence. *Journal of Management Studies*, *23*(1), 88–115.

Hales, C. (1999) Why do managers do what they do? Reconciling evidence and theory in accounts of managerial work. *British Journal of Management, 10*, 335–50.

Hogg, G. and Doolan, D. (1999) Playing the part: practitioner roles in public relations. *Journal of European Marketing*; *35*(5/6), 597–611.

IPR (2003) *Unlocking the Potential of Public Relations*. London: IPR

Moss, D.A., & Green, R. (2001) Re-examining the manager's role in public relations: What management and public relations research teaches us. *Journal of Communication Management*, *6*(2), 118–32.

Moss, D.A., Newman, A., & DeSanto, B. (2005) What do communications managers do? Defining and refining the core elements of management in a public relations/communication context. *Journalism and Mass Communication Quarterly*, *82*, 873–90.

Moss, D.A., Warnaby, G., & Newman, A. (2000) Public relations practitioner role enactment at the senior management level within UK companies. *Journal of Public Relations Research*, *12*(4), 348–58.

Murray, K. and White, J. (2005) CEO's views on reputation management, *Journal of Communication Management, 9*(4), 348–58

(Continued)

(Continued)

Newsom, D., Turk, J.V.S., & Kruckeberg, D. (2000) *This Is PR* (7th ed.). Belmont, CA: Wadsworth/ Thomson Learning.

Pearson, R. (2000) Beyond ethical relativism in public relations. In J.E. Grunig & L.Grunig (eds), *Public Relations Research Annual*, *1*, 67–86. Hillsdale, NJ: Erlbaum.

PRSA (1993) *Public Relations Professional Career Guide*. New York: PRSA Foundation.

PRSA (2006) *The Professional Board*. New York: Public Relations Society of America.

Skinner, C. Von Essen, L. and Mersham, G. (2004) *Handbook of Public Relations* (7th ed.), Oxford: Oxford University Press,

Smythe, J. (2007) *The CEO: Chief Engagement Officer*. London: Gower

Steyn, B. (2003) From strategy to corporate communication strategy: A conceptualisation. *Journal of Communication Management*, *8*(2), 168–83.

Tench, R. and Yeomans, L. (2009) *Exploring Public Relations*. Harlow: Pearson Education.

Toth, E.L., Serini, S.A., Wright, D.K., & Emig, A.G. (1998) Trends in public relations roles: 1990 –1995. *Public Relations Review*, *24*, 145–163.

Van Ruler, B., Vercic, D., Butschi, G, & Flodis, B. (2004) A first look for parameters of public relations in Europe. *Journal of Public Relations Research*, *16*(1), 35–63.

Watson, T. & Sreedharan, C. (2010) *The Senior Communicator of the Future – Competencies and Training Needs*. Florida Institute for Public Relations. Gainsville, FL: Institute for Public Relations.

Yeomans, L. (2009) Internal communication. In R. Tench and L. Yeomans (eds), *Exploring Public Relations*. Harlow: Pearson Education.

Zerfass, A., Moreno, A., Tench, R., Vercic, D. & Verhoeven, P. (2009) European Communications Monitor 2009. Trends in Communication Management and Public Relations – Results of a Survey in 34 countries (chart version). Brussels: EACD/EUPRERA. Available at www.communication-monitor.eu.

Strategy-Making and Planning in the Communications Context

Danny Moss

Key Themes

- Definitions of the concept of strategy and strategic decision-making
- Understanding the process of strategy-making
- Different perspectives of strategy-making
- Corporate, competitive and functional strategies
- Communication and public relations strategy and planning
- Examining the management of communications strategy – applying the C-MACIE framework

OPERATIONAL AND STRATEGIC MANAGEMENT – A MATTER OF PERSPECTIVE

An issue at the heart of this chapter and in many ways underpinning the main theme of this book is the need to distinguish between *operational* management and *strategic* management in the communication/public relations context. Operational management arguably encompasses the routine, day-to-day decisions, controls and actions that enable an organisation to continue to function effectively along the course set out in the organisation's strategic and operational plans. Thus operational management decisions will be made and actions will take place at all departmental/ functional levels. Strategic management, by contrast, is concerned with the key decisions and actions that determine the overall intended positioning and direction of an organisation, and the allocation of the necessary resources to pursue the chosen strategies. In this sense there is a clear hierarchical relationship between strategic and operational management, with the latter normally taking its lead from the former.

Examining the communication/public relations literature and observing how many practitioners operate in practice, it is clear that this distinction between strategic and operational decisions and actions is not always fully understood. Perhaps the most common flaw is the tendency to view all but the most routine of activities as being 'strategic'. This is an error of 'levels' or 'perspective', and of course is not confined to the public relations field – it is also found in other functional areas such as marketing or human resources. This flawed perspective on strategy can generally be attributed to the fact that many manage/practitioners operating at the functional level may have only a partial appreciation of the issues, problems, and opportunities facing their organisation, particularly in large complex organisations. Even with a broader understanding of an organisation's business, it is perhaps only to be expected that functional managers are likely see those issues that appear most relevant to their own function as most important and hence, from their perspective, the decisions or actions relating to those issues may well seem to have strategically important consequences. However, when the same issues, problems, or opportunities are observed from the top management team's perspective – in context of the organisation's overall corporate or business strategy – they may be seen in a quite different light, perhaps being recognised as having important implications at the functional level, but limited 'strategic' significance for the organisation as a whole.

Earlier in Chapter 2 we highlighted the arguments about the 'strategic potential' of the 'boundary-spanning' role of public relations (Aldrich & Herker, 1977), while at the same time recognising that other functions, such as marketing, equally claim to play this role. Moreover, there is a need to distinguish between 'access' to top management and 'participating' in top management decision-making. Over the past decade, in particular, various studies have suggested that there has been a growing recognition of the value of communication/public relations among top management across the corporate sector (see http://www.communicationmonitor.eu). This change has, however, occurred relatively slowly and in a rather piecemeal fashion rather than in the form of a 'wave of change' in organisational attitudes to the role of communication.

Anecdotally, the single most important catalyst for a change in the internal status of the communication/public relations function seems to be where organisations have experienced some form of major crisis or challenge that threatens their position or survival. This type of cathartic experience invariably leads to a fundamental review of 'what went wrong', 'who is to blame' and 'how can we restore our reputation and avoid it happening again'. It is at this point that communication/public relations will often step forward to 'pick up the pieces' and thereby gain renewed recognition and respect within the organisation and among senior management. Whether this translates into a permanent seat at the top table is more problematic and appears to vary from organisation to organisation. Arguably the key requirements to enable the communication/public relations function to gain and sustain greater recognition from senior management is that senior managers themselves need to have a better understanding and appreciation of the value of communication, and that communi-cation/public relations staff need to have a deeper understanding of management and business strategy in order to engage with senior management and better appreci-ate their mindset and priorities. Indeed, one – if not *the* – principle idea behind this book was to re-examine thinking about the various dimensions of communication/public relations function through a managerial 'lens', and to help demonstrate the type of managerial thinking and processes that are needed to ensure that communication/public relations function is taken seriously and recognised as a professionally managed essential function within organisations, rather than a 'Cinderella' function, as has often been the case.

What is Strategy?

One of the major themes that recurs throughout the strategy literature is that of the role of strategy as a 'continuous and adaptive response to external opportunities and threats that may confront an organization' (Argyris, 1985; see also Mintzberg, 1994b; Steiner & Miner, 1977). Within the management literature, a broad consensus exists that strategy is essentially concerned with the process of managing the interaction between an organisation and its external environment so as to ensure the best fit between the two. Thus, for example, Johnson, Scholes, and Whittington (2008) sug-gest that strategy is: 'the direction and scope of an organisation over the long term, which achieves advantage in a changing environment through its configuration of resources and competencies with the aim of fulfilling stakeholder expectations'.

Kenneth Andrews (1987), one of pioneering scholars of strategy, suggested that:

> Corporate strategy is the pattern of decisions in a company that determines and reveals its objectives or goals, produces the principal policies and plans for achieving those goals, and defines the range of business the company is to pursue, the kind of economic and human organization it is or intends to be, and the nature of the economic and noneconomic contribution it intends to make to its shareholders, employees, customers and communities.

Andrews goes on to draw the distinction between corporate and business strategy. The former applies to the whole enterprise, determining the scope of the orgnisa-tion's operations and the areas in which it will compete, while the latter determines how the organisation will compete in its chosen markets – the choice of products, services and the basis on which it will compete.

The emphasis found within many definitions of strategy on the organisational–environment interface, which we highlighted earlier, arguably brings back into focus the potential strategic importance of importance of the 'boundary-spanning' func-tion as one of the key roles that the public relations function can fulfil effectively on behalf of organisations. Here, for example, White and Dozier (1992: 92) argue that 'when organisations make decisions they do so based on a representation of both the organisation itself and its environment', and they go on to suggest that public relations practitioners play an important role in shaping perceptions of the environment and the organisation itself among decision-makers.

However, as White and Dozier also acknowledge, the strategic potential of this boundary-spanning role may often go unrealised, as there are often many competing sources of environment intelligence both within and outside organisations that may have greater prominence and sway over management decisions than the communication/public relations function. Broom and Dozier (1990) suggest that senior managements tend to treat public relations largely as a *tactical* communication function concerned primarily with technical gathering of information and external representation, rather than treating it as an important analyser and interpreter of environment information.

However, before going on to consider what other roles the communication/public relations function can play in a strategic context and how it might contribute to organisational strategy and planning, it is important first to understand how the concept of strategy at both the corporate and competitive level is understood within the management field and what implications this may have for public relations practice.

Perspectives on Strategy

The past 30–40 years have seen the emergence of a growing volume of literature devoted to the subject of strategy. However, a comprehensive consensus definition of strategy has continued to remain elusive. Nevertheless, some broad areas of agreement about what constitutes the basic dimensions of strategy have emerged, particularly in terms of recognising the role of strategy as a means of handling changing environments; in recognising the need to explore issues relating to both content and process of strategy formation; in recognising that strategy exists at different levels (corporate, competitive and operational) and in terms of recognising that strategy-making comprises both conceptual as well as analytical exercises (Chaffee, 1985; Mintzberg, 1994b).

In a wide-ranging review of literature from across the strategy 'landscape', De Witt and Meyer (2004) also acknowledge that it may be impossible to pin down and rely on a single comprehensive definition of strategy, and they argue that it is more important to keep an open mind as to the range of views about what strategy is and how strategy is formulated and managed. They suggest that to capture the breadth and complexity of the subject, a three-dimensional perspective of strategy is needed, encompassing process, content and context (Figure 5.1). Strategy *process* is concerned with how strategies come about – how they are formulated or designed, implemented and controlled, and who is responsible for this activity. Strategy *content* is essentially the product of the strategy process – the elements or activities that make up the strategy. Finally, strategy *context* is concerned with the set of circumstances that surround the strategy process and content – it is essentially the 'where' of strategy, the environment in which the strategy is embedded. De Witt and Meyer emphasise strongly that these 'process, content, context dimensions are not different parts of strategy, but are distinguishable dimensions of strategy' (p. 5).

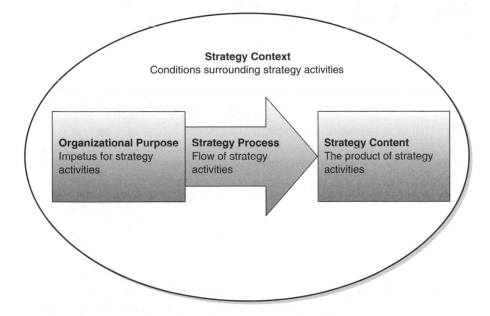

FIGURE 5.1 Dimensions of Strategy: Process, Content and Context

Source: adapted from De Witt and Meyer, 1994 © South-Western, a part of Cengage Learning, Inc. Reprinted by permission. www.cengage.com/permissions.

While acknowledging that some broad areas of agreement about strategy have emerged, Chaffee (1985) argued that there also remain many contentious issues and debates about the nature of strategy and strategic management. Chaffee maintained that while the debate about the nature of strategy remains relatively fluid, some broad clusters of strategy definitions and approaches to strategy-making can be identified. Chaffee identified three distinctive clusters of strategy definitions – linear strategy, adaptive strategy and interpretive strategy – which, when reviewed individually and collectively, reveal something of the contested nature of the current understanding of the concept of strategy. The broad thrust and fundamental assumptions underpinning each of these three strategy clusters are summarised in Table 5.1.

While each of these three models or clusters of strategy definitions represents a quite different view of how organisations approach the task of strategy-making, Chaffee acknowledged that no one model in isolation is capable of explaining adequately all the various nuances of strategy formation that might be found within different industry sectors and organisations. Indeed, Chaffee recognised the need to consider these various strategy models not as alternatives, but as a set of hierarchically related approaches representing different levels of *complexity* and *sophistication* in organisational strategy-making. Thus, for example, some organisations might initially rely largely on linear planning approaches, but might then move to adopt a more sophisticated adaptive and perhaps even interpretive approach to strategy-making as circumstances dictate and as they become more sophisticated and adept at strategy and strategic management. However, even relatively strategically sophisticated

TABLE 5.1   Three Clusters of Strategy Definitions: Emphasis, Assumptions and Processes (adapted from Chaffee, 1985)

Strategy Model	Linear	Adaptive	Interpretive
Emphasis	Methodical, rational, sequential planning approach Aim is the achievement of pre-stated goals	Importance of the link between strategy and changes in the environment Seek to match existing strengths and capabilities to opportunities and risks	Stakeholder oriented Emphasises the role of strategy in shaping the attitudes of stakeholders toward the organisation and its outputs Emphasises idea of managers holding a cognitive map or world view that influences the view of and response to environment change
Assumptions	The company is structured to facilitate the implementation of formal plans The environment is relatively predictable or the company insulated from external forces Managers act in a more or less rational manner	The environment is relatively dynamic and less susceptible to prediction Companies must adapt to environment rather than attempt to impose their will on it Managers forced to take account of to external variables	Strategy strongly influenced by 'politics' and the socio-cultural make-up of the company Success and survival rely on balancing conflicting stakeholder interests Managers seek legitimacy for company policies
Processes	Rational planning approach	Logical incrementalism or emergent strategy	Deal with environment through symbolic actions and communications Emphasizes negotiation and bargaining to achieve consensus

organisations may still rely in part on less complex strategy approaches in some circumstances (why choose complexity when simpler approaches will do the job?). Moreover, Chaffee argued that more complex models of strategy that ignore less complex approaches ignore the foundations on which they must be built if they are to reflect organisational reality. Thus, it may be best to think about these strategy models as offering a menu of options to decision-makers from which appropriate strategy or set of strategies can be selected, or new strategies formed by combining elements of other strategies together.

Johnson (1988), re-examining these three strategy models, suggested they represent two main thrusts in thinking about the *process* of strategy formation:

1. On the one hand, strategy formation can be seen to involve logical, rational processes conducted either through the planning mode or through the adaptive, logical incremental mode (the progressive adjustment of strategies to environmental/market conditions). In both these cases, the role of the strategist is seen as one of consciously seeking to understand and analyse the environment in which the organisation operates so as to configure organisational resources to best meet environmental needs.

2. On the other hand, strategy formation can involve what Johnson terms an 'organisational action approach', in which strategy is seen as the product of the political, programmatic, cognitive, or symbolic aspects of management within the organisation (1988: 80). Here the role of the strategist is as much about negotiation, diplomacy and interpretation as it is about analysis and design.

Thus, the first of these broad themes corresponds generally to the linear or adapted models of strategy, whereas the second theme corresponds broadly to the interpretive model of strategy, where successful strategy-making involves balancing differing stakeholder interests and different internal and external perspectives – in effect, strategy-making as a form of 'accommodation' of interests.

One of the most prolific and influential contributors to the literature on strategy and strategic management is the Canadian academic, Henry Mintzberg, whose work has helped to shape a good deal of the debate around management practice and strategy formation. Recognising the multi-faceted nature of strategy, Mintzberg (1987) advanced his now well-known classification of strategy definitions – five separate, but often interrelated perspectives: strategy as a *plan, position, perspective, ploy* and *pattern* (see the summary descriptors in Table 5.2). Thus, for Mintzberg, strategy as both a position and perspective can be compatible with strategy as a plan and/or pattern. Indeed, management's vision or perspective may emerge from previous patterns of experience and may lead to the formulation of specific plans designed to realise or sustain an organisation's position within the marketplace. Similarly, not all strategies will necessarily follow a entirely pre-planned deliberate path, rather some strategies may *emerge* from unexpected opportunistic developments or by trial an error (Mintzberg, Ahlstrand, & Lampel, 1998). Perhaps one of Mintzberg's (1994a) most significant contributions to the strategy debate has been his emphasis on distinguishing between *strategic planning* and *strategic thinking*. The former, he argues, 'is about analysis whereas the latter is about synthesis'. Mintzberg (1994b: 107) goes on to suggest that 'strategic planning, as it has been practiced, is about strategic programming, the articulation and elaboration of strategies or visions that already exist'. Thus, he argues, planners should make their most valuable contribution *around* the

TABLE 5.2   Mintzberg's Five Ps of Strategy

Strategy type/label	Summary descriptor
Plan	A predetermined, logical course of action, implementation and evaluation
Position	An attempt to locate an organisation within its environment/markets
Perspective	A collective and engraved view of the external world and the organisation's position within it
Ploy	A scheme or manoeuvre designed to outwit opponents
Pattern	A stream of actions that represent a consistent pattern of behaviour

strategy-making process, rather than inside it. Indeed, too much emphasis on planning, according to Mintzberg, may actually be counter-productive and inhibit strategy-making by confusing visioning with the manipulation of numbers.

Despite his criticism of the traditional emphasis on strategic planning, Mintzberg does acknowledge the complementary role of planning and value of planners in translating the output of the 'black box' of strategic thinking processes into actionable programmes and tactics to help ensure the effective implementation of strategies.

Yet a further classification framework for distinguishing different approaches to strategy-making is offered by Whittington (1993), who while focusing principally on business strategy, identified four generic forms of strategy which he argued differ fundamentally along two dimensions: the *outcomes* of strategy and the *processes* by which strategy is made. These four forms of strategy he labels classical, evolutionary, processual and systemic. The distinguishing characteristics of each are summarised in Table 5.3.

In comparing Chaffee, Mintzberg, and Whittington's frameworks for interpreting and making sense of strategy, it is clear that there are a number of commonalities between all three frameworks, but also some notable differences between them, if only in emphasis. All three frameworks acknowledge that strategy can involve both deliberate and essentially rational approaches, as well as emergent forms. The former are reflected in the three authors' linear, planned and classical models of strategy, whereas the latter emergent forms are reflected in the adaptive, pattern, or processual models. All three perspectives also recognise that the relationship between an organisation and its environment – or, more specifically, the key stakeholders within

TABLE 5.3   Whittington's Four Generic Strategies

Type of Strategy	Key Characteristics
Classical	Planned, rational, deliberate
Evolutionary	'Darwinian' in outlook – environmental conditions determine which strategies survive
Processual	An essentially incremental perspective, strategy developed by learning from past actions and experiences
Systemic	Strategy reflects the socio-cultural systems in which the organisation operates

that environment – can and increasingly does figure importantly in thinking about the type of strategies that can or should be adopted. Traditionally, strategy has been seen to focus on organisations seeking to analyse their environments and respond to and/or capitalise on opportunities within them – strategy used to 'fit' or match the organisation to its environment. Increasingly, however, it has been recognised that organisations need to be more sensitive and responsive to the needs of their environments/stakeholders, developing strategies that attempt to balance the organisation and stakeholders' interests. This type of 'more balanced' strategic approach is reflected in Chaffee's interpretive approach, Mintzberg's 'perspective', and Whittington's systemic approach/model.

On balance, there appears to be a general acceptance of the need for a more integrated view of strategy-making that combines or accommodates different models or approaches rather than searching for one dominant model of strategy-making. However, the problem here is that there is little understanding of how such integration may take place in operational terms. One way of perhaps conceptualising the approach to strategy-making is in terms of the notion of a 'continuum' of strategy approaches along which organisations may move, adopting and combining different strategy-making approaches as circumstances and managerial preferences dictate. It also seems evident that the approach to strategy-making may change over time, particularly as organisations grow in size and sophistication and, as Chaffee has suggested, become more adept at strategy, or as they learn to develop appropriate responses to the changing environment/markets they encounter.

Alternative Schools of Thought on Strategy Formation

Perhaps one of the more perplexing questions within the strategy domain remains that of understanding how organisation formulate strategies – the strategy *process*. Reflecting on the range of debates about strategy formation, Mintzberg et al. (1998) distilled what they identified as ten different schools of thought about strategy formation, which they placed into three broad groupings:

1. *Prescriptive approaches* – concerned more about how strategies *should* be formulated rather than how they may actually be formed.
2. *Descriptive approaches* – more concerned with *describing* how organisations do in fact formulate strategy, rather than identifying some form of ideal strategy-making behaviour.
3. *Configurational approaches* – here the emphasis is on integrating the various elements of strategy content, processes and contexts into distinct periods or stages, for example, according to the organisational life cycle, and examining the way strategies enable organisations to leap or progress from stage to stage.

It is beyond the scope of this book to examine each of these ten schools of thought in depth, but a brief summary of the core defining characteristics of each school is provided in Table 5.4; for further details, see the end-of-chapter references. In advancing this strategy formulation framework, Mintzberg et al. acknowledged that not all of the ten schools are readily found elsewhere in the literature, but suggest that they can be found in practice. Moreover, reflecting on question of whether these ten schools represent different approaches to strategy formation or different parts of the *same* processes, Mintzberg and Lampel (1999) acknowledged they have remained deliberately ambiguous, pointing out that:

> Dealing with all this complexity in one process may seem overwhelming. But that is the nature of beast, for the fault lies neither in the stars nor in ourselves, but in the process itself. Strategy formation is judgemental designing, intuitive visioning, and emergent learning; it is about transformation as well as perpetuation; it must involve individual cognition and social interaction, cooperative as well as conflictive; it has to include analyzing before, and programming after, as well as negotiating during; and all this must be in response to what may be a demanding environment. Try to omit any of this and watch what happens! (p. 27)

The authors further argued that the strategy formation process clearly can 'tilt' towards the attributes of one school or another in different contexts and at different stages of an organisation's development. For example, during a business start-up or at times when an organisation needs a dramatic change, strategy formation might lean towards the entrepreneurial school approach; whereas in a mature and stable mass production industry, it is more likely that a rational, deliberate approach would be more appropriate (planning school). What Mintzberg and Lampel recognised is that the approach to strategy formation is not necessarily static, but will evolve over time and circumstances and through the efforts and drive of management: 'Strategy is pushed along by the sheer creativity of managers, because they explore new ways of doing things' (1999: 29).

In many ways, the arguments here can be seen to echo and support De Witt and Meyer's point that to fully understand strategy and strategic management it is necessary to recognise that strategy can only be fully understood when examined from a multi-dimensional perspective, taking in content as well as process and context. Moreover that strategy does not 'happen' of its own accord, it is essentially a human activity, that might reflect the many biases, strengths and failings of those involved.

Looking for the moment only at the context perspective, any attempt to explain organisational strategy-making practices has to take account of the many external environmental influences as well as internal factors, which may shape strategy formation and implementation processes. Here, for example, organisational characteristics such as size, structure, political make-up, and cultural values as well as the cognitive biases that may exist within the strategy-making team may all have a strong influence on strategic decision-making process (Johnson, 1988; Pettigrew, 1992). Equally, an organisation's freedom of manoeuvre with respect to choice of strategy is likely strongly influenced by the nature of the industry or market structures in which they operate (Porter, 1980), as well as by the management

TABLE 5.4 Summary of the Core Features of Ten Schools of Strategy Formulation (adapted from Mintzberg et al., 1998)

School type	Design School	Planning School	Positioning School	Entrepreneurial School	Cognitive School	Learning School	Power School	Culture School	Environmental School	Configurational School
Characteristics										
School category	Prescriptive	Prescriptive	Prescriptive	Descriptive (some prescriptive)	Descriptive	Descriptive	Descriptive	Descriptive	Descriptive	Descriptive and prescriptive
Key descriptor of how strategy formation is viewed	Process of conception	Formal process	Analytical process	Visionary process	Mental process	Emergent process	Process of negotiation	Collective process	Reactive process	Process of transformation
Intended message or focus	Fit	Formalise	Analyse	Envision	Cope or create	Learn	Promote	Coalesce	React	Integrate, Transform
Founding sources	P. Selznick and K. Andrews	H.I. Ansoff	D.E. Schendel, K. Hatten, and M.E. Porter	J.A. Schumpeter, A.H. Cole	H.A. Simon and J.G. March	C.E. Lindblom, R.M. Cyert & J.G. March, J.B. Quinn C.K. Prahalad and G. Hamel.	G.T. Allison, J. Pfeffer and G.R. Salanick	E. Rhenman and R. Norman	M.T. Hannan and J. Freeman, D.S. Pugh et al.	A.D. Chandler, H. Mintzberg, R.E. Miller and C.C. Snow

perceptions of the broad macro-environmental conditions facing the organisation (Duncan, 1972; Mintzberg, 1994b).

Perhaps one of the most extreme examples of how external environment circumstances can force a major change of strategy on organisations, or in this case on whole sectors, can be seen with the recent financial crisis of 2007 which affected banking and financial services sector around the world. Here, it was the unsustainable and, some argue, reckless expansion and investment strategies of many banks, particularly the financing and refinancing sub-prime mortgage lending in the USA, that triggered the global financial crisis that, in turn, led to unprecedented government inventions around the world to try to restore confidence in the banking sector and world financial markets. As a result, banks and financial institutions around the world have had a new set of 'rules of the game' imposed upon them and have had to rethink their future strategies, in some cases radically changing their previous business model. This global banking crisis has also had knock-on effects throughout many economies and industry sectors, not the least being in the building and construction industry where demand for housing has been extremely badly affected by the lack of liquidity in the mortgage market. Other sectors such as home furnishings, automobiles and electrical white goods have also all suffered a decline in demand as a result of the global recession and have had to rethink their business strategies, at least in the medium term.

We have already suggested that strategy is often very much situational and temporal, influenced by a potentially wide range of external and internal environmental factors that may help shape the type of strategies that are adopted. However, in examining the type of strategic decisions and actions that management might consider adopting to respond to these external/internal forces, it is important to recognise that to a large degree the scope of these choice decisions and actions will be determined by the level in the organisation strategy-making hierarchy at which the individual managers are operating. In effect, the scope and purpose of any strategy will vary according to the level within the organisational structure for which it is being constructed.

Levels of Strategy

In order to understand how the scope and focus (content) of strategy as well as the processes of strategy-making may vary, it is important to recognise that strategy and strategy-making take place at different levels within organisations, which in turn need to be linked together so that the strategies adopted at each level are coherent and mutually supporting. In case of most larger businesses, these levels are normally seen to consist of *corporate*, *business/competitive* and *functional* level strategies, which are usually seen to be related in a hierarchical manner. Thus corporate level strategy will set the agenda and determine the direction for the business or competitive strategies, which in turn provide the lead and determine what is required of the functional level strategies to help the higher-level strategies succeed. Some scholars also identify a further higher supra-organisational or *societal level of strategy* – sometimes termed *enterprise strategy* (Schendel & Hofer, 1979) – at which the organisation's position and political legitimacy within society are the key concern. Here the key issues for strategic management are the organisation's relationship to society, the organisation's core values and expectations of it and hence its key relationship with major stakeholder groups.

Corporate strategy is concerned with the overall shape, make-up and deployment of the business resources across what might be a portfolio of separate business units. The overall aim of corporate strategy should be directed towards balancing both external consonance – the fit between the organisation's various activities/business ventures and its environment(s), and internal consistency – the fit between the various parts of the organisation to ensure efficiency of activities and the avoidance of conflicts. For organisations in multiple business sectors, corporate strategy is often directed towards integrating the various business units so as to ensure they are pulling in a coherent direction and represent a coherent whole (both internally and externally).

While corporate strategy determines the make-up and deployment of an organisation's resources and operations – what businesses and markets it operates in – business or competitive strategy determines how it will compete in each of the selected market, product or industry segments. The broad goals and directive thrust set out in the corporate strategy are translated at the business strategy level into more concrete objectives and strategies for each business division or unit. These business strategies normally focus around policies and patterns of activity directed at optimising the business or business unit's competitive position within the specific target markets/industry segments.

Thinking about how organisations can best develop successful competitive strategies has tended to polarise around two broad opposing schools of thought: the competitive positioning approach, associated in particular with the work of Michael Porter (1980, 1985), and the distinctive capabilities/resource-based approach, associated with the work of Prahalad and Hamel (1990), Day (1994) and Kay (1993).

At the functional level, strategy is concerned with the way the various organisational functions – marketing, human resources, finance, operations/production, research and development, etc. – develop programmes of action that support and contribute to the realisation of higher-level business and corporate goals and strategies. Functional level strategies generally take their lead from the higher-level strategies, but must also be aligned with the needs and circumstances in their own operating environment.

The Link between Corporate, Business and Communications Strategy

In examining the area of communication/public relations strategy, we are, of course, essentially looking at an area of *functional* strategy. As such, communication strategy, like all other functional strategies, needs to be aligned with and to support the *higher* business and/or corporate strategies of the organisation. While the logic in this argument might seem obvious, in some cases the communications strategies and plans may be developed without any clear or explicit link to the business or corporate goals the strategy is intended to support. Alternatively, there may be some reference made to the broader business or corporate goals, but there may be insufficient evidence as to how the communications strategy has or can contribute to the achievement of those goals. Here, for example, a frequent criticism over the years of communication/public relations programmes has been the lack of accurate, tangible measurement of results – instead we continue to see outcomes measured primarily in terms of media coverage and its more questionable cousin, 'advertising-equivalent value'. What we have here is essentially a measurement of process – of successful message *execution* and *potential* delivery – but not of impact – that is, behavioural change. We will return to this question of how best to measure communications impact later in the chapter.

What should be clear from the above discussion is that in examining communication strategy in organisations, we need to explore two related questions: first, what is communication strategy is and how it is formulated; and second, how does communication strategy contributes to corporate and business level strategies.

WHAT IS COMMUNICATION STRATEGY?

As was suggested earlier in this chapter, a common weakness found within the communication/public relations literature is a failure to engage critically with debates about our understanding of strategy and its application in the communication context. Indeed, one finds relatively few works that specifically examine the concept of strategy and strategic management in this context. Moreover, when the terms 'strategy' and 'strategic management' have been applied to communication functions and programmes, these terms have often been poorly explained or in some cases applied inappropriately to describe what are essentially tactical programmes or activity. The latter weakness has begun to be picked up and highlighted more prominently in more recent works by scholars such as Cutlip, Center, and Broom (2006) and Gregory (2010), who have called for greater clarity in thinking through what are the *strategic* challenges that communication/public relations professionals should be tackling. Although focusing more on explicating the key elements and stages in the public relations planning process, Gregory nevertheless does make a strong case for distinguishing between *strategy* and programme *tactics*. Gregory accuses many practitioners of rushing into tactics without giving sufficient thought first to establishing a clear and coherent overall communications strategy that might inform and shape the programmes of tactics adopted. According to Gregory, strategy is 'the overall approach taken to a programme or campaign. It is the coordinating theme or factor, the guiding principle, the big idea, the rationale behind the tactical programme.' While welcoming and endorsing Gregory's call for a greater clarity between communications strategy and tactics and agreeing with some of the distinguishing characteristics she identifies with strategy, we suggest that the above 'definition' of strategy does not make a clear enough distinction between *what strategy is* and *what strategy does* (its role and purpose). This distinction is arguably important when we consider later how strategy is formulated.

So how should an organisation's communication strategy be defined? We believe that a well-articulated communication strategy should provide a clear indication of the overall direction, purpose and intended outcome of the activities and resource commitment to the communication/public relations function. Ideally, the communication strategy can be expressed in terms of a unifying 'big idea' that will run through and help integrate all communications activities. So the communication strategy should spell out the *purpose*, *form*, *focus* and *direction* of the communication strategy – how it will contribute to achieving the organisation's overall and specific goals. Another way of thinking about this strategy statement is as an expression of the way the communication function will address and respond to the *issues* that the organisation faces, whether these are at the corporate, business or functional levels. It is important to distinguish between the *strategy* that forms the intended solution to identified and prioritised *issues*, and the expression of those issues themselves, and the associated objectives set in respect of them. This is another common area of confusion when expressing the communication or any other functional strategy, namely confusing issues and objectives with strategy.

In trying to better understand 'communication strategy', we face many of the same challenges encountered when trying to understand and define corporate and business strategy – namely the need to understand both the *content* as well as the *process* of strategy formation. Reviewing and synthesising the relevant literature concerned with theories and models of communication/public relations strategy, a number of essential *themes* can be distilled that help to define the nature of strategy in this context:

- Communication strategy defines the *purpose* and direction for the organisation's communication activities.
- Communication strategy helps to *position* the organisation within the environment/markets in which it operates.
- Communication strategy may be expressed as a *plan* or will contain *planned* programmes of communications activities.
- Communications strategy will reflect and give expression to the prevailing management *perspective* of the organisation – the prevailing ' world-view' of the organisation and its position.
- Communication strategy defines the *deployment* of resources across the communications function.

Here one might detect a relatively strongly correspondence between these 'five themes' and the 'five Ps' definitional framework of strategy advanced by Mintzberg (1987), with a number of his definitional constructs evident in these distilled characteristics of communication strategy. Moreover, as with Mintzberg's original framework, these five definitional themes should be recognised as a set of different but related facets of communication strategy. Thus one can focus on the specific *purpose* behind an organisation's communication strategy, which might be designed to help *position* the organisation in a specific niche within its industry, using a detailed and deliberate communication *plan* to achieve that end. Similarly, the communication strategy might revolve around the senior management's view of the organisation's identity and values (their *perspective*) and may deploy the appropriate resources required to develop a *planned* programme of communication activities to help ensure that the external *positioning* aligns with the internal vision for the organisation.

In addition to these definitional themes or facets of communications strategy, which represent a set of different 'lenses' through which we can examine the purpose, nature and focus of communication strategy, it is also important to understand the essential pragmatic elements that make up the content of any communication strategy. These comprise the who, what, where, when and how of any communication strategy:

1. The 'who' – the key target stakeholders that the strategy is intended to affect.
2. The 'what' – the communication objectives and key messages that the strategy will be seeking to communicate.
3. The 'where' – the chosen set of channels or methods for transmitting the messages.
4. The 'when' – the time scale over which the strategy is intended to work.
5. The 'how' – the specific programme of communication tactics/activities to be deployed to achieve the desired results.

Arguably putting these two 'definitional frameworks' together can help provide a better *basis* for understanding the purpose and essential 'content' or component elements of any communication strategy. But, of course, while these core/generic elements may well be recognisable in any communication strategy, it is equally true to say that communication strategies are essentially situational in nature, reflecting and being shaped by the specific demands and circumstances facing any specific organisation at a unique point in time. However, as we will examine further below, circumstances aside, communications strategy will still tend to vary from organisation to organisation, simply because its design and implementation are shaped by specific individuals or groups of practitioners with their own sets experiences and prejudices, who will bring their own specific mindset and ingenuity to bear on the task of strategy formulation. Consideration of this latter point leads us directly to the second part of the first of the two questions we posed earlier – how communication strategy is formulated.

Communication Strategy Formation

Comparing the extensive range of management literature on the topic of strategy, and more specifically on strategy *formation*, with that found in the communication/public relations literature, one is immediately struck by the predominantly one-dimensional perspective of the *communication/public relations* strategy-making process – namely as a strategic communication *planning* process. Thus, for example, Grunig and Repper (1992) advance a model for the strategic management of public relations essentially comprising a seven-step planning process which approximates closely to a rational planning model similar to those advanced by a number of management scholars such as Johnson and Scholes (1989), Chaffee's (1985) 'linear model', or Whittington's (1993) 'classic strategy model'. This mapping of the Grunig and Repper model of public relations strategic management to the classical linear planning model is illustrated in Figure 5.2. Here we have mapped Grunig and Repper's seven-step model to the three core elements of the Johnson and Scholes (1989) strategic management model, namely *strategic analysis*, *strategic choice* and *strategy implementation*, to which we would logically add *strategy evaluation*. However, while we have shown these elements as forming a linear model, which is perhaps the logical assumption, Johnson and Scholes acknowledge that, in practice, the relationship between these elements may not always follow such a linear path. Indeed, these elements of strategy-making may not even be recognisable as discrete stages, but may overlap with implementation taking place at the same time as choices being made, and strategic analysis is likely to be an ongoing process that continues alongside the other elements of the process. While Johnson and Scholes were concerned with explaining corporate and business strategy-making, these arguments could logically apply equally to functional strategy-making, including communication strategy.

Taking a similar view to Grunig and Repper, Cutlip et al. (2006) see public relations strategy-making and planning as elements of a 'scientifically managed' organisational problem-solving process comprising four key steps:

1. Defining the public relations problems/situation analysis.
2. Planning and programming (what they label as ' strategy').
3. Taking action and communicating (implementation).
4. Evaluation – assessing the outcome.

This 'classical' four-step process model (see Figure 5.3) is, of course, firmly located in what Mintzberg (1994b) what would label the 'design or planning schools of thought, in so far as it sees the process as a rational, largely prescriptive process that is driven by rational analysis of the environment and the issues/problems faced. Indeed, as suggested above, if we look at the treatment of communications strategy-making within the communications literature as a whole, in the vast majority of cases a broadly similar *strategic planning* framework emerges, a typical example of which is shown in Figure 5.4.

C-MACIE AND STRATEGY FORMATION

The communication strategy-making frameworks that we have examined so far broadly portray a more or less similar process of communication strategy-making,

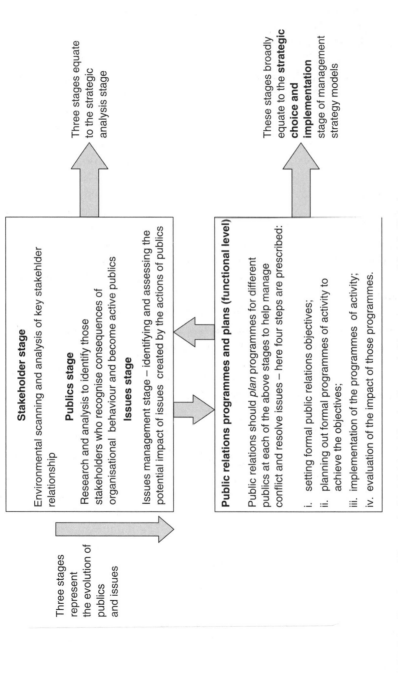

FIGURE 5.2 Grunig and Repper's (1992) Model for the Strategic Management of Public Relations

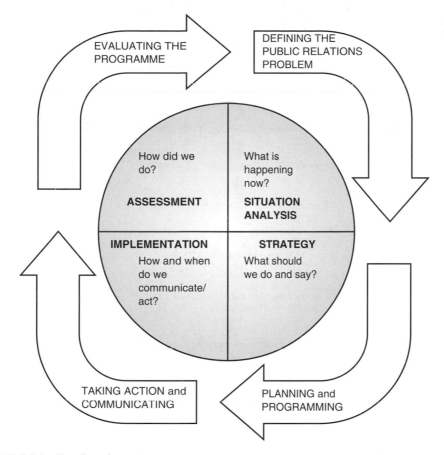

FIGURE 5.3 The Four-Step Public Relations Process Model (adapted from Cutlip et al., 2006)

comprising broadly similar elements. Moreover, these frameworks can be seen to comprise elements broadly similar to those making up the C-MACIE communication management framework we advanced in Chapter 2. Again this close correspondence between these frameworks or models is perhaps not entirely surprising, given that the C-MACIE framework is intended to capture what most commentators would accept are the key component stages in managing the (strategically) important dimension of any communication function's operations. Thus the communications management analysis stage in the C-MACIE model corresponds to and encompasses Grunig and Repper's (1992) stakeholder, publics and issues stage, Cutlip et al.'s (2006) problem-solving, situational analysis stage, and the external/internal and the stakeholder and issues stages in the generic strategic planning model. The communications choice component corresponds to Grunig and Hunt's 'planning stages', Cutlip et al.'s 'planning and programming' stage, and the 'determining of objectives, message(s) and programmes' stage of the generic planning model. The communication implementation

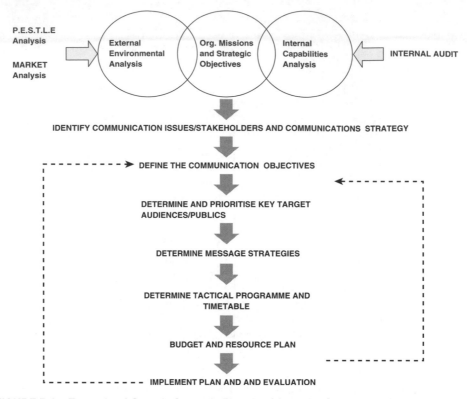

FIGURE 5.4 Example of Generic Strategic Planning Model for Communication

component logically corresponds to the 'programming' and 'taking action' stages of Grunig and Hunt and Cutlip et al.'s models, and to the implementation stage of the generic model; and similarly, the communication evaluation component of the C-MACIE framework corresponds to the evaluation element of the other three models. However, it is important to recognise that the C-MACIE framework was not intended to be simply a rational strategic planning model, even thought it can readily adapted to that purpose. Rather, C-MACIE serves as an *operational* management framework for communication/public relations functions, but its flexibility also enables it to work as an effective model along the strategic–operational continuum.

While the type of rational planning approach discussed above undoubtedly represents the dominant model or approach used to formulate overall business as well as functional strategies, its limitations have been exposed, particularly where organisations are facing new and perhaps rapidly changing environments or markets, in which decision-makers may often have only limited intelligence available to guide strategy formation. Indeed, in the more recent edition of their widely used text, Cutlip et al. (2006) have acknowledged that the fully *planned* mode of communications strategy formation may not always be entirely appropriate or even feasible for organisations operating in rapidly changing environments. Rather, they suggest there is a growing acceptance of an *evolutionary mode* of strategy formation in which 'strategies may develop over time, representing a pattern of decisions that respond to the opportunities and threats in the environment' (p. 310). This dichotomy between planning and evolutionary strategy-making approaches reflects the contrast between the *deliberate* and *emergent* strategy models identified by Mintzberg and Waters (1985) and other management scholars in more recent years. The evolutionary mode of communications strategy-making lies very much in the adaptive, incremental school of strategy formation, or what Mintzberg et al. (1998) term the 'learning school' of strategy formation.

Here we also argue that because the C-MACIE model was conceived as a broad management framework for the communication/public relations function, it is flexible enough to encompass the idea of communication strategy formation taking a variety of different forms other than simply the rational planning approach. Strategic *choice decisions* might take place in a way that could allow communication strategies to be developed incrementally, or may reflect the more 'political' programmatic process that Johnson (1988) termed an 'organisational action approach' to strategy-making. Equally, communication strategies might take the *emergent* form where the strategy is recognised and derived from a pattern of communication and organisational actions that might be recognised with hindsight as forming a coherent strategy. Here the importance of the analytical skills of the communication team will come to the fore, in both capturing the relevant data and making sense of the pattern of actions embedded within it. From this analysis will follow the important *choice and implementation decisions* about whether and how to build on the observed past pattern of actions, and what sort of strategic communication programmes should be put in place to build on them.

Earlier we highlighted Mintzberg et al.'s (1998) examination of ten separate but related schools of thought about strategy formation and their tentative conclusion that, rather than representing entirely different processes or approaches to strategy formation, these different schools might constitute different parts or perspectives of the same process, which itself may change over time. Within the communication/ public relations field, there has been very little consideration of different schools or perspectives of strategy formation, despite the fact that these ideas and debates have been circulating within the management literature for at least two decades. The failure to recognise such debates and to engage with the important question about how communication strategies may be formulated is indicative of a rather blinkered view on the part of many communication/public relations scholars and practitioners who have failed to consider what lessons might be learned from engaging more with the broader evolving field of management theory and practice. The dominance of the 'planning model' of communication strategy formation within the communication/public relations literature is arguably a product of this apparently narrow and 'blinkered' view of strategy and strategic management among traditional public relations scholars and practitioners.

Of course, it would be misleading to view the rational planning approach to communication strategy formation in too negative or critical a light, since it has clearly been used quite extensively and successfully in many different contexts. Moreover, as Chaffee (1985) has argued, the linear planning approach does generally offer a foundation on which more sophisticated approaches to strategy-making will often tend to be built. In this sense, the question to ask is perhaps not whether or not some form of strategic *planning* process is appropriate and effective in the communication context, but rather what its role is or should be in terms of determining the content of the communication strategy. In short, is the planning process capable of encompassing the creative visioning and positioning of the organisation, as well as the prevailing internal perspective of the organisation, and then translating these elements into an appropriate and effective communication strategy? Alternatively, as Mintzberg (1994b) has suggested, does the planning process amount largely to a *strategic programming* process, articulating and elaborating the vision and strategic thinking of others? Clearly, some form of communication plan, however framed, is going to be needed in most organisations, if only as a basis for organising resources and directing the communication staff – determining the *who, what, where, how and when* of any communication strategy. The mistake is to confuse such plans with the genuine visioning and conceiving of the strategy, which is arguably the 'province' of *strategic thinking*.

Strategic Thinking and Strategic Planning

If we accept, as Mintzberg (1994b) has suggested, that strategic planning and strategic thinking represent two related but different processes, requiring different intellectual skills, we need to explore what this means for communications strategy-making. We need to understand who does the strategic thinking within communication/public relations teams, what is the intellectual process involved, and how 'planners' and 'thinkers' work together. There are, however, no simple answers to any of these questions since, as Mintzberg et al. (1998) acknowledge, we are still a long way from fully understanding the process of strategy formation *as a whole*, rather than individual components of it.

Thus if we are to better understanding the process of communication strategy formation, we need to explore further the working processes among the senior communication managers, and the dynamics of the process that occurs as they move from problem/opportunity identification through to the choice of strategies and their implementation. Here the obvious difficulty is to get close enough to observe and understand the process of strategy creation – particularly in terms of the process of conceiving the big unifying ideas. Is this creative thinking process the product of collective or individual thought processes? Are such ideas derived through inspiration or perspiration – sweating the data analysis – or a combination of the two?

We are also concerned with the question of what is a big idea and how the communication strategy should be expressed – what does it comprise and how is this idea translated into a workable plan of action? In essence, we need to try to look behind the various component steps that make up a typical strategic communication plan such as that shown earlier in Figure 5.4 and understand how decision-makers conceive of the ideas or themes that then permeate through the communication strategy. Essentially, we need to examine and perhaps separate the 'thinking component' from the programming or 'doing' components of strategic management.

The DNA of Strategy

Here, we suggest that the *strategic thinking* component of the communication strategy-making process will normally focus around two key components of strategy. The first is determining and articulating the *role* that the communication/public relations strategy can or should play in addressing the issues and problems or opportunities that the organisation faces. This might be about determining the desired positioning of the organisation (or parts of the organisation) in relation to its environment and markets, its stance on a key issue, or response to a key challenge. The second key component of the communications strategy is the determining of a core unifying idea or proposition that can permeate all the organisation's communication activities. This latter component we refer to as creating the *DNA* of the communication strategy. For example, where the challenge is to bring together two merging divisions or companies and to explain the new merged entity to the external world, the communications challenge is to tease out those core values that will resonate with and unite the staffs within the two merging entities and to capture and communicate those values in a meaningful way to the outside world. Here the 'communication DNA' is essentially made up of the way those core values are captured and wrapped up in a succinct communicable message.

Extending this DNA analogy, the core idea should serve as a sort of 'genetic blueprint' – a recipe that informs the design of all the components of the communication strategy, which may also extend to all the organisation's communicative behaviours and not just communication through traditional media channels. The communication plan then serves as a form of 'DNA sequencing', providing the structure and control over the component elements or strategic activities. This DNA analogy also serves to highlight the complexity and challenge of this element of strategy formation. Conceiving of the core communication idea or 'blueprint' is undoubtedly the most challenging and cerebral task in the strategy formation process, which perhaps helps explains partly why this step may often be bypassed or receive only superficial attention as practitioners rush to develop tactical activities. This tendency to rush to technique is understandable because it may enable practitioners to focus on what many will see as what they understand best and are most experienced at doing – namely developing the tangible, most visible element any communications strategy and plan. Moreover, with increasing pressure on all functions to deliver tangible results relatively quickly, communication practitioners may see too much emphasis on thinking through communication strategies as an unnecessary delay in getting to grips with the problems or challenges faced. It is this emphasis on the programme of communication actions at the expense, in many cases, of careful strategic thinking that can lead to the justifiable accusations of a lack strategic understanding on the part of many communication people.

Of course, the implication here is that strategic thinking is necessarily a deliberate *a priori* process, which precedes the articulation and implementation of the strategy. This may not always be the case. As we have discussed earlier in the chapter, strategic thinking may actually focus on identifying and interpreting a developing pattern of organisational activities (communication-related or otherwise), that when viewed with the benefit of hindsight may be recognised as the emergence of a more or less coherent strategy. The challenge then becomes one of distilling the essence of that emerging 'strategy' and then investing resource in strengthened and further developing the strategy. In this sense, rather than determining the core DNA of the communication strategy in advance and using it to guide the programming of the communications activities, it may be more a case of uncovering the embedded communication DNA within the pattern of activities that have been taking place.

Thus in considering communication strategy formation in terms of what Mintzberg and Waters (1985) termed 'deliberate or emergent' modes, arguably the key to successful strategy formation remains the same – the ability of communication strategists to distil the vital 'codes' or recipe – the DNA that will enable communication team to develop powerful, highly relevant and sustainable programmes that will resonate with the core values of the organisation and help position the organisation effectively within its operating environments.

For some commentators this DNA analogy might appear a little contrived, whereas others, particularly those working in the world of advertising, might argue that it only captures what they have been doing for many years – namely distilling core brand values and suchlike into memorable images and slogans. But the communications DNA concept involves more than generating clever images or slogans (although at the programme stage images and slogans may serve as valuable tools in any campaign); as with genetic science itself, the complexity lies below the surface in the careful analysis and teasing out the unique genetic blueprint of the organisation or business that is capable of being integrated into all its communication strategies.

Among organisations whose communication strategy could be seen to be based around a powerful core idea – a genetic blueprint – that resonates through all their communications as a unique corporate DNA signature are iconic companies such as Apple in technology sector, BMW, Rolls Royce and Porsche in the automotive sector, McDonald's, Harrods and Nike in the food and retail sectors, and the Virgin Group in transportation and other leisure areas. It is not just a case of major corporates deploying a large advertising budget to help generate powerful brand recognition. All of these and similarly successful companies have developed a strong core set of values and associated communication propositions – a powerful communication DNA that drives not just their advertising, but all elements of their communication strategies.

Thus, in short, we believe that it is unrealistic to assume that communication/public relations strategy-making will necessarily take any one common form, but rather will reflect the established processes and approaches that communication managers feel comfortable with and which their organisations sanction. Equally, the type of challenges faced within the corporate or business environment, particularly in terms of the degree of uncertainty over the future, will invariably shape the type of communication strategies that might be developed. Perhaps the two constants that will characterise any well-crafted strategy (irrespective of how successful it proves to be) are, first, a clearly articulated and powerful idea that can permeate all communication activities, and second, a well-constructed plan of action that mobilises, directs and integrates all communication resources, activities and personnel towards the delivery of the key communication/public relations goals. Whether such plans are developed incrementally or conceived entirely *a priori* will, of course, depend on the situation facing the organisation, but arguably what there is no substitute for is putting sufficient emphasis on allowing the strategic/creative thinking process to develop the idea(s) that will drive and underpin the communication strategy and plans.

THE CONTRIBUTION OF COMMUNICATIONS STRATEGY

So far we have focused attention on the first of the two question we posed earlier – what communication strategy is and how it is formulated. However, as we also stressed earlier, a comprehensive understanding of communication strategy also requires answers to a second question – how communication strategy contributes to corporate and business level strategies. Indeed, unless the communication function can demonstrate how it is contributing to the corporate and/or business strategy of the organisation, then arguably it has little real purpose in itself. We have already explained the logical, hierarchical link between corporate, business and functional strategies, which implies that the strategy agenda at each level should take its lead from the higher level(s). In the case of communication strategy, this effectively means that its role and agenda will flow from either or both the corporate and business level strategies. While this hierarchical relationship in strategy agendas and strategy formation has been broadly acknowledged within the communication/public relations literature, as Moss and Warnaby (2000) point out, most of the emphasis within the literature has been on exploring how communication/public relations can fit with and contribute to the realisation of corporate goals and strategy, rather than examining the communication role at the competitive strategy level.

What is generally known as the 'Excellence Study' (Grunig, 1992; Grunig, Grunig, & Dozier, 2002) represents perhaps the most extensive examination to date of the role and contribution of communication/public relations to organisational success. In addition to identifying a set of 14 characteristics of excellently managed public relations programmes and departments that the authors argued contributed best to organisational effectiveness, Grunig et al. (2002) also advanced a more refined model – building on the earlier framework advanced by Grunig and Repper (1992) – to explain the strategic management of the communication/public relations function. The central dynamic of the model is the *consequential impact* on the relationship

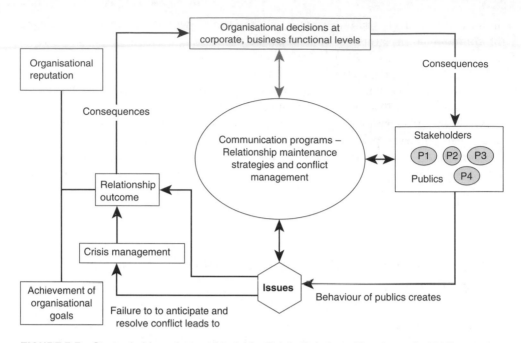

FIGURE 5.5   Strategic Management Model for Public Relations (Grunig et al., 2002)

between organisations and their stakeholders of the decisions and actions taken, on the one hand, by the organisation, and on the other hand, by its stakeholders either in response to or in anticipation of the organisation's actions (see Figure 5.5). Here, Grunig et al. (2002: 145) argued that communication strategy should focus on building and managing relationships and resolving conflicts with stakeholders that may arise from organisational decisions or actions, or as a result of a mismatch of stakeholder and organisational interests.

While this revised strategic management model undoubtedly offers a more complete and more sophisticated interpretation of the strategic role and contribution of the communication/public relations function to corporate strategic management in organisations, it does have a number of notable limitations. First the model focuses primarily on the corporate strategy level and does not examine, at least not explicitly, the role of communication/public relations at the competitive strategy level. Second, while the model suggests the role and purpose to which communication strategies maybe directed, it fails to consider the processes by which corporate and communication strategies themselves may be formulated. Third, like all such models it tends to offer a ' snapshot' view of strategy and strategic management, rather than trying to encompass the possibility of change in strategic focus and approach to strategy-making over time.

Moss and Warnaby (2000) attempted to address the first two of these weaknesses by suggesting a 'nested' model of strategy and strategy-making in organisations as a basis for explaining the potential role of communication/public relations at the corporate, competitive and functional levels, as well as recognising the interrelated nature of strategy-making at all three levels. Focusing specifically on the business or competitive strategy level, it is possible to identify a number of ways in which communication/public relations strategies can contribute to successful competitive strategy development and the achievement of an organisation's competitive goals. Here it is important to recognise that although competitive strategies can take many different forms, thinking about competitive strategy has tended to polarise around two principal schools of thought: the 'competitive positioning school' or 'outside-in perspective' (Porter, 1980, 1985; Day 1994); and the 'distinctive competencies or capabilities-based school',[1] sometimes referred to as the 'inside-out school' (Prahalad & Hamel, 1990; Stalk, Evans, & Shulman, 1992). The former, which has been dominated by the work of Michael Porter, focuses on the need to identify a defensible competitive position within the organisation's target market(s) and develop strategies to exploit and defend that position (e.g., Porter argued for one of two generic competitive strategies – 'low cost leadership ' or 'differentiation' – applied on an industry-wide basis or within specific niche markets when it would become a 'focus strategy'). The 'positioning approach' dominated strategic thinking for much of the 1980s, but was challenged during the 1990s by an alternative school of thought, which saw the source of sustainable competitive advantage lying in developing strategies based around exploiting the distinctive competencies an organisation possesses or has developed, or, in some cases, exploiting the ownership of particular assets that competitors cannot access or match. These two schools of thought about how organisations might develop successful competitive strategies are by no means entirely mutually exclusive, nor may either school alone completely capture the variety of different approaches that organisations may develop to enable them to operate successfully in competitive markets.

It is a beyond the scope of this chapter to explore fully the range of different stratagems that organisations may adopt to compete successfully or to combat competition in the markets in which they operate, and equally to explore the role of communication/public relations strategy across all potential competitive situations and contexts. Indeed, much of the thinking in this area arguably is still evolving. However, an indication of some of the more obvious ways in which communication/public relations strategy may be able to support the achievement of corporate and/or business or competitive goals and strategies is provided in Table 5.5. Further examples of how communication/public relations strategies can support corporate and business strategies can be found in later chapters in this book (see Chapters 6 and 9 in particular).

Measuring the Effects of Communications Strategy

As we have already highlighted in Chapter 2, the measurement of communication outcomes continues to be something of an 'Achilles heel' for the communication/public relations function in terms of demonstrating its 'strategic' value and importance to organisations. Clearly, if communication/public relations is to be recognised as a strategically important function it is essential that it can demonstrate to senior

TABLE 5.5 Summary of the Ways in which the Communication/Public Relations Strategy Might Contribute to Corporate and Business Strategies

Strategy Level and Purpose	Contribution of Communication/Public Relations Strategy
Corporate Strategy Level • Corporate strategy is concerned with the overall shape, make-up and deployment of the business resources across what might be a portfolio of separate business units • The overall aim of corporate strategy should be directed towards balancing both *external consonance* – the 'fit' between the organisation's various activities/ business ventures and its environment(s) – and *internal consistency* – the fit between the various parts of the organisation to ensure efficiency of activities and the avoidance of conflicts • For multi-business sector organisations, corporate strategy is often directed towards integrating the various business units so as to ensure they are pulling in a coherent direction and represent a coherent whole (both internally and externally) **Competitive/Business Strategy** • While corporate strategy determines the scope and purpose of the organisation's operations (what businesses and markets it operates in), business or competitive strategy determines how it will compete in each of the selected market, product or industry segments • The broad goals and directive thrust set out in the corporate strategy are translated at the business strategy level into more concrete objectives and strategies for each business division or unit • These business strategies normally focus around policies and patterns of activity directed at optimising the business's or business unit's competitive position within the specific target markets/industry segments • The source of competitive strategy has tended to polarise around two broad opposing schools of thought – the *competitive positioning approach*, associated in particular with the work of Porter (1980, 1985), and the *distinctive capabilities/resource-based approach*, associated with the work of Prahalad and Hamel (1990), Day (1994), Kay (1993)	• Helps to build and maintain mutually supportive relationships with key stakeholder groups • Providing corporate intelligence and stakeholder analysis to help formulate and validate corporate strategies • Building and maintaining key stakeholder relationships • Building, maintaining and defending the organisation's reputation • Providing issue and conflict management support to corporate management • Communicating and helping to build understanding of corporate policies and strategies internally • Supports business and marketing strategies by building and strengthening the corporate brand and reputation in relevant industry/markets • Building understanding of the organisation and its products/services – creating a more favourable market environment for business strategies to work • Helps to communicate the business strategy across all relevant departments/business units to strengthen internal cohesion • Helps to communicate and support the market/brand positioning across a range of relevant media channels, in design, through word of mouth, etc. • Provides a means of signalling an organisation's low-cost leadership position so as to avoid damaging price wars • Provides communication support for distinctive capabilities/resource-based market strategies: strengthening and differentiating intangible reputational assets; supporting internal and external production and/or distribution networks; helping to educate the market about new innovations

management a tangible contribution to the realisation of corporate and business goals. Arguments that communication is often concerned with bringing about 'softer', intangible changes among target stakeholders attitudes that may then translate more subtly into desired behavioural changes that benefit the organisation need to be substantiated evidentially. It is unacceptable to try to hide behind arguments that measuring such communication effects is difficult or in some cases perhaps impossible. While such 'impact' measurement is undoubtedly complicated and may be impossible to achieve with complete accuracy, this should not be used as an excuse for the dressing up of process measurement in impact clothing. Here criticism has focused on the continued use of media content analysis and the 'advertising-value equivalent' of coverage, rather than genuine impact measurement, in terms of behavioural change amongst the target groups. Cost and time pressures have frequently been cited as the chief reasons for this continued emphasis on media content analysis and the use of advertising-value equivalents as the most common modes of communication programme evaluation. This over-reliance on such metrics arguably continues to hamper the advancement of the communication/public relations professionals within the senior management hierarchy within organisations.

Thus not only do communication strategists need to align themselves with current thinking in the world of management strategy, but evaluation methods also need to be further refined and developed to meet senior managements' increasing demand for proof of value for money and return on investment.

NOTE

1. Some confusion exists within the literature over the use of the term 'competencies'. In some cases it is used as a synonym for 'capabilities'. Durand (1996) suggests that a distinctive competence refers to an organisation's ability to perform in a particular field and is derived from a combination and alignment of the firm's underlying knowledge, capabilities and attitude. Prahalad and Hamel (1990), in contrast, focus more on the firm's collective learning and technologically oriented capabilities. The term 'capabilities' is normally taken to refer to an organisation's potential to carry out a specific activity or activities.

SUMMARY: THE VALUE OF THE C-MACIE FRAMEWORK

Arguably, there is an obvious benefit to be derived from having an organising and explanatory framework such as the C-MACIE model to help make sense of the communications strategy-making process. Clearly, strategy-making, whether at the corporate, business or functional (communications) level, is essentially a managerial responsibility, and the product of a managerial process. However, we have also pointed to a tendency among a significant number of communication professionals to

(Continued)

(Continued)

emphasise the development of communication techniques at the expense of more considered reflection and assessment of the strategic options facing the organisation and the communication team. This 'rush to action', we argued earlier, may be a product partly of pressures on practitioners to be seen to take action, rather than spending time on more careful research and analysis of relevant background data, and on reflection on the best course of action. However, this rush to action might also be a product of the managerial shortcomings of many practitioners in terms of their grasp of strategy and strategic management.

Earlier we considered how the C-MACIE framework might be readily mapped against the more traditional rational planning models of communication/public relations strategy-making, mirroring the key elements in such models of strategic analysis (of stakeholders, publics and issues), choice in the form of communication programmes and activities, implementation and evaluation. However, we also have argued that the C-MACIE framework is sufficiently flexible to encompass more incremental/adaptive as well as interpretive or political/programmatic and even emergent approaches to strategy-making. The adaptability of the framework to encompass different strategy-making approaches arguably reflects the fact that although strategy-making may vary in terms of its outcomes and processes (Whittington, 1993), there are nevertheless a number of common elements found in all strategy-making approaches that are captured in the C-MACIE model:

- Analysis of the external and international environment – problem detection and diagnosis as well as interpretation of patterns of organisational action.
- Choice of how to treat the problem and what communication strategies can be applied or of what programmes of action should be continued/discontinued.
- Implementing the chosen strategy in terms of programming the courses and action and overseeing that the work is done as intended.
- Evaluating the success of the programmes of action and feeding back to management how the implementation of the chosen strategy is progressing.

Other key lessons to emerge from this chapter include:

- The need to understand how the concept and process of strategy-making and strategic management are understood from a managerial as well as a communication/public relations perspective.
- The multi-faceted and at times quite complex nature of strategy and hence the multiple perspectives of how strategy can be formulated – the need to examine strategy form a content, process and context perspective (De Witt & Meyer, 2004).
- The varied ways in which organisations may approach the challenge of strategy formation (Mintzberg et al., 1998) can be contrasted with the relatively narrow perspective on strategy-making found in much of the communication/public relations literature, where the rational planning model has dominated thinking.

(Continued)

(Continued)

- The need to distinguish strategic *thinking* – the creation of the ideas underpinning the strategy – from strategic planning as a form of activity programming.
- Perhaps the key lesson to emerge from this review of the literature is that communication/public relations academics and practitioners need to keep abreast of and be more open to the adoption of new thinking about strategy and strategic management, particularly if they aspire to operate on a level playing field with other members of the senior management team in organisations.
- In short, to be recognised as a significant managerial discipline and organisational function, it is important for practitioners and academics to be able to both 'talk the talk' and 'walk the walk' of contemporary management thinking and approaches to strategy-making.

REFERENCES

Aldrich, H., & Herker, D. (1977) Boundary spanning roles and organizational structure. *Academy of Management Review*, 2, 217–30.

Andrews, K. (1987) *The Concept of Corporate Strategy*. Homewood, IL: Irwin.

Argyris, C. (1985) *Strategy Change and Defensive Routines*. Marshfield, MA: Pitman.

Broom, G. M. and Dozier, D.M. (1990) *Using Research in Public Relations*. Englewood Cliffs, NJ: Prentice Hall.

Chaffee, E.E. (1985) Three models of strategy. *Academy of Management Review*, 10(1), 89–98.

Cutlip, S., Center, A., & Broom, G.M. (2006) *Effective Public Relations* (9th ed.). Upper Saddle River, NJ: Pearson Education.

Day, G.S. (1994) The capabilities of market-driven organisations. *Journal of Marketing*, 59, 37–52.

De Witt, B. & R. Meyer (2004) *Strategy Process, Content, Context: An International Perspective.* (3rd ed.) London: Thomson Learning.

Duncan, R. B. (1972) Characteristics of organisational environment and perceived environmental uncertainty. *Administrative Science Quarterly, 17,* 313–27.

Durand, T. (1996) *Revisiting key dimensions of competence*. Paper presented to the SMS Conference, Phoenix.

Gregory, A. (2010) *Planning and Managing Public Relations Campaigns* (2nd ed.). London: Kogan Page.

Grunig, J.E. (ed.) (1992) *Excellence in Public Relations and Communication Management*. Hillsdale, NJ: Erlbaum.

Grunig, J.E., & Repper, F.C. (1992) Strategic management, publics, and issues. In J.E. Grunig (ed.), *Excellence in Public Relations and Communication Management* (pp. 117–58). Hillsdale, NJ: Erlbaum.

Grunig, LA., Grunig, J.E., & Dozier, D.M. (2002) *Excellent Public Relations and Effective Organizations*. Mahwah, NJ: Erlbaum.

Johnson, G. (1988) Rethinking incrementalism. *Strategic Management Journal* 9(1), 75–91.

Johnson, G., & Scholes, K. (1989) *Exploring Corporate Strategy: Text and Cases*. Hemel Hempstead: Prentice Hall.

Johnson, G., Scholes, K., & Whittington, R. (2008) *Exploring Corporate Strategy*. Harlow: Pearson Education.

Kay, J. (1993) *Foundations of Corporate Success: How Business Strategies Add Value*. Oxford: Oxford University Press.

(Continued)

(Continued)

Mintzberg, H. (1987) The strategy concept: Five 'Ps' for strategy. *California Management Review*, *30*(June), 11–24.

Mintzberg, H. (1994a) *The Rise and Fall of Strategic Planning*. New York: Free Press.

Mintzberg, H. (1994b) The fall and rise of strategic planning. *Harvard Business Review* (January–February), 107–14.

Mintzberg, H., Ahlstrand, B., & Lampel, J. (1998) *Strategy Safari*. New York: Free Press.

Mintzberg, H., & Lampel, J. (1999) Reflecting on the strategy process. *Sloan Management Review* (Spring), 21–30.

Mintzberg, H., & Waters, J.A. (1985) Of strategies, deliberate and emergent. *Strategic Management Journal*, *6*(July–September), 257–72.

Moss, D.A., & Warnaby, G. (2000) Strategy and public relations. In D.A. Moss, D. Vercic and G. Warnaby (Eds.), *Perspectives on public relations research* (pp. 59–85). London: Routledge.

Pettigrew, A.M. (1992) The character and significance of strategy process research. *Strategic Management Journal*, *13*, 5–16.

Porter, M.E. (1980) *Competitive Advantage; Techniques for Analyzing Industries and Competitors*. New York: Free Press.

Porter, M.E. (1985) *Competitive Advantage: Creating and Sustaining Superior Performance*. New York: Free Press.

Prahalad, C.K., & Hamel, G. (1990) The core competence of the corporation. *Harvard Business Review* (May–June), 71–91.

Schendel, D., & Hofer, C. (1979) *Strategic Management: A New View of Business Policy and Planning*. Boston: Little Brown.

Stalk, G., Evans, P., & Shulman, L.E. (1992) Competing on capabilities: The new rules of corporate strategy. *Harvard Business Review*, *70*(2), 57–69.

Steiner, G.A., & Miner, J.B. (1977) *Management policy and strategy*. New York: Macmillan.

White, J., & Dozier, D.M. (1992) Public relations and management decision-making. In J.E. Grunig (ed.), *Excellence in Public Relations and Communication Management* (pp. 91–108). Hillsdale, NJ: Erlbaum.

Whittington, R. (1993) *What Is Strategy and Does It Matter?* London: Routledge.

Public Relations in Practice: Applying Frameworks and Contexts

This part of the book comprises 10 chapters that explore a range of specific specialist areas of public relations practice and context, ranging from corporate branding and reputation management to government communications, work in the not for profit sector, issues management, corporate social responsibility and public relations agency work. In each case authors explore the challenges of working in these sectors and also draw out the managerial implications for public relations professions and organisations.

Corporate Branding and Corporate Reputation

6

Ian Grime

Key Themes

- Examining the relationship between corporate branding, corporate identity, corporate image, corporate personality and corporate reputation
- Understanding the organisation's key stakeholders
- Understanding culture and its impact upon corporate branding
- The role of corporate reputation, ethics and corporate social responsibility
- The use and impact of brand extensions as a corporate brand choice
- Developing corporate brand strategy and communicating to different stakeholder groups

---

INTRODUCTION

In this chapter we will examine the concepts of corporate branding and corporate reputation and will also explore the related concepts of corporate identity, corporate personality, corporate image, while also studying the relationship between these constructs. Here we will review various schools of thought about the nexus between corporate identity, image and branding reputation, examining the value of corporate brands and reputation and exploring the role of communications in their development and maintenance. Finally the chapter explores the process and challenge of corporate brand management through the framework of the C-MACIE model.

WHAT IS CORPORATE BRANDING?

There has been a move from product branding (i.e., branding effort centred solely on one product) to corporate branding (i.e., a consistent branding effort centred on the company as a whole) over the last two decades (Hatch & Schultz, 2001; Keller, 2000). Many people often think of the company as a brand when considering corporate branding (Laforet, 2010). For example, Cadbury's follow a corporate branding strategy whereby all of their individual brands use the Cadbury's name. In contrast, Proctor and Gamble focus on individual brand names such as Flash, Febreze and Gillette in their marketing communications. A corporate brand is different from a product brand in that it can take in far more associations.

A brand is 'A name, term, design, symbol, or any other feature that identifies one seller's good or service as distinct from those of other sellers. The legal term for brand is trademark. A brand may identify one item, a family of items, or all items of that seller. If used for the firm as a whole, the preferred term is trade name'.

Source: http://www.marketingpower.com (American Marketing Association)

A corporate brand might include more general associations that are in common with a number of its products (Keller, Aperia, & Georgson, 2008); for example, BMW is typically seen as being 'well engineered' and Land Rover as 'rugged'. Moreover, a strong corporate or company brand is a valuable asset and can improve a company's presence in the stock market (Bickerton, 2000) and affect brand equity.

Although there is a paucity of definitions of corporate branding in the literature, Bick, Jacobson, and Abratt (2003: 842) define corporate branding as: 'a manifestation of the features that distinguish an organisation from its competitors'. Here the organisation as a whole and its differences from its competitors through positioning are the main focus. Furthermore, corporate brand associations should be *epitomised* by the employees of an organisation. Employees need to understand and buy into the corporate brand, and their behaviours should reflect and communicate its core values and associations. The chief executive officer (CEO) is a vital leader in this communication process. Richard Branson has been excellent in embedding core values and associations into Virgin's employees. However, a CEO who does not embody the corporate brand values can really damage a company. For example, it has been suggested that BP's oil spill in the Gulf of Mexico has not been managed well and that the actions of the CEO can make or break a corporate brand (Meacham, 2010). A poll of CEOs of major companies suggested that BP needs to improve its public relations and crisis management by increasing visibility and making sure that people could see what the company was doing to improve the crisis (Nelson, 2010). However, most CEOs are not always in the public spotlight unless there is some sort of crisis that needs managing. Nevertheless, it is still vital that they embody the core values of the company and lead from the top as they come into contact with a range of stakeholders, where the message needs to be consistent.

CORPORATE IDENTITY AND CORPORATE IMAGE

Hatch and Schultz (2001: 1042) comment that 'corporate branding brings to marketing the ability to use the vision and culture of the company explicitly as part of its unique selling proposition'. They suggest that it is this vision-driven approach to management that optimises corporate identity. Moreover, they talk about a mix of 'mind, soul and voice'. The 'mind' of an organisation refers to its vision, strategy, products and sevices. 'Soul' is all about the core values, culture and internal images that are portrayed by the employees of an organisation. 'Voice' is how the organisation behaves and, in particular, how it communicates.

In recent years, there has been increased interest in corporate identity as its strategic importance has become more apparent (Balmer, 1995; Hatch & Schultz, 2003; Melewar, 2003; Melewar & Akel, 2005). From a managerial perspective, establishing a consistent corporate identity is vital to organisations that wish to differentiate themselves from competitors, to effectively communicate their identity to customers and to achieve a competitive advantage in the marketplace (Doyle, 1990, 2000; Kennedy, 1977; Melewar, 2003). Indeed, a well-established corporate identity can result in consumers having stronger emotional ties to the organisation and greater trust and loyalty (Balmer & Gray, 2003).

However, there is confusion amongst academics and practitioners as to the differences between corporate branding and corporate identity. Corporate identity has been defined as 'the set of meanings by which an object allows itself to be known and through which it allows people to describe, remember and relate to it' (van Rekom, 1997: 411). At first glance there is little difference from the definition of corporate branding identified above, but corporate branding is more about the features of the company brand. The latter are linked to the American Marketing Association definition of a brand in terms of 'its name, term, design, symbol, or any other feature that identifies one seller's good or service as distinct from those of other sellers' (http://www.marketingpower.com). Thus corporate identity is more about how a company brand becomes known through the people and, in particular, the people internal to the organisation (see Figure 6.1).

According to Cheng, Hines, and Grime (2008), Schmidt's (1995) framework for corporate identity is a useful perspective to use as it overlaps with a number of key authors' thoughts in this field. While authors identify and categorise the identity constructs in different ways Schmidt's framework offered below largely coincides with their thoughts.

Corporate Culture

Corporate culture consists of an organisation's values, beliefs and assumptions, such as corporate philosophy, corporate values, corporate mission and ethos,

1	Coca-Cola	70,452 ($m)
2	IBM	64,727 ($m)
3	Microsoft	60,895 ($m)
4	Google	43,557 ($m)
5	GE	42,808 ($m)
6	McDonald's	33,578 ($m)
7	Intel	32,015 ($m)
8	Nokia	29,495 ($m)
9	Disney	28,731 ($m)
10	Hewlett-Packard	26,867 ($m)

FIGURE 6.1 World Top Ten Brands in 2010

Source: www.interbrand.com.

corporate principles, corporate guidelines, corporate historical background, nationality, and any subcultures within the organisation (Melewar, 2003; Schmidt, 1995). Corporate culture is a key facet that helps to shape corporate identity, as an organisation's beliefs, value systems and actions in one way or another are derived from corporate culture. Employees also play a vital role in the development of corporate culture as the sum total of employees' feelings and actions transcend through the organisation to the range of stakeholders. It is essential that the management of the organisation build a favourable corporate culture by leading by example, communicating effectively and training staff in the core values of an organisation. This will minimise conflicts and avoid any dilution of corporate identity (Suvatjis & de Chernatony, 2005).

Corporate Behaviour

Corporate behaviour is 'the sum total of those actions resulting from the corporate attitudes which influence the identity, whether planned in line with the company culture, occurring by chance or arbitrary' (Schmidt, 1995: 36). As shown in PR Briefing 6.1, actions taken by a company will impact upon its identity, image and eventually reputation. BP's initial top management's behaviour and organisational statements regarding the oil spill in the Gulf of Mexico did not reflect the identity of the company (i.e., a company of high standards, integrity and commitment to the natural environment) and the visions and strategies of the organisation. This visual representation of the organisation to the public clearly impacted upon its reputation.

Products and Services

Products and services must also reflect corporate mission and organisational philosophies. A company's portfolio of brands enables it to differentiate itself from

The BP oil spill on 20 April 2010 in the Gulf of Mexico saw a deep water drilling rig explosion that killed 11 people and injured 17 others. BP struggled to control the leek until it was capped on the 15 July later that year. It was estimated that it leaked nearly 5 million barrels of crude oil. This was an environmental and ecological disaster of huge proportions that has cost BP in excess of $32 billion. This global company was facing litigation from damage done to the environment, to the fisheries and tourism industries and to people's lives. But this huge financial loss was potentially nothing compared to the potential damage done to the corporate brand. PR executives are responsible for ensuring that the correct response and actions are taken in line with CSR policies and ideals to ensure that the corporate brand reputation is maintained. How well did BP manage the process?

The BP website has a Gulf of Mexico response home page which includes updates, latest reports, useful contacts, videos of the clean-up, wildlife rehabilitation and how BP is dealing with communities. It also has live feeds from the seabed. BP is using up-to-date interactive social media, including Twitter, Facebook, YouTube and Flickr.

The company's response appears to be a vigorous one, but problems started with their initial reaction to the oil spill when they made a number of public relations blunders without really understanding their corporate reputation and CSR policies. They first had to contain the leak, which took too long. They then had to disperse and remove the oil, which led to a number of health concerns for a number of the clean-up workers. And BP's reputation was tarnished by the action of the CEO. First, he failed to turn up at the scene of the leek for a few days, giving the impression of it not being important. Next, he complained in the press about the pressure he was under, and he was quoted as saying 'I want my life back', when the disaster was having a huge impact upon people's lives. BP also underestimated the extent of the damage in terms of the amount of oil leaking and when they would get it under control. In addition, they stated that they would only pay for appropriate and 'legitimate' claims and failed to bring in outside help early in the process, which led to the perception of them being arrogant. Arguably this could have been controlled by an appropriate crisis management strategy led by public relations experts and delivered through top management who are in touch with the corporate brand, values and identity.

BP's CEO subsequently stood down following criticism of the handling of the leak, but with a reputed £600,000 pension a year. Some observers suggested that the new (American) CEO would be good from a public relations point of view. Apart from rebuilding its tarnished name BP also has to consider the thousands of retail businesses that distribute its products. BP Ameco, for example, considered the possibility of dropping the BP name to prevent any more damage being done to their brand. Only time will tell as to how BP manages the damage done to their reputation and to the full damage done to the corporate brand.

PR BRIEFING 6.1   British Petroleum: a corporate reputation and public relations disaster?

competitors. Companies with a diverse range of products and services may follow a product brand strategy, such as Proctor and Gamble as identified above; while others focus on key values or personality that epitomise the company as a whole. For example, Virgin have a diverse range of products, but the corporate brand is centred around Richard Branson's key qualities such as innovation, quality and caring. The benefits, associations, value, and unique selling proposition associated with the brands and the service they offer all impact upon the corporate brand.

Communications and Designs

Communication plays an important role in corporate identity especially at the internal level. Organisations need to communicate their policies to employees through internal communication channels. Companies can collect feedback from external stakeholders to see if the image they have is in line with the projected corporate identity. This should be a two-way communication channel which transmits and receives information from both within and outside the organisation. The use of corporate designs, corporate advertising, corporate events and corporate sponsoring all impact upon the identity of the company. The corporate design is the visual elements of an organisation; its corporate logo, trademark, symbol, colour, shapes and typeface are sometimes referred to as visual identity (Baker & Balmer, 1997). As seen in PR Briefing 6.2, Haier used corporate design when they changed to the 'two brothers' logo to communicate their identities to the public in America; this had a significant impact upon consumers' perceptions of their corporate brand.

Market Conditions and Strategies

The nature of the industry that a firm operates in (industry identity or market conditions) and the strategic intent of the organisation will have an impact on corporate identity. The industry is characterised by underlying economic and technical factors and the identity of an industry can transfer to the company's corporate identity. For example, the automobile industry is one that relies on quality and reliability, and thus firms need to look at ways in which they can further differentiate their corporate brand identity.

While corporate identity is about the internal perspectives of a company, corporate image is all about perceptions of the corporate brand among those external to the organisation and, in particular, its customers (Davies, Chun, da Silva, & Roper, 2001). Corporate image is defined as 'what people actually perceive of a corporate personality or a corporate identity' (Olins, 1978: 212). It is all of the external stakeholders' perceptions of a company that are important here, and the relationship with or experience of a corporate identity that produces a corporate image in the mind of the public. A strong corporate image is essential for a corporate brand (e.g. Starbucks, BMW) to be successful. It acts as a key differentiating factor for consumers and other key stakeholders, and can also help to recruit and motivate employees. Thus, it follows that the framework offered by Schmidt above helps to capture and conceptualise the relationship between the factors that influence the formation of a corporate image. Figure 6.2 highlights how corporate identity and corporate image are directly related to the reputation that a company has.

Understanding the Organisation's Key Stakeholders

Stakeholders are defined as 'any group or individual who can affect or is affected by the achievement of an organization's purpose' (Freeman, 1984: 25). This definition includes stakeholders internal and external to the organisation. Hatch and Schultz (2001) also suggest that corporate branding influences the images formed not only by

When the Chinese electrical goods manufacturer Haier moved into the US market with a new logo, did they consider the impact of this core branding strategy on corporate reputation? Omar and Williams (2006) carried out case study research into the impact of Haier's new corporate logo in the United States. They assessed consumer attitudes and feelings towards the new logo and the impact of this on Haier's reputation in the US market. Haier is the Third World's largest manufacturer. Haier America has its headquarters in New York and manufacturing facilities in South Carolina. The company manufactures various white goods products including TVs, air conditioners, refrigerators, dishwashers, portable DVD equipment and MP3 players. It currently distributes its products through a number of retail outlets, including Wal-Mart.

In 2002 Haier introduced its new 'two brothers' logo which shows two children, one holding an ice cream and the other giving the thumbs-up. The two main objectives of Omar and Williams's research was to understand consumer perceptions of the new logo and to see how important a logo is for corporate reputation. They randomly administered a face-to-face survey questionnaire to 200 respondents over the age of 18 in Baltimore. The findings showed that half of the respondents were neutral about the logo, with 38% positive and only 18% negative. More importantly, of the positive perceptions, 71% thought that the company was offering children's products. When considering the products that respondents would consider buying, more people suggested products such as ice cream and children's clothing, with electrical goods scoring very low. Respondents were also asked to rank the Haier brand alongside a number of other leading electrical manufactures in terms of brand reputation; Haier scored the lowest, with General Electric being the number one company. Logos also proved vital to consumers with 61% indicating that a familiar logo suggested high quality. The main descriptors of the Haier image was 'childlike', 'friendship', 'fun', 'diversity', 'dependable' and 'quality'. There are clear implications for Haier. The logo has represented distinctive associations and values of the corporate brand. However, there appears to be a mismatch between the image and reputation that a white goods manufacturer would desire, such as 'competence', 'sophistication' and 'reliability'. Any form of communication including the new logo could negatively impact upon Haier's hard-built reputation in China. It is clear that their logo did not provide Haier with a competitive advantage and could potentially confuse respondents as to the reputation of the company. Haier did change their logo in 2004 to just its name.

PR BRIEFING 6.2   The case of the Haier Group logo: Using a logo to communicate corporate reputation gone wrong?

customers but also by a number of other key stakeholders, including employees, investors, suppliers, partners, regulators, special interest groups and local communities.

The challenge for company brands is to make sure that the individual product/ service brands that they represent provide a consistent promise to all stakeholders. Corporate brand managers need to understand that it is not only the external marketing communications that are important, but all the ways in which the organisation

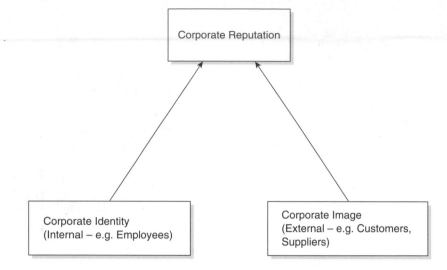

FIGURE 6.2 Corporate Reputation.
Source: Adapted from Davies et al. (2001).

interacts with its key stakeholders. Thus managers need to understand how to align both the internal (i.e., identity) and the external (i.e., image) interactions to achieve a clear and consistent corporate branding strategy. Furthermore, effective public relations are key to successfully approaching these stakeholder groups.

Fiedler and Kirchgeorg (2007) studied customers, employees, shareholders and journalists as important corporate stakeholders. They found that some stakeholder attributes are more appropriate for generic and non-specific branding and marketing approaches, while several other stakeholder attributes are better suited to specific targeting or positioning strategies. More specifically, whilst some associations may be similar for each group, the channels that they are communicated through should be distinct. For example, a company might use a television advertisement to illustrate its ethical stance to customers, but use a press release for news media groups.

Employees are vital to a company delivering its brand promise. Key to the interaction with stakeholders is employees' knowledge of the key values and identity of the corporate brand and application of this to the communication process. This can help corporate brands to improve their relationships and interactivity with stakeholders in everything they do (Hatch & Schultz, 2001).

Whilst employees are vital in delivering the brand promise, they need to be fully aware how corporate social responsibility, ethics and sustainability issues affect a company's reputation.

Corporate Reputation, Corporate Social Responsibility, Ethics and Sustainability

Although there has been a lot of interest in business and marketing ethics, there is a paucity of research in branding ethics.

Ethics refers to 'the moral rules or principles of behaviour for deciding what is right and wrong' (Fan, 2005: 342). For organisations it is difficult to distinguish between ethics and legality, as ethics and values can vary between individuals and organisations. More importantly, Fan (2005) argues there are ethical issues associated with brands relating to moral issues and the right and wrong behaviour in branding decisions. Furthermore, corporate brand image can be affected by non-branding decisions (e.g., where to manufacture or whether to undertake animal testing).

Over the last two decades there has also been an increased focus on business sustainability and the role of businesses in society. Companies have become more socially concerned and aware and have sought to solve the challenges of modern world economies with a view to creating goodwill among their stakeholders (Hagen, 2008). Thus, companies try to appear to be 'responsible' in the public eye. Indeed, the multinationals are spending time, resources and standing within the business world to drive corporate social responsibility (CSR). For example, companies such as Tesco are at the forefront of CSR initiatives such as 'Fairtrade', 'Computers for Schools', automated recycling, and the work they have done with Cancer Research's 'Race for Life'.

However, CSR is sometimes driven by risk management, and for many companies it is used as corporate public relations rather than genuinely attempting to change the way they interact with society. CSR does not show what happens behind the scenes and what is really happening in a company (Fan, 2005).

From the late 1980s there has been a shift of focus from the 'external' view of corporate image and 'internal' corporate identity to 'corporate personality' and, more recently, corporate reputation (Omar & Williams, 2006). Corporate reputation is concerned with how people perceive and feel about a company generally over the longer term, and is defined as a 'perceptual representation of a company's past actions and future prospects that describes the firm's overall appeal to all its key constituents when compared with other leading rivals' (Fombrun, 1996: 72). This definition refers to people's or stakeholders' perceptions of a company which have been formed by its past, present and future actions and describe a company's overall appeal when compared to competitors. Here, of course, it is important to acknowledge that people can buy into and recognise the reputation of companies whose products and services they have never experienced directly (e.g., Rolls Royce, Ferrari) – in such cases the reputation is formed and shared through the images and discourse that surround such companies' products and services.

Thus it follows that it is important for companies to communicate their core mission and corporate values clearly to external and internal stakeholders. It is insufficient to communicate only about products or services, rather companies need to communicate effectively about the range of issues that may affect their operations, their interaction with the environment and industry as well as about their own identity, history and culture (Omar & Williams, 2006).

Whilst much of the corporate reputation research measures the construct using aggregate overall scores, Walker (2010) in a systematic review of the literature suggests that there are five key areas (or attributes) that need to be considered when measuring corporate reputation.

1. The measurement should examine *perceived reputation* – this chapter has highlighted the importance of stakeholders, and it is their perceptions that are important in measuring in corporate reputation and not market share or the number of awards won by the company, as the use of these measures is not consistent.

2. Corporate reputation is related to specific issues and *aggregate perceptions* – it is all of the stakeholders' views that when formed together contribute to corporate reputation. However, this is extremely difficult to do in one measurement and in the main only a small part of the stakeholder perceptions is and can be measured at any one time (usually consumers). In addition, each stakeholder group may have particular issues that are pertinent to them and therefore aggregate scores are important to particular issues and one should measure all of the stakeholders' perceptions on particular instances.

3. The *comparative nature* of corporate reputation need not be limited to other firms – inevitably firms will compare their reputation with their competitors, but this does not have to be done in isolation. It is important for a company to ensure that its reputation is relatively consistent and enduring, and therefore measuring its corporate reputation over a time period is valuable. For example, a company bringing out a new product or brand extension may want to see if this impacts upon their reputation.

4. When measuring corporate reputation it should permit the construct to *be positive and negative* – stakeholders should be able to make judgements about elements of reputation that are good or bad, high or low, and positive or negative. This can give companies clear measurements for reinforcing, repositioning and simply improving corporate reputation.

5. Corporate reputation is *relatively stable and enduring* – while a cross-sectional study of corporate reputation can give a snapshot at one period in time it is important to remember that this is simply what it is. When considering the points made in 1–4 above it is vital to note that a company may be measuring particular instances/issues and with specific stakeholders. Therefore it is the reputation that is imbued from the top management, the vision, mission and culture as represented by the employees and all the marketing communications to key publics that help to form reputation over time.

There are key implications here for companies. It is near impossible to measure all of a company's stakeholders' perceptions of reputation at any one time due to the sheer amount of time and resources needed. Here, specific issues need identifying and the relevant stakeholders need analysing. In addition, the measurement needs to take place at more than one period in time in order to check on consistency. For example, consumer perceptions of image are important to BP. If BP had had an appropriate measure of their image prior to the Gulf of Mexico oil spill, it could then have measured perceptions of image following the oil spill and following the clean-up campaign.

Davies et al. (2001) agree with the above view that reputation is the collective term referring to all stakeholders' views of the company. Furthermore, they suggest that 'image' and 'identity' together (as discussed earlier in this chapter) contribute to overall corporate reputation. Figure 6.2 shows that both internal (e.g., top management's or employees') and external (e.g., suppliers' or customers') perceptions all contribute to corporate reputation. In their research they used the brand personality construct to measure corporate reputation from both internal and external viewpoints. However, the majority of research has used brand personality from an external and usually a consumer perspective. This measurement does fall in line with Walker's (2010) pointers for the effective measurement of corporate reputation.

> Brand personality is defined as 'the human characteristics associated with a brand'. For example, brands can be perceived as 'trustworthy', 'reliable', 'sophisticated' and 'rugged.'
>
> (Aaker, 1997: 347)

Earlier researchers have written about brand personality without really distinguishing between product and corporate brands, with a tendency to focus on the external and mainly consumer perspectives. A distinctive brand personality can help create a set of unique and favourable asociations in consumer memory and thus build and enhance brand equity (Keller, 1993). As a result, brand personality is considered to be an important factor for the success of a brand in terms of preference and choice. Indeed, a well-established brand personality can result in consumers having stronger emotional ties to the brand and greater trust and loyalty which provide an enduring basis for differentiation.

From a managerial perspective, brand personality enables firms to communicate with their stakeholders about the core (or company) brand more effectively and plays a major role in advertising and promotional efforts (Plummer 1985; Aaker 1996). As such, marketing practitioners have become increasingly aware of the importance of building a clear and distinctive brand personality.

This is particularly notable as corporate brands must maintain consistent, desirable and enduring personalities to ensure their long-term success. Whilst previous researchers have relied on *ad hoc* measures of personality, Aaker (1997) developed a psychometrically sound brand personality measure. This consisted of a five-dimensional, 42-trait scale of brand personality (see Figure 6.3). For Aaker, brand personality is an essential component of brand identity and subsequent image that helps create corporate reputation and can enhance corporate brand equity (the value of the brand). Unlike previous measures of the corporate brand that focus on how factors (e.g., brand extensions) can enhance or dilute the core brand values, this interpretation is not possible or appropriate for brand personality. Brand personality is a profile measure and a company may wish to be high or low on the different dimensions. For example, an increase in 'ruggedness' following the introduction of new strategy (e.g.,

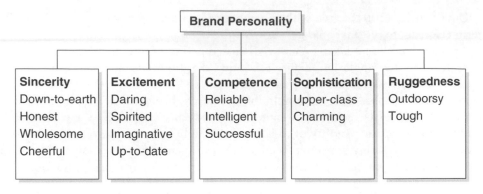

FIGURE 6.3   Aaker's 1997 Brand Personality Scale
Source: Aaker (1997).

an extension to an existing advertising campaign or a new one) could be positive or negative, depending on the salience of ruggedness as a dimension in defining the (original) personality of the corporate brand. As Keller (1998) points out, many brands will *not* wish to be strong on some dimensions as they conflict with other dimensions. For example, ESPN has a rugged personality (reflecting its sports focus) but is weak on the sophistication dimension (in line with its mass market focus). This highlights an important issue when considering factors affecting a brand's personality. It is *not* sensible to consider trying to achieve a high score on all personality dimensions. This is because brand personality is a *profile* multidimensional construct in that its dimensions cannot be combined in some mathematical formula. Its conceptual nature is similar to human personality. Thus, the 'ideal' personality of a brand will depend on the brand's market and its positioning within that market; for example, Advil (a pharmaceutical drug) will presumably be unconcerned by being viewed as unexciting; K-Mart will be unsurprised by its lack of sophistication; and Oil of Olay and Revlon will be most pleased that they are not viewed as rugged (Keller, 1998).

Whilst a number of academics have measured consumer perceptions of corporate (i.e., company or core brand) and product brands using external brand personality and image scales (e.g. Aaker's 1997 scale) there is a paucity of research that actually measures internal (i.e. employee) perspectives.

Keller and Richey (2006: 74) take the debate further by suggesting the corporate brand personality is 'what the company is and how it presents itself to the consumer'. From their perspective it is the internal employees' beliefs and behaviours that define corporate brand personality. More specifically, they define corporate brand personality as 'the human characteristics or traits of the employees of the corporation as a whole' (p. 75). Furthermore, they suggest that it is the sum of actions, words and values of all employees that reflect the organisations corporate brand personality.

They propose that it is the employees' 'heart', 'mind' and 'body' that are important dimensions of corporate brand personality. Figure 6.4 shows that the 'heart' of the corporate brand is characterised by passion and compassion. Employees must

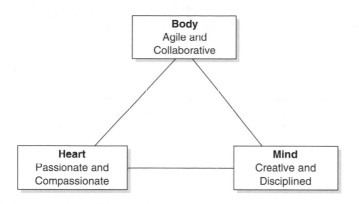

FIGURE 6.4 Corporate Brand Personality

Source: Adapted from Keller & Richey (2006).

have a strong enthusiasm/liking for the company. This passion must be extended to the business, the brands it offers and to its customers. Effective management of CSR strategies, as discussed earlier, is essential to a caring and compassionate company. The 'mind' of the corporate brand reflects creativity and discipline. Firms have to be particularly creative in managing the trade-offs between strategic, tactical, financial and organisational decisions that create synergy. Furthermore the company has to be disciplined in how it deals with these trade-offs.

For example, BP (see PR Briefing 6.1) had a financial trade-off in terms of the cost of the Gulf of Mexico oil leak and associated costs with that of maintaining its reputation. Here BP were caught on the back foot by the US media and lost the initiative in their approach to public relations. This was not helped by the actions of their CEO, Tony Haywood, and has arguably resulted in damage to their reputation.

Finally, there is the 'body' of the corporate brand that is epitomised by being agile and collaborative. It has to be fast moving in today's rapidly changing environment, keeping up with customers' needs and wants. Employees and business functions must work closely together, and companies must collaborate and work on relationships with key stakeholders. In short, it is important to recognise that all parts of an organisation communicate, whether intentionally or not. It is important to try to ensure the consistency in the 'messages' being communicated through explicit communications channels and by the actions and behaviours of employees, partners, sub-contractor etc.

CORPORATE BRANDING STRATEGY

Corporate strategy is defined as the 'blueprint of the firm's fundamental objectives and strategies for competing in their given market' (Melewar & Karaosmanoglu, 2006: 861). All of the organisation's marketing strategies should be able to show how it differentiates itself from its competitors in the industry (Melewar, 2003).

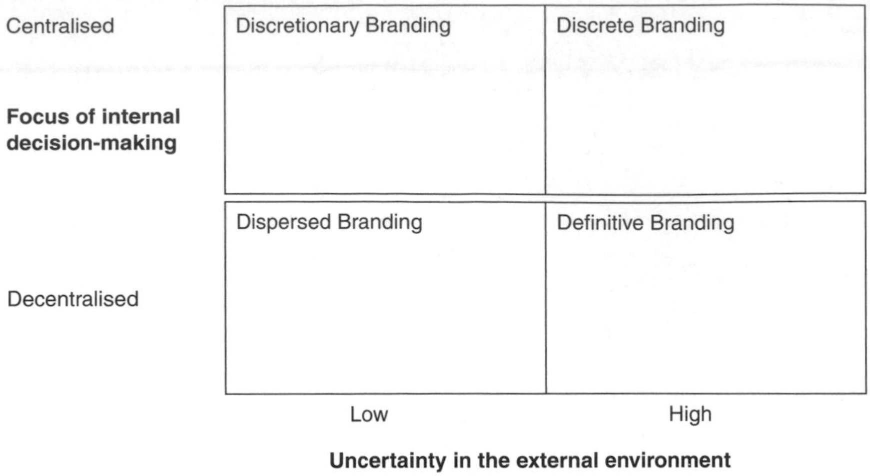

Centralised	Discretionary Branding	Discrete Branding
Focus of internal decision-making		
Decentralised	Dispersed Branding	Definitive Branding

Low   High

Uncertainty in the external environment

FIGURE 6.5   Corporate Branding Strategies

Source: Griffin (2002). Reproduced with permission of Palgrave Macmillan.

Companies have realised that corporate branding is not just about marketing communication activity with customers. It cuts across both functional areas and business units (Schultz & de Chernatony, 2002). Thus, companies need to be clear on their *strategic direction* and must engage all stakeholders with a consistent promise. To enable consistency, companies need to try to align internal and external views of the company. Moreover, due to an increasingly uncertain external environment that is constantly changing, knowledge across business functions needs to be shared and integrated with marketing and public/investor relations. This will enable companies ideally to develop a seamless internal process that presents a consistent message about the corporate brand to the range of stakeholder groups.

Griffin (2002) offers a useful framework that managers can take into consideration when making strategic corporate brand decisions (Figure 6.5). For example, decisions may involve the type of identity and image that is portrayed by the corporate brand or the decision to extend the brand portfolio. The framework identifies internal and external pressures affecting strategic decisions in four main areas. It considers companies that have their decision-making centralised, whereby decisions are made by one person or team of people (normally top-level managers or board members). In decentralised decision-making many members of the firm can make critical decisions. Uncertainty in the external environment can impact greatly on a firm's ability to operate. More specifically, the type of industry, product(s) offered, economic climate, country of operation, legal and political constraints and the type of consumer will all impact upon the level of uncertainty in the external environment.

Griffin (2002) suggests that *discretionary branding* is when there is a stable external environment with centralised decision-making. With this external stability she argues that corporate branding may not be totally necessary for adding value, due to the stable supply and demand and standard operating procedures that centralised decision-making brings with it. This type is generally characterised by industrial firms selling to industrial clients, and it is the top management's decision whether or not to use corporate branding strategies.

Dispersed branding is where there is low uncertainty in the external environment but with decentralised decision-making structures. Here, the corporate branding strategies are likely to be split among the different business functions. Local decisions can be made with little reference to the overall corporate branding strategy. With low uncertainty in the external environment, firms will operate according to standardised rules and procedures with local variations. In this quadrant there is untapped potential for the corporate brand in terms of a resource for competitive advantage. And what if the environment becomes unstable? Business functions may operate alone without consideration of the overall corporate brand strategy. An example of this is BP, where their operations did undermine the corporate brand (see PR Briefing 6.1).

Definitive branding strategies can be used in uncertain external environments where the decision-making is decentralised (e.g., franchise agreements in different countries). Here boundary-spanning specialists are vital to ensure consistency in strategic decisions, resulting from environmental fluctuations.

Discrete branding is where the external environment is changing but decisions are centralised. At this point different brands in a firm's portfolio may be centrally coordinated. Griffin (2002) uses the example of Lever Brothers and Proctor and Gamble that focus on specific brands from a centralised level, but are discretely managed and in some case totally separate from the corporate brand.

The Use of Brand Extensions as a Strategy to Reinforce, Enhance or Change Corporate Brand Perceptions

Although there is confusion in the literature as to the definition of brand extensions, Aaker and Keller (1990: 27) distinguish between two types, namely 'a *line extension*, whereby a current brand name is used to enter a new market segment in its product class (e.g., Diet Coke) and ... a *brand extension*, whereby a current brand name is used to enter a completely different product class (e.g. NCR photocopiers)'. Aaker and Keller (1990) also refer to 'extension' as the general term describing both brand and line extensions, which is the stance adopted here.

The high costs of new product launches have encouraged an increasing number of firms to use extensions for their new product strategy. By using well-known corporate brand names, the costs of launching a new product can be reduced drastically through marketing and distribution efficiencies.

There are a number of benefits and pitfalls of using an extension strategy. Extensions capitalise on the equity built up from the core (company or corporate) brand; thus, the company moves into a new product category and/or market segment from a position of strength. Extensions promote immediate consumer awareness, providing a relatively quick and cheap way to enter a new market. Moreover, the introduction of an extension can lead to enhancement of consumers' perceptions of corporate brand image and reputation through increased communication.

It is well known that the introduction of brand extensions can have positive or negative effects on a core brand's image and subsequent equity (Grime, Diamantopoulos, & Smith, 2002). As identified in Figure 6.2, corporate identity (i.e., internal to the organisation) and image (i.e., externality) constitute an essential part of reputation. Extending the brand can have an impact on the reputation of the corporate brand.

Despite their benefits, extensions can be risky. An extension (either successful or unsuccessful) may potentially dilute the equity built up by the corporate brand (Aaker, 1990). Specifically, the new product may create confusion or negative connotations in the minds of consumers and thus weaken the core values of the corporate brand (Tauber, 1981).

Research has shown that consumers' perception of the fit with the core brand image is a major consideration when attempting to introduce an extension (Boush & Loken, 1991). Perceived fit is achieved when the consumer accepts the new product as consistent with the parent brand. Favourable consumer evaluations of an extension require the core brand to have a good 'fit' with the new product (Aaker & Keller, 1990). Moreover, the better the 'fit' the easier it is to extend to new classes. More importantly, apart from its effect on the extension itself, there is evidence to suggest that fit also has an effect on the corporate brand. Specifically, in extending a brand, good fit has been seen to be important for positive consumer evaluations (i.e., enhancement) of the core brand (Keller & Aaker, 1992). Conversely, a wrong extension decision may create damaging associations and confuse potential customers. For example, when Levi-Strauss introduced their 'Levi's Tailored Classics' range they completely confused consumers by offering a sophisticated and more formal product. They failed with this new brand as it did not 'fit' with Levi's core values. An extension's major strength, capitalising on an established brand name, can also be its greatest weakness: potential dilution of the brand reputation in the long run (Tauber, 1981). These negative changes in consumer beliefs occur when specific extension associations are inconsistent with corporate brand beliefs. For example, when Cadbury's launched their instant mash potato 'Cadbury's Smash', consumers were put off as Cadbury's is synonymous with chocolate.

Extensions can be useful in helping a corporate brand to reposition as an extension may have attributes that transfer to the corporate brand. However, caution needs to be used when following a brand extension strategy as an extension that does not portray the values, image and identity of the corporate brand may indeed damage it.

CORPORATE BRANDING AND THE C-MACIE FRAMEWORK

Along with the concepts and ideas of this chapter, Bickerton (2000) offers a useful perspective of the corporate brand which fits quite neatly with the C-MACIE framework offered throughout this book.

Good communication and effective relations with key publics are essential to building trust for a range of stakeholders, and having good corporate reputation recognises that those relationships with clients are extremely important. This will have a significant impact upon the success of a business and allow a company to distinguish itself from competitors.

Figure 6.6 illustrates the C-MACIE framework through the eyes of corporate brand management. As identified in Chapter 2, the managerial role and process in organisational communications has four key stages that are underpinned by effective communication.

From the corporate brand perspective, communications management analysis is about understanding the context in which the corporate brand operates. Here, an environmental analysis is needed to understand the factors that affect the corporate brand. Internally, all employees need to buy into the company's identity which is formed through its vision, culture and top management philosophy. Employees need to be communicated with from the moment of recruitment right until leaving the organisation. Periodic analysis of employees' perceptions of corporate brand identity and reputation needs to take place to measure employees' attitudes towards the company. Externally, the environment also needs to be monitored to assess all stakeholders' (and not just consumers') perceptions of corporate image.

Next, communication managers need to make choices about which actions they need to prioritise. A company will be doing a number of things – launching a brand extension or a new ethical stance. The communications manager will not only need to prioritise which actions need priority, but also determine the best method of communication. They will also need to account for the intended recipient, the budget and the desired objectives of each action.

Following this, implementation of the communication needs to be done in a timely and effective manner. Internal implementation of communication to employees about the corporate brand can be done through training, briefings, company newsletters and other internal publicity. In addition, action needs to be taken when there are obvious gaps between the perceptions of corporate identity and corporate image. This is especially the case if the company is not delivering on some of its key values. As has been seen with the BP and Haier cases, some of the key problems and decisions taken could have been resolved better with more effective analysis and implementation. All communication is projected through the use of marketing management techniques and effective organisational communications. It is important to remember that a consistent message needs to be sent to all stakeholders for a corporate brand to be truly valued in terms of its identity, image and reputation. The key is ensuring consistency even though different communication media are likely to be used for different stakeholders. For example, a company might employ a public relations or advertising agency to help with the launch of a new brand, but they also need to ensure that employees understand what it is, its values and personality, etc. This is where a philosophy such as that of Clownfish (PR Briefing 6.3) would be useful in understanding all key stakeholders.

Communication management evaluations should be undertaken to ensure that there has not only been a consistency of corporate branding communication, but also a gauge

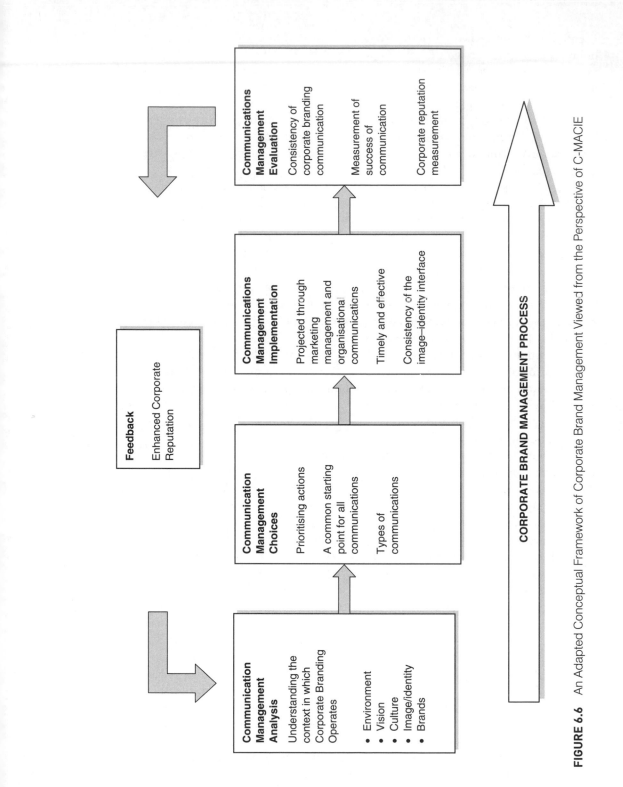

FIGURE 6.6 An Adapted Conceptual Framework of Corporate Brand Management Viewed from the Perspective of C-MACIE

When Diana Verde Nieto founded Clownfish in 2002, at the heart of her business consultancy philosophy were people, planet and profit. Her unique company puts customers and relationships with the corporate brand at the centre of CSR. In today's rapidly changing environment, where marketing communications are integrated using multiple media channels and new technology, consumers have a shorter attention span and make their own decisions about choosing the media that they will consume. It is no longer just about what the brand is saying, it is also about what different publics say about your brand. Her company looks at more than just green marketing, ethics and business sustainability; they consider the brand journey, while also really trying to integrate the customers along the whole process.

Among their clients is Avis, a leading car rental company in Europe, Africa the Middle East and Asia. Clownfish's task was to help Avis launch a campaign for their low-emissions car group. Rather than just thinking about and developing the message that Avis required, Clownfish used a much more integrated approach to developing a strategy. First, they considered a number of key stakeholders' views, both internally and externally. This helped them to develop a clear and consistent message that was credible and realistic. Next, they worked with the marketing team at Avis to design and launch the campaign. This included a launch presentation, back-of-house posters and an eco-pamphlet. Clownfish also connected and launched the range with the press to allow them to experience the eco-collection for themselves. They worked on a number of media channels to make sure that there was a fully integrated approach. They worked directly with Avis in the development of their website, newsletters, blog and Twitter page.

CSR is a 'commitment by organisations to behave ethically and take responsibility for the impact of their business on the environment and society' (Verde Nieto, 2009: 28). It is this attitude towards CSR, coupled with the new 'digitally enabled and interconnected business environment', that connects consumers and brands on an emotional level and can lead to corporate brand differentiation and success. What is important to remember is that CSR is not only about marketing campaigns but also about integrating the efforts of all of the business functions within an organisation, from manufacturing and the supply chain to employee engagement and customer satisfaction. Diana suggests that there have to be 'memorable brand experiences' that really emphasise a company's stance on CSR. Furthermore, it is the 'alignment' of a company's external communication with internal practices that is vital to effective CSR initiatives, and maintaining a constant focusing on continuing the CSR vision is what will keep companies ahead of the game.

PR BRIEFING 6.3   Clownfish and Corporate Social Responsibility

on its success. An evaluation of key stakeholder perceptions should be undertaken and can be compared with the initial analysis carried out through appropriate corporate reputation measures identified in this chapter. For example, when an advertising agency has been employed to develop an advert to raise awareness of a particular ethical stance, the communications manager should not only measure the levels of awareness but also have an understanding of the impact on corporate brand reputation.

Finally, this can be fed back to the initial communications management analysis process, where the goal is to enhance corporate reputation and improve corporate values and associations. Indeed, the C-MACIE framework in many ways simply reflects sound brand management processes in any organisation where the cycle of analysis, choice, implementation of strategies and plans and evaluation represent the logical elements in establishing and maintaining an effective and sustainable approach to corporate branding and corporate reputation management.

SUMMARY

This chapter has examined the relationships between corporate branding, corporate identity, corporate image, corporate personality and corporate reputation. It has shown that corporate branding is quite a complex concept. Corporate identity is concerned with internal (i.e., employees') perceptions, while corporate image is the external perceptions (i.e., a range of stakeholders, including consumers, suppliers and public relations agencies) of the corporate brand. Both corporate identity and corporate image are interrelated and help to shape the reputation that a company has. Brand personality has been typically used as a measure of the product brand and the corporate brand. However, an internal perspective of corporate brand reputation considering the 'heart', 'mind' and 'body' has been presented, while the external view of this construct uses the brand personality scale consisting of 'sincerity', 'competence', 'excitement', 'sophistication' and 'ruggedness'.

There are a number of corporate brand strategies that can be undertaken to achieve a competitive advantage, depending upon the uncertainty in the external environment and the focus of internal decision-making. More specifically, there is discretionary branding where there is a stable external environment with centralised decision-making. Dispersed branding is where there is low uncertainty in the external environment but with decentralised decision-making structures. Definitive branding strategies can be used in uncertain external environments where the decision-making is decentralised. Discrete branding is where the external environment is changing but decisions are centralised. In addition, brand extensions are a key strategic decision for corporate brand managers. However, the impact of corporate brand 'fit' with the extension needs to be considered before embarking upon this strategy as potential dilution of the corporate brand is a real risk, even if the extension is successful.

Finally, the 'C-MACIE' framework identified in Chapter 2 attempts to place corporate branding in the eyes of the communications expert. Moreover, it is vital to remember that there are a number of internal and external stakeholders that impact upon corporate reputation. The communication management process needs to cover a multitude of decisions, ranging from understanding the corporate brand and management choices, to implementing timely and effective communication and evaluating the success of communications. This cycle should result in an efficient corporate brand management process.

REFERENCES

Aaker, David A. (1990) Brand extensions: 'The good, the bad, the ugly'. *Sloan Management Review*, *31*, 47–56.

Aaker, David A. (1996) *Building Strong Brands*, pp. 136–174. New York, London: Free Press.

(Continued)

(Continued)

Aaker, David A. and Kevin L. Keller (1990) Consumer evaluations of brand extensions. *Journal of Marketing, 45* (January), 27–41.

Aaker, Jenifer L. (1997) Dimensions of Brand Personality. *Journal of Marketing Research, 34* (August), 347–56.

Baker, M.J. & Balmer, J.M.T. (1997) Visual identity: Trappings or substance. *European Journal of Marketing,* 31(516), 366–75.

Balmer, J.M.T. (1995) Corporate branding and connoisseurship. *Journal of General Management,* 21(1), 24–46.

Balmer, J.M.T., & Gray, E.R. (2003) Corporate brands: What are they? What of them? *European Journal of Marketing, 37*(7/8), 972–97.

Bick, G., Jacobson, M.C., & Abratt, R. (2003) The corporate identity management process revisited. *Journal of Marketing Management, 19,* 835–55.

Bickerton, D. (2000) Corporate reputation versus corporate branding: The realist debate. *Corporate Communication: An International Journal, 5*(1), 42–8.

Boush, David M. and Barbara Loken (1991) A process-tracing study of brand extension evaluation. *Journal of Marketing Research, 28* (February), 16–28.

Cheng, R., Hines, T. & Grime, I. (2008) Desired and perceived identities of fashion retailers. *European Journal of Marketing, 42*(5/6), 682–701.

Davies, G., Chun, R., da Silva, R.V., & Roper, S. (2001) The personification metaphor as a measurement approach for corporate reputation. *Corporate Reputation Review, 4*(2), 113–27.

Doyle, P. (1990) Building successful brands: the strategic options. *Journal of Consumer Marketing,* 7(2).

Doyle, P. (2000) Value-based marketing. *Journal of Strategic Marketing, 8,* 299–311.

Fan, Y. (2005) Ethical branding and corporate reputation. *Corporate Communications: An International Journal, 10*(4), 341–50.

Fiedler, I., & Kirchgeorg, M. (2007) The role concept in corporate branding and stakeholder management reconsidered: Are stakeholder groups really different? *Corporate Reputation Review, 10*(3), 177–188.

Fombrun, C. (1996) Reputation: Realizing value from the corporate image. *Harvard Business Review School Press,* Boston, MA.

Freeman, R.E. (1984) *Strategic Management – A Stakeholder Approach.* Boston: Pitman.

Griffin, J.J. (2002) To brand or not to brand? Trade-offs in corporate brand decisions. *Corporate Repution Review, 5*(2/3), 228–40.

Grime, I., Diamantopoulos, A., & Smith, G. (2002) Consumer evaluations of extensions and their effects on the core brand: Key issues and research propositions. *European Journal of Marketing, 36*(11/12), 1415–38.

Hagen, O. (2008) Seduced by their proactive image? On using auto communication to enhance CSR. *Corporate Reputation Review, 11*(2)130–44.

Hatch, M.J., & Schultz, M. (2001) Are the strategic stars aligned for your corporate brand? *Harvard Business Review* (February), 129–34.

Hatch, M.J., & Schultz, M. (2003) Bringing the corporation into corporate branding. *European Journal of Marketing, 37*(7/8), 1041–64.

Keller, K. L. (1993) Conceptualizing, measuring and managing customer-based brand equity. *Journal of Marketing, 57,* 1–22.

Keller, K. L. (1998) *Strategic Brand Management: Building, Measuring, and Managing Brand Equity.* London: Prentice-Hall International (UK).

Keller, K.L. (2000) The brand report card. *Harvard Business Review.* February.

Keller, K. L., & Aaker, D.A. (1992) The effects of sequential introduction of brand extensions. *Journal of Marketing Research, 29* (February), 35–50.

(Continued)

(Continued)

Keller, K.L., Aperia, T., & Georgson, M. (2008) *Strategic Brand Management: A European Perspective*. London: Prentice-Hall.

Keller, K.L., & Richey, K. (2006) The importance of corporate brand personality traits to a successful 21st century business. *Brand Management, 14*(1/2), 74–81.

Kennedy, S.H. (1977) Nurturing corporate images – Total communication or ego trip? *European Journal of Marketing, 11*, 120–64.

Laforet, S. (2010) *Managing Brands: A Contemporary Perspective*. London: McGraw Hill.

Meacham, J. (2010) What an umpire could teach BP. *Newsweek*, 14 June.

Melewar, T.C. (2003) Determinants of the corporate identity construct: a review of the literature. *Journal of Marketing Communications, 9*, 195–220.

Melewar, T.C., & Akel, S. (2005) The role of corporate identity in the higher education sector. A case study. *Corporate Communications: An International Journal, 10*(1), 41–57.

Melewar, T. C., & Karaosmanoglu, E. (2006) Seven dimensions of corporate identity: A categorisation from the practitioners' perspectives. *European Journal of Marketing, 40*(7/8), 846–69.

Nelson, J. (2010) BP and Obama tarred by spill. *Canadian Business*, 19 July.

Olins, W. (1978) The corporate personality. An inquiry into the nature of corporate identity. Design Council, London.

Omar, M., & Williams Jr, R.L. (2006) Managing and maintaining corporate reputation and brand identity: Haier group logo. *Brand Management, 13*(4/5), 268–75.

Plummer, J. T. (1985) How personality makes a difference. *Journal of Advertising Research, 24* (December/January), 27-31.

Schmidt, K. (1995) The Quest for Identity: Corporate Identity, Strategies, Methods and Examples. London: Cassell.

Schultz, M., & de Chernatony, L. (2002) Introduction: The challenges of corporate branding. *Corporate Reputation Review, 5*(2–3), 105–12.

Suvatjis, J.Y., & de Chernatony, L. (2005) Corporate identity modelling: A review and presentation of a new multi-dimensional model. *Journal of Marketing Management, 21*, 809–34.

Tauber, E. M. (1981) Brand franchise extension: New product benefits from existing brand names. *Business Horizons, 24*(2), 36–41.

van Rekom, J. (1997) Deriving an operational measure of corporate identity. *European Journal of Marketing, 31*(5/6), 410–22.

Verde Nieto, D. (2009) Corporate social responsibility as part of your brand. *Manager* (Autumn), 28–9.

Walker, K. (2010) A systematic review of the corporate reputation literature: Definition, measurement, and theory. *Corporate Reputation Review, 12*(4), 357–87.

Managing Public Affairs and Lobbying: Persuasive Communication in the Policy Sphere

7

Ian Somerville

Key Themes

- Definitions of public affairs and lobbying
- Understanding the application of the role of specialist public affairs and lobbying techniques in a variety of contexts
- The importance of political intelligence gathering in monitoring the political arena
- Understanding the process of government in different political systems
- Approaches to influencing government thinking and the legislative processes
- Understanding the management of the public affairs function

INTRODUCTION

This chapter examines the specialist area of public affairs and lobbying work.[1] It discusses the importance of intelligence gathering and monitoring the policy-making

---

[1] I wish to acknowledge my debt to several colleagues who reviewed this chapter. I offer my sincere thanks to Danny Moss and Barbara DeSanto for their pertinent comments in regard to structure and organisation. My main debt is to Conor McGrath who, as always, was very generous with his time and expertise and offered encouragement and excellent advice to me throughout the writing of this chapter.

processes in government as well as exploring how organisations can seek to influence government thinking, public policy formation and legislation through the
process of lobbying. Here insights will be provided into how such processes may
vary under different national political systems, as well is in supranational contexts
like the EU or UN. The chapter is divided into two parts. The first part discusses
definitional issues, theoretical perspectives and the influence of political structures
and culture on public affairs and lobbying work. The second part of the chapter
situates the practice of public affairs and lobbying within the management analysis, choice, implementation and evaluation (C-MACIE) framework outlined in
Chapter 2 of this book but develops this framework by considering the practice of
public affairs through the theoretical lens of discourse theory and the concept of
'framing'. Original research data from interviews with senior practitioners is
used to provide illustrative case study examples of the practice of public affairs
and lobbying.[2]

PUBLIC AFFAIRS AND LOBBYING: DEFINITIONAL ISSUES, THEORETICAL PERSPECTIVES AND POLITICAL STRUCTURES

The three sections which make up the first part of this chapter discuss in turn
three key issues in current debates on public affairs and lobbying. In the first section the attempt to provide a coherent and comprehensive definition of public
affairs and lobbying are discussed and the debates surrounding what precisely
constitutes a pressure group or an interest group are examined. The second section outlines some of the key theoretical debates in the field, including the influential contribution from political science which primarily views public affairs
from a pluralist or corporatist perspective. This section also outlines the key features of a 'discourse' approach to theorising public affairs and lobbying. The third
section assesses the impact that differing political institutions, structures and cultures have on public affairs work and briefly discusses these issues from a political
economy perspective.

Defining Public Affairs

Attempts to define the activity of public affairs, who actually engages in it and what
exactly they do, have encountered various difficulties. Harris and Moss (2001: 110)
noted that 'the term "public affairs" remains one that is surrounded by ambiguity
and misunderstanding' and furthermore they suggest that:

---

[2]The interviews cited in this chapter were carried out between March 2004 and December
2009 in London, Edinburgh and Belfast. The interviews were semi-structured and lasted on
average 45 minutes. The participants answered all questions put to them.

Many of those working within the field appear a little uncertain how best to define precisely what public affairs is, or how to delineate the boundaries of the public affairs domain. For some the answer is that those working in the public affairs field handle and advise on organizational relationships with government, while for others, the role is primarily one of lobbying. Those adopting a broader perspective see public affairs as managing a broader range of relationships with organizational stakeholders, particular those which may have public policy implications, in which they may employ a range of marketing communications and public relations tools.'

It is fair to say that many of the definitional problems surrounding public affairs remain unresolved, but for the purposes of this chapter this broader definition articulated by Harris and Moss is utilised. It is clear that public affairs activity cannot merely be limited to advocacy efforts to influence government policy through direct contact with political actors by organisational members or representatives. Public affairs work will almost always involve monitoring and intelligence gathering in the public policy sphere and indeed the wider public sphere. It obviously also may involve indirect engagement such as coordinating with the activities of others engaged in pursuing the same interest or promoting the same cause, and that involves building relationships and alliances with other groups. Depending on the organisation, it may also involve coordinating grassroots activities by members of one's own group.

If we ask who engages in public affairs and lobbying activity, an analysis of most political cultures would suggest it is those actors who have an interest in the development of public policy but are not directly engaged in legislating or governing. These actors are usually described as 'interest groups' or 'pressure groups'. If we examine typical definitions of what constitutes a pressure group, it is clear that the 'pressure' that groups exert is with respect to political influence of some kind, more specifically in relation to the development and implementation of public policy and legislation. Grant (2000: 14), writing in a UK/EU context, states that: 'A pressure group is an organization which seeks as one of its functions to influence the formulation and implementation of public policy, public policy representing a set of authoritative decisions taken by the executive, the legislature, and the judiciary, and by local government and the European Union'. Coxall (2001: 5), in his analysis of pressure group politics, makes a useful distinction between a 'cause' group and a 'sectional' group:

A *sectional* pressure group represents the self-interest of a particular economic or social group in society: examples are the Confederation of British Industry (CBI), the Trades Union Congress (TUC), and the British Medical Association (BMA) ... A *cause* group is formed to promote a particular cause based on a set of shared attitudes, values or beliefs: examples are Greenpeace, the Child Poverty Action Group and Amnesty International.

There is a vast literature attempting to define interest groups and explain interest group activity particularly in studies which focus on the US political context and culture. Thomas (2004) offers a very useful discussion of definitional issues and the problems that occur with attempting to construct a broad all-encompassing definition. Nevertheless – and this echoes closely the definitions of a pressure group which we noted above – he does suggest at the very least an interest group is 'an association of individuals or organizations or a public or private institution that, on the basis of one or more shared concerns, attempts to influence public policy in its favour' (Thomas, 2004: 4). Thomas notes that interest groups work towards achieving their primary goal of influencing public policy through the activity of lobbying. He defines lobbying as: 'The interaction of a group or interest with policy makers, either directly or indirectly, that has a view to influencing current policy or creating a relationship conducive to shaping future policy to the benefit of that group or interest' (Thomas, 2004: 6). His definition has merit in that it does describe the vast majority of groups which engage in lobbying activity but does, as he acknowledges, run into problems with delineating certain kinds of 'interests'. For instance, he would seek to distinguish between an interest group and a social movement, arguing that 'social movements try to champion grand visions of social change (usually for a large, disposed segment of the population)' (Thomas, 2004: 7). One must assume that Thomas is referring here to the historic campaigns for equality and social justice for women, ethnic minorities, the disabled, etc. However, while acknowledging that it may be possible to make some sort of conceptual distinctions, arguably there is such a degree of overlap between such 'social movements' and those that promote and lobby for such causes that it makes little sense to label them as distinct from interest groups. Certainly the connection between broad-based social movements and the various alliances of interest groups that make up social movements means it is probably more coherent to view them as part of the same continuum rather than as discrete entities.

McGrath (2005) offers a succinct and pertinent discussion of definitional issues and points out that in many accounts that attempt to define this area of activity much is made of the distinction between 'public affairs', 'government affairs', and 'lobbying', which, at best, results in a lack of clarity and, at worst, is rather confusing and contradictory. As an example he cites Mack (1997), according to whom lobbying is 'the process of influencing public and governmental policy', whereas 'government relations is the application of one or more communications techniques by individuals or institutions to affect the decisions of government' (cited in McGrath, 2005: 19). McGrath also notes the example of Morris (1997) who explains, if 'explains' is the correct word, that:

> Public affairs is a term rather wider than Government Relations. It is when an Interest Group has a wide range of relationships with government and the political process, locally, nationally and internationally; in the UK, its chief part is about relations between an Interest Group and the Central Government ... Government Relations is dealing with Ministers, Civil Servants, agencies and quangos so as to gain or stop some new thing, to change an analysis or a decision; to increase Government's knowledge or expertise. (cited in McGrath, 2005: 20)

McGrath (2005) returns to Milbrath's, still relevant, 50-year-old definition to describe the essential features of lobbying. Milbraith (1963: 8) notes that 'lobbying is the stimulation and transmission of a communication, by someone other than a citizen acting on his own behalf, directed to a governmental decision-maker with the hope of influencing his decision'.

Ultimately, as is evident from Milbrath's description, in many ways defining lobbying is a more straightforward task than defining public affairs. Lobbying, almost irrespective of where it is practised, is essentially an advocacy activity directed at government/legislators and carried out by actors within or on behalf of a group or organisation. Public affairs is a much broader activity, and those involved in interest group or pressure group politics do more than just lobby governmental decision-makers, although it is fair to say that lobbying is a necessary but not a sufficient element of any definition of public affairs. As noted above, it almost always also involves intelligence gathering, coordinating alliances with other actors, organising ones own grassroots and media relations. Reference to the media leads us into the contentious issue of the relationship between public affairs and public relations which do overlap in significant ways, although the nature of their relationship tends to be viewed rather differently in different political cultures. We will return to this point below; suffice it to say now that in regard to public affairs other functions apart from just lobbying are highly significant. Knowing when to intervene in the public policy formation process and whom to target is of vital importance, but this requires knowledge, analysis and strategic decision-making.

Theoretical Perspectives on Public Affairs and Lobbying

Interest Group Theory and Pluralism

After a comprehensive survey of the literature in the field of public affairs studies Getz (2001: 306) concludes that:

> There is no ... agreed upon theory of public affairs or political strategy. There is a paradigm and there are many models, but theory is hard to find. ... The models are rarely atheoretical, but often they are not firmly grounded in a theoretical base. Rather, they present a series of propositions derived from any theoretical base that seems appropriate *for the proposition*.

She does, however, concede that, while there is no agreed overarching theoretical framework, it is clear that from a political science perspective 'interest group theory' underpinned by a pluralist conception of the relationship between actors in liberal democratic societies is the most widely utilised approach. She notes that 'the dominant theoretical approach to political influence is interest group theory. Interest group theory suggests that the democratic public policy process is an attempt to reach a compromise between the competing goals of a multitude of interest groups' (Getz, 2001: 308). Thomas (2004: 17), in a key work on interest group theory which includes important contributions from a wide range of perspectives, ultimately agrees with Getz that while it is the case that different theoretical approaches make a definitive body of knowledge hard to construct, 'most theoretical approaches utilise 'pluralism' and 'corporatism/neocorporatism'. Pluralism can be defined as 'the idea that modern societies contain all sorts of competing groups, interests, ideologies and ideas and in this context democratic politics is seen as a struggle by interests and ideas to predominate, often by inspiring the formation of political parties or pressure groups' (Budge, Crewe, MacKay, & Newton, 1998: 323).

Corporatist theory, according to Hill (2005: 67), can be viewed as a rather limited version of pluralism which focuses attention on 'the ways in which powerful interest or pressure groups outside the state and groups within the state relate to each other'. He argues that the theory 'tends in a rather generalised way, to develop a single model which gathers the "parties" to this relationship into three overarching groups: *capital, labour and the state*. Much other pluralist theory, however, sees neither capital [nor] labour as single interests, easily brought together in all-embracing institutions' (Hill, 2005: 67).

Some of the literature on public relations has attempted to offer definitions of the related practice of public affairs which echoes this line of thinking. For example, according to Broom (2009: 451), 'Lobbying is an outgrowth of the...democratic system functioning in a pluralistic society'. Many theorists from the pluralist perspective, as is evident from Schwarzmantel's (1994: 50) description below, paint an optimistic picture of what they view as the modern liberal democratic pluralist society:

> Because pluralism takes its starting point to be a modern society in which there are different interests, popular power is realised through group activity, the working of political parties and pressure groups or interest groups, each of which represents one of the many interests into which a developed society is split. Pluralist perspectives salute and emphasise this diversity of interest.

Schwarzmantel here seems not just to suggest that this is an accurate way of describing and explaining how power structures actually work in liberal democratic systems but also to be offering a normative theory. The perspective of pluralism does in some ways provide a useful theoretical perspective for understanding the role of public affairs in a liberal democratic societies, but there are some telling critiques of pluralist theory. Hill (2005: 28) notes that the

> Opposition to the pluralist perspective can take two forms. One is to argue that this is not a satisfactory model for democracy (it is too indirect or it is impossible to realise the 'general will' through such diversity). ...The other is to argue that pluralism provides a misleadingly optimistic picture of the way power is organised in those societies described as pluralist.

This 'pluralist perspective', Hill (2005: 50) notes, is opposed and challenged by a range of theories which identify ways in which power is 'concentrated in the hands of small groups, often described as elites'. Hill notes that in much of the literature these approaches have traditionally been described as 'structural' critiques. The argument is that 'there is a range of institutions – the family, the church, the economy, the state – that are linked together in a structure that has a powerfully determining impact on what gets on the [political] agenda' (2005: 47). However, Hill (2005: 48–9) suggests that when one examines much of this critique,

> It is open to question whether the phenomena being explored should be described as 'structural'. What is being described is divisions within societies, which are maintained and reinforced in various ways … [through] … ideas about society and its culture – discourses if you like – that sustain patterns of power.

Discourse Analysis

Arguably, as we shall see below, Hill dismisses 'structural' issues rather too hastily, but it must be said that his reference to 'discourses' is interesting and important because although there have been some notable attempts (e.g., Fisher, 2003) to apply the discourse perspective to public affairs, this has remained an underdeveloped theoretical lens through which to view the practice. To see what a discourse perspective on public affairs might look like it, is worth turning to the related practice of public relations to examine how discourse theory has been applied there.[3] Historically, public relations, like public affairs, has largely been theorised through variations of a functionalist paradigm (L'Etang, 2008), but as the discipline developed there have been fruitful attempts to theorise public relation through the lens of discourse theory.

Motion and Leitch (1996) suggest that discourse theory can offer valuable insights into public relations practice; in fact, they argue that practitioners can be viewed as 'discourse technologists who play a central role in the maintenance and transformation of discourse' (1996: 298). Arguably the same can be said about public affairs practitioners, and in fact from a discourse theory perspective both practices can usefully be viewed as essentially similar activities though in some senses aimed at different audiences. Motion and Weaver (2005: 50–2) argue that from a discourse perspective,

---

[3]It should be made clear that the author claims only a limited knowledge of 'discourse theory' and its uses in the discipline of language and linguistics. One of the aims of this chapter was to employ several key ideas from this approach and discuss their application in the field of public affairs. For a useful introduction to the method see Wetherell, Taylor, and Yates (2001).

Public relations is theorized as a legitimate tactic in the struggle for and negotiation of power. The task for the critical public relations scholar is to investigate how public relations practice uses particular discursive strategies to advance the hegemonic power of particular groups and to examine how these groups attempt to gain public consent to pursue their organizational mission. ... understanding how public relations represents and promotes selected positions of truth and power is the examination of discourse strategies deployed by practitioners. In public relations, discourse is deployed as a political resource to influence public opinion and achieve political, economic and sociocultural transformation.

Arguably the public affairs practitioner is engaged in a similar endeavour albeit, as noted above, in a more specialist role focused on a more specific audience. Motion and Weaver are suggesting that the ultimate aim of the public relations practitioner is to deploy certain discourses in an attempt to gain a position of power for their client or organisation by establishing what Foucault called a 'regime of truth'. Foucault (1980: 132) suggested that 'There is a battle "for truth" or at least "around truth" ... it being understood also that it's not a matter of a battle "on behalf" of the truth, but of a battle about the status of truth and the economic and political role it plays'. From this perspective a 'discourse' is the vehicle by which public relations practitioners (and public affairs practitioners) attempt to 'establish, maintain, or transform hegemonic power [because] public relations discourse strategies are deployed to circulate ideas, establish advanta-geous relationships, and privilege certain truths and interests' (Motion & Weaver, 2005: 52–3). Viewed in this way public affairs practitioners as well as public rela-tions practitioners should be 'theorised as working to (strategically) privilege particular discourses over others, in an attempt to construct what they hope will be accepted as in the public interest and legitimated as policy' (Weaver, Motion, & Roper, 2006: 18). How does it work in practice? According to Motion and Weaver (2005), a key strategy of how public relations contributes to hegemonic power – where 'hegemonic' means the non-violent struggle to maintain eco-nomic, political, cultural and ideological dominance – is what Fairclough (1992: 93) describes as the 'articulation, disarticulation and re-articulation of elements of a discourse'. Motion and Leitch (1996) suggested that the significance of this strategy for public relations is that otherwise unconnected discourse elements (e.g., images or ideas) can be articulated with pre-existing attitudes or experi-ences with the aim of predisposing an individual to accept these elements. In their study of the genetically modified (GM) technology debate in New Zealand, Motion and Weaver (2005: 64) note that a key strategy of the pro-GM campaign was to try to ensure that the 'issue of GM was disarticulated from the scientific and environmental discourse and rearticulated as an economic discourse'. This echoes other campaigns such as the campaign to ban tobacco, which in the US arguably has become a battle between the discourse of health (and long-term health costs) and economics (jobs).

Framing and Storytelling

As was noted above, there have been explicit attempts to apply discourse theory to the practice of public affairs (Fisher, 2003); however, it should also be noted that, although they do not articulate it in these terms, arguably some recent academic accounts of public affairs do adopt something similar to a discourse analysis of public affairs activity. For example, McGrath's (2007) analysis of the tactic of 'framing', which he suggests involves assessing how 'lobbyists use language consciously to frame policy issues in such a way as to position their organization and its policy preferences to greatest effect' (p. 269), clearly echoes the discourse perspective. McGrath refers to Entman's (1993) definition of framing to explain the concept. Entman notes that the process of framing is in essence 'to select some aspects of a perceived reality and make them more salient in a communicating text, in such a way as to promote a particular problem definition, causal interpretation, moral evaluation and/or treatment recommendations for the item described' (cited in McGrath, 2007: 271). The overlap here with the notion of promoting a hegemonic discourse is evident. The use of storytelling, which obviously involves the construction of a narrative discourse, has been analysed by some researchers in public affairs, although the obvious link between this analysis and discourse theory is seldom alluded to. Terry (2001) has investigated the use of storytelling as an explicit tactic directed towards policy-makers by lobbyists in the US, and Heugens (2002) assesses storytelling as an important corporate and activist tool for gaining the support of various external constituencies in the ongoing semiotic wars over biotechnology. Heugens appears to mean by storytelling the construction of grand narratives (or discourses) about biotechnology by the key opponents in the battle over GM technologies. The corporate interests on one side produce a narrative about scientific progress, human advancement, curing starvation etc. On the other side, the environmentalists construct a discourse focused on potential health risks, exploitation of Third World farmers, corporate greed, etc. Heugens (2002: 68) notes that 'every corporate story that was ever written and performed to gain the support of consumers and legislators for the commercialisation of modern biotechnology was quickly reciprocated by an antagonist story that defied and contested the claims of these earlier variants'. Interestingly, although articulated differently in political terms, the analysis of the battle between the stories, or discourses, surrounding biotechnology offered by Heugens and by Motion and Weaver comes to fairly similar conclusions. This is no surprise as their analyses, despite employing different terminology, are ultimately assessing what are similar strategies by corporate actors and the activists who oppose them.

It is worth pointing out, however, that while deconstructing the use of storytelling is a very useful analytical tool for the public affairs researcher it arguably does not go far enough in assessing and understanding the key role which the political economy context plays in the acceptance or rejection of a 'story' or a 'discourse'. Motion and Weaver (2005: 50) argue 'that discourses deployed for public relations purposes can only be fully understood in relation to the political, economic, and social contexts in which they operate'. As we shall see in the next section, this is also the case with the practice of public affairs.

Structure, Institutions and Culture: Political Economy and Public Affairs

Many textbooks on public policy or public affairs are structured around presenting a list of apparently discrete perspectives such as pluralism, corporatism, Marxism, network approaches, rational choice theory, institutional theory and so on (e.g. Hill, 2005; Sabatier, 2007), all of which have been put forward as theoretical explanations of how public policy formation emerges from the interaction of politics, interest group pressure, and public affairs activity. It is probably fair to say that while it is the case that some of these perspectives are fundamentally oppositional, it is clear that ultimately many of them share common features and assumptions in that all of these approaches do acknowledge the significance of structures, institutions and cultural context.

Political Economy

We noted above the perspective of Motion and Weaver (2005) which argued that the political economy context needed to be taken into account in any coherent under-standing of why some public relations and public affairs efforts are successful and others fail, or, to put it in their terms, why some discourses achieve hegemony and others do not. By the political economy context they appear to mean such factors as the current political landscape (its structure and culture), current economic agendas and relevant existing government legislation. It should be noted that their definition of political economy is broader than that employed in many texts on public affairs. For example, Thomas (2004: 56) outlines a rather narrower view of the concept of political economy when he suggests that 'the political economy explanation of inter-est groups in the public policy process is incomplete. ... The economic interpretation of interest groups suggests that large interests organize, support politicians who pro-mote key programs, and thereby extract collective benefits from government.' Thomas (2004: 67) does, however, acknowledge that the 'types of groups and inter-ests that exist, and the way they attempt to influence public policy are determined by historical, geographical, cultural, social, economic, political, governmental structural and other factors' and makes the important point that in turn 'interest group activi-ties help shape and define the nature of a political system'.

In this chapter the broader conception of political economy is favoured and, fur-thermore, it is argued that in attempting to understand the influential factors which impact upon public affairs practice, the political structures, institutions, and culture are always of primary importance. Their significance is perhaps thrown into sharpest relief when comparisons between political systems are made although, as Thomas acknowledges, comparative studies in this area are rare. Thomas (2004: 75) notes:

> For the most part, however, scholars have only addressed the factor of differences in political and governmental structure incidentally and not as a major focus of their research. Consequently, insights into the influence of this factor must be extrapolated from various studies. Extrapolation

reveals that four factors are particularly important: (1) the constitutional structure, particularly the contrast between the parliamentary and separation of powers systems and federal and unitary systems; (2) the strength of political parties; (3) the power and independence of the bureaucracy; and (4) the degree of centralization or fragmentation of a political system and the extent of corporatism or neocorporatism.

Institutions, Structures and Systems

An exception to this lack of comparative work in public affairs scholarship is McGrath's (2005) important study of lobbying practices in Washington, London and Brussels. McGrath's (2005: 2) starting point is that 'lobbying activities are influenced by institutional architecture and policy-making processes ... lobbying cannot usefully be studied in isolation from the factors which influence it'. A key feature of McGrath's work is that it offers a very useful detailed analysis of the role political culture, institutional frameworks, regulatory environments and executive/ legislative relationships all play in determining differing access points to the policy-making process where lobbyists insert themselves to attempt to influence policy decisions in the three political systems. It is clear that the UK, with its strong party system, is different from the US, with its weak political party control over legislators, and in turn both are very different from the EU, where the key 'policy-making institutions are supra-national, and composed of members or appointees from a range of political parties' (McGrath, 2005: 185). Thomas (2004: 1) also notes the importance of US constitutional arrangements when he points out that 'largely because of its separation of powers system, its weak political parties, and low level of ideological politics, the United States is an aberrant political system in regard to interest group activity'. However, he does go on to suggest that wider socio-political changes may have the effect of leaving the US less peculiar in this regard: 'The decline of ideology across the Western world, and particularly Western Europe, is making the factor of parties less significant and more akin to the situation in the United States by increasing the strategy and tactic options for many groups' (Thomas, 2004: 76). It should also be pointed out that this assumed inverse relationship between political party and interest group influence needs some qualification. For example, amongst UK scholars there is a widespread consensus that attempts by the Thatcher government in the 1980s to curtail the influence of pressure groups ultimately had little impact. Richardson (1993: 99) argues that 'despite attempts to radically change Britain's policy style during the 1980's, interest groups retained their key role'. Jordan (in Thomas, 2004: 303) actually suggests that it is reasonable to claim that pressure groups in many ways exert a more powerful influence over policy in the UK than in the US. It is clear that while the Westminster parliamentary system in the UK means that political parties exert tight control over the legislative process, the decline in party membership and voting figures at election time has seen a certain shift of power in the policy arena toward interest groups. Jordan notes: 'Given the scale of interest group numbers and memberships, the "decline of parties" and their replacement by group participation, interest groups are now taken seriously in Britain' (in Thomas, 2004: 302). Thomas (2004: 72) also makes the point that political and 'cultural differences have also led some countries to regulate interest group activity extensively, as in the United States, while in others it is much less stringently regulated, as in Britain and Germany'. For a useful account of regulatory environments in the US, UK and EU the reader is directed to McGrath (2005: 167–80).

Public Affairs and Public Relations

One final point is worth making in respect to cultural differences, and this in respect to how scholars and practitioners view the relationship between public affairs and public relations in different political cultures. The two activities clearly overlap in several key ways, although the nature of their relationship tends to be viewed rather differently from the US and UK perspectives. A typical US public relations textbook describes public affairs as merely one aspect of public relations work:

> In corporations, 'public affairs' typically refers to public relations efforts related to public policy and 'corporate citizenship.' Corporate public affairs specialists serve as liaisons with governmental units; implement community improvement programs; encourage political activism, campaign contributions, and voting; and volunteer their services in charitable and community development organizations. ... PR counselling firms use the public affairs label for their lobbying and governmental relations services designed to help clients understand and address regulatory and legislative processes. (Broom, 2009: 35)

It is probably fair to say that it is this conception of public affairs as a public relations strategic specialism that is articulated by the majority of practitioners in the US (McGrath, 2005). However, in the UK the relationship between public affairs and public relations is viewed rather differently. In fact in many ways it might be more accurate to say that if one examines much of the UK scholarly literature on this issue the idea that there is any necessary connection at all between the two activities is rejected (or at least downplayed). Moloney (2000: 113) notes:

> Many professional lobbyists reject their inclusion in PR, joining the flight from it as a work title and preferring euphemisms such as government relations, political communications and public affairs specialists. For these separatists, PR is public campaigning via the media, as opposed to private and confidential approaches to persuade powerful persons face to face.

L'Etang (2008: 109), also writing from the UK perspective, suggests that public affairs 'is becoming recognised as a specialism distinct from public relations and experts are beginning to debate issues such as education and qualifications for public affairs consultants'. Ultimately it is clear that although public affairs is frequently described, particularly in the UK, as 'higher status strategic work' (L'Etang, 2008: 109). While there may be some merit in articulating a conceptual difference between the two activities at times, in many ways this is more about cultural difference than the practicalities of public affairs work. As will be explained further in the next section of the chapter, the management of public affairs work in the UK, as in the US and elsewhere, almost always involves much more that just face-to-face 'insider' dealings with those who hold power in public policy arenas. Indeed, ultimately a considerable amount of public affairs practitioner work is indistinguishable from public relations activity. It is also very important to note that shared conceptual understandings and theoretical explanations of both public affairs and public relations can enrich our understanding and analysis of practitioner work.

PUBLIC AFFAIRS AND LOBBYING PRACTICE: THE C-MACIE FRAMEWORK

We now focus on how the practice of public affairs can be articulated within the MACIE framework outlined in Chapter 2. Issues surrounding *environmental analysis, strategic choice and decision-making, implementation of strategy and tactics,* and *the analysis and evaluation of public affairs efforts* are explored. In the sections below interview data with practitioners in the corporate, consultancy and voluntary/ NGO sectors (including British Petroleum, Virgin Media, Amnesty International, Disability Action, Northern Ireland Council for Integrated Education and several public affairs consultancies) are used to illustrate, and provide insights into, key aspects of public affairs work and are theorised utilising the perspectives discussed in the first part of the chapter.

Analysis of the Policy Sphere

Writing about corporate public affairs, Fleisher (2002: 168) argues that in this context 'analysis is the multifaceted combination of processes by which collected socio-political information is systematically interpreted to create intelligence and recommendations for actions'. According to Fleisher, the 'essential responsibility of a CPA [corporate public affairs] analyst is to protect and enhance their company's competitive and non-market interests by providing useful and high-quality analysis about the "4Is", interests/stakeholders, intelligence, institutions and issues' (2002: 168). Although he is writing about practitioners employed in the private sector, Fleisher's point is valid for public affairs across all sectors, and arguably it is frequently pressure groups who put his advice into practice most consistently. Many pressure groups illustrate very well Broom's (2009: 34) point that 'lobbyists spend substantially more time collecting information from government than they do communicating to it, since sound lobbying strategies, tactics, and positions are highly dependent on a strong base of information'. For example, the human rights organisation Amnesty

International (UK) have put a great deal of effort into researching and constructing an up-to-date intelligence database on the elected members and senior officials of every legislature in the UK – Members of Parliament, the House of Lords, the Scottish Parliament and Welsh and Northern Irish Assemblies – to ascertain where they stand on issues which concern the organisation. The Amnesty International campaigns coordinator, who also helps coordinate lobbying efforts, notes that 'we refer to [the database] when we want to know which MP, MLA, Lord or other official is supportive of each individual cause'.

Amnesty International stress that they have identified and work with those actively sympathetic with their cause in all UK parties with elected representatives except one: they have a policy of no discussion with the BNP [British National Party] due to their political and ideological views. From the perspective of a 'discourse approach', the reason for this policy, becomes apparent the BNP does not share or accept the human rights and equality discourse underpinning all other elected parties in the UK. Amnesty International's promotion of this hegemonic discourse – of the right of all human beings to basic human rights – obviously makes it difficult for all major political parties and political institutions – which ostensibly agree with this discourse – to resist appeals to support them. The exception to this is of course the BNP, which is underpinned by and actively promotes racist political policies, thus excluding the possibility of developing a shared discourse and making any attempt at engagement, let alone lobbying, futile. McGrath (2005: 149) cites a US lobbyist who suggests that an organisation must try to engage with all political actors and that 'there should be no enemies in Congress'. In general this is a sensible policy, but it is important also to make the point that, depending on the organisation and its aims or values, sometimes it will not be possible to engage with every political actor, nor should one necessarily try.

In respect to the analytical methods, models and techniques used by public affairs practitioners, Fleisher (2002: 168) readily admits that the 'majority of techniques have been borrowed from related fields like administration, management, marketing, political science, public policy and public relations'. He lists a range of analytical methods and techniques, and particularly those drawn from the disciplines of public relations and management. Others too have noted the use of typical business and management analytical tools such as SWOT (strengths, weaknesses, opportunities, threats) analysis (Shaw, 2005). However, Fleisher (2002: 171) concludes that although these methods exist, a lack of adequate training means that 'analysis will remain underemphasized in … CPA [corporate public affairs] and its practitioners will never exploit the field's vast potential to simultaneously increase both its value and legitimacy'. While Fleisher may be largely correct to point to the lack of a rigorous methodologically grounded approach to analysis, it is clear that practitioners do, of course, make some attempt to analyse and assess their operating environments. Here for example, many do take seriously Van Schendelen's advice about attempting to understand one's opponents in a public affairs battle. Van Schendelen (in Thomas, 2004: 92) warns that 'lack of knowledge of the styles and techniques of the opposition is detrimental to one's own interest'.

An Edinburgh-based consultant whose company is engaged in public affairs work for several large Scotland-based companies claimed that he continually monitored various websites of 'other organizations, pressure groups, or political parties including Friends of the Earth and SEPA [Scottish Environmental Protection Agency] ... to see their view and get a perspective on things, see what's going on on the other side'. The Head of Communication and Lobbying for the Northern Ireland Council for Integrated Education told the author: 'Sometimes it a case of having to do a bit more homework with opponents and try to find out what their opposition is, where its stemming from ... is it a fear of change?'

Clearly, some public affairs practitioners do attempt, sometimes very successfully, to analyse their operating environment and make good strategy decisions based on that analysis. It is equally apparent, however, as Fleisher's (2002) own research demonstrates, that much of what does occur is not based on a coherent or rigorous methodology. This, Fleisher acknowledges, is an issue which needs to be addressed more seriously by current practitioners. It is clear therefore that the identification, monitoring and analysis of legislators, officials, political opponents and other relevant stakeholders is very important in public affairs work, but of course, analysing and assessing the environment are only useful if they enable the development of relevant choices with respect to strategy and tactics and if they aid decision-making with respect to those choices. We can now examine how the second step in the MACIE model – the process of selection and choice of appropriate strategies and tactics – can be applied in public affairs work.

Choice and Decision-Making: Strategy and Tactics

In a key work on the relationship of the business sector to the public affairs process Getz (2001) discusses the key choices and decisions facing private sector companies. The issues she raises face most organisations seeking to influence public policy:

> A clearly important question has to do with the strategies and tactics that might be employed once the decision to participate has been made. Should a firm develop an ongoing relationship with public officials or should it enter and exit the political arena as issues change? Should political decision makers be approached directly or indirectly? Should the approach be intended to inform, to persuade, or both? Which tactics are effective in which situations, and how does one know? (Getz, 2001: 307)

Once an organisation has made the decision to attempt to engage with the public policy process and to try to influence it in favour of its own agenda or cause, the first stage is to analyse the public policy arena to locate the spaces where it might most usefully insert its perspective, or its 'discourse', for maximum influence and to identify who it is most valuable to lobby. Having carried out this analysis and assessment, there are some important choices and decisions to be made about the most appropriate strategies and tactics, which will result in maximum benefit and influence in the public policy sphere.

Showalter and Fleisher (2005) refer to a wide range of public affairs techniques in a discussion designed to highlight 'the necessity for public affairs practitioners to be aware of the various tools at their disposal and to know how, when and where they can be best utilized' (p. 109). They describe and explain a fairly exhaustive list of techniques and tactics including:

> Lobbying, environmental (including issue and stakeholder) monitoring and scanning, grassroots, constituency building, electoral techniques like 'Get out the Vote' (GOTV), issue advertising, political action committees, public affairs and corporate social audits, judicial influence techniques such as Strategic Lawsuits Against Public Participation (SLAPPs), advisory panels and speakers bureaus, voluntarism, sponsorships, Web activism, coalitions and alliances, and community investment. (Showalter & Fleisher, 2005: 109)

Some of these tactics are peculiar or at least fairly exclusive to the US political environment, but many of them are significant options for public affairs in most liberal democracies. In reality, practitioners working for most interest groups will consider a range of techniques, although most of the literature agrees that these boil down to a choice between several key strategies or combinations of these strategies (McGrath, 2005; Thomas, 2004; Showalter & Fleisher, 2005). These strategies are: direct lobbying face-to-face via insider access; indirect lobbying using grassroots pressure; and the formation of coalitions or alliances with like minded groups to exert broad-based pressure.

These key public affairs strategies will be discussed in greater detail below, but before we move on to that discussion it is worth noting that it is frequently argued that web activism can be used to underpin and complement the latter two strategies and thereby transform existing power imbalances that lobbying by powerful groups produces (Kakabadse, Kakabadse, & Kouzmin, 2003). However appealing this sounds, one should be careful of falling into an uncritical technological determinism and assuming that a technology, such as the internet, necessarily subverts traditional hierarchies. As Oates (2008: 155) notes: 'The internet has not radically changed the fundamental relationship between rulers and citizens, but it has provided useful tools for activists to mobilize for specific political causes'. In fact there is evidence to suggest that the internet may actually be reinforcing the status quo. According to Rethemeyer's (2007: 199) research: 'The Internet appears to foster and intensify closed, corporatized policy networks. The solution may not be IT, as the Internet optimists suggest. Rather, it may be to embrace and reform politics-by-organisation. The Internet and other forms of IT have a role – though a small one – in this process.'

It should also be noted that 'choice' of which strategy to adopt may be influenced by socio-economic and ideological constraints. For example, a key choice facing activist groups is whether to engage at all in direct lobbying to try to influence policy or whether to eschew this in favour of protest and pressure from the outside. Some of the more ideologically driven environmentalist and animal rights groups typically have major concerns about compromising their core values by engaging with the governments which perpetuate systems to which they are fundamentally opposed. It is important to bear in mind that some groups may decide to deliberately reject some of the avenues or strategies open to them and choose to remain outside some parts of the public policy arena. Grant (2000: 16) offers a useful definition of insider and outsider groups: 'An *insider* group is regarded as legitimate by government and consulted on a regular basis ... An *outsider* group does not wish to become involved in a consultative relationship with public policy-makers or is unable to gain recognition.' Most interest groups do, however, recognise the importance of putting their case directly to political parties and those holding political office. Fleisher's (2003: 373) advice to public affairs managers is: 'Be prepared to learn as much as you can about the official before meeting them; do not be concerned if the lawmaker is unavailable and a staff assistant is in their place.' A senior practitioner at the Northern Ireland Council for Integrated Education concurs: 'Direct contact is very important...even speaking to the PA of a minister and building a relationship there.'

As noted above, organisations may be excluded from direct 'insider' contact or they might decide other strategies are also required. In these circumstances indirect lobbying using grassroots pressures is likely to be a useful strategy choice. Fleisher (2003: 371) suggests that:

> Grassroots techniques have become essential to the advocacy and influencing toolkit of most sophisticated North American organizations' public affairs operations. These techniques, originated and institutionalised decades ago by activist groups and subsequently modified for corporate application by public policy-savvy businesses, allow an organization's stakeholders the opportunity to work in the public policy process on behalf of an organization who is seeking to establish and impress its position on those elected officials. Very few issues, particularly those captured in the public's attention by the media, escape the onslaught of organised grassroots techniques coming from all sides of the matter.

It is worth making the point that cultural differences need to be acknowledged in respect to strategy choice. For example, in the above quote it is clear that Fleisher emphasises the corporate organising of grassroots lobbying as primarily a Northern American practice. Fleisher's point is backed up by a senior practitioner who works for British Petroleum and has experience of working in both London and Washington. This practitioner stated that in the company's US operation there are pages on the company's intranet 'where you can look up your local congressman. You can also look up his or her voting record. And then BP will also have materials available on subjects of interest to BP that you may or may not wish to use if you were to contact your congressman.' The practitioner acknowledges that it is possible to access this sort of information in the UK and that an employee in a company could petition his/her local MP on behalf of their employer, but the active engagement of the company is a peculiarly American approach. Although this practitioner and Fleisher emphasise this type of corporate engagement is a characteristic of North American political culture, it should be acknowledged that some scholars would argue that it is becoming increasingly important in the UK and European context. Titley (2003) and McGrath (2005) note the increasing importance of 'outsider' tactics, (e.g., grassroots campaigns) which are increasingly supplementing and to some extent perhaps even supplanting 'insider' contact in respect to British and European public affairs. It is clearly a route that is increasingly seen as a useful and legitimate strategy by all interest groups.

Building a public affairs strategy around grassroots campaigning frequently goes hand-in-hand with the strategy of coalition and alliance building with other interest groups. Fleisher (2003: 373) notes that 'Through well-conceived coalitions with other allied interests, various groups have been able to achieve important public policy successes'. On many occasions necessity is also the mother of alliances and coalitions with other groups, with the choice of this strategy being crucial for many groups aiming to reduce the resources cost. Citing specifically recent refugee and violence against women campaigns, the campaign coordinator for Amnesty said:

> It can be very important to work alongside other groups when there is an opportunity to share expertise ... In our regional offices we are quite often forced to work alongside other groups and make alliances as we may not have the resources to complete all of our actions alone or another group may approach us asking if we would like to join them in a specific appeal.

We will examine in more detail the issues surrounding developing an effective coalition in the next section, but what is clear is that when contemplating coalition building as a strategy, establishing clear ground rules and ensuring mutual benefit are of primary importance. As Showalter and Fleisher (2005: 119) note:

> The best coalitions have the involvement and commitment of all stakeholders, clear leadership, group agreement on the vision and mission for the coalition, and assessment of member needs and member resources ... Once these initial building blocks are established, the effective coalition creates short- and long- term objectives, develops an action plan and implements it.

Implementing Public Affairs Strategies and Tactics

For a public affairs manager, choosing which strategy to adopt and which tactics to employ is one thing; successful implementation resulting in policy change which benefits your organisation or advances your cause is, of course, quite another. With respect to direct lobbying efforts a knowledge and expertise of how to engage in and implement traditional face-to-face lobbying still determines the success or failure of many public affairs efforts. McGrath's (2007: 269) point about lobbyists using 'language consciously to frame policy issues in such a way as to position their organisation and its policy preferences to greatest effect' is of key importance in any direct lobbying activity.

The view that direct lobbying is essentially persuasive communication where you simplify your message and frame it in an appropriate and appealing way is echoed by many commentators. Mack (1997) suggests that 'Issues should be framed to show how the public benefits from your side of the argument. Do not go public with a narrow, self-serving issue' (cited in McGrath, 2007: 271). Politics in liberal democracies is ultimately underpinned by utilitarian ideals so it is clear that the 'story' or 'narrative' you present must demonstrate how the policy which your organisation would wish to see accepted is in some way benefiting the common good. This is where an understanding of the role and power of discourse becomes significant for the lobbyist. Being able to demonstrate that your position on an issue is part of a generally accepted discourse which is seen as core to liberal democratic society will always be to your advantage (e.g., human rights, women's rights, freedom, equality, progress). In our discussion above on the battle between the environmentalist lobby and the biotechnology corporate lobby over GM foods we noted that both tried to frame their arguments to appeal to this key societal discourse of maximising the common good. The corporate lobby primarily presented a scientific progress/economic benefits story while the environmentalist lobby employed a corporate greed/citizen disempowerment narrative. Arguably in the above example both sides present simplistic narratives, but in lobbying efforts most commentators would agree that this simplification process is important. A clear coherent message narrative works best. As McGrath (2007: 271) notes, 'public policy issues (the focus of lobbying efforts) tend to be complex, involving an array of both factors and alternatives; framing is an attempt by lobbyists to set the boundaries of debate on a given issue'.

Of course, to actually present your case, access for the lobbyist to government actors or key political figures is a key issue. Several recent studies have revealed the growing importance of party conferences as key forums for meeting and engaging in lobbying efforts with political actors. Thomas (2005: 76) suggests that 'key lobbying efforts take place at party conferences', and Harris and Harris (2005) draw attention to the growth of lobbying activities at political party conferences through the 1990s in the UK. They note: 'The party conference environment acts as a communications conduit for the sharing and swapping of information as well as an opinion exchange and policy positioning forum ... It is perhaps the ultimate network opportunity for those interested in government, political processes, and the formation of policy' (Harris & Harris, 2005: 224). They also note the shifting make-up of the lobbying organisations at these events and specifically point out that:

> increasingly activity by outside groups at conferences is coming from the private sector and 'not for profit' categories ... There has been a steady growth in activities by not for profit organizations over the ten year period of the study and a slow but steady decline among public-sector, unions and professional association interests. (Harris & Harris, 2005: 238–9)

A senior practitioner at the Northern Ireland Council for Integrated Education agrees and views the party conferences of Northern Ireland's political parties as a key target for direct lobbying efforts: 'We would attend their party conferences and take an information stand at their party conferences ... we would be available to talk to people.'

All of the above efforts usually involve a lobbyist communicating face-to-face with key political actors. Grassroots lobbying involves a more indirect approach by organisational lobbyists, but it can be very effective. Writing about corporate sector lobbying, Fleisher (2003: 372) notes that in the US the role of the public affairs manager with regard to managing the grassroots includes 'activities such as motivating employees to meet with and discuss policy concerns with public officials, inviting public officials to organisational sites in order to allow mutual exchange with company employees, get-out-the-vote (GOTV) efforts, voter registration drives, political education of stakeholders and various other forms of government relations supporting activities'. It is fair to say, as we noted in the previous section, there are certain differences in the approach to the deployment of grassroots between the US and the UK/European context. Encouraging members of your company to become effective grassroots lobbyists is perhaps not as common a feature in the UK/European context as it is in US policy debates, but according to practitioners, while not common, it is a growing phenomenon in the UK. A senior practitioner working for Virgin Media pointed out to the author that one of its rival organisations, British Telecom, had in the past actively tried to organise grassroots lobbying by its staff in relation to the policy of providing broadband to all regions of the UK. She noted with regard to encouraging grassroots lobbying by company employees that 'BT actually took that stance and it encouraged its employees to write to their local MP to encourage them to be thinking about the introduction of broadband because they felt it was just so important to the economy. And I think that whole campaign has been hugely successful.'

To some degree, then, the adoption of what were traditionally thought of as US practices in regard to grassroots lobbying are appearing the UK/EU context, although it is probably fair to say that at the present time – for the reasons to do with political culture noted above – in the US many interest groups use grassroots lobbying much more effectively as a political weapon during key legislative debates. Morris (1999: 132), reflecting on the tactics of the National Rifle Association (NRA), notes:

[T]he NRA has become incredibly skilled at using its members as a political tool, unlike many special-interest groups, the NRA does not even aspire to popularity. When it seeks to influence an election, it does not advertise on television or radio. Instead, the NRA sends mailings to its members to urge them to vote for their favoured candidates in elections. The NRA emphasizes its capacity to turn out a disciplined bloc of voters for or against any candidate to strike terror into the hearts of wavering congressmen and senators when gun control legislation comes up for a vote.

Fleisher (2003: 373) makes the important point that 'irrespective of the level of database sophistication, grassroots are only effective if activated individuals are effective in making their views known to public officials'. Many campaigning organisations focus on trying to provide their grassroots with the tools to become effective communicators. The campaign coordinator for Amnesty International regards helping their grassroots members become effective lobbyists as a key strategy for the organisation. She commented:

> Our grassroots level correspondence to MPs is extremely beneficial. We dedicate a page on our website to show activists how to lobby their MP and pinpoint which MPs are good to lobby and when. We highlight that it is best to lobby your MP if they are new to Parliament and that new MPs spend a considerable portion of their time focusing on their constituents.

The power and influence of the grassroots has not gone unnoticed, and some organisations in recent years have engaged in the practice of manufacturing a grassroots campaign to try to influence policy-makers. Although an old practice, the expansion of the internet has led to a significant amount of debate on the creation of 'front' groups created to deceive or mislead policy-makers about public opinion (Showalter & Fleisher, 2005). Also known as 'astroturf lobbying', such front organisations are designed to give the appearance of widespread citizen support, when in reality they often are created to promote narrow interests.

With regard to the actual effective implementation and management of coalition and alliance building, several key issues must be borne in mind by the public affairs practitioner. Coalitions which share a similar ideological position or economic interest, or which belong to the same sector socio-economically probably have the greatest chance of long-term success. This is obviously because they may well share substantive political, economic and social objectives and be able to communicate more effectively because they share a similar world-view or a common discourse. Although frequently overlooked in public affairs literature – Martens (2009) being a notable exception – coalitions are particularly important in human rights lobbying and have been much studied by international relations scholars who have particularly focused attention on the strategy of transnational alliances. Keck and Sikkink (1998) have described the effectiveness of the 'boomerang' model in human rights lobbying. They state:

> Boomerang strategies are most common in campaigns where the target is a state's domestic policies or behaviour ... It is no accident that so many advocacy networks address claims about rights in their campaigns. Governments are the primary 'guarantors' of rights, but also their primary violators. When a government violates or refuses to recognize rights, individual and domestic groups often have no recourse within domestic political or judicial arenas. They may seek international connections finally to express their concerns and even to protect their lives. When channels between the state and its domestic actors are blocked, the boomerang pattern of influence characteristic of transnational networks may occur: domestic NGOs bypass their state and directly search out international allies to try to bring pressure on their states from outside. This is most obviously the case in human rights campaigns. (Keck & Sikkink, 1998: 12)

Although a scenario where transnational advocacy networks put pressure on a specific state government on behalf of coalition partners in that state may be thought of as a strategy to apply only to despotic or totalitarian regimes around the world, the reality is that this boomerang strategy has been used in liberal democracies as well. The campaigns director for Disability Action told the author that they used precisely this strategy to put pressure on the British government to fully ratify the UN Convention on the Rights of Persons with Disabilities and thereby write the provisions into domestic law in Britain. The British government wished to ratify the Convention but with a raft of reservations and opt-outs. Disability Action turned to allied organisations in Australia to get them to petition the Australian government to pressurise the British under a UN mechanism whereby if one government objects to another's reservations then these objections are publicly recorded. In effect it is a strategy designed to expose and embarrass countries into dropping reservations and to comply in full with UN conventions. Disability Actions's campaign's director told the author: 'In regard to UN conventions there is a UN mechanism that we used which stated that another state party to that convention can challenge the reservations on the grounds that they go against the fundamental purpose of the convention.' This strategy was successful up to a point, with the UK eventually reducing the number of its reservations from 30 to just four.

While alliances between ideologically compatible interest groups are more common, it is possible for apparently strange bedfellows such as big business and the voluntary sector to work together for mutual benefit. McGrath (2005) notes the example of the alliance a large Japanese manufacturer of audio equipment and tapes forged with the Royal National Institute for the Blind, among others, to campaign against an increased levy on audio tapes. He cites a senior London lobbyist who helped develop the coalition on behalf of the manufacturer:

> The crucial ally was the blind – if you are blind, you use audio tape in the way that others use pen and paper. Getting the Royal National Institute for the Blind on board was decisive, and yet it was not difficult because this was a genuinely important issue for them: the government was proposing to do something which would substantially increase costs for their members. The RNIB said 'Yes, we absolutely were planning to campaign against this anyway, but we lack resources.' So we told them, 'That's fine. We have resources and you have a powerful argument. Let's put those together.' We decided that what the government was proposing was not a 'levy', it was a 'tax', and we launched a campaign against this tax. Essentially it was funded by manufacturers, but most of the action was provided by other parts of the coalition, in particular the blind. That is why in the end the campaign succeeded, because the blind are a very powerful pressure group and they are not afraid to use their emotional pulling power. (McGrath, 2005: 131)

What is interesting about this example is that the actors in this coalition not only changed the 'frame' of the debate – a 'levy' was rearticulated as a 'tax' – but even more significantly an equality/discrimination discourse was foregrounded and arguably exploited very effectively by the partners in the coalition. Showalter and Fleisher (2005) note that coalitions and alliances are frequently fraught with difficulties but groups can work together, even those with radically different world-views if they can agree on what each can bring to the alliance and what strengths of each partner has. Having discussed the areas of analysis, choice and implementation in the context of public affairs work, the final element of the MACIE model, evaluation, can now be examined.

Evaluation and Assessment of Impact

There have been various attempts to derive evaluation and measurement criteria for public affairs work from what might be described as functionalist frameworks. According to Fleisher (2005: 147), for the public affairs manager, 'Evaluation means determining the relative effectiveness, performance, or value of a public affairs program or strategy, ordinarily done by measuring outputs and outcomes against a predetermined set of objectives'. As he acknowledges, however, things seldom run as smoothly in practice as they do in management handbooks, and, after conducting several major studies in the 1990s and 2000s, Fleisher (2005: 158) concluded: 'Unfortunately, the state of performance assessment in public affairs does not actually look all that much better than it did over a decade ago'. One key trend in the literature on public affairs evaluation which Fleisher identifies is the tendency toward quantitative measurement in recent years, although, as he rightly points out, providing numeric data seems to be being confused with evaluation in much of this work. He notes:

> The dominant view was that all dimensions of performance could be measured, which by default meant that all phenomena could be placed in numerical terms. For those public affairs officers who have attempted to take up the challenge, this has led to their counting most public affairs activities – in terms of things like the number of meetings with key stakeholders, the number of letters sent to key public policy committee personnel, the number of issues being actively monitored, wins and losses, the number of bills being tracked, the number of persons involved in the grassroots programs, etc. Counting is not equivalent to and is only the starting point of measurement ... Also, all the counts that were accumulated by public affairs officers generally only provided snapshot measures of how busy they were. (Fleisher, 2005: 153)

A senior practitioner lobbying on behalf of the Northern Ireland Council for Integrated Education emphasises this focus on the quantitative measurement of meetings, visits and of course press coverage: 'We monitor contact with political representatives, we monitor visits to their offices for meetings, all catalogued, we monitor press ... so we will have a full record of any press articles.' According to Fleisher there has always been great difficulty in measuring or demonstrating the value of public affairs activity. Writing specifically on grassroots campaigns, he notes: 'public affairs does not have a body of procedures established that allows appropriate accounting of the net effect on the investments and uses of public affairs resources as other functions have been accustomed to. In general, public affairs practice and performance have always been more of an art than a science, more qualitative than quantitative, and more conjectural than empirical' (Fleisher, 2005: 145).

Fleisher is largely correct to assert that the effective evaluation of specific strategies and tactics is a problematic area for the public affairs practitioner. Obviously, in a more general sense, the key assessment with respect to any public affairs effort is whether there has been an *impact* on the public policy process and ultimately perhaps legislation, which impacts positively on the organisation or the cause which it promotes. Thus arguably a straightforward way of evaluating any lobbying activity is to examine the legislation adopted in response to the lobbying efforts surrounding an issue. The reality, of course, is that it is seldom this simple because public policy battles may occur over a very long period of time and this needs to be taken into account by the public affairs manager when thinking about evaluation and measurement issues. 'Success' in the policy sphere may not mean the achievement, in the short term, of legislative change at all, instead it may be measured in the gradual transformation of the 'language frame' used to describe the issue. The intimate connection between a language frame and a 'discourse' has been explored in several places in this chapter, and it is clear from research in this area that if your organisation or your interest group can change the language frame used to describe an issue you can change the discourse within which an issue is debated. Once you manage to change the discourse the policy, change and legislation will in many cases follow.

A good example of this can be seen in the lobbying and campaigning efforts pressing for a legal ban on female genital mutilation in East Africa. In the early stages of this campaign in the 1920s, when it was a universal practice undergone by all pre-pubescent girls in Kenya, the term 'female circumcision' was used by all sides in the issue to describe the practice (Keck & Sikkink, 1998). Those in favour of the procedure claimed that it was a 'cultural' practice just like male circumcision and that those who campaigned to ban it were trying to impose 'Western values' upon legitimate 'African culture'. The use of the language frame 'female circumcision' actually reinforced the discourse that this is a cultural issue, and unsurprisingly those who campaigned against the practice had limited success in stopping it and none at all with respect to a legal ban. In reality the practice bears only superficial similarities to male circumcision; as Keck and Sikkink (1998: 67) note, female circumcision 'carries short-term risks and can lead to chronic infection, painful urination and menstrual difficulty, malformations and scarring, and vaginal abscesses; it also reduces a woman's sexual responses and pleasure'. A key change occurred in the 1970s when campaigners against the practice stopped using the term 'female circumcision' and thereby rejected the discourse which opposed 'African culture' to 'Western values'. Keck and Sikkink (1998: 67) note that: 'Modern campaigns in the 1970's and 1980's drew attention to the issue by renaming the problem "female genital mutilation," thus reframing the issue as one of violence against women'. This change in the language frame had a significant impact and there were several attempts to introduce legislation in Kenya's Parliament to outlaw the practice. In the beginning they failed, most notably in 1996, but eventually legislation expressly outlawing female genital mutilation was introduced as part of the Children's Act in 2001. The practice still goes on in secret, but the changing of the discourse to one of human rights, or more specifically women's and children's rights, and the subsequent legislative change have had a big impact in Kenyan society, with a dramatic drop in the number of girls suffering the ordeal over the past generation. Of course evaluation and measurement of this kind of campaign are extremely difficult, and one cannot point to instant results, but what this example illustrates is if increasing numbers of key actors involved in the policy process begin to accept your language frame to describe an issue – have adopted your discourse, so to speak – then you can usually be assured that your organisation has achieved significant progress and is on the way to success in the policy arena. If they wish to evaluate public affairs efforts effectively, public affairs managers and practitioners in all sectors would do well to follow the advice of Mack (1997), McGrath (2007) and others and become much more sensitive to the language and narratives used to describe issues.

SUMMARY

In this chapter we have examined the key issues facing practitioners seeking to manage public affairs across a range of sectors and political, economic and institutional contexts. The usefulness of traditional approaches to managing issues in public policy arena has been examined alongside newer approaches which make use of perspectives based on discourse theory and the concept of linguistic frames. The MACIE framework has been used to structure the examination of the role of public affairs management in contemporary liberal democratic societies and elsewhere. A knowledge and understanding of how to choose public affairs strategies and tactics, how to implement them and how to evaluate success and failure beyond crude quantitative measurement techniques is increasingly vital for all sectors (voluntary, public, private) in their efforts to successfully manage public affairs activity. Managing issues in the public affairs arena is a complex task and, perhaps more than in any other area of professional communication practice, it requires an understanding of the role of persuasive communication and the power of humankind's key symbolic weapons, language and narrative.

REFERENCES

Broom, G. (2009) *Cutlip and Center's Effective Public Relations* (10th ed.). Harlow: Prentice Hall.

Budge, I., Crew, I., MacKay, D., & Newton, K. (1998) *The New British Politics*. London: Longman.

Coxall, B. (2001) *Pressure Groups and British Politics*. London: Politicos.

Fairclough, N. (1992) *Discourse and Social Change*. Cambridge: Polity Press

Fisher, F. (2003) *Reframing Public Policy: Discursive Politics and Deliberative Practices*. Oxford: Oxford University Press.

Fleisher, G.S. (2002) Analysis and analytical tools for managing corporate public affairs. *Journal of Public Affairs*, 3(4), 371–82.

Fleisher, G.S. (2003) Managing the grassroots and assessing its performance. *Journal of Public Affairs*, 2(3), 167–72.

Fleisher, G.S. (2005) The measurement and evaluation of public affairs processes and performance. In P. Harris & C.S. Fleisher (eds), *The Handbook of Public Affairs* (pp. 145–59). London: Sage.

Foucault, M. (1980) *Power/Knowledge: Selected Interviews and Other Writings 1972–1977*. New York: Pantheon.

(Continued)

(Continued)

Getz, K.A. (2001) Public affairs and political strategy: Theoretical foundations. *Journal of Public Affairs*, *1*(4) and *2*(1), 305–29.

Grant, W. (2000) *Pressure Groups, Politics and Democracy*. London: Macmillan

Harris, P., & Harris, I. (2005) Lobbying in the United Kingdom. In P. Harris & C.S. Fleisher (eds), *The Handbook of Public Affairs* (pp. 224–46). London: Sage.

Harris, P., & Moss, D. (2001) Editorial. In search of public affairs: A function in search of an identity, *Journal of Public Affairs*, *1*(2), 102–10.

Heugens, P.P.M.A.R. (2002) Managing public affairs through storytelling. *Journal of Public Affairs*, *2*, 57–70.

Hill, M. (2005) *The Public Policy Process* (4th ed.). Harlow: Pearson.

Kakabadse, A., Kakabadse, N., & Kouzmin, A. (2003) Reinventing the democratic governance project through information technology? A growing agenda for debate. *Public Administration Review*, *63*(1), 44–60.

Keck, M.E., & Sikkink, K. (1998) *Activists Beyond Borders: Advocacy Networks in International Politics*. Ithaca, NY: Cornell University Press.

L'Etang, J. (2008) *Public Relations: Concepts, Practice and Critique*. London: Sage.

Mack, C.S. (1997) *Business, Politics, and the Practice of Government Relations*. Westport: Quorum Books.

Martens, K. (2009) Explaining societal activism by intra-organizational factors: Professionalized representation of human rights NGO's at UN level. In C. McGrath (ed.), *Interest Groups and Lobbying in the United States and Comparative Perspectives*. Lampeter: Edwin Mellen Press.

McGrath, C. (2005) *Lobbying in Washington, London and Brussels: The Persuasive Communication of Political Issues*. Lampeter: Edwin Mellen Press.

McGrath, C. (2007) Framing lobbying messages: Defining and communicating political issues persuasively. *Journal of Public Affairs*, *7*(3), 269–80.

Milbraith, L.W. (1963) *The Washington Lobbyists*. Chicago: Rand McNally.

Moloney, K. (2000) *Rethinking PR? The Spin and the Substance* (2nd ed.). London: Routledge.

Motion, J., & Leitch, S. (1996) A discursive perspective from New Zealand: Another world view. *Public Relations Review*, *22*, 297–309.

Motion, J., & Weaver, K. (2005) A discourse perspective for critical public relations research: Life Sciences Network and the battle for truth. *Journal of Public Relations Research*, *17*(1), 49–67.

Oates, S. (2008) *Introduction to Media and Politics*. Sage: London.

Rethemeyer, R.K. (2007) The empires strike back: Is the internet corporatizing rather than democratizing policy processes? *Public Administration Review*, *67*(2), 199–215.

Richardson, J. (1993) *Pressure Groups*. Oxford: Oxford University Press.

Sabatier, P.A. (ed.) (2007) *Theories of the Policy Process* (2nd ed.). Oxford: Westview Press.

Schwarzmantel, J. (1994) *The State in Contemporary Society*. Hemel Hempstead: Harvester.

Shaw, P. (2005). The human resource dimensions of public affairs. In P. Harris & C.S. Fleisher (eds), *The Handbook of Public Affairs* (pp. 123–44). London: Sage.

Showalter, A., & Fleisher, G.S. (2005) The tools and techniques of public affairs. In P. Harris & C.S. Fleisher (eds), *The Handbook of Public Affairs* (pp. 145–159). London: Sage.

Terry, V. (2001) Lobbying: fantasy, reality or both? A health care public policy case study. *Journal of Public Affairs*, *1*(3), 266–80.

Thomas, C.S. (2004) *Research Guide to US and International Interest Groups*. Westport, CT: Praeger.

Titley, S. (2003) How political and social change will transform the EU public affairs industry. *Journal of Public Affairs*, *3*(1), 83–9.

Weaver, C.K., Motion, J., & Roper, J. (2006) From propaganda to discourse (and back again): Truth, power, the public interest, and public relations. In J. L'Etang & M. Pieczka (eds), *Public Relations: Critical Debates and Contemporary Practice*. Mahwah, NJ: Erlbaum.

Wetherell, M., Taylor, S., & Yates, S. (2001) *Discourse Theory and Practice*. London: Sage.

The Strategic Communication Process in Government: A UK Perspective

8

Anne Gregory

Key Themes

- Exploring the background and principles behind communication by government
- Understanding the nature of government communication
- Identifying the drives behind recent changes in the approach to planned communication by UK government
- Examining the ENGAGE planning framework
- Comparing ENGAGE with C-MACIE
- Applying ENGAGE and C-MACIE to government campaigns

INTRODUCTION

Say the words 'government communication' and most communication/public relations professionals assume that this means how organisations, groups and individuals communicate with governments. This chapter, however, examines how governments communicate with citizens. It is obvious to state that every government has its own particular ways of communicating with citizens because the way civic society is organised and governed in every country is different. Some countries have very centralised governmental structures (e.g., France, India and the United Kingdom), with relatively limited powers and budgets at the local level, although in the UK, Scotland and Wales have achieved a level of autonomy through devolution to the Scottish Parliament and Welsh Assembly. Other countries have federal structures with strong states (e.g., Australia, Switzerland, Germany and the United States). It is salutary to reflect on the fact that the state of California would be the world's seventh largest economy if it were a country. Yet other countries such as Sweden and the Netherlands organise civic society at country regional (provincial) and local (municipal) level.

Apart from what might be regarded as the Western model of liberal democracies, there are of course totalitarian states with dictatorial, theocratic or single-party political regions. Somewhere in between liberal democracy and totalitarianism lie a number of forms of government from failed states, to those in transition from totalitarianism to democratic forms of government, notably those in the former Eastern European bloc.

All these forms of government have communication formats, content and style that suit their purposes. In totalitarian states citizens are usually directed how to behave and communication is essentially one-way. In liberal democracies, structures and processes are in place where the citizen's voice can be heard to a greater or lesser degree. Indeed, deliberative engagement activities in countries such as Australia, Canada and the USA are designed to enable citizens to have a role in defining government policy.

It would be a mistake to think that citizens in liberal democracies are not subject to political propaganda from government. All governments propagandise in varying degrees, for example when making the case for supporting a war or making international political alliances.

This chapter focuses on the communication activities of the UK. However, this should be seen as an exemplar of what is relatively typical in a liberal democracy. Indeed, many of the principles outlined here could and are applied by many different types of regimes in countries around the world, although they all have their own specific systems, processes, emphases, checks and balances. The international case studies later in this chapter illustrate the point.

There is a long history of governments communicating with citizens, stretching back over centuries. However, the purpose here is not to chart that history, but to provide a description of some recent developments in the UK that have led to a more structured approach to communication by government: one that recognisably replicates the process laid down in C-MACIE.

Most standard communication/public relations textbooks, which are admittedly USA- and UK-centric, include histories of the development of the discipline in those countries (e.g., Grunig & Hunt, 1984; Cutlip, Center, & Broom, 2009; Newsom, Turk, & Kruckeberg, 2000 and Tench & Yeomans, 2009). These trace the origins of modern communication/public relations to politics – to the Revolutionaries in the American War of Independence in the USA and to the activity of local government information departments in the UK. L'Etang (2004), Olasky (1987) and Lee (2008) provide more comprehensive overviews.

The term 'public sector' covers a wide range of institutions and organisations which are funded from public taxation and are there to serve a public purpose – for a country's citizens as a whole. These organisations include central and local government, national health services, the armed and civil services (e.g., army, navy, fire and police services), publicly funded education and so on.

The purpose of this chapter, however, is to focus on government communication, that is communication by the elected government, its departments and ministries. This is quite distinct and separate from communication done on behalf of political parties. They too will employ communication professionals, often called special advisors, to promote their ideology and policy objectives, and it is this group of people who have attracted the pejorative label of 'spin doctors' in recent times. It should be noted that the word 'communication' is the preferred term for all public relations and marketing activities in government, so this is used throughout this chapter.

Since 1946, communication for government, government departments, agencies (such and the Border and Immigration Agency) and non-departmental public bodies (such as the Arts Council of England) has been undertaken by civil servants who are politically neutral and whose role is to provide information about and to explain their work. Cole-Morgan (1988), cited by Yeomans (2009: 148), states that the objectives of the information division of each department agency or non-departmental public body are to:

- Create and maintain informed opinions about the subjects with which each department deals.
- Use all methods of publicity, as suitable, to help the department to achieve its purpose.
- Assist and advise in all matters bearing on relations between the department and its public.
- Advise the department on the public's reaction to the policies or actions of the department.

These objectives would find resonance in the departments of the most liberal democracies.

The UK, along with other democratic countries such as Canada, the USA, South Africa, New Zealand and Australia and most Scandinavian and European countries, regards it as a right of citizens that they should be informed about government policies, and the work of government departments generally, and, in particular, they should be informed of the services that are available to them and of their obligations as citizens. Increasingly, governments are encouraging citizens to be involved in the design of those services. For example, in the USA, citizens are encouraged to voice their views on the provision of health services and on policing. It also has to be said that governments of all types wish to exercise power over their citizens, whether that is, for example, to raise taxes from them or to regulate where they can dispose of their refuse. They exercise this power through legislation and through the consensus of citizens to be 'ruled' by the government of the day. The power bargain is that citizens choose who they want to rule them by voting in elections.

In 2008 the US Department of Defense published its *Principles for Strategic Communication*, which includes that they should be credible, responsive and dialogue-based. They also state that they should be pervasive and results-based, tied to a desired end-state. Clearly communication is designed to be purposive, with government deciding the purpose. However, this can be seen to be no different from most communication campaigns in the private sector, which are implemented with the purpose of the organisation furthering its own ends.

THE NATURE OF GOVERNMENT COMMUNICATION

As has been implied, governments and their departments, as well as providing information and explanations, proactively promote or seek to prevent certain behaviours by their citizens. For example, they conduct campaigns on health, road safety, recruitment of teachers and nurses, safety in the home, paying taxes on time, recycling and crime prevention. Coffman (2002), cited by Yeomans (2009) identifies two types of media campaigns in the USA – those aimed at individual behaviour change and those aimed at influencing the 'public will' (see Table 8.1). This approach is again fairly typical in Western-style liberal democracies.

In the past, UK government communication can be seen to be reflective of the public information model elucidated by Grunig (Grunig & Hunt, 1984) which is concerned with the dissemination of information (Gregory, 2003, 2006). There was a heavy reliance on one-way channels of communication, particularly mass media such as television advertising, posters and leaflets. In addition, mindful of their responsibility to explain policy and to provide a public information service which

TABLE 8.1   Two Types of Media Campaigns (Coffman, 2002)

Campaign Type/Goal	Individual Behavior Change	Public Will
Objectives	<ul><li>Influence beliefs and knowledge about a behavior and its consequences</li><li>Affect attitudes in support of behavior and persuade</li><li>Affect perceived social norms about the acceptability of a behavior among one's peers</li><li>Affect intentions to perform the behavior</li><li>Produce behavior change (if accompanied by supportive program components)</li></ul>	<ul><li>Increase visibility of an issue and its importance</li><li>Affect perceptions of social issues and who is seen as responsible</li><li>Increase knowledge about solutions based on who is seen as responsible</li><li>Affect criteria used to judge policies and policymakers</li><li>Help determine what is possible for service introduction and public funding</li><li>Engage and mobilize constituencies to action</li></ul>
Target Audience	Segments of the population whose behavior needs to change	Segments of the general public to be mobilized and policymakers
Strategies	Social marketing	Media advocacy, community organizing, and mobilization
Media Vehicles	Public Service/affairs programming: print, television, radio, electronic advertising	News media: print, television, radio, electronic advertising
Examples	Anti-smoking, condom usage, drunk driving, seat belt usage, parenting	Support for quality child care, after school programming, health care policy

was also accountable, government departments usually housed substantial press offices who provided an essentially reactive service to international, national and local journalists. In line with existing legislation in countries such as New Zealand and the USA, the introduction of the Freedom of Information Act in the UK in 2005 has increased accountability by requiring all public sector bodies, including government departments, to disclose on request the information that they hold, with some exemptions covering areas such as national security.

It can be argued, however, that many government campaigns go beyond mere information provision and that their purpose is to persuade: to change citizens' opinions and or behaviours. For example, campaigns against smoking and anti-social behaviour are directly aimed at behaviour change and can be seen to have all the characteristics of Grunig's (Grunig & Hunt, 1984) two-way asymmetric model, which has scientific persuasion at its heart. These behaviour change campaigns are often labelled 'social marketing campaigns', and employ business marketing principles and techniques to achieve social change.

The Phillis Review

In the early 2000s, under the government of the then prime minister, Tony Blair, there was some blurring of the lines between the role of impartial government communicators and the politically appointed special advisors. Indeed, in 1997, Alistair Campbell, director of communication, who was Tony Blair's special advisor, was given the power to direct civil servants in the Government Information and Communication Service (GICS), and subsequently there were a number of media scandals that reinforced the view that propriety lines were being blurred. For example, a special advisor to the Trade and Industry Secretary told government communicators that they should 'bury' any bad news on 11 September 2001, in an attempt to hide potentially politically embarrassing announcements behind the larger news story of the World Trade Centre terrorist attacks. In December 2002, after denials from the Prime Minister's office, it emerged that the Prime Minister's wife had bought property in Bristol via the fraudster boyfriend of her lifestyle advisor – a fact clearly embarrassing to the Prime Minister, but not something his office should have handled.

It was felt that GICS was being increasingly politicised, and this contributed to the establishment of an independent review of government communication led by Sir Robert (Bob) Phillis, a well-known and respected media executive. The Phillis Review (Phillis, 2004) led to far reaching changes in government communication, the most salient for this chapter being:

- The appointment of a civil servant of the most senior rank to lead the service – a permanent secretary, with a break to the linkage with special advisors.
- A renaming of GICS as the Government Communication Network (GCN), open to all civil servant communicators (GICS had been restricted to those who met certain entry criteria), with a Cabinet Office team providing

learning and development support, and communication tools and best practice guidance.

- 'A redefinition of the role and scope of government communicators' since the Review found that 'as a whole, the Civil Service has not grasped the potential of modern communications as a service provided for citizens' – as a result the Review's 'central recommendation is that communications should be redefined across government to mean a continuous dialogue with all interested parties, encompassing a broader range of skills and techniques than those associated with media relations. The focus of attention should be on the general public' (p. 12).
- 'Each Department's communications activity must clearly contribute to the achievement of the Departments overall policy aims and objectives' (p. 15).
- Greater emphasis and investment in regional and local communication.
- Increasing emphasis on on-line communication.

The impact on the UK government communication community has been significant, with an important manifestation being the diversification of activities now undertaken by GCN members away from the emphasis on media relations (see Figure 8.1).

One of the major undertakings of the Cabinet Office support team was to develop a systematic framework for approaching strategic communication planning. This was to address one of the key findings of Phillis (2004), which was that communication activity across government departments was inconsistent, of variable quality and often tactical in focus. Furthermore, it did not always align with, or support departmental objectives and was not seen as a core capability within departments.

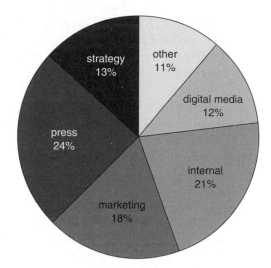

FIGURE 8.1   The Range of Activities Undertaken by GCN Members (the Government Communication Network website (access by membership only) at http://gcn.civilservice.gov. uk. © Crown Copyright, Cabinet Office)

During 2005 and 2006 this framework, called 'Engage', was developed and is now being promulgated throughout government departments (Select Committee on Communications, 2009). Again, it should be noted that although specific to the UK, the approach outlined in Engage is recognisable as having parallels in other countries.

The Engage Framework

The Engage framework 'sets out how Government should approach strategic communication. It takes account of the unique complexity of Government: the sheer scale of most of our initiatives; the complex economic, social and political climate we operate in; the challenge of engaging some of the most hard-to-reach target audiences; the intangibility of some concepts we have to communicate' (GCN, 2010).

Its ambition is not only to provide a strategic planning approach, but also to reposition communication itself as having a critical part to play in intelligence gathering; feeding 'the views of the public into all aspects of policy development and service delivery' (GCN, 2010). Indeed, the *Engage Handbook* (GCN, 2010), states explicitly that the 'framework' will change those who:

- Think of communication tactically, as an ad campaign, or as a press release and a brochure.
- View communications as something that is tacked onto policy and delivery.
- Think of communications only as a function or department and don't recognise that it is at the heart of a people-centred approach.

The Engage framework consists of four main elements: strategic planning process; principles; enablers; and a glossary. It is supported by a substantial knowledge bank, which consists of an explanation of the practical principles behind the framework, application tools, case studies and self-training materials. There are also a series of events, training and development opportunities that supplement and reinforce the learning materials. The four elements of the framework will now be examined, in reverse order, with the first three being covered quite briefly because the focus of this chapter is on the last element, the strategic planning process.

The Glossary

The Glossary aims to provide a common language for communication terms and words across government. It is quite short, but covers some of the key words that permeate the Engage documentation. Some of the most critical words and phrases are *aim, behaviour, core script, customer centric, customer experience, customer journey, insight, objective, proposition, segmentation, stakeholder mapping, strategy* and *targeting*.

These terms are important because they not only establish clear definitions for all government communicators and hence a common language on which to base discussion between themselves and other colleagues, but also provide a clear indication of the orientation of the Engage framework. It is driven essentially by a social marketing philosophy. This was a term first used by Kotler and Zaltman (1971) and relates to the application of marketing principles to social issues. The proposition is that if marketing can be successful in encouraging people to buy products such as cars and drinks, then it can also be used to encourage behaviours that will benefit them as individuals and society as a whole (the purpose of public campaigns referred to earlier).

According to the National Social Marketing Centre[1], social marketing has a number of key features including:

- Customer orientation: with an emphasis on understanding the customer's knowledge, attitudes and beliefs.
- Behaviour and behavioural goals: understanding existing behaviour and developing new behavioural goals which can be influenced over time.
- Insight: gaining a profound understanding of what moves and frustrates people.
- Exchange: an understanding of what is expected of people and the cost to them.
- Intervention mix and marketing mix: using a range of methods and interventions to achieve a behavioural goal.
- Audience segmentation: using segmentation to target people specifically and effectively.

The Engage framework embeds these features, with its main thrust being to achieve behavioural change for social reasons and for the good of society as a whole – an important and possibly debatable critical point since it is government that usually determines what is 'good'.

The Enablers

The Engage framework includes what it calls eight 'enablers' – principles that support the way strategic communication planning is undertaken. These are shown in Figure 8.2 (on p. 201). They are a mixture of *process* enablers, such as 'team working', 'resource optimisation' and 'performance management', and task enablers, such as 'agreeing objectives 'and applying segmentation and insight', These task enablers are repeated in the 'planning process' discussed below, so will not be dwelt on here. It is also noteworthy that the communication approach to intermediaries and partners is one of 'marketing', the clear indication being that government is driving and managing all these relationships and connections.

The Principles

The Engage framework also lays down eight principles, which it states will help communicators engage effectively with audiences (see Figure 8.3 on p. 202). Again, it can be seen that the principles of social marketing, such as 'aim for behaviour change',

---

[1]The National Social Marketing Centre is a strategic partnership between the UK Department of Health and Customer Focus (formerly The National Consumer Council). Some material on social marketing for this chapter was taken from its website at http://www.nsmcentre.org.uk

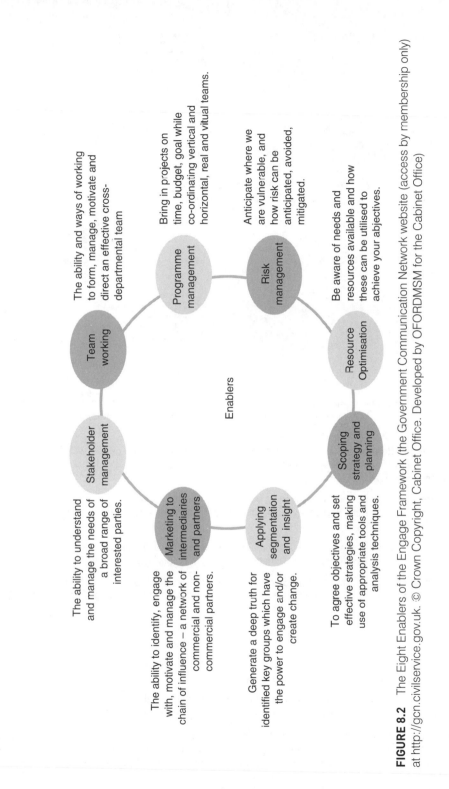

FIGURE 8.2 The Eight Enablers of the Engage Framework (the Government Communication Network website (access by membership only) at http://gcn.civilservice.gov.uk. © Crown Copyright, Cabinet Office. Developed by OFORDMSM for the Cabinet Office)

1. Listening, consulting, understanding, questioning and working together to obtain deep **insight** into people's motivations, needs and barriers is how we become 'people-centric' and help deliver policy successfully.

2. **Segmentation** makes our communication more effective. Identifying people with distinctive shared needs and characteristics and targeting relevant segments gives sharper focus to policy and communication.

3. One of the toughest tasks is achieving **behaviour change**. This isn't always the task for communication. But when behaviour is essential for policy delivery we need to find ways to engage people effectively.

4. **Propositions** express policy in a way that makes sense to the people we are targeting and gives them a clear understanding of just what's in it for them or for society as a whole.

5. Cutting through a **complex communications environment** is increasingly challenging. Not only are there more media channels . . . we have to communicate to and through complex webs of stakeholders, partners and influencers.

6. Communication is part of the **total experience**. The best people experience is achieved when the views of the public are fed into all aspects of policy development and service delivery.

7. Many people contribute to this experience. We need to **collaborate** not only with Policy and Delivery, but with many partners and stakeholders.

8. We must be **open and accountable** in all communication and marketing activities, adhering to our civil service values of integrity, honesty, objectivity and impartiality.

FIGURE 8.3   The Eight Principles of the Engage Framework (the Government Communication Network website (access by membership only) at http://gcn.civilservice.gov.uk. © Crown Copyright, Cabinet Office. Developed by OFORDMSM for the Cabinet Office)

are embedded. The proposition element embraces the 'exchange' concept articulated by the National Centre for Social Marketing referred to elsewhere in the chapter.

The principles also recognise the complexity of the communication environment and the need for communicators to understand this and to work with a range of stakeholders to understand and reach certain groups and to collaborate with them to deliver services. The 'best total people experience' encapsulates the marketing principle that if this is done people are more likely to respond to calls to action for change, but also recognises that public servants are just that, the servants of the people and therefore mandated to provide the best possible service. Finally, the requirement to be transparent and accountable is acknowledged, as is the necessity of being objective and impartial (Phillis, 2004). It is also recognised that communication on its own often cannot achieve desired results. The whole experience, including the quality of the service provided, will impact on the people's experience. While not responsible for every aspect of the service, the communication function can play a vital role in identifying, through research, where any problems in the peoples' experience are, and alerting responsible colleagues to the issues. Thereby they add value beyond their functional role.

The Planning Process

At the heart of the Engage framework is the *planning process*. This provides a systematic template for undertaking programmes and campaigns, and indicates the ideal sequence of activities and their context. It consists of five stages (see Figure 8.4 on p. 204) which are described below, and their application is explained in a case study taken from the UK Foreign and Commonwealth Office (FCO). The case describes the 'Avoiding Penalties' campaign, which comprised a programme implemented to help and protect English football fans travelling to Germany for the World Cup football tournament in 2006. That year's World Cup finals were the biggest ever for travelling England fans. Three hundred thousand fans visited Germany for the tournament, almost four times the number for the Euro 2004 tournament in Portugal. The scale of the event meant that the World Cup was the biggest single issue facing the FCO consular services in 2006.

When reading this case study and any subsequent international cases, it is important to bear in mind that planning is an iterative process and that while the principles governing the process hold, they need not necessarily be followed in the strict sequence indicated. The process is designed to ensure the right elements are addressed to embed rigour in planning, but it is not intended to be a straightjacket. Sometimes the elements involved are given different amounts of attention and sometimes the sequence in which they are taken may be different. The key is that the process should be applied as is appropriate to the situation in which it is being used.

The Five Stages of Engage: Scope

'Scope' means putting together a 'business plan and a communication and marketing strategy which is fully integrated with policy and delivery' (GCN, 2010). The scope part of the processes entails asking three key questions:

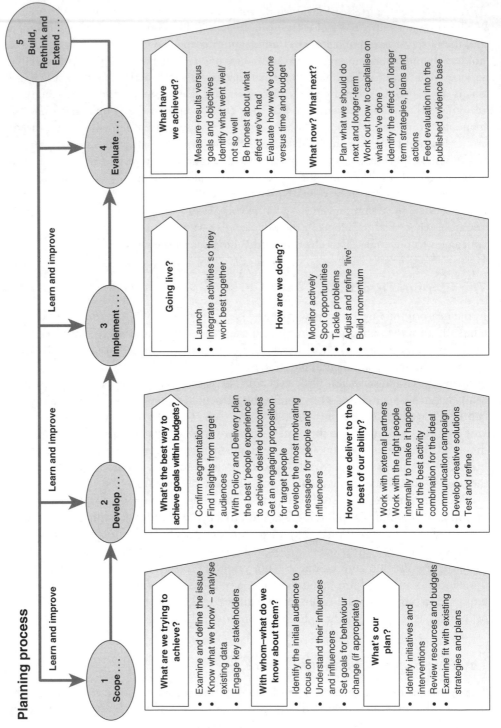

Planning process

1 Scope . . .

Learn and improve

What are we trying to achieve?
- Examine and define the issue
- 'Know what we know' – analyse existing data
- Engage key stakeholders

With whom–what do we know about them?
- Identify the initial audience to focus on
- Understand their influences and influencers
- Set goals for behaviour change (if appropriate)

What's our plan?
- Identify initiatives and interventions
- Review resources and budgets
- Examine fit with existing strategies and plans

2 Develop . . .

Learn and improve

What's the best way to achieve goals within budgets?
- Confirm segmentation
- Find insights from target audiences
- With Policy and Delivery plan the best 'people experience' to achieve desired outcomes
- Get an engaging proposition for target people
- Develop the most motivating messages for people and influencers

How can we deliver to the best of our ability?
- Work with external partners
- Work with the right people internally to make it happen
- Find the best activity combination for the ideal communication campaign
- Develop creative solutions
- Test and refine

3 Implement . . .

Learn and improve

Going live?
- Launch
- Integrate activities so they work best together

How are we doing?
- Monitor actively
- Spot opportunities
- Tackle problems
- Adjust and refine 'live'
- Build momentum

4 Evaluate . . .

What have we achieved?
- Measure results versus goals and objectives
- Identify what went well/ not so well
- Be honest about what effect we've had
- Evaluate how we've done versus time and budget

What now? What next?
- Plan what we should do next and longer-term
- Work out how to capitalise on what we've done
- Identify the effect on longer term strategies, plans and actions
- Feed evaluation into the published evidence base

5 Build, Rethink and Extend . . .

FIGURE 8.4 The Engage Planning Process © Crown Copyright, Cabinet Office. Developed by OFORDMSM for the Cabinet Office

- *What are we trying to achieve?* Answering this involves examining and defining the issue or opportunity, analysing any existing information about the issue and engaging with those most affected.
- *With whom and what do we know about them?* This includes identifying the initial targets of the campaign, understanding what and who influences them and then setting goals for what changes are desired in the target group.
- *What is our plan?* This entails identifying the interventions that are appropriate, securing the right resources for the plan and ensuring the plan aligns with existing departmental strategies and plans.

Avoiding Penalties Campaign

Scope

What are we trying to achieve?
The challenge was to ensure as many fans as possible had a safe and enjoyable tournament and to avoid the consular services being overwhelmed by demand for emergency support. The main requirement was to persuade fans to get travel insurance, check travel advice, abide by local laws and take other simple safe travel precautions.

Two main objectives were set for the 'Avoiding Penalties' campaign:

- *Minimise the number of preventable problems suffered by fans travelling to Germany.*
- *Publicise the fans' hotline number and other details of how FCO staff could help those who needed support.*

With whom and what do we know about them?
Prior FCO research had highlighted that most travelling football fans resist standard government messaging and information, particularly of the 'stay safe' variety. Consequently, the FCO team planned a campaign that would change behaviour, while avoiding traditional channels used by government.

What is our plan?
Understanding the audience led to four campaign principles:

- *Messages needed to be in a form that was attractive and useful to fans.*
- *Use a variety of third party 'mouthpieces' that would be trusted by fans, such as other organisations, brands and celebrities.*
- *Spread the message across a range of different media to reflect the diversity of the target audience and the different ways they access information.*
- *Reach fans as often as possible to overcome resistance to the messaging by creating ubiquity.*

The Five Stages of Engage: Develop

The develop phase of the Engage process asks two key questions:

- *What is the best way to achieve goals within budgets?* To address this question, planners should confirm how they will group their stakeholders, understand the target group by talking to those closest to them and develop 'messages' and an experience that will engage and motivate them based on a compelling 'proposition'.
- *How can we deliver to the best of our ability?* This entails looking in detail at whom and what should be involved in delivering the programme. This includes identifying the right partners and colleagues to work with, and selecting the right combination of activities for the campaign which are tested and refined.

Avoiding Penalties Campaign

Develop

What is the best way to achieve goals within budgets?
A key requirement of the campaign was to keep the message and materials to fans simple, easily accessible and, most importantly, highly portable. The main answer came in the form of a fold-out information card, the size of a credit card, combining safety advice with information likely to be useful to (and therefore retained by) fans (see Figure 8.5). The card itself was promoted as described in the implement stage below.

How can we deliver to the best of our ability?
Central to implementation was a creative approach to building partnerships to gain the widest possible distribution for the card. Each of the initiatives was screened against the campaign objectives and criteria. A very wide range of partners were involved.

The Five Stages of Engage: Implement

Key questions for the implement element of the process are:

- *Going live?* Here the campaign is launched and activities combined correctly so they have powerful effect.
- *How are we doing?* This concerns monitoring the campaign as it proceeds, to adjust it depending on feedback and to ensure it is gaining momentum.

Avoiding Penalties Campaign

Implement

Going live?
The campaign consisted of a whole series of activities, which delivered the cards and other supporting material through the selected partners (see Figure 8.6 on p. 207). These included:

FIGURE 8.5   The Credit Card-Sized Information Leaflet (© Crown Copyright, Cabinet Office)

- *The FA, who sent the card out with tickets and gave distribution access to pre-World Cup England friendlies.*
- *Nine of the UK's biggest airports, where 133,000 cards were distributed using floor-walkers and hand-outs at check-in desks etc.*
- *Through the relevant airlines, British Airways, Lufthansa and British Midland.*
- *Via the police, who distributed over 4,000 cards through ports across the UK.*
- *Through arrival airports in Germany, where fans were given 50,000 cards.*

FIGURE 8.6 Give Away Materials for the 'Avoiding Penalties' Campaign (© Crown Copyright, Cabinet Office)

- A sustained programme of engagement with England fans' groups across the country in the year before the World Cup.
- A partnership with T-Mobile through which text messages were sent publicising the fans' hotline number to every network phone user arriving in Germany – fans could also sign up to receive football news and travel safety alerts on their mobiles while in Germany.
- A mobile internet travel advice service with Pixaya.
- A 'Skinker' (downloadable desktop news alert service), branded and advertised by TalkSport Radio, which mixed TalkSport football news alerts with key safety tips for travelling to Germany, which was installed by 8,000 people.

- *A comprehensive Free Lions Guide to the World Cup including 8 pages of travel safety information co-produced with the Football Supporters Federation (the largest England fans' group) and their sponsors, the Nationwide Building Society.*
- *A dedicated website, http://www.britishembassyworldcup.com.*
- *Press launches with former England footballers Tony Adams and David Platt, which raised awareness of the campaign through widespread coverage including the front page lead of the Sun, a major national newspaper.*

How are we doing?

The main principle of the campaign was to deliver Avoiding Penalties collateral to fans as many times as possible and through a variety of channels to ensure they were aware of and took with them the guidance materials. Mass coverage was key and hence monitoring of the levels of materials given away and taken and of Skinker uptakes was an obvious route.

The Five Stages of Engage: Evaluate

The evaluate stage of the planning process asks:

- *What have we achieved?* The aim is to honestly evaluate whether campaign objectives have been met on time and on budget and examine what has worked well or not, or why.
- *What now? What next?* This requires the planner to look at what should be done in the future and how the campaign can be capitalised upon. Any long-term effects should also be identified and any results of the evaluation captured so that others can learn from the campaigns.

Avoiding Penalties Campaign

Evaluate

What have we achieved?

A very low number of England fans suffered preventable problems during the World Cup. In fact, by the time they came home the German press was calling them 'the best fans in the world'. The 'Avoiding Penalties' campaign played a central role in this as evidenced by:

- *Almost every emergency call during the tournament went to FCO's special fans number, showing its wide awareness among fans.*
- *Fans had very high awareness of issues such as the illegality of Nazi salutes.*
- *Consular staff found a high awareness of FCO's travel safety messages even among those British nationals who did end up needing their assistance.*

The total cost of 'Avoiding Penalties' was less than £125,000. It delivered ubiquity and high impact for very low cost thanks to the partnership approach. Distribution of information cards at airports alone delivered a return on investment (actual costs against commercial rates for the same exposure) of 25:1. It made a significant and measurable positive impact on fans' behaviour during the tournament.

What now, what next?
There were three key learning outcomes that came from the campaign and which can be applied to other projects.

- *Clearly defining the campaign objectives, and also the specific criteria required for the campaign, enables a wide range of implementation initiatives to be screened for suitability.*
- *The persistence required in assembling a wide range of partnerships pays off by stretching a limited budget. In this case, the power lay in selecting a piece of collateral (the card), which could be used effectively across a wide range of partnerships.*
- *Implementation does not necessarily consist primarily of investing money in media outputs. In this campaign the main investment was one of time, involving the FCO team primarily in managing relationships with the key partners identified and motivating them to get behind the key messages in a consistent manner.*

The Five Stages of Engage: Build, Rethink, Extend

This stage ensures the ongoing life of the campaign if required, but also ensures that learning from completed campaigns are captured for future reference.

Avoiding Penalties Campaign

Build, rethink, extend
The campaign was written up and placed in the Engage Knowledge Bank, held on the GCN intranet.

COMPARING THE ENGAGE PLANNING PROCESS TO C-MACIE

It is apparent that the Engage planning process not only resonates with the various planning methodologies and templates proposed in the main communication/ public relations texts (McElreath, 1997; Ferguson, 1999; Austin and Pinkleton, 2006; Cutlip et al., 2009; Smith, 2009; Gregory, 2010), but also aligns well with the planning methodologies used in practice by numerous organisations. For example, the US Department of Defense, whose Principles of Strategic Communication were mentioned earlier, uses the following planning model (US Joint Forces Command, 2010):

- Information Gathering
  - General (for example, who are the stakeholders; what reactions are expected; how are incoming and outgoing messages handled; what are desired outcomes?)
  - Means (for example, which and how will communication channels be used; what capabilities are available; what about the external environment?)
  - Relationships (for example, long-standing and potential partners and stakeholders; how will relationships be built; how will capacity be built through partnerships?)
  - Audience (for example, ally, competitor, adversary; their attitudes, interests, motivations; how will they be segmented?)
  - Networks (for example, formal and informal; social; support)
  - Language/culture
  - Collection (of intelligence and information; gathering, sharing, exploitation)
  - Development (actions, content for segmented audiences)
  - Assessment (for example, monitoring of feedback and progress; unintended effects)
  - Restraints (for example, identifying barriers; rules of engagement; legal)
  - Risks (for example, risk identification and mitigation)
- Planning
  - General (for example, desired end-state; objectives; evaluation criteria; desired behaviour change; partnerships; messages; coordination; mistakes avoidance and rectification)
  - Relationships (for example, roles and responsibilities)
  - Restraints (for example, policies)
  - Means (for example, use of new media; work with agencies, partners)
  - Assessment (for example, programme adaptation, progress measurement; identifying causes of events/issues)
  - Risk
  - Themes, messages, images and actions

Plan Review

- For example, are measurement criteria relevant, responsive and resourced; create feedback loops?

Execution

- For example, what must be done more, less or stopped; how are outcomes assessed, are there new issues or information that needs attention; are there new opportunities?

It is also clear that Engage echoes the C-MACIE approach. Figure 8.7 (on p. 213) provides a comparator. It is evident that there are some elements under the headings of the Engage planning process which are mirrored in C-MACIE, for example aims and objectives comes under scope (the first part of the process) in Engage and under choice (the second part of the process) in C-MACIE, but the thinking behind both processes are clearly similar. However, as mentioned in Chapter 4, the reality is that these processes are not linear, and are often concurrent; hence it is possible to locate certain elements in more than one stage. C-MACIE has budgets under implementation, but it could quite easily be at the beginning of the process because many practitioners either ask for or are given a budget within which to work, from the point where a campaign is first discussed.

There are, however, a number of differences between the two processes, two of which merit some discussion. C-MACIE recommends a more comprehensive scan of the external environment, recognising the role of the communicator as a primary intelligence gatherer and interpreter for the organisation as a whole (see more on this in Chapters 2 and 4). The Engage process appears to focus very tightly on analysis of target groups and this is understandable given the social marketing leanings of the model with its concentration on 'customer-orientation' and changing behaviour.

C-MACIE specifically alludes to strategies, the link between objectives and tactics (Gregory, 2010), whereas Engage appears not to identify this as a key step. That is not to say that strategy is absent in all Engage Process campaigns, but it is notable that it is not explicitly mentioned in the template.

DRAWING INTERNATIONAL PARALLELS

To demonstrate the point that most governments in liberal democracies approach their communication in similar ways, two brief case studies of government campaigns in Italy and New Zealand are presented here, each structured to the Engage/C-MACIE format.

Italy and Government Communication

In Italy, government departments and statutory bodies are able to run their own campaigns, but each year they submit their annual plans to the Department of Information and Publishing of the Presidency of the Council of Ministers who coordinate the communication activities of government. This central department also supports a number of campaigns run by the public sector and works in conjunction with ministries and public bodies on annually agreed programmes. The case outlined below was coordinated by the Department of Information and Publishing.

Abandoned Pet Campaign

There is a major problem in Italy with citizens abandoning their domestic pets. The Ministry of Welfare, along with the Ministry of Tourism, worked with the Department of Information and Publishing to tackle the issue, launching a campaign in 2008.

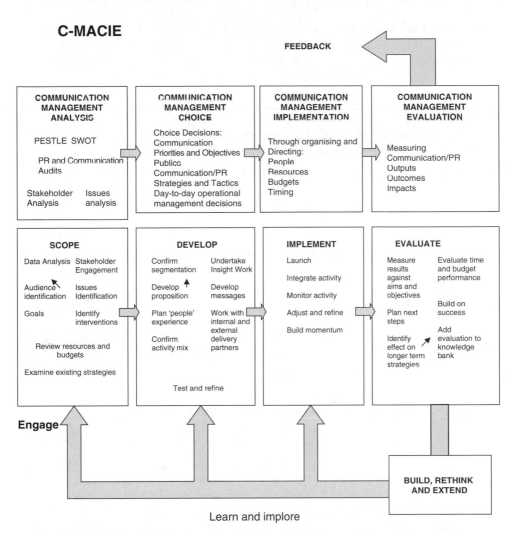

FIGURE 8.7 C-MACIE and Engage Planning Processes Compared

Scope/Communication Management Analysis

Research for the campaign identified that there are over 600,000 stray dogs in Italy and that the largest proportion of them are animals abandoned by their owners. Abandoning a dog is not only socially unacceptable, but also against the law and punishable by imprisonment for up to a year.

One in three families in Italy has a pet at home and summer is the hottest period in all senses. With the annual holidays approaching, people have to either take their pets with them or find them a place to stay. For some owners, abandoning their pet is the solution and this has well-researched hygiene, health and social consequences. Stray, uncared-for dogs can spread diseases to other animals, can gather into packs and cause car crashes, to name but a few problems. The overall aim of the campaign was to reduce the number of abandoned dogs. The Ministry of Welfare was concerned to promote the health and welfare aspects for both the public and for dogs and the Ministry of Tourism was keen to promote the fact that many hotels and holiday centres welcomed pets.

Develop/Communication Management Choice

The Ministries and Department decided that the most appropriate approach (strategy) was to undertake a mass communication campaign about the issue, targeting all the population in order to galvanise opinion to make abandoning pets unacceptable as a whole, but also to ensure they reached everyone who was a dog owner. The specific objectives of the campaign were:

* To spread a culture of responsible ownership, contrasting the abandoning of pets as irresponsible.
* To inform the public that abandoning animals is an offence against the law, with penalties.

The core messages were to stress the inhumanity of abandoning dogs, through the slogan 'Human or Inhuman', and to inform the public that many holiday locations were dog friendly and accommodating of them.

Implement/Communication Management Implementation

The campaign was run at the time when the greatest number of people were thinking about and preparing for their holidays and travelling: towards July and August. The main communication channels were 30-second TV advertisements placed on popular Italian channels, supported by a major poster campaign on all the main highways, petrol stations and cities such as Rome, Naples, Milan, Palermo and Verona. The Ministries also worked with the National Association of Italian Municipalities to promote a poster campaign in the smaller cities, particularly in the Centre and South of Italy where stray dogs are a widespread problem.

All this activity was supported by a national and regional media relations programme. A highlight of the campaign was the national media launch of a website featuring the Minister of Tourism, Hon. Michela Vittoria Brambilla, in June 2010, promoting a project called 'Four-Legged Tourists'. The project gives practical advice about travelling with pets in Italy, and information on thousands of pet-friendly holiday locations and restaurants, dog-care facilities and a variety of animal welfare services. The site is constantly updated with new materials (see http://www.turista-4zampe.it) and a hard-copy guide is available.

The campaign also promotes a competition for accommodation and restaurant owners who provide the most dog-friendly service: dog owners vote for the winners.

Evaluation/Communication Management Evaluation

The campaign has now been running for two years under the auspices of the Department of Information and Publishing. It is a long-term behaviour change programme, so results at this stage are only indicators towards future success. However, the website is becoming increasingly well-known and the TV and poster campaigns have good levels of recognition. A weakness of the campaign is the lack of formal evaluation. This is not untypical of government campaigns, especially since behaviour change often takes several years to achieve and monitoring is both complex and can be expensive.

New Zealand and Government Communication.

In New Zealand, government departments initiate their own campaigns. The case below describes a programme run by the New Zealand Ministry of Health, aimed specifically at minority Maori and Pacific Island women.

Cervical Smear Tests Campaign

The National Cervical Screening Programme was established to reduce the number of women who get and die from cervical cancer. It is managed by the National Screening Unit of the Ministry of Health and is delivered via a complex arrangement of 13 regional services, colposcopy services, laboratories, and more than 5,000 smear takers.

The programme is successful, having contributed to a 50% reduction in incidence and a 65% reduction in deaths. However, 60–70 women still die from cervical cancer each year and there are considerable health inequalities. Incidence among Maori and Pacific Island women is twice the rate, and mortality three to four times the rate of all women. The primary reason is lower rates of screening by Maori and Pacific Island women (47% and 46% coverage of the eligible population having a smear test in the last 3 years), compared to other women (80%).

Scope/Communication Management Analysis

Encouraging women to have cervical smears is not an 'easy sell'. Having a smear test is bothersome, it can be uncomfortable, there is no immediate benefit, and it is a personal issue that many women feel uncomfortable talking about. To develop insights into the attitudes and understanding of cervical screening and cervical cancer among Maori and Pacific Island women, research was undertaken.

The research identified high levels of misunderstanding, lack of awareness, embarrassment and lack of discussion, and a lack of information. All these factors reduced the likelihood of participating in screening. In light of these insights, a number of overall health objectives were developed. These were to:

- raise awareness and 'normalise' the subject;
- increase understanding about screening and its benefits;
- create discussion;

- predispose women towards participating;
- increase calls to the free helpline number;
- increase the number of Maori and Pacific Island women, in particular, who have smears;
- support health promoters by providing a context for their activity.

Given these overall objectives, a number of very specific public relations objectives were set:

- to harness unpaid media;
- to ensure stakeholders were aware of the campaign, its aims, objectives, and how it might affect them;
- to focus the approach to the media on 'setting the agenda' – given negative perceptions of cervical screening in the past, it was essential that the campaign got off to a good start.

The potential target groups were diverse, with more than 1 million women in the programme and an eligible population of 1.2 million. The primary group was Maori and Pacific Island women aged 20–70 who had not had a cervical smear test within the last three years. Secondary groups were:

- family, friends and community members who support and influence these women;
- all women aged 20–70 who had not had a smear test within the last three years;
- stakeholders and the wider sector including government, NGOs, health facilities, smear takers, health promoters, lab staff, professional colleges and groups representing Maori and Pacific Island women.

Messages were developed which aimed at improving awareness and understanding, destigmatising screening and motivating women to go for a smear test. The key facts that were needed to be understood by women were that:

- cervical cancer is caused by a common virus, HPV;
- women can develop HPV without knowing it, even if they are no longer sexually active and regardless of age;
- a smear test can pick up changes caused by HPV that can lead to cervical cancer;
- for those aged between 20 and 70 who have ever been sexually active, having a smear test every three years could save their lives;
- women need to be more open about cervical cancer – talk about cervical cancer with those who they care about and support them in going for their smear tests.

For stakeholders the key messages were:

- the communications campaign aimed to raise awareness of the benefits of regular cervical screening;
- it focused on Maori and Pacific Island women because of their lower rates of screening and higher rates of cervical cancer;
- the campaign would launch on 18 September 2007;
- to visit the website http://www.nsu.govt.nz for more information;
- the campaign had been developed with strong support from providers, to reduce the burden of cervical cancer.

Two different strategic approaches were needed to engage Maori and Pacific Island women. Research identified that direct, compelling messages would work best for Maori and that the strongest motivator was to encourage them to go for a smear test so that they would be around for their *whanau* (extended family). The research showed that direct messages would not work as well for Pacific women. Humour – used carefully – was seen as a way of breaking the ice and introducing discussion of a sensitive subject. The strongest motivator was to encourage them to support their friends in going for a smear test (and they would be more likely to go too).

The project was managed in ten work streams (see below), each with clear objectives, deliverables, responsibilities, and timeframes. The budget in year one was NZ$2.5 million. The first phase was delivered on time, in full and within budget.

Implementation/Communication Management
Implementation

Stakeholders. These were segmented into three groups, all needing differing levels of communication. Meetings were held with key stakeholders, who were then regularly provided with information. A mixture of communication vehicles was used for other groups, including meeting with some, writing to others, providing information for newsletters and websites, carrying information in the National Screening Unit (NSU) and Ministry newsletters, and providing information to health media. A mail-out was sent to 7,000 individuals and organisations involved with the delivery of cervical screening. A pack with the campaign material, media releases and Q&As was sent to 70 organisations close to the campaign launch.

Campaign launch. The Prime Minister launched the campaign in September 2007 at Te Papa (New Zealand's national museum, celebrating its richness and diversity), at a function for 180 people. The focus was on celebrating the success of the programme, and the launch of a new initiative to ensure further success. The launch brought stakeholders together and provided a focus for the media.

Media. The focus leading up to the launch was to introduce the campaign in a low key way, with a strong risk management approach. It was important to maximise pick up of messages by Maori, Pacific Island and regional media. Post-launch public relations focused on continuing to provide information about the campaign to stakeholders and the media. In January, the focus turned to the launch of phase two, which provided an opportunity to update stakeholders and the public on the excellent results in the first three months.

Workforce. Three two-day workshops were held for more than 50 health promoters who are the local champions, the people on the ground dealing with local media and community networks. The workshops included a campaign update, an introduction to social marketing, media training, and practical planning for ways to leverage off the campaign locally. The training gained buy-in, improved the capability of a key workforce and helped to ensure the campaign messages were extended into the regions.

Printed resources. These were updated to ensure consistency of messages and branding. The resources included posters and brochures designed for the general population, as well as versions targeting different ethnicities. A reminder card was developed in response to research indicating that many women forgot when they were next due to go for a smear test. Branding of all resources was revised to make them more consumer-oriented and to ensure increased relevance to Maori and Pacific Island communities.

The free phone service. This was evaluated and opportunities identified for improving accessibility and flexibility. Extended hours were introduced during the launch period. Free cell-phone access was introduced, in recognition of the increased use of mobile phones.

Creative. This involved the development of new creative material, which has been applied to television, magazine, radio, outdoor and medical centre TV.

Advertising. All schedules were developed to achieve maximum reach and frequency with the key audiences.

Quantitative research. A telephone survey of the key audiences was conducted in August to establish benchmarks for awareness, attitudes and understanding of issues related to cervical screening. A monitor survey was undertaken in February 2008.

Monitoring. A national register records the screening histories of women in the programme. Comparison of coverage data, by ethnicity, over time, enables communicators to monitor the effectiveness of the campaign.

Evaluation/Communication Management Evaluation

The results showed significant increases in awareness of cervical screening, that cervical cancer can be prevented and how. Discussion increased from 17% to 37% among the priority audience. Women felt supported to go to screening, and the likelihood of them going rose from 30% to 46%. Recall of key messages was strong. Calls to the telephone line increased by 17% overall, from 3,107 per month in the period a year before, to 3,644 in the first 6 months of the campaign.

In the first 6 months, there were 20,000 new enrolments – 1,700 Maori, 1,700 Pacific, 3,600 Asian and 13,000 from other women. Uptake increased by: 1.6% for

Maori (relative increase of 3%), 2.9% for Pacific Islanders (relative increase of 6%), 1.6% for Asians (relative increase of 3%), 1.3% for other women (relative increase of 2%), and 1.2% overall (relative increase of 2%). These are significant results given the numbers are large, the short time period the campaign had run and the level of behavioural change involved; there was no real change over a number of years before the campaign.

Feedback from stakeholders (and the absence of adverse reaction) indicate that stakeholder relations were effective. Many emails, letters and phone calls were received congratulating the team on the effectiveness of the campaign. Health promoters indicate that the campaign has provided a positive context for their work – it has helped them start conversations with women and has broken the ice for discussion of a sensitive subject.

The approach to media relations was effective. There was good coverage of the launch on radio and in ethnic media, with feature items on Te Karere and Tagata Pasifika. Ongoing positive media coverage is being achieved.

The campaign is a multi-year programme to increase coverage and reduce the incidence and mortality from cervical cancer among Maori and Pacific Island women. Budget is allocated to all areas to reconnect with stakeholders, maximise media opportunities, develop new initiatives and continue to evaluate the programme.

Specific new initiatives include: material targeting Asian women, an ongoing PR programme to reinforce key messages, develop local stories and highlight results achieved at 6 and 12 months; reconnecting with health promoters to get their feedback and to identify new initiatives; making September 'cervical screening awareness month'; and a 12-month survey to inform future communications.

SUMMARY

This chapter has sought to examine the background to circumstances that frame and have driven a new, systematic approach to the communication management process by the UK government. However, this should not be regarded as an approach exclusive to the UK, as the case studies from Italy and New Zealand illustrate. The principles and practices outlined here are very similar to those employed by many liberal democracies, depending on their own contexts, priorities and ways of working. In some countries, for example in Scandinavia, there is greater emphasis on consultation and gaining consensus, while in others governments are much more directive, for example in France and Spain. However, in all these countries the process described in this chapter would be perfectly recognisable.

(Continued)

(Continued)

Furthermore, the parallels between C-MACIE and the UK government Engage planning process are close. This drives two main conclusions: first, strategic planning processes follow a recognisable and similar pattern irrespective of whether this is for organisations generally or for communications/public relations in particular (see Chapter 2 for more on this); second, it can be seen that such an approach has applicability in both the private and public sectors, irrespective of the fact that the motivations and orientations of organisations in these sectors may be very different.

📖 REFERENCES

Austin, E.W., & Pinkleton, B.E. (2006) *Strategic Public Relations Management*, 2nd ed. Mahwah, NJ: Erlbaum.

Coffman, J. (2002) *Public Communication Campaign Evaluation – An Environmental Seam of Challenges, Criticisms, Practice and Opportunities*. Cambridge. MA: Harvard Family Research Project, Harvard Graduate School of Education.

Cole-Morgan, J. (1988) Public Relations in central government. In W. Howard (ed.), *The Practice of Public Relations*, 3rd ed. Oxford: Communications Advertising and Marketing Education Foundation/Heinemann Professional.

Cutlip, S.M., Center, A.H., & Broom, G. M. (2009) *Effective Public Relations*, 10th ed. Upper Saddle River, NJ: Prentice Hall.

Department of Defense (2008) *Principles of Strategic Communication*. Washington, DC: Department of Defense.

Ferguson, S.D. (1999) *Communication Planning: An Integrated Approach*. Thousand Oaks, CA: Sage.

GCN (2010) *Engage Handbook for the Communications Community*. London: Cabinet Office. http://www.wiki.comms.gov.uk/index.php/what_is_Engage...%3F (Accessed 28 July 2010.)

Gregory, A. (2003) The Phillis Review – Government communication under the spotlight. *Ethical Space*, 1(2), 245–54.

Gregory, A. (2006) A development framework for government communicators. *Journal of Communication Management*, 10(2), 197–210.

Gregory, A. (2010) *Planning and Managing Public Relations Campaigns: A Strategic Approach*. London: Kogan Page.

Grunig, J.E., & Hunt, T. (1984) *Managing Public Relations*. New York: Holt, Rinehart and Winston.

Kotler, P., & Zaltman, G. (1971) Social marketing: An approach to planned social change. *Journal of Marketing*, 35, 3–12.

Lee, M. (2008) *Government Public Relations: A Reader*. Boca Raton, FL: CRC Press.

L'Etang, J. (2004) *Public Relations in Britain: A History of Professional Practice in the Nineteenth Century*. Mahwah, NJ: Erlbaum.

McElreath, M.P. (1997) *Managing Systematic and Ethical Public Relations Campaigns*. Madison, WI: Brown and Benchmark.

Newsom, D., Turk, J.V.S., & Kruckeberg, D. (2000) *This is PR,* 7th ed. Belmont, CA: Wadsworth/Thomson Learning.

Olasky, M. (1987) *Corporate Public Relations: A New Historical Perspective*. Hillsdale, NJ: Erlbaum.

Phillis, R. (2004) *An Independent Review of Government Communications*. London: Cabinet Office.

Select Committee on Communications. (2009) *Government Communications Report with Evidence*. London: House of Lords.

(Continued)

(Continued)

Smith, R.D. (2009) *Strategic Planning for Public Relations*, 3rd ed. New York: Routledge.

Tench, R., & Yeomans, L. (2009) *Exploring Public Relations*, 2nd ed. Harlow: Pearson Education.

US Joint Forces Command (2010) *Commander's Handbook for Strategic Communication*.Version 3. Suffolk, VA: US Joint Forces Command, Joint Warfighting Center.

Yeomans, L. (2009) Public sector communication and social marketing. In R. Tench and L. Yeomans (eds), *Exploring Public Relations*. Harlow: Pearson Education.

Business-to-Business Public Relations Agency Practice

Renee A. Robinson

> **Key Themes**
>
> - Overview of business-to-business public relations
> - Various business-to-business agency structures
> - The management of public relations in an integrated business-to-business agency
> - New business and new client acquisition
> - Client development, management and retention
> - Budgeting, estimating and forecasting
> - Evaluation and measurement techniques
> - Staff development and retention
> - Time management

This chapter explores the way a business-to-business public relations practice operates within an integrated marketing communications agency, in which our mission is to serve the communications needs of a select group of clients and provide them with innovative marketing support, creative excellence and superior service. This chapter will also take a comprehensive look at the public relations management function within a business-to-business agency.

INTRODUCTION

Business-to-business public relations aims to transform an organization or company from a mere voice in the crowd to an influential leader by positioning its strongest assets (products, services, people, etc.) as key differentiators that resonate with customers, employees, investors, and business and sales-channel partners – ultimately leading to greater market share, sales and profits.

Common business-to-business public relations services provided by agencies include:

- marketing communications;
- new product launches;
- corporate and product publicity;
- media relations and training;
- trade show planning and programs;
- crisis communications;
- CEO/executive positioning;
- internal/employee communications;
- investor relations;
- social media and other digital services.

In a nutshell, business-to-business public relations utilizes the practice of public relations to build relationships, establish credibility, enhance reputation, sell more products and services, promote an important cause or issue, position an organization as an employer of choice and grow profits.

As an example, consider a tool company that sells drills, saws and fasteners to commercial and residential construction companies, a building products company that sells roofing and decking products to builders and contractors, or an accounting firm that sells its audit and tax services to colleges and universities, health care facilities and small businesses. Each of these organizations has other businesses as its customers and relies on communication to establish awareness among these businesses, build its reputation, sell its products and services, and ultimately grow its business.

Two major developments in the business-to-business public relations arena are impacting virtually every aspect of business. The first is the evolution of the internet, sometimes called Web 2.0, which encapsulates the idea of the proliferation of interconnectivity and interactivity of web-delivered content. Tim O'Reilly, who is widely credited with coining the Web 2.0 term, regards Web 2.0 as the way that business embraces the strengths of the web and uses it as a platform. The second major development is social media, which refers to activities that integrate technology, telecommunications and social interaction, and the construction of words, pictures, videos and audio.

AGENCY STRUCTURE DIFFERENCES

Agencies are structured in various ways depending on their size, areas of expertise and client mix. Some focus on only one discipline (public relations only, advertising only, interactive only, etc.) and partner with other single-focus agencies as needed on projects. Others have a few different disciplines, such as research, public relations and interactive, in their services mix. Then there are integrated marketing communications (IMC) agencies, which represent all of the different communications disciplines that a business or client might need. My experience is with IMC agencies, so I will focus primarily on this type of structure.

The actual term used to describe integrated marketing communications seems to differ depending on whom you ask. In the early 1980s, Young and Rubicam developed the idea of 'the whole egg', which closely resembles today's idea of integrated marketing communications. Shortly after that, Ogilvy and Mather followed with its concept of 'orchestration' (Schultz, 1993). Many other terms, including 'one-stop shopping', 'new advertising', 'seamless communication' and 'integrated brand communications,' are used in the advertising and public relations industries to explain a different concept in marketing communication – the integration of specialized communications functions that previously operated with various degrees of autonomy (Duncan & Everett, 1993).

No matter what you decide to call it, IMC also has a variety of definitions. For example, 'one-stop shopping' implies a range of marketing communications functions with little emphasis on integration of the functions or on the end result of the communication, and 'new advertising' appears a little self-serving for ad agencies as they attempt to reposition themselves as offering something broader than just advertising expertise (Duncan & Everett, 1993).

According to Keith Reinhard (cited in Duncan & Everett, 1993), CEO of DDB Needham Worldwide and former chairman of the American Association of Advertising Agencies, 'the new advertising must encompass all the voices directed towards consumers in a brand's behalf'. Ogilvy and Mather's 'orchestration' and 'seamless communication' seem to follow his definition as they focus more on the process and results of integrated communications.

The definition of IMC used by the American Association of Advertising Agencies is:

> a concept of marketing communications planning that recognizes the added value of a comprehensive plan that evaluates the strategic roles of a variety of communications disciplines, e.g., general advertising, direct response, sales promotion and public relations – and combines these disciplines to provide clarity, consistency and maximum communications impact.

Coming up with a true definition of IMC is difficult because it is both a concept and a process, and the degree of integration within each dimension can greatly vary (Duncan & Everett, 1993). According to Eisenhart (cited in Duncan & Everett, 1993), an organization with an IMC philosophy may or may not physically integrate the people responsible for the various marketing communications functions into one department, although the majority of organizations do.

According to Novelli (cited in Duncan & Everett, 1993), the basic concept of IMC is synergism, meaning the individual efforts are mutually beneficial and the result is greater than if each discipline had selected its own targets, chosen its own message strategy, and set its own media schedule and timing.

As I mentioned earlier, my experience is with a fully integrated marketing communications agency, Nicholson Kovac, Inc., headquartered in Kansas City, Missouri,

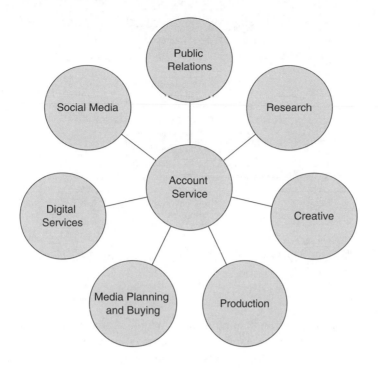

FIGURE 9.1 IMC Agency Stucture

which includes research, account service, creative, media planning and buying, public relations, digital services, social media, direct marketing and sales promotion under one roof as illustrated in Figure 9.1.

I have been with Nicholson Kovac for seven years, starting as a public relations account executive, and am now a public relations management supervisor. I currently work with our vice president/director of public relations and oversee a variety of different client accounts, both business-to-business and business-to-consumer, supervise several members of the public relations team and manage the agency's own public relations efforts.

Nicholson Kovac is a true, full-service IMC agency and is counted among the top independent advertising agencies in the US, serving national and global brands. We utilize a proprietary and comprehensive series of strategic planning models to identify relevant and realistic solutions to our clients' communications challenges. These models ensure that each team member, no matter what discipline he/she is in, is operating according to the same strategic mindset and is focused on maximizing the return that our clients receive from the investment of their marketing resources.

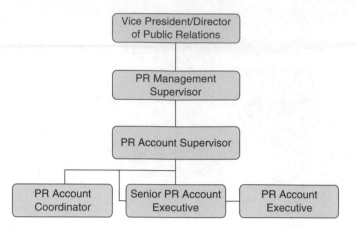

FIGURE 9.2   PR Team Structure

Our mission is to serve the communication needs of a select group of clients and provide them with innovative marketing support, creative excellence, and superior service. We strive to attract these clients with our commitment to help them achieve success and aim to grow with them because we consistently meet or exceed their expectations. Our ultimate goal is to become an indispensable partner with their business.

Although Nicholson Kovac's management team does not formally follow the C-MACIE framework, its components (analysis, choice, implementation and evaluation) are a part of nearly every aspect of our business. We will address these components as we explore the various challenges that face a business-to-business marketing communications agency.

Integration of Various Disciplines

In IMC agencies, one of the primary challenges is how to integrate the various disciplines. This challenge is not new and is common from agency to agency. In fact, after interviewing several advertising executives, Bevan (1996) commented that the relationship between advertising agencies and public relations practitioners has often proven to be an unequal one.

Martin Sorrell, chief executive of WPP Group (parent to Hill and Knowlton and Ogilvy Adams and Rinehart) said: 'People in advertising tend to think because they deal with billings that they are important, whereas we see PR and lobbying as both dealing at a fairly senior level.'

Meanwhile, John Wren, president of Omnicom (parent to Ketchum, Porter Novelli, Countrywide and GPC Market Access) says:

> If you go back ten years in the U.S. and look at the difference between PR and advertising, I think there was misunderstanding about what each side did – there wasn't a great deal of respect. As we went through the recession in the 1990s, communications became more focused and PR really stepped up to the world stage. (Bevan, 1996: 14)

Jones (2003) examined the relationships between advertising and public relations professionals and how they work together in real terms. Cilla Snowball, chief executive of Abbott Mead Vickers, says the relationship between the advertising and PR specialists within the Omnicom Group is only the tip of the iceberg. 'Lots of big integrated accounts operate across every area – advertising, PR, direct marketing, media planning and buying, not just a selected few', Snowball said. 'What we try to deliver on integrated accounts is the quality of people from each discipline. The benefit to the client is increased efficiency and the fact that we know one another and have worked together in the past' (Jones, 2003: 25). She adds that there are obviously 'occasional spats' between the different disciplines, but they share a common goal.

One way that Nicholson Kovac has been able to overcome many of these challenges between advertising, public relations and other disciplines is by operating under just one profit center. Instead, the agency's philosophy is 'success through partnership', or placing the responsibility for profitability on each person in the organization. Under this type of structure, we are accountable to each other, not selfish to our personal – or our department's – gains (see Figure 9.2).

This spirit of partnership is not taken casually by anyone at Nicholson Kovac, as it is the core of the agency's philosophy and was written as the common agreement between the four agency founders several months prior to opening the agency's doors.

SUCCESSFUL MANAGEMENT OF PUBLIC RELATIONS IN AN IMC ORGANIZATION

Though public relations has been a part of Nicholson Kovac's offerings for many years, the idea of integrating it into traditional advertising agencies really surged about 10 years ago, but not without some consternation on both sides.

As public relations agencies' margins begin to outweigh those of their advertising brethren, global marketing services groups were scrambling to bolt public relations onto a range of services traditionally dominated by ad men (Nicholas & Ray, 2001). In 2000, HHCL chairman Rupert Howell and other leading marketers and advertising executives told the public relations industry that it lacked self-confidence, intellectual weight and high-profile leaders, that it did not charge enough but that, despite all this, it had potential to be the lead communication discipline in a new era of 'co-creation'.

Annabel Manwaring, Leo Burnett global creative director, refers to the invaluable role that public relations has in terms of 'building reputation of the product among influencers who can then be used in the advertising creating ambassadors' in campaigns.

Public relations often closes the loop on integrated marketing as more and more agencies go toward the co-creation model. At Nicholson Kovac, for example, account teams with representatives from all disciplines – including public relations– utilize the client brief and present together, agree on strategy and creative, then develop the tactical strategy within the disciplinary teams.

For the first time in quite a long time, leading players are now suggesting that public relations has the potential not only to play on a level playing field, but even to become the lead communication discipline. Public relations should be integrated along with the other disciplines into budgeting and tracking, a concept made more possible by the demise of the commission system in both the United Kingdom and US. This is seen by many in the industry as a starting point to a breakthrough in creative ideas rather than the discipline-based approach that now dominates (Nicholas & Ray, 2001).

'The big issue is the way in which clients' budgets are written, i.e., the fact that there are separate ad and PR budgets, which leads to squabbling. It is structural', Howell said (Nicholas & Ray, 2001: 15). He even goes so far as to claim that public relations should sit at the right hand of power and should coordinate budgets and all other marketing activity.

The fact that public relations, described by Howell as a sub-optimized industry, has to date failed to emerge as the lead communications discipline is attributed to a lack of self-confidence, intellectual authority and high-profile and heavyweight business leaders (ibid.).

'PR is fantastically cheap and you only value what you pay for', Howell says. 'To quote Trollope, "Nobody holds a good opinion of a man who has a low opinion of himself." Where are the real stars and household names? And where are the heavyweight champions?' (ibid.).

Mike Detsiny, former Marketing Society head, claims that public relations people have, for the most part, failed to come to the inevitable conclusion that public relations and communications strategy are the same thing and that the public relations industry does not think 'big' enough or charge enough (ibid.).

Management Analysis

Public relations has been a part of Nicholson Kovac's offerings for many years. The agency was founded as an IMC agency and public relations has been a part of the marketing communications mix virtually from the beginning. One aspect that has changed over the years, however, is the understanding of public relations among other agency disciplines and clients.

When I began working at the agency, public relations seemed to be somewhat synonymous with 'press release'. Others, both inside and outside the agency, had a limited understanding of the various facets of public relations and were most familiar with the media relations aspect of public relations.

While it did not happen overnight, the public relations department's stakeholders now have a more complete understanding of the practice of public relations and utilize a variety of public relations services, including internal communications, CEO/executive positioning, trade show planning and implementation, media training, crisis training and management, and social media.

The public relations department has a representative on the executive leadership team and every account team has at least one public relations representative, which has contributed greatly to prominent position of public relations amid the agency's communications components. Every new agency employee also undergoes an extensive orientation, which includes a one-on-one session with a member of the public relations team as well as members of the other disciplines, so that all employees have a good understanding of what each department does and how to best work with each of them.

New Business Acquisition

To start from the beginning, one ongoing activity that every agency must address, no matter what the size or structure, is new business acquisition, or attracting and gaining new clients. New business can be done in many different ways. One way is through the request for proposal (RFP) process. When conducting an agency search or agency review, many companies send out an RFP to agencies they feel may be a good fit, either geographically or based on industry expertise, for their company. Some will send out an RFP to all agencies in their city to see who responds. Others will select just those agencies who have the industry expertise and the right blend of services that they need. Still others will go based on recommendations or word-of-mouth from friends, associations or other contacts in the industry.

When agencies receive an RFP, they must look at a few factors before they decide whether or not they will move forward. Some of these factors include the RFP company's:

- Financial history. How long has it been in business? Does it have a solid capital base? Does it pay its bills on time?
- Corporate culture. Is it a good fit with the agency's culture? Would the two organizations enjoy working together? Does it treat agencies as vendors or partners?
- Previous agency relationships. How has the company treated its previous agencies? Did it have good working relationships? Why did it end its relationship?
- Budget. Can the agency provide good service, do top-notch work and make money under the proposed budget?

Management Implementation

If the agency decides to move forward after weighing all of these factors, it must provide all of the information required in the RFP – company history, scope of services, agency philosophy, list of current and past clients, case studies or examples of past client work, proposed client team, proposed pricing structure, etc. Once the RFP is submitted, the company will let agencies know if it has been selected to move forward in the process.

If an agency is selected to move forward, it is most often invited to visit the RFP company and make a formal presentation, or new business 'pitch'. These presentations can be capabilities presentations, in which the agency provides an overview of its history, culture, scope of services, clients and case studies; or working presentations, in which the RFP company provides the agency with a scenario or its business and communications objectives, then requires the agency to prepare a comprehensive communications plan, including research, proposed strategies and tactics, and creative execution. If agencies are not invited to visit the RFP company in this phase, presentations are often conducted virtually through a web-based platform.

In most cases, whether in person or via the web, these presentations are designed to determine the agency's overall philosophy or way of thinking, and to gauge the 'chemistry' between company representatives and the proposed agency team. If the company likes the way the agency thinks and feels good chemistry with the agency's team, the relationship will most likely move forward and the agency will gain a new client.

When an agency receives an RFP, it is best to first gather together all of the agency's key players to discuss the RFP and to determine what needs to be done to respond to the issuing company. For example, does the RFP focus more heavily on one discipline over the others? If so, then the discipline of focus should most often take the lead in crafting the RFP response. For instance, if the RFP focuses heavily on public relations, then the public relations department should take the lead in gathering information and putting it together according to the RFP guidelines. If the RFP is balanced among various disciplines, then everyone can divide the responsibilities evenly. The same process can be used to prepare the more comprehensive communications plan, if that is what is requested in the RFP.

Another method that agencies use to gain new clients is active prospecting. Many agencies develop lists of target prospects, most often companies or organizations within their established areas of expertise, which are the right size and have complementary company cultures as well as stable finances.

Once the prospect lists are developed, and the prospects are researched and thoroughly evaluated, agency representatives contact the prospect companies to determine whether or not they are in need of agency services, if they may be planning an upcoming agency review or if they'd be willing to set up an introductory meeting so each group can learn more about the other. Other agencies prefer to establish a series of touch points (direct mails, e-mails, etc.) prior to making initial contact with a company.

If a prospective company is interested in speaking with the agency further after the initial contact or series of contacts, it may decide to conduct an agency review or search, or may decide to have the agency conduct a formal pitch presentation.

FIGURE 9.3 Key New Business Stakeholders

Then the agency will go through a process similar to the RFP response process described earlier.

One additional way that agencies gain new business is by growing current client accounts. This can be done by proposing and implementing new projects for an existing client, by adding new services such as digital services or social media to the client's existing services mix, or by beginning relationships with new business units within a client company.

Management Analysis

New business acquisition, vital to the long-term success of any agency, is an ongoing process that has many different facets and many stakeholders. Let us take a look, utilizing an all-stakeholder perspective, at those associated with the RFP process.

The RFP is initiated by the prospective client, but most have done their research that has touched several other stakeholder groups, including existing clients, past clients, media, agency search consultants and industry associations or organizations (see Figure 9.3).

For example, an animal health company seeking a new agency may work with an agency search consultant to facilitate its search. The agency search consultant's role is to utilize its industry knowledge; experience with various agencies, their principals and their work; and understanding of the agency review process to help the animal health company find the best agency for its needs.

Though companies utilize agency search consultants less these days due to economic pressures, they do serve an important role and smart agencies make sure they consider these stakeholders in their new business process.

Marketing communications representatives within the animal health company may also query their peers to find out about agencies they should include in their RFP process. Their peers may be the agency's current or past clients, who have had day-to-day experience in working with the agency so they can attest to whether or not they would be a good fit for the animal health company's needs. For an agency, it is always the ultimate compliment to have a happy current or past client refer business to it.

Many companies seeking new agencies review media coverage of the agencies working within their industry to determine the type of and quality of work for which each agency is known. They also may look for awards that the agency has won and for demonstrations of thought leadership through bylined articles or other editorial mentions. Some even question media representatives for various industry publications to see which agencies are strategic, detail-oriented, easy to work with, etc. As a result, agencies must consistently work on their own self-promotion efforts and ensure that they see media reps as valued partners.

Prospective clients may also look to industry associations or organizations to see what agencies are involved, which principals are active, and to gather other insights into how the various agencies are seen by their peers. Agencies should be involved in industry associations in which their clients and prospective clients are involved; however, the amount of time and money they invest in all activities must correlate to the importance of each stakeholder group in their overall new business acquisition process.

Client Development, Management and Retention

Once a company has signed with an agency, it must work together to develop a mutually beneficial working relationship. Some agencies conduct an orientation for clients to educate them on how the agency works and the services available, as well as to determine guidelines for moving forward. These guidelines can include:

- preferred account staffing (specific team members, disciplines represented, etc.);
- preferred methods of communication (phone, e-mail, teleconference, web meetings, etc.);
- regularity of communications (daily, weekly, monthly, as needed, etc.);
- status and results reporting methods;

- travel needs and how they will be handled;
- format and schedule of meetings;
- education about company, industry and/or products for agency representatives;
- budgeting and invoicing procedures;
- monthly billing procedures;
- file sharing methods.

Agencies should also develop a method of surveying clients about their level of service on a regular basis. Many send out annual or biannual surveys to explore areas of strength and improvement. Areas of investigation may include: strengths and weaknesses of team members; quality of plans, strategies, tactics, ongoing ideas and day-to-day work; timeliness; responsiveness; and communications.

Regular surveys ensure that agencies learn about any agency–client relationship issues before the relationship suffers. Any weaknesses that are identified can be remedied and strengths can be emphasized. For example, if a client likes working with a specific team member over another, modifications can be made in their day-to-day account team. Or, if they would prefer monthly, rather than quarterly, results reports, then this quick fix can be made as well.

Management Implementation

As stated earlier in this chapter, Nicholson Kovac utilizes its own proven, proprietary set of models to successfully manage client accounts and campaigns. The first is the strategic planning process, which combines left-brain logic with right-brain insights and creativity to identify innovative and integrated solutions to each of our client's unique marketing challenges.

A more expanded version of the traditional, four-step public relations planning model, the following seven steps form the marketing communication planning process at Nicholson Kovac:

1. Information gathering.
2. Intelligence analysis.
3. Issues identification.
4. Innovation/objectives.
5. Strategy development.
6. Tactics/execution.
7. Quality check/evaluation.

Though it may appear complicated and time-consuming, every Nicholson Kovac employee is trained according to the process so it is simply the way that everyone thinks. Though we recommend taking the time to thoroughly complete each step, the process can be simplified to meet tight time constraints if needed.

Once a plan is complete and approved by a client, the implementation phase begins. To eliminate surprises on both the agency and client side, Nicholson Kovac

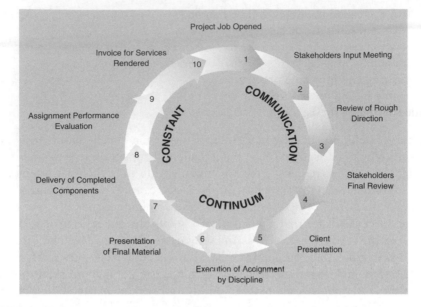

FIGURE 9.4 The Assignment Process Model

developed the assignment process model (Figure 9.4), which detailed each step of a project.

1. **Assignment:** The job is opened, the account leaders and select stakeholders from other disciplines (as needed) review the assignment with the client and all agree on a directional budget.

2. **Pre-planning/strategic planning meeting:** The leader provides and discusses objective(s), preliminary strategies, positioning, initial budgets, initial timelines and creative blueprint with the team. A preliminary budget is allocated by discipline; all agree upon time estimates and specific responsibilities; the initial traffic and production schedule are determined; and team leader and stakeholders conduct a follow-up call with the client.

3. **Review of tactical direction:** Directional roughs, concepts or ideas are approved for final development; specific jobs are assigned; budgets, timelines and traffic schedules are reviewed and finalized; estimates are drafted for client approval.

4. **Stakeholders' final review:** The team finalizes the presentation layout, research, media, public relations, etc., including rationale, impact on estimates and timelines.

5. **Client presentation:** The team presents to the client and client provides approval of the plan/project, estimates and timeline.

6. **Execution of assignments by discipline:** The team completes its assigned tactics and prepares for the final client presentation, which may be

done in a formal presentation meeting or call, or sent via e-mail for client review.

7. **Presentation of final material:** The client reviews and provides final approval of plan or campaign elements. The agency makes final revisions, if necessary.

8. **Delivery of completed assignments:** Various campaign elements are final and ready for delivery. For example: The PR team distributes a news release to targeted media contacts, conducts follow-up calls or e-mails, and tracks placements to determine effectiveness.

9. **Assignment performance evaluation:** Immediately after a job is complete, the team meets to determine whether or not the objectives were met. This includes adherence to project estimates and level of client satisfaction. The team will also determine if a corrective plan of action is needed.

10. **Invoice for services rendered:** The invoice is prepared and delivered to the client.

Because budgeting and estimating correctly and evaluating campaigns and projects are such vital exercises in any marketing communications agency, whether business-to-business, business-to-consumer or both, we will explore those processes in greater detail.

Budgeting, Estimating and Forecasting

According to Croft (1994), the three most common and serious budgeting problems reported by agency principals include under-budgeting, faulty time estimates and incomplete estimates.

In an effort to make clients happy and avoid losing clients or prospects, some agencies will under-budget, or provide estimates lower than what the project will actually cost the agency in terms of time, out-of-pocket costs, or both. While it is a difficult line to walk and sometimes tough to predict, agency managers must work closely with their clients so they can provide estimates within a range that the client is comfortable with, and that their budgets will allow, while also providing the agency with a reasonable profit margin. Estimates should spell out exactly what the client will be getting for its money, nothing more and nothing less.

Another difficult task for many agency managers is properly estimating the amount of time required to complete a project or program. By inaccurately estimating a project, either too high or too low, the agency will either have to write off the overage and take a loss or ask the client for more money. Neither is a desirable outcome.

Write-offs, or not charging clients for time invested on their behalf, can put an agency in a dangerous position. If write-offs become a drain of agency resources, managers must ensure that clients are not continually over-serviced by either providing employees with a specific number of hours to complete their project, or by encouraging employees to have the judgment and confidence to stop work before they invest too much time in a project (Croft, 1994).

To avoid undesirable write-offs or surprising the client with a request for more money, managers must refer back to similar projects to determine how much time and out-of-pocket expenses will be needed to successfully complete the job. If no similar project has been done, managers must work with each team member to determine how much time will be needed for each step throughout the project's development, and also get rough estimates for any out-of-pocket charges that may be needed.

If estimates do not include out-of-pocket costs, such as travel, postage or shipping, and printing, then the agency again runs the risk of getting into a situation where it has to write off the overage or ask the client for more money. If an agency has formal estimating processes, it can eliminate many of these issues.

Evaluation

Every strategic public relations or marketing communications plan should include monitoring and tracking systems to measure overall performance against the campaign or project's objectives. Depending on the client's needs, budget and access to information, measurement can include a variety of different measurement methods, including:

- traditional pre- and post-testing to determine awareness or attitudes;
- share of voice and share of discussion analysis;
- media coverage and return-on-investment reports, including key message penetration, slant and prominence – may also include media and publicity value;
- social media monitoring reports, including number of social media fans/followers and number of quality engagements;
- change in target audience behavior(s);
- sales dollars by customer/division/region;
- sales leads and conversions;
- web analytics;
- impressions;
- e-mail click-through rates;
- perception studies;
- sales insights.

Although it is impractical to utilize each one of these types of measurement for every campaign or project, the agency and client must work together to determine what information is available and the measurement method most appropriate for evaluating the achievement of campaign objectives. The agency and client must also determine appropriate timing for each measurement method. Some types of measurement, like media and social media monitoring, sales leads and web analytics, may be conducted on an ongoing basis and the campaign tactics may be revised or refined based on the findings. Others, like pre- and post-testing for awareness and attitudes, of course, must be conducted at the beginning and end of a campaign to truly determine effectiveness.

In an agency, the client satisfaction is probably the most important measure, as it is one of the key factors in client retention. As mentioned earlier in the chapter, client satisfaction may be measured informally through ongoing client communications or formally through client satisfaction surveys.

Staff Retention and Development

Because investing in existing staff members is far less expensive and much more efficient than replacing them, staff development and retention is one of the major areas to which agency leaders must dedicate resources, time and attention. According to studies by the US Department of Labor and Merck, replacing a staff member is estimated to cost from one-third to one and a half years of a departing staffer's annual salary (Jacobs, 2007). In addition to these hard costs, staff departures can also impact an agency's performance due to knowledge loss, the stress of managing a departed staffer's responsibilities while searching for his/her replacement, and training the replacement. Staff departures also can impact the agency or team dynamic and morale, and can push others to think about career changes of their own. Also, just as with unexpected costs, staff departures can lead to client dissatisfaction.

According to Ken Jacobs (2007), principal of Jacobs Communications Consulting, LLC, which helps public relations agencies grow their business and enhance staff performance and retention through training, a focus on staff development and retention allows agencies to minimize recruiter fees, better manage salaries and benefits, and have more successful teams and satisfied clients, as well as the ability to attract new talent. He says successful retention is driven by agency leaders who listen, communicate regularly, welcome staff involvement, provide competitive compensation, offer a clear vision, provide training and nurture a fun workplace.

Staff development is a crucial element to an agency's success and varies depending on the agency's structure and culture, leadership styles, management styles and staff members. 'Only organizations that think differently about their talent, including how they attract people and create personal and meaningful experiences for them once they start work, have the potential to succeed long term' (Joudene, 2007: 1).

According to Joudene, the organizations that attract the best talent will be those that: continually reinvent themselves against ever-changing business conditions; innovate their employee programs and practices; and create an organizational experience people want to be a part of. Because people are the most important resource in public relations, she says, companies must engage both heads and hearts to achieve any sort of sustainable success.

She suggests that agencies consider and implement community-based practices and programs like wellness activities and resources, flexible work arrangements, sustainable environments and philanthropic efforts, as well as promote each employee's sense of social innovation and responsibility. Managers also must work with each employee to determine what motivates that individual and what he/she needs to become and stay engaged with the agency.

'Sharing the agency's vision and inviting employees to be involved in creating that vision is equally critical,' Joudene said. 'Whether continued employee engagement means working on a new team, feeling a sense of partnership with a manager or being able to balance personal choices alongside professional aspirations, organizations must work to create a meaningful experience – for every employee in every geography' (Joudene, 2007: 1).

Because public relations is continually evolving, professional development is also vital to any agency's business. Many agencies support employee involvement in the Public Relations Society of America or the International Association of Business Communicators, because they offer many avenues for professional and leadership development through monthly educational sessions, daily e-newsletters, monthly publications, networking activities and more.

Agencies also support their employees' learning by providing access to webinars and teleseminars on relevant topics, and by encouraging learning groups to identify, develop or share best practices in various areas of the industry; for example, a lunchtime or brown bag session on best practices in public relations measurement, trade show management or building a Facebook page.

When it comes to staff retention and development, Joudene suggests focusing on creating and maintaining an agency culture to attract, engage and retain top talent. By maintaining this focus, agencies can achieve their vision and ensure their long-term profitability.

Management Analysis

One of the most important aspects of retaining key staff members is to consistently manage their expectations from the very beginning. At Nicholson Kovac, one way we manage our team members' expectations is through a thorough agency orientation. During this orientation, we review the agency's culture and processes, which includes a discussion about the agency's vision and mission. For public relations team members, we also discuss the team's mission and our role within the agency. Depending on which account team we are a part of, we also review how the account team functions, how public relations works as a part of the team, how the team members work together, and expectations for each individual team member as a part of the overall team.

As Mills (2007: 1) says: 'No matter where you find yourself in an organization, you can contribute to the vision and to the success of the collective enterprise.' We operate under this same belief at Nicholson Kovac and utilize our annual career path exercise as just one means to demonstrate this and manage our team members' expectations. The career path, completed for each person within the agency, clearly states each person's long- and short-term goals, his/her contributions to the overall agency goals and specific action steps for achieving these goals. Both the manager and employee complete the career path, which is designed to be a working document that is discussed by both parties and refined throughout the year.

Many managers throughout the agency also believe in serving as an example for the more junior team members and serve as role models for everything from following the agency's strategic planning process and other processes, and functioning as a truly integrated team to working with other agency disciplines and team members, and interacting with clients.

Because an agency is a highly collaborative atmosphere, we encourage everyone to speak up, ask questions and share ideas – no matter their discipline or level. We also believe in listening and an open-door policy, and encourage our team members to come to us with issues or concerns.

Additionally, as managers, we must carefully observe and listen to each employee to determine what motivates him/her and his/her preferred management and communications styles, then make any needed adjustments to our management activities.

Time Management

In my experience on both the corporate and agency side, and according to many public relations agency managers whom I have interviewed, the most difficult challenge we all face is time management. This includes both managing a staff or team's time so you can avoid situations where you are over-servicing clients and not getting paid for all of the time you dedicate to them, and successfully balancing all areas of responsibility, including new business, staff development and retention, and existing client work. It also means finding time to get all of your work done while maintaining an appropriate work–life balance.

One way that many agencies manage time is through the ever-debated time sheets. Killeen and Yellen (2007) recommend reviewing time sheets weekly to determine if you and your team are adhering to approved client budgets. There are many software programs designed to manage time and projects for agencies of all sizes. Team members must know how many hours they are assigned for each project so they can manage their time accordingly. If they need more or less time, they can let you know and the project budget can be adjusted in the beginning.

In a billable hours model, determining an industry average is difficult to pinpoint. Some strive for an average of 80% billability across the agency. For various positions, some use the following as a general rule of thumb: junior staffers, 90–95% billable; mid-level staffers, 70–75% billable; principal or business development persons, 50% billable. Other agencies opt for a per-project fee, in which they set a fee that both the client and agency agree upon, then work until the project is complete.

No matter what billing structure an agency uses, one of the most difficult challenges its managers face is how to get everything done while still maintaining a balanced life. In nearly every agency, many see their work as their life. Marriages, families and home lives are sacrificed for the sake of a successful career. This mentality has changed slightly over the years as the generations in the workplace have shifted and technology has enabled telecommuting or working remotely.

Schofield (2007) recommends working when you are most productive rather than just typical business hours:

> I adopted the attitude that I would do whatever it took to grow and get promoted in my job. That meant that I did not 'do all I could' until 5:30. It meant that I worked until 7:00 p.m., 8:00 p.m. or later sometimes. But since I am not much of a night person, I run out of gas after about 7:00 p.m. So I came into the office much earlier that other people, say 6:30 or 7 a.m.

He also observed that senior managers manage their work more efficiently and suggests working hard to teach and coach subordinates to stand in when you are not available. Overall, the key to a successful work–life balance is to think outside of the 9-to-5 work day and to be flexible.

THE RELEVANCE OF C-MACIE TO BUSINESS-TO-BUSINESS COMMUNICATION PRACTICE

Business-to-business public relations – or business-to-business communications for that matter – is often overlooked and underestimated when compared to its consumer-focused brethren. Many equate business-to-business public relations as not requiring the same skill sets or sophistication as business-to-consumer public relations, but I have found the opposite to be true. Many of my clients have had a business-to-business focus, but we must remember that business-to-business clients' customers are actually consumers themselves.

From a management perspective, the activities of business-to-business and business-to-consumer public relations managers are similar, and the most important thing is the successful mastery and balance of new business acquisition; client development, management and retention; ongoing financial management; staff development and retention; and the day-to-day campaign and project management. Those individuals who can manage and balance these aspects of agency life will be successful in their careers.

The Nicholson Kovac model clearly illustrates the critical role analysis, the first step of the C-MACIE model, plays; indeed, the 'fit' between clients and the agency is entirely based on analysis, beginning with the assessment of whether a client or potential client is a good match with the agency's services and products, evident in the continuing monitoring during the project's duration, and concluding with evaluation, another type of analysis. This is formally demonstrated in the agency's RFP proposal process, where the analysis clearly underpins the thinking and rationale that precedes whether an RFP is best for the agency and the client.

A second interesting analysis feature of the Nicholson Kovac model is its use of informal and formal analysis as expressed in the agency's concern that its method of doing business 'fits' with the clientele it develops relationship with. The indication here is that good business depends on more than just the bottom line; in fact, the bottom line is directly related to the intangible factor of a good rapport and understanding between agency and client.

The Nicholson Kovac model has also developed its choice element, the second part of the C-MACIE model. Developing the 'mutually beneficial relationship' that is a standard phrase in the public relations literature is defined in the list of the agency's guidelines for working with clients, as well as outlining the best strategy and tactics to use to achieve the client's goals, whether that is positioning, branding, advertising, media, public relations, promotion, or marketing strategies and tactics. The attention given to the content of the strategic and tactical plan, along with the expectations of how it will be delivered, creates a solid understanding that can not only be monitored, but also be carefully adjusted if needed, because the choices have been clearly laid out and agreed upon. As noted before, this minimizes 'surprises' in budgets and outcomes.

C-MACIE's implementation component, the most visible part of any project, demonstrates the managerial strength of the agency's model. Leaders from the integrated areas, determined by the goals and objectives outlined in the strategy, are assigned to oversee the implementation and have the expertise, knowledge, and power to make decisions, lead teams, assign tactical elements, and assign the budget numbers to each of the implementation steps and materials. A crucial element of Nicholson Kovac's implementation step is that managers are held responsible for correct budgeting processes, working closely with clients to make sure that estimates are in line with what the actual final figure is calculated to be. Such fiscal responsibility for creative work is key to building and maintaining not only individual client relationships, but the agency's industry-wide reputation. Another key factor that managers are responsible for is time management, overseeing that team members are educated about how their time contributes to the project. As previously mentioned, poor estimates on time will come back to roost at the team managers' doors.

And the final C-MACIE step, evaluation, is also clearly spelled out in the Nicholson Kovac model, which has defined an applicable mix of quantitative and qualitative measures, elements of which can be selected as appropriate to each individual client or project. And, yet again, the partnership between the agency and the client provides clear expectations of how, when, and by whom the project will be evaluated. It is also important to note that client satisfaction is considered a critical part of the evaluation; this has a direct impact on the ongoing relationship of the client to the agency, and also acknowledges that how the client feels about the outcomes of the work that the agency did for it does matter. One of the best reputation management assets is the good name that Nicholson Kovac has earned in its business-to-business work.

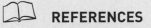

REFERENCES

Bevan, S. (1996) The view from adland. *PR Week*, *9*, 14.
Croft, A.C. (1994) Management by the numbers. *Public Relations Quarterly*, *1*, 20.
Duncan, T., & Everett, S. (1993) Client perceptions of integrated marketing communication. *Journal of Advertising Research*, *33*, 30.

(Continued)

(Continued)

Jacobs, K. (2007) The rewards of retention: Retaining your best and your brightest. *Public Relations Tactics*, *8*, 6.

Jones, H. (2003) PR – at close quarters – how do advertising agencies and PR agencies work together? *Campaign*, *2*, 25.

Joudene, D. (2007) Future forward: Reinventing the way we attract, engage and retain top talent across generations and geographies. *Public Relations Tactics*, *8*, 1.

Killeen, J., & Yellen, I. (2007) Growing your PR practice to increase profitability and compensation during challenging times. *Public Relations Tactics*, *8*, 10.

Mills, D. (2007) Moving up: Five leadership skills to master. *Public Relations Tactics*, *4*, 1.

Nicholas, K. & Ray, A. (2001) Integrated marketing – the poor relation? Can PR take the lead over advertising? *PR Week*, *9*, 15.

Schofield, M. (2007) *The Golden Football: Replacing Account Service with Account Leadership*. http://www.lulu.com.

Schultz, D.E. (1993) Why ad agencies are having so much trouble with IMC. *Marketing News*, 27, 12.

Financial Public Relations

10

Barbara DeSanto and David Bradin

Key Themes

- The traditional role and functions of financial public relations communicators
- The convergence of the roles and functions of financial public relations, analyst relations, and investor relations
- The importance of financial public relations in complicated regulatory, legal, and ethical environments
- The newly complex role of financial public relations in today's tumultuous environment
- Application of C-MACIE to financial public relations

INTRODUCTION

This chapter might perhaps be compared to Dickens's classic *Tale of Two Cities* in that the financial environments have recently displayed both the best of times and the worst of times. The drastic financial upheavals that have been headline news around the world for the past several years have resulted in halogen-light scrutiny on all facets of the financial industry, including banks, insurance companies, pension funds, and corporations. This chapter, therefore, will address two major themes: the responsibilities and activities of financial public relations practitioners; and the opportunities financial public relations practitioners have to contribute their expertise and counsel during these turbulent economic times.

TABLE 10.1　Legislation Governing Financial Markets in the USA and UK

United States	United Kingdom
The Securities Act of 1933	The Criminal Justice Act of 1993
The Securities Exchange Act of 1934	The Companies Act of 1985
Trust Indenture Act of 1940	The Stock Exchange's Listing Rules (Yellow Book)
Investment Advisers Act of 1940	The Take-over Code (Blue Book)
Sarbanes-Oxley Act of 2002 (SOX)	The Stock Exchange's 'Price Sensitivity Guide'
Regulation Fair Disclosure Act (FD)	

FINANCIAL PUBLIC RELATIONS PRACTITIONER WORK

Financial public relations is arguably the most complex and highly regulated environment in which practitioners work. Because of the economic, monetary, financial, and social consequences of decisions made in the financial industry, the industry is highly regulated in most countries around the world. This specialist area of public relations practice concerns itself with managing communication among corporations, financial institutions, investors/shareholders, analysts, financial media, and other stakeholders who have vested interests in the functions of financial markets. Because of the potential sensitivity of markets to the release of information, financial public relations must operate within a framework of laws and regulations governing the public disclosure of company information, particularly any information that is 'price sensitive'.

The overall responsibility for implementing and overseeing financial markets in the United States is the Securities and Exchange Commission (SEC), and in the United Kingdom the Financial Services Authority (FSA). The relevant legislation for each country is listed in Table 10.1.

Both the SEC and the FSA are concerned with:

- Market confidence – maintaining confidence in the financial system.
- Public awareness – promoting public understanding of the financial system.
- Consumer protection – securing the appropriate degree of protection for consumers.
- Reduction of financial crime – as defined by current laws in each country.

While these are common areas of concern, the exact legal requirements and remedies do vary by country. It is imperative that financial public relations practitioners understand the legal requirements under which they operate. However, with the advent of instantaneous global communication and multinational financial operating environments, practitioners must also understand all of the different national financial systems their operations are involved in.

TABLE 10.2 Key Events in the Financial Calendar in the USA and UK

United States	United Kingdom
10-Q Quarterly Report – filed within 45 days of the closing of the quarter	Interim/Half Year Results – filed at the end of each six month period
10-K Annual Report – filed within 90 days of a company's closing fiscal year	The Annual Report and Accounts
Scheduling and conducting the Annual Meeting	Scheduling and conducting the Annual General Meeting
8-K Material Event filings – filed whenever a material event affecting stock prices occurs	Extraordinary General Meeting if special circumstances arise

The Financial Calendar

All financial industry work is driven by the financial calendar, the legally required structure that dictates reporting data and information publically traded companies must provide their regulatory entities. Examples of required documents included on financial calendars include periodic information disclosures at certain times of the fiscal year for public inspection (Table 10.2).

Key Target Audiences for Financial Public Relations

In the USA, Wall Street is the main trade stakeholder group; in the UK London is the financial capital and is called the City. Stockbrokers, stock analysts, merchant bankers, investment advisors and other financial intermediaries and/or market influences comprise this group that Wall Street and the City are concerned with.

Investors and potential investors make up the second key group. These are the organizations and individuals who have invested money into the markets or who could elect to invest capital. These investors are critical because they provide the capital/funds to power the system. Institutions including insurance companies, pension plans, investment trusts, other companies, and private individual investors comprise this group. Potential investors are also important because companies and the market are keen to identify new investment sources.

The financial media are another key target audience. Today's media landscape has certainly expanded beyond the traditional journalists and editors at newspapers, broadcast, and specialized financial press outlets. The advent and widespread use of technology has had an impressive impact on financial media, with blogs, company webpages, and the new US regulations that allow companies to post their required filings simultaneously on their websites as they submit their reports to the SEC all providing more information directly to all stakeholder groups. The USA has cable networks devoted solely to financial news and interpretations, often laced with political opinions and projections of the consequences of different legislation and regulation, thus bypassing more traditional financial sources. Each of these cable channels

also maintains websites, Facebook pages, and Twitter accounts that provide a running commentary, albeit unscientific, of the mood and opinions of anyone with
access to sending a comment.

Employees are an often rather invisible stakeholder group, yet are key to developing and maintaining relationships with customers and investors. In many organizations, employee communication is sorely lacking on business matters and decisions,
and employees often find themselves learning information from media, customers,
or other outside sources, in addition to having to explain these decisions to their
customers. In the financial industry, investors and potential investors rely on financial advisors to help them make decisions about financial planning. The relationship
between financial employees and investors and potential investors is important,
because both parties know that how money and investments are managed is the basis
for decisions, with major consequences if not managed carefully.

Distributors, competitors, and others interested in specific companies comprise
yet another major target audience. Whether cooperating entities that do business
with a financial company or competitors seeking the same investment opportunities,
these groups are affected by each other.

Financial Public Relations Tasks and Duties

Communication among the different stakeholder groups takes two forms: required
communication directed by regulations, and non-required communication determined
by each company as part of its relationship-building. Financial public relations communicators have traditionally been responsible for the following types of communication:

- Preparation of relevant news releases, especially working with the CEO,
  CFO, and legal team on the content, wording and emphasis of the release.
- Distribution of required information to key investors (institutions, brokers,
  and banks) as well as financial media, after or at the same time as filing in
  accordance with appropriate regulations, and to all stakeholders.
- Arranging interviews with and pitching stories to key financial journalists
  in mainstream and trade press media.
- Monitoring and briefing company directors on issues likely to be raised by
  key financial publics prior to interviews.
- In special circumstances, arranging meetings with stockbrokers and analysts
  to explain quarterly, half-term, and annual report results in more detail.

An unpublished content analysis of 25 recent financial public relations job postings
on the PRSA website[1] yielded the following duties for a financial public relations
practitioner:

- Media duties
  - Develop press plans
  - Develop long-term relationships with key financial media

- Translate quantitative data to qualitative information
- Develop issue and trend stories

- Counseling and planning

  - Develop communication plans for strategic stakeholder groups
  - Develop communication strategies and tactics for stakeholder groups
  - Monitor competitors

- Financial communication products

  - Develop presentations and handouts for internal and external events
  - Prepare sales, earnings, and other relevant board-related materials
  - Research investor and media requests
  - Write and/or contribute to: press releases, Q&As, articles, comments & statements, press kits, website content, photo library, annual report, face-to-face meetings

- Other

  - Facilitate and coordinate communication and materials with finance, legal, and accounting functions;
  - Identify and manage corporate social responsibility (CSR) programs
  - Track and analyze shareholder/stakeholder bases
  - Organize formal and informal meetings, including annual and quarterly meetings
  - Create and oversee crisis management programs, especially in the area of media relations.

The above list of duties mirrors Cutlip, Center, and Broom's (1985) list of responsibilities that financial public relations practitioner share with other departments in a publically traded company: (1) monitoring attitudes of key stakeholders ranging from the industry to financial analysts; (2) counseling Executive-level suite executives about keeping communication strategy engaged with company goals; (3) preparing financial literature; (4) arranging and preparing informational materials for financial meetings; and (5) managing financial media inquiries. In financial communication not only do practitioners need to have accurate knowledge of the industry and how to communicate it, they must also be partners and team players, working in concert with the legal and financial officers of the company.

THE DECADE OF THE 2000S AND THE NEW WORLD OF FINANCIAL COMMUNICATION

The world of finance and numbers has never been easy to comprehend. Arguably, it can be said that the majority of people understand their daily routine of paying bills and checking their bank balances, but lack the education and knowledge to make sense of high-level Wall Street or City finance. However, this laissez-faire attitude changed dramatically when the world, and the USA in particular, was hit with not only the corporate but also personal effects of the financial meltdown that developed throughout the 2000s – double-digit losses in people's retirement funds, falling values in their home values, massive job layoffs at worst and stagnant salary increases at best. The question around many of the fabled office watercoolers was: 'How much have you lost?' Several years later, the effects of the meltdown and its subsequent volatile environment are top-of-mind, with people increasingly frustrated, depressed, and, most of all, afraid for their futures. This chapter section will outline the rapidly changing financial environment and the opportunity of financial public relations to rebuild credibility and trust.

The decade of the 2000s began with individual investor optimism and a booming American economy. The environment seemed to burst with relatively easy money, especially in the home sector. Hay (2010: 382) describes this phenomenon of home as an 'investment opportunity' as a manifestation of the 'moral economy', a new way of determining the values used to make financial decisions. Several isolated parts of the American governmental system were nervous about the flush money times, and prior to the American financial meltdown in the late 2000s, enacted several regulations, including the SEC's Regulation Fair Disclosure with the objective of 'equalizing individual and investor access to information' (Clark, 2002: 36), and the 2002 Sarbanes-Oxley Act in response to the Enron and WorldCom financial scandals.[2] In hindsight, While Enron and WorldCom generated their share of media attention, the impact on individual Americans was not felt, because most were not affected by what was perceived as individual 'bad-apple' individuals ruining their own corporations. The systemic infection of the financial system was not even suspected. The shock and direct impact on the entire American population came in September 2008, after the US financial markets experienced a historic technical correction in 2007 that resulted in what has become known as the worst financial crisis since the 1930s. What began as a technical correction in the US credit markets (namely, residential and commercial mortgage-backed securities, and corporate debt) quickly became a fundamental economic recession. The reality of the situation became front-page news in 2008 with the collapse of two of Wall Street's legacy firms, Bear Stearns and Lehman Brothers, along with the failure or near-failure of hundreds of commercial and consumer banks, such as Wachovia, Citi, and Washington Mutual. NAB Research analyst Nancy Bush pointed out that 'America's five biggest banks … now control 46 percent of all deposits, up from 12 percent in the early '90s. Big banks don't have a lot of friends right now' (Lowenstein, 2010: 36).

This front-page news quickly trickled down to millions of individual Americans who saw their own financial worlds crash and burn. Unemployment hit a 26-year high in October 2009 and continued to hover around 10% for all of 2010. The US gross domestic product growth entered negative territory for the first time in 15 years, according to the US Department of Commerce Bureau of Economic Analysis,[3] and related industries such as housing and automotive operated under great pressure just to stay afloat. More than 400 million US mortgages are seriously delinquent (Lowenstein, 2010). As the news developed in the US financial markets and migrated throughout the global economy, it became clear this was a life-changing event.

For the first time, US citizens quickly learned a 'new' financial language with terms including 'too big to fail,' 'bailout', and 'stimulus'. The new everyday vernacular, which most people had no understanding of at all, led to nationwide feelings of betrayal, no confidence, and hopelessness. Debates and decisions made at the federal level in Washington, DC, took on an urgent new importance, impacting not only the economic sector, but playing a huge role in subsequent local, state, and national elections, and in the adjusted social life of millions of Americans. Without a doubt, the financial industry and the US government had their citizens' attention. People continue to ask how this happened and who is responsible.

The firestorm had all the elements to keep it raging long-term, beyond the traditional lifespan of most crises. A new instantaneous mass and personal media world has grown that includes cable 'news' talkshows with partisan pundits shouting half-truths and buzzwords reducing complex issues to simple phrases; the dearth of competent and educated financial press; vocal political activist groups pressuring legislators to 'do something' or they will vote them out; and a traditional two-party majority political system with legislators trying to save their political funding bases, most of which came from PACS, entities created by interest groups to collect money to contribute to election campaigns and candidates, and lobbying groups, while figuring out how to regulate their political piggybanks – a mixture that provides plenty of fuel for this ongoing bonfire.

Impact on the Financial Industry

In general, to those outside the world of finance, the US financial industry continues to seem reluctant to change its ways of doing business. Media coverage continues to paint a dismal picture of continued high unemployment, stagnant wages, home foreclosures gone awry, disappearing pensions, and the potential insolvency of social security. Banks and financial institutions' testimony before a Congress demanding accountability only adds to the growing distrust of any financial entity. Even the US government stimulus funds seem to have been nothing more than the US government rescuing institutions too big to fail, which in turn are supposed to help ordinary Americans borrow money, restructure their mortgages and stay in their homes, and/ or find jobs created by stimulus money. The result has been an immense crisis of confidence that shows little signs of disappearing any time soon.

Financial entities realize that the sense of betrayal and hopelessness was in large part created and continues to exist because of little or poor communication between them and the myriad of groups upon which they depend for survival, including financial, business, and general mass media, stockholders, analysts, legislators and regulators, and potential corporate and individual investors. The financial industry not only survived but thrived for decades under a cloak of incomprehensible language and jargon, complex transactions, and little oversight in an environment of benign ignorance by most investors as long as they were 'making money'. Allon

(2010: 367) cites former US Treasury Secretary Henry Paulson's statement that 'the general terms in which the financial crisis has been understood [are]: excess, speculation, fraud ... conditions which are translated into questions of individual pathology and private morality'.

One of the greatest impact factors is today's technology – no longer is information filtered through the specialized financial mass media; individuals today are realizing they have access to the same information and data that corporations provide through the required SEC EDGAR (U.S. Security and Exchange Commission Mandatory Electronic Data Gathering, Analysis and Retrieval system) filing format, and the new management, discussion, and analysis (MD&A) annual report sections required to be written in understandable English as well as posted to their corporate websites. One result of this legislated transparency is that more individuals realize they have the right to this information, and their experiences with their individual finances and worry about the future give them the incentive to understand it.

Another key factor in the demand for financial transparency has been the US government's Troubled Asset Relief Program (TARP), begun by President George W. Bush and continued by President Barack Obama, under which the government is buying assets and equity to stabilize financial institutions, and stimulus fund economic programs, which inject money into various government and business efforts to put people back to work, which in turn, should see consumers spend more money to boost economic recovery. Two beliefs about this funding are widespread among US taxpayers: (1) that without it a full-blown depression would have occurred; and (2) they provided the money for it.[4] As such, they have great interest in what the bailed-out entities, especially banks and financial institutions, are doing with the money. Little job creation, continuing high unemployment rates, lost pensions, inability to borrow money, lost home values are all placed at the feet of primarily financial institutions. With bailouts and unceasing network mass media coverage, financial cable channels dedicated to pursuing the 'truth' and apportioning blame, and the rise of radio and television financial evangelists for rank-and-file Americans such as Suze Orman, Dave Ramsey, and Clark Howard, all financial entities found themselves painted as 'bad guys', in a mismanaged and selfish industry, regardless of their individual behavior. American financial institutions have suffered. 'Financial firms have been under extreme pressure to redeem themselves with consumers. For the first time in years, they're ranked worse in the industry, behind oil and gas companies', said associate Prophet brand consultant Aneysha Pearce.[5] AIG's widely reported corporate retreat just after it accepted stimulus money and the seven-figure Wall Street bonuses only added to the perceptions that financial people continue to get rich at the expense of the American taxpayer.[6]

A review of the financial and public relations trade press reveals that professionals and academics were sounding the alarm about the missing or diminished role of communication in the financial industry.

Almost a decade ago, Byrun (2002: 44) wrote: 'CEOs need a new strategy. They need to use professional communicators who are trained to perform these duties, who can bring clarity to the most complex financial discussions, and who can translate these to understandable terms for media and shareholders. They need expert communicators who know the value of truth as it plays out beyond corporate walls'.

Silver (2005) outlined three new ways corporations and financial entities could increase their transparency with investors and other stakeholders:

1. In 2003, a circuit court ruling established attorney–client privilege for public relations professionals involved in litigation and under investigation; in essence, giving communication professionals protection in being part of the Executive-suite decision-making (p. 16).
2. In 2004, the SEC attempted to open up communication between investors and companies by allowing companies to use their websites to update prospectuses, conduct media interviews, and provide new stock offering information (pp. 14–15).
3. The term 'full transparency' became associated with 'honesty and accuracy – because it is no longer simply a question of corporate ethics but of serious violations of the law, with potential punitive consequences' (p. 16).

Silver's (2005: 16) conclusion was that 'the company's story and the financial details of that story must be presented to investors, media, and analysts ... with a coordinated strategy. This requires full integration of public relations, investor relations, corporate attorneys, financial officers, and management in a team enterprise'.

Additionally, Silver (2005: 14) warned that 'those that continue to utilize the outdated approach of communicating one message to analysts and Wall Street while communicating another message to the media will suffer in terms of reputations and valuations'.

American financial institutions have suffered. 'Financial firms have been under extreme pressure to redeem themselves with consumers. Although JP Morgan and Chase CEO Jamie Dimon, the high-profile banker trying to set an example of good practice in the financial industry, is concerned about his reputation. 'As more mortgage blunders come to light and anti-Wall Street sentiment grows, even his reputation is at risk of a downgrade' (Lowenstein, 2010: 34).

Goldman Sachs put its concerns about damage to its reputation in its February 26, 2009, 10K B Wall Street filing, calling 'adverse publicity a risk ... it can have a negative impact on our reputation and on the morale and performance of our employees, which could adversely affect our businesses and results of operations'.[5]

Savage (2005: 11) described the importance of financial communicators understanding and implementing new types of financial reporting tools, specifically learning Extensible Business Reporting Language (XBRL). 'This is one of the new tools to "help corporate financial reporting become ... better, faster, cheaper" by streamlining data entry of financial information and sharing it across formats, thus increasing transparency'.

THE CHANGING ROLE OF FINANCIAL COMMUNICATION AND QUALIFIED COMMUNICATORS

Prior to the 2008 crisis, three types of financial communication and communicators were staples of financial institutions: analysts, investor relations professionals, and financial public relations professionals.

Analysts work for firms and provide external third-party specialized information and informed assessment of financial conditions for different companies and industry segments. McCormack (2003: 33) pointed out that 'securing third-party analyst references in media outreach will continue paying significant dividends ... with thinning ranks of reporters struggling to cover more territory in less time, industry analysts ... have become even more desired and reliable sources of credible information'. In fact, McCormack (2003: 34) said, the 'fastest way to determine what's hot and what's not, [is] talk to experienced analysts ...Their professional reputation centers on maintaining credible, educated positions formed on regular access to the most active market players. Most major business and trade publications continue to use research firms and experts to validate and substantiate their coverage.'

Investor relations professionals focus on financial information rather than non-financial information (i.e., numbers), and Laskin (2008) described investor relations as traditionally housed in finance or treasury departments, reporting to a CFO rather than a CEO, and considering information about top management as limited in value. In essence, investor relations professionals are internal communicators, with little contact or interest beyond top management decisions. Typical education background was finance or business.

Traditional corporate communicators are often separate from and defer to investor relations professionals on finance questions. Corporate communicators often focus on external public perceptions and issues, which until recently have not been concerned with financial performance beyond the daily stock market closing-bell numbers. Their understanding of, and often interest in, financial matters was limited. Typical backgrounds for corporate communicators include journalism, public relations, and experience in operations in an industry segment.

The 2007–8 financial crisis spectacularly illustrated the need for (1) transparent communication and (2) integrated communication. In an ongoing slow economic recovery, both transparent communication and multiple targeted messages to different stakeholders are essential to keeping the financial industry under the public microscope. The far-reaching environmental financial changes have forced three important financial sector communicators, industry analysts, investor relations, practitioners and corporate communicators to leave their individual silos of communication that focus on just one area of financial communication and work together to communicate with one voice to key stakeholder groups. Financial institutions found themselves trying to salvage their companies' corporate reputations and financial futures on both internal and external fronts; the most pressing need became that of starting to build credible, believable, relationships worthy of the trust of investors, media, taxpayers, and legislators/regulators.

The result is that transparency and intelligible and open communication about all facets of the financial industry's dealings with all internal and external appropriate and interested stakeholders is not only essential, but demanded.

EXPECTATIONS FOR TODAY'S FINANCIAL PUBLIC RELATIONS COMMUNICATORS

Inside the Financial Industry: Demonstrating Value in the Business of Numbers and Money

Financial communication requires that communication managers take a systems' approach to corporate responsibilities. According to McElreath (1993: 13), systems theory is best explained through an analogy: 'an organization is a living entity because it has boundaries, inputs, and outputs, "through-puts," and enough feedback from both internal and external environments so that it can make the appropriate adjustments in time to keep on living'. From an investor relations perspective, this provides investors with accurate and timely information for evaluating the economic fundamentals of financial institutions and how the stability and health of the entire financial institution may affect their financial decisions. An organization's acceptance of a systems approach will further increase transparency, because the organization's executives know that they have considered all factors in constructing their messages to their stakeholder groups.

According to Robbins (1990), organizational effectiveness is only enhanced when the organization concerns itself not only with the internal functions of the organization, but also with the external environment in which the organization operates. 'Systems theory emphasizes the interfaces between organizations and their environments, as well as between subsystems within the organizational system and between subsystems and the organizational whole' (Grunig, Grunig, & Ehling, 1992: 71). Effective organizations operate in an open system as opposed to a closed system. Closed systems are not likely to change and are not open to considering options other than those from inside the organization, whereas open systems allow information to flow in from outside the organization and are open to new ideas (McElreath, 1993). Open systems will proactively seek information and feedback from the external environment in which the organization operates, and make adjustments based upon the feedback (Cutlip, Center, & Broom, 2000). As a result of the role that the US government played in the financial markets in 2007–8, financial institutions were forced to operate as open systems. This provided a level of transparency into the internal decisions of the institution's directors and senior management. The creation of Sarbanes-Oxley is a perfect example of a measure created and implemented to demand accountability from chief executives. Before the advent of Sarbanes-Oxley, many companies' chief executives said they did not exactly know what their accounting firms or required SEC documents contained. The result: the Sarbanes-Oxley legislation that made CEOs acknowledge with their signatures that they had reviewed and accepted responsibility for what those documents stated.

CEOs and CFOs also need reasons to support what 'intangible assets' – things like good corporate reputations and high-level name recognition, think Coca-Cola and Nike. 'The CFO will determine if the department's contribution to the bottom line is actual or perceived. If a line item has actual value, it can be directly correlated with the bottom line ... perceived value occurs when no direct correlation can be made' (Savage, 2005: 46). Here public relations has the opportunity to create and use metrics outside the organization to illustrate perceived value through the efforts of an organization operating in an open system to look outside the organization for feedback on the organization's performance, credibility and legitimacy (McElreath, 1993). Boundary spanning includes many public relations research activities, including content analysis, media analysis, and general market analysis to determine whether the organization is competitive or operating within market parameters. Lerbinger (1977), describes one technique, environmental monitoring, which is a prominent boundary-spanning technique, used to identify changes in the markets or public sentiment towards an organization's product or practices. Together, these techniques allow organizations to stay in tune with public discourse and provide feedback regarding a company or organization about its practices and activities. This feedback is even more valuable when it is translated into some type of numerical information, the language of the dominant group in any financial service organization.

Internal Counseling and Strategy for the Executive-Level in the Age of Transparency

The challenges and opportunities for public relations professionals to become trusted and valued members of the Executive-level suite executives hinge on articulating and demonstrating contributions to the organization's financial goals. Communication managers within financial institutions manage the relationship and the transparency between the senior management and directors of the financial institution and the key stakeholders. Freeman (2010) describes a stakeholder as a person or group of people who can either influence and/or be influenced by an organization. According to this definition, stakeholders include any individual or group with direct or indirect contact with an organization: totally internal groups including company executives, managers, and employees; group with a foot in both internal and external camps, including vendors, suppliers, and investors; and groups that are external to the company itself, including citizens, politicians, potential investors and customers, and media. As the social, economic, and political landscape of financial institutions was challenged between 2007 and 2009, these organizations were challenged to identify the firm's stakeholders and determine if their position within or toward the organization had changed. Further, communication managers were charged with determining the change or lack of change in the firm's relationship with their stakeholders and subsequently working with the firm's directors to communicate with the various stakeholder groups so that the firm's message would be accepted. The following practitioner views are representative of what they believe are the CEOs and CFOs most important considerations:

Tsang (2005) offers the following insights:

> Public relations can affect a business in two distinct ways. The first is by creating a reaction in the marketplace that leads to a more desired perception. The second is by reporting on perceptions in the marketplace to affect the decision-making of senior executives...[creating] a window to the marketplace perceptions of the company. (p. 18)
>
> The CFO's primary concerns include corporate reputation, shareholder value, revenue, profitability, and spending. If PR results do not speak to these five categories, most CFOs will not consider them significant. (p. 19)
>
> The question PR practitioners should ask themselves, as they commonly do for their external constituencies, is how do I convert what I do into something that person cares about? (p. 19)
>
> When working with the CFO, you can bet it will be a story of numbers. (p. 46)

Boundary-Spanning between Internal and External Stakeholders

Dougherty (1992) identifies four different categories of stakeholders: enabling publics, functional publics, normative publics, and diffused publics. Enabling publics, according to Stephens, Malone, and Bailey (2005), include shareholders, regulatory agencies, and boards of directors, and provide the ability and direction which allow the organization to exist. Functional publics, an organization's employees, unions, suppliers, and customers, provide inputs and receive outputs from the organization. Political groups, professional societies, and trade unions are defined as an organization's normative publics. Finally, diffuse publics – media, environmentalists, residents, and the greater public – are externally affected by an organization's activities. According to Polonsky and Hyman (2007: 6), 'failure to consider all relevant stakeholders (1) can increase the probability and magnitude of unsuccessful activities, and (2) can be viewed as irresponsible, given that some groups' interests are omitted'.

As previously explained, stakeholders, through direct or indirect contact with an organization, can affect or be affected by an organization. Through communications and public/investor relations, financial organizations can increase the efficiency of the communication process. Springston, Keyton, Leichty, and Metzger (1992) echo Grunig and Grunig's observation that public relations is responsible for increasing organizational effectiveness by managing publics that impede its ability to function as it sees fit. Further, Springston et al. (1992: 82) conclude, 'the management of relationships with relevant organizational publics constitutes the core of public relations practice'. After identifying an organization's core public, the communication manager must determine the best approach for communicating with its members based upon the desired outcome.

Although the turmoil in the credit markets between July and August 2007 was not definitively a crisis, a key area to gain insight into communicating with investors would be to look into research dealing with communicating with stakeholders during a crisis. Ray (1999: 395) states that 'the purpose of communication during a crisis is to influence the public's perception of the organization and maintain a positive image or restore a damaged image among stakeholders'. Further, according to Patel, Xavier, and Broom (2005: 2), 'for public relations managers to be effective in establishing and maintaining mutually beneficial relationships with stakeholders, they must understand and negotiate the many environmental influences on the organization that impact its survival'. As organizations maintain relationships with many different groups of stakeholders, managers must realize the current boundaries of the relationships with all groups. This might include having to negotiate with two or more different groups at the same time, on the same issue, with the goal of finding a mutually benefiting result. As such, the intense media coverage of the US financial institutions in that began in 2007 and continues today created an environment of 24-hour coverage of the deterioration of the financial markets, increasing skepticism and an environment of negative reaction toward anyone identified as a financial market participant, and this coverage continues as the recession drags on. The role of the communications manager in this situation is to manage the message that the institutions want to disseminate and work with the firm's directors to ensure that the proper messages are disseminated to the myriad of stakeholder groups ranging from direct investor inquiries to media inquiries, as well as participating in constructing written and verbal messages to the regulatory agencies and government officials. In every circumstance, as a result of regulatory rules and rules governing statements from publicly traded institutions, this message must be factually based and transparent, so that all stakeholders, including the institution's directors and employees, are aware of and understand relevant information and that nothing is concealed or misrepresented.

Information Management: Language, Words, Numbers and Money

Although the finance industry is not necessarily a technical industry marked with complex technological innovations and high-tech wizardry, professionals working in finance must have a complex understanding of the overall economy and fundamental operation of complex investment vehicles. Accompanying this understanding is industry-specific jargon. Stakeholders who have some understanding of broader finance may or may not have a complete understanding of financial fundamentals or the accompanying jargon. According to Einsidel and Thorne (1999), various publics have the ability to understand scientific concepts and accept the uncertainty associated with such concepts. Other scholars have found that when communicating with the broader public, organizations need to make scientific information more explicit, not implicit (Levy, Robinson, & Davis, 1986). This conclusion was supported by Rogers (1999), when she found audiences wanted information placed in a broader context, specifically how it will affect them, decreasing uncertainty. Further, Zehr (1999) introduces public science, where scientists discuss scientific topics with a crowd of nonscientists. Based on these findings about communicating with audiences on a technical level through a public relations approach, communication managers within a financial institution should likewise communicate with their investors on a very technical level. Investors range from banks, hedge funds, pension funds and other sophisticated investors, to mutual fund and retail investors who have an understanding of their investments and risks associated with their investments. Accordingly, communication managers using the public relations relationship approach should explicitly communicate the fundamental financial health of the financial institution and how the performance, whether positive or negative, impacts the stakeholders. As a result of the previous research, the best content to be included within the communication strategy is measurable performance results of the organization, as well as commentary, similar to the MD&A, on the financial condition and results of operations section of a public company's annual 10K. According to the SEC website, the MD&A of financial condition and results of operations section of a 10K should address, among other things, the amount of liquidity and capital resources available to the institution.[7] This section is the written statement from the directors of the company that states the company's fundamentals as well as the direction in which the directors see the company moving in the near and long term. Further, statements to stakeholders should be, and are required to be, factually based, be written in understandable English rather than industry jargon, and should provide a transparent view of the organization.

Before the financial meltdown, public relations practitioners had to speak the language of numbers and data, with little regard to the words and language used. Two years before the first hints of the 2007–8 troubles, Silver (2005: 16) wrote that this focus on numbers needed to change:

> Intangibles such as trust, credibility, and confidence are essential in the investment process, and financial PR professionals are central to strengthening them. These professionals should not just communicate dry numbers, but share values and insights, visions, inspirations, and raw financial data with shareholders or potential investors, hard-line institutional investors, sophisticated analysts, Wall Street, employees and customers.

This was the beginning of realizing that companies and organizations had to begin to tell their stories, the idea that companies and organizations are more than just numbers. Laskin (2008) points out that investor relations 'is also predominately an interpersonal function. The most frequent channels of communication are one-on-one meetings … [paving] the way for relationship-building'. Vice president of marketing and professional development for the American Bankers Association Maggie Kelly agrees: 'Instead of promoting products and rates, banks are talking about the future, how they are helping the recession and that it's OK to trust them again' (Irving, 2009: 36). 'Today, and during the past year, individual banks are communicating their own stories – but the industry as a whole has inadvertently come together with many of the same messages ... Banks share a common challenge right now: to save the industry's reputation' (Irving, 2009: 37).

Because financial institutions have not had to think about or defend their 'stories', this is a new opportunity for communicators to help them develop, tell, and measure the effects of their stories. Brown, 2008 chair of the Public Relations Society of America's Financial Communications Professional Interest section, advocates this approach: 'You can be a source of new information to the management team ... ' (Elasser, 2008: 6).

The technological capabilities provide the potential for any individual interested and willing to learn the language of business to tap into industry-specific data and behaviors readily available to external audiences. And external stakeholders are interested – witness the popularity of financial channels and programs on cable television. It is up to communicators to take the lead on developing the language and words – and the stories – about their financial institutions as a key reputation and communication strategy.

While an organization should strive for consistency and directness in creating messages to communicate with stakeholders by telling its story, it is necessary to recognize that this storytelling must have a strategic base: 'The company's story and the financial details of that story must be presented to investors, media and analysts – indeed everyone – with a coordinated strategy. This requires full integration of public relations, investor relations, corporate attorneys, financial officers, and management in a team enterprise' (Silver, 2005: 16). In short, all pieces of the story must be coordinated and presented as the company's one story. Conflicting episodes of stories will only do more to damage already fragile reputations and stakeholder perceptions.

The idea of storytelling as a corporate strategy has come during a time of what some have called a crisis, and others, a risky time to navigate through with both words and numbers. The Three Mile Island crisis offers some background into risk/crisis communication. Ultimately, the effects of the Three Mile Island nuclear disaster were exacerbated by the use of different and uncoordinated communication strategies and messages to the media and the broader public (Farrell & Goodnight, 1981). As a result, the public and federal government reacted to inconsistent information in a way that could have further damaged the nearby geographic public. The situation escalated when less skilled communication technicians disseminated information that was either inconsistent or too complex for the broader public to comprehend.

Similarly, in an investigation of audience acceptance of messages from organizations after a crisis, Cowden and Sellnow (2002: 215) found that 'audiences are likely to reject organizational messages during a crisis that are inconsistent with past actions'. To maintain organizational legitimacy before, during, or after a crisis, an organization's messages must remain consistent; or if changed, the change in position or strategic focus should be shared with the public in both an explicit and public format.

Communication managers must keep detailed records of all historical communications to the various defined stakeholder groups to ensure that messages remain consistent. While the economic environment can quickly change and a firm's position in their industry can change, the historical content of messages must be considered before new messages are sent. To be transparent, an organization must record all communications and be prepared to publicly restate reports. As such, the communication manager must be able to inform the firm's directors of the contents of previous messages and how any subsequent messages will be perceived as consistent or inconsistent.

Risk communication, as it relates to public and investor relations, has relevant theoretical applications to the economic situation. Palenchar and Heath (2006) explain that when you multiply an outcome's probability by its degree of severity the product is risk. This is similar to the math used by investors when making a strategic investment decision, as investors analyze the suitability of an investment based upon its potential return to the investor and the risk the investor is taking in making the investment. Additionally, Covello (1992) defines risk communication as 'the exchange of information among interested parties about the nature, magnitude, significance, or control of a risk'. An organization's effectiveness at communicating risk, as explained by Reynolds and Seeger (2005), allows the public and investors to know hazards and risks, which in turn can strengthen their relationship with the organization and aid in the decision-making process over more than just one transaction.

For risk communication to have a positive impact on investors, the information communicated about current or potential risk to an investment should be, as explained by Egbert and Parrott (2001), communicated to match the needs, values, backgrounds and experiences of the audience. In the current situation, this would require the information to be presented in a way and through means the audience will understand, primarily through the presentation of quantitative data, such as financial statements, demonstrating the health or strength of their current investment and relative market indices. The need for information about the investment, the background, as it pertains to the investors' knowledge of the general investment and understanding of the way the performance of the investment can be measured, and the experience relates to how the investor perceives the current market and whether the message agrees with their current assessment.

While the overall strategy of telling an organization's story is a key strategy to (re) building reputations, one important technical tool is also imperative for financial communicators to master: Extensible Business Reporting Language. Savage (2005: 22) describes it as 'an SML-based standard that permits the automatic exchange and reliable extraction of financial information across all software formats and technologies'. What this means in simple terms is that every word in a financial document has a tag, which is automatically put into a correct cell in an Excel file. Thus, anyone with access to Excel will be able to get the exact information from any financial institution's required public filings and any other financial information that companies choose to share with the public. 'By creating XBRL documents and distributing them as widely as possible, companies will do their share in helping to restore investor confidence. XBRL is expected to benefit all members of the financial information supply chain: public and private companies, accountants, regulators, analysts, the media, institutional and individual investors, capital markets and lenders, as well as key third parties such as software developers and data aggregators' (Savage, 2005: 12).

Similarly, Laskin (2008) warns investor relations professionals that 'It won't take long before investor relations officers will face negative and even obnoxious postings in their electronic communication channels'. What this means is that the financially savvy communicators will have to learn how to 'translate' their data-based information into communication vehicles – stories – that external audiences such as investors, potential investors, and media will understand and, more importantly, believe.

THE RELEVANCE OF C-MACIE TO CURRENT FINANCIAL COMMUNICATION PRACTICE

The traditional and new roles and opportunities for financial communicators are well suited to the C-MACIE model. No other industry has the potential to have far-reaching impacts and/or consequences than the financial industries sector. Financial matters have become the topic of everyday conversation for a majority of people around the world, no longer confined to the boardrooms and Executive-level offices of companies, organizations, and financial institutions. While the outlook for the financial industry remains under great scrutiny, there are opportunities to gain access to the Executive-level suite for those financial communicators who have mastered the financial industry knowledge and can combine the best communication management and leadership skills with it.

The management of analysis stage of the C-MACIE model not only speaks directly to the communicator's role in gathering and interpreting the perspectives and opinions of all major stakeholders. Stakeholders, from corporate investors to individuals, are at best wary of the fragile economic environment, and at worst too paralyzed by indecision to make any financial moves. Communicators as boundary spanners are exceptionally important as qualitative information collectors and interpreters for their organizations. While CEOs and CFOs speak the language of numbers, those numeric decisions must be translated into words that will reassure and rebuild credibility with stakeholder groups even considering financial relations with these companies. Communicators who are bilingual in numbers and words are essential to helping all stakeholders understand each other.

The choice component of the C-MACIE model focuses on aligning the communication strategies with the company's business objectives and overall strategy. Stakeholders are now very aware that there is trouble in financial paradise, and in general they are leery of any messages coming from financial institutions. What companies and organizations put forth as their business objectives must be communicated clearly, accurately, fairly, and in a timely fashion. While transparency can be considered a buzzword, actions are going to speak far louder than words for a very long time. Here communicators have the opportunity to lead and educate senior executives about the power of transparent communication. Indeed, skillful communicators using their knowledge of stakeholder perceptions and concerns should be able to assist senior executives to define transparency, which, in turn, should result in better-targeted communication addressing the concerns and questions of the various stakeholders. Further, communicators should also demonstrate how carefully developed communication strategies and tactics are critical components tying directly into the business's goals and objectives. To paraphrase Lasswell's timeless thought: it does matter what is said to whom in what fashion.

Implementing, monitoring, and maintaining strategies and tactics is the third step of the C-MACIE management model. This component assumes a new importance in today's digital world, where messages take on an eternal life through channels like YouTube. Selecting channels and placing messages is perhaps the best-known role of communicators. In traditional times this included newspapers, magazines, radio, and television as well as personal face-to-face encounters. Add the new media forms such as Facebook, YouTube, company and personal websites, and apps for personal media devices, and the potential to reach stakeholders through multiple channels instantaneously is at hand. Financial communicators must be able to proactively select the best channels and then manage their messages through the myriad of possible trails. It can be argued that today's financial communicator has even greater pressure to not only be aware of the myriad of new digital channels that meet the regulatory and legal environments, but figure out how to use these channels to build lasting relationships with key stakeholder groups. For example, the SEC now allows US companies to post the required disclosure documents to their websites at the same time as the documents are submitted to the SEC. This gives companies an opportunity to proactively interact with the stakeholder groups they know will be most affected. In addition, this opportunity to add more information has the potential to engage stakeholders and media in conversation, another way of building trust and credibility.

And, finally, although evaluation is included in every public relations model, it is arguably critical in the financial industry. The events of the past decade are constant reminders of what can – and has – happened when evaluation was either not done or not heeded. This is another area where financial public relations managers have the great opportunity to assist senior executives, especially by putting the numbers into words that convey the perceptions, meanings, hope, and fears of stakeholder groups. In March 2010 two major US companies, Goldman Sachs and AIG, listed 'adverse publicity' as a risk in their 2009 10K reports; their major concern is damage to their corporate reputations. Evaluation is a crucial part of making sure that the company's business and communication efforts are appropriate to the various stakeholder groups and that the strategies and tactics are moving beyond just awareness to the process of rebuilding attitudes and, ultimately, encouraging financial behavior that will benefit both the industry and its investors.

NOTES

1. This content analysis is a work-in-progress for a future article on public relations roles and functions.
2. Definition of Sarbanes-Oxley Act retrieved from http://www.Searchcio-techtarget.com
3. Figures from the US Department of Commerce Bureau of Economic Analysts retrieved from http://www.bea.gov
4. http://www.investopedia.com/terms/t/troubled-asset-relief-program-tarp.asp
5. E. Morris, Financial services community tries to rebuild trust. *PRWeek US*, 1 February 2010. Retrieved from http://www.prweekus.com
6. P. Whorisky, After bailout, AIG executives head to resort. *The Washington Post*, 7 October 2008. Retrieved from http://www.washingtonpost.com
7. Securities and Exchange Commission, http://www.sec.gov/rules/other/33-8056.htm

SUMMARY

The economic turmoil of the past decade has resulted in a demand for transparent and understandable communication of financial information to a myriad of target groups around the world who have watched their seemingly safe, reliable invest-ments take a wild ride through the 2000s. These new demands for financial informa-tion provide an opportunity for public relations managers well versed in financial matters to demonstrate the role effective, well-informed, and well-managed commu-nication can play in restoring investor confidence.

REFERENCES

Allon, F. (2010) Speculating on everyday life: The cultural economy of the quotidian. *Journal of Communication Inquiry*, 34(4), 366–81.

Byrun, R. (2002, Fall) Corporations: Come clean with communications. *Public Relations Strategist*, 43–4.

Clark, C. (2002, Fall) Information disclosure: An update on Regulation Fair Disclosure. *Public Relations Strategist*, 8(4), 36–9.

Covello, V.T. (1992) Risk communication: An emerging area of health communication research. In S.A. Deetz (ed.), *Communication Yearbook*. Newbury Park, CA: Sage.

Cowden, K., & Sellnow, T. L. (2002) Issues advertising as crisis communication: Northwest Airlines' use of image restoration strategies during the 1998 pilots' strike. *Journal of Business Communication*,39, 193–219.

Cutlip, S.M., Center, A.H., & Broom, G.N. (1985) *Effective Public Relations*, 6th ed. Englewood Cliffs, NJ: Prentice Hall.

(Continued)

(Continued)

Cutlip, S.M., Center, A.H., & Broom, G.N. (2000) *Effective Public Relations*, 8th ed. Englewood Cliffs, NJ: Prentice Hall.

Dougherty, D.J. (1992) Interpretive barriers to successful product innovation in large firms. *Organization Science*, 3, 179–203.

Egbert, N., & Parrott, R. (2001) Self-efficacy and rural women's performance of breast and cervical cancer detection practices. *Journal of Health Communication*, 6, 219–33.

Einsiedel, E., &Thorne, B. (1999) Public responses to uncertainty. In S.M. Friedman, S. Dunwoody, & C.L. Rogers (eds), *Communicating Uncertainty: Media Coverage of New and Controversial Science* (pp. 43–58). Mahwah, NJ: Erlbaum.

Elasser, J. (2008, Fall) Wall Street Woes: An interview with Timothy S. Brown, APR, 2008 Chair of PRSA's Financial Communications Professional Interest Section. *Public Relations Strategist*, 14(4), 6–7.

Farrell, T.B., & Goodnight, G.T. (1981) Accidental rhetoric: The root metaphors of Three Mile Island. *Communication Monographs*, 48 (Dec.), 271–300.

Freeman, R.E. (2010) *Strategic Management: A Stakeholder Approach*. Cambridge: Cambridge University Press.

Gordon, R. (2010, March 5) Bad publicity new 'risk' factor on Wall St. (Electronic version). *PRWeek*. http://www.prweekus.com.

Grunig, L.A., Grunig, J.E., and Ehling, W.P. (1992) What is an effective organization? In J. Grunig (ed.), *Excellence in Public Relations and Communication Management* (pp. 65–90). Hillsdale, NJ: Erlbaum.

Hay, J. (2010) Too good to fail: Managing financial crisis through the moral economy of realty TV. *Journal of Communication Inquiry*, 34(4), 382–402.

Irving, C. (2009, Fall) Adding it up: Public relations is at the forefront of banks' recovery. *Public Relations Strategist*, 15(4), 36–7.

Laskin, A. (2008, November 14) *Investor Relations*. Retrieved from http://www.instituteforpr. org.

Lerbinger, O. (1977) *The Crisis Manager: Facing Risk & Responsibility*. Hillsdale, NJ: Erlbaum.

Levy, M.R., Robinson, J.P., & Davis, D.K. (1986) News comprehension and theworking journalist. In J.P. Robinson & M.R. Levy (eds), *The Main Source: Learning from Television News* (pp. 211–28). Beverly Hills, CA: Sage.

Lowenstein, R. (2010, December 5) The stress-testing of Jamie Dimon: America's Least Hated Banker. *New York Times Magazine*, 34–41, 54, 62, 66, 68, 70.

McCormack, J. (2003, Spring) Capturing the lasting influence of analysts: How AR will strengthen PR. *Public Relations Strategist*, 9(3), 33–4.

McElreath, M. (1993) *Managing Systematic and Ethical Public Relations*. Dubuque, IA: Wm. C. Brown.

Palenchar, M.J., & Heath, R. L. (2002) Another part of the risk communication model: Analysis of communication processes and message content. *Journal of Public Relations Research*, 13, 127–58.

Patel, A.M. and Xavier, R.J., & Broom, G. (2005) Toward a model of organizational legitimacy in public relations theory and practice. In *Proceedings International Communication Association Conference* (pp. 1–22). New York.

Polonsky, M.J., & Hyman, M.R. (2007) A multiple stakeholder perspective on responsibility in advertising. *Journal of Advertising*, 36(2), 5–13.

Ray, S. J. (1999). *Strategic Communication in Crisis Management: Lessons from the Airline Industry*. Westport, CT: Quorum.

Reynolds, B., & Seeger M. (2005) Crisis and emergency risk communication as an integrative model. *Journal of Health Communication, 10,* 43–55.

(Continued)

(Continued)

Robbins, S. P. (1990) *Organization Theory*. Englewood Cliffs, NJ: Prentice Hall.

Rogers, C. L. (1999) The importance of understanding audiences. In S.M. Friedman, S. Dunwoody, & C.L. Rogers (eds), *Communicating Uncertainty: Media Coverage of New and Controversial Science* (pp. 179–200). Mahwah, NJ: Erlbaum.

Savage, M. (2005, Winter) New standards in communicating to financial audiences: Why you need to understand XBRL. *Public Relations Strategist*, *11*(1), 10–2.

Silver, D. (Winter 2005) Creating transparency for public companies: The convergence of PR and IR in the post-Sarbanes-Oxley marketplace. *Public Relations Strategist*, 11(1), 14–7.

Springston, J.K., Keyton, J., Leichty, G., & Metzger, J. (1992) Field dynamics and public relations theory: Towards the management of multiple publics. *Journal of Public Relations Research*, 4(2), 81–101.

Stephens, K.K., Malone, P.C., & Bailey, C.M. (2005) Communicating with stakeholders during a crisis: Evaluating message strategies. *Journal of Business Communication*, *42*(4), 390–419.

Tsang, Y.M. (2005, Winter) Selling public relations to the CFO and other executives. *Public Relations Strategist*, 11(1) 18–19, 46.

Zehr, S.C. (1999) Scientists' representations of uncertainty. In S.M. Friedman, S. Dunwoody & C.L. Rogers (eds), *Uncertainty: Media Coverage of New and Controversial Science*. Mahwah, NJ: Erlbaum.

Non-Profit Communication Management

David Therkelsen

11

Key Themes

- Influence of the specialized education of the organization's principles
- Importance of the employee base as the organization's community information providers
- Importance of volunteers in achieving the organization's goals and objectives
- Importance of direct, non-mediated communication with the organization's key stakeholders
- Importance of developing and maintaining a public policy voice

---

INTRODUCTION

In the United States, according to the National Center for Charitable Statistics, nearly 1.5 million entities are legally organized as non-profit corporations. They range in size and scope from implementing the vision of one person to mammoth multi-program organizations such as the YMCA. Non-profit organizations (NPOs) have two common identifying characteristics: all have been exempted from paying federal income taxes; and all are eligible to receive contributions that are tax-deductible to the donor. They receive this treatment because for generations it has been US public policy to support organizations that exist to serve a charitable purpose and not to earn a profit. Similar entities exist in most countries in the world, but with a wide range of legal organization methods and tax treatment.

This chapter will consider public relations management in the non-profit sector from the perspective of just one of the tens of thousands of NPOs that have the size and scale to support public relations activity. It is an organization where this chapter's author was privileged to oversee the public relations function for 23 years, either directly or from higher senior management positions. It is an organization which, because of enlightened top-management values in place for decades, 'got it right' in its public relations activities, and thereby earned the consistent support of its stakeholders.

The organization – the American Red Cross based in St. Paul, Minnesota – is, strictly speaking, two divisions of a larger organization that will be described more fully shortly. The St. Paul Red Cross organization is recognized by its shorthand acronym, 'SPRC'. There is no formal representation here that the public relations methods of SPRC were 'typical'. Both by reputation and results, however, SPRC may be regarded as a best demonstrated practice for public relations management and programming in the non-profit sector. While this agency's approaches probably were not typical, neither were they unique; there are likely hundreds of other non-profits which also operated then, and today, under best demonstrated practices.

About SPRC

The remainder of this chapter will consider the public relations function of SPRC from 1978 through 2001.[1] Like most large entities, the American Red Cross is dynamic and constantly changing. The resulting table of organization was not always neat and tidy. But for most of these years two divisions coexisted under a single board of directors and management, including public relations management. One division is referred to as 'human services'; this group provided disaster relief, health and safety training, senior transportation, and other social services in St. Paul and immediately surrounding suburbs, serving a population of about 700,000 residents. The other division is the 'biomedical', responsible for assuring a safe, adequate blood supply for a population of about 1.9 million people in much of Minnesota and parts of Wisconsin, Iowa, North Dakota, and South Dakota. For many years it was also part of its region's network for organ transplantation and for bone marrow transplantation.

SPRC accomplished its work through about 700 staff members, in addition to thousands of volunteers. It sought, and usually achieved, a leadership position within the national American Red Cross organization. Its management culture, significantly influenced by physicians and scientists, emphasized high professionalism in all functions, public relations among many others.

The public relations unit itself changed and evolved, but for most of the period in question consisted of nine or ten professionals. This was a sufficiently large staff to be reasonably specialized – some staff members developed communication products such as brochures, newsletters and annual reports; others focused on media relations; and there was an in-house graphics design group. Additionally, the director and one or two top assistants routinely counseled the CEO and other top executives on the public relations aspects of program and policy decisions.

The high standard of professional excellence that was consistently imposed from the top would make many senior public relations executives envious, but there was a hard edge to this. For example, top public relations leaders were always 'at the table' when key decisions were made, but they did not get there automatically. Their place was earned only after positive results of a highly professional approach were demonstrated.In many non-profits public relations research is seen as an unaffordable luxury at best, and as a waste of resources at worst. In contrast, at SPRC, public relations programming would not be supported and funded by top management and claimed results would not be believed unless they were well supported by data, usually derived by research of sufficient rigor to be persuasive and actionable.

A Nod to Key Scholars

Perhaps because the 'dominant coalition' of SPRC was so influenced by physicians and scientists, most of whom also had academic appointments at the nearby University of Minnesota, scholarship was valued in all of its management functions, whether considered 'line' or 'staff'. Top leadership wanted to be well prepared intellectually for all situations and all decisions. To the extent that public relations leadership – or that of any other function – could assist with this, they were at the table. But they needed to be truly prepared, with research, data, and a track record of results.

Some of the key themes of this textbook were also salient in the SPRC environment. The American Red Cross is, of course, very much in the business of crisis and disaster response, and it is worth noting that Mintzberg (1973) was one of the first scholars to recognize the role of top management in crisis leadership and as organization spokespeople. It is a short leap from defining top management's responsibilities in this fashion to grasping the central role of public relations in supporting the CEO and others.

Additionally, the tenets of the C-MACIE formula, the framework of this text, was the operating practice basis at SPRC. As this chapter recounts, analysis, choice, implementation and evaluation were large responsibilities of the agency's public relations leaders.

PUBLIC RELATIONS MANAGEMENT PROPOSITIONS

The public relations function at SPRC operated under several clearly articulated principles. They were not handed down on tablets; they were arrived at through trial and error and through an ethic of continuous learning. They include:

There are more similarities than differences between public relations in the non-profit sector and other sectors. This was one point of significant departure from the views and practices of many other non-profits. At SPRC, leaders did not believe there was anything particularly 'special' about the non-profit sector. Like any organization in any sector, it was necessary to identify key stakeholders, do the hard work of building relationships with them, and then communicate in a highly professional fashion. While some non-profits believed they would be excused if, for example, their communication products were not of high quality, SPRC believed its communication products are in the same competition for the attention, interest and ultimately behavior of its key constituencies as any other entity. A brochure or newsletter would not somehow get through the psychological filters of its audiences without compelling graphics and writing, would not leap ahead of the hundreds or thousands of other messages aimed at those same audiences every day, just because SPRC was a 'deserving' non-profit.

One difference that SPRC did acknowledge was that in the non-profit arena any given entity is likely to be accountable to more stakeholder groups. A corporation may recognize its customers, employees, and sources of capital as its most important constituencies. A non-profit will have all of these or their equivalents, plus volunteers, funding sources, units of government and more. If SPRC considered changes in, for example, its blood drive scheduling practices, it would need to understand the impact of these changes on employees, volunteers, blood donors, local community leaders, blood drive sponsors, and regulatory agencies.

The highest aim of public relations is long-term, mutually beneficial relationships with those constituencies that can directly affect the success or failure of the enterprise. This construct, a consistent theme in the work of American public relations practitioner/scholar Patrick Jackson, was fully embraced by general management, and public relations management, of SPRC. It led to a tough-minded view of how to deploy public relations resources. The agency rarely, if ever, did anything aimed vaguely at 'building awareness'. While it recognized that there was a role for media relations in its public relations repertoire, most of the time it looked for ways to go directly to its key audiences without intermediaries. While SPRC probably never fully realized the two-way symmetrical ideal as defined by Grunig et al. (1992), the agency nevertheless understood that relationships, by definition, involve mutual exchange of influence. In the interests of maintaining 'long-term, mutually beneficial relationships', it conducted a series of informational/recognition seminars each year, for volunteers in local communities throughout its five-state area who led the organization of blood drives. A more conventional, but arguably far less effective, non-profit approach might have eschewed the relationship-building seminars in favor of public service advertising campaigns.

The top public relations manager should advise the CEO and other senior managers on policy and program decisions before they are made. For many senior public relations executives who aspire to strong influence with the dominant coalition, this is the gold standard, and SPRC consistently achieved it. The agency rarely, if ever, decided its posture and its actions on complex, controversial matters without full airing of impacts on all key constituencies, and with public relations leadership not just at the table, but fully engaged. There were always serious issues like these, commanding the serious attention of SPRC leadership, including its public relations leaders, such as: how to conduct educational efforts to reduce HIV infection among public school populations; how to build a registry of unrelated bone marrow donors that would do enormous social good, but would introduce a higher level of risk to volunteers in society; and how to communicate with blood donors about that rare but real test result that not only means their blood cannot be given to others but may indicate serious health issues previously unknown to the donor.

What was key in this was the proposition that the public relations executive needed to function in a collegial fashion, as part of the senior team, and must win the right to be there and be heard by consistently contributing valuable, actionable, insight.

Public relations strategies should be constituency-based, not institution-based. Strategy development always began with identification of constituencies of interest. Typically these were community leaders, employees, volunteers, blood donors, financial contributors, and regulators. SPRC would focus on its key constituencies, and the desired behavioral outcomes from each. As a consequence, the framing of strategic questions would typically be: 'How can we demonstrate to financial contributors the quality of stewardship of SPRC?', not 'How can we convince our contributors to write bigger checks?' Or 'How can we create a benefits package that maximizes our attractiveness as an employer?', not 'How can we get the employees to accept an increase in their share of the health care insurance premium?' Or, 'How can we assure that community leaders know and will convey to others the impact SPRC has on community well-being?', not, 'How can we get Mr. or Ms. Mover-Shaker on our board?'

Research and planning should precede all important public relations programming, and evaluation should follow. A key word here is 'important'. No organization works with unlimited resources, and sometimes an initiative will be undertaken just because it makes sense to the decision-makers. But SPRC almost never initiated any major public relations activity without undertaking at least informal research to validate its assumptions about the situation at hand. For example, there was belief within the American Red Cross that World War II veterans and their families held the organization in low regard because of questionable policies undertaken under pressure from the US government during the war. The belief took hold because Red Cross officials would frequently run into, and get an earful from, veterans who were unhappy with the policies, and who may have waited 30 years or more until they found an opportunity to vent their displeasure on some unfortunate Red Cross leader who may have been in grade school when the alleged offense occurred. Research, however, demonstrated unambiguously that the vast majority of those who could influence success or failure of American Red Cross in the local community had never even heard of the incidents in question. Even the World War II veteran population was, in the main, favorably disposed toward the agency. This kind of research, aimed at improving understanding of the true situation, prevented SPRC from investing in public relations programming to address a non-existent problem.

Similarly, when significant resources were put behind public relations activity, evaluation was almost always conducted afterwards: did we reach the intended audience? To what extent were key messages heard and retained? To what extent can we demonstrate that desired behavior, or at least propensity in the direction of the desired behavior, followed? Only by evaluation could public relations and agency leaders know which efforts were effective, which were not, and then practice an ethic of continuous improvement.

> Preventing a crisis is more important than managing one. (But you will get less credit.) SPRC aimed to make program and policy decisions in consultative fashion, so that those decisions would have the best chance of earning the support of its key constituencies. When US public health authorities made decisions in the 1980s to exclude sexually active gay men from blood donation, protests and demonstrations followed in many communities around the USA. Gay activists by and large understood that blood bank organizations did not make this decision, but they also knew the local blood banks were high-profile symbols of this new policy, and thus more subject to pressure than distant federal bureaucracies. There were no such crises in the SPRC area, because the agency worked constructively with local activist organizations and local public health agencies whose rapport with the gay community had been well established.

The paradoxical corollary of this proposition has been noted. In the public relations field, sometimes larger careers get built by those who overcome the crisis once it has already occurred. But those who are instrumental in preventing its occurrence in the first place bring greater value to their employer or client.

> Mass media does not matter very much. But to the extent it does matter, use it to advance overall reputation, not to promote the next event. This principle goes against much non-profit sector orthodoxy. But SPRC leadership was well aware of research conclusions that media coverage rarely has any direct influence on behavior, and thus placed much less emphasis on media relations than the typical NPO. Even so, the agency organized its public relations activity so it could be highly responsive to media inquiries (e.g. having 24/7 spokesperson availability for community disasters), and it practiced full transparency in responding to media controversies such as blood safety. Thus media tended to seek out agency leadership as spokespeople, and media coverage was commensurately positive.

Public service advertising (PSA) matters even less. This principle was even more controversial and against the grain of NPO thought. NPOs are led to PSA campaigns in the first place because they cannot afford (or think they cannot) paid advertising. SPRC did not have big budgets to put behind paid advertising, either. But its leaders did not leap mindlessly to the PSA tactic, involving advertising that is not really advertising at all – since you cannot control whom you reach nor the frequency with which you reach them. Instead, the agency deployed its resources in other ways altogether, often involving going directly to its key audiences rather than through intermediaries of any type.

While these eight principles were appropriately tough-minded, and differentiated SPRC from many other NPOs, one paradox should be noted here. Many have already argued that the public relations function must be performed rigorously, and with quantification, to earn standing with the dominant coalition – that proverbial place at the table. These principles are well aligned with that view. Yet SPRC, along with the authors of this text, also understood that the public relations function, to a greater extent than accounting or finance or training or other staff functions, *does* involve the human element, and thus in important ways this work is less subject to precise analysis and quantification.

THEORY MATTERS

Because of strong academic and scientific influence on the overall management culture, the dominant coalition was naturally attuned to theory, and desired that leaders of all functions know and apply the body of knowledge developed in their fields; they must know the most critical concepts and how to apply them. To be sure, this management team, like most others, spent most of its days confronting the day-to-day pressures of successful operation, not studying the latest journals.

In 2001, several years after I had left more direct public relations management responsibilities in favor of broader, general-management accountability, along with colleague Christina Fiebich, I published the much-cited message to action model (Therkelsen & Fiebiech, 2001).

While this was to a significant degree a meta-study pulling together strains of research from many of the behavioral sciences, and while it drew minimally on my own professional work, it can also be considered a retrospective road map of how SPRC managed and practiced public relations. The message to action consisted of two arguments:

- That for a message to succeed it must overcome each of six hurdles, none of which can be assumed. It must be received, attended to, understood, believed, remembered … and then, at a 'moment of truth', acted upon.
- That to accomplish this very ambitious set of tasks, the architect of the message must have command of the social sciences, communication, psychology, and marketing, and subdivisions of each.

In order to be effective, a message must be:

Field	Discipline	Received	Attended to	Understood	Believed	Remembered	Acted on
Marketing	*Demographics*	1	3	9	13		
	Psychographics	2	4		14		
Psychology	*Persuasion*				15		21
	Information processing		5			18	22
Communication	*Linguistics*			10			
	Writing		6	11		19	
	Design		7	12		20	
Social Sciences	*Sociology*				16		
	Anthropology				17		
	Economics		8				23

Just to get a message from here to there, from sender to receiver, requires a reasonable command of the social sciences, communication, psychology, marketing – and subdivisions of each. To be successful, a message must be *received* by the intended individual or audience. It must get the audience's *attention*. It must be *understood*. It must be *believed*. It must be *remembered*. And ultimately, in some fashion, it must be *acted upon*. Failure to accomplish any of these tasks means the entire message fails. It fails because it does not accomplish the purpose for which it was created.

FIGURE 11.1   The Message To Action Model

Source: Therkelsen and Fiebiech (2001).

One does not need expert knowledge in these fields, nor can even the most intellectually broad-gauged public relations leader hope to be an expert in all, but working knowledge and access to the current themes of scholarship is necessary.

While SPRC and its public relations leadership strove to know and apply the most important ideas from these fields, colleagues drew especially on the conceptual models of Patrick Jackson, who in both practice and scholarship regularly challenged conventional wisdom.

Arguably one of Jackson's (1990) most important scholarly contributions to the public relations field involves his insistence on the primacy of the employee public. SPRC was one of the first NPOs, and ahead of many in other sectors as well, to recognize the strategic importance of the employee constituency. Like many other authors, Jackson helped organizations understand that it is the employees who are in a position to advance the marketplace and strategic goals of the organization, and to advocate for its public policy goals, among other positive outcomes. Unlike many authors, particularly from the public relations field, Jackson rejected the idea that employee communication was about newsletters and emails and CEO meetings with 'the troops'; he insisted that the key to effective relationships with employees was empowered, trained, front-line supervisors. The public relations role, Jackson argued, was to forget the employee newsletter, and spend the same energy equipping immediate supervisors to become superb communicators.

Jackson was also one of the few who amplified the darker downside of marginalizing the employee public: this will drive turnover. An organization that tolerates, say, 25% employee turnover will, every 4 years, create a constituency of those whose experience with the organization was not satisfying throughout the actual employee population.

SPRC took these lessons to heart, and forged leadership partnerships among general managers, human resources leadership, and public relations that emphasized the employee public as a key to organizational success, and emphasized the role of the front-line supervisor as communicator.

Jackson's arenas of practice model (Table 11.1) also had strong influence on public relations structure and programming at SPRC. The model defines the public relations role in sales support, public policy, and organizational effectiveness. Many NPOs only solidly recognize the first role – in effect, marketing communications. Not only do they squander their public policy voice and their opportunity to engage other key constituencies such as employees, retirees, vendors, and their industry, but they also can fall victim to the 'seamless web' Jackson warns about: that failure in any of the arenas can provoke failure in either or both of the other two. This is part of the reason why, as noted previously, SPRC implemented national public health policy direction in selection of blood donors only after engaging in its own public policy relationships in its own local community. Failure to so engage in public policy could (and in other communities did) lead to failure in the sales support arena, through reduced success in collecting blood that could be distributed to hospitals.

TABLE 11.1 The Three Arenas of Practice: A Public Relations Model

	Sales Support	**Public Policy**	**Organizational Effectiveness**
FUNCTIONS	Customer relations	Constituency relations	Employee/retiree relations
	Sell products and services	Issues anticipation/ tracking	Recruitment
	Publicity and promotion	Crisis management	Shareholder relations
	Other marketing support	Damage control	Financial relations
		Lobbying/governmental relations	Supplier relations
		Community relations	Industry relations
		Social responsibility	
GOALS	Sales and profits	Maintain a hospitable environment	Teamwork, motivation, productivity, loyalty, morale
	Brand preference	Create a cadre of active supporters	Cost-effectiveness
	Market share		One Clear Voice
CLIENTS	Sales and marketing	CEO, Board	CEO, CFO, COO, HR
COLLABORATORS	Sales and marketing	Law	Human resources
		Strategic planning	Corporate secretary

Source: Adapted from full model by Patrick Jackson, as published in *PR Reporter*, February 13, 1989.

In a last nod to Jackson (1990), the behavior communication model speaks especially to NPOs, in its primary assertion that awareness almost never leads directly to behavior (Figure 11.2). While well supported by research, this impeaches the basic strategies of many if not most NPOs, whose mindset all too often is 'if only the public (whoever that may be!) knew all about the great things we do it would support our work'. Fortunately, Jackson offers two alternative routes to desired behavioral outcomes. The latent-readiness portion of BCM builds the understanding of practitioners that publics advance along a continuum of readiness to exhibit any given behavior, and reaching audiences or subsets at their moment of readiness is far more likely to yield the desired result than an 'awareness' campaign. One way SPRC applied this learning was in its promotion of organ donation through its relationship with the Minnesota state drivers license bureau. It made the case for becoming an organ donation within every-four-year license renewal notices. It reached one-fourth of Minnesota adults every year, at the time they were ready to make a decision about this important but emotionally sensitive behavior.

BCM's other route to behavioral influence is through triggering events. Jackson and others have identified at least six categories of triggering events, but his particular contribution is the understanding that when a triggering event occurs, such as a significant lifestyle change, individuals will not move directly to a final behavior, but instead to an intermediate behavior, such as consulting with trusted friends or colleagues. This understanding powerfully validated a relationship-building philosophy of public

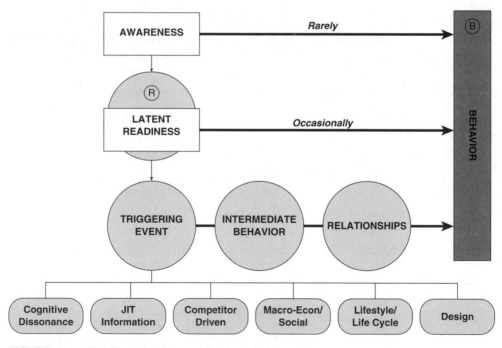

FIGURE 11.2 The Behavior Communication Model

Source: Reprinted with Permission. www.jjwpr.com.

TABLE 11.2 Relationship between Marketing and Public Relations

	Marketing	Public Relations
Scope of interest	Customers	All key constituencies
Aim	Transactions; maximizing business success	Long-term, mutually beneficial relationships
Highest methods	Discover customer needs and satisfy them	Align organization's policy with the interests of its publics
Common techniques	Market research	Public opinion research
	Segmentation	Issues management
	'Four P's'	Crisis management
	• Product	Public policy
	• Price	Media relations
	• Place (distribution)	Employee relations
	• Promotion	Communication development and
	Customer contact	production

Adapted from Kotler (1986) and others.

relations. When a couple became empty-nesters, for example, this triggering event created an opportunity for them to volunteer as a couple, perhaps traveling to Red Cross disaster assignments around the country. But they would first talk not directly to their Red Cross chapter, but to others who do this work. If what they heard was positive (and, through a relationship-based view of practice, SPRC could influence this), their own propensity seriously to explore this option became much higher.

It is common in NPOs to mix both titles and functions between marketing and public relations. While both of these functions were of critical importance to SPRC, its leaders tried to maintain great clarity as to which was which. To do this, the agency developed its own model, but drawn from the constructs of Kotler (1986) and others, to educate itself about when it was engaged in public relations activities, directed at accomplishing a long-term, mutually beneficial relationship with its publics, versus when it was undertaking marketing activities, aiming for a specific transactional result in its marketplace (Table 11.2). The former set the relationship tone and direction, the latter 'closed the sale.'

Results Matter the Most

The best test of approaches chosen in any management discipline is whether, in the long run, they contribute to better results than had they not been chosen. For SPRC the verdict was unambiguous. From the late 1970s into the twenty-first century the agency quadrupled in size. It led its peer organizations within the American Red Cross in business growth, innovation, and contribution to science. It led its own local community of NPOs in these same categories. Special recognition came one year when the St. Paul Chamber of Commerce named SPRC the 'Small Business of the

Year'; perhaps the first time a non-profit had ever been so honored.[2] None of these results were solely the achievement of the public relations function, of course; high-performing organizations achieve because all general and functional management leaders work in a highly unified way to achieve desired results.

But over a period of years much evidence accumulated that organizing and practic-ing public relations as laid out in this chapter consistently delivered results well beyond the norm of other NPOs or other American Red Cross field units.

Perhaps the single most dramatic example was a case involving public relations research. In the mid-1980s, following steady growth in blood donation since the 1950s, the upward growth curve abruptly flattened, locally and nationally. No mat-ter what SPRC or any other blood center did, collections stayed flat. This influenced blood shortages locally and nationally, because medical advances were increasing the need for blood products.

A theory emerged that previous growth trends halted because of rising fears that blood donors could acquire HIV infection by giving blood. Most blood centers around the USA embraced this theory, and launched campaigns to convince donors that they could not contract any infectious disease by donating blood.

One of the few blood centers that paused to investigate the theory was SPRC. After a series of research studies, the strategic team came to realize that the HIV hypothesis was entirely incorrect: that blood donors, or potential blood donors, had fully informed themselves and knew giving blood was safe. Only those who were not prospects anyway had any safety concern. In retrospect, this should not have been so surprising. Under elaboration likelihood model theory (1986), blood donors and potential blood donors would inquire much more fully into the consequences of a behavior that could affect their own safety than those who had minimal likelihood to exhibit the behavior in the first place.

So if the HIV hypothesis was incorrect, what was the true reason why donations were flat, and what could be done about it? After additional research, SPRC con-cluded that the trend lines were driven by age demographics. A generation that fought World War II and came back to build many civic institutions, including local blood donation, was reaching the upper age limit to donate blood that was in place at the time. Yet the youngest baby boomer reached the minimum age to donate in 1981. Thus, older donors were leaving and were no longer automatically replaced by boomers. A flat trend line was the result.

Understanding this, SPRC did not spend its scarce resources trying to convince donors of what they already knew. Instead, the agency developed upgraded strate-gies: aiming to get its donors to give three times a year instead of twice, or twice a year instead of once. Through these strategies, it developed one of the highest rates of blood donation in the USA, and in fact was able to collect blood for other communities around the country, which, perhaps because of ill-chosen beliefs about causes of flatter growth trend lines, were not able to collect enough for their own needs.

Another success involved SPRC's community leader strategy. It identified community leaders as a key audience, and devoted significant resources, including a specialized publication, monthly cultivation meetings, and a board of directors strategy to reach them and gain their advocacy for the agency's mission. Research showed that those community leaders who did engage with SPRC's efforts were more likely to weigh in on Red Cross' behalf when a major grant was being awarded, or a major new program was being initiated and funded.

Also in the 1980s SPRC became Minnesota's coordinating agency for procurement of organs for transplantation. In cooperation with several other entities and supported by original research, SPRC fundamentally changed the message strategies for encouraging organ transplantation. It undertook intricate 'social engineering' to stimulate conversations within families so members knew one another's beliefs and wishes abstractly, rather than thinking about them for the first time in that terrible moment after a death when families have to make a decision on behalf of a loved one. After a four-year campaign based on the newer strategies, Minnesota had moved from the middle of the pack to second in the nation in the consent rate obtained for organ donation.

Employee relations were another area of great success. SPRC had a bipolar turnover curve: about 25% of its new hires in a large and critical job function left within two years. Yet if they passed that crucial milestone, they then stayed for a very long time. The first-two-year turnover was highly expensive, because due to extensive training and proficiency monitoring, new employees usually did not work independently and at full productivity for at least six months. To replace them within another year or so resulted in large recruitment, hiring and training costs.

The agency undertook a comprehensive employee retention program, including the aforementioned development of front-line supervisory skills. But the program included improvement of communications at all levels, more accountable employee suggestion systems, highly transparent access to agency information, as well as other reforms. Turnover declined to about 10% in the critical first two years, resulting in major gains both in effectiveness and cost reduction.

THE RELEVANCE OF C-MACIE TO NPO COMMUNICATION PRACTICE

Effective communication/public relations practice in NPOs is not, as pointed out in this chapter, different from other kinds of communication practice. What is evident is that four elements – analysis, choice, implementation, and evaluation – are just as critical as in for-profit organizations.

Analysis is evident from the management 'place at the table' that the SPRC senior communicators earned through making contributions to strategy through research and fact-finding, even in the face of commonly held assumptions, such as the example of why fewer blood donors were available. St. Paul Red Cross (STPR) communicators realized they were responsible for, and equipped to, conduct the research necessary to build effective campaigns, which in turn, provided the messages to help the organization reach its business goal of rebuilding the donor base. It is also interesting to note that while it was critical for the communicators to bring quantitative research to the table, qualitative research also made valuable contributions to the strategies developed.

Equally evident in this chapter is the choice element of the C-MACIE model, especially in the choice of channels to use to communicate with which key stakeholder groups at what times. The example of creating specialized direct communication with key community leaders, who in turn provided support to other community entities, including legislators and funders, demonstrates the power of coalitions and relationships with partners. Another example is SPRC's choice to bypass traditional media and focus on more direct communication with other key groups, thus helping ensure their messages were presented in ways that were direct and complete from the chapter, thus limiting the selective 'pick-and-choose' tactics of traditional media coverage. Similarly, the communication with employees and the all-important volunteer base upon which the SPRC depended, were based on the idea of direct, continuous, and open communication with these two groups.

Implementation naturally followed from what the research indicated and the choices made from the research results. The partnership with the Minnesota state license bureau renewal program, for example, shows how the SPRC capitalized on the natural opportunity to 'add value' by incorporating the simple decision, made at an unemotional business transaction time, with the result that the number of donors substantially increased.

No discussion of the non-profit industry segment is complete without considering evaluation. As indicated in this chapter, the SPRC dovetailed evaluation with research, continuously collecting information and carefully considering what it 'meant'. As previously mentioned, quantitative did not trump qualitative – the SPRC's understanding that both types of information provided valuable data was understood. The key point here is that this information was the one key element that earned – and ultimately kept – the communication management team at the senior management table.

NOTES

1. Because of a merger in 2006, there is no longer a 'St. Paul' Red Cross chapter; a St. Paul-based biomedical unit does remain.
2. To this author's knowledge, no other NPO has achieved the best small business status in Minnesota.

SUMMARY

Devoting a chapter to non-profit public relations appropriately recognizes the size and social impact of this sector of the economy, as well as the large arena of public

(Continued)

(Continued)

relations practice that it has become. It also recognizes there are meaningful differences between the non-profit and other sectors, though this chapter argues that those differences can be exaggerated; that the professional principles that build and maintain relationships with those who can help or harm an organization be successful are universal.

As in other sectors, a highly professional approach to public relations begins with being 'at the table', but that place is not automatic or conferred by job title, it must be earned by public relations execution, and public relations counsel, that truly contributes to the success of the enterprise.

The Minnesota-based non-profit for decades did most things right in its public relations activity, and it had consistently positive results as a consequence – in program and financial growth, in strength of relationships with key constituencies, in its community and national leadership profile.

SPRC rejected some of the conventional wisdom of NPOs. Its public relations programming de-emphasized mass media and public service advertising campaigns. Rather, it aimed to reach its constituencies directly without intermediaries. To the extent that it did this through communication products, it emphasized quality, not to be 'slick', but rather out of recognition that its messages competed with hundreds or thousands of others every day, and the human mind does not particularly differentiate, or 'forgive,' the message initiated by a non-profit whose pockets may not be as deep as another entity.

The very growth and success of the non-profit sector in recent decades is evidence that SPRC was hardly unique in managing public relations and all of its other functions by applying best practices. Those studying public relations or general management or both, can learn from this and other best practices documented in the literature.

REFERENCES

Grunig, J.E., Grunig, L.A., & Dozier, D. (1992) *Excellence in Public Relations and Communications Management*. Hillsdale, NJ: Erlbaum.

Jackson, P. (1990) *PR Reporter* 33(32).

Kotler, P. (1986) *Principles of Marketing*, 3rd ed. Upper Saddle River, NJ: Prentice Hall.

Mintzberg, H. (1973) *The Nature of Managerial Work*. Upper Saddle River, NJ: Prentice Hall.

Petty, R.E., & Cacioppo, J.T. (1986) *Communication and Persuasion: Central and Peripheral Routes to Attitude Change*. New York: Springer-Verlag.

Therkelsen, D., & Fiebiech, C. (2001) Message to desired action: A communication effectiveness model. *Journal of Communication Management*, 5(4), 374–90.

Therkelsen, D., & Fiebiech, C. (2003) The supervisor: The linchpin of employee relations. *Journal of Communication Management*, 8(2), 120–9.

Internal Communication as a Function of Public Relations

12

Michael Board

Key Themes

- Internal communication is essential to company/organizational survival
- Employees are key stakeholder groups with specific communication needs
- Managers are key internal communication who must develop, implement, and evaluate internal communication strategies and tactics
- Multi-directional communication and 'inside-out' communication are important internal communication strategies

INTRODUCTION

Whether the term 'employee communication' or 'internal communication' is used, public relations professionals are or should be involved in all the facets of communication inside an organization. Be it top-down, horizontal or down-up, all communication within an organization is ultimately a public relations function and the responsibility of the public relations professional. In relation to the C-MACIE management framework presented in Part One, internal communication will seek to identify and understand the key forces that shape an organization from the inside out. For the purposes of this chapter, we will use the term 'internal communications' to cover a variety of communications topics, including, but not limited to: employee expectations, superior–subordinate communication, customer satisfaction, goal setting and strategic planning, performance reviews and evaluations, and the free flow of internal business communication. We feel the term 'internal communication' supersedes 'employee communication' in the depth and breadth of topics to be covered in this chapter, and dealt with on a daily basis by today's typical public relations professional. The purpose of this chapter is to better prepare you for some of these functions by identifying the key issues, pitfalls, strategies and tactics of solid, foundational internal communications.

THE IMPORTANCE OF INTERNAL COMMUNICATION

As the world decreases in size due to communication technologies such as the internet, more businesses pop up through entrepreneurial ventures, and the economy fluctuates with the increase and decrease in interest rates, it becomes increasingly important to capture every bit of business one can to ensure maximum success over time. Although there are various external factors that can significantly impact the success of any organization, there is no factor more important than its internal communication framework.

At a surface level, internal communication may not appear to be such a do-or-die issue, but upon further examination it is obvious that it is fundamental for sustained success. There are a number of organizational factors that hinge on thorough internal communications, including employee morale, employee retention and performance, customer service and satisfaction, inter-organizational goals and objectives, and employee relations. The best laid external communication campaigns would be impotent and ineffective if once the customers entered the business they were treated poorly, noticed low employee morale, or were given misinformation. In fact, it could be argued that it is counterproductive to deal with customers before an organization is ready for the interaction internally.

To reach long-term goals, most organizations understand the need for external marketing communications plans; however, few put proper emphasis on the equally important internal communications methods that serve as the grease of the organizational machine. The C-MACIE management framework emphasizes that people management is one of the fundamental tasks of management, 'yet is also generally acknowledged to be one of the most potentially problematic and unpredictable elements affecting functional performance' (see Chapter 2). Internal relationship management, which is a major function of internal communication, is a required skill in many organizations to help get things done through the various internal struggles and politics that commonly exist. Many organizations are plagued with age-old internal communication practices that need serious revamping. Many mid-level managers do not communicate with upper management on a consistent basis, and top-down communication is often kept to a minimum. Barrett (2002: 220) states that 'under-communication' is one major reason why change and success do not occur in many organizations. 'Employees will not make sacrifices, even if they are unhappy with the status quo, unless they believe that useful change is possible. Without credible communication, and a lot of it, the hearts and minds of the troops are never captured' (Barrett, 2002: 220). Organizational goals are often left to stand alone, without planning, objectives or evaluation to support them. Goals are also not communicated to all employees regularly, leading to average employee output and attitude. In partial concordance with Gatley and Clutterbuck (1997: 108), many organizations appear to have several communication gaps, including a 'lack of accountability for communication, ... lack of formal planning and integration, ... lack of shared processes for ensuring fast cascade of core messages and relaying upward feedback, and a lack of simple, shared messages on vision and strategy'.

Why Internal Communications?

The purpose of internal communication is to *internally* reposition the organization through communications principles such as branding, relationship building, employee relations, and customer loyalty and satisfaction. There is no doubt public relations has considerably changed the way organizations communicate with their external publics; however, 'communication with a company's own employees is only now achieving the status and resources that PR departments have commanded since the late 1970s' (Blakstad, 1995: 35). Organizations are slowly realizing their employees *are* the business, from the person answering the initial incoming phone call to the follow-up after a sale.

According to Sprague and Del Brocco (2002: 33), 'internal communications encompass every interchange between human beings within an organization' and 'may be the single most influential factor in your organization's success or failure'. The only true goal of internal communications is to 'change employee behavior in order to further the goals of the organization' (Sprague & Del Brocco, 2002: 34). Other researchers suggest that solid, quality internal communication methods offer a variety of benefits to the organization internally, as well as externally. Clampitt and Downs (1993: 23) suggest that 'the benefits obtained from quality internal communications include improved productivity, reduced absenteeism, higher quality (of services and products), increased levels of innovation, fewer strikes and reduced costs'. Scholars suggest, however, that all internal communications programs need not be overly complex or complicated. One researcher suggests 'that internal communications programmes which effect significant improvements are often characterized by their simplicity' (Tourish, 1997: 109). An effective internal program, depending on particular organizational size and structure, could be as simple as more strategic and planned face-to-face communication methods.

One key component of any truly successful internal communication program should be two-way, symmetrical communication (Grunig & Hunt, 1984; Grunig, 1992; Cutlip, Center, & Broom, 2000). Internal communication is too often a top-down message, composed by executives and management in an effort to inform the ranks about an issue they may not even care about. 'Frontline employees are specialist', Sprague and Del Brocco (2002: 35) state. 'They are passionately interested in their own pay, benefits, working conditions, advancement prospects, tools, and quality of life, and they are equally uninterested in overall company direction and performance.' They further argue that internal communications need to be employee-driven, not management-written. 'It's not what we want to tell them, it's what they want to know. Messages that are driven by priorities that do not match those of the target audience are doomed to fail' (Sprague & Del Brocco, 2002: 35). In true business verbiage, 'internal communications that serve as part of the typical "top-down" or "cascade" model are unlikely to deliver ROI' (Sprague & Del Brocco, 2002: 36). Regardless of the organizational type, return on investment is ultimately how communications professionals and internal programs prove their worth. The goal of any internal communications program should be to add value to the organization by increasing the quality and quantity of communication that occurs from day to day (Cook, 1991; Hause, 1993; Howard, 1996).

Why Not External Communications?

The study of internal communications at an organization is not to suggest that external communications are not important, are functioning at 100%, or do not need adjustments. Although the external communications at most organizations could be improved, research suggests that to reposition any organization, efforts should truly be worked from the inside out. 'Companies often spend millions of dollars on external marketing but give little time and attention to internal marketing' (Davis, 2001: 132). However, all the external efforts to win new customers would be in vain if they were not treated properly once in the business. Customers are also extremely difficult to satisfy when the employees themselves are not satisfied. Additionally, without individual, departmental, and organizational goals, measuring the efficacy of an external plan would be exponentially more difficult.

The internal communications needs of any organization are intrinsically linked to the external needs. 'The increasing visibility of insiders to outsiders means that employees are under pressure to interface with the customer as representatives of the organization in the way they think, feel and behave. This requires that they sign on to the organizational paradigm' (Kiriakidou & Millward, 2000: 50). Research also shows that employee satisfaction leads to greater customer satisfaction, and more thorough communication internally leads to better communication externally as well (Abbott, 2003). Also, many of the same paradigms that exist for external communication campaigns can be applied to internal campaigns. 'Like external marketing programs, internal marketing can be used to inform, educate, persuade, motivate or build relationships. Claims made in internal marketing programs are no different from claims made in advertisements to external customers' (Davis, 2001: 128). Davis (2001: 129) also concluded that the 'managers of service businesses need to market the company to employees before marketing the company to customers'. Management must have buy-in and support from the employees before a business can operate efficiently and successfully.

INTERNAL COMMUNICATION NEEDS

All organizations need a plan to communicate more effectively among employees. 'If organizations suffer from poor upwards, downwards, horizontal and diagonal flow of information … odds are that the inhibited behaviours concerned have been promoted by managers (consciously or unconsciously)' (Tourish, 1997: 113). Employees need, and in most cases want, to know what changes are occurring, the company's objectives, and how those changes and goals affect them. 'People are not just interested in how they do their job – they are passionately concerned with the broader environmental context in which that job occurs' (Tourish, 1997: 113). According to Lippitt (1997: 19), 'effective internal communication enables people to align their actions to support organizational goals, to coordinate and maximize resource use, and to stay motivated'. Internal communication is key to sharing and coordinating goals, promoting inter-departmental problem solving, business planning and goal setting.

A SWOT analysis is a common business technique that is widely used in marketing to analyze an organization's strengths, weaknesses, opportunities, and threats. 'Primary and secondary research is used to identify competitive advantages by recognizing how to leverage strengths, dampen weaknesses, avoid the threats and capture the opportunities' (Harris, 1998: 235). Clarke Caywood coined the 'TOWS' analysis in an effort to place 'the importance of threats and opportunities in keeping with the [integrated marketing communications] principles of substituting 'outside-in' thinking for 'inside-out' thinking' (Harris, 1998: 236). A TOWS analysis is widely held as a valuable tool to measure an organization's external communications issues, but let us not forget its internal value as well. When we follow Harris's ideal of inside-out thinking, a TOWS analysis can answer some valuable questions regarding the workings of an organization's internal communications as well.

THE PITFALLS OF POOR INTERNAL COMMUNICATION PROGRAMS

No one wants to dwell on the negative and take a pessimistic point of view, but let us all agree that public relations professionals are often faced with the task of proving their worth and value to the organization. Public relations programs are frequently the first to be cut when economic times are tough, but thankfully often the first to be hired back once the absence of public relations is seen and felt. There are some clear, strategic steps to be taken to correct an organization's internal communication woes, but the best public relations manager should want to dig deeper into the problems and pitfalls before any corrective actions are taken. After careful analysis of a broad range of internal communication research and programs, three predominant themes surface throughout the literature. The three main themes, or internal communication problem areas, are:

1. A severe lack of internal communication between managers and non-managers.
2. A feeling of lack of respect and value from non-managers to managers, and likewise from managers to non-managers.
3. A critically low level of employee morale across all levels of employee hierarchy, including both managers and non-managers.

Now that the major themes and problem areas are identified, a more in-depth look at the underlying issues is needed to further evaluate the problems to help a PR professional to offer some solutions.

Lack of Internal Communication

A lack of internal communication between managers and non-managers, as well as with other employee-to-employee groups, presents the opportunity for many other problems and issues to surface and grow. Other common organizational issues are often caused by a lack of communication, including: a lack of understanding of individual, departmental, and company goals and strategies; the non-existence of a formal performance review process; a shallow understanding of what is occurring in other areas of the business besides one's own; and low levels of supervisor–subordinate communication as a whole.

Goal Setting and Strategic Planning

A lack of internal communication in an organization can foster many problems, but one of the most likely is a lack of goal setting and strategic planning. It could easily be a problem when you have too many leaders and not enough followers, but the problem seems to lie deeper in many organizations. A lack of clear, timely, management-defined goals causes a downward spiral, where employees do not understand macro-level organizational goals. Most of the employees in an organization believe that the organization is functioning at an adequate level, but also that it could also improve in many areas or departments. The underlying principle in strategic planning and goal setting is that no one can get to the top of an industry without leadership and the help of others. Leadership needs to come from the owners, through the management, and trickle down to the non-managers to facilitate a successful organization.

Many managers are concerned that too much information would have as many negative effects as too little information, but this is more often an issue with managers who are uncomfortable communicating goals and objectives, or uncomfortable with the management of other people as a whole. While too much information is a valid concern, it is equally important that employees do not get their information from an outside or non-management source. The ideal situation would be for all employees, particularly in a small business, to contribute to goal setting and give feedback on what they see on the frontlines of the business. For instance, the employees who work with customers on a daily basis should know more about customer concerns, praises, or complaints than the managers do, because they see and hear them daily. Managers should use that knowledge and experience to help the business and its employees improve their performance.

Another common issue in many organizations causing a lack of internal communication is that the managers are often too bogged down with other duties to truly manage through goal setting and strategic planning. This can only be changed in one of two ways: delegate the management duties that they do not have time for, or delegate the duties that bog them down so they can manage more. The best managers are able to decipher and utilize their own strengths and weaknesses, as well as those of their management team. Many managers see delegation as a admitting that 'I can't do this and I need help', whereas nothing could be farther from the truth. Only skilled and seasoned managers are capable of determining who in their team is best suited for particular duties, helping to set their goals and motivating them to accomplish those goals through communication.

Performance Reviews and Evaluations

Much like organizational goal setting, individuals also need direction to increase their level of performance. If nearly half of the team does not know what goals there are to achieve, how can an organization expect to achieve success? It would almost be impossible to achieve those goals with any type of consistency. This points to a breakdown or lack of communication from the managers who should set the goals for the non-managers who should work to achieve the goals.

As mentioned above, employees cannot improve what they do and how they do it if management does not communicate on what the employees need to improve. Potentially, an employee could remain employed for years, thinking he or she is doing all he can to help the organization succeed, yet be totally off-base with regard to what management wants. A planned, consistent performance review and evaluation process is a guaranteed way to communicate face-to-face with employees about their strengths and weaknesses. Performance reviews also allow management a way to grade their employees and help them improve their individual performance, as well as the performance of the organization as a whole. Many performance review programs are not well received, and that lack of success could be for a variety of reasons, including the ability of the employees to perceive the fact that the managers do believe in the idea. Anyone can sense when another person is not sold on an idea, and if the employees realized that, or if there was inconsistency with the review process, the reviews are often ineffective. Additionally, many performance review programs are sporadically given, leaving employees to guess about whether or not the process is going to stay or go. But how would the employees know what their performance should be if their manager has not reviewed it with them? It is simply unfair to place expectations on employees without giving them an explanation of those expectations. A consistent, planned periodic performance review program is a key element for a manager to build a solid internal communication framework from the ground up.

Free Flow of Business Information

A simple employee survey (discussed later in this chapter) could serve as confirmation, but most organizational employees prefer face-to-face communication versus any other method. Face-to-face communication methods could include meetings with various employee groups, group discussions and/or reviews. However, whether face-to-face or some other method, employees need to communicate more and allow a free flow of business information among all levels of the organization. This is not to say that the people in the mail room need to know the budget for office supplies for the CEO, but they certainly need to know about all issues affecting them. One respondent stated in the comments section of a survey instrument administered at an equipment dealership in North Carolina: 'If we don't talk and work better as a company, I don't see future goals and objectives being met the way they should be.'

One example of poor internal communication and its effects was a health insurance premium increase at the equipment dealership mentioned above. For years the company paid 100% of every full-time employee's insurance, including his or her dependents. The company had endured several insurance premium increases, yet continued to pay 100% of the total. Although the company paid the increases to help the employees, management did not communicate with employees on what was being done for them. So, when insurance premiums increased to a level the company could not pay in full, it passed on the extra to the employees, which upset everyone. There was no warning and little explanation of the insurance changes, so employees got angry, vented to the general manager, and morale decreased. Better internal communication methods could have lessened the impact of the insurance benefits change. If the company had communicated in the past that the insurance premiums were increasing, but the company would absorb those increases, it would not have been such a shock when the company could no longer pay the entire premium. Also, if management had given a warning as to the changes to come in the future with the premium increases instead of making a sudden, drastic change, it would have no doubt been more accepted by the employees. In short, a little communication can go a long way and keep morale high, even if the communication is about something that does not positively affect the employees.

Manager–Non-manager Communication

Related to the free flow of business information is the communication between manager and non-managers, or supervisors and subordinates. From the research described earlier in the chapter, it is obvious that many employees prefer a method of communicating different from what management currently uses with them. Although word of mouth is perhaps the easiest form of communication, it is also the most misinterpreted and leads to more disinformation among employees. Written communication is probably the quickest method and leaves a paper trail for reference; however, it lacks the interpersonal aspect of being able to pull from the group's knowledge base for problem-solution sessions. Written communication also lacks the ability of question-and-answer sessions, which could greatly affect the efficiency of the messages and

> **Manager to Non-manager Communication Must Employ this T.A.C.T.I.C.**
>
> T – TIMELY
> A – ACCURATE
> C – CONSISTENT
> T – THOROUGH
> I – IMPORTANT
> C – CLEAR

FIGURE 12.1   T.A.C.T.I.C. Sidebar

make the communication process more difficult. Face-to-face group communication often gives the most credibility to a message, allows questions to be answered promptly and ensures that all members of the group hear identical messages. Group meetings, when conducted efficiently, often give all members the chance to voice their ideas and get immediate evaluation by management.

If employees are not getting the information they want or need from management regarding the organization as a whole or its individual departments, problems will undoubtedly surface. Additionally, if any information they received from management is not believed to be clear, timely or accurate, the credibility of those communicating the internal messages at the organization will be severely damaged. It is imperative that manager–non-manager communication is timely, accurate, consistent, thorough, important and clear. Figure 12.1 spells out what the TACTIC example contains.

Non-managers do not need to be bogged down with the financial demands and goals of the department or business, but they do need to know where they have been, where they are going, and that their job is secure.

Lack of Respect and Value

Weak internal communication will often trickle down into interpersonal relationships and cause other problems – and this happens in many organizations, regardless of size. A common issue caused by poor internal communication is a lack of respect and value among all employees, including managers and non-managers. Two key issues dealing with this theme are the managers feeling as though they are not appreciated and valued for what they give and do, and the non-managers feeling as though they work diligently but with little reward or recognition from the managers.

The Value of Managers
It is a natural tendency to stop going above and beyond the call of duty if no one appreciates it, which is what many managers feel from their employees. Respect is a two-way street, and if either party feels slighted, there will be major internal communication and interpersonal communication problems. However, respect must be earned. It may be impossible to 'make' someone respect you without causing resentment or fear, which would be counterproductive in any business or organization.

Management does not have to prove itself to the non-managers, but it does have to lead by example. For instance, if a manager asked an employee a question related to a customer, and the employee said he or she would find out the answer but never did, the manager would have a valid complaint. Likewise, when an employee goes to his supervisor but is brushed off, ignored, or lied to, the relationship is damaged and the communication effort was a failure. Like respect, communication is a two-way street, and it is common for very little traffic to travel down that road between managers and non-managers. Non-managers want the managers to do what they say, and managers want non-managers to do what they are supposed to do.

Timely, accurate, and consistent communication efforts from the managers down through the non-manager ranks would greatly increase the level of respect for and value of the managers. Most likely, it is not that the managers are not liked as people on an interpersonal level, but more that there is a breakdown of respect due to a lack of communication. If more managers would step up and communicate like managers should, the respect and value they desire and deserve would develop over time. It is truly not the job of managers to evolve in accordance with the non-managers' perceptions, but rather to communicate thoroughly and consistently on business matters.

The Value of Non-managers

Just as many managers do not feel valued by their employees, many non-managers feel neglected and taken for granted by their superiors. Even if employees believe they are treated ethically with regard to their employer, they can also feel unimportant and unappreciated because their ideas are not heard, valued or considered by management. A positive correlation is often found between the employees who feel their ideas are heard and valued by management and those with the highest morale levels. Although there is no way to statistically determine that fact with the anonymous survey instrument found later in this chapter, there is a strong possibility that the non-managers who feel most appreciated and valued as employees are also those with higher levels of morale and performance.

When it comes to non-managers feeling valued as employees, pay raises and rewards cannot be overlooked. If an employee group does not feel valued or appreciated by managers, incentive programs built to reward employees could bridge the gap caused by a lack of internal communication. Instead of simply giving more paid time off or pay raises, organizations could offer continuing education and employee development programs as well. However, implementing an incentive plan just to appease non-managers is not a method for showing a belief in the value of an organization's employees. There is nothing wrong with an incentive plan or extra vacation, but employees should have to earn those extras by performing at a superior level. Non-managers should be rewarded for what they do, just as the organization should be rewarded for having more efficient employees with better morale. If the organizational culture is one where all benefits, pay and incentives are the same regardless of performance or years of service, non-managers will feel undervalued and deliver a comparable performance. If the employees of an organization are its most valuable public, as many scholars believe, it is extremely important for employee issues such as these to be handled quickly and succinctly by management to avoid internal communication meltdown.

Lack of High Morale

The third problem area caused by poor internal communication is a lack of high employee morale, which may, in fact, be caused by the first two problem areas. If the employees believe there is no future for them at an organization or there are no advancement opportunities in the future, there is good chance morale will be low and turnover high. Also, low levels of employee morale typically cause the employee group to stagnate and become dissatisfied in his/her jobs, which can cause low performance and low customer satisfaction.

Whether your organization is the smallest in the industry, or the world-wide leader, customer satisfaction and employee performance should be two of the most important issues on your people management agenda. 'Deere & Company, founded in 1837 (collectively called John Deere), has grown from a one-man blacksmith shop into a corporation that today does business around the world and employs approximately 56,000 people' (Deere & Co., 2010). John Deere simply could not have grown to become one of the world's most recognized brands without a strong internal emphasis on employee–customer relations, employee performance and customer satisfaction. John Deere believes so strongly in customer satisfaction that the company developed its own internal program, Satisfaction First™, to monitor every major customer experience (Deere & Co., 2004). This has 'statistically documented the positive benefit that maintaining satisfied customers, or restoring disgruntled customers to satisfied status, has on repeat purchases' (Mangen Research Associates, 206). If the following three problems are left uncorrected, it is a safe bet that the organization will not experience the type of repeat business, company growth and customer satisfaction John Deere has been enjoying for more than 160 years. For an example of a typical equipment dealer customer survey instrument, see the John Deere survey at the end of this chapter.

High Turnover

One of the goals of any manager and internal communication program should be to reduce the turnover rate. Organizational culture can often dictate the feel of the employee workforce, be it a survival of the fittest atmosphere, a family atmosphere or a team atmosphere. Moving away from smaller, more intimate businesses to larger, more profit-minded conglomerates, most organizations leave the family atmosphere at home when they drive or walk to work. Our fast-paced societies leave organizations to thrive on team and survival atmospheres, where only those who possess the greatest business skills excel. Regardless of the culture an organization purports, ideally management should want to foster an atmosphere where their non-managers could thrive, instead of just survive. One obvious reason for high turnover rates is poor hiring decisions. It is always possible that the wrong person was hired for a particular position, which clearly shows the importance of the hiring and selection process. However, it is also possible that a poorly chosen person could develop into a superb employee if both the employee and his/her manager are willing to work on it together through solid internal communication.

Customer Dissatisfaction

Regardless of the type of organization, customer loyalty is extremely important for long-term success. Every organization has 'customers', even if they are not thought of as such. Becoming more customer-focused is key in attracting and retaining customers, and the lifetime value of a customer is far greater than many organizations realize. Customers can sense if the employees with whom they are interacting do not truly like their jobs. Low morale is a tell-tale sign of employee dissatisfaction, which translates to customer dissatisfaction. Other causes of dissatisfaction include interpersonal issues, job-related stress, and personal matters interfereing with job performance among others. Regardless of the reason, employee dissatisfaction and customer dissatisfaction are directly linked and can become a cancer inside an organization.

Low Performance

A major concern with low morale in an organization is low performance. High employee morale produces high levels of employee performance. With sustained high employee performance their organizations are more positively received by their publics, and consequently more successful. Employees with higher morale levels also tend to be friendlier and more willing to satisfy customers, or go the proverbial extra mile. Low performance causes the inverse of all the positive attributes mentioned above. A symptom of low morale, sustained low employee performance negatively affects an organization's reputation with its publics and harms long-term relations. Customers want and need a friendly atmosphere where employees make them feel welcomed. When customers look forward to coming to a business or organization, it is much more beneficial for all involved parties.

PUBLIC RELATIONS STRATEGIES TO IMPROVE INTERNAL COMMUNICATION

Internal Agenda Setting

According to Smith (2002), an organization's goals are rooted in its mission and/or vision. Mission and vision statements do more than state the idealistic view of an organization. They can give direction and purpose, motivate employees, increase morale, and effectively show customers that the organization is looking to continually improve. Many organizations develop a mission statement, vision statement and/or core values when the organization is in its infancy, never revisiting those ideals as the organization matures and evolves. Just as personal goals need to be reevaluated on a regular and ongoing basis, so do the goals of an organization. As a fundamental tenet of internal communication, an organization's leaders have an opportunity to pick the direction and set the course via internal agenda setting through mission statements, vision statements and/or core values. Just as public relations functions externally to guide media toward particular issues and topics by agenda setting, internal agenda setting can help to mold an organization's atmosphere and culture from the ground up.

Mission statements as a form of internal agenda setting should describe the organization's purpose, how to achieve its vision, provide focus to the organization, compel and motivate employees, and differentiate the organization from the competition. With a more futuristic view, vision statements should describe an ultimate goal and business achievement, and clearly identify the organization. The vision statement should describe where the organization will be in within five years if it continuously achieves its mission. In addition to vision and mission statements, a set of core values can further instill the purpose of the organization into employees and customers alike. These core values should be customer-focused, and prove to be fundamental for the ultimate success of the organization. These ideals should be displayed for all customers and employees to see regularly. As these ideals become engrained, employee performance and customer satisfaction will increase. Core values are there to help guide employees in their daily jobs and help the managers set the path for strategic trailblazing. Like a fingerprint, every organization is different, therefore, these goal statements will vary greatly from one organization to another. However, for the purposes of this chapter and to present the general idea of these agenda setting tools, sample vision, mission, and core value statements can be found in Figures 12.2–12.4, as well as an example set of statements.

Our Vision

XYZ Corporation will be the clear leader in territory sales, and hold a dominant position as the preferred source of automobiles, service and parts the greater Charlotte-metro area.

FIGURE 12.2   Vision Statement

Our Mission

XYZ Corporation exists lo provide outstanding parts, sales and service for all consumer and commercial customers that will help them succeed in their enterprises. We will strive to maintain fair prices and margins that allow our business to innovate and grow, while enabling our customers to purchase locally from a reputable and trusted business. We will work to ensure that the expectations of our customers are always exceeded at each interaction and by each employee.

FIGURE 12.3   Mission Statement

Our Core Values

- Friendly – We are friendly, courteous, and respectful to others.
- Helpful – We are happy to help our co-workers and customers find solutions.
- Fair – We are fair and honest in our dealings with others.
- Teammates – We are a TEAM. "It's not my job" is not in our vocabulary.
- Flexible – We are easy to do business with.
- Clear – We communicate with our customers and with co-workers directly, concisely, and effectively.
- Focused – We are customer driven.
- Over-Achievers – We exceed our customers' expectations.

FIGURE 12.4 Core Values Statement

Strategies

In essence, a strategy is an organization's overall plan that determines 'what and how it wants to achieve' (Smith, 2002: 69). Based on the list of common internal communication pitfalls mentioned above, three primary strategies are suggested below. These three strategies are not intended to be an exhaustive list, but rather a starting point for an organization to get back on the road to recovery with its internal communication program. Intentionally broad, these strategies and their concurrent tactics are proven methods for strengthening internal communication at a variety of organizations world-wide. However, even though they appear simple on the surface, do not underestimate the actual difficulty of completing these strategies and tactics, as each comes with an internal communication checks and balances system with an organization's success at stake.

- *Strategy 1*: To develop more open channels of communication to encourage a free flow of internal business communication among all levels of the organization and all levels of the employee hierarchy.
- *Strategy 2*: To develop a rewards and recognition plan to encourage an increase in employee morale through goal setting and performance-based incentives.
- *Strategy 3*: To develop an internal awareness campaign on customer satisfaction to encourage an increase in employee performance, customer satisfaction, and customer retention.

Tactics

Harris (1998: 247) states: 'Tactics are the methods, actions, and activities used to achieve objectives'. Based on the previously identified strategies, several tactics have been developed that will support each strategy as it relates to organizational success. These tactics can help to position any organization to develop a healthier internal communication program and become a success from the inside out.

Strategy 1: To develop more open channels of communication to encourage a free flow of internal business communication among all levels of the organization and all levels of the employee hierarchy.

Tactic 1 – Communication Training

According to Harshman and Harshman (1999: 18), the seven Cs of communication 'allow the organization to build powerful, ethical communication processes that mirror the stated values. The characteristics are not like items on the supermarket shelf such that one can pick and choose which to implement. They are tied together'. All managers in an organization need to become trained and knowledgeable on the seven Cs of effective communication (see Figure 12.5 on p. 294), and empowered to train the non-managers. If all the employees at an organization, managers and non-managers, become better individual communicators, then the organization will likewise become more efficient in its communication.

Tactic 2 – Employee Meetings

Employee meetings at many organizations are poorly organized and poorly executed. Employees often see meetings as sporadic and non-productive, in addition to commonly used to convey 'bad news'. If past meetings at an organization are viewed as unproductive, then all parties involved need to work to change the meeting format to make them more valuable from a communication viewpoint. If employees prefer face-to-face communication, which is frequently the case, meetings should be one of the best mediums for communicating on a variety of issues. Perhaps only one issue at a time

---

1   Central – Communication is central to the business and the performance of the business.
2   Consistent – Communication comes out regularly rather than on an intermittent basis.
3   Congruent – Communication is congruent with actions and does not send mixed signals to employees or customers.
4   Coordinated – Communication activities are content and coordinated; that is, they fit together versus being a random pattern of disbursing information.
5   Courageous – Communication is courageous rather than being seen as timid and safe.
6   Collaborative – Communication is done in conjunction with employees rather than being controlled by top leaders independently of the employees or as something done 'to' employees.
7   Credible – Communication is seen as credible by stakeholders rather than viewed as selfserving to the needs ofthe owners and/or the people at the top of the organization.

Adapted from Harshman, E.F. & Harshman, C.L. (1999). Communicating with employees: Building on an ethical foundation. *Journal of Business Ethics, 19*(1), pp. 3–19.

FIGURE 12.5   The Seven C's of Communication

should be discussed in a problem-solution format, or perhaps small group meetings would work better instead of larger ones. As a starting point, weekly managers' meetings should be implemented to discuss organizational goals, departmental direction, and employee issues or concerns. Also, monthly employee meetings should be implemented to discuss general business issues, employee issues, and any problems internally or externally. Harris and de Chernatony (2001: 447) state: 'to gain employees' commitment to a brand's identity it is important to establish staff communication

Who:
- Evaluations should be conducted by the employee's immediate supervisor.
- Senior management should evaluate other management personnel only, i.e. – not nonmanagers.

What:
- A plan of action should be stated, in writing, to help all employees improve their performance between evaluation periods.

When:
- To begin the process, all employees should have a minimum of two evaluations per calendar year, to be held in January and July (For a period no less than three years; Subject to change based on employee and organization performance).
- All new employees should have an informal evaluation 30 days after hire, a formal evaluation 90 days after hire, and then begin their regular evaluation schedule at the next calendar evaluation meeting, January or July.

Where:
- Copies of employee evaluations should be placed in their respected employee files and reviewed prior to each evaluation period to determine any performance changes.

Why:
- All employees should be held accountable for the issues discussed in their evaluations, with clear rewards and penalties.
- All incentives, salaries, bonuses and commissions should be negotiated at the set review period only.

How:
- An evaluation form should be completed by the responsible manager prior to conducting employee evaluation assessments.
- After evaluation forms are completed by department managers and reviewed with the senior management, evaluation meetings should be conducted in a timely fashion with all employees (senior management not included in actual review meetings).
- Employees should be allowed to read their own evaluations, and given time and space to respond to any issues, good or bad.
- After three years-of semi-annual reviews, an adequately performing employee may be reduced to annual reviews at the discretion of their immediate supervisor.

FIGURE 12.6 The Who, What, When, Where and How of Performance Reviews-Employee Performance Evaluation Process & Procedures

programs. Internal organizational communication is crucial for providing and obtaining information, achieving understanding and gaining employees' commitment'. These meetings should serve as a way for non-managers and managers to communicate symmetrically and consistently.

Tactic 3 – Performance Reviews

A performance review plan should be implemented to give the non-managers a better understanding of what their manager and the organization expects from them as employees, not just a random review occurring once every couple of years. Pay raises will be an issue in any organization, so the management should let the employees know what is expected to earn a pay raise, and that is all part of the performance review process. It is a vicious communication cycle to not give employee performance reviews. Managers complain because their employees are not performing to management expectations and goals. Non-managers complain because they feel that their performance is good, but that they are not being rewarded for it and they do not really know if management notices their efforts. Neither party is satisfied with the other, and morale continues to decrease until an employee or several employees leave the organization, and the cycle starts anew. A simple performance review schedule, clearly communicated to employees, should solve some of these issues (see Figure 12.6 on p. 295).

Tactic 4 – Newsletter

An employee newsletter is one of the easiest and most inexpensive ways to communicate with an employee group on simple issues. It can be used to reiterate organizational performance goals and the status of those goals, human resource issues, and other timely information. As a monthly communication medium, it offers another channel of communication with the added benefit of longer shelf life. A newsletter can be printed and distributed or mailed, or produced and distributed electronically. There are benefits to each, therefore, the organization must decide which is more beneficial for its internal communication program. By printing and mailing the newsletter to the employees' places of residence, employees' families are encouraged to be involved with the organization and understand a little more about where their family member works, if they so choose. By electronically distributing the newsletter, the organization is encouraging the timely distribution of information and encouraging employees to read it while on the job. This internal publication can be simple in format and internally produced, while offering another way for managers to effectively communicate with non-managers.

Tactic 5 – Employee Suggestion Box

Something as simple and easy as a suggestion box can offer non-managers another way to communicate with management on sensitive issues. All organizations should purchase, install, and use an employee suggestion box so that employees can anonymously make comments and suggestions about their departments, the organization, or other pertinent issues. This box should be placed in an area accessible to employees only, such as the break room. The managers should be responsible for checking the suggestion box weekly and, most importantly, responding to the non-managers' suggestions and comments in a timely fashion. If the non-managers were to use the suggestion box but the managers failed to respond, the communication would be a failure and more damage could be done to the internal communication in the organization. Responses to the suggestions should be posted for all employees to read, perhaps on a bulletin board in the break room.

Strategy 2: To develop a rewards and recognition plan to encourage an increase in employee morale through goal setting and performance-based incentives.

Tactic 6 – Goal Setting

The managers need to work within the parameters of the organization's mission, vision, and values to develop clear, timely and specific goals for individual, departmental, and organizational improvement. The goal-setting initiative from the managers is extremely important for organizational success, in that it should be one of the primary measuring tools for performance evaluations. Just as Harris and de Chernatony (2001: 447) found, 'employees need to know what is expected of them and how they can contribute to the brand's identity through their behaviour'. A simple yet thorough goal-setting campaign should be conducted to clearly state the goals and the corresponding desired outcomes.

Tactic 7 – Rewards and Incentive Plan

Many employees at various organizations receive sporadic rewards and pay raises without any true evaluation to support those incentives. From the employees' viewpoint, it can be difficult to determine why a pay raise was or was not received because there are no related performance goals on which employees are measured. With the implementation of a performance evaluation process and formal goal setting, a rewards and incentive plan for meeting stated performance goals should be implemented to increase employee morale. Perhaps a multi-faceted incentive plan to reward for individual and/or departmental improvement would be the best plan. Many organizations invest large amounts of money on employee training, yet do little to reward employees for more knowledge or to keep those highly trained employees. Perhaps part of the pay raise scale should be tied to the amount of training and experience an employee brings to the organization. It is probable that each department will have a different reward and incentive plan, due to the fact that each department will have its own set of goals and objectives.

Tactic 8 – Benefits Package

To help reduce the threat of a high turnover rate, a benefits package needs to be developed to reward employees for longer terms of service, achieving goals and objectives and exhibiting organizational values. There are innumerable options for benefits packages, including extra paid time off, cash and gift card rewards, education credits to be used on advanced degrees, etc. An increase in the number of paid vacation days would be one way to thank employees for their dedication to the organization. For instance, once an employee reached 10 years of service, he/she could earn one extra paid vacation day for each additional year of employment. This could be a valuable benefit because many organizations limit the number of paid vacation days regardless of how many years an employee has worked there. Benefits packages are a valuable tool to increase employee morale and retention, thereby increasing customer satisfaction and organizational performance. Packages are also a valuable tool to attract top-performing recruits from other organizations.

Strategy 3: To develop an internal awareness campaign on customer satisfaction to encourage an increase in employee performance and customer satisfaction.

Tactic 9 – Employee Training

Managers in most organizations are probably well aware of the cost of business and the cost associated with trying to attract new customers, but non-manager employees probably are not. To foster a deeper understanding of customer service, customer satisfaction, and customer retention, employee training should be given to help all employees understand the importance of satisfying the organization's existing customers, as well as how difficult and expensive it is to gain new customers. It is possible that internal training can help an organization's employees become customer satisfaction experts.

Tactic 10 – Satisfaction Surveys

As a way to check on the effectiveness of the employee training mentioned above, as well as reward employees for good customer service skills, surveys could be sent to random customers after their interactions at organization. The customers could be asked to rate their experience at the organization, as well as how satisfied they were with the level of service they received. The more specific the survey, including the name of the employee with which the customer interacted, the more the employees will feel their individual experience with each customer is important and will be evaluated. These surveys could also be used later to help further train the employees on what customers expect when they bring their business to the organization.

THE BENEFITS OF IMPROVED INTERNAL COMMUNICATION

The benefits associated with a fully functional, employee-driven internal communication campaign are limitless in terms of immediate organizational impact and long-term relationship building and credibility among the organization's publics. As with many public relations and communications efforts, an accurate measurement of the full impact on an organization is difficult, to say the least. This section briefly discusses three key benefits of improved internal communication: increased customer satisfaction, improved employee performance and strengthened business stimulators.

Improved Employee Performance

The phrase is often overused, but it makes common sense that well-informed, connected employees with a clear understanding of their personal, departmental and organization goals will do an overall better job. Whether they are assembling widgets in a industrial factory or negotiating the terms of a major corporate acquisition, all employees want to be informed, and ultimately most want to do a good job for the organization. With a thorough, employee-driven internal communication program, all employees, regardless of their position in the organizational hierarchy, will increase their performance level as their individual-job congruence also increases. And as everyone in the proverbial boat begins to individually row harder, the entire organization begins to excel too.

Increased Customer Satisfaction

Customer satisfaction is the goal of business. Although many marketers will argue that the goal of business is to make money, it is simply a fact that without satisfied customers an organization will not make much money, or at least not for long. All businesses want satisfied customers; otherwise they would not exist. 'A brand's emotional values are communicated not just by advertising, but also through employees' interactions with different stakeholders', according to Harris and de Chernatony (2001). 'Employees represent a source of customer information and action needs to be taken to ensure this is compatible with the way senior management wishes the organization to be perceived' (Harris & de Chernatony, 2001: 442). In other words, management is responsible for how customers are treated, as well as communicating organizational goals to the employee. 'It is therefore crucial to look inside the organization to consider how employees' values and behavior can be aligned with a brand's desired values' (Harris & de Chernatony, 2001: 442). Stressing how important employee–client interactions are, Harris & de Chernatony (2001: 442) state that 'through their interactions, employees significantly affect a brand's relationship with its consumers'.

Better Business Stimulators

Like the individual–job congruence model previously discussed, employee–client interactions are more likely to be favorable and pleasing to both parties if there is a higher level of congruence and consistency within the interchange. 'People respond more favourably to brands and companies they perceive as being consistent with their self-concepts', stated Harris and de Chernatony (2001: 442). They further explain that 'both advertising and employees' interactions with consumers contribute to the symbolic meaning of a brand'. Business stimulators, or to phrase it another way, the factors which cause you to do business with a particular organization, are the keys to success that are painstakingly sought after by many of the top organizations in the world. Customers love doing business with people they like, and employees who are happy in their jobs give better customer service. How many times have you not returned to a restaurant because the customer service was poor, even if the food was fantastic? Likewise, how many times have you highly recommended a restaurant, or other business, because their employees went the extra mile to make your experience there the best it could be? We have all been there, but few organizations realize that these business stimulators are rooted in a foundational internal communication program. Many organizations attempt to increase customer service, boost employee morale or reduce turnover, which are all noble tasks. But if the organization does not proactively promote better internal communication at all levels of the organization, those customer service programs will fall on deaf ears.

USING KEY INTERNAL COMMUNICATIONS TO UNLOCK EMPLOYEE EXPECTATIONS

Most managers assume they know the expectations of their employees, but that assumption is a dangerous one for the organization. If an organization is failing to use internal communications to meet or exceed the expectations of its employees, it is failing as a whole. To simplify the process of understanding employee expectations, and through the reading and analyzing of countless articles written by some of the greatest researchers in the communications field, five key expectation areas were determined and listed below. Many of these areas of expectations are as simple as our own inherent needs as human beings, such as meaningful personal communication, realistic future career goals, and admiration for a job well done (Heath, 2000: 8–10; Tourish, 1997: 111–12; Barrett, 2002: 220–25).

With regard to expectations, 'if employees ... were prodded to work for the ... [company] ... and if they saw themselves as effective contributors to the company's goals, they would, in theory, be more likely to perform at a higher level' (Nicoll, 1993: 35). Further, Goris, Pettit, and Vaught (2002: 664) state that the 'Job Characteristics Model suggests that high levels of performance and satisfaction should result from a match between the growth needs of an individual and the motivating characteristics of the job being performed'. Their research shows the need to seek out and interpret the desires of the employee population in all organizations, including their personal, relational, company, career, and reward expectations, in an effort to increase job satisfaction and organizational performance. The researchers continue to show that 'pay, security, interpersonal relations, and supervision influenced individual-job congruence association with job performance' (Goris et al., 2002: 665). Through the above researchers and others, five key areas of interest in relation to internal communication and employee expectations were decoded:

1. Personal expectations – what employees expect to gain from their employment on a personal level.
2. Relational expectations – how employees prefer to relate to coworkers while on the job.
3. Organizational expectations – how employees feel about the organization and its communication as a whole.
4. Career expectations – what employees expect to gain from the organization with regard to their career path.
5. Reward expectations – how employees would like to be rewarded for superior performance.

Just knowing and understanding the five areas of employee expectations is not enough for a manager to be successful in his/her pursuit of a fruitful internal communications program. To better comprehend the rationale behind the areas, the following questionnaire is suggested as a tool for management to strengthen and build its relationship with employees. When teamed with a Likert-type scale, this questionnaire can and will open a wealth of knowledge about your employees and set the organization down the path toward a sustainable internal communications foundation, on which holistic organizational success can be built. For a full rationale of the meanings behind each individual statement, see the survey at the end of this chapter.

- *Statement 1*: I am valued by management as an employee.
- *Statement 2*: I am treated fairly and appreciated as an employee.
- *Statement 3*: I believe my opinions and ideas are heard and evaluated when voiced.
- *Statement 4*: My performance as an employee could be better.
- *Statement 5*: My morale as an employee could be better.
- *Statement 6*: I prefer word-of-mouth communication (Ex.: So and so said this …) to learn about departmental goals, duties and business information.
- *Statement 7*: I prefer face-to-face communication (Ex.: Meetings, group discussions, reviews) to learn about departmental goals, duties and business information.

- *Statement 8*: I prefer written communication (Ex.: Memos, e-mails, company newsletter) to learn about departmental goals, duties and business information.
- *Statement 9*: My manager recognizes employees for good performance (Ex.: Rewards, pay raises, atta-boys).
- *Statement 10*: My manager shares information about my department and/or the organization as a whole regularly (Ex.: Meetings, memos, e-mails).
- *Statement 11*: My manager follows up promptly on employee questions and concerns.
- *Statement 12*: I am aware of the organization's goals and objectives.
- *Statement 13*: I am aware of what is going on in other areas of the organization besides my department or area.
- *Statement 14*: I do all I can to ensure our customers/patrons/volunteers are serviced and satisfied.
- *Statement 15*: I understand the importance of my role in customer service and customer satisfaction.
- *Statement 16*: My understanding of the organization's goals and objectives is important for its success.
- *Statement 17*: Overall, internal business communication is clear, timely and accurate.
- *Statement 18*: I am aware of my job-related goals and objectives.
- *Statement 19*: I am aware of my departmental goals and objectives.
- *Statement 20*: I believe there are advancement opportunities for me here.
- *Statement 21*: I believe I could make a profitable career here.
- *Statement 22*: My expectations as an employee are being met.

Statements 1–5 related to personal expectations, 6–11 to relational expectations, 12–17 to organizational expectations, and 19–22 to career expectations. Other than Goris et al.'s (2002) job characteristics model which deals with individual–job congruence, there is little or no pertinent research relating to employees' reward expectations. Because of the lack of literature to call upon, we were left to call upon the collected professional experiences at various workplaces of friends and colleagues and the known reward programs at other organizations. Through that collected knowledge, the following reward expectation categories were devised in effort to cover the most popular areas consistently. The purpose of this part of the internal communications questionnaire is to help managers learn how to gain support from their employees and what would motivate them to want to make personal communication changes and/or help to increase their morale. This also helps the organization learn how it can compensate and reward employees for superior performance, in addition to typical pay raises.

It is suggested that managers ask employees to rank-order six reward expectation statements from 1 to 6, with 1 being most desirable. The rewards are purposefully generalized, but include the following six areas: public recognition; extra paid vacation; quarterly luncheons; gift certificates; organization-sponsored events; and pay raises.

- *Statement A*: I prefer public recognition as a reward for achieved goals and objectives (Employee of the Month, atta-boys, etc.).
- *Statement B*: I prefer extra paid vacation as a reward for achieved goals and objectives (A half-day or whole day of paid vacation).
- *Statement C*: I prefer quarterly luncheons or meals as a reward for achieved goals and objectives (Organization sponsored, catered lunches).
- *Statement D*: I prefer gift certificates as a reward for achieved goals and objectives (Restaurant certificates or gift cards).
- *Statement E*: I prefer an organization event as a reward for achieved goals and objectives (Amusement park trip, sports event, etc.).
- *Statement F*: I prefer pay raises as a reward for achieved goals and objectives (Higher wages, bonuses or commissions).

Again, tying in with Goris et al.'s (2002) job congruency model, employee–employer expectations are key to operating a successful business, maintaining a faithful and trained employee base, and increasing customer satisfaction.

C-MACIE RELEVANCE TO INTERNAL COMMUNICATION

In this chapter we have sought to examine the basic principles of internal communication as it relates to the function of management-level public relations. We have explored many of the underlying issues of internal communication, including some pitfalls of poor internal programs, fundamental public relations strategies and tactics to better the internal environment, the benefits of those improved programs, as well as a method for managers to determine the expectations of their employees, thereby increasing employee satisfaction and retention. We believe it is clear how internal communication stands as a cornerstone to the C-MACIE management framework in terms of people management and the relationship-building process within an organization.

One example of how internal/employee communication uses the analysis step of the C-MACIE model is illustrated by the TOWS analysis. Developing a TOWS analysis can provide managers and supervisors with a benchmark about the status of internal communication and provide insight into what areas of internal communication need to be addressed. Further measures, such as employee surveys and face-to-face meetings with employees, can reveal areas where things are going well as well as areas where improvement is needed. Managers conducting such analyses will find that engaging employees in the internal communication process can also avoid rumors, grapevine gossip, or outright misinformation.

Following the analysis step, managers do have choices as to what their strategies and tactics should be for creating consistent, clear, and fair communication in their organizations. Organizations deal in different types of information, ranging from the very sensitive or highly technical, to the traditional political and organizational culture information. The choices managers make to create, develop, and implement employment communication plans have great impact on developing and/or maintaining employee loyalty and trust. Managers should realize that the choices made here should be tailored to the different types of employees, upward, downward and sideways in the organization. An important consideration here is also that employees have some 'say' in what information they want and/or need to do their jobs and feel like a valued part of the organization.

The choice and implementation steps of the C-MACIE model are closely tied in employee/internal communication. Asking employees for their views, ideas, and feedback creates the expectation that they are partners with all levels of the organization, and it is the manager's duty to make sure that when communication is asked for, it is at least recognized, and, at best, incorporated into the organization's life. Setting up suggestions boxes, meeting with groups of employees to gather their ideas and concerns, or sending out surveys without actually intending to use the information often causes more dissatisfaction and distrust among employees than never implementing it to begin with. Another consideration with implementation is to make sure that the most appropriate number of employee communication tactics are used – avoiding overkill – and that the types of communication tactics are appropriate to different kinds of employees.

The final step of the C-MACIE model – evaluation – is generally discussed in terms of evaluations of individual employees and their job performance. The C-MACIE evaluation section suggests that simple job performance can be enhanced by clear, accurate, timely, well-managed communication on an ongoing basis with employees throughout the organization. Evaluation does not end with the individual employee and how well he/she has fulfilled her individual job expectations. It must include evaluation of how well informed and satisfied employees are with their knowledge of the organization's goals and objectives and its place in its respective industry sector. In today's world of higher-than-normal unemployment and underemployment, how employees are engaged in communication throughout the organization can be a critical factor in how well the organization does in today's economy.

SUMMARY

Although internal communication is often neglected in lieu of external communication programs, through the findings of various researchers we believe it is clear that an organization must first position itself internally before it can begin a successful external campaign. Employees are the most valuable, and perhaps the most overlooked, public of any organization. A strong, employee-driven internal communication

(Continued)

(Continued)

program is key to helping increase customer and employee satisfaction, employee performance and retention, as well as improved future business stimulators. Early in this chapter we posed the question, why internal communication? We hope it is now clear that in most organizations internal communication acts as the glue to bind all employees together in terms of goal setting, strategic planning and the free flow of internal business communication as a whole.

 ## REFERENCES

Abbott, J. (2003) Does employee satisfaction matter? A study to determine whether low employee morale affects customer satisfaction and profits in the business-to-business sector. *Journal of Communication Management*, 7(4), 333–9.

Barrett, D.J. (2002) Change communication: Using strategic employee communication to facilitate major change. *Corporate Communications*, 7(4), 219–31.

Blakstad, M. (1995) Getting the message on internal communication. *Human Resource Management International Digest*, 3(5), 35–7.

Clampitt, P., & Downs, C. (1993) Employee perceptions for the relationship between communication and productivity: A field study. *Journal of Business Communication*, 30, 5–28.

Cook, R. (1991) Communicating bad news to employees. *Compensation and Benefits Review*, 23, 13–20.

Cutlip, S.M., Center, A.H., & Broom, G.M. (2000) *Effective Public Relations* (8th ed.). Upper Saddle River, NJ: Prentice Hall.

Davis, T.R. (2001) Integrating internal marketing with participative management. *Management Decision*, 39(2), 12–132.

Deere & Co. (2004) Satisfaction First. Retrieved February 1, 2010, from https://satfirst.deere.com/en_US/References/Surveys/dealer_experience_surveys.htm

Deere & Co. (2010) General Information. Retrieved February 1, 2010, from http://www.deere.com/en_US/compinfo/generalinfo/index.html

Gatley, L., & Clutterbuck, D. (1997) United Distillers: A planned approach to employee communication. *Training & Management Development Methods*, 11(3), 107–10.

Goris, J.R., Pettit Jr., J.D., & Vaught, B.C. (2002). Organizational communication: Is it a moderator of the relationship between job congruence and job performance/satisfaction? *International Journal of Management*, 19(4), 664–72.

Grunig, J.E. (ed.). (1992) *Excellence in Public Relations and Communication Management*. Hillsdale, NJ: Erlbaum.

Grunig, J.E., & Hunt, T. (1984) *Managing Public Relations*. New York: Holt, Rinehart, Winston.

Harris, F., & de Chernatony, L. (2001) Corporate branding and corporate brand performance. *European Journal of Marketing*, 35(3/4), 441–56.

Harris, T.L. (1998) *Value Added Public Relations: The Secret Weapon of Integrated Marketing*. Chicago: NTC Business.

Harshman, E.F., & Harshman, C.L. (1999) Communicating with employees: Building on an ethical foundation. *Journal of Business Ethics*, 19(1), 3–19.

Hause, D. (1993) Giving employees bad news. *Public Relations Journal*, 49, 18–23.

Heath, K. (2000) A prescription for employee satisfaction. *Total Communication Measurement*, 2(8), 6–11.

Howard, C. (1996) Face-to-face communications: Payback is worth the effort. *Public Relations Quarterly*, 41, 11–14.

Kiriakidou, O., & Millward, L.J. (2000) Corporate identity: External reality or internal fit? *Corporate Communications*, 5(1), 49–58.

(Continued)

(Continued)

Lippitt, M. (1997) Say what you mean, mean what you say. *Journal of Business Strategy*, *18*(4), 18–20.
Mangen Research Associates (2006) *John Deere Satisfaction First*. Retrieved February 1, 2010, from http://www.mrainc.com/sat1st.html.
Nicoll, D.C. (1993) Corporate vale statements and employee communications. *Management Decision*, *31*(8), 34–41.
Smith, R.D. (2002) Establishing goals and objectives. In *Strategic Planning for Public Relations* (pp. 69–81). Mahwah, NJ, and London: Erlbaum.
Sprague, R.W., & Del Brocco, S.F. (2002) Calculating the ROI on internal communications. *Employment Relations Today*, *29*(1), 33–44.
Tourish, D. (1997) Transforming internal corporate communications: The power of symbolic gestures and barriers to change. *Corporate Communications*, *2*(3), 109–16.
Yrie, A.C., Hartman, S., & Galle, W.P. (2002) An investigation of relationships between communication style and leader-member exchange. *Journal of Communication*, *6*(3), 257–69.

APPENDIX A: RATIONALE OF EMPLOYEE EXPECTATIONS SURVEY

Personal Expectations

Statement 1: I am valued by management as an employee.

This statement was derived in part by Harshman and Harshman's (1999) underlying values of successful internal communications. A list was constructed which includes: 'Trust one another; treat each other with respect; and recognize the value of each individual' (Harshman & Harshman 1999: 14). Considering oneself to be valued on the interpersonal level is key to successful communication patterns.

Statement 2: I am treated fairly and appreciated as an employee.

Following Barrett's (2002) thoughts on supportive management, 'managers must model the behavior they expect of their employees, the adage of 'walking the talk' (Barrett, 2002: 222). In other words, managers should not ask their employees to do something that they would not do, which would be unfair and show a lack of respect and appreciation for the employees.

Statement 3: I believe my opinions and ideas are heard and evaluated when voiced.

Many actions 'can influence the level of success of a change communication program, but at the end of the day, complete success depends upon … immediate follow-up on employee ideas and rewards for good ideas and good communications' (Barrett, 2002: 224). For employees to voice their ideas and opinions honestly and consistently, they must know that those thoughts will be considered and evaluated.

Statement 4: My performance as an employee could be better.

According to Harshman and Harshman (1999:5): 'In working with a large number of public and private sector corporations and agencies over the last seventeen years, we have seen a high positive correlation between performance problems and communication problems'.

Statement 5: My morale as an employee could be better.

Closely related to employee performance, low morale is often another indicator of communication problems in an organization. The role of thorough communication should be to 'impact positively the attitudes of employees' (Harshman & Harshman, 1999: 24).

Relational Expectations

Statement 6: I prefer word-of-mouth communication (Ex.: So and so said this ...) to learn about departmental goals, duties and business information.

In support of Barrett's (2002) thought on effective media, 'effective communication uses all vehicles to reach its audiences, but most importantly, it relies on direct, face-to-face communication over indirect, print or electronic media', which does not include employee-to-employee word-of-mouth communication.

Statement 7: I prefer face-to-face communication (Ex.: Meetings, group discussions, reviews) to learn about departmental goals, duties and business information.

According to Davis (2001: 124): 'The most credible source of communication for most employees is one-to-one, face-to-face communication. It is indispensable for relationship marketing. It can be used to discuss issues, communicate confidential information, transmit bad news, and test out ideas'.

Statement 8: I prefer written communication (Ex.: Memos, e-mails, company newsletter) to learn about departmental goals, duties and business information.

Davis (2001: 124) says: 'Impersonal, one-way communication media such as memos, letters, company magazines, newspapers and videotapes often lack credibility in the eyes of employees. These media may be useful for communicating detailed information and maintaining a permanent record. But the extensive use of these media is consistent with a "directive controlling" style of management influence. They may be more effective when the objective is to inform people without inviting a reply'.

Statement 9: My manager recognizes employees for good performance (Ex.: Rewards, pay raises, atta-boys).

According to the literature, 'modern, high performance, successful organizations tend to reflect ... embedded reward systems that are connected to the performance of the business' (Harshman & Harshman, 1999: 15).

Statement 10: My manager shares information about my department and/or the organization as a whole regularly (Ex.: Meetings, memos, e-mails).

According to Harshman and Harshman (1999: 15), one of the fundamental tenets of solid, open employee communications is 'if you cannot tell employees something, at least tell them why you cannot tell them'.

Statement 11: My manager follows up promptly on employee questions and concerns.

Yrie, Hartman, Galle (2002: 259) said that 'there may not be one best way for supervisors and subordinates to communicate, but rather that the kind and quality of communication required may vary across situations. For example, each situation is unique and the receiver and their perceptions are part of the sender's environment therefore the ways in which communication occurs may also be diverse'.

Organizational Expectations

Statement 12: I am aware of the organization's goals and objectives.

The influence for this statement is echoed through many articles and research projects on the topic of internal communication. Barrett (2002: 220) clearly describes the importance of goal setting: 'If management can be coached into realizing that employee communication is a key ingredient in becoming a high-performing company, they will more likely give it the time and energy it needs and deserves', and one of the characteristics of a high-performing companies is 'clear performance goals'.

Statement 13: I am aware of what is going on in other areas of the organization besides my department or area.

Harshman and Harshman (1999: 15) say that successful, high performance businesses often have 'high involvement of employees in the conduct of the business'.

Statement 14: I do all I can to ensure our customers/patrons/volunteers are serviced and satisfied.

According to Harris and de Chernatony (2001: 442), 'with the recognition of corporate branding, and therefore the critical role staff play, they need to be included in the internal debate about defining a brand's values. While management will still be required to initiate the process, staff should be encouraged to contribute to discussions', which directly leads to increased customer satisfaction.

Statement 15: I understand the importance of my role in customer service and customer satisfaction.

According to Harris and de Chernatony (2001: 441), 'employees constitute the interface between a brand's internal and external environments and can have a powerful impact on consumers' perceptions of both the brand and the organization'.

Statement 16: My understanding of the organization's goals and objectives is important for its success.

Harshman and Harshman (1999: 15) state that one principle of communication is 'that all employees understand the business', including the 'rationale for, and details of, strategies, decisions, and actions'. Furthermore, Davis (2001: 130) states that 'decision making in organizations is political and emotional as well as logical and rational. How managers introduce ideas will affect their acceptance. Managers mistakenly assume that others will automatically see the merit and logic in their ideas'.

Statement 17: Overall, internal business communication is clear, timely and accurate.

This statement comes directly from Harshman and Harshman (1999: 15), who identified several characteristics of solid internal business communication, including: 'Two-way; relevant to employees' needs; understandable; useful; timely; and mature'.

Career Expectations

Statement 18: I am aware of my job-related goals and objectives.

According to the strategic employee communication model, 'meaningful communication is communication that accomplishes two primary objectives: informs and educates employees at all levels in the company's strategy; and motivates and positions employees to support the strategy and the performance goals' (Barrett, 2002: 220).

Statement 19: I am aware of my departmental goals and objectives.

Employee communication regarding goal setting is vitally important for business success. 'In high-performing companies, employee communication reinforces the company's strategic objectives. There should be a one-to-one correlation between what the company has established as its strategic objectives and what is listed as the objectives for the communications' (Barrett, 2002: 221). Additionally, 'the communications must be structured to translate the central strategic messages (from vision to performance or financial goals to income) to all employees' (Barrett, 2002: 221).

Statement 20: I believe there are advancement opportunities for me here.

Statement 21: I believe I could make a profitable career here.

Statement 22: My expectations as an employee are being met.

Statements 20, 21, and 22 are most closely linked to the literature that discusses the need for employees to feel secure and valued. To reiterate Goris et al.'s (2002) job characteristics model, the highest levels of job performance occur when an individual's needs are most closely matched with a given job or career. These survey statements align themselves with the individual–job congruence factors of 'pay, security, interpersonal relations, and supervision' (Goris et al., 2002: 665).

Public Relations Consultancy Practice

Jane Tonge

> **Key Themes**
>
> - Examining the nature and growth of the public relations industry
> - Exploring different types of consultancies
> - Understanding the work of consultancies
> - Examining the nature of consultancy–client relationships
> - Exploring consultancy management

This chapter will examine the way in which public relations consultancies are organised and managed in order to respond to client organisations' needs and to deliver public relations services and support for corporate and business strategies. The chapter will also examine how consultancies themselves are managed as businesses in their own right and how they manage client relationships.

INTRODUCTION: THE NATURE AND GROWTH OF THE PUBLIC RELATIONS INDUSTRY

Public relations is a multi-billion pound industry entrenched in both business and political life (CIPR, 2009b) with organisations outsourcing a broad range of public relations activity to consultancies (DTI/IPR, 2003). The importance of the marketing communications industry has grown significantly during the past two decades and led to the emergence of both national and multinational public relations consultancies within the communication sector. This continued success can be witnessed in the public relations industry's resilience in the face of the recessionary storm. (CIPR, 2009b; PR Week, 2010a).

The public relations industry has grown significantly in recent years, both in the UK and worldwide. The 1990s in particular witnessed significant spending on public relations services – for example, in Australia overall annual spend on public relations services was estimated as A$170 million in 1996, of which A$50 million went to public relations consultancies, with the top eight consultancies taking A$32 million in annual fee income (Tymson & Sherman, 1996). In the US there was also a significant increase – in 1999, the Council of Public Relations Firms, representing America's leading public relations organisations, reported that the 50 largest PR firms saw a record 32% growth and billed US$2.8 billion. Indeed, over an 11-year period there was an increase in revenues of over 300% for the top 50 US public relations firms, with combined revenue increasing from $1.1 billion in 1990 to $3.7 billion in 2001 (CPRF, 2004). By 2002, the estimated size of the industry worldwide was approximately $5.4 billion (CPRF, 2002).

Such unprecedented growth was then followed by a plateau, with the International Communications Consultancy Organisation (ICCO), an umbrella organisation for 1,400 public relations consultancies in 28 countries, reporting little overall growth in the world public relations industry in 2004 (ICCO, 2004). The recent economic downturn has also affected the industry. Yet there are signs of resilience, with the worldwide public relations consultancy sector showing continued revenue growth of an average of 8.5% in 2008, according to the ICCO World Report covering 22 countries (ICCO, 2009). Russia posted the biggest annual increase at 33%, while the world's two biggest markets for communications, the US and the UK, grew at 4% and 7% respectively, outpacing growth in gross domestic product in both countries.

In the US, growth in consultancy revenue was reflected in a CPRF (2009) survey where the majority of US public relations firms reported revenue growth in 2008, with 61% of participating firms growing their top line at an average rate of 4%. Examining a broader audience of public relations professionals, a 2009 State of Public Relations Survey reported results which demonstrated that despite the gloomy economic news, more than two in three practitioners surveyed (67%) were optimistic for the public relations industry (CPRF, 2009). 'The public relations industry enjoyed a healthy and steady expansion mid-decade but experienced a slowdown in business toward the end of 2008', said Kathy Cripps, president of the Council of Public Relations Firms. 'We are realistic about what to expect in 2009. However, our members are continuing to help corporations maintain visibility and manage issues, while also helping them to better communicate with their employees during turbulent times. Helping to navigate these issues is what public relations firms do best, and will continue to do this year despite a difficult economic climate' (CPRF, 2009). This statement is echoed by survey data which identified a noticeable slowdown in hiring staff, while public relations tactics such as special events (60%) and celebrity spokespeople (44%) were most likely to be cut from campaigns due to economic concerns, with social media (79%) and digital content creation (55%) topping the list for items with the most growth potential.

Recent results suggest that the global public relations industry has weathered the economic storm well. Statistics indicate that the majority of top international marcoms groups with public relations interests such as Omnicom (US), WPP (UK), Publicis (France), Interpublic (US), Havas (France), Huntsworth (UK), and Photon (Australia) have increased their market capitalisation, which offers signs for optimism (PR Week, 2010a). Many consultancies have seen generic growth, underpinning the view that the global public relations industry is emerging from a tough time in overall good shape (PR Week, 2010a).

UK Public Relations Industry

Turning to the UK, the public relations industry is the most highly developed in Europe and recognised as 'a major centre of the European public relations industry' and 'a centre of excellence for marketing communications services (including advertising, public relations, direct marketing, market research, exhibitions, conferences and sales promotion' (DTI, 2004: 1). The industry has more than doubled in size in the last two decades, increasing from 19,500 public relations professionals in 1988 to nearly 48,000 practitioners as identified by the Centre for Economics and Business Research (CEBR, 2005) for the Chartered Institute of Public Relations (CIPR). This comprises managers, principals and officers who work in-house and also consultancies and freelancers. Of these professionals, most (82%) are in-house specialists employed directly by companies, government or not-for-profits, leaving 18% to include those working for public relations consultancies. The rate of growth in the number of jobs in public relations at all levels has been higher than that of any management function over the last fifteen years (CIPR, 2005) and the leading professional body for the UK public relations industry, the CIPR, has seen its membership increase more than fourfold from 2,000 in 1990 to 9,000 members in 2009, making it the largest public relations institute in Europe.

CEBR (2005) research estimates that the imputed turnover of the profession as a whole is £6.5 billion. It contributes £3.4 billion to UK economic activity as well as generating £1.1 billion in corporate profits, if the contribution of in-house public relations workers is valued at the same rate as that of public relations consultants. Further, the revenue of public relations consultancies in the UK is estimated in the region of £1.2 billion (CEBR, 2005), with consultancies whose clients lie primarily within the public, health and charities sectors accounting for over a third (36%) of turnover of all public relations consultancies.

Similar to the global public relations industry, a recent survey of 2,000 CIPR members revealed that the UK public relations industry has remained resilient in the face of the recent recession (CIPR, 2009a, 2009b). For many UK consultancies, despite the economic circumstances, there has been generic growth. The total amount of work billed by the UK's top 150 consultancies in 2008 was £858 million, dipping slightly to £814 million in 2009. A closer look at the top ten consultancies in the UK by the end of 2009 also reveals that despite dark financial predictions with reports of redundancies and client losses in the first six months, overall UK consultancies endured a rollercoaster ride with few patterns emerging and an estimated average growth of 0.75% (PR Week, 2010a). Although the industry appears to be 'flat', nevertheless 'twice as many consultancies showed growth as ... showed a decrease' (PR Week 2010a: 4). Bell Pottinger Group and its collection of corporate entities continue to top the UK consultancy league with a fee income close to £60 million and 8% growth, while the UK's top independent consultancy, Edelman, also showed some small growth. Thus it appears that consultancies in the UK at least are coping with the recession, both in terms of business stability and client new growth. As reported by CIPR (2009a, 2009b), 33% of consultants retained more than 10 regular clients and 60% added between two and five new clients, with 60% of consultants continuing to work with budgets of under £50,000, a constant figure over the last five years.

Challenges and Opportunities

As with the majority of industries, and despite indications of growth, the ICCO predicts a tough time ahead for public relations consultancies, with six key challenges to overcome – shrinking client budgets, staffing, maintaining growth and profitability, client expectations, competition and price pressure, and keeping up with industry change. However, a number of opportunities for public relations consultancies are also on the horizon. These include a rising demand for crisis management work and expansion of the public sector in many countries, coupled with established factors which continue to favour the practice of public relations, namely a rapidly changing media environment that drives a loss of control over messages, and the pressing need to build direct conversations with customers and stakeholders, leading to the conclusion: 'Given this environment, ICCO is confident that public relations consultancy is well positioned to ride out the downturn and to exploit the upturn when it comes' (ICCO 2009).

In terms of specific practice areas, growth in income for consultancies has been driven globally by corporate and consumer communications, with marketing and brand communications to consumers proving to be the largest revenue producing area for consultancies in both the US and the UK, and technology services not far behind (ICCO, 2009). Healthcare communications also continue to prosper in the US, the largest healthcare market in the world, as well as in Russia, Greece and Austria. Furthermore, work in crisis management plays an increasingly significant role throughout continental Europe, where the business climate in most of the mature economies has become dominated by news of corporate restructuring and record losses as well as a plunge in consumer confidence and spending (ICCO, 2009).

Despite this difficult environment, many areas of the industry have continued to expand throughout the recession. The greatest growth has been experienced in digital public relations and the use of social media, with digital communications now seen to underpin public relations development. Reputation management, crisis management and strategic planning are also growth areas, evidence that the current economic landscape means that now, more than ever, company performance is contingent on managing reputation (CIPR, 2009b). Potential for growth in the coming years is also forecast. Lord Chadlington, chief executive of Huntsworth, which holds one of the largest and most geographically diverse UK portfolio of public relations consultancies, advises:

> In a recession, clients often cut advertising budgets and to compensate, consumer public relations booms. We saw double-digit organic growth in many of our consumer brands and sectors. The crossover between consumer public relations and medical education drove healthcare public relations forward and leads us to expect strong growth in these sectors in the next five years ... the real growth driver, however will be the creative use of digital media. Clients should increasingly turn to us as a natural source of digital counsel. (PR Week 2010a: 5)

DEFINING A PUBLIC RELATIONS CONSULTANCY

The words 'consultant' and 'consultancy' derive from the Latin *consultare*, meaning 'to discuss', from which we also derive words such as *consul* and *counsel*. A consultancy is a professional practice giving expert advice in a particular field (OED, 2009). In terms of public relations, various definitions of a consultancy abound, ranging from simple statements to more detailed explanations. One broad definition sees the concept of consultancy as a process in which a consultant provides a service to a client – which could be an organisation, an individual acting on behalf of an organisation, or a unit within that organisation – for the purpose of meeting the client's needs, whereby service implies paid expertise (Williams & Woodward, 1994). Others portray public relations consultancies in contrast to management consultancies, advertising and corporate design agencies by describing public relations as offering services predominantly in corporate image-building to various external constituencies (Schultz & Ervolder, 1998). Yet others suggest that, on the contrary, public relations consultancies and those offering services in the areas of public affairs and corporate communications are actually management consultancies, albeit with a number of significant differences, including their business base and approach to client problems (White, 2000). Indeed, a number of scholars focus on problem solving when defining public relations consultancies, maintaining that these fall within the area of 'professional services' (e.g., White 2000; Boojihawon & Young, 2001) 'Professional services firms such as management and public relations consultancies offer services directed at the solution of client problems. These may involve difficulties or opportunities, but services provided are aimed at problem solving' (White, 2000: 82). Some argue that all public relations practitioners are 'consultants' regardless of whether they work in-house or for a public relations consultancy firm:

> In both cases, the approach to the delivery of professional services is similar. An issue or situation is analysed, the desired outcome interpreted as quantifiable objectives, the critical audiences to whom messages will be addresses identified, the messages themselves translated as a communication strategy, an action plan developed and implemented, and results monitored and evaluated against objectives. (Wade, 1995: 111)

In the UK, professional bodies such as the CIPR (2009c) define 'consultancy' as externally hired public relations services, either an individual consultant or a public relations consultancy. The Public Relations Consultants Association (PRCA, 2004) offers a more comprehensive view:

> Public relations consultancy practice is the provision of specified technical and creative services by an individual or a group of individuals, qualified to do so by reason of experience and training, and having a legal corporate identify registered for the purpose in the United Kingdom. The whole or principle income of the corporate body so formed will be by way of professional fees paid for its services by clients under contract to the consultancy.

Public relations consultancies operate within a complex and expanding macro-environment (see Figure 13.1) and thus manage a wide variety of stakeholders. Although they differ in size and structure, they tend to have one common factor – the public relations firm or consultancy consists of one or more public relations professionals whose purpose is to counsel others in their communication and relationship-building activities in exchange for a fee (Hinrichsen, 2001). The companies that consultancies represent are called 'clients', and a client's programme or project is called an 'account'. There are many reasons why a client might seek public relations services, whether to access senior-level counselling or gain additional personnel to assist on a project, but generally the consultancy has expertise that the client cannot access internally (Hinrichsen, 2001). Clients are central to the activities of consultancies, as employers are central to in-house practitioners. As such, clients' needs and requests determine public relations practice, to a large extent. Many clients ask consultancies to assist with their strategic planning and do much more than handle media relations (Lages & Simkin, 2003) thus exposing the consultancy to the strategic needs of clients.

Agency or Consultancy?

The terms 'agency' and 'consultancy' are commonly applied to a public relations business and are often used interchangeably by many, including practitioners. However, some argue that the term 'consultancy' is not only preferable but more accurately reflects the type of services offered. Jefkins (1992) points out that 'PR agency' is an ambiguous expression and an abuse of language, as it is physically, legally and financially impossible for a public relations consultancy to be an agency. Confusion may have arisen with comparisons to the 'advertising agency', which is the agency of the media, receiving remuneration by way of commission on media purchases. However, a public relations consultancy is not an agent, and is not paid commission, least of all by the media (Jefkins, 1992).

Exploring Types of Public Relations Consultancies

Public relations businesses tend to fall into the category of small specialist consultancy firms (Ram, 2000). The UK public relations industry mainly comprises small or

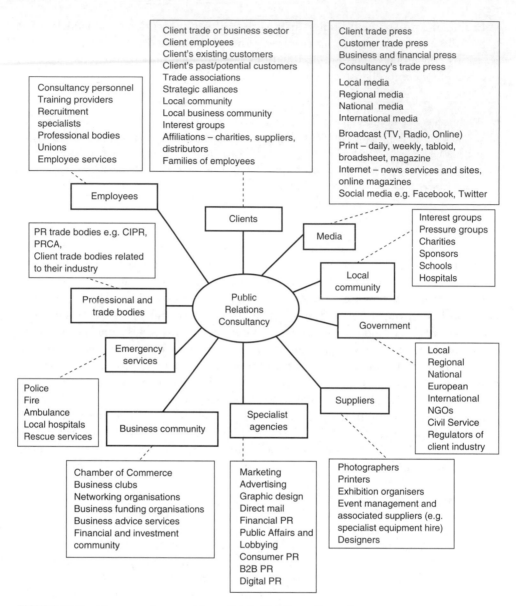

FIGURE 13.1   Macro-environment for a Public Relations Consultancy

micro-firms where 65% have up to six employees and 67% have turnover below £500,000 (Lages & Simkin, 2003). Although some of the world's largest public relations consultancies are British, public relations firms in the UK are amongst the 3.2 million small and medium-sized enterprises in the country, and are no different than any other small business in that their structure and organisation can vary widely depending on the size, sector and individual nature of the services they offer. Virtually all public relations consultancies are different, with structures ranging from large complex international companies with offices throughout the world to small geographically based firms and specialist independent consultants, as well as vertical and horizontal segmentation and a trend towards integrated communications (Wade, 1995). While the top international marcoms companies own a range of consultancies, a large number of public relations businesses remain independent. Those in the UK have also witnessed some growth despite the economic pressures, for example with top independent consultancy Edelman bringing in over £25 million fee income and its closest rival, Engine, securing an impressive 47% growth (PR Week 2010a). However, not all independents remain immune to the recession, with several showing little growth and some a considerable fall in fee income.

WHAT DO CONSULTANCIES ACTUALLY DO?

Organisations are now outsourcing a broad range of public relations activity to consultancies, but what services can they actually offer? As the PRCA (2004) suggests: 'Public relations consultancy practice is the provision of specified technical and creative services'. These services may include a whole raft of activities and functions: advice or services related to political, government or public affairs; establishing channels of communications with the client's public or publics; financial public relations; management communications; marketing-related activity; media relations; and employee and industrial relations. Similarly, the CIPR (2009d) identifies many different communications functions which are covered by the public relations umbrella. Consultants will offer to provide or advise on a 'full service' basis, which may include media relations; marketing of products, services and issues; copywriting; press office functions; online and digital communications; media and presentation training; sponsorship; event and conference management; research; evaluation; corporate identity, image and reputation; and strategic planning. The plethora of skills required and the need to keep pace with technological advances and expanding client demands is reflected by practitioners' experiences. Di Burton, managing director at Cicada Communications, explains:

PR consultancies are changing. The increase and speed in communication channels, social networks and so on are pushing public relations consultancies to learn quickly, reflect on their skills and become more agile. Many are still focusing on specialisms such as media training or event management. Boundaries are also blurring around what is considered traditional PR and business consulting. Consultancies have to become more disciplined and brave about taking on bespoke work of higher value to survive. As a consequence, all staff need business advisory skills and to become much more savvy about a bigger business picture so they can take PR into the board room, and be part of the dominant coalition.

Despite the potential and demand for growing diversity in public relations services, however, not all public relations consultancies can claim proficiency in every area. Some confine their practices to certain industries or interests, while others offer consultative but not executive services. Confusion sometimes arises when public relations consultancies offer a number of marketing communication services, such as marketing, design or website production, while there are advertising agencies that have public relations departments or subsidiaries. However, an 'independent' public relations consultant is one who has no connection with an advertising agency.

Structure and Roles

Most consultancies are organised along the lines of at least a three-tiered hierarchy, as illustrated in Figure 13.2, generally in the format of account directors, managers and executives. Here the most senior member of the public relations team may be the owner-manager, company director or account director, depending on the size of the consultancy and the extent to which senior management wish to have a 'hands-on' role. Their function will be more strategic and financial, involving winning the account and agreeing budgets, fees and contracts and the subsequent public relations strategy. They may be involved in campaign planning, act as a senior point of contact for the client within the consultancy, and provide guidance to the team allocated to work on the client's account, offering creative input if necessary. The account manager's role is one of both strategy and implementation, often acting as a linchpin between the consultancy and the client. Working with the account director, they will help to plan the public relations strategy and media schedule, as well as implement it. They will oversee the budget and check spending and time allocated to client work, as well as liaising with the account director and client on progress. Within the consultancy, the account manager will also supervise one or more account executives on a range of client accounts, providing guidance and creative ideas as well as planning, organising and producing many aspects of the strategy or campaign. Here they are supported by the account executive, whose role is mainly one of implementation, liaison and research. Supervised by the account manager, the executive will work on a range of client accounts, providing support and researching information. They will frequently liaise with the client, the media and suppliers, and assist in all aspects of public relations activity from drafting press releases to event management support, as well as providing creative input. Key skills for all of these roles – and thus for public relations practitioners in general – are strong time management and the ability to handle the complex requirements of multiple accounts at any one time, as well as adept interpersonal skills and the capability of liaising with clients, media, suppliers and a range of others on researching, planning, delivering and evaluating the public relations strategy. In addition, public relations practitioners need to be capable across a wide

FIGURE 13.2 Consultancy Structure and Roles

range of competency areas – verbal communications, integrity, influence, persuasion and diplomacy, writing and editing skills, critical judgement and enthusiasm, motivation and curiosity (DTI/IPR, 2003). Such skills are required at all levels within the consultancy, where practitioners may have a varied and multi-function role (see boxed text).

TWO PUBLIC RELATIONS PRACTITIONERS AT A LARGE CONSUMER PUBLIC RELATIONS CONSULTANCY IN MANCHESTER EXPLAIN THEIR ROLES

Natasha, the managing director, explains her role and the types of public relations work she gets involved with, often at a strategic level: 'As managing director, I'm responsible for day-to-day operations at the business, from financial performance to client satisfaction and retention to staff recruitment, training and retention. I'm involved in new business generation as well, writing pitches, preparation, planning, strategy and creativity. I also do client work selectively, and lead on two thirds of clients' businesses. I work on top level planning with two or three clients, which can be anything from looking at acquisition strategy to internal communications or career guidance. On a day-to-day level, I liaise daily with 50 per cent of clients at senior planning level. I network with a lot of people on a regular basis, keep them abreast of issues, challenges or problems on client side or problems on our side. We also have our own profile to maintain, so I liaise with editors that are important to us, trade press and where we have key clients, such as in construction, I keep in touch with editors to make sure they are up to date with the right issues and angles.'

Greta, an account executive, describes her more 'hands-on' role as a junior employee: 'I'm the account executive and work on four accounts, including a DIY store, brewery and automotive client. My role is to handle the press office, organise events, do everything that needs doing for two accounts, where I'm the main contact. For the other two, I get involved in *ad hoc* projects that need more manpower, like organising events where I'll take over the logistics side of it. Daily tasks are press releases to trade press, and I'm responsible for lots of store openings. We might have four in one day so I'm organising photographers, celebrities, running competitions for schools to get them there, and getting the store set up and ready. I liaise with the store manager and run competitions in local newspapers and radio stations. There's a lot of work and pre-planning goes into that. It's very time-consuming. One client has a very busy press office and makes a lot of proactive calls to journalists and I take a lot of calls from journalists requiring product information, images or prices. It's a very busy process and it all comes through to me, so I'm always making calls, fielding calls and involved in event organisation day-to-day.'

For micro-consultancies with fewer than 10 employees, these demarcations may become blurred and practitioners will take on a variety of roles depending on the client – for example, acting as account executive on one account while a colleague takes the lead as account manager or director, and alternating as the lead practitioner on a different account while the colleague takes a more junior role. In this way, responsibilities and activities can be shared out more equitably among a small team, ensuring that the direction and pressure do not always fall to the same person. Often a small consultancy is established by an entrepreneurial and experienced practitioner who leaves a larger consultancy to set up their own business, usually taking with them one or more clients with whom they have developed a close and successful working relationship. The entrepreneurial practitioner or owner-manager will adopt a lead role managing these key accounts to ensure continuity and reassure the client that they will continue to receive high service levels from the same reliable public relations expert they have previously entrusted with their business. New clients joining the smaller consultancy may thus be allocated to a different practitioner as the lead contact, since these come fresh to the business with less need for continuity or a 'familiar face'.

For small to medium-size consultancies (10–250 employees), as with any developed or established business, additional organisational layers will develop as the company thrives and expands. For example, larger consultancies may have a board of directors overseeing the company's operations, including the owner-manager, partners or managing directors in the consultancy. As consultancies expand, they can also split into specialist divisions – digital communication, community relations, investor relations and so on – each headed by an expert account director and backed by a team of managers and executives. Added to this may be any number of support personnel with a wide variety of functions and job titles – junior account executive, media assistant, business development manager, finance manager, analyst, strategist, freelance journalist and so on.

However, not only does size influence the organisation of the consultancy but also the sector in which it operates. This may differ depending on whether a consultancy specialises in consumer, business-to-business or financial public relations, or a combination of these; whether it has a dedicated public relations offering only, or operates as a full service agency providing marketing, advertising, digital and graphic design or other communications services.

Vertical and Horizontal Consultancies

Public relations consultancies can also be identified in terms of the range of services offered. For example, Wade (1995) draws the conclusion that there are no hard-and-fast rules about the nature of public relations consultancies nor how they should be used, but rather argues that the situation is entirely fluid and develops in fresh directions to meet changing needs. As the nature and style of consultancies has altered, so the practice of public relations has become more specialised and the value of specialist advice and support is more readily recognised. It can be argued that public relations consultancies fall into two broad groups – vertical consultancies and horizontal consultancies. A vertical consultancy is a firm that has chosen to specialise in a field, practice or a type of client. This might include consumer consultancies that concentrate on clients whose aim is to reach the mass market, public affairs specialists, business-to-business consultancies and others who specialise in areas like high technology, the environment, employee relations and other fields. Horizontally structured consultancies offer a range of services and may well embrace both consumer and business-to-business communication (Wade, 1995). Here, there is an increasing trend for consultancies to stretch their range of services beyond the traditional 'below-the-line' limit of public relations practice and offer integrated communication services.

Range of Public Relations Consultancy Services

Thus public relations consultancies specialise in a variety of different areas and operate in numerous ways. Table 13.1 offers a comparison of several main types – financial, full service, business-to-business, consumer and public affairs consultancies – providing a flavour of what each may focus on in terms of services and offerings and how they can position and differentiate themselves with regards to their mission. In particular, they may draw their personnel from differing backgrounds so as to widen their expertise and offering to clients – whether from the law, banking or accountancy for financial public relations firms, or journalists, designers and marketers for full service consultancies. Similarly, the consultancy's mission will be carefully adapted and targeted according to their client group and its needs, ranging from high-level strategic investor relations to sustained media relations campaigns or high-impact communication programmes and strategic counsel.

The range of services provided also gives an indication of the very wide variety of public relations and communication activities that consultancies are now embracing and offering to clients, and which require continually updating and adapting to meet changing client needs and the emergence of new markets and the latest technologies. Within the five examples shown in Table 13.1 – all real and existing UK consultancies – a huge variety of services are described. These include traditional public relations activities such as media strategy and management, research, events management, crisis management, corporate social responsibility, charity public relations, corporate identify and branding, financial communications, public affairs advice and lobbying, strategic communication and campaign delivery. Yet also on offer are design-led services including artwork, type-setting, copywriting, photography, exhibition design, print buying, as well as sector-specific services such as property and planning, political project management, Select Committee training, party conference engagement programmes, investor relations, mergers and acquisitions, and litigation support. More common now are those services encapsulating new technologies such as digital media, online marketing, web design, viral marketing, and social networking strategies. Some consultancies also step into the management arena and offer bespoke training, such as in thought leadership. Others broaden their reach and provide wider communications expertise in advertising and marketing – which moves them from pure public relations consultancies to integrated communication firms, especially as the range of services on offer grows and diversifies.

Competition from Freelance and Specialist Consultancies

The growth in public relations practice has led to increasing competition for consultancies from a number of quarters. There is a growing tendency for advertising, sales

TABLE 13.1   Variety of Public Relations Consultancies

Type	Size	People	Mission	Services	Location
Financial Consultancy	Global network stretching across Europe, the USA and Far East.	Backgrounds in journalism, banking, accountancy and the law. Attracts people of many nationalities and conducts business in a wide variety of languages.	To help any company, or organisation, communicate to best effect with all its different financial audiences, providing high-level strategic media and investor relations consultancy. We have a global reach, working across all the world's major business centres to provide clients with best practice communications solutions.	Financial communication, investor relations, mergers and acquisitions, IPO/share offers, emerging markets, debt markets, litigation support, crisis communications, business-to-business communication, thought leadership, digital media, and research.	London
Full Service Consultancy	Small, independent full service marketing and public relations consultancy.	Backgrounds in business, public relations, journalism, design and marketing. Creative environment for PR and design people.	We provide a full range of public relations activity in order to build the campaigns you deserve. As a public relations consultancy we make sure all our clients get recognised. At the centre of our service is a sustained media relations campaign that captures headlines.	Public relations, advertising, new media, events, design, print/production, crisis management, corporate social responsibility, charity public relations, corporate branding, and marketing strategies.	Manchester
Consumer Consultancy	Independent consumer PR consultancy, for example specialising in food and drink.	Provides training in skills needed to develop a career in public relations and pay for courses in other areas from languages to cooking to guitar playing, believing that creativity fosters creativity.	We are thinking people who swear by good ideas, and our clients hire us because our campaigns make a difference. Our client list includes some of the UK's most iconic FMCG food and drink brands.	Fully integrated consumer public relations and digital campaigns that dovetail with existing marketing campaigns or offer one-off, bespoke digital executions. Digital services include: online marketing; Web design; viral marketing; and social networking.	Cardiff

(Continued)

TABLE 13.1 (Continued)

Type	Size	People	Mission	Services	Location
Business-to-Business Consultancy	Business-to-business public relations consultancy focusing on long-term relationships	Backgrounds in business, public relations, journalism, design and marketing. Entrepreneurial environment and in-house PR training scheme.	We understand the press and the publishing process because that's where we come from. We match that knowledge with an understanding of how industry works, the commercial processes by which products and services are created, marketed, communicated and delivered to customers. We understand a l of these things, and we bring them together.	Public relations, design, artwork, typesetting; copywriting, photography, exhibition design and management, media strategy, print buying and management, events management, conferences, and marketing consultancy.	Edinburgh
Public Affairs Consultancy	Specialises in political, corporate and planning communication. Associates based around the UK.	Wide range of employees including associates. Team includes consultants who combine years of political and media experience with sound business acumen.	Our passion is the process of communications which can strengthen relationships and enhance reputation. We do this by providing tailored, high-impact communication programmes and strategic counsel for our clients to enable them to secure their strategic business objectives.	Public affairs advice, property and planning services, local political project management, political campaign delivery, political surveying and auditing, Select Committee training, strategic communications, and party conference engagement programmes.	London

promotion and management agencies to offer public relations skills (White & Mazur, 1995). Low barriers to entry and often low entry standards for qualifications enable many small firms to set up with relative ease (Lages & Simkin, 2003), leaving the public relations industry very permeable to new entrants. It is also perceived as an easy start-up business since it is not a registered profession in the UK and anyone may call themselves a practitioner.

Consultancies also face competition from undercutting freelancers (ICCO, 2004). As the business environment becomes more complex, consultancies may find it hard to provide consistent quality in the large range of public relations activities demanded, each one requiring increasingly specialist knowledge which freelancers can offer. Consultancies have responded with a growth in specialisations, including the niche market sectors of healthcare and digital communication – the main private sectors fuelling growth in world public relations markets (ICCO, 2004) although not without problems:

> The issue of competing, or even surviving, through specialisation is a major challenge facing the executives of many PR consultancies. The expectation was that to succeed there was only one option, but in two guises: niching either for smaller PR firms concentrating on narrowly defined market sectors, such as health or agrochemicals, or the large PR consultancies creating specialist teams or departments within their firms. (Lages & Simkin, 2003: 302)

Such specialisation is evidence of the maturity of public relations and the increasing strength of its areas of expertise.

CONSULTANCY–CLIENT RELATIONSHIPS

Relationships between clients and consultancies are complex and have long been the source of tension and bemusement on both sides. This complexity is not without historical precedent. George Michaelis' Publicity Bureau, the first recognised public relations consultancy, experienced a variety of conflicts in their relationships, such as clients not paying, consultancy staff changes, questions regarding the consultancy's integrity, and consultancy–client lack of agreement on objectives. Over 45 years ago, Bernays (1965: 312) similarly detailed the complexities of client relationships:

> Professional relationships, I have learned, are not enduring in an impermanent world. They are like railroad timetables – subject to change without notice. Even with a contract, relationships often change, by renegotiation. A new policymaker in the firm, a change in the economic climate, a wave of cutting expenses – any of these can end what appears to be a permanent and fruitful relationship.

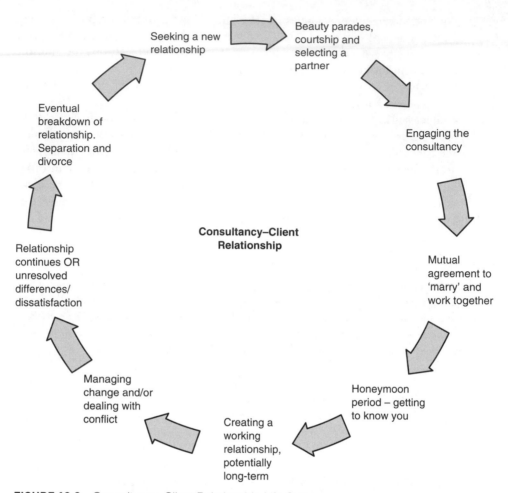

FIGURE 13.3 Consultancy–Client Relationship Life Cycle

The consultancy–client relationship can be viewed as a cycle of events in much the same way as any relationship may start, proceed and eventually end. Figure 13.3 shows several key stages in this 'marriage' of organisations which begins with a client deciding a relationship is required, identifying appropriate consultancies – for example, through a 'beauty parade' of eligible firms pitching for the account by displaying their wares and offering solutions to the organisation's communication needs. The client will be attracted by virtues such as credentials, personnel, creativity, strategy ideas, the portfolio of current clients, media contacts and networks, costings and promises leading to selection of the 'right' consultancy. Once engaged by the client, the two parties agree to 'marry' and work together. There follows a honeymoon period, often of 3–6 months, during which the two organisations get to know each other, their personnel and practices, and establish the foundations of a working relationship. The consultancy will also begin the process of research, analysis and planning. As time moves on, sustaining a long-term business relationship can become the focus, especially if the two organisations work well together, and strategies and campaigns have been successfully implemented. However, as the relationship matures, changes will inevitably take place within both organisations and the external environment, and familiarity can breed contempt. The repercussions may result in tensions or even conflict, which if not anticipated and carefully managed can lead to separation and eventual divorce with the breakdown of the consultancy–client relationship. The cycle may then begin anew for the client organisation. However, the consultancy will face a more complex situation as it will be engaged at various stages of the cycle with any number of clients and thus need to simultaneously manage a range of client relationships at different points and with conflicting pressures and demands.

Embarking on a Consultancy–Client Relationship

Clients and consultancies will have a variety of reasons for starting a relationship. Oliver (1990) distinguished six major motives for relationships in his overview of inter-organisational research:

- necessity based on some authority;
- potential to exercise power and control over the other;
- reciprocity of benefits;
- efficiency of operations;
- increase of stability and predictability in an uncertain environment;
- enhancement of organisational legitimacy.

In the area of marketing, where exchange theory traditionally had a strong influence (Halinen, 1997), researchers have stressed the reciprocity of benefits as the most critical motive. Certain assumptions have been made – that the scarcity of resources induces cooperation rather than competition, that relationships are characterised by harmony and mutual support rather than by conflict and domination, and that organisations expect the benefits of a business relationship to far exceed potential drawbacks.

A business relationship can be defined as a 'mutually oriented interaction between two reciprocally committed companies' (Håkansson & Snehota, 1995: 25). Two principal forms of business relationships are the 'market exchange relationship' and the 'relational exchange relationship' (Dwyer, Schurr, & Oh, 1987; Frazier, Spekman, & O'Neil, 1988), and within public relations both types exist between clients and their consultancies. Market exchange relationships arise when the client purchases primarily on price, uses multiple sources of supply – or a raft of consultancies – and tends to switch consultancies frequently. Such relationships are not uncommon, for example in large organisations where different consultancies may be responsible for public relations work on competing brands, or for consumer, business-to-business, financial, regional and even international public relations activities. Relational exchange relationships emerge when the client and consultancy develop a longer-term relationship. Relational exchange is less price-driven and based on greater recognition of mutual commitment between trading partners than is found in market exchange relationships. Here again, clients and their consultants may build up long-term relationships over time, with a consultancy often focused on nurturing, building and maintaining a client account over many years.

In business and service contexts such as public relations, client–consultancy (or buyer–seller) relationships are interactive relationships that involve not only the exchange of products and services for money but also necessarily social interaction and other interactive processes (see Grönroos, 1982; Gummesson, 1987; Ford, 1990). As such, it may be misleading to use the 'exchange relationship' concept when referring to buyer–seller relationships in business-to-business and service markets, and instead adopt the term 'business relationship' as more appropriate to indicate the specific nature of buyer–seller relationships in professional business service sectors (Halinen 1997) such as public relations.

Consultancy Selection

Organisations now outsource a broad range of public relations activity to consultancies, and selecting the right consultancy to act on behalf of a business can be a difficult process. A range of stages need to be broached, and here a comparison with the C-MACIE model can be made in the phases that occur. As seen in Figure 13.3, the consultancy–client relationship life cycle may see the client conduct initial market analysis to identify the type of consultancy suitable for the campaign or public relations activity required; choose and engage a suitable consultancy, often via a competitive pitch process; and, once selected, implement the public relations strategy, manage the consultancy–client relationship, and evaluate the outcomes.

The commission process can be a major problem area for both client and consultancy. Consultancy selection is often a source of anxiety and concern for both parties, each of which may have experienced both good and bad practices in previous pitch processes (see PR Week, 2010b). Consultancies often complain that the pitching process is too onerous and expensive in terms of investment of staff time and creative input, as well as costs such as credential packs, strategy plans, graphic design, and travel. Further concerns are too many competitors on the short list, and the real potential that unscrupulous clients may use the pitch to steal ideas. Some public relations consultancies also believe that the quality of brief and public relations objective setting provided by clients is often poor, leading to the argument for greater training and development in the area of public relations procurement and its management (DTI/IPR, 2003).

On the client side, dislikes in the pitching process range from consultancies that seem uninterested or regurgitate old campaigns to those who arrive with senior personnel who are unlikely to work on the account and fail to either bring along account executives or let them speak when they do. Also frustrating for clients are consultancies that fail to explain what skills and experience the potential account team will bring, present a pitch that is off brief, are unable to answer questions, lack creativity or offer ideas that are unfeasible, impractical, inappropriate or just too expensive.

Clients have a range of ways in which they choose consultancies (PR Week, 2010b) such as recommendations from industry colleagues, using intermediaries to identify suitable candidates, practitioner networks, word of mouth, reading the trade press to identify successful campaigns and the consultancies responsible for them, and checking consultancy websites for previous work and clients, areas of expertise and sector specialisation. In examining consultancy selection, compatibility may also be an issue, with larger firms preferring associations with consultancies similar in size and capability as themselves (Cagley & Roberts, 1984).

Sustaining Long-Term Business Relationships

Long-term business relationships are common in professional business service areas such as public relations, as well as legal, financial, consulting and advertising professions (Levinthal & Fichman, 1988; Michell, 1988; Yorke, 1990; Sharma, 1994; Zabkar & Rojsek, 1998). Business relationships can be characterised by continuity, commitment and their long-term nature, where continuity is seen as a key element (Heide & John, 1990) with each exchange event viewed in terms of its history and anticipated future (Dwyer et al., 1987), while commitment involves a future orientation and refers to the stability and durability of a relationship (Håkansson & Snehota, 1995).

Consultancies and their clients can gain many potential benefits from long-term business relationships. They may lead to a deeper understanding of marketing relationships and a clearer picture of how to respond to changes in order to build mutually beneficial relationships (Zabkar & Rojsek, 1998). It is generally less costly for a service firm such as a public relations consultancy to maintain and develop an existing client relationship than to attract a new one (Grönroos, 1990), and there may also be considerable strategic and social benefits. A long-term business relationship may produce strategic benefits for the consultancy in its own marketing efforts, by generating referrals and credentials, or create competitive advantage by building barriers which 'lock in' the client and so deter it from switching consultancy. The client can make transaction cost savings by developing a long-term relationship with a consultancy, and enhance the quality of services it offers. The progression of a relationship to the commitment stage is an indication that the rewards of the existing relationship are much higher than the rewards of alternative relationships for both client and consultancy, while a long-term relationship also denotes that its establishment was a positive experience for both sides from which they continue to benefit via the trust and satisfaction derived from a quality affiliation (Zabkar & Rojsek, 1998).

Complexity in Public Relations Consultancy–Client Relationships

Understanding the relationship between professional service clients and their advisors is complicated by the diversity in professional roles and services (Schell & Wood,

1998). The consultancy–client relationship is central to successful public relations programmes and campaigns, yet public relations is not alone as a field in seeking to understand how its business relationships work. Studies have attempted to identify this in a range of areas including services marketing (Gummesson, 1978), financial and legal firms (Yorke, 1990), advertising (West & Paliwoda, 1996; Silversides, 2001) and design consultancies (Shaw, 1998).

Bourland (1993) identified a range of issues which recurred in studies on public relations consultancy–client relationships, including concerns over finance, knowledge, work products, management and communication. In particular, three key issues were:

- the need for chemistry, variously described as a good fit, rapport, compatibility, a fitting of the cultures or philosophies, and quality relationships;
- the need for mutual understanding of objectives; and
- conducting meetings that are on time, with clear objectives.

Mutual concerns for client and consultancy involved knowing each other's business, contributing to the flow of communication between the parties involved, and maintaining financial obligations, whether billing or payment. Expertise, maintaining the relations through communication, and payment also presumed that the two parties 'liked' each other or had compatibility.

Conflict in Public Relations Consultancy–Client Relationships

Not all relationships are plain sailing, and conflict can arise in any consultancy–client association. Its source may be a combination of unresolved issues and ongoing problems, but communication – or lack of it – emerges as a key conflict generator for both consultancies and their clients (Bourland, 1993). In particular, consultancies may need to work on communication issues such as reporting to the client and listening, while clients must focus on ensuring a consistent flow of information and initiating feedback. Further sources of conflict attributed to consultancies include the consultancy not fulfilling its promises, not being an objective resource, lacking professionalism or integrity, lacking excitement about the client's business, and failing to meet deadlines. For consultancies, the client-originated conflict issues include clients not providing sufficient time, a lack of trust in the consultancy, being too demanding, for example by setting impossible deadlines, and being indecisive, including backtracking on plans, as well as needing hand-holding and reassurance (Bourland, 1993). While neither party is infallible, such issues can gain momentum and prove disastrous to a consultancy–client relationship if left unchecked.

Comparison with Advertising

While there are a few studies on consultancy–client relationships in public relations, other communication and media-related areas have a rich source of literature on this area, particularly the advertising industry. Research demonstrates that advertising consultancy–client relations literature can be used, with caution, as a basis for studying conflict in public relations consultancies (e.g., Bourland, 1993), bearing in mind that advertising is tied more directly to tangible products and results (sales) whereas public relations deals with building awareness and understanding, and influencing long-term relationships. Five categories for consultancy–client relationships have been identified in public relations: factors leading to satisfaction/dissatisfaction with current relationships; description of the selection and/or pitching process; 'ideal' criteria for successful consultancies or consultancy CEOs; consultancy issues or trends; and miscellaneous (Bourland, 1993). Prominent sources of conflict include lack of knowledge of the client's business, insufficient research, not reporting to the client, unfair billing practices, and client dissatisfaction with work products.

Comparing these to advertising consultancies (e.g., Hotz, Ryans, & Shanklin, 1982), a number of correlations between conflict issues in both public relations and advertising consultancy–client relations can be seen, including a 'lack of cost consciousness' in advertising consultancies which recommend expensive national television advertising, comparable to public relations consultancies failing to bring communications programmes and projects in on budget or not working economically. Overall, four potential consultancy-based conflict issues were identified for public relations (Bourland, 1993, adapted from Wackman, Salmon, & Salmon, 1986):

- **Work Product** – representing issues related to output and potential output, such as research.
- **Work Pattern** – factors affecting how work is accomplished such as productive meetings, accessible account executives and adherence to deadlines.
- **Organisational Factors** – encompassing structure, policies, politics and personnel.
- **Relationships** – internal and external chemistry with factors including low consultancy personnel turnover, good relations with account service people, and strong leadership.

The conflict between client and advertising agency is a well-documented struggle (Simkin & Dibb, 1998), with disagreement about who should resource and be responsible for effectiveness research, whether this is at the developmental, confirmatory or evaluative stages of producing and running a campaign, although the need for developing techniques to objectively assess the effectiveness of advertising usually meets with no disagreement. This could similarly be true in the public relations industry where the same issues are prevalent (Dibb, Simkin, & Vancini, 1996; Grunig, Grunig, &

Vercic, 1998), with practitioners acknowledging the need for public relations to defend more robustly its output and contributions through evaluation.

Breakdown of Public Relations Consultancy–Client Relationships

Consultancy–client relationships are a very complex topic with many differing opinions on what makes a successful or unsuccessful relationship. A number of variables have been identified as leading to disaffection within these relationships (Michell, Cataquet and Hague 1992). Ghosh and Taylor (1999) found six different studies on why there was dissatisfaction or failure in consultancy–client relationships, each with a different explanation as to why the relationship was unstable. Not only does this reflect the intricacy of the consultancy–client relationship, they argue, it implies that each has its own unique problem which makes it difficult to generalise. The high level of involvement with each other is often the 'cause' of many consultancy–client relationship problems (Ghosh & Taylor, 1999) making communications and role defining – particularly between account executive and the client marketing department – more difficult (Weilbacher, 1981), leading some to suggest that conflict is characteristic of consultancy–client relations (Michell, 1988).

As these relationships are a partnership where both contribute towards the end result, it is likely that performance and personal problems contribute towards most break-ups (Ghosh & Taylor, 1999). But is the partnership an equal one? Some argue that consultancies are not equal partners because it is their job to keep clients happy (Michell 1986) and so they must be highly attuned to client dissatisfaction, although 'consultancies seldom appeared to formulate strategies to prevent the break' (Michell, 1988: 10). As the consultancy usually has the most to lose if a relationship fails, it is important that they identify their client's unique needs and respond appropriately.

When a consultancy–client relationship breaks down, either the consultancy or the client has decided to part ways (Ghosh & Taylor, 1999), yet maintaining a relationship can be more desirable for a client than breaking up with the consultancy. For example, in presenting the case for long-term consultancy–client relationships, Hanscombe (1984: 409) gives a persuasive argument for preventing consultancy–client relationship break-ups and argues that one gets 'continuity of approach' by keeping the same consultancy. Michell (1988) concurs and points to his study of advertising consultancies where larger firms consistently keep their consultancies for longer than small firms, implying that a long-term relationship with an advertising consultancy contributes to larger companies' success. However, 'many clients make it unmistakably plain that they are always on the lookout for a new consultancy' (Ogilvy, 1971: 37) – an attitude that continues to exist today and which is ultimately counter-productive for the client, as the consultancy becomes frightened they will lose the account, and 'frightened' people are powerless to produce good work (Ogilvy, 1971).

But why do some consultancy–client relationships fail? Consultancy performance can be one factor in the relationship breakdown (Hodgson, 1991). More specific areas of poor performance are creative product, account servicing, personal relationships, personnel turnover, organisational structure and the role definition of consultancies and clients. Some consider inadequate creative work the biggest problem in consultancy–client relationships (Verbeke, 1988/89), although clients may evaluate the consultancy's creative work based on 'gut feeling' or the level of trust and good 'chemistry' they have with consultancy personnel rather than a straight 'scientific' evaluation (Weilbacher. 1981). Poor staff continuity can help erode consistency and deplete trust in the relationship, and personality conflict may affect the length of relationships and lead to a parting of the ways (Higgs, 1986). Consultancies which are insensitive to signals of client dissatisfaction and fail to anticipate emerging crisis in relationships with clients may see their accounts ended (Doyle, Corstjens, & Michell, 1980), while those which lack a developed marketing orientation towards clients and fail to recognise impending client dissatisfaction (Michell, 1986) may also find their relationship terminated.

However, the causes of relationship fractures and breakdowns are not always transparent. Clients can easily criticise consultancy performance, and consultancies may claim that it was some intangible 'personality problem' that caused the relationship break-up, thus both may avoid taking blame. Consultancies may rate personality problems considerably higher than clients do, pointing to contradictory evidence on whether personal relationships or performance variables are the main cause of failed consultancy–client relationships (Hodgson, 1991).

These are among the major reasons for account switching in advertising consultancy–client relationships, and some are recognisable in the field of public relations, with the importance of positive personal relationships a recurring factor in the maintenance or dissolution of client accounts with a consultancy. However, consultancy–client relationships are a multifaceted issue, with both parties indicating many different sets of reasons for a break-up, offering a mix of inadequate consultancy performance, lack of client cooperation or access to timely information, changes in consultancy or client management or policy, and personal relationship problems – all of which may lead to account switching by the client or indeed, albeit rarer, the consultancy sacking the client.

MANAGING A CONSULTANCY

In relating public relations consultancies to the C-MACIE framework, the four areas – management analysis, choice, implementation and evaluation – are clearly evident, applying to strategically important decisions but also more routine matters involving running the organisation. A consultancy is in a unique position, having a dual role – operating as an entity in its own right and managing and guiding its business, and simultaneously acting in *loco parentis* for its clients. In both roles, practitioners analyse, choose, implement and evaluate. Their effectiveness in conducting and combining these functions has a direct impact on the survival of the consultancy and the success of the client's communications strategy, with similar tasks conducted for each organisation.

Analysis

In terms of analysis, consultancies undertake a range of activities that enable them to analyse the public relations industry and sector they operate within, and also their clients' markets to determine the issues and challenges they must address. This may be deemed even more essential in turbulent economic times when the fate of both consultancies and clients is more uncertain. As particular industries are hardest hit by recession – such as construction, recruitment and the public sector – the consultancies serving them will need to continually scan, analyse and interpret their external environment to pre-empt such trends and, in anticipating them, seek ways to protect their business from being over-exposed in sectors where markets are constrained and communication budgets tighten or disappear entirely. Thus a consultancy will need to examine market conditions, competition, financial positions and key challenges to identify trends and their implications for the business. Such trends may well affect the business's competitive effectiveness. For example, the rise of digital technology has placed pressure on consultancies to understand, develop and offer digital, online or 'new media' services to meet client demand, and both retain and acquire clients with digital needs in the face of firms that have entered the digital market more quickly and with greater expertise, thus posing a significant threat to the consultancy's competitive position. Also essential is analysing key stakeholder groups to identify attitudes and behaviours – of employees, the media, current and prospective clients, suppliers, competitors and the business community – that will impact on the consultancy's continued successful operation. As Figure 13.1 indicates, such environmental scanning and analysis may encompass a wide range of stakeholders for any public relations consultancy.

Similarly, a consultancy conducts analysis for its clients, researching their sector and markets and those of their customers to understand the environment in which they operate and identify communication opportunities. Such scanning may involve using analytical techniques such as stakeholder mapping and analysis or communication auditing, so as to fully comprehend the key challenges and issues the client faces and identify the stakeholder relationships which need to be maintained or enhanced through a public relations strategy.

Choice

Consultancies armed with analysis findings and an in-depth understanding of both their own and their clients' environments can then move to 'management choice' and take informed decisions about the strategy options for their business and the route they wish to take. Such choices may centre on which markets to enter, which services to provide, the personnel they need to recruit, which clients or pitches to pursue, whether to expand their business, whether to remain a pure public relations consultancy or move into a wider communication offering, or whether and how to embrace ethical, digital or other new services. And with each of these decisions comes a plethora of choices about the issues involved, the challenges they pose and how they might be overcome, identification of potential strategies and tactics which could be adopted, selection of staff to lead them, and deciding where new responsibilities lie, whether current resources are sufficient or more are required, and which actions to prioritise. Such choices may be calculated using a number of criteria – previous experience, professional judgement and entrepreneurial ability of the owner-manager or directors of the consultancy, strength of personnel and current skills base, available resources and budget, buoyancy of client sectors, competition activity, client needs and demands, opportunities for growth, threats to the consultancy's survival, and potential risk factors. As with all businesses, such issues will need to be weighed carefully before a consultancy chooses which strategy to adopt and how to implement it.

Choice is also a key element of the work a consultancy undertakes for its clients, and, after conducting a thorough analysis of the client's environment, decisions then need to be taken regarding the most appropriate communication or public relations strategy to devise, recommend and implement. Again, choices are required concerning the direction to take, setting of key objectives, identifying stakeholders to prioritise, selecting suitable public relations tactics and carrying out a successful campaign or relevant strategy to meet the client's communication needs. Such activity is the shared responsibility of the account team allocated to the client, although as suggested above, the choices for which each practitioner is responsible may differ, with the director focusing on strategic decisions and managers and executives more likely to make tactical choices surrounding implementation techniques and timings.

Implementation

Implementing the choices made for the consultancy business is as vital to the success of the firm as the strategic decisions themselves. This often lies in the success with which the decisions are communicated to and accepted by the consultancy personnel and in turn the degree to which they are willingly and successfully implemented by those same staff. Such decisions and changes may impact on the structures, processes and relationships within the consultancies. As skilled practitioners are the key resource any consultancy possesses, managing personnel via 'people management skills' or human resources skills can be a delicate area, especially in small firms where people work very closely together, and even minor changes can have significant repercussions on established working practices and relationships. Taking a new direction to incorporate services such as ethical or digital public relations may result in the need for new staff with relevant expertise, fresh offerings and restructured campaigns to existing clients, as well as the pursuance of new business in unfamiliar sectors. Account teams may be restructured, new practices brought in, additional skills required to be learnt, and new relationships will need to be established, not only internally among consultancy personnel but also externally, incorporating them into existing client relationships or within the business's network. All of this will impact on those working in the business. While such changes may elicit a positive response and be welcomed as the way forward, they may equally create unease among staff who feel the status quo shifting as new people and practices are brought into their workplace, the structure of the consultancy alters as teams are reorganised, responsibilities and reporting lines are modified, and uncertainty about their own place and role creeps in. Such unease can be overcome in part by involving staff in decisions about the direction the business must take, consultation on the proposed changes and ensuring that people are aware of what is happening and why from an early stage rather than introducing changes at the last minute as a *fait accompli*. While such changes may be desirable to keep the consultancy fresh and dynamic – and even essential to ensure its survival – nevertheless, they can be unsettling and may take time to bed in until new people, structures, processes and relationships become established, familiar and the accepted norm once more.

Implementation of choices is also central to the activity which a consultancy undertakes for its clients – implementing the public relations strategy, campaign or media schedule is a large part of a practitioner's work and requires concerted and coordinated effort by the whole account team. Implementation is required on a number of levels – requiring successful and ongoing liaison with the client on the campaign direction, gathering timely information and feedback and using these to create many of the tactical elements – whether content for press releases, feature articles, press packs, speeches, presentations and a variety of promotional literature or exhibition and event material, or web and digital content. Such tactics are then implemented to target key stakeholders. Here the media is often an important vehicle for communication with a range of publics, whether for business, consumer, community or political campaigns, and ongoing and successful liaison with media contacts and networks can form a cornerstone of the implementation of the chosen strategy. Yet broader campaigns will pursue other avenues at the same time, with media relations often conducted in tandem with activities focusing on community liaison, lobbying, internal communication or social networking where the media may not be directly or deliberately involved.

Evaluation

Often the source of much lamenting that practitioners fall short in this area or do not pay it sufficient regard in strategy or campaign planning, evaluation is a key part of the C-MACIE framework and one which most successful businesses undertake within their own practices, even if not formally or via any specific evaluation tools. Few businesses can survive and grow without at least reflecting on, learning from and adapting the choices they have made and their implementation and consequences. Consultancies may evaluate their own practices in a number of ways to determine the extent to which policies, strategies and programmes of change have achieved their aims and objectives. Internally, the effects on personnel can be identified via personnel reviews and the extent to which changes have been harmonised and accepted into everyday working practices, and through early identification and resolution of potential conflict areas. Business objectives can be reviewed to ascertain how far they have been achieved – examining client retention and the growth of existing accounts through offering new services, the flow of referrals, invitations to pitch for new business, and the acquisition of new clients – whether in the consultancy's traditional sectors or newer, more diverse areas. Ultimately, the bottom line will indicate the extent to which plans and strategies are bearing fruit and enabling the consultancy to survive and grow. Externally, the perceived reputation of the consultancy can be researched, via survey or focus groups, and industry rankings provide a useful indicator of the business' position in relation to competitors. The longevity of client–consultancy relationships may also indicate that the consultancy is working on the right lines, providing high-quality creative public relations services at competitive rates that lock in the client and build barriers to account switching or poaching, although no business can afford to be complacent with a long-standing customer when operating in a highly competitive environment in times of economic uncertainty.

Consultancies can and should also be involved in evaluating the communication programmes and campaigns they implement for clients, although here they are often criticised for failing to incorporate evaluation into their activities or for conducting measurement of processes only – such as media coverage and use of advertising value equivalents (AVEs) – rather than evaluation of impact. While many reasons for this lack of activity are proposed – often centring around lack of time, expertise and budget, and perhaps also a combination of low motivation to engage in evaluation and little willingness to pay for such work from clients with hard-pressed budgets – one area which is seeing growth in evaluation may lead the way for other public relations services to follow. Within digital public relations, practitioners frequently employ analytical software tools to monitor and evaluate campaigns, social network sites, blogs, Twitter, Facebook and the like to track the extent to which they are engaging with online communities. While it can be argued that such tools are easier to implement at a technical level and are focused on very specific activities that are more cost-effective to monitor, nevertheless the growing trend for evaluation in this area may influence client expectations and consultancy practice within other public relations services.

SUMMARY

This chapter has reviewed public relations consultancies and explored a number of key areas. It has examined the nature and growth of the public relations industry both in the UK and globally, and considered the effects of the recession and the challenges it faces, as well as opportunities and new areas of growth. Different types of consultancies have been considered together with the macro-environment in which they

(Continued)

(Continued)

operate, as well as their structure, role and functions. Exploring types of public relations consultancies has revealed a variety of forms and purpose, and a growing list of services and areas of expertise which they may claim to offer. In particular, the consultancy–client relationship has been explored and a life cycle of events suggested by which this business association may commence, proceed and eventually end, while acknowledging that this complex area still requires research and understanding – whether of consultancy selection criteria, attributes determining long-term relationship sustainability, or factors which lead to relationship conflict and breakdown. Finally, public relations consultancy management has been explored with reference to the C-MACIE framework, and in examining management analysis, choice, implementation and evaluation, the dual role which a consultancy undertakes is recognised in managing and sustaining its own business in an increasingly competitive marketplace while also acting on behalf of clients and conducting similar activities to help sustain their business via strategic communication programmes and strategies.

Such activity combines with a whole host of issues currently facing public relations consultancies – an increasingly competitive marketplace, the growing complexity of technology, the rise of digital communication and social media, demanding clients, economic pressures, tightening budgets, the blurring of responsibility between different marketing communication disciplines, the desire to become more professional – and the need to retain, maintain and acquire clients as well as run a commercial operation. Challenging but interesting times are no doubt ahead for the sector, and how consultancies rise to meet these challenges and move forward will be fascinating to watch.

REFERENCES

Bernays, E.L. (1965) *Biography of an Idea: Memoirs of Public Relations Counsel*. New York: Simon and Schuster.

Boojihawon, D.K. & Young, S. (2001) Understanding international strategy in professional services industries'. In: McDonald, F., & Tüselmann, H. (eds), Proceedings (Vol. 1) of the 28th Annual Conference of the UK Chapter of the Academy of International Business: 'International Business in the 21st Century: Change and Continuity – Strategies, Institutions, Regulations and Operations', April 2001. Academy of International Business, Manchester Metropolitan University, UK.

Bourland, P.G. (1993) The nature of conflict in firm–client relations: A content analysis of *Public Relations Journal* 1980–89. *Public Relations Review, 19*(4), 385–98

Cagley, J.W., & Roberts, C.R. (1984) Criteria for advertising agency selection: An objective appraisal. *Journal of Advertising Research, 24*(2), 27–31.

CEBR (2005) *PR Today: 48,000 Professionals; £6.5 billion Turnover. Summary Document: The Economic Significance of Public Relations*. Centre for Economics and Business Research Ltd Report for the CIPR. Available at www.cipr.co.uk/research

CIPR (2005) *What is Public Relations?* Chartered Institute of Public Relations. Available at www.cipr. org.uk

(Continued)

(Continued)

CIPR (2009a) PR industry remains resilient in recession. Chartered Institute of Public Relations press release, 2 December. Available at www.cipr.co.uk/News (accessed on 29 December 2009).

CIPR (2009b) *2009 CIPR membership survey: The state of the PR profession*. Chartered Institute of Public Relations and ComRes survey report, December. Available at www.cipr.co.uk/News/research

CIPR (2009c) *PR Jargon Buster*. Chartered Institute of Public Relations. Available at www.cipr.co.uk/direct/lookingforpr (accessed 28 December 2009).

CIPR (2009d) *What is Public Relations?* Chartered Institute of Public Relations. Available at www.cipr.org.uk

CPRF (2002) *2002 Public Relations Industry Revenue and Performance Data*. Council of Public Relations Firms. www.prfirms.org (accessed 10 February 2005).

CPRF (2004) PR industry rebounding: first half surveys show revenues up from last year – new business on the rise. Council of Public Relations Firms press release, 10 August. www.prfirms.org (accessed 10 February 2005).

CPRF (2009) U.S. public relations industry expanded in 2008; '09 projected to be flat, according to the Council of Public Relations Firms. Council of Public Relations Firms press release, 26 February. Available at www.prfirms.org.

Dibb, S., Simkin, L., & Vancini, A. (1996) Competition, strategy, technology and people: The challenges facing public relations. *International Journal of Advertising*, *15*(2), 116–27.

Doyle, P., Corstjens, M., & Michell, P. (1980) Signals of vulnerability in agency–client relations. *Journal of Marketing*, *44*(4), 18–23.

DTI/IPR (2003) *Unlocking the Potential of Public Relations: Developing Good Practice*. Department of Trade and Industry and the Institute of Public Relations joint report, November. Available at www.ipr.org.uk/unlockpr/index.asp.

DTI (2004) Business services overview: Marketing communications. Department of Trade and Industry. Available at www.dti.gov.uk/sectors

Dwyer, F.R., Schurr, P.H., & Oh, S. (1987) Developing buyer-seller relationships. *Journal of Marketing*, *51*(2), 11–27.

Ford, D. (1990) *Understanding Business Markets: Interaction, Relationship and Networks*. London: Academic Press.

Frazier, G.K., Spekman, R.E., & O'Neil, C.R. (1988) Just-in-time exchange relationships in industrial markets. *Journal of Marketing*, *52*(October), 52–67.

Ghosh, B.C., & Taylor, D. (1999) Switching advertising agency – A cross-country analysis. *Marketing Intelligence and Planning*, *17*(3), 140–6.

Grönroos, C. (1982) *Strategic Management and Marketing in the Service Sector*, Research Reports 8. Swedish School of Economics and Business Administration, Helsinki.

Grönroos, C. (1990) Marketing redefined. *Management Decision*, *28*(8), 5–9.

Grunig, L.A., Grunig, J.E., & Vercic, D. (1998) Are the IABC's excellence principles generic? *Journal of Communications Management*, *2*(4), 335–56.

Gummesson, E. (1978) Towards a theory of professional service marketing. *Industrial Marketing Management*, *7*, 89–95.

Gummesson, E. (1987) The new marketing – Developing long-term interactive relationships. *Long Range Planning*, *20*(4), 10–20.

Håkansson, H., & Snehota, I. (1995) Analysing business relationships. In H. Håkansson & I. Snehota (eds), *Developing Relationships in Business Networks*. London: Routledge.

Halinen, A. (1997) *Relationship Marketing in Professional Services: A Study of Agency–Client Dynamics in the Advertising Sector*. London: Routledge.

Hanscombe, P. (1984) Choosing an agency: the advantages of fidelity. *ADMAP*, September, 409–12.

(Continued)

Heide, J.B., & John, G. (1990) Alliances in industrial purchasing: the determinants of joint action in buyer-seller relationships. *Journal of Marketing Research*, *27*(February), 24–36.

Higgs, R. (1986). Getting the best out of the agency – A client's view. *ADMAP*, April, 217–22.

Hinrichsen, C.L. (2001) Best practices in the public relations agency business. In R.L. Heath (ed.), *Handbook of Public Relations*. Thousand Oaks, CA: Sage.

Hodgson, D. (1991) Perceptions of Mattingly & Partners in the Auckland advertising market. 40,499 Project, University of Waikato.

Hotz, M.R., Ryans, J.K. Jr., & Shanklin, W.L. (1982) Agency/client relationships as seen by influentials on both sides. *Journal of Advertising*, *11*(1), 37–44

ICCO (2004) *World Report June 2004*. International Communications Consultancy Organisation. www.iccopr.com (accessed 10 February 2005).

ICCO (2009) Global public relations consultancy robust despite economic downturn. International Communications Consultancy Organisation World Report 2009, Press Release 12 May 2009. Available at www.iccopr.com/news-event (accessed 29 December 2009).

Jefkins, F. (1992) *Public Relations* (4th ed.). London: Pitman.

Lages, C., & Simkin, L. (2003) The dynamics of public relations: Key constructs and the drive for professionalism at the practitioner, consultancy and industry levels. *European Journal of Marketing*, *37*, 298–328.

Levinthal, D.A., & Fichman, M. (1988) Dynamics of interorganisational attachments: auditor-client relationships. *Administrative Science Quarterly*, *33*(3), 345–69.

Michell, P. (1986) Auditing of client–agency relations. *Journal of Advertising Research*, *26*(6), 29–41.

Michell, P. (1988) Where advertising decisions are really made. *European Journal of Marketing*, *22*(7), 5–17.

Michell, P., Cataquet, H., & Hague, S. (1992) Establishing the causes of disaffection in agency-client relations. *Journal of Advertising Research*, March/April, 41–8.

OED (2009) *Oxford English dictionary*. Oxford: Oxford University Press.

Ogilvy, D. (1971) *Confessions of an Advertising Man*. New York: Athenaeum.

Oliver, C. (1990) Determinants of interorganisational relationships: integration and future directions. *Academy of Management Review*, *15*(2), 241–65.

PRCA (2004) Public Relations Consultants Association. Available at www.prca.org.uk

PR Week (2010a) Top 150 consultancies. *PR Week*, 23 April.

PR Week (2010b) Client/agency relationships: The good and the bad. *PR Week*, 23 April, 20–3.

Ram, M. (2000) 'Professionals at work – transition in a small services firm.' *Journal of Small Business and Enterprise Development, 7*(1), 69–77.

Schell, C., & Wood, D. (1998) *Professional Services Relationships and Client Loyalty*. Working Paper No. 386, Manchester Business School, University of Manchester.

Schultz, M., & Ervolder, L. (1998) Culture, identity and image consultancy: Crossing boundaries between management, advertising, public relations and design. *Corporate Reputation Review*, *2*(1), 29–50.

Sharma, D.D. (1994) Classifying buyers to gain marketing insight: A relationship approach to professional services. *International Business Review*, *3*(1), 15–30.

Shaw, E. (1998) Networks as a strategic entrepreneurial marketing tool – A review of the evidence. In B. Hulbert, J. Day, & E. Shaw (eds), *Academy of Marketing Symposia on the Marketing and Entrepreneurship Interface 1996–1998*. Northampton: Nene University College.

Silversides, G. (2001) Networking and identity: The role of networking in the public image of professional service firms. *Journal of Small Business and Enterprise Development*, *8*(2), 174–84.

Simkin, L., & Dibb, S. (1998) Key business dilemmas and the marketing remit in business-to-business marketing services. *International Journal of Research in Marketing*, *8*(4), 283–99.

Tymson, C., & Sherman, B. (1996) *The New Australian and New Zealand Public Relations Manual*. North Shore City, New Zealand: Tandem Press.

(Continued)

(Continued)

Verbeke, W. (1988/89) Developing an advertising agency-client relationship in The Netherlands. *Journal of Advertising Research*, December-January, 19–27.

Wackman, D.B., Salmon, C.T., & Salmon C.C. (1986) Developing an advertising agency-client relationship. *Journal of Advertising Research*, 26(6), 21–8.

Wade, N. (1995) Consultancy public relations. In S. Black (ed.), *The Practice of Public Relations* (4th ed., pp. 111–26). Oxford: Butterworth-Heinemann.

Weilbacher, W. (1981) *Auditing Productivity: Advertiser–Agency Relationships Can Be Improved*. Association of National Advertisers Inc.

West, D.C. and Paliwoda, S.J. (1996) Advertising client–agency relationships: The decision-making structure of clients. *European Journal of Marketing*, 30(8), 22–39.

White, J. (2000) Innovation, research and development in professional services firms: A comparison of management and public relations consultancies, drawing implications for public relations practice. *Journal of Communications Management*, 5(1), 82–8.

White, J., & Mazur, L. (1995) *Strategic Communication Management: Making Public Relations Work*. Wokingham: Addison-Wesley.

Williams, A., & Woodward, S. (1994) *The Competitive Consultant*. London: Macmillan.

Yorke, D.A. (1990) Developing interactive approach to the marketing of professional services. In D. Ford (ed.), *Understanding Business Markets: Interactions, Relationships, Networks*. London: Academic Press.

Zabkar, V., & Rojsek, I. (1998) Commitment in relationships among clients and advertising agencies in a country in transition. In *Proceedings of the 14th IMP Annual Conference: Interaction, Relationships and Networks: Visions for the Future*, Volume 1. Turku School of Economics and Business Administration, Finland.

A Managerial Perspective of Public Relations: Public Relations and the Internet – The Impact of the Social Web

Rob Brown

14

Key Themes

- How management of the public relations function is changing in response to the rapid growth of on-line communication
- The impact of so-called Web 2.0 technologies and social media
- How the traditional 'rules of the game' for public relations practitioners have changed
- How these changes are forcing practitioners to re-evaluate how they approach communications with the media and with stakeholders.

INTRODUCTION

In this chapter we explore how the rapid expansion of internet usage and internet-based activity and services over the past decade in particular has presented organisations in both the private and public sectors with new opportunities and challenges in engaging with and building relationships with their respective stakeholders. Here it is the communication/public relations professionals who are often at the forefront in developing effective stakeholder engagement strategies. However, with the emergence of the so-called Web 2.0 technologies and the rapid growth of social media usage, particularly across the developed world but increasingly globally, professionals have been forced to rethink their often tried and tested methods of communicating with different stakeholder groups. In some cases, the solution has been to hire specialist digital communications staff or to take over and absorb fledgling digital media consultancies. In other cases, departments have undergone intensive training to help them understand the potential of Web 2.0 technologies and social media. Of course, the media environment has evolved and is continuing to evolve, and because of this constant change, it is important for practitioners to be alert to whatever new opportunities or challenges might emerge. In this chapter we consider the implications of these important changes in the communication environment, and particularly in web-based technologies, for the management of the communication/public relations function in organisations. Here we have used the MACIE model as an organising framework to explore this topic area.

COMMUNICATION MANAGEMENT ANALYSIS – WHAT HAS CHANGED?

An Explanation and Understanding of the Social Web

The biggest current challenge to public relations managers is the delivery of effective PR programmes on-line as the content of the internet becomes increasingly socialised and fragmented. The 'social web' is the term that has come to describe the current iteration of the internet, in which the content is largely created by the users. To some extent it is a misnomer because the internet has contained user-generated content ever since it was conceived in academic circles in the 1960s. Many people date the emergence of the social web to 2004 and the highly influential Web 2.0 Conference run by the US publishing company O'Reilly Media. The term Web 2.0, often regarded as interchangeable with the term 'social web' was first used by Dale Dougherty, a co-founder of O'Reilly Media. Nothing really changed in 2004 from a technological point of view. Most of the tools that were available to create Web 2.0 environments were already available. There has, however, been a continuous and rapidly increasing change in the way that people view the internet. It is now organic and driven by ordinary internet users.

Web 2.0 has a range of definitions and interpretations. It is a simple concept. Instead of just browsing the web and consuming content, users add their own content. They do this in 'blogs' and 'forums' (see Terminology Box 1), in social networks like Facebook and LinkedIn, on photography and video sites like Flickr, YouTube and Vimeo, among many others. They can effectively stream their aspects of lives, regularly commenting on thoughts and actions through the microblogging network, Twitter. With blog platforms like Wordpress (see Terminology Box 2), it is incredibly easy for individuals with only very limited technical skills to create the sites into which they can add content that they themselves produce or that they gather from

TERMINOLOGY BOX 1

Blogs and Blogging

The word is a contraction of the term Weblog. The first bloggers were effectively online diarists, keeping a running account of their lives. Blogging took off towards the end of the 1990s when a specific publishing platform 'Blogger' was launched from August 1999. It quickly became the most popular and simple to use blogging tool and allowed mainstream Internet users with little specialised knowledge to start their own blogs. The rapid expansion in the number of blogs can be gauged by the fact that, at the time of writing, the monitoring tool Technorati tracks over 112 million blogs and if the word 'blog' is typed into Google it produces over 3 billion hits.

Blogs have some defining characteristics. They have a date stamp in the title and normally allow comments to be attached. Blogs are usually maintained by an individual, although in some cases organisations or corporate bodies may produce blogs. Some blogs focus on specific issues or topics whereas others are more like personal online diaries.

See Brown, R (2009) *Public relations and the Social Web*, Kogan Page for more details.

TERMINOLOGY BOX 2

Blogging Platforms

Blogging platforms offer a range of services and applications based around specialised content management systems which are themselves specifically designed for creating and regularly updating blogs. In addition to allowing bloggers to answer, the body copy and headline loading platforms essentially facilitate the automatic publication of all blogs on a regular basis and also allow for comment or feedback.

WordPress, which started in 2003, has become the largest self-hosted blogging platform in the world. It is used by millions of bloggers every day.

The rapid emergence of *Twitter* in recent years has become the leading micro blogging site in the world allowing users to write short blogs of a maximum 140 characters. These micro-blogs can be uploaded by SMS text, or directly from any computer.

See Brown, 2009. *Public Relations and the Social Web*, Kogan page for further details.

around the web. Though simple in concept, in practice this growing trend signifies the transfer of control of the internet, which is now the central platform for communication, from the few to the many.

In particular, we can see how the delivery and consumption of news information is being democratised. There are already some iconic examples where Twitter has supplanted the role of major news organisations in breaking stories. When the story broke on the 2008 terror attacks in Mumbai, much of news was first channelled via Twitter. Details of the siege were reported minute by minute by people who were there. In January 2009, within minutes of US Airways flight 1549 ditching in New York's Hudson River, the social web was distributing information about the crash and even reassurances about the survival of all 155 passengers and crew. Commuter Janis Krums was on a New York ferry that had been diverted to the crash site to pick up the stranded passengers. He used his cell phone to take a photograph of the plane floating in the Hudson and and uploaded it to TwitPic (a Twitter picture service) with the comment 'There's a plane in the Hudson, I'm on the ferry going to pick up the people. Crazy.' The image was forwarded in seconds to web users across the world. After the contested elections in Iran in June 2009, when the world's mainstream media were being blocked from reporting the Mousavi-led uprising in Iran, video, photographs and on-the-spot reportage were sent out by ordinary people. There is no doubt that the the availability of these channels and the concurrent surge in citizen journalism have provided a new layer of news sourcing where information comes fast and direct.

If the social web has impacted so dramatically on the dissemination of news, then it must surely have a commensurate impact on the practice of public relations, a discipline that is inextricably interwoven with the process of generating news and features.

The Evolving Media Landscape

Newspapers gave public relations practitioners an early taste of the evolving media landscape when towards the end of the millennium they began to produce internet editions. The early titles were essentially on-line mirrors of the printed versions, but they then started to create content that was unique to the web versions. The way public relations stories were released was very quickly affected by news organisations that were now able to publish stories literally within minutes of receiving them. In the intervening years major newspaper organisations have gone about the business of reinventing themselves as news brands delivering across a variety of platforms and using audio and video content in addition to the written word.

The very concept of the printed newspaper is now under considerable financial pressure. Take the example of Boston's main daily newspaper, the *Boston Globe*, serving a conurbation of 4.5 million people. The *Boston Globe* is regarded as a bastion of fine journalism that has been the recipient of 20 Pulitzer prizes. The newspaper was acquired by the *New York Times* in 1993 for $1.1 billion, but by the middle of 2009 was losing over $1,000,000 per week. In the UK weekly newspapers have been closing regularly and the whole newspaper model is under scrutiny, and this extends to the national daily newspapers. The *Guardian*, for example, no longer regards itself as just a newspaper. It is a trusted media brand that delivers podcasts, video content, web content that is open to its users as well as a the traditional daily, 'dead wood and ink' version.

When the *Guardian* relaunched itself in the UK in 2005 with the smaller sized Berliner print format Alan Rusbridger, the editor, said he believed the *Guardian* website was cannibalising newspaper readership and that this had been a factor in the prior fall in the paper's circulation, something that we have witnessed across national newspapers. He provided another fascinating insight into the future of national daily newspapers. The *Guardian*'s new print format had necessitated the purchase of new printers at some considerable cost, £62 million. The initial budget had been £50 million and Rusbridger apparently said that they would likely be the last printers that the paper bought.

There have been significant changes to the way we watch television. This has been possible since the invention of the video recorder, but innovations like Sky+, Hulu and the BBC iPlayer have made the practice commonplace. Television viewing is also no longer platform-specific – that is to say, you no longer have to watch television on a television. PCs, laptops, mobile phones and gaming devices all allow us to watch both recorded and streamed TV content. This means that content which comes from traditional broadcasters and that which comes from a range of other sources, including those that incorporate user-generated content, the ubiquitous *YouTube* for example, are converging.

Radio programmes that have never been broadcast in a traditional sense are becoming more and more popular – we just do not refer to them as 'radio' any longer, but as 'podcasts'. They are relatively cheap and easy to produce and simple to make available.

The internet provides a platform that allows the delivery of traditional media content but has also provided a forum through which consumers and organisations can interact. This interaction, two-way communication and the blending of content created by mainstream media companies with content originated by a previously passive consumer cohort signifies the biggest change of all.

Impact on the Public Relations Industry

In the light of these changes in media consumption habits and, more particularly, in the structure and nature of the media organisations that provide content to the consumer, it is critical that public relations managers adapt to the new environment. We must not presume that the practice of public relations will continue on the same scale in its current form.

The core tasks for public relations, namely media relations, are more difficult due to the greater complexity of news distribution; however, there are new opportunities. The new channels and networks through which messages will flow will increase the prospects of reaching highly targeted audiences defined by specific interests. The conventional definition of public relations refers to communicating with 'publics' defined by broad demographics. Now because of the plethora of digital media we can target groups based on very specific interests, narrow demographics and precise geographical locations.

Given that the media is becoming disparate and fragmented, the question arises as to where in terms of managing public relations programmes we should be focusing our energies. In fact. more than ever we find that the answer is in the description of the 'public relations' function. Public relations people need to be talking to the public, now more than ever.

The nature of communication must also change from mono-directional to multi-lateral and from didactic to dialogue. Conversations are taking place about organisations and brands all of the time, and these discussions are often taking place in public – a Twitter search will establish that. Public relations practitioners need to understand that if they do not participate, the conversations will not stop and so ultimately brands, businesses and organisations will have to participate in dialogue in order to have an influence on how they are perceived. The consumer now demands it.

Reversals of Influence

The owners of the means of communication no longer exclusively control content. That is what the concept of Web 2.0 represents. The movement away from deference and one-way communication is embodied in the architecture of Web 2.0.

Newspapers have realised that breaking news is now no longer the preserve of journalists. Many traditional news organisations create spaces where individuals can post news and comment. In the UK, the *Guardian*'s 'comment is free' section represents one of these 'open access' news spaces and by mid-2008 the *Guardian* was receiving 10,000 postings a day to their site. There is a gradual ceding of control over news agendas. As soon as the demonstrations started to occur after the Iranian election of 2009, most major news organisations covered the events. During the first weekend however, CNN failed to give the events any prominence in its news coverage. The social web was up in arms and within 24 hours CNN had revised its editorial agenda and made the situation in Iran its main story. It was generally agreed that Twitter was one of the key sources of eye-witness coverage for several days. Later in 2009 the editor of the *Guardian*, Alan Rusbridger, used Twitter to highlight an injunction that had been served by the law firm Carter Ruck to prevent the reporting of Parliamentary questions about the activities of Swiss multinational company Trafigura and their alleged dumping of toxic waste in the Ivory Coast. Subsequent responses on Twitter and the publication of information by bloggers resulted in the injunction being overturned and widespread reporting of the case through conventional media channels.

It is not just the news makers who are giving up control. The degree to which brand identities can be managed is being significantly eroded, and this has created concern in boardrooms around the world because corporate communicators can no longer control the conversations around their brands, products or businesses in they way did.

Thus while it has always been necessary to examine carefully the publics/target audiences, the media available and the specific context in which any particular communications campaign is to take place, this type of analysis has become all the more complex because of the marked changes that have taken place in recent years in the both the availability of social media and the impact that this has had on conventional media consumption patterns.

COMMUNICATION MANAGEMENT CHOICE – HOW PUBLIC RELATIONS CAN EVOLVE

Conversations with the Audience

Managers are faced with the need to evolve thinking and practice within the industry. The traditional role of public relations can be adapted and is actually well suited to an environment where a multitude of conversations are taking place. Public relations, unlike (say) advertising, has always considered the target audiences for communication programmes to be a plurality of publics; different groups with different ideas and with whom we need to converse in different ways. The challenge of influencing the journalists and broadcasters who control the media, and therefore the means of communication, is being eclipsed by a new problem; namely that of identifying which of the plethora of new channels carry influence and authority with different audiences. This challenge is a key part of the evolution of the discipline of public relations.

Determining the channels for a public relations strategy was a relatively straightforward management task. We have had easy access to the reach, peak audiences and demographic breakdown of the media. Now, the challenge for those developing public relations strategies is to make sense of the myriad of audience channels. To give some sense of the scale of the internet, it is interesting to note that in July 2008, Google reached the milestone of indexing 1 trillion pages, and since then the web has been growing at a rate of several billion pages per day.

It is, however, in the nature of the social web to provide us with the tools with which to measure it. Some of these are well established and others are emerging on an almost daily basis.

Public relations managers have at their disposal tools that can measure not only the number of hits that particular websites or communities get but also the influence and authority of sites on the web. For example, sites like Technorati and PostRank will measure the level of trust and influence across blogs and many other forms of web content. PostRank measures RSS feed items, blog posts, articles, and news stories and provides a score based on how interesting or relevant people have found an item to be. Technorati, which has been around for considerably longer, measures the authority of blogs by establishing who links to a site or blog.

If we simply want to measure the number of visits that a particular website gets, then Alexa.com will give us a pretty reliable indication. Perhaps the most useful tool of all available to us is that of search ranking, which for most of us means still means Google. The front page results for a Google search will provide us with a very useful indication of the most important websites for any given topic.

New Channels

The biggest interest in the social web from a public relations and marketing perspective has been around the concept of social networking. However, as a concept this is

not new at all – it is exactly what the internet was created to provide. The first iteration of the internet was to link four US Universities (University of California at Los
Angeles, Stanford Research Institute, University of California at Santa Barbara and
the University of Utah), so that they would be able to more easily share information.

Social networks have evolved into communities used by millions of people every day.
Networks, like Facebook, Bebo, MySpace and LinkedIn are not just popular in terms
of the number of users, there is a very high level of engagement with the sites, which is
one of the many reasons they have become of interest to us. Brands and organisations
with commercial interests should engage with social networks with some caution.
There are types of businesses and organisations whose presence on Facebook and other
social network science would be better tolerated than others. Sectors that involve participation work better, for example sport, music, fashion, leisure and even politics.
There are an increasing number of social networks that are built around shared interests, and these, where relevant, can be particularly useful channels of communication.

Blogs represent a significant and growing facet of the social web. A blog is similar
to a website but with some defining characteristics. They usually have date stamps
and allow comments to be attached to each individual post. Blogs are usually maintained by an individual, and where a blog is maintained by an organisation it is made
clear who the individual contributors are. Posts are frequent and usually listed in
reverse chronological order. It is the blogs that focus on specific subjects that are of
most interest for public relations.

Many bloggers are conducting a form of participatory journalism; some are journalists who use blogs to publish content without editorial interference. We can
approach some bloggers in the way that we approach journalists. In addition to
pitching ideas to bloggers off-line, we can converse with them by adding comments
to their blog. The social web also provides us with tools for engaging with bloggers
that were unavailable to us in our dealings with journalists. A good example is the
use of Twitter to pitch a story.

Organisations are increasingly incorporating their own blogs into their public relations and communications strategies. Because search engines favour regularly updated
content, blogs will boost a company's presence in search rankings. However, some
businesses can be nervous about the open discussions that take place in and around
blogs.

Twitter has evolved into a really powerful public relations tool. Media organisations have Twitter streams that are often faster with news than their other channels.
You can opt to follow a selection of them and by doing so create your own personal-
ised news-wire. A straightforward way to do this is to create a group using the Twitter
client, Tweetdeck. Twitter can also facilitate business networking. The network essentially requires conversation, and conversation builds relationships. Google is the dominant search engine, but if you want a mixture of opinion as well as fact or you can
ask questions and get replies on Twitter. If you are promoting a client, say so. Linking
to a site or blog will be self-explanatory and Twitter can be a good way to drive traffic
to a site. There are several corporate bodies that have achieved over a million followers on Twitter in less than a year. Twitter is also a very powerful monitoring tool that
that allows you to search on key words using a variety of Twitter applications.

Really simple syndication (RSS) has become a useful pillar for many public relations campaigns. RSS allows users to subscribe to information headlines provided by a web host. By posting press information that is RSS enabled, all those individuals who have chosen to receive the information we send out, receive it automatically. By combining RSS feeds with Twitter you can tweet your headlines and push your blogs. RSS feeds directly via Twitter, effectively providing an easy route for 'breaking news'.

Public Relations and Search

Understanding the increasing relationship between public relations and search on the web is important for managers working in the public relations industry. Thompson (2007) identified a major new challenge for the public relations industry – the need to consider and deliver against the results of relevant search. He wrote:

> Google is not a search engine. Google is a reputation-management system, and that's one of the most powerful reasons so many CEOs have become more transparent. Online, your rep is quantifiable, findable, and totally unavoidable. In other words, radical transparency is a double-edged sword, but once you know the new rules, you can use it to control your image in ways you never could before.

Public relations content has become very useful for creating searchable content, and public relations managers need to ensure that written content is delivered in a way that is optimised for search. The industry needs to utilise some of the approaches that were previously the domain of search engine optimisation (SEO) businesses. The language that we use needs to take account of terms that are likely to be used for search, but at the same time we need to avoid jargon and phrases in favour of straightforward and descriptive text.

From the point at which Google arrived on the web the SEO business found ways to manipulate search, and SEO became a key part of digital marketing. High rankings have a commercial value. SEO techniques have been generally divided into those that are regarded as being either good design and practice, which search engines approve of (white hat), or they are attempts to trick search engines (black hat). As a result there is a tension between SEO and search engine providers. Over time search engines have consistently elevated the importance of news in search rankings. Public relations has always been concerned with delivering news so from that point the public relations business has acquired a new importance.

That importance continues to grow. For many years it was believed (and this belief was fuelled by the search industry) that a key element optimisation for a web page was the use of key words or meta tags. But in September 2009 Matt Cutts, a software engineer at the Search Quality Group in Google, said that the world's leading search engine 'disregards keyword meta tags completely. They simply don't have any effect in our search ranking at present.' The reason was that they had been abused so extensively is the past. Essentially this means that Google regards tagging as 'black hat'.

With the pressure to populate copy with keywords the most important thing was sometimes forgotten. Copy needs to well written, interesting and relevant. Now that we know that tags are less significant, it becomes clear that engaging content has an even more direct impact on search engine rankings and consequently on traffic. The quality of the content therefore is critical to receiving high rankings, because it will affect the number of pages viewed and the *stickiness* of the site. Crafting words is a core skill for the majority of public relations people. We also need to consider how to deliver quality content in all of its other forms including still images, audio and video.

The challenge for managers is to capitalise of the opportunities that natural search provides.

The Architecture of Digital Public Relations

Managing public relations in the digital context remains the same as conventional public relations in most respects, but there are new challenges.

Blogger engagement has similarities with media relations, but bloggers are not journalists (although many journalists also blog). There are no editors to manage the content or maintain quality control. Great blogs, and there are many, are popular and influential. I believe that the way we approach these bloggers should be similar to the way in which we approach good journalists – with a strong idea or a piece of useful insight or information – but we need to understand the medium and its differences, so as well as providing words and images we need to provide where relevant, audio video and critically hyperlinks to other relevant web content.

The internet does not merely add another dimension to our channel strategy; it is so vast and complex that on-line public relations campaigns should be built up using a variety of different on-line channels in a way that is suited to the communications challenge at hand. As part of the planning of a digital public relations campaign you should decide which elements of the social web would the most suitable and build ideas around how you harness those elements in delivering your programme.

The critical thing is to understand exactly what you are doing. The bold assumption that engaging with the social web simply means developing the techniques of traditional public relations is wrong. The level of complexity that we now face is daunting. If we go back to a time before the explosion, it seemed that the media was entirely quantifiable. Every good public relations person could name every national daily and Sunday newspaper and probably had a pretty good understanding of the editorial stance and range of content for most of them. Now we are dealing with a communication architecture that is far more complicated to map out. There are digital channels appearing all the time, with others disappearing or declining in importance. We need to accept this state of flux and we must constantly seek out new intelligence and information.

Managers need to recognise that 'link building' has become a core skill. Hyperlinks are central to the concept of the World Wide Web. To increase traffic to our on-line content, we need to find ways of creating links that will take people to it. Practitioners need to build link strategies into digital public relations programmes. Links also elevate Google rankings. Search engines give sites with good genuine links a higher ranking.

Maximising links must be done strategically. There must be quality content that other sites might wish to link to in the first instance. Reciprocal linking works well, but not all sites are equal. Securing a reciprocal link from a site that ranks highly on Google will deliver more traffic. By selecting a few good sites, emailing them individually with details of exactly what you can offer and where you think a link might fit in with their existing content, you will get a greater response rate.

Thus as we have shown, while the media landscape and people's media consumption habits have changed quite markedly over the past decade and these changes have accelerated with the advent and rapid expansion of new media channels and social media usage, the fundamental basis of effective public relations strategy and management arguably have not changed that radically. What has of course changed quite dramatically is the range and type of options that public relations managers have available to them in communicating and engaging with various stakeholder groups. Moreover, what has to be factored carefully into any public relations campaign strategy is the changing nature of the roles and balance of power in the information/news gathering, and news/information transmission/sharing between, on the one hand, traditional news media and the new generation of citizen journalist, bloggers and other information providers, and, on the other hand, news/information seekers and consumers. It is the change in this dynamic that perhaps represents the most significant impact of the social web, and it is these changes that have arguably driven the need for a marked change in nature of operational public relations practices.

COMMUNICATION MANAGEMENT IMPLEMENTATION – THE IMPERATIVE FOR CHANGE

It is well observed that whenever changes take place that necessitate a complete re-evaluation of practice within an industry, there are those who respond, those who wait to evaluate and those who choose not to recognise the need for change. Managers within the public relations industry have been confronted with such profound and relatively rapid change within the newspaper and broadcast industries that it is virtually impossible to ignore the need for changes to the practice of public relations. Moreover, the accelerating pace of these changes in the media environment has made the case for change all the more pressing. Remaining doubts that practitioners might harbour about the need for fundamental change can be answered by using one of the tools made available to them to measure social activity on the web. Using Google Insight for Trends to evaluate searches over time for the description 'PR agency', they will see a steady and consistent decline in the total number of searches. The total fell by half in the five years from 2004 to 2009. The phrase 'social media PR', however, has seen a rapid increase in searches since it was first requested via Google in 2006.

The Impact for Public Relations Managers

Whether the changes are evolutionary or revolutionary – and I believe they have characteristics of both – the management impact is significant. Change in the broad practice of public relations will require a cultural shift as well as practical solutions, including training and day-to-day guidance for staff. In organisations where managers are slow to respond to change, public relations departments will see their effectiveness decline, and for agencies their competitive edge will be eroded.

As for any change management situation, there will be opposition among practitioners, and a key task of the management function will be to overcome this opposition. Organisations will require champions and thought leaders from within their ranks to assist with the transition.

Using New Tools and Embracing New Skill Sets

Public relations people have always supplied content in the form of written words and commissioned images to support the copy. This continues to be a core part of the practice of public relations. It has always engaged with influential opinion formers and sought to persuade and influence. This will also remain at the heart of the industry. We will continue with most of the most of the methods we currently use. For example, media briefings will continue, and despite journalist complaints we will still be using email, but the most effective practitioners will also use the new tools available via the web and social media.

Some organisations have started to use what they call the *social media release* in place of conventional press releases. Whether you choose these instruments or not, increasingly practitioners are sending more than just words. Increasingly communication with the media may include audio, video and images. These communication materials should include relevant links either as postscripts or preferably embedded in the text. Online or social media newsrooms are increasingly used by agencies to host content as well as places that journalists can be directed to in order to obtain rich content.

Managers need to consider the role for creating broader digital assets in the form of photography, audio, video production and web design. Increasingly public relations campaigns will utilise social networking assets as elements of campaigns, and the public relations function will be expected to be capable of creating and managing a Facebook fan page and running a Twitter presence with an evolved understanding as to how to build relevant followers.

A killer aspect of the web is that it is infinitely measurable. Social web public relations has the potential to do away entirely with the imprecision in evaluation that has always dogged the public relations industry. It is in the area of measurement and evaluation that the most rapid advances in the use of new tools and skill sets are occurring.

COMMUNICATION MANAGEMENT EVALUATION

The internet provides us with a range of tools for measuring online public relations. Many provide in-depth analysis and the majority are entirely free to use. We can target our audience far more effectively than ever before and we can feed intelligence back into our campaigns in a cycle of constant improvement. The measurement of key message delivery, pre- and post-campaign quantitative and qualitative research and measurement against benchmark data are all available to us.

What we also need to observe and evaluate is how our public relations functions, whether internal departments or agencies, adapt to new practises.

Evaluation of Public Relations in a Digital Age

There is an argument that the most important objective of most public relations programmes, particularly in a digital media context, should be to impact on the search ranking. We could regard Google page ranks as a proxy for brand influence or an organisation's importance, and the difference that occurs over a period of time will give us a strong indication of momentum.

Using a variety of tools in conjunction with one another can provide robust results:

- *Google Alerts* provides updates of the latest search results – which could, for example, be the name of a client or product.
- *Google Trends* is an extremely powerful tool that allows you to monitor activity on virtually any subject or organisation and show results over a specified time frame or region.
- *Google Analytics* is a free service that generates detailed statistics about visitors to your own website or blog. Google Analytics can track where visitors are coming from, whether the hits are generated by search engines, by referrals from other sites (and what sites these are) or from public relations or other marketing campaigns.
- *News readers* have become infinitely more adaptable and many will let you adapt and manage the content using RSS feeds so that you get exactly the kind of news that you want.
- *Twitter* is becoming highly effective in both monitoring and disseminating news. The *New York Times*, BBC and the *Guardian* were among the early adopters.
- *Alexa* allows you to track the performance of a website over time with the advantage over Google Analytics, for example, that you that you can track any website, not just your own.
- *Compete and Quantcast* are among sites that provide information on traffic history, volume and quite detailed demographics.

Where accurate evaluation is an essential part of the delivery there are arrays of suppliers that can provide effective measurement of social media. The services that they provide include web-based computer dashboards showing information in real time about your company or brand. They will include engagement scores and share of voice compared to major competitors.

Evaluating Organisational Change

The most obvious measure of success in organisational change is the continuity in the effectiveness of the public relations function. However, we are unlikely to want to wait to find out whether campaigns win awards or an agency continues to be profitable in order to assess success. There are a range of other measures that managers might choose to apply. One of these would be to incorporate tests into training programmes to measure the effectiveness of the training modules. Perhaps more effective would be to monitor the behavioural changes and changes to the structure of public relations programmes that occur when the techniques and approaches described earlier in this chapter are embraced and implemented.

For example, the linear approach to campaigns will tend to be replaced by more continuous cycles. Rather than following a process of research, objective setting, campaign implementation and evaluation, campaigns will tend to do all of these things concurrently, with constant re-evaluation and improvement. That is because research and evaluation will be continuous, and therefore refining objectives and feeding this into implementation can be done at any time.

Media consumption habits will change. It is a good to ask practitioners whether they are aware of breaking news in the middle of the afternoon, say. If they consume news using social media channels they will be. If they rely on conventional channels they are less likely to be equally well informed at all times of the day.

Ultimately, it is the test of a good manager to be observant. If their organisation is responding to the imperative to adapt, the manager will know.

SUMMARY

In this chapter, the aim has been to examine how the fundamental basis of public relations practice – and consequently its management – has been changed and continues to evolve as a result of the radical changes that have and continue to take place in the media environment. Here in particular we have focused on the impact of the rapid growth and use of the social web and its impact not only on conventional media providers, but also fundamentally on how people around the world are able to source, gather and consume information and news.

(Continued)

(Continued)

Drawing on the C-MACIE framework, this chapter has sought to show how the social web poses new challenges and opportunities for managers in terms of understanding new media and media consumption patterns and how these influence and reflect different people's behaviours. We have then taken the analysis further to show how this analysis and understanding of this new 'digital media environment' leads to a variety of choice options that managers need to consider and decide upon in terms of how best to communicate and engage with stakeholders. These choices in turn give rise to a set of operational decisions and actions needed to put plans into action. Finally, we have examined how working in this new digital and social media environment has helped practitioners address the perennial question of how to measure the impact of campaigns effectively. Here we examined a range of tools that are available to help practitioners monitor and evaluate the impact of their campaigns almost as they are taking place, rather the traditional model of waiting until the campaign strategy has been delivered before attempting to assess the impact. Of course, the fundamental process of public relations – that of managing relationships between organisations and stakeholders so as to enhance the organisation's situation, reputation and or ability to realise its specific goals – does not change, but what the internet and social web have done is to radically change the channels, and the balance of influence within the various channels, through which stakeholder engagement and communications take place. It is this fundamental lesson that tomorrow's public relations manager needs to acknowledge and respond to if he/she is to functional effectively on behalf of their organisation or agency.

📖 FURTHER READING

Brown, R. (2009) *Public Relations and the Social Web: How to Use the Social Media and Web 2.0 in Communications*. London: Kogan Page.

Golden, M. (2010) *Social Media Strategies for Professionals and their Firms: The Guide to Establishing Credibility and Accelerating Relationships*. Oxford: Wiley.

Meerman Scott, D. (2011) *The New Rules of Marketing & PR: How to Use Social Media, Online Video, Mobile Applications, Blogs, News Releases, and Viral Marketing to Reach Buyers Directly* (3rd ed.). Oxford: Wiley.

Phillips, D., & Young, P. (2009) *Online public relations: A Practical Guide to Developing an Online Strategy in the World of Social Media*. London: Kogan Page.

Qualman, E. (2010) *Socialnomics: How Social Media Transforms the Way We Live and Do Business*. London: John Wiley & Sons.

Thompson, C. (2007) The see-through CEO. *Wired, 15.04*.

Strategic Issues Management: The Importance of Reasoning

John Arthur

Key Themes

- Understanding how issues management emerged and has been defined
- A critical review of the failings of some prevailing approaches to issues management
- Examining the key elements of the issues management process using a life-cycle narrative approach
- Understanding the challenges/barriers for organisations to embed the issues management process
- Examining an exemplar of ineffective issues reasoning for prioritisation
- Examining attributes of effective systems-based reasoning for issues prioritisation
- A review of the C-MACIE framework

INTRODUCTION

The Issues Management Conundrum

On 1 July 2010, I (a manager in one of the world's largest companies) met with a group of people from company X (a prestigious global consulting group). They offered to tell me about their risk services and they showed me a diagram including the excerpt shown in Figure 15.1.

(Continued)

(Continued)

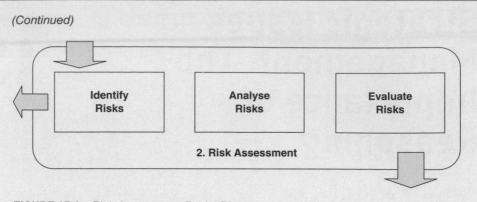

FIGURE 15.1 Risk Assessment Partial Diagram

I commented on the presence of three words: assessment, analysis and evaluation. As these were in separate boxes and the boxes were alluding to some kind of holistic process, I probed gently as to how they were different. I went on to suppose that the evaluation activity would, as the meaning of that word suggests, return some values pertinent to the business in question. I asked how those values would typically be calculated. I asked what metrics were being used in the analysis phase. I was reassured that a 'likelihood–impact plot' was at the heart of understanding which risks were the priority ones.

I probed a little further. How precisely were likelihood and impact being measured? The agent went on to describe how, at a meeting, people would give their opinions and these would be resolved into a place on the scale. 'Yes, but what scale?', I asked, 'What is the measurement unit? What is it that you are asking people to measure?'

I have shortened the conversation for you. My consultant friend began (rather passionately) to defend the need for organisations to have a systematic way to examine threats and, once they had discussed them, to find a method to summarise that discussion in a way that could be communicated to busy senior management and so on. And he is perfectly right. People do need to do this.

The thing is, though, I do not think that the sort of discourse he described is measurement. I think it is journalism. I do not think the result of that process belongs in a mathematical housing. I do not think the 'likelihood–impact plot' means anything at all. It imparts no knowledge. It is an intellectual placebo for people who feel the need to measure but cannot stand the pain of actually doing so. It is a complexity reduction technique that bypasses the need for the complexity.

One recurring question that communication professionals and management should ask is whether issues management processes and tools can be scientific. It is this debate that we explore in more detail in this chapter, drawing on the author's experience of the issues management approach in one of the world's largest multinational companies. This consideration will be in three distinct, but related, parts.

First, we look at some of the wider external and internal design contexts for modern issues management systems. Stopping to highlight what we see as some of the drawbacks of current approaches in this area, we will define our understanding of some of the key process, organisational and technology transfer challenges.

Second, using real examples from Unilever's own issues prioritisation system as a test case, we describe what we see as the essential measurement and analytical features of a reasoning platform for strategic issues management.

Finally, in keeping with the context of this book, we discuss the broader challenge of 'strategic issues management reasoning' through the lens of the C-MACIE framework. Drawing on applied examples, we wrestle with some of the principles over a more detailed discussion of issues management thinking.

We conclude this chapter by asserting that strategic managers would do well to accept the benefits of reasoning for 'complexity reduction'. This cannot be driven by a policy of intolerance of complexity masquerading as an appetite for simplification. Rather it must be done through having processes and tools which embrace complexity. However, these processes and tools need to be of a sufficiently elegant and purposeful design as to be able to produce tailored outputs which meet the specific reasoning support needs of a range of users and strategic audiences.

CONTEXT FOR ISSUES MANAGEMENT SYSTEMS DESIGN

In order to appreciate fully the challenges of establishing and maintaining an effective issues management approach, we need first to explore the context for issues management process design. Here we perhaps need to ask fundamental questions: what issues management is, how the discipline is positioned, and the key challenges facing those engaged in it.

The Origins of Issues Management

It is generally acknowledged that the founding figure in the field was Howard Chase, a public relations professional who is credited with having coined the phrase 'issues management' in 1976 to describe the process by which organisations attempt to monitor, analyse and manage the social, political, and economic concerns that affect their strategic future and viability. In this sense issues management arguably was originally a public relations concept and responsibility.

How Has Issues Management Developed?

A review and synthesis of some of the mainstream public relations literature (e.g. Heath, 2001; Grunig & Hunt, 1984) reveals a broad consensus about the chronological development of the modern issues management concept. In the 1970s, perhaps sparked by growing hostility to corporations, issues management grew out of a restructuring of corporate communication. During the 1980s, companies focus on the strategies that would protect them from increasingly organised stakeholder activists (assisted by new media). Issues management thus became corporate communication plus public policy. Then, in the 1990s, with burgeoning global communication, increasing fears (in some quarters) over globalisation and periodic environmental or social disasters, issues management becomes corporate communication, public policy and social and environmental responsibility (with or without crisis management attached). At the end of the 1990s public policy becomes an interplay between government, the media, the public and corporations. Issues management becomes part of a powerful advocacy engine to influence and drive public policy. According to commentators like Hainsworth (1990a), companies had grown wise to the idea that: 'Where legislation and regulation are concerned, issues are always resolved to someone's advantage and someone's disadvantage.'

An Alternative Lens?

An alternative lens, one could argue, is that modern issues management was not the result of this rarefied and elegant awakening process but rather the result of companies absorbing the impacts of long-term trends they themselves had caused and benefited from. These trends include:

- The move from corporate philanthropy to corporate social responsibility.
- The move from environmental compliance to sustainability (sourcing and production).
- The globalisation of physical supply chains and mass marketing communications.

In the postmodern boardroom one could speculate that the trends argument holds the most attention with boards who perennially purchase high-level 'barometer survey' evidence to help them reflect on the impact of trends on meta-constructs like 'reputation capital'. Arguably the trends themselves, responding to the corporations they describe, have become globalised 'mega-trends' now:

- The end of abundance – sustainability goes mainstream.
- Consumer control – truly global connectivity.
- Pushing boundaries of science and technology – genetic and 'nano'.
- Economic growth of the BRIC nations (Brazil, Russia, India and China) – increasing competition for global resources.
- From corporate entity to corporate digital identity – social media.

Whichever interpretation you prefer, there seems little doubt that issues management is increasingly being called upon to deal with globally relevant strategic decision making. We see issues management increasingly moving from a public, or corporate, affairs domain to a cross-functional 'total business strategy' domain. However, the key question is whether issues management itself has become a discipline. Has issues management developed adequately to meet these larger challenges? Are the models, tools and processes fit for this purpose?

Equally, we should be asking whether management models, such as C-MACIE, provide an adequate theoretical framework in which to ground and build an issues management system which supports strategically relevant decision making.

These are particularly important questions when modern issues management is a potentially rather entrenched discipline. Many of the approaches, which date back to the late 1970s and early 1980s, speak to a context far different than the one we have today (Jones & Chase, 1979; Chase 1984). As suggested earlier, issues management did not develop within a robust and 'scientific' disciplinary field but developed within early forms of the public relations 'domain'. This may explain the positioning of issues management itself, often still confused with public relations/government relations, and the challenge of demonstrating its strategic business value.

Critical Weaknesses in Extant Approaches

Certainly, to deliver strategic business value, issues management has to reduce the complexity of the many corporate relationships and interactions that may play out and affect an organisation's strategies and operations over time. This is not a trivial task, indeed quite the opposite, but there appear to be a number of critically intertwined weaknesses in the attempt to apply mainstream management science principles to this area, for example:

- Complexity reduction is being confused with simplification.
- Issues management processes and tools are used for description not explanation or prediction.
- The overall approach to measurement is insufficiently scientific.

Basic plotting tools, such as the 'Boston box', are used as simplification devices. These tools, however, are by no means the only form of simplification. It has, unfortunately, become typical of this area that the 'accepted norms' for discourse and modelling are themselves often simplifications and given to being less scientifically rigorous than might be wished. In their desire to simplify, these models err on the side of description over explanation and, in some cases, fail on both fronts. Palese and Crane (2002) offered an 'integrated model' which placed issues management in a corporate governance framework (see Figure 15.2).

Without being overly critical of what is essentially a descriptive model advanced by the authors, this is rather typical of the reductionist/simplistic depictions we see in issues management texts. This model is claiming to identify 'the optimal relationship between the key internal players' in an integrated corporate governance framework. Yet, as is clear, it is not a sufficiently sophisticated exposition to back up such a claim.

Where these models do increase in sophistication tends to be in two key directions: first, when they describe a process; and second, when they use quasi-mathematical

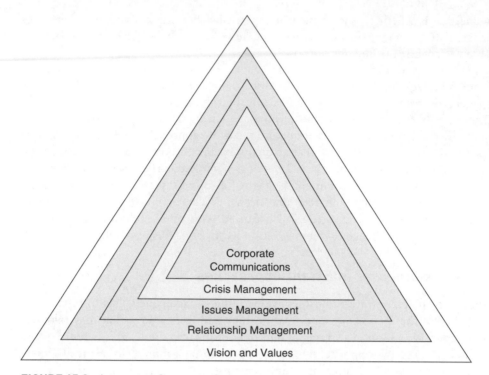

FIGURE 15.2   Integrated Corporate Governance Framework (Palese & Crane, 2002)

imagery. In the process case, there has been the occasional voice of dissent – see Bronn and Bronn's (2002) discussion of Ehling and Hesse's (1983) criticism of such models being 'nothing more than everyday management activities that all managers do'. However, such criticism is rare.

A long-running example of what we would call quasi-mathematical model building is the frequently cited 'risk issue lifecycle' model, often attributed to Hainsworth and Meng (1988). Potentially Hainsworth and Meng were building on the very similar but simpler Tombari (1984) lifecycle model (see Mahon & Waddock, 1992). Wartick and Mahon (1994) may have simplified this model to create their three-stage issues lifecycle which is based on similar constructs.

Where this quasi-mathematical reasoning gets taken a little too far, arguably, is when you see highly subjective constructs reduced to a 'formula'. Thus, for example, Coombs (2002) suggests the following as a reasonable method to assess issues with respect to the internet:

$$\frac{\text{Threat} = \text{Impact} \times \text{Likelihood}}{(\text{Issue Legitimacy} + \text{Issue Manager Power})}$$

How this formula is supposed to 'work' is not clear. 'Impact', from the accompanying text, can be financial (direct or indirect) or it can be one of another 150 means (not

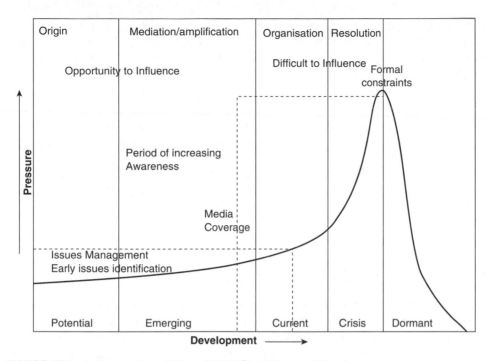

FIGURE 15.3 Hainsworth and Meng (1988) Risk Lifecycle Model

listed in the paper) of measurement. The determinants of '*likelihood*' are 'issue legitimacy' (an 'extent') and 'issue manager power' (an 'ability') based upon evaluations on 1–10 scales. It is hard to understand how these 'variables' also serve, as they appear to, as the denominator in the above formula.

We would argue that examples of 'issues management formulas' and plots, such as those discussed in the early parts of this chapter, demonstrate a misappropriation of mathematical models. This is complex because these models are being used both in the formation of judgements (during evaluation/assessment processes) and in the representation of models/outcomes (during the simplification/communication process). We would argue that mathematical constructs being applied are in fact a convenient 'housing' for complexity. That is to say, they provide a commonly accepted shorthand built on concepts we are all familiar with from secondary education mathematics lessons. What they absolutely do not do is reduce that complexity according to any observable rules of mathematics.

To give just one example of why this is the case, let us just briefly look into the technicalities of the above statement and pose three questions of the mathematical diagram (issues lifecycle) shown in Figure 15.3:

- How can this plot be predicated on axes without any scales?
- Where is the formula for the complex function needed to create this curve?
- Where is the measurement data required to validate the complex variance of the construct shown?

For each question the answer should be clear. Here the use of linear mathematical constructs (essentially normative science) is really a *narrative device,* and this is a common flaw in many such models. This sleight of hand might not be without reason, but it is certainly without rationale.

Thus with the illusion (or implied 'authority') of 'measurement' assumed within these models, their authors need to add that rationale. This leads to the models in question being heavily qualified with labels. These labels are referring to 'stages', 'events' or 'processes'. Some of these capitalise on a further benefit of false linearity to dramatically suggest a 'threshold', for example something like the omnipresent, but never adequately defined, 'crisis tipping point', or, as is the case here, an arbitrary 'release point' for the whole argument. In Figure 15.3 an issue simply plummets to becoming 'dormant' at a single point in time without nuance or explanation.

Positive Factors in Common Approaches

In the face of all this criticism, one has to ask: if these models are so limited, so terribly unscientific, why are they so successful? Why are practitioners in this discipline, time and time again, so uncritically accepting of such poor-quality reasoning? Why do many management science publications appear to accept a proliferation of complexity reduction models when it can be argued that these do not begin from a point of adequate complexity? The answers to these questions are themselves, ironically, very complex, but for our purposes a simple one will suffice: they *are* really useful, since they get the job done.

So, while it is important to expose the limitations of these quasi-scientific approaches, nevertheless we also need to explore how the advantages of these approaches can be used and built upon.

Consider a standard issues management 'tool', such as the 'likelihood–impact plot' discussed at the beginning of this chapter. There are clearly a number of benefits that this tool offers to senior management engaged in strategic decision-making. These include:

Speed: The first thing is that it is quick form of 'measurement'. A group of senior thinkers can deliver judgements through democratic debate in a short space of time. It is a common mode for them. If they are facilitated in this process by simple graphics on the wall and sticky notes upon which to write so that they can see their ideas take shape, they will perceive this to be quite focused. If measurement is no more taxing than making rank-order comparisons, it will not take long to do. There are clearly significant advantages to a system that facilitates such speedy decisions.

Acceptance: The use of techniques like this across a range of strategy-setting meetings is reported to be very common. When people study the technique on an MBA course, for example, and then see it used as they climb up the ladder of organisations it becomes a sort of 'given'. It is familiar, the measurement burden is never onerous and it does translate across contexts. This is an easy approach to 'sell in'.

Expedience: When the technique is quick, familiar and portable it also becomes expedient. Senior decision makers' time is always at a premium. Their patience is legendarily short on two levels that concern issues management – they dislike time-consuming processes, and they dislike having to learn 'a new language' in order to do their job. If they can cover a whole range of complex strategic prioritisation tasks by falling back on various clones of the probability impact plot, this is highly expedient.

Flexibility: A quick, easy, familiar, portable, expedient system that management are very comfortable with is going to be a popular choice among senior managers. This has the effect of making it a lingua franca for other functional players who wish to communicate with members of management. That fact has created a proliferation of similar devices, making this single technique more and more ubiquitous.

Transferability: Any approach or technology which achieves this level of acceptance, use and endorsement becomes what can be called the 'reference grammar' for reasoning in the decision spaces in question. This is the shorthand we will use going forward to denote both the considerable (perceived) benefits and the convenient metaphors for assessing and talking about complex issues or risks.

The technical name for this acceptance and endorsement phenomenon is 'technology transfer'. The very robust, and very similar, tools and processes available across mainstream issues management today have achieved a critical level of application. This goes some way to explaining why they keep 'getting transferred'.

In short, these models are too attractive to stop them turning up everywhere, which is a shame for strategic decision makers in the long run because, as we have already noted, they constitute extremely weak reasoning. Whilst there can be no doubt that strategic decision makers eschew complexity at the decision point, there is also no doubt that they want intelligent information processing to lie behind their reasoning. After all, they are reasoning, in the very largest of companies, with hundreds of millions of dollars at stake.

So how do we take full advantage of the enviable penetration of these models without suffering from their limitations? The answer is simple. We strengthen them. We make them more scientific.

The first step to strengthening our approach is differentiation. If the key weakness of these models is that they are hypothecation posing as extrapolation (English pretending to be mathematics) – we need to separate these parts of the story again and pay attention to their individual credibility.

To provide strategic support for strategic decision makers, it is time for the issues management discipline to concentrate its efforts on modelling *and* measurement. This is far from easy, but perhaps this ought to characterise the 'strategic decade' in the issues management story. Issues management is, after all, a management *science* discipline.

Strategic Issues Management Decision Support

In the next section we use real applied examples to bring some of the arguments above into clearer focus. These examples are taken from a real global company (Unilever) and examining how an actual issues prioritisation tool (*Descartes*) works. Three aspects of how we will explore the actual process of issues management are worth noting:

1. The use of small, helpful models is encouraged but the emphasis should be returned to a narrative form. Such a narrative should be the 'controlling story' for reasoning about the design of processes and tools.
2. Completely scientific mathematical measurement is considered impractical. However, usable but more formal measurement can be realised.
3. A mathematical housing for issues management reasoning/communication is not inappropriate. However, its legitimacy can be increased if the reasoning is based on meaningful values.

Recapturing Narrative Reasoning: A Lifecycle Model

A 'controlling story' is to issues management process design what a 'user scenario' or 'use case' is to technology design. It simply creates a sensible narrative to describe the objects upon which you intend to act in their proper context. In the modern industrial application the story cannot be over-complicated. The language has to be made up of bold and simple concepts.

Figure 15.4 shows a basic lifecycle model, using a 'sunrise to sunset' metaphor, to represent the typical stages in the emergence and development of an issue. Importantly, each stage can support an expanded narrative about what is uniquely happening at each particular point, as is summarised in Table 15.1.

Much of this story should be very familiar to most people working in this field. As a model Figure 15.4 also has the flavour of a mildly self-fulfilling prophecy. This is because it is not really a model at all, but rather a diagram depicting a train of thought supported by a narrative. The real usefulness of this narrative emerges when we seek to understand the origin and causes of mistakes that might happen at any stage. It is this facility diagnose process errors which turns a good controlling story into a good process.

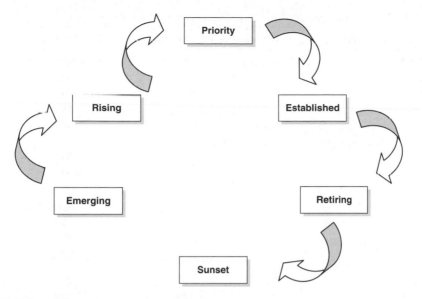

FIGURE 15.4 Unilever Lifecycle Controlling Story

TABLE 15.1 Issues Lifecycle Expanded

Stage	Description	Consideration
Emerge	Issues emerge from the pool of pre-suppositions, be these public opinion, legislative intent or contingent upon scientific discovery, etc.	When issues are being defined in their emergent state, time-frames should be assessed, but are often untrustworthy
Rise	From that pool of issues, at any given point some issues will rise in actual/potential impact or in perceived importance.	No domain-independent model would seem to be able to predict which issues will rise
Priority	Actual and perceived priority (and resource) is given to some issues	It is important to acknowledge that priority issues, should have a target shelf-life
Established	Priority issues will be established (and accepted) when a management plan, in month-on-month operational terms, is in place	It is important that priority issues should be defined as operational outcomes, not a set of woes
Retirement	As this month-on-month extraordinary effort loses the features which distinguish it from 'normal' business, the original issue goes into retirement – the 'issue status' is put away	The advocacy plan, risk assessments, etc. around the issue should be actions towards a solution, not the solution themselves
Sunset	The issue 'sunsets' completely when its management has no distinguishing features over and above company policy, practices or commitments	Issues should never therefore have 'permanent' status

TABLE 15.2   Examples of 'Mistakes' in Issues Lifecycle Reasoning

Mistake type (by stage)	Example of implication	Example solution space
Emergence No long- or medium-range radar system to identify issues that are emerging – internally and externally – around present and future business interests	In today's often over-hyped, high-speed digital communications arena, the company will have to play catch-up to its own critical issues and be on the back foot	A cross-functional team within your business (supported by one of the many commercially available IT systems) should develop and benchmark a system proportionate to the risks
Rising Having no system to understand how (and why) emerging issues are rising in their importance/impact	This will leave the business in a reactive mode, expending effort on defining position statements reacting to the audiences who are 'pushing' the issue. This premature definition may focus on the wrong business impact	Quick and fluid classification, keep the definition fluid by identifying the 'courtyard of rising influence' – business impact, key data sources, key opinion formers, etc.
Priority Having no coherent, data-driven and rational system for issues prioritisation is inexcusable for a modern corporation	The absence of a coherent system for prioritisation leads to a default e.g. democratic (often political) activities emphasising the organisation's existing hierarchy.	A systematic process which is rational and flattens the hierarchy, taking care to avoid one which only appears to, e.g. voting spreadsheets or sticky note exercises.

Three Mistakes Mapped to the Lifecycle Stages

To illustrate this last point it may be useful to explore a breakout of just three of the stages in our lifecycle as summarised in Table 15.2.

Where Does a Lifecycle Model Get You?

The use of a lifecycle model should not be viewed as over-complicating a simple business threat assessment. Whatever process is developed, above all else, it must be fit for purpose. A good 'controlling story' is a narrative technique that helps do this and should make one's process:

- More coherent and concise to communicate convincingly to senior management.
- Able to create role and task differentiation, so that it is simple to understand who does what, when and with what aim.

- Able to quantify the business values at stake (difficult and rare for preventative systems).
- Defensible from classic industrial 'Ludditism', i.e. accusation of being 'paralysis by analysis'.

Moving from Controlling Story to Embedded Process

Once the 'architecture' of the process for issues management activity has been defined, the hard part will be embedding this into the existing organisation. Organisational factors are possibly the single biggest source of failure in technology transfer and the adoption of new methods of working.

This next section discusses briefly examples of some organisational factors that could account for failures in the successful adoption of effective issues management systems. We will do this by giving just a single example from three broad classes of factors: (i) definition levels (ii) technology transfer (iii) people. There are a host of other factors that might be examined, given more time to discuss them. Nevertheless, the three factors selected here do go some way to illustrate the necessity to understand the organisational context for the issues management process.

Definition Level Trouble

Issues management, and issues prioritisation in particular, presents a recurring problem – how to equate the significance of different (incomparable) types of issues. For example, how does one judge the importance of accusations of the use of child labour compared with volatile organic compound (VOC) legislation? Clearly, the frame of reference for these is wildly different.

Example pitfall: Too high a level. Defining all strategic issues at too high or too broad a level is a good way to get them onto 'the same playing field'. Senior audiences may initially like this approach as it seems momentarily aligned with strategy. However, in reality this is just mimicking the rhetoric of strategy. Operationally more pragmatic players will not be able to 'use' issues which have not been adequately defined in terms of their operational impacts.

The partial answer to how one compares child labour and VOC legislation is in providing definitions of the issues that are *very rigorous*. That way any reasoning around them, comparative, content or personnel, will be grounded in a palpable narrative which comes to the forefront of any analysis or dispute. This is probably the best one can hope for.

Technology Transfer Trouble

The desire for technological support for issues management efforts can come about for a range of reasons, three of which stand out: the proliferation of issues to be managed can easily get out of hand, making it impossible to decide on priorities; the cross-cultural complexity of issues in today's globalised markets linked by globalised communications requires huge sensitivity to sustain a position; the advent of a crisis.

Example pitfall: Unsustainable system. The reaction to the challenges outlined above (issue numbers, cultural complexity, crises) is often to have detailed positions, questions and answers (Q&A) and key messages ready to go. Only a technological solution, such as a database or an issues tracking system makes this really feasible. However, providing and maintaining integrated, comprehensive and up-to-date content for such an issues management tool becomes extremely time-consuming. This is further complicated when the audiences who receive the benefits, for example senior leaders in a crisis, are not the people who have to do all the hard work in keeping it fit for that (rare) purpose.

The partial answer to this technology transfer problem might be a lesser tool, a simpler process, a less data-hungry and more easily maintained system. Alternatively, the full power tool could deliver different (agreed) benefits to different players.

People Trouble

Even when the issues management system has helped to embed a good definition and workable, usable tools, there is still a further hurdle to overcome – namely the status, position and authority of people involved. A key problem for the communications people (normally the designated issues managers) is whether they have the authority to command the roles of other organisational players convincingly.

Example people pitfall: Internal competitors. Groups from other functions or geographies may already provide an issues management service focused around their own senior 'champion'. These competitors may resist over-centralisation or over-engineering of the system – often this is simply an example of old-fashioned internal politics. This competition may be from audit and finance, investor relations, technical/regulatory and risk management, all of whom have a claim on the subject matter of issues.

The partial answer to these people troubles lies in the constant reinforcement of the strategic alignment of your issues management system to, and by, senior champions. It also lies in understanding how internal competitors can be allowed a stake in your approach.

Addressing Definition, Technology and People Challenges Overall

The above examples represent a very small subset of the many challenges of any serious industrial systems design. Issues management systems are not alone in operating in such a complex environment. It is the reality of that complexity that drives the need to reason about process, content, technology design and organisational factors before one can sensibly measure issues in a way that will support strategic decision making.

Much of the solution to these and other problems lies in how the role of the *designer* of the strategic issues management system is defined. The person in that role has to actively define the issues management process, actively design the tools and have a marked ability as a communications manager in his/her own right. Here the way the *communication strategy* is defined – in terms of its relationship to corporate and business strategy – is crucial to launching a modern strategic decision support system.

Having explored the underpinning theoretical background to the development of issue management, and some of the problems with the common approaches/models of issues management, the next section goes on to examine an alternative. This is a working issues management system that addresses many of the weaknesses identified in traditional approaches. Here the chapter draws on the author's experience of designing an issues management system for one of the world's leading consumer goods companies.

HIGHLIGHTS OF A LIVE ISSUES MANAGEMENT SYSTEM

Just how do you prioritise issues meaningfully? That is a core question at the heart of an issues management process and the basis of our next discussion.

A Negative Example

Figure 15.5 is one example of one of the issues prioritisation approaches in Unilever eight years ago. This picture was generated as the output of a 'sticky note exercise'. A group of managers came to a consensus on the relative rank of key issues affecting a major business using two axes: likelihood and impact. The chart is presented here is actually the output of the process.

Here, a number of the key, but not uncommon drawbacks of this 'sticky note technique' can be identified. The main problems can be summarised as: the starting point; the approach; the legitimacy of scaling; the modelling method; and the coherence of output.

> **Starting point:** The starting point for the analysis output shown here was a desire to create this issues 'bubble diagram'. The quality director of the business, having seen this graphic in another context, was convinced it was the right vehicle to simplify his own problem – to describe relative importance of the issues in a portfolio approach on one page. This is obviously a communication starting point, not an analytical one.
>
> **Approach:** Leaving aside the weaknesses of brainstorming techniques (the technical complexities of which are beyond the scope of this text) it is useful to focus on the rationale for the choice of the measurement attributes. The two axes (likelihood and impact) are a clear graft from the (not unrelated but illegitimately deployed) area of risk assessment, but it is not clear why they are being used here. The fact that it is common for the same communities to be concerned with risks, quality, safety, etc., goes some way to explaining it. We are seeing them display a kind of reasonable synergy with the way these other concepts are measured. When directly questioned about prioritising issues (not risks) in this way, the creators of this diagram could

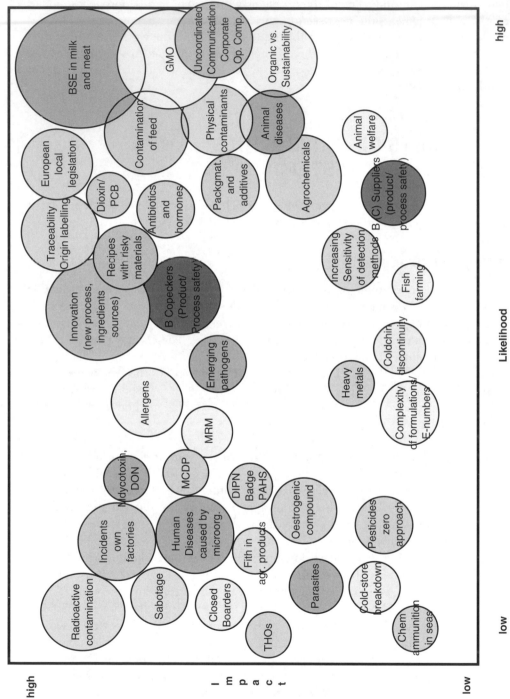

FIGURE 15.5 Unilever Historical Bubble Diagram

offer no clear rationale for why these two attributes (likelihood and impact) would be meaningful.

Legitimacy of scaling: The scales in our example will struggle to provide rationally informed reasoning, suffering as they do from four main failures:

1. The issues are not defined on a common template, they are merely named.
2. Generic 'likelihood' or 'impact' cannot carry a fixed (and therefore comparable) definition to cover the diversity of issue scale.
3. The participants have placed the issues into a range from 'high' to 'low' which is not quantified.
4. The results of the measurement are displayed (notwithstanding the labelling) in a continuous scale (illegitimately so).

Coherence of output: The measurement choices in the example above are, from a scientific perspective, all but incoherent. On the surface, at least, the approach taken appears to represent a mathematically calculated output. However, when examined more closely, the resulting plots of issues, where different sized plots are taken as indicators of relative significance of the issues, have no mathematical basis. They have in fact been generated almost entirely on the basis of collective, subjective judgement.

Indeed when the owners of the Unilever visualisation were asked to explain the meaning of size and colour in their plot they said: 'we can't remember, but they seemed like a good idea at the time'.

Managers are doing two things with a system like this. First, they are engaged in the issues assessment process itself. Second, they (sometimes another group entirely) are also relying on the outputs of the issues assessment processes to inform their decisions. While both activities depend, for the integrity of the strategic decision support they produce, on coherent reasoning, the approach fails to pass that test. It only gives the appearance of underlying coherence from the mathematical housing of the output. Of the flaws in this technique we can summarise three simple challenges for issues prioritisation tools:

1. Is it well understood upon which common scales the issues in question can, in fact, be best measured on?
2. Has the trade-off between facilitation of an easy measurement process and sufficient rigour to support strategic decisions been made explicit?
3. Is the execution of the measurement activity as (scientifically) robust as the end result makes it appear to be?

Of course, the Unilever (of old) was not, by any means, the only business relying on this type of largely subjective, judgemental approach to issues analysis and prioritisation. As Figure 15.6 illustrates, the World Economic Forum clearly used to have similar advisors.

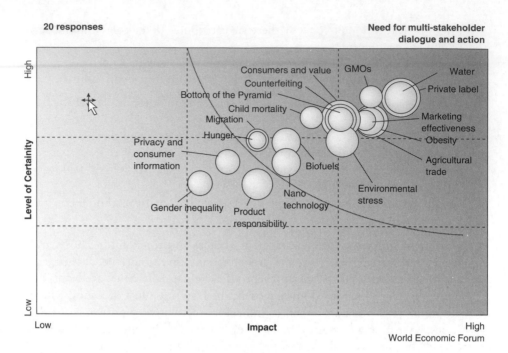

FIGURE 15.6   WEF Example of Issues Priority Output

Source: Internal Unilever communication (Pestana, M. V. (2007) FMCG Partners Issues Priorities Exercise Output).

A Positive Example: Introducing Descartes

Unilever's prioritisation tool, *Descartes,* was designed to improve upon the kind of (often flawed) reasoning described above. Importantly, as we have already alluded, the starting point in developing this new tool was the 'reference grammar' of the traditional reasoning technique – for example, the use of a Cartesian plot summary, the reduction of complexity to two scale scores, and the clustering of items into significance bands. Moreover, the end product of the process remained unchanged.

The real challenge was to make the approach, the measurement, the tool and the outcome *more rational*. Consequently *Descartes* is neither a scoring tool nor a decision-making tool, it is a *reasoning platform* to support strategic decision making (and communication) around issues.

Descartes has been developed iteratively over a number of years in a research-led process and has become a powerful system. A full description is beyond the scope of this text, but also is not necessary in order to explain its benefits. The system involves three key processes which are outlined in the opening screen shot shown in Figure 15.7.

1. **Scoring:** Purpose built score-cards (on an analysis by analysis basis) are 'sent out' (via an internet system) to experts throughout the business.
2. **Visualisation and analysis:** Leaders and managers bring together scores from experts to compare, combine and interpret (in a unique visualisation).

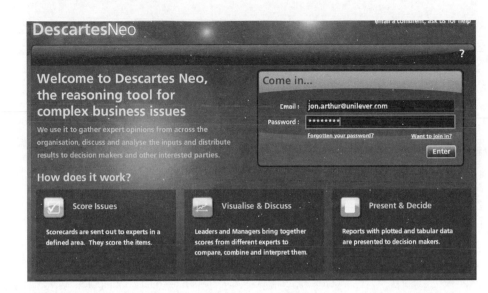

FIGURE 15.7 *DescartesNeo* Startup Screen

3. **Reporting and communication:** The finalised data is visualised in graphics supported by a structured commentary based around the core proposition of the analysis approach.

Space and commercial confidentiality do not permit a detailed treatment of *Descartes'* design and the process which houses it. What we can do is two things. First, we can exemplify the benefits of an approach like *Descartes* by summing up in a highly simplified manner (see Table 15.3) how it addresses (or does not address) the criticisms of other issues management approaches discussed in this chapter so far. Second, taking two items from that table, we can examine examples of *Descartes* being used in more detail.

A Best Practice? Worked Examples from Descartes

The basic critical premise of this chapter has turned on the problems of complexity reduction, explanatory (and predictive) power and scientific measurement in traditional issues management systems. Against these standards current issues management, it is arguable, is not rigorous enough to support strategic decision making.

Importantly, counter to these 'scientific' objections, we note that many extant systems have an enviable degree of popularity, perceived value and penetration in modern business. Thus we have dubbed these techniques (measurement in particular) the 'accepted reference grammar' for issues reasoning.

If *Descartes* is a reasoning platform for issues prioritisation therefore, we should be able to show that it is not just a more sophisticated system. Rather, it should be one that can bridge this gap between scientific rigour and acceptance into the existing reference

TABLE 15.3 Summary Criticisms of Traditional Issues Management Approaches and *Descartes'* Solutions

Problems/challenges	Solution in *Descartes*
Process rigour	
Not rigorous enough	The tool is in support of a comprehensive governance process linking cross-functional teams into a detailed and systematic scoring exercise
Not strategic	The tool has 'technical' (i.e., operationally focused) and 'strategic' (i.e., high-level, objective-focused) scoring systems which are linked
Should support the lifecycle	The issues management lifecycle described in this chapter is the formal annual planning round (globally and in business units)
Description not explanation	Due to detailed score-cards, multiple score and review rounds and a full analysis, explanation of the global and local status of issues is available in the data
Speed, acceptance, expedience, flexibility, transferability	The analysis is slower, acceptance is high (due to value and track record), expedience is lower (when used fully and rigorously), flexibility is significantly higher (it can assess any sensible prioritisation task), transferability is arguably far higher
Competitor systems or needs	Due to the above, competitor systems can be compared and even absorbed
Measurement rigour	
Too high-level definition of issues	The system is linked to a sister database which ensures a pre-existing, detailed definition of issues is used
Not strong enough, not scientific enough	The scoring is still heuristic but is based on formal, proven techniques from the social sciences (e.g., behaviourally anchored rating). Variables made up of multi-attribute scores (multiple questions) allowing for greater depth of meaning
The use of 'high' and 'low' not quantification	A 1000-point scale is used, all data is presented numerically in a coherent interval-level form
Not dealing with bias or conflict	A key analytical step is the interrogation of any data which contains high variance between scorers/groups
Uncritical acceptance of measurement variables	Is still possible, but each analysis begins with a core proposition and custom-defined attributes and score-cards
Strategic support utility	
Over-simplification from the start	Simplification is a result of a combination of complexity reduction and targeted communications
One size fits all, no tailored output	'Vertical audiences' (technical to strategic) and a 'horizontal audiences' (national to global) have dedicated analysis and results propositions
Linked to communication strategy	The prioritised portfolio serves as an input to the annual target and performance setting of communication
Benefits goes to a different audiences than those who work to input	Each participant (scorers) and recipient (leadership teams) gains significant planning and action advantages from their input

grammar. In the following section we will use just two examples, one from the measurement side and one from the reasoning side, to support the assertion that it does.

Improved Multi-attribute Scaling

A tendency common in consensus-based issues prioritisation techniques (e.g., group sticky note exercise) is to operate at too high a level. For example, can the notion of high or low 'business impact' really be worthwhile in the absence of any real data? Reasoning at this sort of level is restricted to categorising issues as more or less important.

Descartes uses a detailed scoring proposition made up of multiple questions coupled to a mathematical basis for priority. The score-cards are the result of a research process akin to questionnaire development. The resultant scale items are not single metaphors (like business impact) but multi-attribute scales (up to ten quantitative attributes per scale) of specific business constructs. Importantly these are still in the reference grammar, they are still reasonably high level. Table 15.4 shows examples of (single) items from two different score-cards.

Having business-relevant scale items like 'competitive advantages' or 'fit with strategy' broken down into differentiated criteria is a first step towards increased rigour. How these are then scored, however, is still the key variable for the quality of your assessment.

Descartes rejects the generic 'three-zone' approach (high–medium–low) in favour of a questionnaire design technique found in research psychology, the use of Behaviourally Anchored Rating Scales (BARS). Simply put, the rating scale points (high, mid and low) for every question are anchored to a different measurable/verifiable behaviour. Figure 15.8 illustrates this with an example of a question from a recent stakeholder prioritisation exercise.

How Does Multi-attribute Scaling Support Reasoning?

Three key improvements can be highlighted: captured reasoning; reduced bias; and standardised definition for priority.

> **Captured reasoning:** Multi-attribute score-cards support reasoning by capturing it. The priority of an issue is still being rolled up into two single variables to allow plotting (adopting the reference grammar). However, the reasoning for these values is not lost to memory, it is codified in data. The logic of priority can be revisited (or challenged) at any time and changes can be tracked over time. Figure 15.9 shows, in summary form, an example of how you can replay the story of why this issue is a priority.

TABLE 15.4 Example Items Tactical and Strategic Score-cards

Typical tactical question areas	Typical strategic question areas
Competitive Advantages	**Fit with Strategy**
– Level of control over key business impacts	– Impact on optimisation of supply chain
Reputational Advantages	**Unilever Influence**
– Internal Stakeholders Confidence	– Benefit from high visibility in the issue

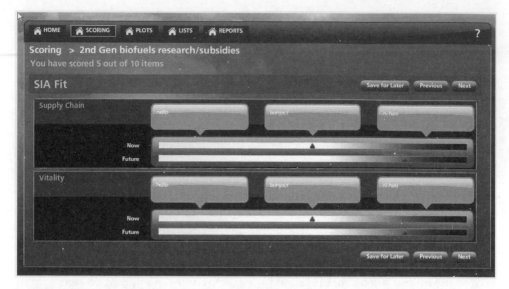

FIGURE 15.8 *DescartesNeo* Question Screenshot

Unilever Interest			External Pressure		
Licence to Operate	Now		Intensity of Law-making	Now	
	Future			Future	
Competitive Advantage	Now		Public Interest	Now	
	Future			Future	
Financial Impact	Now		Customer Pressure	Now	
	Future			Future	
Innovation Priority	Now		Failures and Challenges	Now	
	Future			Future	
Scale	Now		Trade	Now	
	Future			Future	
			Spill-over	Now	
				Future	

FIGURE 15.9 *DescartesNeo* Expanded Scoring

Reduced bias: This offline scoring approach greatly reduces bias associated with the social psychology of consensus formation processes. It also allows scorers to create a more sophisticated proposition for why they think something is a priority, rather than suggesting that priority is absolute. These nuances, we would argue, can serve to structure subsequent advocacy planning and strategy debates.

Standardised priority: In *Descartes* the definition of 'a priority' is standardised for every issue. This is because it is an agreed multi-attribute construct. In short, people trust that it is not a guess. This constrains the influence of politicised debates both in settling the individual issue priorities and discussing the map of all issues.

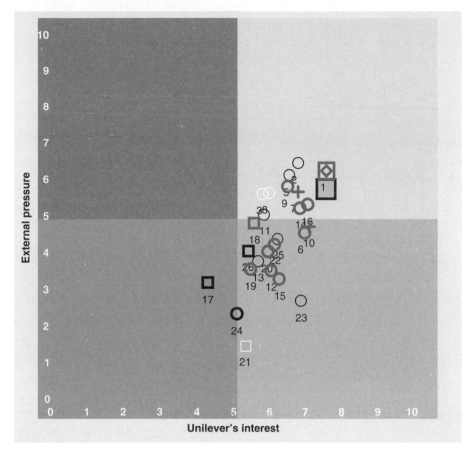

FIGURE 15.10 *DescartesNeo* Overall Plot

A common score-card, made up of multi-attribute scales, based on BARS does not just create 'a score' for priority. It makes the rationale for a priority transparent. This is achieved by rejecting high-level metaphor for fears, like 'impact', and using meaningful criteria, like 'supply chain costs', appropriate to the business audience in question. It is more effort to create and use, but the benefits to rationality are self-evident.

Dynamic Assessment Environment/Conflict Resolution Capability

A key benefit of the more traditional and more ubiquitous 'sticky note approach' is that, at the end of the exercise, the data is summarised as one overarching illustration/ diagram. This is enormously helpful. Such a visualisation is the key to the sorts of reasoning that these tools and approaches should be supporting and the sorts of communications platforms which are the reference grammar for strategic briefing.

Figure 15.10 shows a typical full overview from a live *Descartes* analysis (the variable key is not shown). The ability to see all of the organisation's issues in a

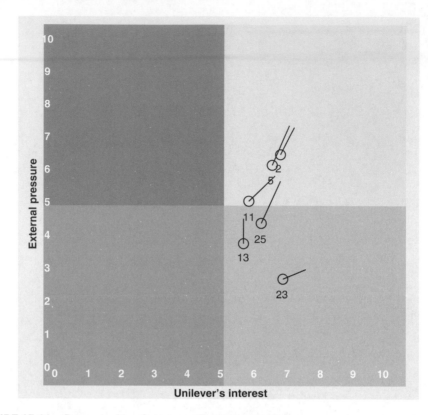

FIGURE 15.11   *DescartesNeo* Sub-group Plot Now and Future

single display is a great help to strategic advisors and thinkers, aiding overview and communication.

Where *Descartes* scores over its alternatives of course is that this is a big picture one can interrogate dynamically. Figure 15.11 shows another view of the same data, but now there are key differences. The first is that we can summon bespoke subgroups of data across qualitative and quantitative criteria set by the user. The second is that, due to a more coherent underlying questionnaire, we can plot a dynamic view covering scorer beliefs about priority now and in the future. A whole world of reasoning now opens up.

One final reasoning benefit to highlight is that we can use the visualisation to explore conflict. Figure 15.12 shows a group of scorers' ratings on the same issue (Figure 15.12b shows the rolled-up data). Two things are very clear. First, the rolled-up data is not meaningful enough, it is obscuring the conflicted state of affairs. Second, this round of issues scoring is not informative enough to enable conclusions to be drawn about on priorities. It requires further investigation about why scorers are taking opposed positions.

Reasoning using the codified score-card now comes to the fore. Scorers 1 and 3 are not diametrically opposed. In fact, they agree substantially on some attributes (ability to influence and level of risk). Where they disagree is also obvious. For example, look

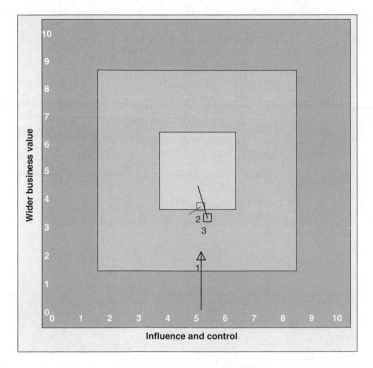

FIGURE 15.12a *DescartesNeo* Single Issue Multiple Scorers

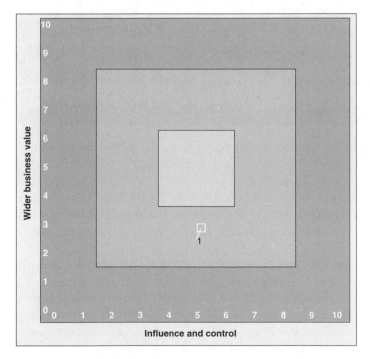

FIGURE 15.12b Rolled Up Single Score

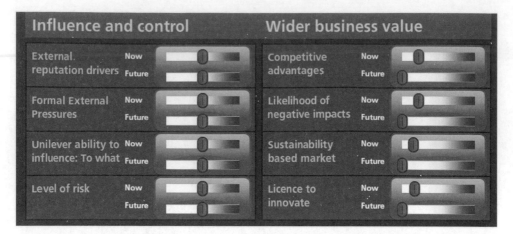

FIGURE 15.13a *DescartesNeo* Score-cards Comparison Between Two Disagreeing Scorers

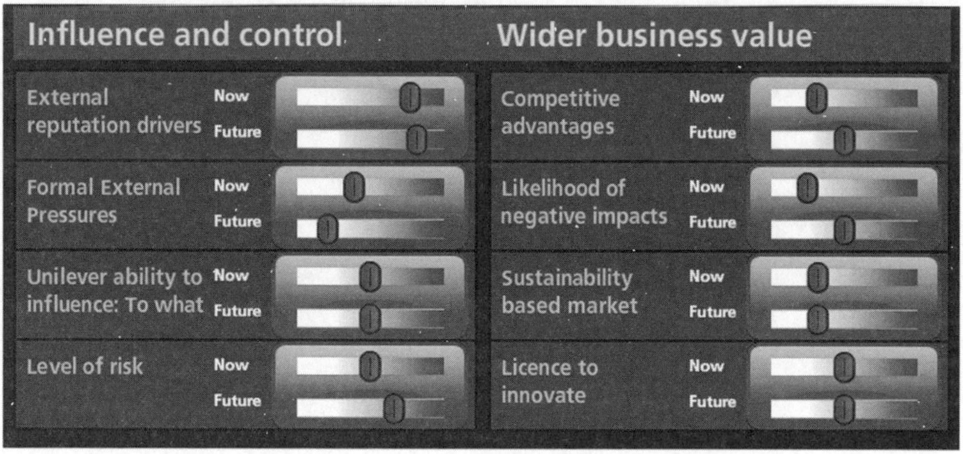

FIGURE 15.13b *DescartesNeo* Score-cards Comparison Between Two Disagreeing Scorers

at the differences in 'external reputation drivers' and 'formal external pressures'. One of the things we can deduce is that these two scorers have a reason to perceive the external environment differently. The reasons for this can be explored further.

How Does Dynamic Assessment Improve Reasoning?

Descartes is a flexible reasoning device. It can fully realise the same type of two-dimensional scale found in the 'Boston box' matrix (a key form of 'reference grammar' for this area). It can reason more deeply about why something is a priority and provide a data-driven and dynamic answer. If the reasoning task actually requires a very deep look at how people are scoring and thinking and how an issue appeals dynamically to different stakeholders, this too is fully supported. This enhanced reasoning power comes about by a rejection of three common attributes of lesser systems:

- consensus-based approach;
- over-simplified scoring/measurement proposition;
- quick and easy (but extremely limited) analysis capability.

One obvious criticism of the *Descartes* approach will be the cost (mainly in time) of setting up unique scales, attributes anchors and scoring propositions. We would argue that this cost is experienced as a start-up cost. This cost is massively offset not just by the overarching advantages exemplified above, but also by the fact that any further rounds of issues prioritisation will be highly informed by the previous data.

What we see in just these two examples of the power and flexibility of a tool like *Descartes* is that the complexity of prioritising issues has been embraced, not avoided.

Business Benefit Examples

At the end of this technology transfer argument for *Descartes* over simpler alternatives it is plain that the resultant technology is formidable. For tools to support strategic decision making (issues prioritisation in particular) we feel they should be based around the highest *feasible* quality of reasoning. Accepting this is fine but there has to be evidence of business benefit. Here we give two real examples of communication about *Descartes*. The first is from Unilever's global issue leader

Through the first issue prioritisation process in 2006, which was initially designed as a pilot, Unilever narrowed an initial portfolio of over 70 issues down to around 25 high priority issues by incorporating the input of 111 issue leaders and team members using *Descartes*. This was then narrowed through discussion to 11 specific key issues and presented the results to the Unilever Executive and Board. They endorsed the results in their entirety and since that time, the model has been used to support decision-making and resource-setting at European and Americas regional level, and in many countries, including the UK – where the Public Affairs plans (2008–2010) have subsequently been based on *Descartes* analysis.

The second is from the strategic regulatory affairs director. He refers to 'associations' and not issues – issues are not the only thing a modern business has to prioritise.

Over a period of 3 months we evaluated over 854 industry associations in more than 80 countries based on 1,124 individual contributions. We did all this without a single face-to-face meeting using *Descartes* and supporting teams only by telephone and web-conferencing. With *Descartes* the actual time spent amounts to 281 hours of work – about 0.15 FTE plus a coordination 'overhead' of 0.5 FTE, a total of 0.65 FTE.

Had we used conventional face-to-face discussion we estimate this exercise would have taken a total of 4.2 FTE, some 550% more expensive, excluding travel and other costs. In addition to these huge resource efficiencies, *Descartes* ensured, through the use of a single global score-card, that all data is comparable irrespective of origin.

As is obvious from these statements, the returns for Unilever from adopting a complexity reduction approach which first embraces complexity are considerable.

C-MACIE AND MODERN ISSUES MANAGEMENT

The C-MACIE framework, discussed at the beginning of this book, asks communication professionals to discharge four key strategic roles seen through the lens of the unique contribution of communications:

1. Analysis of the forces shaping the licence to operate.
2. Choices in relation to strategy alternatives selection.
3. Implementation of policy, strategy and programmes through people and processes management.
4. Evaluation of the business impact of communications effort.

Using issues management as our core example, the following discussion examines some of the strengths and limitations of this management model. The chief strength, in our estimation, is the effect that communication can have on the quality of the reasoning – and complexity reduction in particular – which underpins the strategic choices of others. The chief limitation, one which has been highlighted elsewhere in this book, concerns the real sphere of influence and locus of control of communication professionals. Are they 'interventionist agents' in the execution of company strategy or are they knowledge brokers in support of it? Key points in our argument here are as follows:

- On the need for communication analysis: this as a key role, but a deeper and more incisive definition of 'strategic' is needed.
- On implementation and evaluation: the modern environment suffers from a need for greater subtlety and greater interest, respectively.
- On communications choices: communication strategy and operational strategy seem insufficiently differentiated.
- On understanding forces shaping business: we would broaden the definition of forces, the strategy should shape the outside world rather than just react to/defend against it.
- On operational stakeholders support: this fails to address cases where operations are in a more complex relationship with corporate strategy.
- On the helicopter view: we find this metaphor insufficiently intervention-focused to support C-MACIE's other claims.

On Greater Clarity

While we would broadly agree that in advocating the C-MACIE approach it is right to pursue 'greater clarity in communication management', when it comes to the case of issues management we would strengthen that idea. Greater clarity should not just be in the communicator's comfort zone of 'better communication' (although it is clearly not impeded by it) but should broaden in scope to include the greater challenge of better reasoning.

For issues management this reasoning has to be about integration (context, process, people, technology) of a system into the organisation. This reasoning also has to be about implementation (legitimate measurement, coherent reasoning, dynamic approach), that is, demonstrating how this system delivers 'added value' in a common currency with other strategic limbs of the business. This value proposition has to be justified over and against the effort needed to deliver better reasoning.

Greater clarity can be found if the complexity reduction tasks (definition, measurement, analysis, conflict resolution) in this sphere are a separate reasoning activity from communication about their results. In this way the common desire to communicate simplified propositions will not be allowed to drive and weaken the reasoning approach. Likewise the desire to have powerful and coherent reasoning system will not dictate complex (read 'audience-independent') communication.

As the usual owners of issues management systems, communication managers have to proactively address these problems, not just communicate with clarity within or about them. If there is a skills gap in this area, care should be taken, e.g. in the choice of consultants, to ensure that the right professional expertise in the right field (the human factors of reasoning) supports business strategy.

Communication Implementation and Evaluation

Coupled to greater clarity of reasoning, we would argue that implementation and evaluation ought to be two primary concerns of any issues management model before it is built. Implementation – how an issues management system will affect strategic choices – ought to be a design aim for a system, not an interesting observation. Likewise, evaluation is always left to the end of models like C-MACIE. While this recognises timing – you cannot evaluate what you have not done – it fails to recognise good design. If you do not have evaluation criteria you cannot steer the success of the design.

In terms of being able to implement, we would argue that the position of the communications function is more subtle than that afforded by C-MACIE. Thus, this role for communication managers – people management, in pursuit of operational objectives – is rarely what the communications function does. Communicators are more likely to implement through influencing their knowledge brokering networks.

Likewise, communication evaluation is not the strong suit of many applied communicators who tend to live in a more immediate universe, nor is it often the strong suit of many of the consultants they charge with the responsibility. The day-to-day pressures and the ever changing game of the modern industrial strategy mitigate against any longitudinal view.

Fixed objectives are a necessary corollary of effective performance measurement. These are rare beyond the extremely general case. That is why communication functions often struggle with the twin challenges of having a coherent strategy and demonstrating the value added to the business from their 'intangible ridden' remit.

The solution to this problem is better knowledge capture and a business impact assessment far in excess of the simple guessing behaviour of the probability impact plot or even a modelling environment like Descartes. This remains such a complex challenge that it is perpetually on the long-term 'to do' list of communication. This is something that C-MACIE merely confirms.

Communications Choices

We agree that a chief driver for communications managers should be to advise the dominant coalition on the right communication choices. However, we disagree that the authority of such a role extends, as C-MACIE suggests, to making communication managers responsible for resource allocation at the strategic execution. This places communication managers' choices at the hub of the business. This clashes with the very clear knowledge broker role elsewhere in the C-MACIE model and, we would argue, the reality of the strategic positioning of many communication managers.

The C-MACIE model arguably would benefit from differentiating between choices to do with communications (i.e., ones under the purview of a communication function role), and those to do with directly delivering the strategy of the company.

On Communication Analysis

C-MACIE calls for communication managers to be able to: analyse what is facing the organisation; interpret challenges and opportunities internally and externally to anticipate forces shaping the operating environment, etc. A source of bias here, however, has to be a weak/absent definition of 'communication strategy' itself. A communication strategy to manage the live issues, however coherent, makes no sense if it is divorced from the long-term 'strategic' communication needs of the business:

Example: Unilever, as the owner of the Birds Eye brand, established the Marine Stewardship Council, working for many years with cross-sector private and public organisations to understand the challenges of sustainable fisheries. This very complex arena called for considerable issue-led communications effort. However, the communication strategy for this issue would have been all but wasted had the strategic intent of the company – to sell Birds Eye to a buyer who would maintain the effort to fish sustainably – not been included.

It is insufficient to 'interpret challenges' and take an 'all-stakeholder perspective' from a mandate to manage live issues for a business. Care must be taken to explicitly marry this to business intent. That can only be achieved if the mandate is expanded for communications managers to be included in the long-term strategic reasoning of the business. As C-MACIE points out, this remains rare.

On Communication Analysis and 'Forces'

C-MACIE considers it a desirable role for communication 'to understand the forces shaping an organisation'. This is the classical 'bringing the outside in'. For today's issues management this discourse is too unilateral and limits the communication managers to helping the company to react to the outside world. Shaping the outside world via strategy and interpreting the interaction of outside and inside to change operating assumptions are also necessary for a truly strategic role.

In effective modern issues management the forces shaping the business are dialogical in nature. The notion of effectiveness has to include the degree to which the strategy of the company can be served by actively shaping the definition of the issues in the outside world. This is referred to as 'taking the inside out'.

Example: Unilever has a long and impressive history in tea production and remains one of the world's largest tea producers. It is, and has been, one of the world's most ethical tea producers also. With the advent of greater public interest in fair trade there was perhaps a natural assumption that an Anglo-Dutch multinational would, almost by definition, be ripe for criticism.

Anticipating this trend, Unilever was able to create a reversal of this issue by re-emphasising its exceptional pre-existing credentials in the area through forging a certification partnership with a third party. Importantly, the mission of this third party and the objective of the partnership covered not only the key topic of fair labour but also the wider social and environmental aspects of the whole product lifecycle. These issues were of great interest to Unilever's global strategic position, and through this strategy Unilever significantly refocused the external debate in its favour.

Bringing the outside in and taking the inside out, however, are still not enough. A third set of 'forces' should be of interest to the C-MACIE driven communication manager: changes to the operating environment itself to keep it in step with strategy and the wider world. This operational influence is where the sphere of influence and locus of control of communication come up for question.

Example: Unilever's code of business principles ensures that its suppliers understand and respond to international pressure on pre-defined social and environmental criteria – for example, the international prohibition of unfair (but nationally legal) labour practices. As everyone knows, going ethical is often a more costly alternative. Unilever's supply chain is, of course, fixated with optimisation in order to deliver the business results that maintain shareholder confidence. It does not take a PhD in business science to see a complex conflict of interests when the markets are tighter.

To lay claim to an effective input for communication managers in this arena, C-MACIE would have to enlarge on how communication managers can gain an influential operational connection. This is a stronger definition of communication management and expertise allocation than we see in C-MACIE at present.

On Operational Stakeholders

C-MACIE suggests that creating the day-to-day interpretation of the outside world for operational stakeholders is a key activity for communication managers. This presumes that communicators are more connected to the operations than may be the case. Often the 'strategic communicators' in a large business tend to be focused not on operations but on public affairs and corporate reputation spaces (e.g., policy lobbying, NGO and stakeholder partnerships). Issues management itself can be skewed in this direction.

Where issues management meets operations there can be, particularly for large multinational companies, a clash with the diversification of operational intent, i.e. what is good for the company might be bad for the business or vice versa.

Example: The Ben and Jerry's ice cream company built its reputation on hardheaded ethical stances on key issues. Defining supportive day-to-day interpretation from an operational stakeholder perspective becomes a complex trade-off depending on where the communications manager actually works.

Put rather simply, imagine a case where Ben and Jerry's adopt a free-range sourcing policy. Strategic communications managers (wider Unilever) might be lobbying for Ben and Jerry's to understand the operational impact of that policy on a number of other brands also owned by Unilever. Communication managers in Ben and Jerry's, however, could potentially be providing very different input on the 'corporate reputation capital' of the brand's stance.

As both sets of communication professionals are working for the same company there has to be an active definition of the 'day to day' as part of some 'total communication strategy' before managers using C-MACIE can claim to deliver 'strategic effectiveness'.

Communications Analysis and 'the Helicopter'

C-MACIE is a proponent of 'the helicopter view' as a key strategic delivery of communications. This is a serene state where a detached communication professional is able to survey a whole business scene, inform key opinion and influence decision makers. C-MACIE seems to be recognising that communication managers are not in the dominant coalition – placing them outside of this strategic role – but suggesting that they need to be effective within it. The helicopter approach is insufficient to achieve this.

If anyone is going to be in a helicopter it really ought to be the authors of the strategy, not the communicators who support the strategy. The helicopter view, in issues management terms, would allow you to get away with simply specifying what the issue was and leaving it there. Good strategic issues management therefore places communicators as tank commanders – a direct and interventionist approach.

Example: When Unilever, along with the whole industry, discovered some years ago that its raw material supply chain for sunflower oil had been illegally contaminated by lower-grade oil, a serious incident team swung into action. The authorities, lacking an adequate scientific model for consumer safety under these conditions, had no option but to ban on all products as a precautionary measure. The business impact of such a ban would have been enormous, running to literally hundreds of millions of euros across the whole industry.

Unilever communication managers in this case were not intent on getting into a helicopter and providing a view of how all the stakeholders interrelated and creating communications around that. Using a firmly established live network of contacts with the authorities, Unilever was in a position to provide the missing scientific model, courtesy of its own independent Safety and Environmental Assurance Centre. Not only was this model accepted but it became an industry standard for all such cases. A ban on products, this time using a consumer safety threshold, was introduced and the potentially massive impacts were greatly reduced.

What a case like this demonstrates is that adequately placed and connected communication managers, who have an interventionist perspective, often hold the key to the strategic solution, not just the keys to the helicopter.

SUMMARY AND RECOMMENDATIONS

There is little doubt that modern issues management now has to deal with globally relevant strategic decision making. Whether issues management – as a discipline – is developing adequate models, processes and tools to do so is a key question. Weaknesses of some approaches include: an inappropriate use of summary mathematical housing for modelling and 'measurement'; a failure to reduce the complexity of the challenges in the definition, technology and people spaces; and poor quality reasoning about process, technological and organisational factors. The answer to these challenges, however, is not simply more sophisticated systems but systems which bridge the gap between the need for scientific rigour and acceptance into the existing reference grammar for reasoning.

The subtitle of this chapter is 'the importance of reasoning'. This is simply because when one looks at what is on offer in the marketplace of ideas, when one reviews some of the mainstream management science, when one really stops and thinks 'what are we actually doing?' when it comes to issues management, we are confronted with a question about the quality of our reasoning.

For too long now, it seems we have avoided that question in industry. Too high a premium has been placed on simplification. The arguments for this are straightforward – people are too busy to commit to a detailed analysis, too inexpert with complex concepts, too senior to afford the time, too used to cutting to the one-slide summary, and too compliant to a mainstream complicit with a lingua franca of the Cartesian plot split neatly, but arbitrarily, into four and 'measuring' unsubstantiated concepts.

In the modern world globalised corporate reputation clashes with globalised consciousness raising. The globally aware village is characterised by the dual forces of inequity and discontinuity of culture and psychology. In a pan-global governmental arena there are plural conceptions of 'rights' to resources, to work, to markets, to the licence to operate a business. These and other forces call for increasingly complex and interconnected strategic decisions to be made by managers. All this is under the gaze of expert regulators and commentators and critiqued by powerful detractors.

The fact that the really effective decision support processes, the really valid issues management reasoning systems, the legitimate coherent and verifiable measurement

(Continued)

(Continued)

types, and the clever communication strategies that support strategic decisions are all propositions of complexity should not cause us undue anxiety. With the right infrastructure and the proper application of science this complexity can be reduced. This is not through simplification but through complex reasoning followed by elegant communication. This is the real challenge facing modern communication managers working with today's issues.

That 'complex reasoning–elegant communications' challenge has a dual focus. First, it must be coherent and valid so that it can be commensurate with the importance (financial, social, ethical and environmental) of the decisions it purports to support. Second, it must be acceptable to the decision makers in question, to the managers who have to wield it, to the scientific community that has to refine it.

As you reflect on this chapter, one of the key lessons we hope to instil is the need to think about the substance of the analysis and advice you offer to the management team. Will you offer the accepted brain candy of the day wrapped in graph paper, or will you confront management with the importance of reasoning? The following recommendations are intended as a guide to developing coherent and more potentially relevant and powerful issues management reports for senior management:

1. Embrace complexity. The starting point for meaningful issues prioritisation has to be to understand their complexity, not a desire to simplify them. Have processes and tools which do embrace complexity reduction but do not confuse it with an intolerance of complexity itself. Use metaphor as a narrative tool to understand the governing concepts.
2. Communication. How the output will look is not the right starting point to define an issues prioritisation tool, but it is not an illegitimate question at a later time. Judiciously judge the appetite for complexity in different bits of your business and build your story (but not your tools) around it. Aim to produce multiple, tailored outputs which meet the reasoning support needs of a range of audiences.
3. Make it work. Expect issues management to have to lobby for its importance, have an advocacy plan to maximise penetration and acceptance, emphasise evidence for a fit with strategy rather than just using the same language. Understand your organisation's and your senior stakeholders' pre-existing 'reference grammar' for strategic decision support and deliver a system which involves and improves it. Work with a cross-functional team and make them designers and ambassadors for your whole approach.
4. Reasoning is key. Remember how to use narrative techniques to creatively reason about your process and to define your issues meaningfully. Strategic issues management should be based upon high-quality, transparent data where participants are defending their reasoning not their scores. The 'reasoning platform' approach is therefore the most strategically effective and worthwhile one for modern strategic issues management.

📖 REFERENCES

Bronn, P.S., & Bronn, S. (2002) Issues management as a basis for strategic orientation. *Journal of Public Affairs, 2*(4), 247–58.

Chase, I I.W (1904) *Issues Management: Origins of the Future*. Stamford, CT: Issue Action Publications.

Coombs. W.T. (2002) Assessing on-line issue threats: Issue contagions and their effect on issue prioritisation. *Journal of Public Affairs*, *2*(4), 215–29.

Ehling, W.P., & Hesse, M.B. (1983) Use of issue management in public relations. *Public Relations Review, 9*, 18–35.

Grunig, J.E., & Hunt, T (1984) *Managing Public Relations*. New York: Harcourt Brace Jovanovich.

Hainsworth, B.E. (1990a) Issues management, An overview. *Public Relations Review, 16*(1).

Hainsworth, B.E. (1990b) The distribution of advantages and disadvantages. *Public Relations Review, Spring*. Cited in Regester, M., & Larkin, J. (1997) *Risk Issues and Crisis Management*. London: Kogan Page.

Hainsworth, B., & Meng, M. (1988) How corporations define issue management. *Public Relations Review, 14*(4), 18–30.

Heath, R.L. (ed.) (2001) *Handbook of Public Relations*. Thousand Oaks, CA: Sage

Jones, B.L., & Chase, H.W. (1979) Managing public policy issues. *Public Relations Review, 5*(2), 2–23.

Mahon, J., & Waddock, S. (1992) Strategic issues management: An integration of issue life. *Business & Society, 31*(1), 19–33.

Palese, M., & Crane, T.Y. (2002) Building an integrated issue management process as a source of sustainable competitive advantage. *Journal of Public Affairs*, *2*(4), 284–92.

Iombari, H.A. (1984) *Business and Society: Strategies for the Environment and Public Policy*. New York: Dryden.

Wartick, S.L., & Mahon, J.F. (1994) Toward a substantive definition of the corporate issue construct: A review and synthesis of the literature. *Business & Society, 33*(3), 293–311.

Public Relations and Specialist Contexts

3

This final part of the book comprises four chapters which explore further the specialised areas of public relations practice and some of the governing constraints under which practitioners work. The chapters deal with the ethical considerations and constraints on practitioners, the legal framework that determines what practitioners can and cannot do within the law, areas of corporate social responsibility, andthe considerations when operating on an international or global scale.

Ethics and the Public Relations Management Process

Mel Powell

16

Key Themes

- Ethics and the communication manager
- Why the ethics of communication are so complex
- Codes of practice and their limitations
- Brief introduction to utilitarianism and Kantian ethics
- Specific ethical issues affecting persuasive communication
- Proactive ethics management: ethics and the C-MACIE model
- Reactive ethics management: the management of decision-making about ethical problems

---

INTRODUCTION

This chapter examines the type of ethical considerations that face public relations practitioners in their everyday work settings and explores the ethical dilemmas that practitioners can sometimes face in their work. It looks at the type of theoretical debates that surround a consideration of the ethical context for public relations decision making and action and considers the relevance of professional codes of practice in this context. Finally, the chapter seeks to examine the way ethical considerations may manifest themselves in the context of the C-MACIE management framework that has been advanced as a basis for understanding contemporary management practice in the communication/public relations context.

THEORETICAL OVERVIEW: ETHICS AND THE PUBLIC RELATIONS MANAGER

Ethics are the moral systems we hold as individuals. They are important because they guide our actions, not just as individual people, but in our role in organisations and society. Ethics have to be a part of the management process for *all* managers, but for communication managers, this area is particularly important.

Because of the importance of this impact, most organisations and professions arrive at a set of agreed ethical principles in the form of codes of practice, spelling out what they consider to be the main ethical considerations for their own area of work and, in some cases, *how* they should be addressed. Many people think of these sets of guidelines as 'business ethics' and think that following their recommendations will in itself ensure ethical behaviour. But codes simply set out a *current consensus* on what is best practice or simply acceptable; *only individual people have ethics,* and the wider the impact of their choices and actions is, the more important their personal ethics are.

This idea that one person's actions have a wider impact on others and society as a whole is why ethics are such an important area of knowledge for all managers, and why having a code of ethics is widely accepted as an important requirement for professional status in any area of work (Grunig & Hunt, 1984; Cutlip, Center and Broom, 2005; Elton, 1993).

For communication managers, though, ethics are increasingly seen as even more important and certainly more problematic. To understand why this is, and to make ethical decisions in a reasoned and professional way, every communication manager needs some understanding of ethics and how they apply to communication and public relations. The first part of this chapter aims to supply this, before the following sections examine how this knowledge can be applied both to proactive and reactive communication management.

Ethics are important for the communication manager for the same reason as for managers in other professions: *power*. French and Raven (1959) listed five key sources of power. Information, along with the skills and resources needed to communicate it effectively, is the sixth, added later. Just how important it can be is seldom fully realised by those who possess it. But information is a valuable commodity in itself, and all the more so because having or not having information affects the decisions people made about their lives. Hence simply *having information* and being able to decide whether to release or withhold it is in itself an enormous source of power. Having the skills to judge how and when best to communicate it, and the ability to choose whom to include and whom to exclude is a further source of *expert power*, included in French and Raven's original listing. In addition, there is the more widely recognised power which is associated with influence – in this case, to influence people's attitudes and change their behaviour through persuasive communication – undoubtedly the area of public relations which is the focus of most ethical issues and concern. And it is axiomatic that with power comes the responsibility to use that power wisely and well.

There are a number of reasons why ethics is a particularly problematic area in communication and public relations. Briefly, these are power, different views of public relations. and the conflicting duties of the practitioner.

Power

Why is power a problem? To see why, you might need to take a step back and ask some very fundamental questions about public relations: is it a good or a bad thing? What is its effect on society? And in particular, the 'grail question' – whom does it serve?

These are the questions about public relations asked by theorists who take a critical perspective based in Marxist theory and are concerned with questions of power and inequality in society. L'Etang (2006) points out that because communication expertise is a resource like any other, there is an inherent risk that it will be used by those who are already wealthy and powerful to manipulate audiences in order to maintain and strengthen the status quo. In addition, as we will see later, power imbalance between the parties in a communication carries ethical risks in itself because of some of the considerations which arise from ethics.

Different Views of Public Relations

The second complicating factor is that there is no universally agreed definition of what public relations or communication is, or is for. This means that it is much more difficult for public relations than for other professions to define what a practitioner's duties are, the ethical issues that arise from these, and the best way of addressing them.

Grunig and White (1992) points out that these different views of communication come from something as fundamental as the *worldview* of individuals or organisations. Drawing on both systems theory and communication, he characterised the ideal type of communication as two-way or dialogic, proceeding from an open systems worldview and aimed at ensuring the maximum information flow between the organisation and its stakeholders, in order to bring about mutual understanding. Accordingly, the 'four models' (Grunig & Hunt, 1984; Grunig and Grunig, 1992) view of types of communication evaluated communication approaches not only on how far they used dialogue, but also to what end, with genuine open-ended discussion and negotiation (two-way symmetric communication) being viewed as more advanced than persuasive or rhetorical approaches, in which the significance of feedback is only to ascertain whether the persuasion has been effective (one-way asymmetric).

There has been considerable debate about whether or not this approach is realistic or consonant with different worldviews, with critics such as Pieczka (2006) and L'Etang (2006) pointing out that its inherent weakness is that it assumes an essential benevolence in organisations and that issues in society are resolved through consensus rather than being contested. However, it appears relatively straightforward in ethical terms. Given both a benevolent, open systems organisational worldview and processes which will facilitate genuine dialogue, ethical outcomes will follow.

The questions it raises, though, for the communication manager are about the difference between personal and organisational ethics and whether a well-intentioned practitioner can genuinely shape or influence these. Curtin and Boynton (2001: 420) conclude: 'If management does not support proactive public relations ... then tension develops between the norms of ethical theory and what practitioners can achieve pragmatically, resulting in a lack of motivation for practitioners to advocate ethical stances.'

The second, opposing worldview assumption identified by Grunig and White (1992) is the *asymmetrical* view, in which the underlying supposition is consonant with the stance of a closed-systems organisation: that the purpose of communication is to shape the environment in a way which suits the organisation's interests. This gives rise to what Grunig describes as 'two-way asymmetric communication' or persuasion. Many of the ethical issues which affect public relations are linked with this view of communication as persuasion or rhetoric. This is where people's main fears of public relations come from – a view which sees it as a spectrum of persuasive communication ranging from 'spin' and manipulation to propaganda and even brainwashing. Because this is the form of communication in which the explicit aim is to influence people to change their attitudes and therefore their behaviour, it is here that the issue of power (which should alert us to the possibility of the abuse of that power) it at its highest. It is no coincidence that George Orwell, who arguably loved and respected the power of words more than any other twentieth-century author, feared the power of persuasive communication harnessed for the wrong ends so greatly.

Many practitioners and academics view persuasion or rhetoric as the better or the 'natural' way of conducting communication (Andersen, 1978; Miller, 1989; Jaksa and Pritchard, 1994; Moloney, 2000). This view sees persuasion as 'simply the way things are' in acknowledging that self-interest is usually a motive for communication. It also argues that persuasion fits well with a modern, diverse society because it accepts that there are different points of view, and allows for the testing and exploration of these ideas through debate. The idea is that poor ideas and arguments will be exposed through debate, and that eventually this process of informed debate will have a result which is much the same as that of symmetrical communication (Heath, 1992). In essence, this view reassures public relations practitioners: 'You represent your client to the best of your ability, I will represent mine, and the outcome will be ethical' (Gregory, 2002).

However, L'Etang (2006) makes similar ethical criticisms of the rhetorical school of public relations to those she advances against Grunig's dialogic model. While she acknowledges that rhetoric, because of its links with dialectic, is apparently a more morally sound and realistic model for a society in which rights and views are and must continue to be contested, she points out that the optimism of the rhetorical school about its powers for social good is subject to a fundamental flaw. Because in a capitalist society, public relations expertise is a commodity which is for sale like any other, it will necessarily be available to the highest bidder. Hence the poor and disfranchised will struggle to win a voice in public debate, whilst governments and multinational organisations will dominate it (L'Etang, 2006).

Arguments for and against the persuasion model are summarised by Curtin and Boynton (2001). They note that supporters of this model point out that in a democratic society, based on free expression, persuasion is acceptable and necessary for the emergence of truth. They also point out, however, that persuasion is considered unethical when the truth is compromised by deliberate lying or distortion in the interest of organisational profit rather than the public interest (2001: 414), and note also the more fundamental Marxist perspective of L'Etang (2006) mentioned already.

Debates over the ethical nature of rhetoric remain unresolved. Paradoxically, its key strength – its pragmatism about the operation of human self-interest within a pluralistic society – can also make it a threat in the hands of public relations practitioners who have little understanding of ethics. The risk is that a rhetoric view of public relations may lead practitioners to oversimplify or dismiss the ethical issues inherent in their profession – an approach which arguably puts both their personal reputation and that of the profession at stake.

Duties

The third complicating factor about ethics in the field of public relations is that of handling duties to a number of different stakeholders which may conflict with one another. These duties are summarised by Seib and Fitzpatrick (1995: 16) as duties to self, the client organisation, employer, profession and society.

Managers in all professions are expected to observe a duty to society as a whole and to reconcile this with duty to their client or employer. For public relations practitioners, though, the picture is more complex. As with any consultancy-based profession, there may be a conflict of duties to the employer and to the client. Arguably, though, it is because – in the persuasion model of communication at least – the whole *purpose* of communication is to influence or manipulate society in a way which suits the client, and because of the degree of power wielded by the communicator in doing this, that these issues are seen as being much more difficult for public relations professionals. In addition, there are arguably many duties not considered by these listings – for instance, to provide truthful information to news media and to safeguard the interests of vulnerable stakeholders – which may also conflict with the duty to put the interests of the client or employer first.

More recently, as public relations has developed as a profession, there has been a growing awareness that professional competence is also an ethical duty, which arguably impacts on all of the other duties (Parsons, 2004). In other words, keeping your skills and professional development up to date is more than a self-interested activity – it can also be seen as a necessary means to uphold your ethical duty to ensure that the advice that you give and actions you initiate are competent and soundly based.

It can be seen, then, that public relations managers have to handle more, and more complex, ethical issues than those in other professions – and often have to do so under public scrutiny. What is available to help them?

CODES OF PRACTICE

In recent years, the Chartered Institute for Public Relations has taken steps to emphasise the crucial nature of ethics to the public relations profession. Principles of good practice and ethical behaviour have been given increasing prominence in successive revisions of its Code of Conduct. These have also been moved to the forefront of other published material. This is arguably an important step: many industry associations have adopted a similar code in order to provide guidance for their members (Curtin & Boynton, 2001).

Ethical issues covered by the current code include the following:

- **Integrity**
  - Honest and responsible regard for the public interest.
  - Checking the reliability and accuracy of information before dissemination.

- **Confidentiality**
  - Safeguarding the confidences of present and former clients and employers.
  - Not disclosing confidential information unless specific permission has been granted or the public interest is at stake or if required by law.

But codes and rules do not make an ethical profession, for a number of reasons. These include the practical problem that compliance with rules or the law is not the same as being ethical; as well as the operational issues that rules apply only to those who have chosen to be members, and the difficulties of policing and enforcing sanctions on members who do break them. Then there are ethical considerations about the motives for adopting such codes: should public relations professionals agree to act ethically in order to advance the profession's status and therefore their own, rather than because it is the right thing to do?

The final and arguably the most important limitation is a logical one. No code can reflect all eventualities. In issues management, Regester and Larkin (1997) suggest that an issue that is allowed to escalate until it reaches the notice of powerful bodies will eventually reach a stage of *codification*, in which rules are put in place to deal with such a situation should it arise again.

In many individual sectors, codes of practice are examined and strengthened after a particular professional has faced a crisis and their judgement has been found wanting. There will always be a time when a public relations practitioner will be the first to face a particular ethical dilemma. In this eventuality, only a knowledge of the principles of ethical decision-making and the ability to apply them to a new problem will protect them. In the end, at the practical level, ethical decision-making in public relations relies on the personal judgement of the practitioner (Huang, 2001; Day, Dong, & Robins, 2001).

So what does the professional public relations manager need to know in order to take on this heavy responsibility? The short answer is that there are no easy answers and no shortcuts. Ethical judgement entails having enough knowledge about ethics to evaluate and if necessary supplement your own personal moral codes, and the ability to recognise, evaluate and decide how to act on ethical issues in much the same structured and logical way as you tackle other managerial problems. The next section gives a much condensed and simplified overview of the key ethical systems you need to do this.

A BASIC INTRODUCTION TO ETHICAL SYSTEMS

There are two main philosophical systems which are used to recognise and evaluate ethical dilemmas and decisions which have an ethical dimension. Neither is a stand-alone system: they are used together to sieve out and consider the ethical issues in a situation. Rather than introduce them as abstract philosophies, though, we will introduce them through the characters and concerns of their originators and the historical contexts that brought them about. Then we will move on to consider the implications when both systems of thought are applied to communication issues, and then finally to look at how these can be applied to the C-MACIE process.

Jeremy Bentham and Consequentialism – an Ethic of Welfare

Jeremy Bentham was an English philosopher whom most people remember best from history lessons as the founder of utilitarianism whose stated aim was 'the greatest happiness of the greatest number'. As a philosopher concerned with social justice at the time of the British Industrial Revolution, his concern was essentially with social welfare, and in particular how the increased wealth generated by rapid industrialisation could be made to benefit the many rather than the fortunate few. Therefore he tended to focus on material benefits, and in particular on the ideas of 'happiness' and of usefulness or 'utility'. (His concern with usefulness and wish to continue to be useful even after his death extended to providing in his will for his body to be stuffed by a taxidermist and left to University College, London, in whose foyer he can be seen sitting to this day.)

His philosophy of utilitarianism therefore was a consequentialist philosophy, whose emphasis was on the outcome of any action. The key question in considering whether an action was good or not was: had it been, or was it likely to be, of benefit or harm? If the outcome was beneficial, then the outcome was a good one, and the more widespread the benefits, the better the action.

There are obvious flaws in this approach. One of these is the question of motives. It sometimes happens in life that an action which was intended to be selfish or destructive accidentally results in good consequences. Does that therefore make it a good act? At its simplest, utilitarianism would tell us that it does: demonstrable material benefits, especially if they accrue to many people, are by definition good.

The consequences for the moral being of the individual responsible are less important in this way of thinking.

Another flaw is that in its simplest form, utilitarianism overlooks the rights of vulnerable or minority groups to 'happiness'. The easiest example of this is that of bullying at school. It may well make for the greatest happiness of 29 pupils in a class to bully the thirtieth – but what about the happiness of that particular pupil? Bentham himself came to address this in a later revision of utilitarianism, which took account of the problem of the suffering of minority groups or individuals through an injunction to take into account the level of distress of such groups when considering whether the 'greatest happiness' had been served.

A more obvious corrective to both of these flaws can be found in the other key ethical system: that of Immanuel Kant.

Immanuel Kant and Non-consequentialism: an Ethic of Duty

In contrast to Bentham, Immanuel Kant's ethical philosophy was derived from religious principles, and particularly from Christian ethics. Not surprisingly, then, his focus was less on the outcomes of actions, and more upon the moral and spiritual status of the individual responsible. Hence his ethical viewpoint is described as non-consequentialist – determining whether an action is a good one not from the outcomes, but from the motives which prompted it.

Kant's key principle was that an action is a good one only if it is performed for reasons of duty or principle – in other words, if it is done 'just because it is right'. In order to weigh up which duties were particularly important, he put forward the principle of universality. To test whether an action was a good one or not, he suggested asking the question: 'What if everyone behaved like that?' The answer, he suggested, would be found in picturing the kind of world which would result if the action were universally adopted.

One of the highest duties which Kant identified from this principle was that of telling the truth: an area which raises particularly difficult questions when applied to communication, as we will consider later. He argued that the universality of this principle could be tested by envisaging a world in which everyone routinely told lies all the time. Life in such a world, he argued, would be untenable because it would be impossible to be certain what the consequences of any action to be, and therefore to plan ahead or to act rightly.

The flaw in this principle is easily exposed by the question: what if telling the truth resulted in something evil? Or what about the 'necessary lie' needed to prevent evil from happening? The answer within Kantian ethics might be that in some circumstances, there are duties which are even greater than telling the truth, and it is up to the wisdom of the individual to judge when this might be.

Immanuel Kant is the source of another principle which forms an important balance and corrective to consequentialism and which has very important resonances for the ethics of communication: the idea of 'respect of persons'. Kant adopted from Christian thought the principle which arguably gave it the greatest distinction from the Roman worldview which it initially opposed and eventually superseded: that idea that every human being has an intrinsic value, simply because they *are* human.

On the surface of it, 'respect of persons' appears to be a very familiar principle to us in modern times, and some of its import is now enshrined in many national constitutions in the concept of 'human rights'. Kant's original idea went much further, however. For him, 'respect of persons' meant not only recognising the intrinsic value of every human being, but also that it was wrong to use other human beings instrumentally or as a means to an end, as we might use an object. 'Not using people' is clearly an important principle for humanity in general, but particularly when we consider the power of communicators. How can we be sure that, in persuading people to do something they might not originally have chosen to do, we are not simply using them as a means to an end?

As we have seen, neither ethical system on its own is without flaws, and neither has all the answers. Used together, though, they can be used to identify and analyse the morality of any course of action. At the individual level, they can be used through ethical decision-making models to guide your decision-making. At the organisational level, they can enable you as a communication manager to act as a well-informed ethical voice in advising policy. And at the campaign planning level, they can be used to help you to plan and evaluate an ethical campaign.

To help communication managers address this, Parsons (2004: 21) suggests five 'pillars' or principles, which draw on both Kantian and utilitarian principles:

- Veracity (tell the truth).
- Non-malfeasance (do no harm).
- Beneficence (do good).
- Confidentiality (respect privacy).
- Fairness (to be fair and socially responsible).

These can act as a useful checklist for communication managers, and in a later section we will consider Parsons's advice on how to use them in ethical decision-making in reactive situations.

Firstly, though, we need to consider the particular issues which arise when these ethical principles are applied to communication – and in particular, to persuasive communication.

ETHICS AND PERSUASION

Academics have made a wide range of different claims about the ethical status of persuasion. On one side, persuasion is characterised by Grunig and Hunt (1984) as 'asymmetric PR' and a less historically and morally advanced form of communication than the two-way symmetric ideal, whilst others argue that persuasion is both natural and potentially beneficial (Andersen, 1978; Miller, 1989; Jaksa and Pritchard, 1994; Moloney, 2000).

From its early origins, research into persuasion tended to focus only on determining its effectiveness. This scientific approach takes an objective stance on the concept of persuasion, arguing that it is a neutral skill which can be applied for both good and evil ends (L'Etang, 2006).

In recent years, however, there has been an increasing awareness of the ethical issues inherent in persuasion. Fawkes (2006) identifies four key concepts in evaluating whether persuasion is ethical: free will, truth, autonomy of audiences, and intent. The first three of these are rooted in Kantian or non-consequentialist ethics.

Free Will and Autonomy of Audiences

Many academic definitions of ethical persuasion refer to free will, which along with autonomy of audiences derives from Kant's idea of 'respect of persons'. In the context of communication, free will implies that the means of persuasion must allow the receiver the possibility of dissent, and by implication, rational rather than emotional means of persuasion are likely to be more ethical in nature. 'Autonomy of audiences' refers to two linked ideas: the communicator being respectful of the receiver and taking steps to redress any imbalance of power between them, and the motive for communication being benevolent rather than exploitative.

Truth

Truth also derives from deontological ethics, being identified as a categorical imperative by Kant. Many codes of practice for public relations practitioners emphasise the duty to tell the truth at all times. Truth and truth telling are, however, difficult and contested issues. In everyday life, truth-telling tends to be relative and seldom practised fully all the time. As Oscar Wilde said: 'The truth is rarely pure and never simple.'

A simple injunction to 'tell the truth' ignores the theoretical complexities of public relations. Seen as rhetoric, it must argue for a particular perspective or version of the truth. In such a relativist view, the client organisation's version of the truth may differ from that of others; indeed, there may be several different versions of the 'truth' within the same organisation, and the communication manager may have to judge which one is the most convincing before, in communicating it more widely, they make it 'the organisation's truth'.

There are further complications for public relations practitioners because of the nature of their work. From the point of view of duty ethics, they have a wide range of responsibilities which may be difficult to reconcile. These include duties to their employer, to their client (if in an agency setting), to their staff, to their profession, to their own principles and to the public. The duty to tell the truth may well conflict with all of these at times, and the other duty may sometimes be judged by practitioners to override it.

In addition, the power of public relations over the dissemination or withholding of information can also raise questions about telling the truth. One can decide not to tell the truth by simply withholding information, but what about 'being economical with the truth' or giving limited information which gives an impression which is more advantageous to the organisation? The power to decide the timing of information, in other words, to place it in the public domain at a time which maximises advantage or limits damage to the organisation, also has a bearing on this issue.

Intent

The final factor, intent, is raised by a number of academics, including Taylor (2001), who start from the scientific view that persuasion itself is neutral and that its moral status derives from the motives of the communicator (Fawkes, 2006), a view which would be endorsed by both main ethical systems – consequentialism because of its emphasis on the objectives, or potential for good, of actions as well as their actual outcomes, and Kantian ethics because of its concern with the moral status of the individual.

Baker and Martinson (2002) offer five principles for ethical persuasive public relations, which they call the TARES test:

1. Truthfulness – commitment to honesty.
2. Authenticity – personal/professional integrity.
3. Respect – for the rights of the audience.
4. Equity – persuasion by fair, not manipulative means.
5. Social responsibility – awareness of the effects on society as a whole.

Most of these factors derive from Kantian ethics, whilst the final one, in its reference to social good and the 'greatest happiness of the greatest number' principle, stems from utilitarian principles. It is also linked with the idea of duty to society which a number of authors have identified as one of the responsibilities defining public relations as a profession.

From this discussion, it can be seen that both the rhetorical model of public relations and its linked area of persuasion raise a number of complex ethical issues, whose existence and implications are acknowledged by the very academics who endorse this model as more realistic for a pluralistic society (Heath, 1992; L'Etang, 2006).

ETHICS AND DIFFERENT MODELS OF PUBLIC RELATIONS

The fact that there are different views and models of public relations complicates the task of defining public relations ethics for practitioners and academics alike for a number of reasons. How public relations is defined and understood by practitioners will affect how they define and recognise ethical dilemmas, as well as how they attempt to resolve them. For instance, a practitioner who endorses the persuasion model may not recognise that pressure from his client to publish misleading material, or to publish accurate material for ulterior reasons, poses an ethical dilemma (Bivins, 1987; Gregory, 2002a). Even if he does so, is he likely to possess the sophisticated level of ethical judgement to achieve in practice the 'checks and balances' identified by Heath (1992) as necessary to make the rhetorical model of public relations compatible with social good?

Seib and Fitzpatrick (1995) also highlight this latter issue which is common to concerns about the ethical status of both views of public relations: that of the degree of autonomy of the individual practitioner, implicit in the distinction between being an 'advocate' and a 'mouthpiece' for the organisation. This issue is also highlighted by Bivins (1987), and coincides with the view of Windahl, Signitzer and Olson (1992: 28) in their discussion of relationships in the communication process. They put forward the idea of the communicator's stance being equally balanced between the needs of the client organisation and the receiver, and not unduly influenced by either of them, identifying this impartial position with the idea of a 'professional orientation'.

Arguably this concept of personal autonomy is also crucial to the issue of ethical practice in both the dialogic and the rhetorical models of communication. Within the dialogic model, the public relations practitioner would need considerable judgement and strength of character to perform the boundary role, which necessarily means acting as the organisation's advocate in the external context, and voicing the needs of external and often opposing groups on the inside. Similarly, even those in favour of the rhetorical model of communication (such as Heath, 1992; L'Etang, 2006) acknowledge the complexity of the issues it raises, and therefore the heavy responsibility it places on both the profession and the individual practitioner.

So how, in practical terms, can a manager be sure of putting into practice this ethical responsibility?

The following section explains how this knowledge of ethical principles, in *proactive* communication, can inform each step of the C-MACIE planning process.

Equally, though, ethical issues arise in *reactive* communication contexts such as media relations or crisis communications. The final section of this chapter considers these and introduces some of the ethical decision-making models and processes put forward by Parsons and others as a useful guide in these situations.

PROACTIVE ETHICS MANAGEMENT: ETHICS AND THE C-MACIE PLANNING PROCESS

Communication Management Analysis

This first step in the process is concerned with analysing the situation facing the organisation and determining the issues and challenges to be addressed. It also involves boundary spanning in order to understand the forces which affect the organisation, particularly in terms of relationships with stakeholders.

Not all communication managers are aware that this stage of the planning process may involve an ethical as well as a strategic element. Traditionally, the emphasis at this stage has been upon identifying and prioritising those stakeholders who have the greatest potential impact upon the organisation and its ability to achieve its goals, in order that communication efforts and resources can be concentrated on those stakeholders. Such a view has informed models for stakeholder prioritisation such as those of Johnson and Scholes (1993) and Mitchell et al. (1997). Mitchell's widely used model does identify legitimacy and urgency as well as power as the variables which can be used to identify key stakeholders. Nevertheless, a group of stakeholder lacking in power is not going to be able to fulfil all three attributes and therefore be identified as the all-important definitive stakeholder which will automatically command the attention of the dominant coalition and have their claims attended to.

In contrast, if we look at this stage of the process from a Kantian point of view, we can see that the public relations manager is likely to have an ethical responsibility at this stage to give special consideration to powerless stakeholders purely *because* they are powerless, and there is otherwise a risk that the imbalance of power between them and the organisation may lead the organisation to fail in its duty of 'respect of persons' towards them. Minority and vulnerable stakeholder groups are also at risk of being either forgotten or excluded, or even used instrumentally in managed communication specifically because of their lack of power.

For some organisations, this step will be far more clear-cut than for others. Managers in public sector organisations are likely to be very clear that their remit is specifically to include, inform and empower vulnerable and minority groups, and are likely to be practised in ways of achieving this. However, organisations have a way of becoming inward-focused and complacent, and it can take bravery on the part of a public relations manager to speak up for unregarded stakeholders outside the organisation and their communication needs.

On the other hand, communication managers in the private and commercial sector may need to make an effort to look further than the major financial and commercial stakeholders suggested by their organisation's view and their own initial analysis. This is especially true when the organisation is sufficiently powerful that its actions and communications may have an impact on society as a whole or on sections of society.

This point is particularly important in ethics as regarded by the other key school of thought, that of utilitarianism. Its genesis as an ethic of social welfare and its emphasis on the good as 'the greatest happiness of the greatest number' point clearly to the importance of taking a broad rather than a narrow view in stakeholder analysis, and an awareness of the wider social impact of any campaign.

Here it becomes apparent that the broader, *all-stakeholder* perspective for environmental analysis recommended in Chapter 2 is important not only from a strategic, but also from an *ethical* point of view. Even when (or especially when) the organisation itself insists that a narrow perspective is the appropriate one, the communications practitioner who advises it has an important duty to take a 'helicopter view' of the situation and advise senior management accordingly. Significantly, *not* doing so means that a practitioner risks failing not only in their duty to serve society as a whole (as Bentham would have pointed out), but in their more obvious duties of professional competence and serving the best interests of their employer.

Communication Management Choice

This stage of the communication management process is perhaps the most crucial ethically as well as strategically. For the way in which we make an informed choice about what 'the nub of the problem' is, as well as the broad strategy for using communication to address it, has to be informed by our idea of what the organisation is about, what the world is like and what could and should be achievable by communicating with people – in other words, our *worldview*, as Grunig and White (1992) described it. And as Grunig has pointed out, our worldview, whether personal or organisational, has profound consequences for why we communicate, what we hope to achieve by doing so, and how we communicate.

The first two steps in the communication management choice stage of the C-MACIE model, both the *selection of key issues* finally resulting from a broad and far-sighted approach to environmental scanning, and a considerate and inclusive approach to the *selection of stakeholders*, take the same ethical issues considered at the analysis stage a step further. The implications here are those of 'firming up' and final choices.

Choice of Communication Strategy

In the next step, though, the *choice of communication strategies to be adopted*, different ethical issues and choices face the communications manager. From the initial overview of the ethics of communication at the beginning of this chapter, we can see that the choice of *how* communication will be used and *what it is to achieve* are freighted with ethical responsibility for the person in charge. It is perhaps at this moment in the planning process that the power of the communications manager, and the responsibility which goes with it, are at their highest.

The two different approaches to communication – persuasive and two-way – and the ethical arguments associated with them have been discussed briefly in the introduction. The big question for the communications manager at this stage, though, is how these two different approaches might be used as ways of tackling a problem or issue which faces both the organisation and its publics. Shall the organisation 'solve' the issue, and then attempt to inform its stakeholders of its actions and persuade them that these were right and the actions taken were effective? Or shall the organisation communicate with people in order to involve or empower them, and therefore make them partners in solving the issue together?

A recent example which might help in envisaging what these different approaches might look like in practical terms can be seen in how two different UK local authorities used communication to deal with the issue of elderly people being targeted by dishonest or 'cowboy' traders. A 'Beat the Cowboys' information campaign to make the elderly target audience aware of the problem, and of its own efforts to resolve it. Council B took a more dialogic approach. First, it carried out research with elderly people to find out what their main concerns were, and found that fear of being cheated meant that many left household repairs outstanding rather than try to find a reliable trader. It then worked with local traders to set up an 'accredited trader' scheme, and then ran an informative campaign explaining how to find and use a trustworthy trader. Both approaches were effective in terms of meeting their objectives, but it can be seen that Council B's dialogic approach took a different view of its stakeholders. Instead of seeing them purely as victims or villains, it gave them dignity by involving them as fellow problem-solvers. As Kant would say, it gave them 'respect of persons'.

Of course, the choices of communication managers in reality are often constrained by considerations such as time and money. Arguably it may take longer and cost more to organise and run a campaign which empowers people by involving them in dialogue, and it is notoriously the case that public relations is often called into the planning process too late to be able to influence overall strategy. But it is one thing to have to choose consciously an informative or persuasive strategy rather than a two-way one for good reasons and to be able to justify the choice, and another to be unaware of or unwilling to consider the option of using a dialogue-based strategy. There may be no difference in 'real' terms, but the difference in the ethical awareness of the practitioner and the effect their life and work will have is considerable.

Of course, in many cases, many of the choices are defined by the senior management of the organisation and by their view. This will be particularly true of corporate objectives, which may well be set before the communication manager is approached for help with communication. However, an area where the manager is likely to be called upon to exercise choice is that of setting communication objectives in support of a chosen strategy.

Once again, worldview is important here. Communication objectives, at their simplest, can be described as answering the question 'how is communication going to fix this?' for each of the key issues which have been identified. The answer will depend partly on the manager's view of what issues are capable of being fixed by communication, and what sort of communication will do the job best. Again, there is an ethical as well as a strategic dimension to these considerations.

Objective Setting

Setting the objectives for a campaign is a particularly crucial step in terms of ethics when viewed from a utilitarian point of view. Bentham, you will remember, was primarily interested in the *outcomes* of actions and took the view that if an outcome was good (by which he meant beneficial to the largest possible number of people), then the action itself was a good one. Acknowledging though that good intentions can go wrong in practice, he was also interested in analysing the goodness of people's *motives*. In other words, in judging whether an action was good or not, he wanted to look at not only whether its results were good, but also whether at the outset the planned action had the *potential* to do good.

We would suggest that there is a very clear parallel between Bentham's interest in motives and potential good and the aim and objective setting stage of the communications planning process. He would have asked at this planning stage whether the aims and objectives were being set with the intention of bringing about the greatest amount of social benefit, or whether the focus was too narrowly set on the increased happiness of a select few.

Bentham though, in his revision of utilitarianism to take account of levels of unhappiness or distress, would have raised another important question at this stage – that of the degree of potential benefit to the various stakeholders. In other words, even in an apparent 'everybody wins' scenario, his view as an ethicist of social welfare would also raise the question of who benefits the most and the amount of power the different stakeholders have. Kantian thought would add a further consideration – that of the risk that the less powerful might be used instrumentally, as a means to an end, by the more powerful – in this context, the instigator of the communication. This consideration means that some types of communication strategy which have been used so frequently that they are simply accepted as part of the communication landscape need to be given further consideration from an ethical point of view rather than simply being adopted without question. For example, cause-related marketing has long been accepted as a useful communications tool, frequently described as being a 'good' strategy in ethical as well as effectiveness terms, because 'everybody wins'. But when you view it in terms of ethics, the question is raised about who is the greatest winner – usually the instigator of the scheme – and whether the valid concerns of the less powerful are being exploited to drive increased consumer spending and customer loyalty which they can ill afford. Such a strategy might be successful in the organisation's eyes, but would leave them open to valid criticism from a wider social standpoint.

Immanuel Kant would have added to this the consideration of the motives for communicating the question of duty. If an action took place for reasons of duty or an over-riding moral imperative, he regarded it as a good one. Hence he would have viewed any form of communication which fulfils a duty as by definition a good one. Because of his view of telling the truth as a universal moral imperative, he would have regarded a campaign to make truthful information more widely available as an inherently good one: a principle which informs the objective setting of many public sector communications in particular, where there is often a duty to inform a very large number of stakeholders not because they are powerful in strategic terms, but because they are seen as having an entitlement to the information. Here it is important to consider that a one-way informative campaign, although regarded as less advanced than dialogic communication by Grunig and Hunt (1984) and Grunig and Grunig (1992) can, in some circumstances, be a very ethical way in which to communicate.

Given the clear and direct link between setting the objectives at the start of a campaign and evaluating the outcomes at the end, it is clear that having a clear focus at the outset on objectives which are ethically sound as well as strategically correct can have huge implications for the campaign's eventual effect. They are the structure on which the whole campaign will be built, and a weakness at this stage will run right through it like a crack in the fabric of a new building. Parsons's (2004) five pillars of public relations, as discussed earlier, combine both utilitarian and Kantian considerations, and we have suggested below how you could add to them in order to use them as an ethical check-list at this stage:

1. Veracity – tell the truth. Does the campaign set out to make truthful information more widely available?

2. Non-malfeasance – do no harm. Could the objectives you have set result in harm to any groups or individuals?

3. Beneficence – do good. Do the objectives you have set have the potential to bring about good results? Is there an opportunity to do good here that you might have missed?

4. Confidentiality – respect privacy. Will individuals' confidentiality or privacy be compromised in any way?

5. Fairness and social responsibility – are the objectives you have set likely to treat everyone involved fairly? Are they socially responsible, and are the results likely to benefit society as a whole?

Using these ethical principles as a checklist at the objective-setting stage will help to ensure that your campaign and your organisation are not open to criticism over the aims of the strategy.

Choice of Specific Tactics and Implementation

With the overall communication strategy and the objectives to support it in place, the focus moves on to the next stage – the selection of the specific tactics that will deliver the strategy through communication with the key target audiences. It has already been explained how both creativity and risk analysis have a role to play at this stage in a two-step process. Firstly, creative techniques such as brainstorming can be used to generate a wide range of possible communication techniques. This is essential to find ways in which the key ideas behind the campaign in a way which is new and unusual, and therefore memorable – a major factor in achieving the long-term awareness or persuasion which often form the objectives of a campaign, and therefore its overall effectiveness. It also forms the 'wow factor' which clients often see as the main added value which they achieve from using professional public relations, and provides the elements of fun and creativity which, for many public relations practitioners, make the job interesting and worthwhile.

However, the essential thing about successful communication management is that it combines creativity with analytical and managerial thinking, and that creative inspiration is used to help to achieve strategies which are carefully planned and carried out. Hence the creative step is followed by a further analytical stage, in which the exciting ideas generated are subjected to careful analysis against a number of criteria to determine their suitability for use. There are many different approaches to this. Some experts such as Green (2001) think of this as the second step in a two-step brainstorming process, and therefore part of the creative process itself, whilst others view it as a separate analytical stage. In summary, though, the criteria considered by these different routes usually include:

- compatibility with brand/corporate values;
- compatibility with objectives/strategy;

- legality;
- budget and timescale;
- assessment of the commitments and risks involved – to stakeholders as well as the communicator and the client organisation.

As mentioned in Chapter 2, consideration of the ethical status of the ideas generated may also form part of this stage. We will now look in more detail at what type of considerations may be needed, and suggest some ways of doing this.

Perhaps because it is the tactics used by public relations campaigns that are most visible to the public and familiar to practitioners at all levels, irrespective of their knowledge of the strategic thinking and management behind campaigns, discussion of the ethics of public relations has tended to focus on this particular step. Given that the key tenet of utilitarianism is that it is outcomes, and by extension motives, that really matter in ethical terms, it is not surprising that most of the ethical considerations associated with this stage, about *how* the communication is carried out, are derived from a Kantian viewpoint.

Looking at Kant's key principles of the importance of moral imperatives, especially the key ones of telling the truth and 'respect of persons', we can see a number of implications for ethical communication. The issue of truth raises a range of important questions, in particular where to draw the line between showing a favourable view of an organisation or product and blurring the truth. There are also important ethical considerations about the balance between truthfulness and creativity in campaign planning – for example, how far is it acceptable to use tactics such as 'sexing up' a story to fit in with the news values of particular media, images or statements which show a partial or distorted view of reality, or manipulating the availability or timing of information.

'Respect of persons' raises particular questions about the relationship between the communicator and the audience and the balance of power between them. Kant's emphasis on the wrongness of using people as a means to an end raises the question of whether the intended audience are being treated with respect or used instrumentally. 'Respect' encompasses a number of different areas, including the assumptions made about intelligence, attitudes, ability to think and arrive at a decision independently, and the right to privacy and lack of intrusion or distress through communication. 'Instrumentality' includes the duty not to coerce or exploit. Both of them involve the idea of the sacrosanct nature of free will – in the communication context, the freedom to choose whether to attend to, consider or be persuaded.

Fawkes (2006) summarises these principles in her analysis of key issues in ethical communication, as intent (which we have considered earlier at the choice of strategy stage), free will, truth and autonomy of audiences – all of which derive from a Kantian point of view.

We will now consider each of these areas, giving examples, and then suggest useful ways of checking for them at the Choice of Tactics stage.

- Free will

The issue of free will is usually considered in relation to persuasion, and at its simplest can be tested out by the question 'could the audience decide *not* to be persuaded?' If the answer is 'no', then the tactics are clearly edging into the area of propaganda or coercion.

A useful practical touchstone in relation to the issue of free will is the idea of 'self-persuasion' – that people decide to be persuaded by spending enough time thinking a communication message over and comparing it with and relating it to their existing beliefs (Petty & Cacioppo, 1983; Shimp, 2002). At the centre of this idea of voluntarily engaging with persuasion is the concept that people can choose to engage intellectually with information or an argument and can decide, rationally and of their own accord, if they find it convincing. On the other hand, when campaigns rely on appeals to the emotions alone, there is a risk that people may be 'steamrollered' into a response which they would not have arrived at if allowed to consider the facts dispassionately. Hence persuasive campaigns which set out to persuade through rational argument rather than emotional appeals are more likely to stand up in reasoned debate with those who have other views, as well as to ethical scrutiny. For this reason, communicators who have plenty of material capable of fuelling an emotional response may deliberately decide to eschew 'quick hit' emotional persuasion tactics in favour of reasoned factual argument. One example of this was the Body Shop's early communications explaining its policy on avoiding ingredients tested on animals. Many would have regarded it as a key example of a campaign in which cute or distressing pictures of animals might have been used to discredit competitors without similar policies. Instead, the Body Shop chose to use text-only leaflets highlighting and explaining the key points of their policy in a logical sequence, the implication being that the facts alone should be enough to persuade a reader of the merits of their argument.

In case clients or employers need further convincing of the merits of this approach, it is worth noting that persuasion that is ethical in observing free will can also be effective persuasion; in fact, there is evidence to show that in some circumstances, communications which consider both sides of an argument can be more convincing to their audiences, especially those who were initially undecided (Bettinghaus & Cody, 1994). In journalistic terms, treating your audience like 'broadsheet readers' supplying them with the facts and trusting in their ability to make up their own minds, rather than tabloid readers who need very clear guidance on what to think, may be the most effective way to persuade as well as the most ethical, both in terms of allowing for free will and of 'respect of persons'.

- Truthfulness

The issue of truthfulness in public relations is most often considered in relation to reactive media relations, but also raises important considerations in the proactive planning of a communications campaign. On the surface of it, the issue should be a simple one: most professional bodies' codes of practice include a statement similar to the wording in the Advertising Standards Authority's Code of Practice (2003) which states: 'All marketing communications should be legal, decent, honest and truthful.' But in practice, when

does 'talking up' your organisation or its products or services become blurring the truth? And since, as discussed earlier, truth is relative, whose version of the truth is to be considered the definitive one and communicated?

Because of the degree of power wielded by public relations practitioners in setting the media agenda, there are other related issues to do with 'telling the
truth', such as giving or withholding information and the timing of the
release of information.

One particular issue about truthfulness and telling the truth in tactics is that of
truthfulness *about the identity and motives of the communicator*. One
example of this is the idea of setting up 'arm's-length' groups to act as
apparently independent third-party endorsers. Recently, the increasingly
varied and complex communication landscape of on-line media has allowed
many more similar tactics, for example, attempting to influence the discussion on chat rooms without disclosing the real identity of the communicator; setting up bogus websites to publicise films, or to influence the volume
of 'e-traffic'; modifying Wikipedia entries to improve the exposure or reputation of clients; and setting up fake blogs which are not actually written by
the apparent communicator.

Another tactical issue involving truth is that of 'teaser' campaigns which do not
reveal the full information that is being communicated, or its purpose, until
the receiver's attention is already engaged. In operational terms, this is frequently accepted as a valid and effective tactic, but in ethical terms, how far
is it acceptable to mislead a target audience – even if this is for their own or
a wider social good?

We think the position is very clear: if your client wants to hold the moral high
ground, it is imperative that all communication is truthful as well as effective. If it is
not, then any advantage the client gains through an effective campaign may be eroded
by criticism of its behaviour in ethical terms. If you have a reputation to maintain, how
you communicate as well as what you achieve by communicating is vitally important.

Respect of Persons

We have already discussed the importance of taking a broad view of stakeholders
when planning a campaign, and of considering the needs of minority, low-power and
vulnerable groups of people at this early stage. It is the tactics you choose as a communication manager, though, that speak loudest about your real understanding and
opinion of your target audience. Will your communication methods show that you
and your client accord them consideration and respect? Or will it be obvious from
the content and tone of your communication that your interest in them is only as a
means to an end in achieving what the client wants?

One of the key questions here is that of the power balance between you as the
organisation's communicator and them as the receivers of communication. The
greater the imbalance between you, the more risk there is that they might be ignored
or exploited. In practical terms, the more you can to empower them by making them

partners in the process of communication rather than passive receivers of it, the more ethical the outcome is likely to be. Therefore as Grunig and Hunt (1984) and Grunig and Grunig (1992) originally suggested, two-way tactics which involve dialogue with the receiver are more likely to be ethical.

Even when your intentions towards a disadvantaged target audience are entirely benevolent, it is still important to take an involving and dialogue approach. Your perception of what their needs are may not be the reality, and the most straightforward way to address this is simply by asking them. Equally, even the most vulnerable groups are not happy to be characterised as victims who are in need of help and protection, but would rather be regarded as partners in problem solving whose contribution is sought and valued.

Another aspect of 'respect of persons' in the selection of tactics is that of respect for both their feelings and their privacy. There is a growing consensus that particular groups of people, such as elderly people, have a right to protection from unwanted, intrusive communication such as door-knocking or hard-sell direct mail. The question about whether communication should cause unwarranted distress or shock is a more complex one. In particular, the debate about whether and when it is justifiable to use shock tactics in communication, and particularly in persuasion, is continuing. The most convincing arguments are those which justify its use for particular moral purposes. For example, public information campaigns which set out to persuade people of something for their own or for the public good, such as those targeting smoking or drink–driving, rely on shock techniques to draw people's attention to a message which might otherwise become hackneyed, and to bring about emotional as well as rational persuasion. Campaigns by organisations such as Barnardo's and Save the Children also justify their use of shock tactics to galvanise the support of a public which might otherwise be too jaded or suffering 'compassion fatigue' to help some of the most vulnerable in society. It would be hard to justify the use of shock tactics for less important issues though, and particularly for campaigns for commercial gain or which benefit only the client organisation.

Communication Management Evaluation

Evaluation is important in ethical as well as managerial terms – not least because what is evaluated at the end of a campaign tells the story of what the campaign was *really* about. Evaluation measures which concentrate only on the experience of the client organisation and do not include the voices of other stakeholders are the clearest possible indication of the real motives for communicating.

Traditional evaluation approaches, especially for persuasive campaigns, have tended to use feedback from the recipients of communication only to establish whether the client's objectives have been met – at the most basic, whether target audiences have been persuaded to a particular point of view. A more ethically concerned approach would take into account their experience of the communication, their assessment of how fair or otherwise it had been, and their perception of how their relationship with the communicator had changed as a result.

Where communication objectives have been set in a way that is ethical and inclusive, obviously the evaluation measures set to assess the achievement of those objectives will reflect this. However, when making a final assessment of the success of a campaign, communication managers might wish to add to the consideration of whether and how far the objectives were achieved an assessment of how ethical the campaign was. Baker and Martinson (2002) provide a checklist of factors for evaluating how ethical a persuasive communication has been, which may be useful at this stage:

1. Truthfulness – was the commitment to honesty apparent?
2. Authenticity – was the campaign in line with your own personal and professional integrity?
3. Respect for the rights of the audience.
4. Equity – was the persuasion achieved by fair, not manipulative means?
5. Social responsibility – was there an awareness of the effect on society as a whole, and were the final outcomes socially beneficial?

The first four points here are derived from Kantian ethics, and we have already considered how they affect a number of stages of the campaign planning process. The final one, appropriately, comes from a utilitarian view of the final outcomes of a campaign, and asks what for Bentham was the key question in assessing whether any action was a good one – did it result in the greatest happiness of the greatest number? Did it benefit society as a whole? If the answer is 'no', it could not be considered a good campaign in ethical terms, however effective it was in achieving the intentions of the client.

This section has suggested how, from start to finish, the communications manager can take account of ethical considerations at each step of the C-MACIE planning process. Figure 16.1 attempts to summarise the guidance and to provide a quick ethical flow-diagram for C-MACIE planning using utilitarian and Kantian principles.

REACTIVE ETHICS MANAGEMENT: THE MANAGEMENT OF DECISION-MAKING ABOUT ETHICAL PROBLEMS

Many, if not most, of the ethical issues for public relations managers arise in a *reactive* context, in areas such as media relations and crisis communications, which often require a difficult decision to be made under time pressure. Many of the texts on ethics which are aimed at the public relations practitioner offer step-by-step ethical decision-making models to help with this: Seib and Fitzpatrick (1995), Gregory (2002, 2006) and Parsons (2004) all devote detailed coverage to this approach. Parsons (2004) gives an insight into the reason for this, highlighting one of the main advantages for public relations practitioners, which is that they combine consideration of ethical principles with initial steps of research and analysis with which they will already be familiar from business strategy models in general, and public relations planning models in particular. In the C-MACIE model, these are the steps of analysis and then choice.

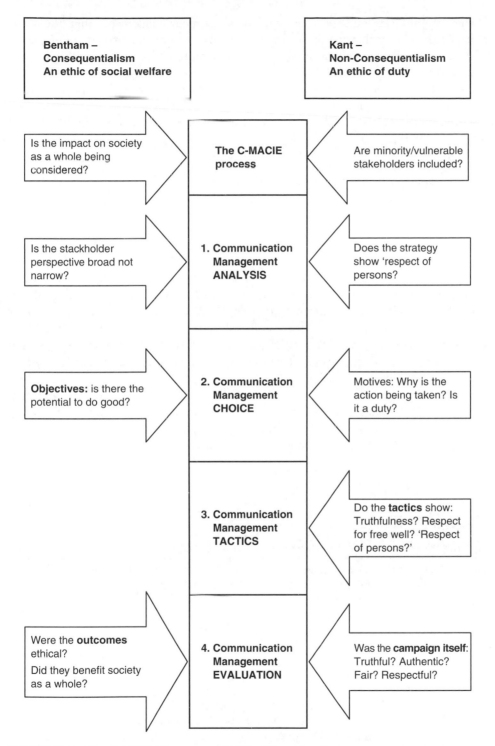

FIGURE 16.1 The C-MACIE Process and Ethical Considerations

She observes that ethical decision-making is a similar process, but that 'the tricky part is recognizing that we are facing an ethical issue in the first place' (Parsons, 2004: 142). She suggests that the first step is therefore to recognise whether there is an ethical issue involved in what may simply appear to be an organisational or tactical issue. Based on her suggested five 'pillars' or principles for use in ethical decision-making in public relations (2004: 21) – veracity, non-malfeasance, beneficence, confidentiality and fairness – she suggests the following check-list to identify ethical issues (2004: 142):

- Is there harm involved?
- Is there a missed opportunity to do good?
- Could anyone be misled in any way?
- Will anyone's privacy be invaded?
- Is it unfair to assume?
- Does it feel wrong?

Parsons (2004) then goes on to introduce the key decision-making models themselves, providing an expanded and updated version drawing on the strengths of earlier versions such as the 'Potter box' (Potter, 1972) and those put forward by Sims (1992), Trevino and Nelson (1993) and Seib and Fitzpatrick (1995). Table 16.1 shows how it lines up with the initial steps in the C-MACIE planning process and also identifies the other steps in the process which are common to most step-by-step decision making models.

Most of the steps are clear and self-explanatory. In Step 7, in which Parsons suggests further reflecting on your decision, it is useful to use the techniques for this step from the Sims (1992) process. Sims suggested two quick tests at this stage for checking the course of action on which you have decided:

- What would my family think?
- What if I read it in a newspaper?

TABLE 16.1   C-MACIE process

Step description	Planning stage	Parsons (2004)
CM Analysis	**Research step**	1. Gather all pertinent information
	Analysis step	2. Clearly define the problem
	Values step	3. Identify the professional values
		(the 'five pillars' are suggested)
	Ethics step	4. Apply the principles of ethical decision-making
	Stakeholder/duty step	5. Analyse your loyalties
CM Choice	**Strategy step**	6. Make a decision
CM Evaluation	**Checking step**	7. Second-guess your decision
CM Implementation	**Action step**	8. Take action
	Documentary step: record your decision	*Record your decision*

This works so well because it exposes the chosen course of action first to personal ethics (by reference to their most likely source, within the family) and then to the wider social ethics, through the mechanism best known to public relations practitioners, the mass media. These two tests are both effective and fast. Most communications managers must have reflected at some time that if their clients regularly used the second one, their jobs would be made much easier.

The 'action step' added by Parsons and other later theorists is arguably an important one, since, as Nash (1993) points out, the ability to use reason to work out what is the right thing and the ability to actually do it are two different things. Our view is clear: the whole reason why the personal ethics of managers are important is because they affect their actions. Unless we put into practice, or at least attempt to put into practice, what we have worked out to be right, ethics will remain at the level of an interesting intellectual game to play, instead of doing their job in the real world.

We have added a final step to Parsons' process: *record your decision*. This is because from our own experience in teaching and in practice, we have learned that one of the most important uses of these processes is in documenting the thinking behind an ethical decision. If a difficult decision is questioned later, in the context of an internal or public inquiry or legal proceedings, you can then explain the reasons for the decision clearly and demonstrate your own ethical integrity and due professional diligence. This will mean that you can undertake ethical decision-making with greater confidence, in the knowledge that your decision can be justified if necessary. At the very least, it should help you to sleep better at night!

SUMMARY

In this chapter we have set out to show that although ethics as it affects the communication manager is often thought of in conjunction with reactive work, it also has many logical links with the communication planning process in general, which have been illustrated here by relating it to the step-by-step C-MACIE process. Several important points arise from this.

Firstly, ethical decision-making, like the C-MACIE process, can be attempted step by step, with the initial steps lining up with the analysis and choice stages. We can see ethical choices not as a personal preference or as an afterthought, but as a mainstream and valid communications management activity.

Secondly, if ethics are built into the communication planning process, than it is likely that the resulting strategic approaches will be morally sound as well as effective, and therefore that you, as a communications manager, will have fulfilled your duty to give good-quality counsel to your client or organisation in a broader, more holistic way. Ultimately this will result in your helping the organisation to improve not just its image, but its reality, which Grunig (1993) has pointed out is the *real* duty of a strategic communication manager.

📖 REFERENCES

Andersen, K (1978) *Persuasion Theory and Practice*, 2nd ed. Boston MA: Allyn & Bacon

Baker, S., & Martinson, D.L. (2002) Out of the red light district: Five principles for ethically proactive public relations. *Public Relations Quarterly*, *47*(3).

Bettinghaus, E.P., & Cody, M. J. (1994) *Persuasive Communication*. Fort Worth, TX: Harcourt Brace College Publishers.

Bivins, T.H. (1987) Applying ethical theory to public relations. *Journal of Business Ethics*, *6*(3), 195–200.

Curtin, P.A., & Boynton, L.A. (2001) Ethics in public relations: Theory and practice. In R.L. Heath (ed.), *The Handbook of Public Relations* (pp. 411–22). Thousand Oaks, CA: Sage.

Cutlip, L., Center, A., & Broom, G. (eds) (2005) *Effective Public Relations*, 8th ed. Upper Saddle River, NJ: Prentice Hall.

Day, K.D., Dong, Q., & Robins, C. (2001) Public relations ethics: An overview and discussion of issues for the 21st century. In R.L. Heath (ed.), *The Handbook of Public Relations* (pp. 403–10). Thousand Oaks, CA: Sage.

Elton, L. (1993) University teaching: a professional model for quality. In R. Ellis (ed.), *Quality Assurance for University Teaching*. Buckingham: Open University Press.

Fawkes, J. (2006) Public relations, propaganda and the psychology of persuasion. In R. Tench & L. Yeomans (eds), *Exploring Public Relations* (pp. 266–87). Harlow: Pearson Education.

French, J.R.P., & Raven, B. (1959) The bases of social power. In D. Cartwright (ed.), *Studies in Social Power*. Ann Arbor: University of Michigan Press.

Green, A. (2001) *Creativity in Public Relations*. London: Kogan Page.

Gregory, A. (2002) 'To spin or not to spin': The ethics of public relations. Lecture at the Annual General Meeting of The Institute of Public Relations, 2 May.

Gregory, A. (2006) Ethics and professionalism in public relations. In R. Tench & L. Yeomans (eds), *Exploring Public Relations* (pp. 288–305). Harlow: Pearson Education.

Grunig, J.E. (1993) Image and substance: From symbolic to behavioural relationships. *Public Relations Review*, *19*, pp.121–39.

Grunig, J.E., & Grunig, L.A. (1992) Models of public relations and communication. In J.E. Grunig (ed.), *Excellence in Public Relations and Communications Management*. Hillsdale, NJ: Erlbaum.

Grunig, J.E., & Hunt, T. (1984) *Managing Public Relations*. New York: Holt Rhinehart Winston.

Grunig, J.E. & White, J. (1992) The effect of worldviews on PR theory and practice. In J.E. Grunig (ed.), *Excellence in Public Relations and Communications Management*. Hillsdale NJ: Erlbaum.

Hazelton Jr, V. (1989) *Public Relations Theory*. Hillsdale, NJ: Erlbaum.

Heath, R. (1992) The wrangle in the marketplace: A rhetorical perspective of PR. In E.L. Toth & R.L. Heath (eds), *Rhetorical and Critical Approaches to Public Relations*. Hillsdale, NJ: Erlbaum.

Huang, Y. (2001) Should a public relations code of ethics be enforced? *Journal of Business Ethics*, *31*(3), 259–70.

Jaksa, J A and Prichard, M S (1994) *Communicator Ethics: Methods of Analysis*, 2nd ed. Belmont, CA:Wadsworth

Johnson, G., & Scholes, K. (1993) *Exploring Corporate Strategy*, 3rd ed. London: Prentice Hall.

L'Etang, J. (2006) 'Corporate responsibility and public relations ethics. In L'Etang, J., and Pieczka, M. (eds), *Public Relations: Critical Debates and Contemporary Practice*. Mahwah, NJ: Erlbaum.

L'Etang, J. (2006) 'Public relations and rhetoric. In L'Etang, J., and Pieczka, M. (eds), *Public Relations: Critical Debates and Contemporary Practice*. Mahwah, NJ: Erlbaum.

Miller, G.R (1989) Persuasion and public relations: Two 'Ps' in a pod . In Botan, C. and Hazelton Jnr, V. (eds), *Public Relations Theory*. Hillsdale , NJ: Erlbaum.

Mitchell, R.K., Agle, B.R., & Wood, D.J (1997) Towards a theory of stakeholder identification and salience: Defining the principle of who and what really counts. *Academy of Management Review*, *22*(4), 853–86.

(Continued)

(Continued)

Moloney, K. (2000) *Rethinking Public Relations*. London: Routledge.

Nash, L. (1993) *Good Intentions Aside: A Manager's Guide to Resolving Ethical Problems*. Boston, MA: Harvard Business School Press.

Parsons, P.J. (2004) *Ethics in Public Relations: A Guide to Best Practice*. London: Kogan Page.

Petty, R.T., & Cacioppo, J.T. (eds) (1983) *Social Psychophysiology: A Sourcebook*. New York: Guilford Press.

Pieczka, M (2006) Paradigms, systems theory and public relations. In L'Etang, J., and Pieczka, M. (eds), *Public Relations: Critical Debates and Contemporary Practice*. Mahwah, NJ: Erlbaum.

Potter, R. (1972) The logic of moral argument. In P. Deats (ed.), *Toward a Discipline of Social Ethics*. Boston: Boston University Press.

Regester, M., & Larkin, J. (1997) *Crisis and Risk Management*. London: Kogan Page.

Seib, P., & Fitzpatrick, K. (1995) *Public Relations Ethics*. Fort Worth, TX: Harcourt Brace.

Sims, R.R. (1992). The challenge of ethical behaviour in organisations. *Journal of Business Ethics*, 11.

Shimp, T. A. (2002) *Advertising, Promotion and Supplemental Aspects of Integrated Marketing Communications*. Cincinatti: Dryden Press.

Taylor, P. (2001) 'What is propaganda?' www.ics.leeds.ac.uk/pmt-terrorism/what-propaganda.pdf.

Trevino, L.K., & Nelson, K.A. (1993) *Managing Business Ethics*. Chichester, New York: Wiley.

Windahl, S., & Signitzer, B., with Olson, J. (1992) *Using Communication Theory*. London: Sage.

Corporate Social Responsibility: Balancing Business and Social Priorities

17

Richard Warren

> **Key Themes**
>
> - Definitions of the concept of CSR
> - Understanding the development of CSR
> - The drivers behind the growth of CSR activity
> - Benefits to organisations of CSR engagement
> - Types of CSR programmes
> - Managing the CSR activity

This chapter examines the increasing importance attached to the concept of corporate social responsibility (CSR) within the corporate world, and the degree to which such concerns have led to a rethinking and reshaping of business priorities and strategies in recent years.

INTRODUCTION

The roots of the concept of corporate social responsibility are traceable back to earlier times and perhaps notably to ideas that were circulating in the nineteenth century if not earlier. However, arguably it is only in the second half of the twentieth century that CSR has come of age, attracting the attention of businesses and business leaders across the developed world. Indeed, the recent rapid growth of interest in and engagement with CSR has left many business schools struggling to catch up with latest developments in this area.

The concept of CSR embraces the idea that companies should consider the interests of society and the natural environment rather than their own vested interests when making decisions. CSR is now a well-known expression for what, in the recent past, has been a collection of different and yet related terms: corporate philanthropy, corporate citizenship, business ethics, stakeholding, community involvement, corporate responsibility, socially responsible investment, sustainability, triple bottom line, corporate accountability and corporate social performance. On the surface, at least, some of these terms might seem to be closely related, but many have other connotations as well. Indeed the lack of consensus over how to define and explain CSR has seriously hampered theoretical development as well as research into the implications of these related policies and practices. A great deal of imaginative, innovative and energetic activity is taking place in the field of CSR all over the world and researchers have been keen to understand and account for this phenomenon, and to see whether it can, over time, become a movement which fundamentally changes the institutionalisation of business practice.

This chapter explores the development of CSR and its role in modern society. We also seek to advance a theory of CSR which arguably will bring greater clarity and direction for both those engaged managing corporate activities that may well have implications for CSR; and for those who may have direct responsibility for managing the CSR policies themselves. Such a theory may help managers to understand better what to do, how far to go, and how to evaluate and account for the results they are achieving in their endeavours to implement CSR policies. To understand the CSR movement several questions need to be addressed: why the demand for CSR has arisen; how it manifests itself in business practice; whether it can be understood in theoretical terms; and whether it will become institutionalised in an accountable way.

OLD WINE IN NEW BOTTLES

While there has always been concern about the social impact of business upon society, most notably from Ruskin (1860) onwards, the debate within orthodox business theory is more recent. A general concern about the greater engagement in CSR activity began in the post-war period as part of the 'social responsibility debate', which started in the USA and radiated outwards to Europe in the 1950s and 1960s. Bowen (1953) explicitly enjoined a debate on the wider social responsibilities of business to the community, a debate started by the work of Peter Drucker, whose seminal study of General Motors questioned the purposes and responsibilities of the large corporation (Drucker, 1946). In the 1960s, environmental concerns about the impact of business in terms of pollution and the depletion of natural resources was kick-started by Rachel Carson's *Silent Spring* (Carson, 1962). The impact of the social responsibility debate on company practice in Britain was slow to ignite, but Kempner, Macmillan, and Hawkins (1974) raised many of these growing concerns in the context of British business.

The social responsibility debate in the USA in the 1970s provoked some classic statements of the difference of opinion between liberals and social democrats about the purpose of business in society. Notably the economic liberals von Hayek and

Friedman stood opposed to the earlier views of the social democrats Berle and Means. The liberals argued that businesses are to be understood as private property and are as such instruments of their owners, designed primarily to make money. The common good is served by this narrow focus because the pressure of unintended consequences ensures that each business seeks out efficient allocations of resources, so generating the maximum amount of wealth in society and the maximum amount of opportunity to engage others in the wealth creation process. This argument is encapsulated in the title of Friedman's article published in the *New York Times Magazine*, 'The social responsibility of business is to increase its profits' (Friedman, 1970). The other advantage seen in this argument about the role of business is the emphasis on business avoiding the temptation to stray into other areas of activity such as politics or law making; this restriction of the scope of business power in a democratic society is thought to be a great virtue. The danger in the broader notion of social responsibility is that managers may see this as an open invitation to begin making political decisions and exercising power for their own purposes. This considerably loosens the notion of accountability to shareholders and increases the managers' prerogatives.

Writing in 1932, Berle and Means asked if shareholders were becoming less influential in the conduct of corporate affairs, and whether the control function of ownership was now being superseded by that of management (see Berle & Means, 1968). They noted in their study of these issues that, as companies grew larger, the proportion of shares held by the largest shareholders decreased so that the company was increasingly becoming 'managerially controlled'. Indeed, they estimated that in the USA in 1932, 65% of the top 200 largest non-financial corporations were managerially controlled (defined as individuals controlling less than 5% of the voting stock). The implication of a growing divorce of ownership from control was, they argued, considerable. For example, if it could no longer be assumed that managers were effectively being made accountable to shareholders, then to whom were they accountable, and to whom should they be accountable? On what criteria should managers be selected for office, and what objectives would they and should they be pursuing? Interestingly, Berle and Mean assumed that because management were not significant shareholders, they would be guided in their behaviour by a sense of responsibility to society, and there would be a softening in the aggressiveness of capitalism and the beginnings of a managerial revolution in the operation of a 'people's capitalism'. This would require changes in corporate law to reflect the new contract between business and society. In essence, what Berle and Mean were suggesting is that stakeholder management would replace shareholder joint stock companies. Instead of managers being accountable only to the shareholders under the law, two new types of accountability would supplement this check on mismanagement: the development of a 'corporate conscience' which would restrain management from acting in their own self-interest, or in a socially irresponsible manner, and then the requirement to be answerable to the 'public consensus' or public opinion. Clearly, this would imply the development of a professional management conforming to a professional code of conduct and in touch with and prepared to justify their actions before the court of public opinion.

However, it was not until the final decade of the twentieth century that this argument seemed to find a receptive climate in business, and new calls for business to exercise a degree of CSR came to the fore. A movement in the direction of the views of Berle and Means in the last twenty years is noticeable around the globe, and is now widely detectable in business practice. To understand why the climate has become more receptive towards the acceptance of CSR we need to consider some of the explanations that have been offered by commentators on these events.

WHY HAS CSR BECOME PROMINENT IN THE NEW MILLENNIUM?

The internationalisation of business and the process of globalisation raise many ethical issues about acceptable norms of conduct on the part of business. The core concerns of CSR today include: human rights, labour standards, poverty, bribery and corruption, environmental protection, product safety, and financial probity and the control of money laundering (Kline, 2005). Racism and discrimination are also a universal problem for global business ethics (Chua, 2004). Multinational companies (MNCs) are increasingly being challenged by non-governmental organisations and the media to justify their conduct and legitimacy in ethical terms. Activities that undermine human rights and visibly damage the environment are being particularly strongly challenged by pressure groups. The US firm Arco has been forced to sell its interests in Burma by the pressure from the Western consumer lobby in response to the Burmese military dictatorship's persecution of democratic opposition parties and human rights abuses. The Deepwater Horizon oil spill, involving BP in the Gulf of Mexico, flowed for three months in 2010. The environmental impact of the oil spill continues since the well was capped. It is the largest accidental marine oil spill in the history of the petroleum industry. The spill has caused extensive damage to marine and wildlife habitats as well as the Gulf's fishing and tourist industries.

In recent years nation states and international institutions such as the United Nations have begun to call upon companies to respect human rights, seek sustainable business practices and take up other ethical initiatives. In 1999, the UN Secretary General launched the idea of a Global Compact, covering human rights, labour, and the environment, and invited companies to embrace and enact a set of nine principles in their operations. Businesses that are willing to sign up to these principles have to send the UN a letter from the chief executive officer (CEO) setting out the company's commitment to the principles, and then be prepared to publicise, once a year, one example of how they have put these principles into practice. Businesses that comply are allowed to use the UN Global Compact logo on their company publicity. Over 2,300 businesses from over 87 countries have signed up so far.

The adoption of a 'CSR vocabulary' and activity in business is now substantial and widespread. These changes are an indication that there has been a response by business to social, political and ecological pressures that are largely instinctive, *ad hoc*, with hitherto little guidance or direction from a justifying theory. In initiating policies and activities demonstrating concern for CSR business has made all the running, with business school academics often struggling to catch up, the business schools being mainly content with describing and categorising these initiatives rather than directing them.

In a world of nation states the assumption is that the state will be the locus of regulatory activity in regard to the operation of the company. However, the growth of many businesses into corporations that operate in many states and across states means that the regulatory powers of any one state have been much attenuated, and the jurisdiction of one state over an MNC is often limited. Moreover, the wealth and financial power of the MNC mean that politicians are often competing against each other to gain the support of the corporation for inward investment and support for their political party. States can therefore be in a position where they are competing with each other for foreign direct investment and to provide the most favourable regulatory regime to attract MNCs to invest in them. Consequently, this conflict of interest between acting as the regulator of corporations and recipient of their investments is weakening the control of the state in relation to business. The power and scope of many companies means that the welfare and prosperity of many citizens in a nation state can be affected by the decisions taken by the management of the corporation. The speed of communications and mobility of finance and investment through international markets and the outsourcing and globalisation of the supply chain of the MNCs enhance this power still further. Corporations can choose where to be registered, and so can shape in many ways the legal regime that will govern their operations. Nation states are often, in effect, engaged in regulatory competition. Without some degree of self-regulation or restraint there will be fewer and fewer restrictions placed upon the conduct of the MNC besides those of the market.

THE CONCEPT OF CSR

As has already been suggested, CSR is the idea that companies should consider the interests of society and the environment when making decisions and setting policies. However, authoritative definitions of CSR are hard to come by in this developing area of responsibility because there is, as yet, so little orthodoxy in the theories and practice of CSR (Carroll, 1999). There seems to be no general theory of CSR, although many academics have sought to establish the fact that such a responsibility exists, and some academics are leading advocates and campaigners for its adoption in business (Zadek, 2001). In fact, CSR is perhaps better understood as a new concern or activity that has been pioneered by business, and then discovered by the academic world, and finally recommended to the state for validation and endorsement. This process has now moved on a stage further, beyond the academic world and the nation state, to the supranational level in Europe and the United Nations.

The European Union has embraced CSR, and the Commission of the European Communities (2001: 6) has defined CSR 'as a concept whereby companies integrate social and environmental concerns in their business operations and in their interaction with their stakeholders on a voluntary basis'. There are three points to note in this definition: (i) this activity on the part of companies is held to be a voluntary initiative; (ii) these social and environmental concerns should be integrated; and (iii) all businesses should interact with their stakeholders. Let us consider these points in turn.

First, the EU, at the moment, is encouraging firms to embrace CSR as a voluntary activity, which is a move above and beyond what is required by company law. Firms are urged to do this as a matter of enlightened self-interest; but as yet, most states and in particular the supranational EU do not want to force this responsibility onto firms or require that it becomes legally enforceable. This reflects a political compromise within the EU, as firms in some states are now finding that certain aspects of CSR are now almost mandatory and are increasingly becoming integrated into some states' frameworks of company law. For example, CSR reporting is now virtually compulsory for UK firms that want to maintain stock market listings and the approval of large investment funds. So, whilst the EU definition defines CSR as an added value or voluntary activity, this may be a transition phase prior to its incorporation into the regulatory framework of business. On the other hand, CSR may just be a passing fad, as it has been in the past, which the EU is happy enough to endorse and encourage at present but which will in due time be allowed to drop away so that its incorporation in to company law will not then arise. The voluntary character of CSR will also allow it to be dropped by business in a few years if the public pressure for CSR begins to subside. The designation of CSR as voluntary in the EU definition indicates, then, that it is still a tentative and a contested political issue that has succeeded in gaining the attention of the EU but has not yet managed to become an institutional fixture in business.

Second, the EU definition indicates that two responsibility agendas ought to be integrated: the social and the environmental. The environmental agenda for business has been around since the 1960s, and in Europe some states are much further along the road of making business more environmentally conscious than others. The movement towards 'sustainable business' has a long way to go, but consciousness of the perils of ignoring this agenda is clearly evident in the many ways in which the actions of businesses are impacting on many aspects of people's daily lives. Here the question of what constitutes 'sustainability' in the business context was addressed in the Brundtland Report (World Commission on Environment and Development, 1987; see box), which claimed that sustainability is about three interrelated concerns regarding the welfare of people, a concern for the planet, and the need to make profits. Sustainable businesses try to balance all three through the triple-bottom-line concept, using sustainable development and sustainable distribution to satisfy these different stakeholders.

Many of these requirements have been steadily making their way into state and EU regulations, but once again business is being urged to take this responsibility further than mere compliance. The social responsibility agenda that is being integrated with the environmental or green agenda has arisen more recently, but represents the growing need for business to act ethically, transparently and responsibly in its dealings with customers, and in the communities where it operates. The integration of these two agenda reflects the globalisation of business and the fact that the social and environmental are ultimately connected and must be embraced as a single concern for sustainability in business.

THE BRUNDTLAND REPORT

In 1987 the Brundtland Report, *Our Common Future*, alerted the world to the urgency of making progress towards economic development that could be sustained without depleting natural resources or harming the environment. Published by an international group of politicians, civil servants and experts on the environment and development, the report provided a key statement on sustainable development, defining it as 'development that meets the needs of the present without compromising the ability of future generations to meet their own needs'.

The Brundtland Report was primarily concerned with securing a global equity, redistributing resources towards poorer nations whilst encouraging their economic growth. The report also suggested that equity, growth and environmental maintenance are simultaneously possible and that each country is capable of achieving its full economic potential whilst at the same time enhancing its resource base. The report also recognised that achieving this equity and sustainable growth would require technological and social change.

The third element of the EU definition of CSR, the notion of stakeholders, is also referred to in the definition, and this reflects some of the debate in business that developed in the 1990s about the different ways to embrace capitalism: sometimes characterised as a choice between the Rhenish (stakeholder) and the Anglo-Saxon (stockholder) view of the firm. The term 'stakeholder' is contrasted with 'shareholder' (or in the USA 'stockholder') as the signifier of the differing perspectives at issue. Shareholders are often held up as the beneficial owners of the company because they are the major risk bearers and are therefore entitled to the profits of the business after all other contract payments have been made. The creation of shareholder value is said by many commentators to be the *raison d'être* of the business and is therefore the primary duty of the shareholder's agents, the managers of the company. The substitution of the term 'stakeholder' for 'shareholder' is an explicit questioning of this first duty assumption, effectively redefining the duties of management as pluralist or multiple. Stakeholder advocates are seeking to define business as a shared endeavour with many participants, all of whom have a stake in its success, and in the firm's good governance. The development and adoption of CSR thinking has been paralleled by a growing and changing adoption of the stakeholding concept within the business world. Indeed, there is now a push to see this conception of stakeholder responsibilities incorporated into company law. In the so-called 'Rhenish model' firms, in countries such as Germany and the Netherlands, stakeholder representatives drawn from the workers have boardroom seats. The demand to enfranchise more stakeholders in the company would substantially alter the institutional nature of business and the model of governance that that sets its purpose and function. The introduction of stakeholder language into the EU definition is indicative of the radical potential the CSR concept has and indicates that this will be a contentious and momentous change in the institutional structure of capitalism should this view come to prevail.

Before we consider whether there can be a theory of CSR that guides its development, it is important to understand the variety and range of activity that needs to be brought under the orbit of such a theory.

THE RANDOM NATURE OF THE PRESENT ACTIVITY IN CSR

Many companies have developed policies on CSR in response to these legitimacy pressures. A quick reading of the report and accounts for many large companies will reveal that 'stakeholders', 'accountability' and 'sustainability' have become the slogans of the new millennium. Many companies are now publishing operating and financial reviews alongside their mandatory accounts, and some have actively welcomed independent auditors and pressure groups such as Friends of the Earth as verifiers of their sustainability statements and achievements. The failure of a company to take swift action in the face of social pressure can be enormous, it is much harder for managements to get these decisions wrong than right. For many companies, the attention that has had to be devoted to social responsibility issues is proving to be costly and time-consuming. Most companies now allocate some of their budget to social responsibility issues. What was once perhaps treated as something of a public relations stunt is now a serious part of many firms' business strategy (Silberhorn & Warren, 2007). For example, Ford Motor Company handles its CSR through an environment and public policy committee led by the company's chairman. At Pfizer, the full board takes decisions on CSR and periodically reviews the company's policies and practices. At BT, the board has created a social policy unit.

In the context of the developing world, CSR often takes the form of compliance with basic expectations about the conduct of business and in reducing public hostility towards business enterprise. In a study of CSR in Russia this concept is much more about creating productive firms that provide real jobs and that generate wealth and pay taxes. By showing that business can act independently of the state, business CSR policies are hoping to build the social legitimacy of business as an honourable and respectable occupation. If this were to be successful, it could be seen as a real achievement in the context of a society where 70 years of communist propaganda attempted to portray business as rapacious and immoral enterprise that exploited the working class and impoverished the Third World (Kuznetsov, Kuznetsova, & Warren 2009).

A new trend in CSR is for companies to work together alongside governments and development agencies on problems that are too big for any one company to handle, such as the HIV/Aids pandemic, poverty and corruption. The UN is helping to forge some of these collaborations with its initiative called 'Growing Sustainable Business for Poverty Reduction in Africa'. This initiative aims to encourage businesses to target poor consumers and improve the links between big and small companies on the continent. This could extend the scope and impact of CSR quite considerably and is an initiative that business is itself promoting. The Shell Foundation is also exploring collaborative solutions to social and environmental problems in Africa (http://www. shellfoundation.org). It has set up two investment funds that provide loans to small businesses in Uganda and South Africa. The fund is trying to tackle two common problems in Africa: the lack of access to energy among poor rural households and the fact that small business growth is often hampered by poor governance, corruption and the unwillingness of banks to make risky loans. Using the Royal Dutch Shell group's reputation, the Foundation is encouraging local banks to put up capital alongside its own finance. Other micro-finance initiatives are also focusing on poor people as a potential market for goods and services. Most recently, the Shell Foundation has suggested that international development aid should be focused more closely on enterprise and small business development using business principles to evaluate the success of these investments.

REASONS WHY WE NEED A THEORY OF CSR

These trends towards the embracing of CSR, particularly on the part of big business, have not been without their critics in recent years (Vogel, 2005). As was noted earlier, these tendencies attracted criticism when they were raised in the 1970s by the Nobel Prize winning economists Friedman and Hayek. In recent years, the CSR movement has criticised by the noted economist, David Henderson, and the business ethicist Elaine Sternberg (Henderson, 2001; Sternberg, 1994) They view the CSR movement with utter dismay. CSR is regarded as a danger to clarity and accountability derived from the theory of shareholder value maximisation in business. This simple theory of shareholder value maximisation provides clear direction to company management and accountability criteria for the shareholders. In neo-liberal terms the corporation's purpose is, within the rules of the business game (lawful, and according to custom), to produce maximum shareholder value. The measures of this goal are profits, dividends and share price. Here the argument is that if we are to go against this theory, we need good reasons to do so, and a better theory of business purpose to provide guidance on policies and practice.

What counter-argument can be put up to this neo-liberal criticism? First, we need to acknowledge that there is a lot more to business than return to shareholders on the capital invested. We now know that other forms of capital are at least as important for business to prosper. Besides financial capital we need 'human capital' in the form of education and training; but in recent years we have also come to recognise the essential requirements for social and natural capital as well.

'Social capital' is the building of trust, and corporations can accumulate this in two ways: by adhering to rules of moral conduct, which build trust and are not aimed at another purpose; and by building or maintaining a democratic dialogue upon which all transactions between the corporation and its stakeholders depend. Social capital can be measured and its increase or decrease accounted for in balance sheet terms.

'Natural capital' refers to the natural resources and ecosystem services that make possible all economic activity, indeed all life. These services are of immense economic value; some are literally priceless, since they have no known substitutes. Yet current business practices typically fail to take into account the value of these assets, which is rising with their scarcity. As a result, natural capital is being degraded and liquidated by the wasteful use of such resources as energy, materials, water, and topsoil.

Let us briefly look at the vital importance of social and then natural capital in modern business practice.

CSR Develops and Builds Social Capital

It is increasingly recognised that the trajectory of global capitalism will be different from its past, and that the nature and form of the company is likely to change under pressure from the market, and as the result of changes in knowledge and technology. However, these are not fully determining processes; besides the economic and the informational dimensions of society, there are the political and social dimensions that will also play a part in shaping the company of the future. One argument that has gained increasing support is that the role of social capital in furthering the development of the information age could prove to be decisive.

'Social capital' is a term that has been coined by many commentators to describe the norms of trust and social reciprocation that are essential to maintain a civil society. The work of Francis Fukuyama (1995, 1999) has brought it to a much wider audience, but he, in turn, acknowledges that the concept is derived from the sociological theory of James S. Coleman (1990), the writer on architecture and urban affairs, Jane Jacobs (1992), and more recently the political scientist, Robert Putnam (1993). If capital is understood to be property and money, human capital is the investment in human knowledge and skills, and social capital is the term now used to describe the relationships of trust which bind people together. Social capital is intangible and relational but no less important for social welfare than property capital. Fukuyama's definition of social capital is 'the existence of a certain set of informal values or norms shared among members of a group that permit co-operation among them' (Fukuyama, 1995). He points out that the sharing of values and norms does not necessarily produce social capital because the values may be perverse and the cooperation used for malign purposes, as for example in the case of the Mafia. The bonds that produce social capital must be more virtuous (such as truth telling, promise keeping, and reciprocation), and must be directed towards worthy ends. Social capital is not a pervasive feature of all societies; it tends to reside in affiliation groups and is distributed in various amounts in different societies. The family is a very important source of social capital generation, and this is so in many other types of centres of affiliation – clubs, churches, trade unions, political parties, and importantly, companies.

Robert Putnam's interesting study of civil engagement in different regions of Italy showed that the quality of governance was determined by the long-standing traditions of civil engagement, or its absence (Putnam, 1993). He measured voter turnout, newspaper readership, membership in choral societies and football clubs as the proxy indicators of a successful region. He concluded: 'In fact, historical analysis suggested that these networks of organised reciprocity and civic solidarity, far from being an epiphenomenon of socioeconomic modernisation, were a precondition for it.' When he returned home he set about trying to measure the degree of civil engagement that existed in contemporary America. His now famous book, *Bowling Alone*, announced that the quality of collective life in the USA was in decline because the post-war generations were weaned on television and were forsaking the traditional forms of organised activity (bowling clubs, etc.) on which their parents and grandparents had spent their free time (Putnam, 2000). Whether television is the simple cause of this decline is debatable, but his general thesis, even if partly correct, has serious implications for society because membership of networks comprising formal associations or informal patterns of sociability is a vital component of social connectedness. A connected community can alleviate many social problems and facilitate the implementation of various kinds of public policy, for instance by using trade unions to administer social welfare schemes. If social capital is depleted then society looses a valuable resource that can help to ameliorate the social disruption and disconnection that capitalism tends to cause in its wake.

The task of maintaining and generating social capital is an important challenge that faces all social institutions, and particularly business institutions, for they are the main engines of creation and destruction in the global market.

The Importance of Natural Capital

To build natural capital companies need to radically increase resource productivity. Implementing just this responsibility can significantly improve a firm's bottom line, and can also help finance the other natural capital deposits such as eliminating waste and reducing the use of non-renewable energy sources (Porritt, 2005).

There are a variety of different systems of environmental reporting in European companies at the moment. Reports produced by some companies in these countries not only describe the firm's environmental policy and its production of eco-friendly products but also try to show the resources used and the efficiency with which they were employed. In other words, they set out a kind of input-output analysis, showing all the inputs of energy and raw materials and then the outputs of products and emissions to the environment. In some pioneering companies they have attempted to account for their environmental impacts by putting a financial cost on them. In terms of quantitative environmental reporting, which attempts to provide a more comprehensive picture of the companies environmental impact, the most innovative reports to-date are from German, Swedish, Danish and Austrian companies. Reports produced by some companies in these countries not only describe their environmental policy and its production of eco-friendly products but also show the resources used and the efficiency with which they are employed.

Another factor putting pressure on companies to increase their levels of environmental reporting is the growth of ethical and environmental investment funds in the USA and Europe. Fund managers have declared to investors that they will adhere to certain investment criteria in addition to rate of return; typically the performance factors considered are heavily weighted in favour of environmental issues. Fund managers have to conduct or rely upon expert research to guide them in their investment choices; consequently, the more companies are prepared to disclose and provide verification of their environmental claims, the more attractive these firms will be to the fund managers. As these investment funds grow in size, more and more companies will probably want to be the recipients of this kind of investment, creating a self fulfilling cycle of environmental and sustainability reporting.

A CANDIDATE THEORY OF CSR

What might a theory of CSR look like? It needs to be a normative theory of business as its purpose is to provide guidance on corporate conduct. This is different from positivist theory, which formulates a law to cover what businesses do in practice. A normative theory has a moral component to provide a direction in matters of values and conduct, and helps in the making of judgements about what is valid in terms of CSR policies.

A candidate theory of CSR might be as follows: the purpose of the corporation is to produce maximum sustainable value for stakeholders, within and upholding the rules of ethical business. The measure of this is profits for shareholders and deposits of social and natural capital for other stakeholders. This might be more appropriately called a theory of corporate sustainability and responsibility (CS&R) to reflect the need to contribute to both social and natural capital building and maintenance.

How Might Corporate Sustainability and Responsibility Develop?

Social and natural capital recovery and moral arguments may not be persuasive enough, however. Political and ideological considerations based upon property interests are probably more powerful forces shaping company institutionalisation. Some of the impetus towards a greater concern with business ethics, and the demand that companies learn to become more socially and sustainable responsible, will be countered by calls for business to become more innovative, risk-taking and, ultimately, wealth generating. Supporters of the capitalist ethos and interests will argue strongly that the restoration of shareholder power over their property rights in the company, and management accountability to shareholders regarding how this property is used, are still essential prerequisites for the generation of wealth in society and ultimately for the preservation of political freedoms. This position can also be defended in democratic terms because it is claimed that we are all, in some form or another,

TABLE 17.1 The Four Possible CS&R Policy Trajectories

	Liberal	Communitarian
Low contribution to social and natural capital	Limited CS&R Shareholder value	CS&R Stakeholder value
High contribution to social and natural capital	Selective acts of philanthropy	CS&R The common good

shareholders now. Widespread vicarious shareholding in the form of pensions, insurance policies and savings gives most people a stake in the efficient management of the capitalist system, and, it is argued, the best way to serve the interest of everyone with such a stake is to ensure that more attention is paid by the company's management to delivering shareholder value.

The new joint-stock politics regarding CS&R may well in its essentials revolve around the debate about property rights versus the need to rebuild and maintain social and natural capital (Warren, 2000). If we put these together as two dimensions and divide each dimension into two positions, there are four possible scenarios that will indicate what the possible trajectories of CS&R policies may be. These can be mapped out in a 2 × 2 matrix as shown in Table 17.1.

The Four Possible Future Trajectories of Institutionalised CS&R

The first dimension is the degree to which property rights are considered to be held under social conditionality. At one end of the dimension there is the liberal view that property is to be the exclusive and unalienable possession of the individual. That this right is absolute because it was acquired either by a contractual exchange under the law in the market place, or the property has been brought into being by an act or effort of the owner and therefore has become his property. Or the entitlement is long-standing and of proven provenance, so that a challenge to such ownership would be doubtful and ultimately fruitless. In other words, the holding of property by the owner is exclusive and final. It follows from this that the holding of such property shall be also unconditional: that the property is to be undivided and the owner's right of use or appropriation of the property is only to be challenged if it interferes with the property or personal rights of other people. Owners shall be at liberty to destroy, change, and increase their property at will, and be under no restraint from the public or other citizens. In the case of property in the company, owners can buy and sell shareholdings at any time, and without prior consultation with others. Shareholders may then create or wind up companies at will under company law without reference to employees, customers, communities or other parties. And the principal relationship between the owner of company shares and the management of the company is a fiduciary one of the agent principle sort. The form of the company is best understood in the liberal view as a nexus of contracts.

At the other end of this dimension is the view of a more communitarian political philosophy that maintains that property is to be owned and appropriated under various degrees of social and environmental conditionality. Personal property (cars, stereos, wrist watches, etc.) is to be held in an unconditional and exclusive sense. But then other types of property which have a bigger impact upon social and environmental life are to be held under various conditions of restraint and forbearance. These will restrict the degree of ownership and the rights of the owner to appropriate and do what they wish with this property. For example, owners of large tracts of land will be able to sell the land under certain conditions but will be restricted in whom they can sell it to, what uses it can be put to, and who can or cannot be allowed access to the land. When it comes to the company form, this could mean that while shareholders are entitled to dividends and nominal ownership of the company the sale of shares is a conditional process that will involve consultation with various stakeholders, rights of veto and delay to the sale and perhaps even the denial of sale in certain circumstances. Indeed, it might involve the separation of shareholders' property rights and ownership and the collective ownership of the company form which is constituted as a trust with overriding powers over the shareholders.

The second dimension is the degree of social and natural capital maintenance that the company is expected to contribute towards and help recover: a low contribution or a high contribution. Low social and natural capital contributions on the part of the company will involve moderate changes to the form of the company, which will modify its present constitution under the law but not substantially change its function in society. Low levels of social and natural capital maintenance might moderate social discontent to some extent and help to relegitimise the company in society in the short term, but will not necessarily undermine its destructive tendencies in the longer term. High aspirations for business organisations in the rebuilding of social and natural capital, based upon their taking a greater role in supporting the social communities of society and in reducing environmental impact, will be more difficult to achieve, but would in the long run change the institutionalisation of capitalism more fundamentally. Which view comes to prevail will to a large extent depend upon which political processes and structural drivers gain dominance during periodic legitimisation crises, where the powers of the state are often invoked to appease democratic discontent and the force of property interests in society is at its weakest.

MANAGING CSR

Very few companies have set up full CSR management systems. Creating and building a successful system is a complex, long-term project for any company. This is because it involves a shift in the way a company conducts business and is very much like trying to implement a total quality management approach. The commitment to CSR starts with assigning responsibility for CSR within the company, then a process of engagement with stakeholders to discover what their concerns are, and how they can be worked with to create partnerships. Many companies have made CSR a boardroom responsibility either by appointing a new director with CSR expertise, or by creating a committee to oversee this area of responsibility. However responsibility for CSR is organised, it is important that a company builds mechanisms for communication between its business functions and units. In this respect, cross-functional teams can play an important part in integrating CSR and can encourage feedback from supporters and sceptics.

The involvement of the human resource management function in CSR is particularly beneficial because employee involvement in helping to determine the CSR agenda and what causes are to be pursued helps counter the danger of these causes being chosen solely by the management of the firm. Accusations of managerial self-indulgence and personal aggrandisement or political bias can then be avoided, and it could be argued this gives the CSR agenda more legitimacy as it has been made more democratic. Engaging employees and their representatives in implementation means focusing on awareness (employees need to be made aware of CSR directions, strategies and commitments). Employees should be given the context for and background on the firm's approach to CSR, including the motivation for engaging in it, why the approach was adopted, its relevance to the organisation, how it fits with existing firm objectives, how it changes current approaches, and other implications. Involving employees in discussions of how CSR commitments are implemented is a way for these stakeholders to develop a sense of ownership of and pride in the firm's CSR activities. Employee procedures to support CSR might include: incorporating CSR performance elements into job descriptions and performance evaluations; providing regular updates on progress (in meetings or the company newsletter); developing incentives (such as rewards for best suggestions); and removing or reducing disincentives (e.g., competing interests such as premature deadlines that encourage employees to choose non-CSR options).

Developing CSR capability in a company presents many challenges for the management. The following characteristics need to be developed in the organisation's members: awareness of stakeholders and their needs, the capacity to create partnerships, being open to new ideas and creative ways of thinking, taking a strategic view, and taking action on the variety of CSR initiatives. The CSR training can help managers and employees understand the role of different stakeholders and how to implement CSR policies in many different ways. For example, the retailer, Tesco, actively offers employment opportunities to people who have been out of work for several years, lone parents, older people made redundant, and young unemployed people. This initiative both enlightens store managers and staff regarding the good characteristics of these, often marginalised, workers, as well as creating goodwill in the local community. The Co-operative Bank engages its customers in fully-fledged campaign programmes demonstrating the bank's stance on a range of important issues that its customers have helped to determine in the first place. Lloyds TSB has developed well in advance of the legislative requirements a specific strategy to eliminate any form of discrimination faced by disabled people across the organisation. This policy, the bank claims, has led to more business from disabled customers, and has widened the choice and availability of jobs for people with disabilities.

Some companies are using their appraisal and compensation systems to encourage CSR awareness in employees. For some managers bonuses and share allocations depend partly on how well they perform on various measures of corporate citizenship that are seen as essential to protecting or enhancing the reputation of the business. Statoil, the largest Norwegian oil company, links indicators related to health, safety, environment and employee satisfaction to managers' remuneration packages. The most commonly assessed aspects of CSR at the moment are employee safety and diversity, followed by ethics and the environment.

For all companies, raising awareness of the importance of CSR at all levels is a key priority, especially at middle management levels and further down. The preferred tools seem to be internal newsletters and press reviews. However, conferences and briefings are also used, especially at senior, country and middle management levels. Activities initiated by employees are further seen as helpful in raising awareness. Knowledge and skills development for employees is starting to get more attention. Secondments and project assignments seem to be the preferred tools for achieving this, at least partly.

Companies' total engagement with CSR needs to be both transparent and accountable. It is therefore particularly important that shareholders and other stakeholders are informed about these policies so that the effectiveness can be monitored and enhanced through a feedback process.

In discussing the type of consideration and challenges of developing an effective CSR management system arguably we can see that the processes and considerations involved can be related to the C-MACIE management model explained in Chapter 2. Indeed, most of the element of this model are essentially generic to any functional management system in that all functions are based on elements of analysis and choice that then flow to specific operation strategies, the implementation of those strategies and the evaluation of the results. The potential complexities of the stakeholder relationships and associated issues that need to be carefully balanced if organisations are to achieve and maintain the type of responsible positioning and reputation that a commitment to CSR engagement demands, inevitably place considerable emphasis on careful situational and stakeholder analysis. Here tools such as stakeholder mapping and issues management systems come into their own in assisting managers to interpret and weigh the relative importance of different stakeholder groups and positions and the issues associated with them.

Thus while analysis of stakeholder and issues may be a complex task, interpreting this analysis and drawing out the implications for CSR-related strategies can be equally difficult, often requiring a significant degree of subjective judgement. Indeed, choice decisions may sometimes require an incremental trial-and-error approach as the organisation explores the impact and reaction of stakeholders to particular strategies adopted. Here of course it is important to recognise that for business organisations there is always a commercial imperative, an obligation to shareholder and creditors that has to be balanced against any wider stakeholder concerns. Thus choice decisions are often something of a delicate balancing act, particularly where the commercial imperative is a pressing one. The danger here is that the CSR goals and positioning may get lost or overridden by the pressure to deliver on the commercial, investment front. Thus, for example, there has been a noticeable decline of emphasis on CSR strategies and activities as the impact of the current world-wide recession has been felt in corporate boardrooms around the world.

However, it would be a mistake to assume that CSR is something of a 'luxury' or 'fair-weather' activity that organisations can chose to turn on and off as their fortune rise and fall; rather it is perhaps better recognised as an increasingly embedded corporate activity that is subject to the type of budgetary pressures that every function faces during difficult times.

Implementing and evaluating CSR policies can often prove more challenging than other mainstream business strategies simply because of the complexity of outcomes that CSR policies may be intended to achieve. Often CSR policies may have a relatively long gestation period and their impact may be only partly under the control of the organisation, which may be working with a range of agencies and public bodies where the CSR policy is seeking to have longer-term social benefits in one or more countries/regions of the world. Equally, any attempt to evaluate the longer-term benefit of a CSR policy to the organisation itself may be difficult to quantify and may only be realised in terms of the long-term reputation of that organisation with particular groups or in particular regions.

In short, the development of a CSR policy is not something that can be expected to have some immediate quantifiable payback to the organisation in question. However, this does not mean CSR has to be written off as largely 'philanthropy'. Changing societal and political expectations of the role of businesses, coupled with changing customer and wider stakeholder expectations, have meant that CSR has increasingly become an integral part of the total corporate offering and positioning that all major corporations have recognised they need to develop to sustain their ongoing success and growth.

📖 REFERENCES

Berle, A.A., & Means, G.C. (1968) *The Modern Corporation and Private Property*. New York: Harcourt Brace.

Bowen, R.H. (1953) *Social Responsibilities of the Businessman*. New York: Harper.

Carroll, A.B. (1999) Corporate social responsibility. *Business & Society, 38*(3), 268–95.

Carson, R., (1962) *Silent Spring*. Boston: Houghton Mifflin.

Chua, A. (2004) *World on Fire*. London: Arrow Books.

Coleman, J.S. (1990) *Foundations of Social Theory*. Cambridge, MA: Harvard University Press.

Commission of the European Communities (2001) *Promoting a European Framework for CSR*. Brussels: CEC.

Drucker, P. (1946) *The Concept of the Corporation*. New York: Mentor.

Freidman, M. (1970) The social responsibility of business is to increase its profits. *New York Times Magazine*, 13th September 1970, pp 32–3, 122, 124, 126.

Fukuyama, F. (1995) *Trust: The Social Virtues and the Creation of Prosperity*. London: Hamish Hamilton.

(Continued)

(Continued)

Fukuyama, F., (1999) *The Great Disruption*. London: Profile Books.

Henderson, D. (2001) *Misguided Virtue*. London: IEA.

Jacobs, J. (1992) *The Death and Life of Great American Cities*. New York: Vintage.

Kempner, T., Macmillan, K., & Hawkins, K. (1974) *Business and Society*. Harmondsworth: Penguin.

Kline, J. (2005) *Ethics for International Business*. London: Routledge.

Kuznetsov, A., Kuznetsova, O., & Warren, R. (2009) CSR and the legitimacy of business in transition economies: The case of Russia. *Scandinavian Journal of Management, 25*(1), 37–45.

Porritt, J. (2005) *Capitalism: As If the World Matters*. London: Earthscan.

Putnam, R. (1993) *Making Democracy Work: Civic Traditions in Modern Italy*. Princeton, NJ: Princeton University Press.

Putnam, R. (2000) *Bowling Alone: The Collapse and Revival of American Community*. New York: Simon and Schuster.

Ruskin, J. (1860) *Unto This Last*. London: Dent.

Silberhorn, D., & Warren R. (2007) Defining corporate social responsibility: A view from big companies in Germany and the UK. *European Business Review, 19*(5), 352–72.

Sternberg, E. (1994) *Just Business: Business Ethics in Action*. London: Little Brown.

Vogel, D. (2005) *The market for virtue*. Washington, DC: Brookings Institution.

Warren, R. (2000) *Corporate Governance and Accountability*. Bromborough: Liverpool Academic Press.

World Commission on Environment and Development (1987) *Our Common Future*. Oxford: Oxford University Press.

Zadek, S. (2001) *The Civil Corporation*. London: Earthscan.

Public Relations and the Law: Managing Your Way through the Maelstrom of Potential Legal Pitfalls

18

Ann Rodriguez

Key Themes

- Reviewing the history of interaction between public relations and the law
- Introducing new avenues of interaction between the two professions
- Understanding the key areas where public relations activities come into contact with legal public relations principles
- Determining the key choices public relations practitioners must make to successfully navigate the pitfalls associated with the intersection of public relations and the law
- Understanding the long-term implications of those choices
- Evaluating the success or failure of the interaction of public relations and the law, given various factual scenarios

---

INTRODUCTION

While it may be hard for most to comprehend just how intricate a relationship holds between public relations and the law, it is vitally important that public relations managers gain an understanding of how and why they and their clients might run afoul of the law. Public relations practitioners must be aware that there are many points at which the law and public relations intersect, and therefore many opportunities for costly errors, both financially and in terms of adverse publicity.

Under the area of law called conspiracy, public relations practitioners need to be know that they can be held legally liable for providing advice or implied support for any sort of illegal activity of an employer, or even a client. A public relations practitioner could be named as a co-conspirator with others if he/she aided in illegal activity, whether knowingly or not, covered up such activity, counseled another to engage in such activity, or cooperated in any other way to further an illegal action. Additionally, public relations practitioners cannot count on a veil of protection because they have simply created and distributed materials under the direction of and on behalf of clients. Courts have ruled against public relations firms in just such a situation on more than one occasion and have insisted on the legal responsibility of practicing due diligence with regard to the type of information and documentation supplied by the client (e.g. Guth, 2009; Wilcox et al., 2003).

In today's litigious environment, almost everything organizations do is under intense public scrutiny. Public relations practitioners are often thrust into the limelight when their organizations' actions face legal challenges. It is imperative that they have a keen understanding of the laws governing what they may or must say or do in a variety of situations. And yet, at least one study has suggested that many public relations practitioners have no real grasp of such relevant laws and regulations. More than half of the practitioners surveyed indicated that they had no familiarity with Securities and Exchange Commission (SEC) regulations, 45% were not familiar with laws governing financial public relations, and 40% were not familiar with laws pertaining to commercial speech (Fitzpatrick, 1996).

HISTORY OF INTERACTION BETWEEN PUBLIC RELATIONS AND THE LAW

Early interactions between public relations and the law generally consisted of charges of defamation, invasion of privacy, and violations of copyright and trademark laws. Defamation charges stem from the freedoms guaranteed by the First Amendment to the US Constitution and account for a large number of lawsuits involving public relations practitioners both historically and still today. The legal debate over an individual's right to privacy is complicated and forever evolving through the work of the judiciary. And while the US Constitution does not specifically mention such a right, it has been judicially crafted over the years and is often referred to as a modern communication tort (civil wrong) (Parkinson & Parkinson, 2006). Copyright and trademark protections are also rooted in the US Constitution, Article I, and in general protect against the unlawful use of an individual's or organization's intellectual property.

Some early and seminal defamation cases include *New York Times Co. v. Sullivan* (1964), *Curtis Publishing Co. v. Butts* (1967), *Gertz v. Robert Welch, Inc.* (1974) and *Hutchinson v. Public Proxmire* (1979), all of which helped to define the rules in place today regarding who can successfully be sued for defamation and for what types of communications. The cases and their progeny have further defined a judicial standard of review and therefore help public relations practitioners today to understand how particular communications will be classified and judged if those communications should lead to litigation.

Early and continuing privacy cases, including *Roberson* v. *Rochester Folding Box Co.* (1902), *Melvin* v. *Reid* (1931), *Virgil* v. *Time, Inc.* (1976), *Onassis* v. *Christian Dior – New York, Inc.* (1984) and *Cinel* v. *Connick* (1994), helped develop privacy law, especially with regard to what type of communication would constitute a violation, how that would have to be published, and what harm must come from that publication. As mentioned earlier, this area of law, particularly involving public relations practitioners, given their various publicity roles and responsibilities, is still evolving in many ways.

Judicial decisions involving copyright and trademark law, including *Burrow-Giles Lithographic Co.* v. *Sarony* (1884), *Morrissey* v. *Proctor & Gamble Co.* (1967), *Apple Computer, Inc.* v. *Franklin Computer Corp.* (1983) and *Feist* v. *Rural Telephone Service Co., Inc.* (1991), have operated in concert with several significant statutory modifications of US copyright law to further define which created works merit copyright protection and which organizational marks can be legally protected to the benefit of the organizations that own them. Of particular importance to public relations managers should be an understanding of such laws to best protect the economic interests of their employers and clients.

MORE RECENT DEVELOPMENTS

In recent years, significant technological advances have encouraged a change in the way that the mass media, and therefore public relations managers, have come to deal with legal issues of great interest to a variety of publics. In particular, the immediacy and authenticity provided by television cameras in the courtroom give various interested publics a new and unique perspective on a plethora of high-profile legal cases. Their presence, therefore, can and does impact the public relations efforts of both sides involved in the litigation and, at a minimum, needs to be well-planned for and managed. Further, both sides should decide how to capitalize on the presence of cameras and indeed control for beneficial use as the trial progresses.

Additionally, the now widespread use of the internet offers public relations managers interesting opportunities while it poses potential problems when trying to keep a handle on the legal effects of such unfettered communication possibilities. Finally, an entire new area of public relations and the law has emerged as the value, and indeed necessity, of public relations is further appreciated by the legal community. Litigation public relations, as it has come to be known, provides fertile ground for public relations managers to interact with lawyers, help them to best frame their cases in the media and ultimately to persuade public opinion in their favor with the hope of affecting positively the outcome of their case. We will look at each new development individually.

Cameras in the Courtroom

While it feels commonplace in today's society to turn on CNN or truTV (formerly CourtTV) and be able to watch so-called gavel-to-gavel coverage of a trial, that has certainly not always been the case. In fact, after a brief period of fair judiciary acceptance, we have seen judges less willing to accommodate such electronic coverage requests since the circus-like atmosphere that surrounded the OJ Simpson trial in 1995.

The US Supreme Court first considered the idea that cameras in the courtroom might deprive a criminal defendant of his due process protections under the Fourteenth Amendment to the Constitution in the 1965 case of *Estes* v. *Texas* (1965). In that case, the trial had been moved to a new venue because of the notoriety created by massive pre-trial publicity. The defendant asked that the judge ban radio transmitters and television cameras from the courtroom. The judge refused the ban, the defendant was found guilty, and appealed based on the fact that he did not receive a fair trial because of the presence and disruptive nature of the recording equipment in the courtroom. Ultimately, the Supreme Court decided that the defendant indeed did not receive a fair trial because the recording equipment in the courtroom created a distraction and potentially led to altered testimony, destruction to the defendant's reputation, sensationalism for financial gain and the swaying of public opinion.

Interestingly, the Supreme Court seemed to change its mind when it decided the 1981 case of *Chandler* v. *Florida* (1981), because it could find no evidence that the presence of cameras had hampered the defendant's case or deprived him of an impartial jury. The state of Florida had, however, limited the broadcast coverage of the trial, which the Court approved of. The Supreme Court recognized that under the concept of federalism, it has no supervisory authority over state courts and therefore limited its ruling to the finding that the Constitution does not prohibit a state from allowing cameras in the courtroom as it sees fit. As a result, a number of states have experimented with allowing such courtroom access, while others have chosen not to.

The implication for public relations managers, especially those working with a party to the case, is that a great deal of planning needs to go into decisions regarding how best to control and/or manage how the media portrays the events of the trial. So, for instance, if cameras were allowed in a case in which you were involved, you should counsel your attorneys even more stringently on courtroom behavior, dress, and demeanor than you would if just the courtroom onlookers were viewing the trial. Further, it is imperative that you find a way to get your trial team heard in front of the media early and often, as the public tends to inherently side with the prosecution unless well-persuaded otherwise, especially during the other side's presentation of evidence and witnesses. This type of proactive damage control could in fact have quite a positive impact at verdict should it be managed appropriately.

The Internet

The extraordinary and rapid pace at which the internet has entered the process and now dominates human communication in general and the public relations profession in particular has created a variety of legal issues about which the public relations manager needs be keenly aware. The internet is demanding new regulation in the areas of copyright, defamation and privacy especially, though the law is notoriously slow to respond to such demand. Therefore, it can be confusing for a public relations manager to anticipate and plan for such potential problems. And potential problems abound as public relations practitioners take more and more advantage of the ability to speak directly with stakeholders through this immediate and compelling channel of communication.

Public relations practitioners are using the internet to send and receive a variety of messages about their clients and to receive and evaluate valuable stakeholder feedback in a timely, almost immediate, manner. Even though these messages are conveniently available via the internet, most are still copyright-protected and therefore public relations professionals should be quite cautious about how and when they use them. While the primary concern with copyright is unauthorized reproduction, the unfettered access to information that the internet provides creates new concerns regarding displaying copyrighted material in multiple locations and digital transmissions of copyrighted work. The public relations implications are many, but a public relations manager can best prepare for potential problems by planning to create and control the electronic dissemination of client materials as best he/she can, and to counsel clients to take great care when creating websites and using them for the valuable two-way discourse with publics.

Though the law is still evolving in the areas of defamation, the internet and responsibility for libelous communications online, public relations managers need to be aware that, in general, public relations practitioners will be held liable for defamation should they use the internet for the troubled communication, since the practitioner controls the message sent. In this instance, the public relations manager is functioning as publisher and therefore responsible for the veracity and lawful nature of the organization's communications.

Issues of privacy and the internet ought to be of even greater concern to public relations managers as they plan both the substance of their communications and the methods of dissemination. In terms of substance, public relations managers need to make sure that, especially when using photographs or any arguably personal information, they obtain the appropriate explicit (written) consent. That consent should clearly address the unique issues of the internet, for instance, multiple display points, digital downloads and reproduction with or without the use of desktop publishing enhancements.

The dissemination issue is of particular concern to public relations managers when they decide to utilize e-mail or any other interactive feature of the internet as a medium for their messages, paying special attention to the protection of the personal information of their publics. Because internet communications can easily be traced and authors identified by a variety of unscrupulous users, stakeholders have a strong desire to have personal information protected, especially as the internet provides greater avenues for unwelcomed intrusions. So, the important managerial decisions implicated involve weighing the vast benefits the internet provides in terms of reaching publics and building and maintaining important relationships through increased communication opportunities, against the numerous ways in which stakeholders can feel intruded upon, even violated, as a result of those very communications.

Additionally, in the legal communications wars, many advocates have quickly learned the public relations value of the internet and particularly the use of search engine optimization (SEO), ensuring that search engines such as Google, Yahoo! and MSN find organizations early and often in the litigation process. That ability to communicate widely and easily can impact significantly the case and trial as it progresses through the legal system, so SEO becomes an indispensable weapon in that communications effort. Online sources gain instant credibility, often simply by existing. As a result, the internet has essentially begun to favor the side that is pursuing an aggressive SEO strategy.

Litigation Public Relations

Litigation public relations, or litigation communications as it is sometimes known, is the management of the communication process during the course of any legal dispute or actual trial, so as to positively affect the outcome and/or the reputation of the client at issue. Born in the early 1980s, it is quite a new practice as communication professions go. And while the media has for many years covered legal cases of particular interest, and certainly parties to such cases have informally attempted to influence public opinion in their favor, it is the formal practice and organized and strategic methodology of litigation public relations that best define it today and differentiate it as a discipline from the haphazard activities of the past.

Many observers believe that litigation public relations began during the now famous libel suit of William Westmoreland against CBS News. Essentially the trial was about allegations that CBS News, through a *60 Minutes* segment with Mike Wallace, stated that Westmoreland, while in charge of US forces in Vietnam, knowingly exaggerated enemy casualty numbers to convince both the Johnson administration and the American public that the US was winning the war. Westmoreland sued CBS for libel and a media circus ensued. John Scanlon, a well-known public relations practitioner in New York, masterfully managed the media coverage on CBS's behalf. Scanlon's efforts even caught the attention of the venerable *New York Times* (Haggerty, 2003). In an article in late 1984, the *Times* reported that Scanlon was 'fighting with the uncodified art of public relations' (Kaplan, 1984). It raised the question of the propriety of the use of public relations tactics during litigation, particularly as Scanlon was feeding the media much of the information that they were then reporting each day. However, the *Times* also interviewed two distinguished law professors about the practice and neither seemed to object to it. '[U]nless you get your side of the story communicated, people lose their faith in CBS News', said Harvard Law School professor Arthur Miller. 'Both sides are seeking a public opinion verdict as well as a jury verdict', stated Yale Law School professor Geoffrey Hazard (Haggerty, 2003: 11). Scanlon's tactics must have worked and indeed seemed to cement the practice of litigation public relations because Westmoreland dropped his $120 million libel suit against CBS News and settled the case with no real vindication and without receiving any money from CBS. The two sides issued a joint statement that read in part: '[we] now agree that the court of public opinion, rather than a court of law, is the appropriate forum for deciding who was right in this case' (Farber, 1985: 1).

While the Westmoreland case might have been the beginning of litigation public relations, there has been case after case over the years further defining and refining its role in the legal process. Today, it is expected that both sides, particularly in a high-profile case, will reach out to the media via a public relations representative on a daily basis. In fact, if one side did not do so, it might not be providing the best representation for its client.

Organizations should always consider whether and how relationships with their publics would be affected should they find themselves embroiled in any sort of legal public problem. The mere fact that the organization has been implicated in some sort of questionable activity, sometimes even after it has been completely exonerated, often means that the organization is found to be less credible and trustworthy by its publics. It is therefore important that a public relations manager understand the need for early and strategic public relations activity working hand-in-hand with the legal strategy, so as to minimize as much as possible any of that potential negative press or publicity. Though not a typical business case, an interesting example of this lies in the Duke University Blue Devil lacrosse team and the false allegations of rape against it in 2006.

Initially, while the team members implicated denied any wrongdoing, the University and the city of Durham (which houses it) waged a campaign of harassment, imposed discipline and issued statements, all of which signaled the players' guilt. Even the district attorney got involved and made inflammatory pretrial statements to the media immediately following the rape allegations. These statements were so ethically questionable that they helped bring about the district attorney's disbarment a year later. When it was finally determined that the team members were in fact not guilty of the crime of which they had been accused, the damage to the team's reputation had already been done. And, as it turned out, one of the first things they did after filing a civil suit against the University and the city of Durham, was to hire a well-known public relations firm not just to handle media enquiries, but to put together a full-scale public relations program designed to provide up-to-date information about the lawsuit, providing commentary aimed directly at discrediting the defense and swaying public opinion back toward the team members allegedly wronged, through the use of public press conferences, media releases and most importantly, a website.

While some criticized such a move as prejudicial to a possible jury pool, legal commentators noted that the information only prejudices a jury if it is untrue (Khan, 2008). The team utilized litigation public relations late in the process, but at a time arguably most beneficial for its own legal goals.

Of course corporations have also realized the benefits of litigation public relations, especially when litigation attracts extensive media coverage. Microsoft and its chairman, Bill Gates, not only hired a number of lawyers to battle the US Department of Justice when faced with monopoly and antitrust charges, but also hired public relations firms to present the company's case to the public. Experts say that good public relations is necessary because studies show that nearly one-third of the public believes an organization is automatically guilty after being accused of wrongdoing (Wilcox et al., 2003).

While the previous examples represent cases with a high public profile and intense media attention, it is important for public relations managers to realize that litigation public relations is not all about press conferences on the courthouse steps and evening summaries of court proceedings on late-night TV talk shows. The fact is that most cases settle before they ever reach the courtroom (Dessem, 2001). Therefore, litigation public relations most commonly takes place early in the legal process, often becoming most effective if it can, in fact, get the matter settled before a case is even filed. Often this happens as a result of a public relations manager planning a strategic appeal to the reputation protection of the other side; the mere suggestion that the media might be interested in the dispute may very well lead an unwilling foe to negotiate an amicable end to the issue at hand.

Once a case has been filed, however, why can't the lawyers simply handle the media involvement in their case themselves? Simply, because communication is not the lawyers' expertise, the law is. The lawyers should concern themselves with legal strategy and utilize communication professionals, those trained in public relations strategy, to handle the media relations and public attitudes toward the case. Public relations managers should be able to intelligently explain to lawyers the value of the service they provide with respect to litigation public relations and how vitally important a part of the overall trial strategy that communications messages, crafted the right way, disseminated through the right media, and aimed at the right publics can be. Only public relations professionals can provide that type of valuable service during a given legal dispute.

Finally, it is important for public relations managers to realize that litigation public relations is not the same as crisis communication. Crisis communication is about immediate response in an attempt to limit the damage to a client's reputation from a media story or event regarding some negative incident or event. In contrast, litigation public relations is much less time-restrained, often taking place over months and years, rather than days. In fact, part of the managerial challenge with litigation public relations is to put together such an often long-term strategy with various goals in mind at key points as the trial develops. Litigation public relations is also less event-driven in that big media events are less effective, especially given the time frame discussed above. Additionally, with litigation public relations the issues are often much more complex than with traditional public relations activities, even those associated with crisis communications. For public relations managers, the process of whittling down the complex issues into manageable and interesting pieces of information for reporters is often quite a challenging endeavor. And finally, in most crisis communications situations a high-ranking official from the client organization is called upon to address key publics, but with litigation public relations the client is not always the best choice to speak regarding trial issues – the public wants to hear from the 'experts', who usually are the attorneys themselves. The public relations function plays out behind the scenes as those same attorneys are counseled in what, how and when to say what they must.

KEY AREAS OF INTERACTION

There are seven key areas of interaction between public relations and the law where problems are likely to occur. Public relations managers with the most knowledge not only of the individual areas of law, but also of where public relations activities are most likely to intersect with legal principles such that a problem could occur, will be the best prepared to plan for such contention and address any real legal problems in as proactive a manner as possible. Let us look at these seven key areas one by one.

Defamation

Defamation is any false statement that creates public hatred, contempt, ridicule or inflicts injury on reputation (Guth & Marsh, 2009; Parkinson & Parkinson, 2006; Wilcox et al., 2003; Lattimore, Baskin, Heiman, & Toth, 2009). It takes the form of either slander or libel. We define the defamatory statement as slander if it was spoken, and as libel if it was written. For a party to successfully sue your client organization for defamation, he or she would have to prove all four elements that define a defamatory action. The first element is communication or publication – the statement must have been communicated to a third party. Second, the statement must clearly identify whom the speaker is talking about, called identification. Third, the statement must have defamed the party bringing the case (called the plaintiff), which means it must have caused some sort of injury. The injury is usually to the plaintiff's reputation, and most often the plaintiff must also show that the damage caused to his or her reputation is compensable or financially measurable. The fourth element needed to prove a defamation case is fault. Often referred to as intent, the plaintiff must prove that the one making the defamatory statement did so with one of two levels of intent, negligence or actual malice.

Negligence means not being as careful as one should be. Actual malice is a legal standard first outlined in the pivotal case of *New York Times Co.* v. *Sullivan* (1964). It provides that a particular party suing for defamation may not prevail unless he or she proves that the statement was made 'with knowledge that it was false or with reckless disregard of whether it was false or not' (*New York Times Co.* v. *Sullivan*, 1964: 279–80). The primary element that a public relations manager should concern himself or herself with is the last one, intent. For most individuals to win a defamation case, they need only prove intent as negligence. However, if the plaintiff in question can be classified as a 'public figure', then he or she must prove intent as actual malice. A public figure is defined as any public official or 'person who voluntarily puts him or herself in the public interest' (Parkinson & Parkinson, 2006: 269). Actual malice is a much harder burden to meet and therefore cases brought by public figures are generally less successful.

From a public relations management standpoint, areas with activities that could result in a defamation suit against your client organization are all external and internal communications such as news releases, press conferences, newsletters and feature stories. Other areas of concern include active involvement in matters of public controversy and kindred integrated marketing communications activities such as advertising and sales promotions. The best way for a public relations manager to take precautions against his/her organization becoming a defendant in a defamation suit is to disseminate only honest and accurate information, to use delicate language concerning oneself with political correctness, to avoid comments about competitors altogether, and to use 'puffery' (claims that express subjective rather than objective views, understood not to be taken as measureable truth) rather than specific and measurable claims.

Organizations will sometimes find themselves in the position of plaintiff, suing another for defamation against them. In this situation, generally the organization is treated as a private citizen and therefore need only prove intent as negligence. However, organizations can be considered public figures, particularly if they have involved themselves in matters of public controversy and utilized their heightened access to the media to respond to some issue or charge, or if the defamatory statement comes from public relations/advertising activities communicated to the public for commercial purposes.

The last important thing for public relations managers to know about defamation is that there exist two primary and important defenses. One is truth. Truth is an absolute defense, it always wins. So, if the allegedly defamatory statement can be proven to be true by the defendant, the case is over. Another defense exists called 'fair comment', which states that if the allegedly defamatory statement was 'a subject of legitimate public interest' (Pember, 2002: 227), then the odds are that a judge would rule in favor of the defendant, as public policy dictates that as a society we want to encourage public discourse regarding issues of public concern – the democratic ideal of seeking public consensus.

Copyright and Trademarks

Article I of the US Constitution grants Congress the power to promote science and the arts by giving authors and inventors exclusive rights to their writings and discoveries. Copyright protection is given to authors and patent protection is given to inventors. Collectively, patents, copyrights and trademarks are called 'intellectual property' (Parkinson & Parkinson, 2006). As property, copyrights may be bought and sold with valid permission, just as any other form of property.

Copyright law serves as protection of a created work from unauthorized use. To create such protection, several key elements must be met: the work must be original (intellectually creative) and fixed in a tangible medium of expression (permanent or stable medium, including but not limited to, writing, painting, photography, magnetic recording or any other tangible medium later developed) (Parkinson & Parkinson, 2006). Copyright law does not cover ideas, facts or pure information, but instead covers the unique way that information is expressed. Copyright protection extends from the moment of creation in a fixed medium. It does not require notice or registration; however, to successfully pursue an action for infringement, one does need to meet both notice and registration requirements. Most copyrights established today are valid for the life of the author of the copyrighted material plus 75 years. It is important to note that simply purchasing a work does not give the new owner a copyright in the work. The copyright must be sold separately. Therefore, buying an original Mark Twain manuscript, for instance, does not give the purchaser the right to copy or to publish that manuscript (*Chamberlain* v. *Feldman*, 1949).

To sue successfully for copyright infringement, one must show that a valid copyright exists, that one actually owns the copyright, and that the person being sued reproduced, distributed, displayed or manipulated the copyrighted work so as to create a violation. To prove the violation is relatively simple; one must show that the person had access to the original work and that the person produced something that is substantially similar (*Ferguson* v. *National Broadcasting Co.*, 1978). Additionally, intent is not required, so that one could be sued for copyright infringement if he/she profited from another person's misuse of copyrighted material. Called 'vicarious infringement', this applies when owners of media outlets hire others who use copyrighted material inappropriately. And, while it may seem that internet service providers (ISPs) would be in danger of such litigation, they are actually exempt because, while they may charge for their services, courts have ruled that they are merely charging for the use of their system, not for the transmission of specific images, much the same as all common carriers (Parkinson & Parkinson, 2006).

PR PRACTITIONERS AND THE WORK FOR HIRE DOCTRINE

What is 'work for hire' and why should a public relations practitioner care? Simple. Public relations people should always know when what they are concepting, creating and presenting constitutes their own intellectual property or is owned by the client for which they are working at the time of creation, therefore, the public relations professional creator cannot copyright the work nor can he/she benefit from a sale of the copyright.

The law is as follows. Anything produced by an employee while working within the scope of his/her employment is a work for hire. The US Supreme Court has ruled that an employee is anyone acting within the scope of his/her employment who is doing the normal work of his/her job while under the supervision and control of an employer. Specifically, the courts look at three factors to determine if a person is an employee: first, an agreement for payment; second, the employer's right to assign tasks to and control the work of an employee; and third, the employer's right to set working hours. Independent contractors who are not employees tend to own their own tools, set their own hours, and are free to hire assistants. The Supreme Court's definition of employee would cover most public relations and advertising practitioners.

In practical terms, independent public relations or advertising professionals may not be employees. However, they still may produce work for hire. Such contract work produced by an independent contractor is work for hire only if the work was done under a written contract and if it also fits in one of the following ten specific categories:

- Contributions to collected works
- Parts of motion pictures or audiovisual productions
- Translations
- Supplementary works like forewords, illustrations, and prefaces
- Compilations of other works
- Instructional texts
- Tests

(Continued)

(Continued)

- Answers to tests
- Atlases
- Sound recordings

If there is no written contract or if the work does not fit in one of these specific ten categories, the work is not work for hire. The status of work by independent public relations or advertising professionals depends entirely on the existence of a written contract and the type of work being done. Interestingly, news releases have been held to not be work for hire, but many other types of public relations communications might be considered so.

In fact, Kaufman (2009) indicates that questions regarding ownership of copyrightable public relations material can particularly arise when considering fairly creative work such as logo or website designs. Her advice? Draw up specific contracts with a limit on the transfer of ownership to only one specific design chosen by a client so as to protect other concepts presented but discarded by the client. This further allows the public relations professional to retain ownership of these ideas for potential use with future clients as well.

There are defenses to copyright infringement actions. The most common of these is fair use. Others include parody, satire and news. There are four criteria generally used to determine what is and is not fair use: the purpose and character of the use; the nature of the copyrighted work; the public portion of the work copied/used; and the economic impact of that use. All four will be considered in unison by a court to justify use of the copyrighted work. When courts consider the purpose of a work and the economic impact of the use, they are looking at motives – was the copyrighted material taken to gain profit? If so, it is not a fair use. However, generally if the motive is educational, criticism, or involves news reporting, then it is a fair use. When considering nature of the work, courts will often allow copying of reference materials, databases and directories as fair use because these are more works of diligence than creativity (Parkinson & Parkinson, 2006). With regard to proportion, courts consider both the quantity and the quality taken – what may not be taken is the most 'valuable portion' or 'heart' of the work, that which makes it memorable (*Williams & Wilkins* v. *United States*, 1973).

A trademark is a word, symbol or slogan, used singly or in combination, that identifies a product's origin – the Nike 'swoosh', the McDonald's golden arches, the white-script 'Coca-Cola' against the red background. While also considered intellectual property, trademarks are different from copyrights in that they are primarily regulated by state law, not federal, and one cannot sell a trademark without it significantly affecting the product or service to which it is attached. Also, the ability to legally protect a trademark only attaches if the trademark is registered with the US Patent and Trademark Office, if the trademark is used by the owning organization, and if there has been some establishment of an association between the mark and a particular product or service (*Thrifty Rent-A-Car System* v. *Thrift Cars, Inc.*, 1987).

In general, a trademark registration must be renewed every 10 years to avoid abandonment of the trademark, making it available for use by another. However, some trademarks may not be registered. If the mark is already in use by another product or company, or if the mark proposed is so similar to an existing mark that confusion in consumers' minds would necessarily result (called antidilution), then registration cannot occur. Additionally, if the mark is merely a descriptive term, like 'parking lot' or 'safari', a geographic description, a surname or is obscene in some way, it cannot be registered. Courts will look at a variety of issues when determining trademark infringement, including similarity of the marks, similarity of the product categories, strength of the existing mark and actual consumer confusion. It is also important for organizations to actively protect their trademarks so as not to risk abandonment. Companies accomplish this by discouraging generic use of the mark (consumers' use of 'Kleenex' to mean facial tissues or 'Xerox' to mean photocopy), by publicity of ownership of the mark, use of the mark in all public relations and advertising activities, and actively searching for instances of infringement and protesting such.

'Privacy' Torts

A tort is essentially a civil wrong, as opposed to a criminal wrong. There are four so-called privacy torts at issue when public relations activities and the law collide: publication of private facts, false light, appropriation, and intrusion. Public relations managers need to be educated in the area of privacy torts because most public relations plans at some point will involve the dissemination of information about people, well known or not, and the make-up and presentation of such information could lead to legal troubles if not be handled appropriately.

Publication of Private Facts

In a civil action against a defendant for publication of private facts, it is alleged that the defendant revealed a private fact about the plaintiff, a fact which a reasonable person would have kept private, which the plaintiff actually did keep private, and which is not newsworthy. For a plaintiff to win such a case, he or she must also prove that the private fact was about the plaintiff, was a fact that would be highly offensive to a reasonable person, and was intentionally communicated or published to a large group by the defendant. Private facts cases turn often on issues of newsworthiness, which is not always clearly defined. In general, however, courts look for matters of legitimate public interest and do not encourage 'prying into private lives for its own sake' (*Virgil* v. *Time, Inc.*, 1975: 1129), but will consider newsworthy most instances of public interest such as would be covered by a local press organization.

Also of interest to public relations managers should be the publication element – any plaintiff suing an organization for publication of private facts need only show that some medium of mass communication released or broadcast the information to meet the communication element, which is a fairly easy threshold to reach. The best way for any public relations manager to avoid such suits is to make sure proper consent is acquired. The best form of consent is express consent where the plaintiff gives consent for information to be used for a specific purpose and in a specific medium. Even then, the consent is limited by its specific terms and public relations practitioners should not then use that same information in any other manner without securing express consent for the next purpose. Implied consent can also be argued by a defendant organization in such a suit, where the plaintiff participated in 'conduct which is reasonably understood by another to be intended as consent' (*McCabe* v. *Village Voice, Inc.*, 1982: 529). Issues leading to private facts suits most often occur for public relations managers in publicity activities, especially when employee information is utilized. The lesson here is *always* to obtain consent!

False Light

Cases involving false light deal primarily with the use of a photograph taken in one situation to illustrate another situation or where the individuals in a photograph are inaccurately identified. False light is intended to protect the plaintiff from emotional distress or mental anguish. To win a false light lawsuit, a plaintiff need only prove that a false impression of the plaintiff was created, that it was presented to the public by the defendant with malice or reckless disregard for the truth, and that the false impression would offend a reasonable person (Parkinson & Parkinson, 2006). Public relations managers will come into contact with potential false light actions through publicity materials, internal newsletters and annual reports. While there are a variety of ways to defend such suits, as with private facts cases, the best way is via consent. However, an organization could also win by showing of an absence of malice (no intent to harm), truth, and sometimes fair comment.

Appropriation

The tort of appropriation protects against improper use of one's name or likeness by others. Sometimes referred to as the 'right of publicity', that is really a misnomer as it does not guarantee anyone the right to secure news coverage/publicity or other public relations attention. What it does is essentially prevent the use of names or likenesses for commercial purposes without consent. Unlike the aforementioned privacy torts, with appropriation, intent is generally assumed, so a plaintiff need only prove the use of his or her likeness without consent, from which the defendant benefited financially.

From a public relations standpoint, appropriation will be implicated particularly in public relations or advertising campaign materials. Cases tend to turn on whether the plaintiff can easily be identified by the general public and whether or not some financial benefit was gained by the defendant. With regard to identification, the plaintiff need not be well known and his or her 'likeness' might be from a voice, profile, or the use of lookalikes or soundalikes (quite often misused in publicity materials). Further, the financial benefit element need not be in the form of defendant profit, but could be the fact that the plaintiff's ability to profit from his/her own image has been diluted. A public relations manager embroiled in such a suit can defend his/her actions by arguing incidental use – small or trivial use neither valuable to the medium nor damaging to the plaintiff – or newsworthiness.

Intrusion

Actions for intrusion are based entirely on how information is gathered, not on the information itself nor how it is communicated. If a communications professional gathers information by intruding upon physical space where the plaintiff had a reasonable expectation of privacy or by obtaining information that the plaintiff reasonably expected was private, that is intrusion. While public relations managers need rarely concern themselves with this particular privacy tort, it is interesting to note that if not the law, then ethics dictate that public relations managers be keenly aware of who they are employing and what those people are up to. The Public Relations Society of America Code of Ethics should guide such activity, but where that fails, the law may succeed.

Contract and Agency

Much of what we do as public relations managers involves the use of contracts – in fact, from the selling of our own services to the drafting of releases as discussed earlier, the practice of public relations revolves around contracts. Therefore, it is useful for public relations managers to at least have a basic understanding of the legal principles that guide contract law and how various public relations activities might be implicated. At a minimum, it is important to know when you are forming a contract and when to seek legal advice on drafting a contract or evaluating a contractual obligation.

A contract is a legally enforceable agreement between two or more people. The elements required to create a contract are a 'meeting of the minds' (parties consent to be bound by a specific agreement) and consideration (something of value given to the agreement by each party). That meeting of the minds is often defined as an offer by one party and an acceptance of that offer by the other party. Some contracts are implied by conduct, many are written down, but many are not. Yet all are enforceable forms of a contract. In a few specific situations, however, contracts cannot be enforced unless they are written down. This requirement is called the Statute of Frauds. And while the contracts covered under the Statute of Frauds vary from state to state, most contracts dealing with suretyship (contract to answer for another), the sale of land, performance of duties to take place more than 1 year later, the sale of goods more than $500, or executing the will or estate of one who has died fall under its guidelines (Parkinson & Parkinson, 2006). In general, for public relations managers, a good rule of thumb is always to reduce your contracts to writing. It simply protects both parties and encourages mutual understanding of the terms from the outset.

It is also useful for public relations managers to realize that some people cannot legally contract with them. Those under the age of 18 in particular can legally disaffirm any contract they enter into and therefore avoid its obligations. That means for public relations professionals that if a minor has signed a release, he/she could disaffirm that contract, even after having been paid to appear in a public service advertisement, for example, and then even sue for one of the privacy torts mentioned above if the advertisement ran anyway. Contracting with minors is a tricky area and public relations professionals should *always* be wary of such activity.

'Breach' is the legal term for one party not meeting his/her obligations under the terms of a contract. Most often the remedy for breach is some level of monetary award, but occasionally a court will order 'specific performance', which means that the breaching party must do whatever the contract originally called for – not compete as agreed, provide exclusive information, model or perform as agreed, etc. It is an uncommon remedy, but available should money not solve the problem that the breach created.

Another closely related area of the law that public relations managers should concern themselves with is agency. Agency law, and particularly employment law, deals with the responsibilities employers and employees owe to one another. While general employment law is always important for managers of any type to understand, it is the specific elements of employment law, that deal with human resource issues like termination and the creation of an agency relationship, that are of the utmost importance to the public relations manager.

Public relations practitioners deal directly with the clients who pay their employers. Under a principle called *respondeat superior*, the employers can be held liable for the public relations practitioners' misconduct and might be forced to honor their contractual agreements as well. And, since public relations firms are often quite visible, they have a greater potential than most businesses for being embroiled in a high-profile lawsuit, with potentially long-term damaging effects to their reputations. So it is critical that public relations managers know how to tell when their actions or the actions of their employees may create legal obligations for their firms or even their clients (Parkinson & Parkinson, 2006).

Most employees are employed 'at will', which means at the discretion of their employer, and therefore can be fired at will. The few exceptions deal with discriminatory practices and with situations where actual employment contracts exist. Employees may also be terminated for cause – business or economic reasons – or for 'just cause', which is misconduct or inadequate performance.

Employees are most often viewed by clients and customers as representing their employer. For the most part, public relations managers should expect that this will be the case with their employees and, in fact, they usually encourage their employees to cultivate relationships with clients on the organization's behalf. This status, however, has given rise to the set of laws described as agency law, which has evolved to cover all kinds of situations where one person acts as the agent or representative of a principal. The agent is obligated to act primarily for the benefit of the principal and, therefore, people doing business with the agent may legally assume that the principal will stand behind the actions and agreements of the agent. Particularly relevant to the practice of public relations, agents are often the only ones from a given public relations firm with whom the clients and other target public members will interact. Therefore, the agent not only speaks for the firm, but legally binds its obligations as well.

While the agent–principal relationship with regard to employees is easy to understand, it is significantly less clear how the agency relationship develops with regard to independent contractors. An independent contractor is someone who agrees by contract to do something for another, but is not generally controlled by that other person while he/she is engaged in fulfilling his/her end of the contract. In other words, an independent contractor is one who is not working on behalf of the principal. In the typical scenario, an independent contractor is not considered an agent of the principal. However, there are exceptions to this rule that could very well impact the legal responsibilities of public relations managers. These exceptions are when the principal has hired the independent contractor to perform inherently dangerous activities, or solely to escape legal duties imposed by the activities that the independent contractor is performing. In both cases, courts will find that an agency relationship exists and therefore hold the public principal responsible for the legal consequences of the agent's actions. Another issue to be aware of is that if the public relations organization has as its business form a partnership, then each partner is by definition an agent of the others. However, this ability to bind the partnership can be restricted by some form of limited liability partnership agreement.

When obligations arise for the principal via the agent, a court will force the principal to be responsible only if the agent was working within the scope of his or her agency. So, if a public relations practitioner detours from his or her agency and interacts with another while on this detour, then arguably the public relations organization would not be responsible for any legal liabilities incurred during that interaction. Further, the principal can always terminate the relationship with the agent and immediately stop the agent's ability to obligate the principal in any way.

Aside from obligations, the other concern for public relations organizations as principals should be the rights of third parties as against the principal for any actions of its agents. Here public relations managers need primarily be aware that any tort (civil wrong, as opposed to criminal wrong) committed by the agent becomes the liability of the principal. Therefore, any legal damages are the sole responsibility of the principal. This situation can arise in a variety of ways, including plant tours, open houses, press conferences, and any sort of promotional event, in addition to any number of individual acts of the agent.

Investor Relations

Because communication is so important in helping to determine the market price of securities, the areas of investor relations and financial reporting are two of the most lucrative areas of communications practice. They also have in recent years garnered significant public attention for the legal and ethical misconduct of practitioners.

Accurate information about securities has a profound impact on their value, but the delivery of such can be a daunting task. Public relations managers may be charged with the production of documents and other communications used to encourage stock purchases, to report the activities of the corporation, and to influence the elections that determine how publicly held organizations will be managed. Both state and federal laws regulate these communications activities. The SEC enforces those laws and regulations, requiring 'full and fair disclosure of the character of securities' (Lattimore et al., 2009), and attempts to help secure adequate publicity of those facts necessary for an interested investing public to make an informed decision regarding the honest investment potential of a given security at offering. The SEC requires submission of annual reports, quarterly reports and current reports, and often a public relations manager will be responsible for making sure that the final products speak with flair to a multiplicity of publics, including current stockholders, financial analysts, and potential investors. These publications have real strategic communications value in that they seek to cast the organization in the best light possible so as to maintain or increase support, both financial and otherwise, for the organization.

Some of the highest-profile legal problems associated with investor relations deal with insider trading claims. 'Insider trading' refers to the use of information only available to those inside an organization to guide purchasing or sale decisions about securities. It is not uncommon for public relations practitioners to have access to such inside information as a matter of course when preparing releases, reports, etc. The most important thing to remember as a public relations manager is to never make personal investment decisions based in any part on information gained through SEC reporting duties for a client. Martha Stewart certainly was made keenly aware of the impact of an insider trading scandal in 2004 as she not only spent time in jail for her actions, but her brand suffered greatly and to date has never quite regained the heights of the stellar reputation it once enjoyed. Though she continued throughout the ordeal to employ a positive public relations presence, she still suffered through terrible reputation damage, ultimately having her previously quite successful prime time television show moved and then cancelled, having two quite unflattering TV movies produced about her, being forced to remove herself from the boards of directors of several high-profile companies, including her own, Martha Stewart Living Omnimedia, and being forced by the SEC to comply with significantly elevated and harsh financial disclosure rules (Garrett, 2006).

PR PRACTITIONERS AND LAWYERS: WORKING TOGETHER FOR THE GOOD OF THE CLIENTS

The world of PR needs lawyers. PR practitioners may not relish the idea of attorneys, who in their minds only tell them what they cannot do, but with the variety of issues today which can create peril for client organizations, the PR folks need the lawyers, make no mistake.

Dealing with issues from product and safety recalls to organizational mergers and acquisitions, not to mention areas ripe for crisis communication, investor and community relations, PR practitioners need the guidance and expertise that lawyers bring. And, the wise practitioner realizes that a healthy and proactive approach to the often difficult partnership is the best way to protect, and indeed further, the client organization's best interests. However, the real challenge lies in the ability of the two very different perspectives to find common ground and learn to speak a common language.

Wilcox, Cameron, Ault and Agee (2003), citing an attorney and a PR professional, both from the same PR firm in California, compiled the following list illustrating the differences between the two perspectives:

(Continued)

(Continued)

What Attorneys Do that Drives PR Practitioners Crazy

- Focus almost exclusively on the inner workings of the trial, the judge and jury, forgetting about the outside world.
- Withhold information from the PR team.
- Use 'legalese' when speaking to the press and others as spokespersons.
- Take too long to review documents and forcing too many changes in the PRwork product.
- Attempt to restrain communications from the client organization such that too often important information cannot get out.

What PR Practitioners Do that Drives Attorneys Crazy

- Disclose too much information.
- Mistakenly cross boundaries of privileged information.
- Oversimplify.
- Overstate.
- Inadvertently impact litigation negatively by sharing inappropriate information.

So, given this great divide, how can a client organization hope to have valuable interaction between the two parties? While it is useful for an organization's PR and legal counselors to work together on a regular basis, developing and refining strategies to help avoid legal trouble, it is imperative that they do so when a legal case is pending. In this situation, the client organization would be wise to put together what one commentator has referred to as a core Legal Communications Team or LCT. Its purpose is to facilitate cooperation between the two differing groups, both with their own distinctive ways of analyzing issues and tactical approaches to problem solving.

Who should populate this Legal Communications Team? While it obviously depends somewhat on the size of the client organization, it always should consist of individuals who are committed to working across lines – organizational, philosophical and cultural – to ensure that both the legal components and the communications components are working in tandem. It also must have the support of upper-level management and a clear mandate from the very top of the client organization's management structure to support both legal and communication goals. Ideally, a LCT might include the following:

- The General Counsel or another corporate legal representative.
- Other corporate lawyers preferably with some understanding of and sensitivity to communications issues.
- The leader of the outside law firm's litigation team.
- At least one senior internal or external communications professional with an understanding of and sensitivity to legal issues.

Finally, it is important to keep it as small a group as possible so as to ensure that there are not too many differing views and that negotiation and compromise are kept paramount as the client organization's best interests are always at the forefront of planning and execution of the LCT's strategies.

(Continued)

> *(Continued)*
>
> PR Practitioners and Lawyers can get along and certainly must on occasion work together to successfully represent their client organizations. While different perspectives and priorities are certainly present, with good management both entities can learn to not only work well together, but to be proactive in their efforts such that the client organization can benefit in many and varied ways.
>
> *Sources:* Wilcox, D.L., Cameron, G.T., Ault, P.H. and Agee, W.K. (2005) *Public relations: Strategies and Tactics.* Seventh Ed. Boston, MA: Allyn and Bacon; James F. Haggerty, Esq. (2003) *In The Court Of Public Opinion*, Hoboken, NJ: Wiley & Sons, Inc.

Trial Strategies

It is incumbent upon public relations managers to know that, just because a legal dispute with which they have been recruited to help has finally gone to trial, the public relations role does not necessarily change. In fact, it is at this moment in the public relations management process that a manager ought to remind himself/herself that he/she must not sacrifice the strategic vision or course just because the case is now at trial and it may seem that the rules have changed. The scenery may have changed, but the rules and strategy have not. In fact, they cannot.

What is different is the feel, the sense of urgency, perhaps the media attention. Everything about the dispute, now a trial, is escalated, but it is of the utmost importance that the public relations manager remains consistent, clear and on track with the strategy already established. To change course at this juncture would be both foolhardy and potentially damaging to a client. After all, decisions made in haste or in times of crisis generally lack the strategic value and strength of wisdom that those made in calmer times possess.

What the public relations manager will need to do, however, is prepare for daily contact with the media, paying particular attention to how best to control the tone and direction of the messages. This becomes much more of a challenge as almost everywhere your client and legal team will go in and out of the courthouse will be monitored and manned by the media. Pay close attention to logistics; how will your client enter and exit the courthouse, what will your client's clothing say about the seriousness with which he/she is taking the case, does your client look or act guilty somehow, and finally, what will you prepare to say publicly each day, addressing all of the above and then some, and how will that message be presented to the media?

At least one commentator feels strongly that the typical courthouse steps press conference that gains so much media attention that it becomes a spectacle rather than a controlled medium through which your client's message gets heard, is *not* the answer (Haggerty, 2003). This is certainly what we see on television – programs like *Shark*, *Law & Order* and *CSI* all invariably have a courthouse steps press conference in each episode. But in the real world they can often do more harm than good. Many times that is because what is typically a quite controlled medium in a heated trial environment becomes uncontrolled – too many media personnel asking too many questions at once, often feeding off of one another and thereby sending the whole event spiraling toward a frenzied conclusion.

What the public relations manager ought to do instead is try to maintain one-on-one contact with key media representatives throughout the trial. This approach has a multitude of benefits, including a calm and controlled atmosphere and the ability to choose with whom to speak so as to best take advantage of the media relationships already cultivated and nurtured. Finally, if you must hold a press conference, consider moving it from the courthouse steps across the street to a park and set clear ground rules at the start as to length of time for questions, prepare a statement to be read first by your client or counsel, and then stick to those ground rules. It will make for a much more beneficial communications experience.

Control is the real key to the successful use of litigation public relations and the management of trial strategy. The public relations manager needs to understand what is happening at any given moment in the trial (motions, issues, judgments); coalesce and prioritize messages for the next moment, hour, or day; then prepare those messages, making sure that when the moment arrives to communicate them, he/she is fully and calmly prepared to do so. The public relations manager needs to formulate a communication strategy and then stick to it, even when the whirlwind of trial swirls worst; a multi-faceted strategy encompassing overall goals and effective methods to pursue those goals, all inextricably linked to the legal strategy and the case itself, particularly the milestones of the case, the points at which the media will be most interested and, therefore, demanding.

CHOICES

Public relations managers must make a myriad of choices daily, particularly when dealing with issues potentially involving the law or related legal problems. Some of those key choices include with whom to communicate, what to say and how to say it, and to what ends. Often, these choices are dictated in some measure by regulations put in place to protect individual freedoms of speech and press, or those intending to encourage a free market environment promoting healthy competition and natural price adjustments. Some of the regulatory bodies with which public relations managers ought to be familiar are the following:

The Federal Trade Commission (FTC) – governing all commercial advertising and product or service news releases, typical media used for many public relations activities. Essentially, this type of communication is illegal if it deceives or tends to mislead the public in any way. The FTC requires that unsubstantiated or false claims be stopped immediately, and some advertisers may also be required to run corrective advertising – an expensive and damaging punishment to any organization's communications reputation.

The Federal Communications Commission (FCC) – regulating all electronic media to ensure that licenses are operating in the public interest. FCC regulations are of particular concern to public relations managers working in the political field as they require that all candidates and issues have an equal opportunity to be heard. Further, the candidates and their parties are accountable for the content of their messages. Public relations managers should pay particular attention to political requirements and proscriptions by the FCC, especially as alternative forms of electronic media proliferate.

The Securities and Exchange Commission (SEC) – regulating the trading of stocks of publicly owned organizations. The SEC requires full and fair disclosure of the character of securities, and the prevention of fraud in the sale thereof. It also requires the submission of reports as discussed above, especially the annual report which has significant strategic value to a multiplicity of public relations publics. Public relations managers should also be aware of the Sarbanes-Oxley Act of 2002, passed partially in response to the Enron collapse, which requires public companies to be much more 'transparent' in their communications with key publics, including investors and employees. Public companies must now provide greater information about their officers, financial transactions and specific codes of ethics. Public relations managers are particularly affected as they are called upon to assist in strategically disclosing corporate decision-making to a vast number of important and influential publics.

Many other federal agencies have important oversight responsibilities when it comes to public relations communications, such as the Food and Drug Administration, Bureau of Alcohol, Tobacco and Firearms, United States Postal Service and National Labor Relations Board (Lattimore et al., 2009). Therefore, public relations managers should learn to anticipate how federal laws and regulations could be broken when an organization seeks to communicate with any and all of its publics, and then adjust public relations plans accordingly.

When public relations managers make the wrong choices, there are often dire and long-term consequences. The Enron example is a good one as it exemplifies how mistakes compound and become seemingly systemic, leading in this case to complete collapse. Enron was an energy company based in Houston, Texas. It was a well-respected and successful company by all accounts, especially its own, with claimed revenues of nearly $101 billion in 2000, until its bankruptcy in 2001. It was eventually revealed that Enron's reported financial condition was sustained by institutionalized, systematic and creatively planned accounting fraud. It has since become a popular symbol of willful corporate fraud and corruption. Enron grew wealthy due in large part to its marketing and promotional activity, which was almost exclusively misleading or simply untrue. As a result, not only did Enron itself go bankrupt, but also the well-established accounting firm of Arthur Andersen, representing Enron, was caused to dissolve, due in large part to the damage done to its reputation (Bryce, 2002).

APPLICATION OF THE C-MACIE MODEL TO PUBLIC RELATIONS IN LEGAL ENVIRONMENT ANALYSIS

By definition, the legal profession is concerned with fact-finding and information-gathering as the basis of presenting their cases to win in the courts of law and public opinion. The descriptions of the public relations managerial duties in this chapter illustrate that public relations practitioners and attorneys must work hand-in-glove in their respective environments, sharing information and determining what the best courses of action in the realms of public opinion and courts of law should be. Analysis in the legal world is certainly not confined to just the beginning stage of any case; it must be continually addressed and monitored as new information, including public perceptions, media coverage, and court proceedings, becomes available.

In addition to the courtroom environment, public relations managers should also be aware of their legal responsibilities in any area where fairness, accuracy, and truth are important. In essence, that is every area in public relations operates, from not-for-profit agencies to highly regulated industries. Public relations managers are charged with being aware of, complying with, and reminding and advising their organizations and senior executives of the laws and ethics of communication that must be followed and the consequences of their actions.

Strategy and Implications

There are numerous examples of public relations tactics in action with regard to legal issues – in some situations the interaction works well, in others it does not. It is often hard to predict what an outcome of such interaction will be, though if the public relations manager follows some key principles of public relations and maintains a clear understanding of the legal issues and implications as well, he/she can certainly anticipate success. How you might measure success is a different question. In one instance success might mean simply that a threatened lawsuit is never filed; in another, a problem with a company might go away because of a successful public relations strategy of negotiation coupled with a keen understanding of the other side's greatest concern, that of reputation maintenance. And the legal issues do not have to involve high-profile companies or well-known celebrities to warrant use of public relations tactics. Such was the case of a little boy who walked with a brace on his left leg. He was 5 years old and about to enter kindergarten and his brace was old and worn, needing desperately to be replaced. However, the boy's father had recently changed jobs and as such his new insurance company would not cover the cost of the brace.

The insurance company told the boy's parents to check back in six months when their coverage for 'special services' would begin. This upset the parents greatly, fearing that their son would have a hard time making friends and keeping up with them in kindergarten, with such a rickety leg brace. Their attorney told them that they could fight the insurance company through administrative appeals and the court system, but that even if they won it would take years. The attorney instead decided to call the insurance company's general counsel to discuss waiver and payment, but met with resistance when the general counsel stated that he did not feel that the situation called for an override of the rules. After a bit of an argument, the family's attorney told the insurance company's general counsel that the boy would start kindergarten the following Tuesday with a new leg brace paid for by the insurance company, or with his old rickety leg brace and a television news camera crew. The very next day the boy's mother got a call saying the insurance company had reconsidered the claim and a new brace would be delivered that afternoon. Such is the power of litigation public relations (Haggerty, 2003)!

Often, however, the outcome is not so successful. O.J. Simpson can attest to that. Even his vast celebrity status could not protect him from lingering doubt and absolute shunning by the commercial enterprises that had just shortly before his murder trial made him a celebrity spokesperson extraordinaire. All the spin, all the litigation public relations efforts, nothing could salvage Simpson's reputation, and his celebrity status went from that of a superstar professional athlete before the trial, to that of a bad boy criminal after. And while Simpson's legal team, themselves celebrity attorneys, tried every public relations tactic in the book before, during and after the trial, ultimately there was no way to salvage Simpson's reputation. And, though O.J. Simpson was found not guilty of murder, he was shortly thereafter found liable for the two deaths in a civil suit brought by the families of the victims. Today, nearly 15 years later, he finds himself once again behind bars, this time convicted of armed robbery, kidnapping and assault, a situation arguably caused by his own now infamous celebrity status.

The Simpson murder trial essentially ushered in the era of litigation public relations and heightened the debate surrounding cameras in the courtroom. The debate still rages today and litigation public relations has become entrenched as a vital part of the overall legal strategy of many counselors at law. The Simpson legacy is an important one, as much for its impact on public relations as its impact on the legal system.

Evaluation

So how does a public relations manager measure the success of his/her public relations strategy as it plays out in the legal arena? The answer really depends on what legal issues are implicated and how you have chosen to utilize public relations strategy to deal with those issues.

Preparation is paramount. A public relations manager ought to have an environmental scanning process in place that periodically allows for him/her to become readily aware of environmental factors that could cause legal issues in the future for his/her clients. At that point, the public relations manager can choose to be proactive, learning as much about the situation as possible and setting in place plans to deal with potential problems or avoid them altogether, or reactive, waiting until the problem has risen to the level of a crisis and then implementing a hopefully well-defined and well-thought-out crisis communication plan. Clearly, the proactive option is the better one and will almost certainly yield more positive results. However, environmental factors and organizational culture may simply dictate a wait-and-see strategy which can still be managed effectively by the well-prepared public relations manager.

The actual measurement of success or failure will necessarily be subjective. One way to measure it is to simply review the press that your client has received after your public relations efforts have concluded to see how much is positive and how much is negative, or perhaps merely how much the negative coverage has dwindled.

However the public relations manager chooses to measure the results of the public relations effort, the most important consideration ought to be what lessons can be learned from the situation and its outcome. The public relations manager should be most concerned with this because by evaluating and then applying lessons learned to the next public relations planning process, the true two-way communication model of public relations is implemented and the public relations process public is improved for the client in that either the legal problem is avoided altogether the next time or its effect on the client organization is lessened considerably.

So what constitutes success? For the most part, it is salvation of reputation. As for O.J. Simpson, he seemingly did not learn much from his murder trial and subsequent civil case. As mentioned above, he found himself once again behind bars for attempting in 2007 to steal some of his own sports memorabilia from a collector at a Las Vegas hotel (Cable News Network, 2008). Ironically, it seems as if his attempt to salvage his own memorabilia, and with it perhaps a glimmer of his football glory days, operated to instead bury his already tarnished reputation. No amount of public relations, it seemed, could salvage that reputation, if for no other reason than Simpson and his public relations partners had never been able to overcome the taint of the murder trial, and therefore the O.J. Simpson brand held very little commercial value, even before its death knell in 2008.

In contrast, Kobe Bryant, who faced sexual assault charges in 2003, managed over the course of five years to salvage and perhaps improve his reputation and therefore the commercial value of his brand. In 2003, the Los Angeles Lakers professional basketball team star had sex with a female hotel employee and was accused days later of sexually assaulting the 19-year-old woman. Bryant claimed that the sex was consensual, essentially admitting he was an adulterer at a press conference with his wife by his side, but denying that any sexual assault occurred. Almost immediately several big-name companies that had endorsement deals with Bryant dropped him, including McDonald's, Coca-Cola and Nutella. The losses to Bryant as a result amounted to between $4 and $6 million (Sports Illustrated, 2004). However, the accusation proved to be just that, as the alleged victim refused to testify and the charges were dropped in 2004. A civil suit was earlier initiated against Bryant, but that too was settled out of court with a hefty payment to Bryant's accuser and an apology by Bryant himself.

With the public relations efforts to repair his reputation in full swing, endorsement opportunities began to return – Nike and Upper Deck (trading cards), which had endorsement contracts in place with Bryant prior to the incident, began to run ads featuring him again in both print and TV campaigns (Salazar-Moreno, 2008). Sina.

com, a Chinese language portal used for blogging, signed a deal with Bryant in early 2008 and Coca-Cola returned to Bryant by offering him an agreement to endorse its Vitamin Water brand in late 2008 (Street & Smith's Sports Business Daily, 2009). So it would seem that while O.J. Simpson's reputation was irreparably harmed by his legal troubles, Kobe Bryant's run-in with the law was just a minor speed bump in the road to his building a commercially successful reputation brand.

Whether it is the salvation of your client's reputation that is on the line or simply attempts to avoid legal troubles for your client organization as a result of its public relations program efforts, a public relations manager will be best prepared to handle such situations if he/she is well trained in the intricacies of the law, especially as they apply in a variety of communication settings. Education and preparation are key for a public relations manager to understand how to plan for and implement strategic initiatives when his/her client organizations are faced with legal obstacles. Evaluation and integration of lessons learned into the public relations planning process after the legal issues have been resolved will dictate the level of success or failure the public relations manager ultimately achieves.

SUMMARY

Attorneys realize that the 'court of public opinion' is often as powerful as the 'court of law' in which they represent their clients. Attorneys also recognize that their expertise is the law, and so increasingly are hiring public relation practitioners to represent their clients in the court of public opinion. Because high-profile court cases garner prominent news coverage, public relations managers play an important role in managing the media covering the trials, giving rise to the emerging practice of litigation public relations.

The other arena in which public relations practitioners and attorneys work together is in any organization that must adhere to government regulation, policies, and laws. The emphasis here is again on partnership, as public relations practitioners have the same responsibilities for truthful, accurate, and transparent communication as the attorneys. Like all other organizational managers, public relations managers cannot claim ignorance of the law as a defense.

REFERENCES

Apple Computer, Inc. v. *Franklin Computer Corp.*, 714 F.2d 1240 (3rd Cir. 1983), cert. dismissed 464 U.S. 1033 (1984).

Bryce, R. (2002) *Pipe Dreams: Greed, Ego, and the Death of Enron.* New York: Public Affairs.

Burrow-Giles Lithographic Co. v. *Sarony*, 111 U.S. 53 (1884).

Cable News Network (2008, December 5) O.J. Simpson to serve at least nine years in prison. Retrieved March 11, 2009, from http://www.cnn.com/2008/CRIME/12/05/oj.simpson.sentencing/index.html

Chamberlain v. *Feldman*, 300 N.Y. 135, 89 N.E.2d 863 (Crt. App. N.Y. 1949).

(Continued)

(Continued)

Chandler v. *Florida*, 449 U.S. 560 (1981).

Cinel v. *Connick*, 15 F.3d 1338 (5th Cir. 1994).

Curtis Publishing Co. v. *Butts*, 388 U.S. 130 (1967).

Dessem, R.L. (2001) *Pretrial Litigation: Law, Policy & Practice*. St. Paul, MN: West Publishing.

estes v. texas, 381 U.S. 532 (1965)

Farber, M.A. (1985) Suit against CBS is being dropped by westmoreland. *New York Times*, February 18: 1.

Feist v. *Rural Telephone Service Co., Inc.*, 499 U.S. 349 (1991).

Ferguson v. *National Broadcasting Co.*, 584 F.2d 111 (5th Cir. 1978).

Fitzpatrick, K.R. (1996) Public relations and the law: A survey of practitioners. *Public Relations Review*, *22*(1), 1–8.

Garrett, A. (2006, August 7) Martha Stewart settles with SEC. Retrieved March 11, 2009, from http://internationalcorpgov.blogspot.com/2006/08/martha-stewart-settles-with-sec.html

Gertz v. *Robert Welch, Inc.*, 418 U.S. 323 (1974)

Guth, D.W., & Marsh, C. (2009) *Public Relations: A Values-driven Approach*, 4th ed. Boston: Allyn & Bacon.

Haggerty, J.F. (2003) *In the Court of Public Opinion: Winning Your Case with Public Relations*. Hoboken, NJ: Wiley.

Hutchinson v. *Proxmire*, 443 U.S. 111 (1979).

Kaplan, P.W. (1984) Public relations a facet of Westmoreland trial. *New York Times*, October 23: B5.

Kaufman, N.L. (2009) *Why 'guns for hire' should scrutinize 'work for hire' provisions*. www.wisecounselpress.com/articles/hired_gun.html, retrieved February 6, 2009.

Khan, N. (2008, March 14) Media again a player in lax case. Retrieved August 29, 2008, from http://www.public relationscg.com/pages/TheChronicleOnline031408.htm

Lattimore, D., Baskin, O., Heiman, S.T., & Toth, E.L. (2009) *Public Relations: The Profession and the Practice*, 3rd ed. New York: McGraw-Hill.

McCabe v. *Village Voice, Inc.*, 550 F.Supp. 525 (E.D. Pa. 1982).

Melvin v. *Reid*, 112 Cal.App. 285 (1931).

Morrissey v. *Proctor & Gamble Co.*, 379 F.2d 675 (1st Cir. 1967).

New York Times Co. v. *Sullivan*, 376 U.S. 254 (1964).

Onassis v. *Christian Dior – New York, Inc.*, 122 Misc.2d 603, 472 N.Y.S.2d 254 (Sup.Ct. 1984).

Parkinson, M.G., & Parkinson, L.M. (2006) *Law for Advertising, Broadcasting, Journalism, and Public Relations: A Comprehensive Text for Students and Practitioners*. Mahwah, NJ: Erlbaum.

Pember, D.R. (2002) *Mass Media Law*, 12th ed. New York: McGraw-Hill.

Roberson v. *Rochester Folding Box Co.*, 171 N.Y. 538, 64 N.E. 442 (1902).

Salazar-Moreno, Q. (2008, May 12) Endorsements Coming Back to Kobe Bryant. Retrieved March 11, 2009, from http://www.blackvoices.com/blogs/2008/05/12/endorsements-coming-back-to-kobe-bryant/

Sports Illustrated (2004, August 29) Kobe's marketing power is in danger. Retrieved March 11, 2009, from http://sportsillustrated.cnn.com/2004/basketball/nba/08/29/bc.bkn.bryant.sfuture.ap/index.html

Street & Smith's Sports Business Daily (2009, January 16) Kobe Bryant inks multi-year deal with Chinese web site sina.com.. Retrieved March 11, 2009, from http://www.sportsbusinessdaily.com/article/126975

Thrifty Rent-A-Car System v. *Thrift Cars, Inc.*, 831 F.2d 1177 (1st Cir. 1987).

Virgil v. *Time, Inc.*, 527 F.2d 1122 (9th Cir. 1975), cert. denied 425 U.S. 998 (1976).

Wilcox, D.L., Cameron, G.T., Ault, P.H., & Agee, W.K. (2003) *Public Relations: Strategies and Tactics*, 7th ed. Boston: Allyn & Bacon.

Williams & Wilkins v. *United States*, 487 F.2d 1345 (Ct.Cl. 1973), aff'd 420 U.S. 396 (1977).

Managing Global Public Relations

Robert I. Wakefield

19

> **Key Themes**
>
> - Understanding the management challenges in the global communication/public relations context
> - The key environmental considerations and challenges faced by organizations operating on an international/global basis
> - Frameworks for the management of global communication/public relations
> - Exploring the process of international communication/public relations management through the C-MACIE framework

INTRODUCTION

In the last 20 years or so, virtually everything in the world has been affected by the forces of globalization – including the public relations industry. Professionals in the field are finding their work impacted by the global economy, the pervasive and instantaneous social technologies, and the increasing interconnections and frictions of diverse societies. Often these things take place inside practitioners' own countries. At the same time, more and more organizations – and not just corporations – have expanded operations beyond their own nations of origin, and this has fostered increased complexities and challenges for their public relations staff members.

After years of relative neglect, discussion of public relations across borders has become more prevalent in practical and scholarly literature (Molleda, 2009). But given the variation of thought in these treatises, it is difficult to grasp what is meant when we refer to *global public relations* – or, for this chapter, what does it mean to 'manage' or facilitate a global public relations program? Does a public relations activity automatically become global if it appears on the internet, or does its globalization require other political or cultural factors? Is global public relations a process limited to governments or businesses that address publics across borders, or does it now include the myriad non-profit or special interest organizations, or even individuals, who disseminate their own messages, build relationships, or press for societal change in the global arena? Has the internet rendered communication so all-encompassing that *all* public relations is now global (Falconi, 2010; Grunig, Grunig, & Dozier, 2002)? If so, do its management processes differ from the traditional public relations efforts, or is it all the same now?

In previous research, the author of this chapter labeled the practice of public relations across national borders as *international public relations*, and defined such practice as 'a programme or practice that has the opportunity of affecting or being affected by publics in more than one country' (Wakefield, 1997: 11). Wilcox, Cameron, Ault, and Agee (2007: 516) similarly defined international public relations as 'the planned and organized effort of a company, institution, or government to establish mutually beneficial relations with the publics of other nations'. However, Falconi (2010: 2) argued that virtually all public relations is now moving into the global sphere. He maintained that 'a growing number of organisations and professionals have begun to ... transition from traditionally *international*, to *global* communication practices, and this because it is today increasingly evident that communication ... may no longer be approached from a local, national, regional or even an international perspective, but only from a global one, even if and when its activities are local'.

It may be true that all organizations today can encounter social communication directed at them from anywhere in the world – even if this consists of one angry person spouting false information from a computer and sparking the interest of other individuals from any number of nations or cultural groupings. Because of this possibility, certainly every organization needs to acknowledge this global social context and be prepared to deal with it. However, those kinds of possibilities seem much different from the daily realities faced by organizations which have physically extended their operations into many nations, with multiple offices or divisions, thousands of staff members, and other resources scattered around the world. These transnational entities constantly encounter differing political and cultural systems, time-zone challenges, local and global activist groups, and other publics who live in the many host nations in which they operate. Molleda (2009) argued that transnational organizations must account for this much greater complexity than those entities – community institutions, local hospitals or care centers, public school systems, and the like – whose publics and daily communication concerns usually are limited to a fairly small geographical context.

Because of these increased complexities, much can and should be learned by studying public relations programs in transnational organizations. Vercic (2003: 487) said: 'Corporate public relations in the world stage is the forerunner of the best in public relations ... therefore, to study the best in public relations we need to focus on transnational public relations'. The organizations that operate around the world are those that most need to understand how to organize and operate their public relations programs on a truly global basis – but it also is hoped that the challenges the transnational entities face and the manner in which they organize to handle those challenges can be instructive to everyone who practices in the public relations industry.

This chapter, then, specifically examines the management of global public relations within transnational organizations. The focus may be mostly on corporations, but the discussion could also be relevant for governments, not-for-profit organizations, the large non-government organizations, and any other institutions that spread their physical presence, reach and influence over many nations. The chapter looks at how public relations programs in these organizations can or should function to best build relationships and preserve reputations around the world.

To this end, the chapter examines the theoretical frameworks for managing and practicing public relations across borders. It looks at the evolution of these frameworks and applies them in today's environment. The chapter will also discuss the structuring of public relations in global organizations, communication between a worldwide public relations staff, response to publics of various nations, and other relevant considerations. It will explore the various facets of globalization that may have impacted public relations management over the past decade, which include the expansion of the internet, the concurrent spread of activism, and the changes in traditional mass media. Finally, drawing upon the C-MACIE framework outlined in Chapter 2, the chapter will assess current challenges facing organizations and international public relations managers operating in an increasingly competitive global marketplace, and the key managerial decisions and processes involved in global communications.

THEORETICAL FOUNDATIONS FOR MANAGING GLOBAL PUBLIC RELATIONS

Most of the early writing on international public relations was more anecdotal than scholarly (Angell, 1990; Dilenschneider, 1992; Epley, 1992), and theory building in the global realm did not really start to develop until the late 1980s or even early 1990s. In the book *Experts in Action* (Cantor, 1989), a few chapters examined public relations across borders, including one by Anderson (1989) that attempted to distinguish between centralized and localized managerial strategies. As far as this author knows, the first book to attempt to impose theoretical insight entirely into the international scene was edited by Nally (1991) and published in the United Kingdom. Yet, even that book included significant anecdotal insight and little actual theoretical construction.

The early attempts to bring theory into the global realm of public relations called upon theoretical foundations from other social science disciplines, such as sociology and global society, political science, business management, cultural anthropology, and development communication (Pavlik, 1987; Wakefield, 1996). Global society theories, for example, examined whether the world was integrating (described as *convergence*) through advancing technologies, travel, intercultural interactions and the like, or pulling apart through local attempts to protect cultures, languages, and local ways of life (referred to as *divergence*). Epley (1992) explained how this debate affected public relations practice. Various cultural theories also guided theory building in global public relations, perhaps beginning with Hall's (1959: 191) assertion that 'culture is communication and communication is culture'. Sriramesh and White (1992) adapted this worldview into public relations research, and then added elements of

Hofstede's (1980) cultural dimension research. This foundation looked at basic cultural values related to power in societies, societal tendencies to value communal or individualistic order, their views and behaviors related to uncertainty and risk, and whether they were prone toward masculine tendencies of competition and aggressiveness or the more feminine virtues of cooperation and compromise. Alternative cultural foundations, such as that described by Adler (1983) which assesses the way cultures view their relationship to time, space, good versus evil, etc., also contributed to early worldviews of global public relations and continue to provide insights today.

Over the past two decades, other research avenues have been added to the global public relations mix. For example, Molleda (2009) noted several theoretical foundations for global public relations research and practice: environmental perspectives including but not limited to culture, cultural competence theories, public relations for and in emerging economies, global public diplomacy, and other paths of research. In addition to this, a few public relations scholars have chosen to reemphasize the early roots of public relations as a relationship function in the broader community context, rather than going with the prevalent focus on the message production and dissemination machine that seems to dominate the practice today (Ledingham and Bruning, 2000). Kruckeberg and Starck (1988: xi) noted that 'Only with this goal [of community building] as a primary objective can public relations become a full partner in the information and communication milieu that forms the lifeblood of U.S. society and, to a growing extent, the world'. This was important to global public relations because it served to remind practitioners and scholars that analysis of effective public relations activity should not be limited to organizations, but that it should be viewed from within the framework of the broader global community in which organizations operate.

Global Versus Local

One of the earliest discussions on the actual practice of public relations in the global scene – one of the research paths outlined by Molleda (2009) – was patterned after inquiries in international business on how to account for the various cultural differences around the world and balance the global and local imperatives faced by organizations operating among these differing cultures (Adler & Doktor, 1986; Baalbaki & Malhotra, 1993; Bartlett & Ghoshal, 1989). Anderson (1989), for example, noted a preference among the authors toward one of two poles: establishing standardized programs at headquarters and implementing them in all markets with minor adaptations; or placing resources and autonomy in the local markets where native communicators best understand their publics. Yet, in practice, adhering to either of these poles was problematic. Centralization could impose programs that were inappropriate for local conditions (Botan, 1992). Complete local autonomy indicated that the transnational perceived little need to protect its reputation through global consistencies. When problems surfaced somewhere, there was no way for the organization to respond rapidly or to avoid the spread of the problem to other places – thus risking 'a public relations disaster' (Kinzer & Bohn, 1985: 5).

Some authors proposed that transnationals must respond to both global and local demands. Traverse-Healy (1991) said that international public relations should centralize policies and messages and then create strategies to adapt to local language, customs and politics. He offered suggestions for reaching this balance. Likewise, Morley (2002: 29) added that 'a good product, service, or communications strategy can achieve global success as long as it is customised to meet local tastes' (p. 29).

If it was true that the right combination of the global and the local was needed for successful global public relations, the key was to discover how that combination should be weighted to be most effective. Potential answers to this puzzle were contained in a few related models. The first was Brinkerhoff and Ingle's (1989) *theory of structured flexibility*, created for the development management domain. It suggested a combination of factors that were *generic* to effective global management – that could be universally applied – and those that affected *specific* local contingencies. The generic realm included overall objectives and strategic plans, consensus on policies, and establishment of responsibilities. The specific allocated flexibility to implement the broader, centralized themes in specific regions or countries.

The Global Research Process

This early research on the global and the local has evolved into a few significant studies and research tracks, as outlined by Molleda (2009). For one, Falconi (2006) called for a 'managerial dashboard tool' that would address public relations issues between global and local managerial levels. In response, Sievert and Porter (2009) created a 'heuristic analytical grid' that included four 'contexts' under which global programs should function: *standard* context, including the various external political, economic and media systems; *function* context, which takes in the various cultural dimensions among other local factors; *structure* context, which incorporates the financial and power structures within the organizations themselves; and *role* context, which brings in the various global actors who can help achieve communication goals. The grid can be used to assess communication and its various contextual factors, and therefore offers utility for future research – and, in fact, Sievert (2010) already has used the grid for a preliminary study in Europe. However, the grid is based on journalistic models instead of the relationship-building models that Kruckeberg and Starck (1988) and Ledingham and Bruning (2000) advocated. Perhaps because of this focus, the model highlights actors who can support communication goals while ignoring those actors and other factors in today's rapidly changing society that can damage organizational communication.

THE GENERIC/SPECIFIC THEORY

Falconi (2010) recently advocated a stakeholder-based theory that balances the global and the local: the generic/specific theory of global public relations. He defined it as a 'normative framework ... based on best practice cases and participant observation by a growing cohort of scholars and professionals from many corners of the globe' (p. 10). Interestingly, Falconi cited the 'governance of stakeholder relationships as the new global frontier of public relations' (p. 4), and referred to the generic/specific theory as a 'new framework' developed 'in these last ten years' (p. 10). While it does seem that too many public relations practitioners have devolved into a one-way message dissemination approach to communication, the stakeholder relations worldview is not nearly so new, at least in the scholarly community, as shown with the Kruckeberg and Starck (1988) and Ledingham and Bruning (2000) treatises mentioned above. Furthermore, the generic/specific theory arguably was conceived two decades ago (Grunig, 2006), and then was spread globally through considerable research and dialogue, as Falconi (2010) stated.

Although the roots of the generic/specific theory trace back into theories on management, dialogue, culture, and other constructs, the theoretical foundation among public relations scholars was the study on excellence in public relations management (Grunig, 1992), which identified variables that contribute to exemplary public relations practice in any given organization: positioning of the senior public relations practitioner within senior executive ranks; integration of the public relations function rather than spreading it into several different organizational units; distinction from instead of incorporation into the marketing function; equity in hiring and retention practices; and the like (see Table 19.1). While Grunig (1992) did not emphasize global organizations, much of the model was drawn from theories that had originated or been accepted outside the United States; therefore, it was seen as a valuable point of departure for an exploration into global practice (Verčič, Grunig, & Grunig, 1996; Wakefield, 1997).

The generic/specific project borrowed distinctions on global and local management from Brinkerhoff and Ingle (1989), and then incorporated 14 variables from Grunig (1992) into propositions for global effectiveness (Grunig, 2006; Wakefield, 1997). The eight generic variables proposed that a transnational should continually foster trust and interaction from publics worldwide; public relations implements strategic communication at headquarters *and* in each local unit; an integrated public relations staff cooperates with but is not subordinate to marketing, legal, or other functions; all public relations officers worldwide are trained in strategic thinking; and public relations is structured to rapidly adapt and respond to threats and opportunities anywhere in the world that could affect the entity's reputation. The specific factors that were seen as affecting local markets were level of development, the political and cultural environment, language differences, the potential for activism, and the mass media.

As Falconi (2010) pointed out, these propositions have since been examined through various studies and treatises originating from different parts of the world. In the 1990s, Verčič et al. (1996) tested the application of the specific variables in Slovenia and found applications even in newly emerging democracies. Wakefield (2000) then conducted three additional studies: a Delphi study testing both the generic and specific principles among senior practitioners from 18 nations; a survey of experts in 12 more countries, replicating an instrument from the original Delphi;

TABLE 19.1 Extension of the Grunig (1992) Model of Excellent Public Relations Management into the Global Realm through the Generic/Specific Theory

Grunig's (1992) Variables of Excellent Public Relations		Extension into Generic Principles of Global Management
1. Communication is strategically managed	→	Strategic communication is global in scope
2. Communication units foster symmetrical relationships with internal/external publics	→	… in every organizational unit around the world
3. All communication functions are integrated	→	… Globally
4. Communication plays separate role from marketing or other functions	→	… to scan and interact with the stakeholder environment around the world
5. Chief communication officer reports directly to senior management	→	… in every organizational unit around the world while also working as an integrated communication team with other units and headquarters
6. Communication staff members are qualified to perform their roles	→	… according to universal standards of PR and understanding of local practices
7. Requisite diversity exists within the communication function …	→	… to interact with publics all over the world in culturally appropriate ways
8. The communication program will be flexible and adaptive to the organization's environment	→	… so as to proactively interact and adapt to the dynamic global environment and publics

Specific Variables in Global PR Programs that Demand both Local and Global Interactions

1. The political and economic factors of each host nation
2. The varying cultural impacts of public relations practice around the world
3. The development and infrastructures of various nations around the world
4. The potential for activism on both global and local levels
5. The variances in media coverage, locally, regionally, and globally
6. The global influences of the Internet

and a project for Edelman Public Relations that investigated the philosophies and activities of 25 transnational corporations from 12 countries using the generic/specific principles as the measuring stick for effective public relations practices.

As these studies have moved into the global realm, they have evolved into two distinct yet equally important aspects of global public relations. Culbertson and Chen (1996) said that there are two main research tracks in the global public relations environment: *comparative*, or studies of the practice from country to country; and *international*, or studies of public relations practices specifically within international organizations. At that time both of these tracks were lacking in research, and the latter, the organizational track, was particularly non-existent. Given the increasing number of transnational firms, there was a need to launch both of these types of research to guide public relations efforts. As the years pass, these gaps are slowly being filled.

Analysis of the Specific: Country Studies

To date, research in Culbertson and Chen's (1996) comparative category seems to be much farther advanced than investigations focusing on organizations. Dozens of articles and book chapters can be found discussing public relations in one country or another. Many of these studies are contained in two volumes of a book edited by Verčič and his colleague Sriramesh: *The Global Public Relations Handbook* (Sriramesh & Verčič, 2003) and *The Global Public Relations Handbook, Revised and Expanded Edition* (Sriramesh & Verčič, 2009). Using mostly the specific factors of the generic/specific theory – political, cultural and economic environment, media system, and activist environment – as the framework for the books, each edition contains more than a dozen examinations of public relations in various nations. These chapters are beneficial in building the body of knowledge about public relations practices and environmental factors around the world. However, for the most part, the descriptions do not address the implications for transnational entities operating in each country.

One of the most important specific factors outlined in Sriramesh and Verčič (2003, 2009) is culture. While other specific variables certainly exist, culture serves as the societal foundation that usually fosters these elements. For example, political and economic systems often arise from cultural moorings, and media systems and activism also are strongly affected by culture. Therefore, culture and its impacts around the world are addressed liberally in each of the volumes.

The books also contained a section which examines public relations issues in governments, the United Nations, and public relations firms that service corporations, in addition to two chapters in the first edition that specifically examined transnational corporations. In one of these chapters, Verčič (2003) thoughtfully outlined the challenges and opportunities faced by practitioners who are trying to organize and carry out public relations in transnational firms. He viewed this outline as important to the field because 'corporate public relations in the world stage is the forerunner of the "best" in public relations. It demands more work in a more complex environment. Therefore, to study the "best" in public relations we need to focus on transnational corporate public relations' (p. 487). Verčič's (2003) contribution to the debate serves as one of the few thoughtful treatises on public relations in the transnational entity, but much more is still needed to offer guidance to those whose public relations work carries them across sociopolitical lines.

Organizational Analysis: Model of World-Class Public Relations

While Sriramesh pursued research in the comparative realm, along with Verčič's organizational input, Wakefield organized his 1990s research mentioned above into a model for public relations management in the global organization. Certainly, there is no overriding prescription that fits every organization operating around the world. Entities will always differ in philosophy and structure depending upon the industry in which they operate, their culture of origin, size and financial resources, and other factors. However, organizations of any type can benefit from a broad guidebook for successful public relations. Therefore, Wakefield (2000) proposed a model of world-class public relations. The term 'world-class' was borrowed from Kanter's (1995) book *World Class*, in which she argued that successful transnational entities incorporate the best thinking and resources from anywhere in the world, not just from the home country. She referred to such entities as *cosmopolitan* or *world-class*. Similar reasoning was incorporated into the model of 'world-class' global public relations excellence.

The 'world-class' model highlighted the need to balance the global and the local discussed above. It was premised on the belief that neither exclusive standardization nor autonomy was appropriate for a comprehensive global public relations program. Standard catch phrases like 'think global, act local' (Morley, 2002: 29) also seemed insufficient. Rather, as has been reiterated in subsequent writing, the key guiding principle behind an effective global program is the need to *think globally and locally* and *act globally and locally* – all at the same time (Wakefield, 2009). With that foundation, the model identified six factors determining the effectiveness of a global public relations program:

1. *Purpose* – a program that emphasizes relationships instead of just a product marketing or messaging focus.
2. *Executive support* – or the extent to which senior management supports public relations efforts.
3. *Teamwork* – qualified public relations people in all units around the world who share information and strategic input rather than being structured as a top-down, imposed work force.
4. *Adequate training* of staff in public relations or a related field.
5. *Communication style* – whether communication was based on simple one-way dissemination of messages or two-way interaction and information sharing with both internal and external publics.
6. *Response preparedness* – the extent to which a public relations staff is prepared to anticipate and rapidly respond to any issues or crises that may arise anywhere in the world.

From these six factors, it was then possible to assess the public relations pro-grams of any transnational organization and to classify the programs into one of four categories of effectiveness: *dormant, emerging, sophisticated,* or *world-class.* The categories ranged from virtually no resources or qualified personnel and little global interaction at the dormant end of the spectrum (which would render an organization vulnerable to potentially serious public relations crises) to full global staffing of highly qualified personnel who actively cooperate to accomplish mutual communication goals at the world-class level.

Current Status of the Models

Today, the generic/specific models and their evolutionary offshoots still seem to be valuable to the public relations community. Of course, like any theory, they have their weaknesses. First, the generic/specific theory has almost always been tested through qualitative methods, and often through snowball samples of perceived 'experts' in the field, albeit experts from many different nations. Although these experts have great combined experience, it is possible that that they were selected from the same community of ideas and worldviews about public relations and do not represent the perceptions of the entire realm of public relations practitioners and academics. By the same token, the model of world-class public relations was tested only once, through lengthy telephone conversations that looked for patterns and outliers. While this process was instructive, and even though the opinions expressed in the study held up against the various factors of the generic/specific theory, it is always possible that what was reported could be quite different from what actually was happening inside the organizations being reported. Therefore, much more test-ing is needed to strengthen the validity of both models.

Despite their weaknesses both of the models remain, after one or two decades since their inception, in the conversation among academics and practitioners world-wide. As mentioned by Falconi (2010), the generic/specific theory holds great prom-ise for future study, and the comparative research of Sriramesh and Verčič (2003, 2009) has helped to extend the dialogue about the environmental factors that affect global public relations practice. Wakefield's (2000, 2007) model still serves as one of the few that actually delves into how organizations should structure their public rela-tions programs to account for these environmental factors and organize global com-munication efforts to maintain solid relationships in any given location.

One of the challenges with either of these generic/specific evolutions, as well as any model that purports to guide practitioners in the global arena, is the rapidly changing dynamics of the world and how they affect these models. For example, globalization has fostered four main influences on public relations practices across borders. The first is an alteration from the traditional, center-to-periphery notions of globalization into what Sirkin, Hemerling, and Bhattacharya (2008) called *globality.* Today, they said, 'business flows in every direction ... Western business orthodoxy entwines with eastern business philosophy and creates a whole new mind-set that embraces profit and competition as well as sustainability and collaboration' (pp. 1–2).

Three other factors that have certainly influenced public relations practice are: the advent of the internet and social media; changes in the reach and power of activism throughout the world, both within and between national boundaries; and the nature and reach of the traditional mass media. Therefore, when proposing principles for effective management of global public relations, an updated model should address these influences.

THE C-MACIE FRAMEWORK FOR GLOBAL COMMUNICATIONS

One concern in building theory in public relations is to make it relevant to the practical realm. This is particularly the case in global public relations, where theoretical guideposts are still relatively rare. The remainder of this chapter, therefore, will suggest ways to convert the theory into the practical. The C-MACIE framework emphasized at the beginning of this book helps to achieve this process.

Step 1: Analysis

The first step in the framework is to conduct a careful analysis of communication management efforts. This begins inside the organization. Many organizations seem prone to examine their communication by identifying various publics in the external environment and determining how communication is progressing with those publics. However, as Broom (2008) explained, thorough analyses need to include not only a broad look around but also a deep look inside the organization. Similarly, earlier in this book organizational communication was defined as *both* external and *internal* communication on behalf of the entity. A comprehensive communication framework is formed by linking together internal and external communication, but the two realms were still seen as distinct by the editors of this book. This is particularly critical in the global realm, where even internal communication can create great tensions and competing interests. Therefore, to succeed in global communication efforts, transnational organizations must align internal communication before addressing external communication issues.

The alignment of internal communication is particularly salient with the public relations staff members located in host nations throughout the world. Artz (2007) stated that the worldviews and values of host country employees align more naturally with their own cultures than with their distant employers. 'This transnational working class still lives primarily on a national level ... and [is] socially susceptible to nationalism, patriotism, and localism', he added (p. 152). Yet public relations staff members are in a position to facilitate cultural differences between their own community and the transnational organization. Often this means explaining to their employers the local cultures and their inherent ways of doing things – or defending the behaviors of the transnational to their own family members, acquaintances, and communities. If the transnational is insensitive to host country behaviors and needs, or if communication efforts seem too centralized and heavy-handed, it can create dissonance within these local public relations staffers and lead to increasingly pent-up frustrations.

Perhaps the best way to align internal communication, then, is to recognize and accommodate the balance of the global and the local, as the generic/specific theory proposes. Long-time practitioner Thornton (2010) explained that global public relations staffs must 'keep an open mind as you begin to consider and plan for global strategic and local tactical execution. While headquarters may lead the charge in most global business plans, it is the regional and country operations that will truly validate the concept and legitimize the strategy behind those plans' (p. 1). Thornton then outlined how this balance plays out in an actual global team:

> Every team has a leader, in one form or another, sometimes as a result of a direct reporting relationship or indirectly through a matrix-reporting relationship – or in some organizations a combination of both....Regional and country communicators need to be appreciated for their collaboration and value – and should be recognized as being part of the extended global communications team.... The process is multi-pronged as there is a defined process for sharing information and results through individual update calls, weekly conference calls, frequent country visits, global communications meetings and informal gatherings (p. 1).

Step 2: Choice

The proper balance between the global and the local presupposes a variety of important yet difficult choices, as suggested in the second step of the C-MACIE framework. These choices begin at the executive level of the organization, and then cross into structuring, planning, and implementation of communication efforts. Research conducted by Wakefield (2007) suggested several decisions that need to be made to help facilitate a solid communication program. These choices include:

- Senior executives view organizational communications as a core international function and support it completely by allocating proper funding and resources.
- Public relations seeks to protect the reputation or brand of the organization first, and then supports marketing and promotional efforts.
- Public relations officers function as an integrated, horizontal global team, with frequent, purposeful interaction between headquarters and all local units.
- The global team constantly shares information, ideas and solutions, and cooperatively sets global communication guidelines.
- Every unit creates and carries out strategies based on those guidelines and on their own assessment of local needs and conditions.
- The global communication team anticipates and is prepared to expedite, even across borders, any contingency that arises.

When public relations units in transnational organizations have proper support from senior executives and are attuned to each other's needs and activities, they can construct reputation programs that do not simply mirror or support marketing efforts, but locally and globally build relationships to help preserve corporate interests. As the generic/specific theory suggests, such public relations efforts can be attuned to local politics, socioeconomics, and culture, to media differences, to the formation and changes in public opinion, and to activist possibilities around the world. They also can respond to instantaneous and constant global internet communication about their organization.

Still, many corporations persist in seeing the world only in terms of their global products and marketing efforts. Too often this worldview carries the misconception that transnational firms can influence publics simply by modifying centralized products and messages. They then inevitably focus on their own interests while ignoring the interests and attitudes of publics located not just where they operate but, in today's internet society, anywhere in the world. The firms then become vulnerable to crises because local values and perceptions extend beyond mere choices over products and product messages. When publics are harmed by the actions of transnationals, they retaliate. For this reason, a centralized marketing mindset can be woefully inadequate for long-term relationships. What is needed is a more complex way of conducting global public relations – for the organization to think simultaneously in both global *and* local terms and to act globally *and* locally, constantly integrating and reinforcing these levels of strategy and action.

Step 3: Implementation

As suggested earlier, implementation of communication programs in a global environment is invariably complicated. Organizations must first consider their different publics. This includes not just those publics that are important natural targets for organizational messages – customers, potential customers, government and civic officials in the various host nations, vendors, and employees around the world – but also those publics and individuals whom Esman (1972) referred to as *diffuse*, as difficult to identify or to even predict that they might become publics. These generally are publics who are not selected by the organization but who choose to communicate with the organization – usually around an issue that has arisen because the organization has failed to meet the expectations of the given publics (Grunig & Repper, 1992).

With the global communication technologies of today, it is even more difficult to identify where publics may arise than it was when the generic/specific theory was created. Individuals and activist groups can use the internet to constantly monitor the activities of corporations and governments, and they can more easily create their own communication networks to pressure the large organizations with more power and speed than ever before. As Soutus (2010: 1) said: 'Messages now zip around the world in the blink of an eye. Local issues are more frequently morphing into global issues. Company reputations and brands are built, debated and scrutinized by hordes of online bloggers and citizen journalists. Millions of stakeholders organize and discuss issues on new social media platforms.' The global arena also exacerbates the differences in ethical frameworks and the various concerns that motivate publics to scrutinize and communicate with organizations (Lieber & Higgins, 2010).

All of these differences in global communication have mandated a change in the basic purposes and techniques of organizational communication programs – from the one-way message dissemination mechanisms that have dominated public relations in the past few decades to the need for continual interaction in online conversation. Many organizations are not prepared for this change, and make their relationships with publics even worse when they attempt some centralized, one-way response to these online demands for communication. As Falconi (2010) argued, today's communication environment requires that organizations enter into dialogue *with* their stakeholders, rather than trying to talk *to* them as they have long been prone to do.

Despite the added challenges of today's global environment, transnational entities have a great opportunity to use the same technologies to improve their implementation of communication around the world. When this author conducted research for Edelman (Wakefield, 2000), the corporations involved were still using the telephone and periodic meetings to communicate with public relations staff members around the world. E-mails were being used, but the instantaneous reach and interaction of today's mobile phones, Facebook, Twitter, YouTube, and other tools were still non-existent. What was decided and communicated at a global level trickled slowly throughout the employee ranks, and what was decided and conducted in each location got back to headquarters and to other units in hours if not days. Today, while pressures from publics can arise instantaneously, there also is an opportunity to communicate frequently within the public relations staff and to respond fairly instantaneously when the need arises. Once organizations get used to the need for continual dialogue with their stakeholders, the opportunities for them to engage in such conversation will remain unprecedented. Overall, this will help create more genuine communication and better long-term relationships with stakeholders, both at the global level and in the various host nations around the world.

Step 4: Evaluation

Evaluation is perhaps the most important phase of the global communication process, as the C-MACIE framework suggests. Yet, it is probably the most difficult step to achieve in the organization – partly because of the expense involved in conducting meaningful evaluation and also because practitioners are not well enough versed in the principles of research to conduct evaluation efforts. Until relatively recently, as well, measurement of communication programs was significantly lacking in the public relations literature. However, these conditions have changed in the past decade, as scholars such as Hon and Grunig (1999), Huang (2001), and Noble and Watson (2007), as well as researchers such as Paine (2007) and Scott (2007), have addressed the issue of evaluation. In addition, institutes and associations like the Global Alliance for Public Relations, the Institute for Public Relations, and the International Association for Measurement and Evaluation of Communication have increased the focus on communication measurement through ongoing commissions and summits on the topic.

The critical need in global public relations is to reduce reliance on communication *outputs* and begin to evaluate the *outcomes* or impacts that make an actual difference in relationships with stakeholders. While it can be useful to count the number of news releases that were picked up by mainstream media or the number of hits that a website or YouTube video received, the real concern is what these numbers mean for better dialogue, better perceptions of the organization, or more generation and preservation of revenue, particularly in the long term. In today's global context, the need is to reliably measure these outcomes in a way that can offer an accurate picture of how this is affecting relationships. Paine (2007: 3) explained:

> PR researchers need to rethink their approaches as well. The normal maxim for measurement is, 'If you can't measure it, you can't manage it.' The problem with measuring … is not how to do it, but rather that the nature of [social media] renders management impossible. You simply can't manage what 100 million independent-minded, opinionated people are going to say.

One way to approach evaluation of outcomes is through Hon's and Grunig's (1999) guidelines for measuring relationships. They explained, 'In order to answer the much broader question – "How can PR practitioners begin to pinpoint and document for senior management the overall value of public relations to the organization as a whole?" – different tools and techniques are needed' (p. 1). The authors then outlined six key components of long-term relationships between organizations and their various publics: mutuality of control between the organization and its publics; mutual trust; mutual satisfaction; commitment to the relationship; an exchange relationship (where one party gives benefits to the other only because the other has provided benefits in the past or is expected to do so in the future); and a communal relationship (one in which both parties offer benefits to each other out of concern for the welfare of the other, even when they may get nothing in return – and the authors considered this relationship to be more beneficial than an exchange relationship). Later, Huang (2001) tested the measurement of these relational elements in multiple cultural contexts and found that the elements held up across cultures.

SUMMARY

Developing theory in such a vast and ambiguous domain as global public relations is not easy. Still, considering that the roots of globalization began in the 1960s or so and that public relations officers have been connected to transnational organizations since then, it is remarkable that theory building in this domain is still relatively scant

(Continued)

(Continued)

(Molleda & Laskin, 2005). But now that public relations has moved into an internet-induced global communication era, the need for theoretical guideposts has become increasingly crucial. While traditional public relations practices may offer some benchmarking for the global realm, the more challenging dynamics and complexities are now requiring something more specifically pertinent to cross-border practice.

Falconi (2010: 3) explained: 'In absence of … a global and relationship based perspective, a professional communicator is no longer able to effectively perform at any level (local, regional, national, international)'. He then proposed his 'new' framework for global public relations – one based not on a 'communicating-to' (p. 9) or message dissemination approach which he said has dominated public relations (particularly in the US) for more than half a century, but based on stakeholder relations and dialogue. In his own words, 'This framework is the *generic principles and specific applications* one' (p. 10) – a framework which, as mentioned earlier, has existed for nearly two decades.

Hence in this chapter we have focused attention back on the generic/specific theory and its offshoots of comparative research and the 'world-class' model as useful theories for global public relations, theories worth additional assessment and discussion. The models advocate global consistencies and cooperation but eschew top-down, centralized management approaches. The models preserve the need to apply communication principles and stakeholder engagement at both the local and the global levels, in accordance with Falconi's (2010) current admonitions. Yet the models also offer enough flexibility to accommodate different philosophies and structures of organization and communication. What the models do most is to encourage organizations to have in place a structure that accommodates both the global and the local, which utilizes all the public relations talent available around the world for their communications programs, and at the same time encourages listening, issues anticipation, and global flexibility.

In today's increasingly complex and interrelated business operating environments, global public relations is not just a matter of what to do at the global level and what to enact at the local level, as though each level operates in some separate universe. Instead, it should be considered a *global fusion of competencies and creativity* in all areas of the public relations function throughout the organization. Many organizations today have public affairs, media relations, community relations, product publicity, and other related functions in separate silos, geographical units, or divisions. Others have combined them all, but under a marketing communication umbrella. This author would submit that both of these philosophies can be problematic. The first is because the various functions are not coordinating activities enough to maintain the kind of consistencies necessary for effective relationship building. The second is problematic because the focus of the communication then becomes the consumer – and often only the consumer – instead of the more diverse base of stakeholders that are important to the success of the organization.

What is needed is for all relationship-building functions in the transnational organization to work cooperatively as equal team members, with information sharing, input, idea banks, issues anticipation and all other functions performing equal, horizontal roles. These should be guided by a team leader who has constant access to and complete support from senior executives, a great listening mindset, and an ability to encourage and persuade. When this global team is supported by senior executives of the organization, positioned in the decision-making ranks at both the global and the local levels, with necessary budgets and resources, the opportunity for effective programming of global public relations should significantly increase.

📖 REFERENCES

Adler, N.J. (1983) Cross-cultural management: Issues to be faced. *International Studies of Management and Organization, 13,* 7–45.

Adler, N.J., & Doktor, R., with Redding, S. (1986) From the Atlantic to the Pacific century: Cross-cultural management reviewed. *Journal of Management*, 12, 295–318.

Anderson, G. (1989) A global look at public relations. In B. Cantor (ed.), *Experts in Action*, 2nd ed. (pp. 412–22). White Plains, NY: Longman.

Angell, R. (1990) 'International PR': A misnomer. *Public Relations Journal, 46*(10), 8.

Artz, L. (2007) The corporate model from national to transnational. In L. Artz & Y.R. Kamalipour (eds), *The Media Globe: Trends in International Mass Media* (pp. 141–62). Lanham, MD: Rowan and Littlefield.

Baalbaki, I., & Malhotra, N. (1993) Marketing management bases for international market segmentation: An alternate look at the standardization/customization debate. *International Marketing Review, 10*(1), 19–44.

Bartlett, C.A., & Ghoshal, S. (1989) *Managing Across Borders: The Transnational Solution*. Boston: Harvard Business School Press.

Botan, C. (1992) International public relations: Critique and reformulation. *Public Relations Review, 18*(2), 149–59.

Brinkerhoff, D., & Ingle, M. (1989) Between blueprint and process: A structured flexibility approach to development management. *Public Administration and Development, 9*(5), 487–503.

Broom, G. (2008) *Cutlip and Center's Effective Public Relations*, 10th ed. Upper Saddle River, NJ: Prentice Hall.

Cantor, B. (1989) *Experts in Action*, 2nd ed. White Plains, NY: Longman.

Culbertson, H.M., & Chen, N. (1996) *International Public Relations: A Comparative Analysis*. Mahwah, NJ: Erlbaum.

Dilenschneider, R. (1992) *A Briefing for Leaders: Communication as the Ultimate Exercise of Power*. New York: HarperCollins.

Epley, J. (1992) Public relations in the global village: An American perspective. *Public Relations Review, 18*(2), 109–16.

Esman, M.J. (1972) The elements of institution building. In J.W. Eaton (ed.), *Institution Building and Development* (pp. 19–40). Beverly Hills, CA: Sage.

Falconi, T.M. (2006) Moving towards a global dashboard of local public relations infrastructure? Retrieved July 14, 2010, from *PR Conversations* online blog post, at http://www.prconversations.com/?p=99.

Falconi, T.M. (2010, April) *Global Stakeholder Relationship Governance*, White paper for Institute for Public Relations. Retrieved May 15 from http://www.instituteforpr.org/files/uploads/Global_Stakeholder_Relationship_Governance.pdf.

Grunig, J.E. (1992) *Excellence in Public Relations and Communication Management*. Hillsdale, NJ: Erlbaum.

(Continued)

(Continued)

Grunig, J.E. (2006) Furnishing the edifice: Research on public relations as a strategic management function. *Journal of Public Relations Research*, *18*(2), 151–76.

Grunig, J.E., & Repper, F.C. (1992) Strategic management, publics, and issues. In J. Grunig (ed.), *Excellence in Public Relations and Communication Management*. Hillsdale, NJ: Erlbaum, 117–58.

Grunig, L.A., Grunig, J.E., & Dozier, D.M. (2002) *Excellent Public Relations and Effective Organisations. A Study of Communication Management in Three Countries*. Mahwah, NJ: Erlbaum.

Hall, E.T. (1959) *The Silent Language*. Garden City, NY: Doubleday.

Hofstede, G. (1980) *Culture's Consequences: International Differences in Work Related Values*. Beverly Hills, CA: Sage.

Hon, L.C., & Grunig, J.E. (1999) Guidelines for measuring relationships in public relations. Institute for Public Relations, Gainesville, FL. Retrieved Jan. 15, 2009, from IPR website, http://www.instituteforpr.org/research_single/guidelines_measuring_relationships.

Huang, Y.H. (2001) OPRA: A cross-cultural, multiple-item scale for measuring organization-public relationships. *Journal of Public Relations Research*, *13*, 61–91.

Kanter, R. (1995) *World Class: Thriving Locally in the Global Economy*. New York: Simon and Schuster.

Kinzer, H., & Bohn, E. (1985) Public relations challenges of multinational corporations. Paper presented to the International Communications Association Conference, Honolulu, HI.

Kruckeberg, D., & Starck, K. (1988) *Public Relations and Community: A Reconstructed Theory*. Westport, CT: Praeger.

Ledingham, J.A., & Bruning, S.D. (2000) *Public Relations as Relationship Management: A Relational Approach to the Study and Practice of Public Relations*. Mahwah, NJ: Erlbaum.

Lieber, P.S., & Higgins, C. (2010) Communicating with global publics: Building a theoretical framework for international public relations. In G.J. Golan, T.J. Johnson, & W. Wanta (eds.), *International Media Communication in a Global Age* (pp. 366–379). New York: Routledge.

Molleda, J.C. (2009, March 19) *Global public relations*. Online white paper for the Institute for Public Relations Essential Knowledge Project, Gainesville, FL. Retrieved on January 15, 2010 from http://www.instituteforpr.org/essential_knowledge/detail/global_public_relations/.

Molleda, J.C., & Laskin, A.V. (2005) *Global, International, Comparative, and Regional Public Relations Knowledge from 1990 to 2005: A Quantitative Content Analysis of Academic and Trade Publications*. Miami: Institute for Public Relations.

Morley, M. (2002) *How to Manage Your Global Reputation: A Guide to the Dynamics of International Public Relations*. Basingtoke: Palgrave.

Nally, M. (1991) *International Public Relations in Practice*. London: Kogan Page.

Noble, P., & Watson, T. (2007) *Evaluating Public Relations: A Best Practice Guide to Public Relations Planning, Research and Evaluation*. London: Kogan Page.

Paine, K.D. (2007) *How to Measure Social Media Relations: The More Things Change, the More They Remain the Same*. Gainesville, FL: Institute for Public Relations. Retrieved on June 10, 2010, from IPR website, http://www.instituteforpr.org/research/measurement_and_evaluation/P10.

Pavlik, J.V. (1987) *Public Relations: What Research Tells Us*. Newbury Park, CA: Sage.

Scott, J. (2007) Relationship Measures Applied to Practice. In E.L. Toth (ed.), *The Future of Excellence in Public Relations and Communication Management* (pp. 263–73). Mahwah, NJ: Erlbaum.

Sievert, H. (2010) First tests of the dashboard in Europe: An empirical contribution to the global navigation of international corporate communications. Working paper for the meeting of the Global Commission on Public Relations Research, Institute for Public Relations, Miami, FL, March.

(Continued)

(Continued)

Sievert, H., & Porter, S. (2009) An expanded view from the corner office: Further discussions and research on the global navigation of international corporate communications. Presentation at 16th annual BledCom International Public Relations Research Symposium, Bled, Slovenia, July 1.

Sirkin, H.L., Hemerling, J.W., & Bhattacharya, A.K. (2008) *Globality: Competing with Everyone from Everywhere for Everything.* London: Headline.

Soutus, S.H. (2010, April) Serving coke to Dr Frankenstein. *IPRA Frontlineonline Journal,* http://www.ipra.org/frontlinedetail.asp?articleid=1472

Sriramesh, K., & Verčič, D. (2003) *The Global Public Relations Handbook.* Mahwah, NJ: Erlbaum.

Sriramesh, K., & Verčič, D. (2009) *The Global Public Relations Handbook*, revised and expanded edition. Mahwah, NJ: Erlbaum.

Sriramesh, K., & White, J. (1992) Societal culture and public relations. In J.E. Grunig (Ed.), *Excellence in Public Relations and Communication Management* (pp. 597–614). Hillsdale, NJ: Erlbaum.

Thornton, G. (2010, February) Relationship-building for global stakeholder engagement. *IPRA Frontlineonline Journal*, http://www.ipra.org/archivefrontlinedetail.asp?issue=February+2010&articleid=1436

Traverse-Healy, T. (1991) 'He corporate aspect. In M. Nally (ed.), *International Public Relations in Practice* (pp. 31–39). London: Kogan Page.

Verčič, D. (2003) Public relations of movers and shakers: Transnational corporations. In K. Sriramesh & D. Verčič (eds.), *The Global Public Relations Handbook: Theory, Research, and Practice* (pp. 478–89. Mahwah, NJ: Erlbaum.

Verčič, D., Grunig, L., & Grunig, J. (1996) Global and specific principles of public relations: Evidence from Slovenia. In H. Culbertson and N. Chen (eds.), *International Public Relations: A Comparative Analysis* (pp. 31–65). Mahwah, NJ: Erlbaum.

Wakefield, R. (1996) Interdisciplinary theoretical foundations for international public relations. In H. Culbertson and N. Chen (eds.), *International Public Relations: A Comparative Analysis* (pp. 31–65). Mahwah, NJ: Erlbaum.

Wakefield, R. (1997) *International Public Relations: A Theoretical Approach to Excellence Based on a Worldwide Delphi Study.* Dissertation published by the University of Maryland – College Park.

Wakefield, R. (2000) World-class public relations: A model for effective public relations in the multi-national. *Journal of Communication Management, 5*(1), pp. 59–71.

Wakefield, R. (2007) A retrospective on world-class: The excellence theory goes international. In E.L. Toth (ed.), *The Future of Excellence in Public Relations and Communication Management* (pp. 545–568). Mahwah, NJ: Erlbaum.

Wakefield, R. (2009) Public relations in a globalized world where even 'glocalisation' is not sufficient. *Public Relations Journal, 3*(4). http://www.prsa.org/Intelligence/PRJournal/Archives.

Wilcox, D.L., Cameron, G.T., Ault, P., & Agee, W.K. (2007) *Public Relations Strategies and Tactics*, 8th ed. Boston: Pearson Education.

Index